IInd Deya International Conference of Prehistory

Recent Developments in Western Mediterranean Prehistory: Archaeological Techniques, Technology and Theory

Volume II:

Archaeological Technology and Theory

Edited by

W. H. Waldren, J. A. Ensenyat and R. C. Kennard

TEMPVS REPARATVM

BAR International Series 574
1991

B.A.R.

BAR, 122 Banbury Road, Oxford OX2 7BP, England

The current BAR catalogue, with details of all titles in print, post-free prices and means of payment, is available free from the above address.

All volumes are distributed by BAR.

BAR − S574

Waldren W H, Ensenyat J A and Kennard R C (Eds)
IInd Deya International Conference of Prehistory Volume II

© The individual authors 1991

ISBN 0 86054 727 2

Tempvs Reparatvm Volume Editor: David P Davison

British Archaeological Reports are published by

TEMPVS REPARATVM
Archaeological and Historical Associates Limited

All enquiries regarding the submission of manuscripts for future publication should be addressed to:

David P Davison MA MPhil DPhil
General Editor BAR
Tempvs Reparatvm
29 Beaumont Street
Oxford OX1 2NP

Tel: 0865 311046
Fax: 0865 311047

IIº CONGRESO DE PREHISTORIA DE DEIA
Técnicas, Tecnología y Teoría Arqueológica

BAJO LA PRESIDENCIA DE HONOR DE
SU MAJESTAD LA REINA DOÑA SOFIA

Museo Arqueológico y Centro de Investigaciones de Deià
del 23 al 30 de Septiembre de 1.988

ACKNOWLEDGEMENTS
****

CONSELLERIA DE CULTURA DEL GOVERN BALEAR

CONSELLERIA DE CULTURA DEL CONSELL INSULAR DE MALLORCA

AJUNTAMENT DE DEIÀ

AJUNTAMENT DE SOLLER

AJUNTAMENT DE VALLDEMOSSA

AJUNTAMENT DE MANACOR

MUSEU DE SOLLER

UNIVERSITAT DE LES ILLES BALEARS

FOREWORD

*A*mong the most essential qualities in scientific investigation are those of tolerance and respect for the ideas and works of fellow scientists; despite the possible differences these may demonstrate from one's own. We are at a point of departure- and indeed we have been for some time- when it is not enough to limit one's interests to a narrow geographic or single disciplinary sphere of investigation. At the same time, it is paradoxical that isolation within personal parameters ocassionally may be both productive and necessary , and hence must be respected, it can be counterproductive to shut ourselves off academically or otherwise, too completely, from the exposure and enterprise of other routes of investigation and communication. However, in what we like to feel is an enlightened world, it is indeed remarkable how often these qualities of tolerence and respect for one's peers are forgotten or only partly taken into consideration as we travel about in our isolated personal worlds. It is also important, as part of our task as scientists, not to narrow our interests, no more than our tolerence of respect, but to consider any number of possible optional approaches to our individual disciplines and the methodology and interpretations they contain, or for that matter despite the often esoteric nature and direction that some of those avenues of investigation may take compared to our own accustomed ones.*

Another purpose of serious research-one also forming another essential ingredient, applicable in the present case to the archaeological process-is the free-flowing and widest possible interexchange of data and information, the result of our research. It also stands to follow, I believe, that the more varied and different the avenues of researsh are, the more regularly and fully descriptive they should be reported, and that only in that way can they be more meaningful and productive as research.

As part of a series of three confrences with different themes, but similar objectives and dedicated to the rapid interexchange of data and information, the first two conferences: the Ist Deia Conference of Prehistory, Early Settlement in the Western Mediterranean Islands and their Peripheral Areas (1984): and the Oxford International Conference , Bell Beakers of the Western Mediterranean (1986) have been already published and distributed. While these first two conferences were more chronologically and geographically oriented and therefore perhaps of a broader and hence of a more general interest than the present conference, the current colloquium, the IInd Deia Conference of Prehistory, Archaeological Techniques, Technology and Theory, is designed to place emphasis on new means of archaeological interpretation along with the quantitative and qualitative analysis of contextual materials, and is therefore more specialised than that found in conventional excavational report approaches; being more experimental and in certain respects more controversial.

As perhaps a new (state of the art ?) breed of archaeologist and prehistorian, we are living in a particularly exciting and interesting age, when the computer- especially the personal gender- is today available and even common among us. This is in contrast to as short a time as a decade ago when the computer was available only to specialists, and a mystery to most of us. As a tool, the personal computer makes possible for the first time numerous tasks, applicable equally to the field, laboratory and library, which have been otherwise impossible until now and opening avenues and approaches to analysis and interpretation formerly only possible to the selected few.

The availability as well as versatility of the computer is particularly efficient and effective when dealing with the enormous quantity of artefacts and other archaeological remains usually found on richer sites; artefacts that up until now have been destined only for museum storage. The computer's availability and versatility also opens the road to innovation and widely different avenues of scientific approach. This is especially so in dealing with statistical arrangements and other experimental analyses. In short, the computer offers us the opportunity to view archaeological materials, their composition and even physical contexts from often completely new perspectives as well as significantly increasing the number of available variables with which we can work. In fact, the time has become nigh when to work without this new tool is in many ways to overlook the initial principles of archaeology itself; limiting ourselves to antiquated as well as very restricted viewpoints.

As a final contribution made by the personal computer, it is of course the tremendous possibilities it opens up in the area of media communication; especially in all forms of publishing. Examples of this can be found in the last two conferences where the preparation and publication of papers took place inside a year of conference meetings. This has been true for the current proceedings' volumes. In many respects, the availibility of the personal computer and the software created for it have resulted in what is without a doubt the rebirth of an old discipline ... in our case that of the archaeological sciences.

On the part of the organisational committee, I would like sincerely to thank the individual conference contributors for their prompt response to the first call for papers, as well as the prompt submission of their final papers. Regarding the present volumes, as in the actual conference itself, there are no doubts many areas of investigation where there are absences of important and innovated work; work currently being carried out within the three archaeological "T"s; works that are not included, but perhaps should have been. This is indeed unfortunate. This is due to a number of logical and unfortuitous reasons: the matter of a more convenient or appropriate time for the conference, other obligations on the part of potential participants, lack of available travel funding or in the odd case more personal or professional reasons.

Despite any shortcomings, the present conference is certain to prepare us better for what is to be expected in forthcoming conferences of this sort and therefore helps to give us each some advance background to the different avenues of research encompassed, and hence serves its original purpose.

Finally, I believe that the papers published here are a good cross-section of the most modern as well as up-to-date, techniques, technology and theoretical approaches being used by a productive group of recognised professionals for the interpretation of both protohistory and prehistory.

ABOUT THE CONFERENCE PAPERS

Originally, the division of the conference papers were grouped into three clear cut categories: Techniques, Technology and Theory. The final publication of the conference proceedings is such that the currently published papers are in two separate volumes: Techniques and Technology, Volume I and Technology and Theory, Volume II.

This has been carried out for two logical reasons which deal with the nature of the published papers. Firstly, the final compilation of the various contributions resulted in a single volume too unwieldy and too costly to produce. The second reason is that the nature and character of the papers better lent themselves to two volumes, forming a more natural division and bridge between the three subjects of techniques, technology and theory, which can be frequently fundamentally interrelated.

As the work exists in two more modest sized volumes, Volume I is dedicated to papers dealing with (1) techniques used in the analysis of materials and the analytical results themselves or (2) techniques used in the description and explanation of ancient technology ; for example, the analysis of the ancient metals and demonstrartion of the technological methods used. Volume II deals (3) with papers that bridge the two aspects of techniques and technology, seeking in physical and statistical analyses to explain and interpret change and innovation in hypothetical terms of economy and resources; the papers on theory (4) deal more directly with theoretical discussion of acknowledgeable archaeological problems.

W.H.W
Organisational Committee

PREFACIO

*U*na de la cualidades esenciales en cualquier tipo de investigación cientĭfca es la tolerancia y el respeto hacia las ideas y trabajo de los miembros de la comunidad científica, a pesar de las posibles diferencias que puedan existir con nuestro propio trabajo. Generalmente es mal sano y poco científico el cerrarnos ya sea académicamente o de otra manera, al aire fresco, libertad y espíritu emprendedor de otras rutas de entendimiento presentes en el trabajo de nuestros colegas investigadores. Donde nosotros creemos ver un mundo avanzado, es remarcable cuán a menudo estas ideas no se toman en consideración. Al mismo tiempo, estamos en un punto de partida, y en el que sin duda alguna hemos estado durante algún tiempo, donde no es suficiente el aislarnos dentro de un a estrecha esfera geográfica o disciplinaria, aunque paradógicamente aislamiento de este tipo puede ser, en ciertos momentos, periódicamente necesario y debe ser respetado. De la misma manera, es igualmente importante el considerar cuantos más sistemas metodológicos, de interpretación y definición en nuestras disciplinas individuales como se nos ofrezcan. De nuevo, ello debe realizarse a pesar de la frecuentemente dirección y naturaleza esotérica que algunos métodos de investigación pueden tomar comparados con el nuestro propio.

Otro objetivo de cualquier investigación seria, y que forma una de sus partes más importantes, en este caso dentro del proceso arqueológico, debe ser la libre circulación, lo más amplia y rapida posible, del intercambio de datos e información relacionados con hallazgos y otra evidencia. Además, en mi opinión, cuanto más variados y diferentes sean los caminos que tome la investigación, y cuanto más regular y descriptivamente se informe de el los, más fructíferos y significativos serán los resultados de la investigación.

El presente Congreso forma parte de una serie de tres congresos con objetivos similares, los dos primeros: I Congreso de Prehistoria de Deia, Asentamiento Inicial en las lslas del Mediterráneo Occidental y sus Areas Periféricas, y el Congreso lnternacional de Oxford, la Cultura Campaniforme del Mediterráneo Occidental que ya han sido ampliamente difundidos. Estos trataban temas relacionados con problemas específicos de significación cultural, social y económics, y tenían una mayor orientación cronológica y geográfica que el actual. Quizás por ello despertaran un interés general más amplio. El presente congreso, II Congreso de Deia, Tecnicas, Tecnología y Teoría Arqueológicos, pone un especial énfasis en las nuevas formas de interpretación y analisis del contexto arqueológico, mas especializado que los métodos arqueológicos convencionales. Aunque, al mismo tiempo, el presente Congreso si bien tiene su origen y unos objetivos fundamentalmente similares, incluso tratando en gran medida el área del Mediterráneo Occidental se diferencia de los dos anteriores en que los métodos tienen carácter basicamente experimental.

Como arqueólogos y prehistoriadores; estamos vivieodo una era particularmente interesante y apasionante, en la que el ordenador - que sólo estaba a disposición de especialistas es, hoy en dia, común entre nosotros. Como herramienta, el ordenador hace posible por primera vez numerosas tareas que de otra forma serían irrealizables para el investigador de orientación acadamica y de campo; abriendo caminos y accesos a análisis e interpretaciones que anteriormente sólo estaban al alcance de unos pocos. Esto es particularmente cierto cuando tenemos que trabajar con la enorme cantidad de artefactos y otros resos arqueológicos que normalmente se hallan en yacimientos ricos. Esto también es aplicable a los resultados *obtenidos por métodos experimentales ya que nos permite una visión más ampli a de los resultados experimentales. Resumiendo, el ordenador nos ofrece la oportunidad de observar estos materiales y contexto arqueológicos así como los modelos experimentales desde nuevas perspectivas. En efecto, próximo está el dia en que trabajar sin esta nueva herramienta sea, por muchos motivos, pasar por alto los propios principios de la misma arqueología. una de las últimas aportaciones del ordenador personal son, desde luego, las tremendas posibilidades que ofrece la área de la comunicación; especialmente en todas las formas de publicación de resultados. Los mejores ejemplos de ello lo representan los dos últimos Congresos en los que la publicación final de las ponencias estuvieron disponibles al año de su celebración, así como lo evidencia la presente publicación. En pocas palabras, la disponibilidad del ordenador y de los programas existentes hacen posible un total renacimiento disciplinario... en nuestro caso en las ciencias arqueológicas.*

Sin duda alguna, muchos trabajos importantes que actualmente se están llevando a cabo en muchas areas de las tres "T" de la arqueología están ausentes en esta publicación. Ello se debe a una serie de razooes lógicas: la cuestión de unas fechas más adecuadas, otras obligaciones contraídas con anterioridad, problemas para afrontar los gastos que ocasiona la participación en un congreso y los casos más extraños, cuestiones personales. En cualquier caso, creo que los articulos aquí publicados son una buena representación de la más moderna y avanzada metodología utilizada en la actualidad para la interpretación de la proto y prehistoria.

W.H.W
Oxford 1989

SOBRE LAS PONENCIAS DEL CONGRESO

Originalmente, la división natural de las ponencias se correspondía con las tres secciones que constituían el congreso: Técnicas, Tecnología y Teoría. Sin embargo, la publicación final de las actas del congreso se divide en dos volúmenes: Técnicas y Tecnología en el volumen I, y Tecnología y Teoría en el volumen II.

Ello es debido fundamentalmente a dos motivos que afectan a la naturaleza de las ponencias publicadas. En primer lugar, la compilación final de las ponencias en un solo volumen hubiera constituido un volumen demasiado abultado y difícil de manejar, y además hubiera sido demasiado costoso. El segundo motivo para la división de las ponencias en dos volúmenes reside en las propias características de las ponencias que permiten dicha división. De esta manera, se cosigue una división más acertada de los temas y además se constituye un nexo de unión entre los tres temas, es decir, Técnicas, Tecnología y Teoría.

El resultado final han sido estos dos volúmenes de dimensiones más modestas. El volumen I está dedicado a las ponencias que versan sobre (1) técnicas utilizadas en los análisis de los materiales y sus resultados y (2) técnicas utilizadas en la interpretación de cualquier tipo de tecnología prehistórica, por ejemplo, análisis de metales y los métodos tecnológicos utilizados en su producción. El volumen II incluye aquellas ponencias (3) que de alguna forma constituyen el nexo de unión entre los dos aspectos de técnicas y tecnología, cuyo objeto es, a través de análisis físicos y estadísticos, intentar explicar e interpretar de forma hipotética los cambios e innovaciones que se producen y su efecto económico; y aquellas ponencias (4) que tratan más directamente las cuestiones teóricas que afectan a la arqueología.

ARCHAEOLOGICAL TECHNIQUES, TECHNOLOGY AND THEORY

PRESENTACION DE LAS PONENCIAS

Dr Antonio Arribas Palau

En la presentación de las ponencias y comunicaciones de este Symposium, de Deià hemos optado por distribuir los temas según los siguientes apartados: (1) *Teoría*, (2) *Metodología y aplicaciones a casos concretos*, (3) *Arqueometalurgia*, (4) *Paleoecología y Arqueobotánica*, (5) *El Sudeste de la Península Ibérica*; (6) *La labor del equipo de Deià*, (7) *Otros trabajos realizados en Baleares*, (8) *Varia*.

Acaso pueda objetarse que esta distribución es aleatoria y subjetiva pero nuestra intención es mostrar la realidad de la investigación y por ello el gran peso de documentación de tipo teórico, metodológico y analítico que ocupan algunas de las áreas geográficas reflejadas en el Symposium ofrece la oportunidad de calibrarlas muy especificamente.

TEORIA

Según él hay que configurar una posición teórica cuyos conceptos operativos tengan su punto de mira en el acontecimiento y en la discontinuidad junto con una reformulación de las categorías de tiempo, espacio y proceso y de una valoración adecuada del papel que juega el azar (siguiendo las ideas de Foucault).

Juan A. Barceló (*Consecuencias teóricas del uso de la Estadística compleja en Arqueología*) pone de manifiesto que la Arqueología Estadística es una forma de entender las relaciones matemáticas que subyacen a un pequeño espectro de la realidad, especialmente lo que se refiere a la Cultura Material como forma de estructurar la vida humana en el espacio y en el tiempo.

John Castleford expone las dificultades que conlleva la definición del Mesolítico (*Mesolithic Europe*) y considera las implicaciones de las limitaciones y las ventajas de varias soluciones (enfoques particularistas, teoría general de sistemas, etc.) con el fin de lograr solventar esas dificultades.

METODOLOGIA Y APLICACION A CASOS CONCRETOS

En un área como es el Peloponeso Central y Oriental, falto de estructuras de carácter monumental que no permite reconstrucciones de tipo histórico, E.J. Krigas (*L.H. socio-political and economic activity in Central and Eastern Peloponese*) pone de relieve que durante las últimas fases del dominio de Pylos en el S.E. del Peloponeso hubo movimientos de tribus hasta áreas tan alejadas como Arcadia, donde se puede propugnar una teoría de continuación de la cultura micénica.

Cruz Auñon, Moreno y Rivero exponen sus (*Experiencias arqueológicas en la provincia de Sevilla*) , basadas en el descubrimiento de una gran concentración de cuevas artificiales en una rica área entre el Guadalaquivir y el Sudeste. Resultado de prospecciones con el magnetómetro protónico, cartografía automática y excavación alcanzan a descubrir la funcionalidad de un tipo especial de habitación semiexcavada y la presencia de silos a basureros.

ARQUEOMETALURGIA

Con respecto a las operaciones matalúrgicas destinadas a la obtención del cobre, Ayala, Polo y Ortiz (*Arqueometalurgia de yacimientos de la región de Murcia*) indican las tres fases: concentración, tostación y reducción y señalan la utilización del método analítico de espectrometría de fluorescencia de Rayos X.

Ruiz Delgado, Barranco y Respaldiza ofrecen los resultados obtenidos en objetos de bronce mediante los métodos de Fluorescencia de RX y PIXE (particle induced XR emission) discutiendo ambos métodos en sus limitaciones y su aplicabilidad a la arqueología.

El *Analisis arqueometalúrgico de los exvotos ibéricos* llevado a cabo por L. Prados con espectrómetro de XRF y con metalografías dá por resultado una diversidad de aleaciones según se trate de piezas coladas o trabajadas. Por ello es de gran interés el conocimiento técnico de las ventajas que cada una de las aleaciones puede aportar.

Con el *Estudio de piezas de orfebrería pre-romana mediante la técnica de microscopía electrónica de barrido y microanálisis por dispersión de energía* , Aballe, Perea y Adeva han llegado al análisis de soldaduras en oro de piezas antiguas pre-romanas de Iberia y a la observación de rasgos tecnológicos que permiten la reconstrucción de técnicas de fabricación antiguas y la identificación de los talleres.

Por último Queiroga y Pinto da Silva (*As Corrosoes Metalicas Sue Potencial No Estudo Dos Metais Da Cultura Castreja*) hacen hincapié en al interés de las corrosiones antiguas y su potencial en el estudio de los metales de la cultura de los Castros.

PALEOECOLOGIA Y ARQUEOBOTANICA

Un conjunto de estudios sobre este apartado llevan la impronta de las directrices que el prof. J.-L. Vernet de Montpellier ha sabido imprimir a un grupo de investigadores del área mediterránea y andaluza de la Peninsula Ibérica.

Asi Mª. Oliva Rodríguez y J-L. Vernet, inmerso dentro del proyecto de Los Millares, presentan los resultados paleoecológicos sintéticos obtenidos de los carbones dispersos del poblado y del Fortín I de este yacimiento (*Paleoécologie au Chalcolithique a Los Millares d'après les charbons de bois*). Las medidas de crecimiento realizadas sobre el olivo parecen implicar la utilización de las dos variedades: salvaje y cultivado (estas medidas se distribuyen controversialmente a lo largo de la linea de las 1000 milésimas de micra).

Respecto al desarrollo de yacimiento indican como causas la proximidad de la etapa mediterránea (Q. faginea, Q. suber) del mismo modo que la presencia de un bosque riverino bien desarrollado, mientras que el deterioro de las condiciones ecológicas-aridez, explicarían su abandono.

Teniendo en cuenta que en la antracología, o sea el estudio de carbones de madera prehistórica, se ha hecho esencial una metodología de obtención de muestra, E. Badal y Chr. Heinz

(*Méthodes utilisés en Anthrocologie por l'étude des sites préhistoriques*) exponen la metodología empleada por ellas en los yacimientos de El Abeurador y en la Cova de les Cendres.

Un estudio arqueológico-antracológico corre a cargo de M.J. de Pedro y E. Grau (*Tecnicas de construcción en la Edad del Bronce: la Lloma de Betxi, Paterna, Valencia*) y en que se destaca como la distribución de los carbones del nivel de destrucción y del suelo y por otro lado de los del techo y postes indica la existencia de unas actividades agrícolas, textiles, metalúrgicas, de la madera y de cestería.

Rivera y Obon de Castro (*Vegetal remains in archaeological contexts. Taphonomy and recovery techniques*), considerando que la arqueobotánica sienta las bases para una interpretación paleo-etno-botánica, incluyen técnicas de identificación y sistemas de análisis ecológicos y etno-botánicos.

EL AREA DEL SUDESTE DE LA PENINSULA IBERICA

R. Chapman, M. Picazo, V. Lull y E. Sanahuja (*The development of Complex Societies in S. E. Spain*) nos ofrecen las primicias del "Proyecto Gatas" cuyo propósito estriba en esclarecer los problemas planteados por los diversos modelos teóricos de Chapman, Lull, Ramos, Gilman y Mathers que parten de diferentes supuestos sobre el cambio cultural: cambio climático-vegetacional, naturaleza de la intensificación, complejidad e integración de las culturas, grado de interacción, etc.

INVESTIGACIONES DE W. WALDREN Y EL EQUIPO DE DEIÀ

En torno al Centro de Investigación de Deià, dirigido por el Dr. W. Waldren, se inscribe toda una serie de investigadores que aportan sus resultados al Symposium, ya sea desde el campo de la teoría, de la metodología, de la analítica y que en el momento actual han logrado dar una coherencia muy eficaz a los estudios efectuados en el área de Sóller-Deià-Valldemossa y que, a la larga, permiten su ampliación para una visión sintética de la Prehistoria de Mallorca. Se trata por lo tanto de un programa amplio e integrado que debe ser enfocado en su totalidad.

W. Waldren (*Age determination, Chronology and Radiocarbon Recalibration in the Balearic Islands*), tras la serie de análisis de C14 que ha venido realizando en los yacimientos de la región, llega a la conclusión de que para alcanzar una interpretación de la Prehistoria balear hay que huir de la idea de que nos enfrentamos ante un fenómeno insular y aceptar el papel que la recalibración ha de jugar siempre que queramos alcanzar una interpretación local o de correlaciones en la búsqueda de contextos continentales más amplios.

J. Ensenyat (*Island Colonization in the Western Mediterranean: The Balears*), siguiendo los principios de biogeografía insular de Cherry, que brindan un patrón válido para la colonización humana de las islas (en especial dos formas implícitas en la insularidad -tamaño limitado y aislamiento-) toma en consideración las características peculiares de cada una de ellas: condiciones de navegación, tamaño, topografía, geología, clima, recursos naturales: agua, flora, fauna, potencial agrícola etc.

Se llega a la idea de que la colonización humana de Mallorca a partir de la tierra firme es resultado de migraciones planificadas, cuyo proceso se rastrea como una serie de oleadas debidas a la presión de la población en las áreas de la tierra firme adyacentes.

Para C. Hoffman (*The metals of Son Matge. Technology as cultural activity and behavior*) las actividades y la cultura material tienen un papel activo a la hora de dar un sentido a un contexto cultural. En el caso de la metalurgia examina las relaciones humanas y las actividades involucradas en la fabricación de una pieza desde que el mineral aflora de la tierra, se procesa y funde, se moldea y se termina. Su análisis de los metales del abrigo de Son Matge le permite (1) reconstruir las técnicas de producción, (2) discutir los patrones de obtención, producción y distribución a través de un paisaje cultural y (3) interpretar los objetos y los grupos de técnicas utilizados en la producción de los útiles dentro de un contexto cultural.

W. Waldren en *Simple approaches to the analysis of prehistoric pottery* describe las líneas maestras de su metodología en el desarrollo de técnicas de análisis de la cerámica de los yacimientos excavados en la región. Se basan en especial en el exámen fisico, análisis químico de carácter cuantitativo y en experimentación de orden práctico.

Siguiendo el tenor de los estudios de Stuiver-Waldren y Van Strydonck-Waldren, en esta ocasión la ponencia de Van Strydonck y M. Dupas (*The classification and dating of lime mortars by chemical analysis and C14 dating*) interesa en especial para plantear sobre nuevas bases el tema de los enterramientos post-talaióticos de Mallorca y Menorca.

Waldren-Ensenyat y Cubí (*Son Mas. A Mallorcan Prehistoric sanctuary circa 2000-1750 B.C.*) aportan un informe preliminar de los resultados de la excavación de este santuario, uno de los mejor conservados de las Baleares, cuya fachada cóncava le relaciona con los recintos de taulas menorquines. La secuencia estratigráfica-cronológica (C14), dentro y fuera del recinto, permite asegurar una actividad desde el 2000 a.C. hasta el 200 a.C. con un contexto inicial rico en campaniforme situado por debajo y adyacente a los cimientos talaióticos (que se fechan a partir del 1000/800 a.C.).

OTROS TRABAJOS DE MALLORCA

Tan sólo se presentan a este Symposium tres trabajos sobre la isla de Mallorca realizados fuera del ámbito del grupo de Deià.

M. Orfila, A. Esteban y A. Vallespir (*Palynological analysis in Mallorca*) dan cuenta de la metodología empleada para el estudio de la paleovegetación de una zona (Santa Ponça) mediante el análisis del polen de los "cores". Desde el 8000 a.C. hasta el cambio de Era se detectan movimientos de las dunas que modifican la línea de la costa.

M. Diaz-Andreu y M. Fernández Miranda (*Cuevas sepulcrales pretalaioticas de Mallorca*) efectúan un ensayo de clasificación de 150 cuevas naturales y artificiales basado en análisis matemáticos y tipológicos de cerámica y de las cuevas.

VARIA Y MISCELANEA

Un grupo de comunicaciones que se apartan por entero de los bloques señalados hasta ahora quedan englobados en este último epigrafe.

R. Formentini (*L'immagine femminile nelle statue-menhirs*) en su análisis de las estatua-estelas, al menos hasta la Edad del Hierro, considera que ha sido un error considerar como arma -y no como instrumento- el tipo definidor del guerrero cuando hay una gran cantidad y variedad de atributos y símbolos femeninos en las estatuas-menhires. La motivación de sus autores sería la de conseguir una imágen femenina cuya función hubo de consistir en aplacar por seducción el espíritu inquieto del muerto que amenazaba con regresar al mundo de los vivos.

A. Arribas Palau

T. Chapa (*Análisis comparativo de las esculturas mediterráneas pre-romanas: las representaciones de leones*) intenta con sus estudios de comparación en los aspectos formales, determinar áreas de contacto o de convergencia y relaciones genéticas utilizando técnicas que permiten establecer las relaciones morfológicas y las evolutivas. Así se intenta evaluar la dinámica de la evolución interna y los contactos exteriores de este tipo de producción artística.

A. Muzzolini (*L'evolution technologique du bige au quadrige en Mediterranée oriental, au Maghreb et au Sahara: quand et pourquoi?*) llega a la idea de que, tanto en el caso del carro de guerra como en el de carrera, la sustitución de la biga por la triga o cuádriga es resultado del intento de asegurar la estabilidad de la plataforma. Cuando se haya conseguido este objetivo se añadirá la rapidez, necesaria para romper a la carga las falanges y para trasladar los trofeos a los santuarios.

Por último Hoskin en su comunicación *Elementary archaeoastronomy* pone de relieve que la arqueología astronómica requiere el conocimiento de temas astronómicos y una sensibilidad a consideraciones de carácter estadístico. Dado que los arqueólogos no suelen poseer esos conocimientos y los que trabajan en arqueología astronómica no conocen los problemas de los arqueólogos, el autor propugna salvar ese foso. De un gran valor ilustrativo es el ejemplo de las taulas de Menorca en el que esperamos valiosos resultados, si bien está aún apenas iniciado por el propio Hoskin.

PALMA DE MALLORCA, BALEARES, ESPANA
1989

VOLUME II
CONTENTS

THE CLASSIFICATION AND DATING OF LIME MORTARS
BY CHEMICAL ANALYSIS AND RADIOCARBON DATING: A REVIEW

MARK VAN STRYDONCK
Royal Institute of Cultural Heritage
Jubelpark 1
Brussel 1040, Belgium

M. DUPAS
Royal Institute of Cultural Heritage
Jubelpark 1
Brussel 1040, Belgium

RESUME

Among the numerous works treating the conservation of historic monuments, most are devoted to the study of their stone, the various factors which provoke its alteration and the treatments to apply in its conservation. This is certainly justifiable as stone is the ground material of most historical monuments. However, the important role played by motars in constructions has gone mostly neglected, and this lack of knowledge concerning mortar has been the source of many technical and aesthetical errors occurring during restoration works. At the same time, this lack of data concerning mortars has also deprived historians and archaeologists from an important source of information in the study of the chronology of various kinds of constructions.

Conscious of the opportunity to mend this lack of attention, ICCROM organised a symposium in 1981 devoted to mortars, cements and grouts used in buildings. It organised a reunion of specialists anxious to exchange their knowledge and to set the groundwork for a research programme dealing with this area of investigation.

Mortars in constructions have been used for a long time, even before the Christian Era. Greeks and Romans used the first lime mortars for the construction of walls. They were made of fat lime and sand. To make them harder the Greeks added earth from Santorin to their mixtures, while the Romans added pozzolana. Sometimes these components were replaced by ground brick. Mortars prepared in these manners became less sensitive to the action of water, were harder and presented properties comparable with those of hydraulic mortars. The exceptional quality of Roman mortars was not only due to the addition of volcanic ash but primarily to the very elaborate technique used during the preparation of the lime and the mixture of all the components. With the abandonment of Roman techniques and traditions, mortars from the beginning of the Mediaeval Period presented poor quality, and it is only at the end of the XIVth Century that one finds again mortars with a good cohesion and care in their preparation.

Hydraulic limes appear during the XVIII Century, and mortars prepared with this type of matrix become harder, more coherent and more resistant to water than mortars prepared with fat lime. Discovered at the beginning of the XIXth Century, cements became more progressively used, substituting hydraulic limes in modern construction, because of their faster hardening property.

Both conservators and archaeologists are deeply interested in the various techniques used and the composition of mortars. This is especially so for the conservator who needs to reproduce an equivalent of the original mortar and whois not, only, interested in its original composition but also in its physical and mineralogical characteristics. The discovery of hydraulic matrices being rather late, the archaeologist will be mainly interested in lime mortars. He will want to find criteria which allows him to classify them in regard to dated mortars and will do this from analytical results realised using a great number of samples taken from the same site. The research as presented here will be centered on the character of the material, the nature and the proportions of the components.

Among the different limes used in construction, we can distinguish fat lime as being obtained from burning of pure limestone and that hydraulic lime was obtained by burning argillaceous limestone. Fat limes harden by absorption of atmospheric carbon dioxide: hydraulic ones contain a more of less important part of silicates and aluminates which harden in the presence of water.

Younger mortars are generally more hydraulic than older ones. The hydraulic index , which in fact is the ratio between the clay and lime faction, seems to be a useful parameter for classifying mortars.

Besides lime, mortar also contains sand. Often a mineral or organic aggregate is added to the mixture. Sands can either be argillaceous or calcareous. Aggregates are used to increase the volume of the mortar and to avoid cracks during the hardening. They are made up of left-over bricks, gravels, pebbles, stones (calcareous or not). Organic matter like blood, eggs, sugar, etc have also been added to the lime to increase the hardness of ancient mortars.

The chemist who has to analyse such a complex material is confronted with a lot of problems and one can realise that it is difficult to find a normalized analytical procedure capable of satisfying conservators and archaeologists. Each laboratory tries to apply a methodology best suite to funstion and selected in regard to the elements and criteria necessary.

There are many procedures to analyse mortars. They all have their advantages and drawbacks. Some are simple, being oriented to the determination of the principal components in the sample. If precautions are taken in the use of this method, it facilitates the examination of a great number of samples, and hence their rapid classification. While other more complex method are more informative to conservators and archaeologists and permit a better identification and determination of the type of lime used in the mixture, these methods take longer and are more expensive. The chemist in these cases has to evaluate each of the components and select the best method for satisying the requirements of the conservator or archaeologist.

It is well known that radiocarbon dating does not date archaeological events but only the materials found in an archaeological context. Hence, there may be an important interval between the age of the material and the archaeological event. A classical example of this is the ^{14}C dating of wooden beams used in construction. The ^{14}C dated tree rings can easily be a century or more older than the building itself. This problem becomes even more severe if we consider the possible re-use of material. This problem can be avoided by using mortar where present as a dating material.

Although lime mortars do not belong to the normal type of materials used in radiocarbon dating, such as bones, charcoal, peat, etc.,there is no theoretical objection for its use as a dating material. During the hardening process fat lime absorbs carbon dioxide (CO_2) from the atmosphere and is transformed into calcium carbonate $(CaCO_3)$. Although this chemical is completely different from the photosynthesis by plants, the result is the same: atmospheric carbon dioxide is incorporated in the material. After the absorpion is ended there is no exchange anymore with the atmosphere and the concentration of ^{14}C in the mortar will decrease due to the radioactive decay. Since the absorption time is normally very short compared to the statistical error on a radiocarbon date, the radiocarbon content is a good measure of the age of the construction. It is however true that the error on a (calibrated) radiocarbon date is rather large compared to dating methods used by historians. On the other hand, most of the big constructions (castles, churches, cathedrals) were built above older structures, and at the same time it took several hundreds of years to complete them. Historical records are mostly very vague about the exact location of earlier structures. By dating remains of older and younger parts of the building, it is possible to trace the original plan of construction and distinguish the younger parts, thus making dating possible by relative chronology.

Since 1964, several laboratories have tried to date mortar. A first attempt by Delibris and Labeyrie in France gave good results. However, in England Baxter and Walton as well as Stuiver and Smith in the United States tried the method and found the results were sometimes a thousand years too old. They traced the failure to the fact that calcareous sand (with an infinite old age) was used as an aggregate. The aggregate is in fact the main problem in mortar dating. A pollution of about 5% fossil or dead carbon increases the sample age by about 400 years. A second problem is the incomplete burning of the carbonate. Due to insufficient heating of the limestone, some old carbonate can remain in the produced lime. Besides the problem of fossil carbonate other minor problems in mortar dating are the incomplete carbonisation of the mortar and the use of reworked material.

In an attempt to eliminate the fossil carbon, Valastro found that there is a difference in appearance between atmospheric CO_2 and the fossil rock carbonate. The former tends to react faster with an acid solution than the latter. So by dating only the first CO_2 from the reaction, good results can be obtained. Still the results obtained by this method are questionable since the isotopic fractionation of the sample was normalised to the ^{13}C value of the atmosphere (-7°/oo) and not the standard value of -25°/oo.

Based on the same principle Van Strydonck et al dated not only the first CO_2 from the acid reaction, but several fractions. By doing this the presence of faossil carbonate in the sample could be made visible. The method has the advantag of being self-controlling. The slope of the curve representing the radiocarbon activity versus the % of CO_2 released by the acid reaction gives an indication of the amount of fossil carbonate in the sample. If this amount is particularly large then the radiocarbon date of the first fraction is in most cases unreliable.

Special attention is given to the isotopic fractionation. On theoretical grounds it should be possible to calculate the percentage of fossil carbonate in a mortar sample by measuring the ^{13}C value of *the sample. However due to kinetic effects the isotopic equilibrium between the carbonate and atmosphere is seldom reached. A systematic study of this effect was first undertaken by Pachiaudi et al on a laboratory scale and by Van Strydonck et al on a test site. The results showed that the partial pressure of the atmospheric CO_2 in the freshly made lime and the compactness of the mortar are dominant factors in the isotopic shift.*

Related to the mortar dating are other studies undertaken by Stuiver and Waldren and Van Strydonck and Waldren on the Post Talayotic prehistoric lime burials from the island of Mallorca. The Balearic islands of Mallorca and Menorca are the only known places where quicklime burials occur in prehistory and where the custom of inhumanation in quicklime was quite popular during the Iron Ages. Although the lime in these burials and in conventional mortar are made by the same process some differences do appear in the radiocarbon and ^{13}C curves. These differences are caused by the fact that the burials are an open system, much more effected by rain and groundwater, along with the fact that they contain a very large volume of lime.

The Classification and Dating of Lime Mortars
By Chemical Analysis and Radiocarbon Dating: A Review
M. Van Strydonck and M. Dupas

INTRODUCTION

For many years the conservation of monuments and archaeological sites has been the subject of a vast number of research projects. The continuous degradation of the world architectural patrimony urged scientists to concentrate their efforts on the study of the construction materials and their behaviour, primarily, in a polluted atmosphere. As a result of their research a lot of papers were presented during international conferences on the chemical, physical and biological factors that influence the alteration of stone and on the techniques of stone conservation.

Although a lot of attention was drawn to the study of construction materials one has to admit that the important role of mortar has been overlooked for many years. However, these materials contribute essentially to the life of a building, its stability, its harmony. It cannot be denied that this lack of knowledge sometimes brought about errors, technical as well as aesthetical, since the restorer - ignoring the original composition of the mortar and its properties - was not capable of reproducing the original mortar. This lack of interest for mortars deprived historians and archaeologists from an important source of information in the study of the chronology of building construction. The characterization of well located and dated mortars helps the archaeologist as well as the restorer to establish a classification of the mortars and distinguish the different construction campaigns.

Aware of the urgent need to fill this gap, ICCROM organized a symposium in 1981 on mortars and binders used in ancient buildings.

In this paper the different types of mortar used in ancient construction will be presented. Their composition as well as the possibilities given to the analyst to characterize the mortar will be reviewed. Radiocarbon dating of mortars will also be discussed. Although the principle of radiocarbon dating will not be explained, an initiation in the basic isotope geochemistry of mortar carbonate will be given. The limitations of this dating method as well as the aims of further research will be described. This critical examination of the different methods will enable the researcher to choose the methods best suitable to his purpose.

THE HISTORY OF MORTAR

The use of mortar in construction goes back to ancient times. Before the advent of the Grecian and Roman civilisations walls were assembled by means of a mortar that consisted primarily of clay and earth. This earth sometimes contained remains of burned bones and plaster

$(CaSO_4.0.5\ H_2O)$. In order to agglomerate the whole, water and sometimes organic material was added to this mixture. It is almost certain that lime didn't occur in those rudimentary compositions (Furian and Bissegger 1975).

Lucas found that the ancient Egyptian mortar taken from the Sphynx and the pyramid of Cheops (IVth dynasty, c. 2600 BC) consists of plaster. The analytical results of about 15 samples indicated the presence of a sometimes even important quantity of calcium carbonate, which can also be found in Egyptian plaster made at the beginning of this century. From these analyses it was clear that the Egyptians didn't use lime in their preparation, but that the presence of $CaCO_3$ in the mortar was due to an impurity in the plaster (Lucas 1906).

The first real use of lime mortars in the construction of buildings goes back to the first century BC. Those early Greek and Roman mortars were made of lime and fine sand. To make the mortar harder, additives like volcanic ash were added to the mixture. The Greeks used Santorin earth while the Romans used Pozzolana (Furlan and Bissegger 1975). When these materials became exhausted they were replaced by baked clay, tiledust and crushed brick which, as an additional effect, gave a special colour to the composition. Mortars made in this way were less sensitive to water and showed properties comparable to modern day mortars based on hydraulic binders. For this reason they were used to assure the water-tightness of cisterns in the construction of aqueducts, etc. Although the Greeks only occasionally used mortars, in the Roman Period it became an essential part of the architecture, as shown in the solidity of the buildings.

It is mainly through Vitruvius that the first recipes of Roman mortar fabrication came to us. Sand and slaked lime were the primary constituents of the mixture. Vitruvius describes the conditions required for the use of these components and insists that care be taken with the preparation of the mixture. He also describes the properties of the Pozzolana which makes the mortar much harder and resistant against water.

Many authors have studied Roman mortars. Like most of them Frizot concludes that the exceptional quality of those mortars is not only caused by the use of volcanic ash, but also due to a very elaborate fabrication of the lime, to the choice of the constituents and to the care that was taken in making a very homogeneous mixture of aggregate and binder (Frizot 1977). This high quality Roman mortar is not only found in building but also in supports of wall paintings of that epoch (de Henau and Dupas 1982).

Although there exists a great number of documents informing us about the Grecian and Roman mortars, archives hardly tell us anything about Medieval mortars. For this reason scientists had to call in chemical analyses to give or to complete the information about the composition of these mortars.

Due to the abandoning of Roman techniques and traditions the early Medieval mortars are in general friable and of a mediocre quality. Inside the walls the mortar was not compressed in the way the Romans did, which made the structures rather fragile.

The use of organic materials in Medieval mortars is contested. It is supposed that the ancient builders used organic additions to make the mortar more compact and less exposed to the action of water. However, German research effected on mortars from the XIth to the XVIIth century didn't show any trace of animal proteins in Medieval mortar (de Bouard 1975). It seems that the mortar quality becomes better from the XIIth century to the end of the Middle Ages. But it would be imprudent to say that a mortar of mediocre quality is necessarily an old one. In Poland for instance, mortars from the Xth and XIth century are often well preserved. They consist of lime and calcium carbonate which replaces the sand as an aggregate. But at the same time, in the beginning of the XIth century, some mortars were made of lime and very fine sand, which are also preserved very well (Jedrzejewska 1960).

In general, mortars have a better quality when the preparation technique of the lime and the mixtures are very elaborated. Usually we find this only from the beginning of the XIVth century on, when mortars regain a good cohesion and are made with sands that contain no earth or clay.

Although it is doubted that organic material was used, it is very certain that Medieval mortars contain tiledust and crushed brick. The hydraulic properties of these materials were known by the Medieval constructors. The investigation of a great number of archaeological mortar samples from the choir of the church at Theux (Belgium) shows that bricks were used in the preparation of Merovingian and Carolingian mortars (Dupas 1986).

It is in the beginning of the second half of the XVIIIth century that hydraulic binders appear. The hardening of these binders is provoked by water while fat limes harden by absorption of carbon dioxide from the atmosphere. Mortars made with a hydraulic binder have better cohesion and have a better resistance to water than those made with fat lime.

The discovery of cement in the beginning of the XIXth century was an important step ahead in the search for better construction materials. Cement mortars present a very important mechanical resistance and are very stable against water. Thanks to these properties cement replaced hydraulic lime in modern construction. However, its use in restorations is not recommended, since cement is not very porous and prevents the passage of water vapour through the joints. This can cause damage to the construction materials. The dirty grey colour of the cement is also seldom in harmony with the old construction. Above all it provokes the appearance of soluble salts, which is dangerous for the conservation of the stone (Peroni *et al.* 1981).

THE MORTAR CONSTITUENTS

Mortars are made by mixing sand with a paste of water and a binder. This binder can be fat lime, hydraulic lime or a cement (Anstett 1948).

THE BINDERS

Fat limes are obtained by heating at 850-900°C more or less pure limestone, that contains no more than 6% of clayey materials ($CaCO_3$ + heat = CaO + CO_2gas). The quicklime (CaO) is then slaked with a minimal quantity of water and transforms into hydrated lime (CaO + H_2O = $Ca(OH)_2$). The hardening happens during the absorption of carbon dioxide from the atmosphere ($Ca(OH)_2$ + CO_2atm. in presence of water = $CaCO_3$ + H_2O). Mortars from fat lime have a poor mechanical resistance. They harden very slowly and superficially. For this reason their use is nowadays limited to restoration works (Peroni *et al.* 1981).

Hydraulic limes are obtained by heating calcareous stones that contain an important clay fraction. During the heating the lime reacts with the clay fraction and gives hydraulic silicates and aluminates. According to the clay content, more or less hydraulic limes are obtained. The hydraulic part of this type of lime hardens due to a reaction with water and not by the absorption of carbon dioxide.

Cements are the ground products obtained by heating at high temperature a mixture of limestone and clay in well defined proportions. These binders have a very high hydraulicity.

They harden essentially in the presence of water. By mixing with different additives, different types of cement can be made.

THE SANDS

Different types of sand can be used in the preparation of mortars.

Calcareous sand derives from limestone and can contain a certain amount of clay.

Siliceous sand is mainly quartz.

Granitic sand contains, besides quartz, feldspar and micas.

The quality of the mortar depends not only on the nature but also on the shape of the sand grains and most of all on the granulometric composition. Mortars made with very fine sand are mostly very porous and not very resistant. It seems that the best mortars are made with sand in which the volume of the large grains is twice the volume of the small ones. Sand containing clay dust and earth is not recommended (Anstett 1948).

THE AGGRATE

Apart from a binder and sand, mortar may contain additional products, either from organic or mineralogic origin. The most common mineral aggregates are: volcanic ash (Pozzolana), gravel, pieces of brick, and small stones (calcareous or not). They were used to increase the hydraulic properties of the mortar, to enlarge the volume and most of all to avoid cracks. These mortars look very much like concrete.

In different periods, even after the Middle Ages, organic materials were added to the mixture. It ensured a better cohesion and made the mortar harder. The most common natural products added were ox blood, sugar, glair, urine, etc. (Sickels 1981). The addition of organic matter into the mortar is now replaced by synthetic resins appropriate to the specific use of the mortar.

THE CLASSIFICATION OF MORTARS

The question to reproduce an old mortar or plaster usually arrives during restoration works. The restorer wants to know not only the composition of the mortar, but also its mineralogic and physical properties: nature of the binder, nature and granulometric properties of the sand, porosity, etc. The archaeologist is not so interested in the technical aspects of the mortar. He wants to find, from the examination of different samples taken on a site, criterions that make it possible to distinguish different construction phases.

The chemist will focus his examination on the analyses of the most important components of the mortar. This investigation is not simple and one has to be careful not to draw conclusions too easily. Differences in composition do not always mean a different construction period. It is very well possible that during the construction materials were used from a different origin and location. Of course this makes the research very complex and the problems can only be solved when there is good cooperation between the archaeologist and the analyst (de Bouard 1975).

The validity of the analyses depends in the first place on a carefully executed sampling. Some old mortars are very heterogeneous. This makes sampling sometimes a very delicate operation. Isolated samples, which are not representative of the whole have no scientific value. H.

Jedrzejewska has defined the condition of sampling in a paper which is a very important reference for the analysis (Jedrzejewska 1967, 1981).

In spite of the fact that Roman mortars have a certain hydraulicity due to the Pozzolana or tiledust, it has been noticed that, in general, younger mortars are more hydraulic than older ones. This is because the hydraulic binders, invented in the XVIIIth century, little by little replaced the fat lime in mortar. The hydraulic index that gives the ratio between the clay fraction and the lime fraction is in fact an excellent criterion to classify mortars (Leduc and Chenu 1912) (fig. 1B).

$$\text{The hydraulic index} = \frac{Al_2O_3 + Fe_2O_3 + SiO_2 \text{ soluble}}{CaO + MgO}$$

The ratio CaO/MgO is also a criterion to classify mortars. Since these products are the basic components of a mortar, a change in the ratio means a change of the raw materials used. Although this change does not always indicate a change of period it surely gives important information about the construction (fig. 1A).

Other criteria for classification don't rely on the chemical composition but on visual aspects. A petrographic examination makes it possible to indicate the amount of limestone in a sand and define the aggregate. Microscopic analyses can give information about the constituents and prove the presence of hydraulic products. The macroscopic examination, although very simple, gives very precious information about the granulometry and the nature of the sand, the colour and the form of the aggregate, the homogeneity, the cohesion and the general aspect of the mortar.

THE MORTAR ANALYSES

THE VISUAL ANALYSIS

The visual analyses sometimes contribute more to the classification of mortars than the chemical analyses. Let's illustrate this with an example. During the examination of the archaeological mortars from the church of the Saints "Hermes et Alexandre" in Theux, it has been found that the Merovingian and Carolingian mortars were made with a river gravel, characterized by small round pebbles. It is only from the romanesque period on that one finds well defined sands in the mortar, to which angular stones were added. In more recent samples black calcareous waste is added that came from a nearby quarry (fig. 2).

In the Merovingian and Carolingian mortars some remainders of bricks were found, proving that perhaps the Roman tradition was not abandoned completely (Dupas 1986; Charola *et al.* 1984).

In general one can say that within one group of samples, all kinds of visible properties can be used as a criterion for classification.

THE CHEMICAL ANALYSIS

It is clear that ancient mortars are very complex materials. This makes it extremely difficult for the analyst to define a normalized analytical procedure. As a consequence, each laboratory uses its own methodology, oriented to its proper needs.

A common method is making a melt with sodium potassium carbonate ($NaKCO_3$). With this technique it is only possible to obtain limited information. The results are given as oxides of the different components (e.g: CaO, MgO, etc.). One cannot tell whether those elements come from the binder or from the aggregate. It is also impossible to trace down the origin of the silicon and therefore the hydraulicity remains unknown.

Methods using hydrochloric acid (HCl) to decompose the mortar are much more interesting. The dissolution can be carried out with a cold or a hot solvent.

The last method uses a 10% (vol.) HCl solution, that is heated rather fast until a yellow colour appears. After filtration of the hot solution a residue is left on the filter. This residue is attacked by a sodium carbonate (Na_2CO_3) solution. The residue of this attack is then treated with sodium potassium carbonate to determine the insoluble silicon. The soluble silicon, which is one of the parameters in the hydraulic index, is obtained by subtracting the soluble silicon from the total silicon. This last one is measured in a melt with sodium potassium carbonate on an aliquot sample. This method is very accurate, but very elaborate (Voinovitch *et al.* 1962)

The methods using a cold solution are the most common. The sample is attacked by a diluted hydrochloric acid solution. The insoluble is considered to be quartz and clay. The soluble silicon, needed to calculate the hydraulic index, is only obtained in very specific conditions. The most simple "cold" method is the one used by Jedrzejewska. Only three parameters are defined: the amount of carbon dioxide, the amount of sand and soluble materials. As reagent a solution of 50% (vol.) hydrochloric acid is used. The amount of carbon dioxide (CO_2) is given as calcium carbonate ($CaCO_3$) and the residue is considered to be the sand. The soluble materials are the difference between 100% and the sum of the two other components (Jedrzejewska 1960). This method made it possible to analyse a lot of Polish mortars and to classify them according to different periods from the Xth to the XVIth century. However, this interesting method has some drawbacks.

> It does not take into account the presence of $MgCO_3$, which can be very important in Dolomite limes.

> The hydraulic silicates are not the only components of the "soluble" fraction as this author makes us suppose.

Magnesium and soluble salts can be a part of this fraction and may thus be wrongly considered as an hydraulic constituent.

Another very simple method is the one developed by E.B. Cliver. Three values are measured by gravimetrical analyses: the soluble fraction, the sand fraction and the fine residue fraction. The colour of this fine fraction enables the author to determine the nature of it. The method makes it possible to calculate the percentages of three fractions, namely the lime fraction, the sand and one of the three following constituents: Portland cement, natural cement or clay (Cliver 1974). J. Stewart and J. Moore tested this procedure on synthetic mortars. The results are not very encouraging. There seems to be qualitative as well as quantitative errors and the method is not very reliable (Stewart and Moore 1981).

The more elaborate methods all use more complex chemical techniques and apparatus.

D. Dufournier from the "Centre de Recherches archéologiques médiévales de Caen" developed a method which takes 10 parameters into account: 4 determining the properties of the carbonate, the sand, the clay and the stones, the other 6 are established from the granulometric composition of the sand. A microscopic examination of the sand or even of the raw mortar gives information about the constituents and completes the analyses. The chemical analysis is limited to the determination of the carbon dioxide fraction, expressed as calcium carbonate. The fraction of the untreated, broken mortar lumps that doesn't pass a 2mm sieve is considered as stones. An acid treatment is applied to the fraction that passed the 2mm sieve. The residue of this attack is considered to be the sand fraction. The amount of clay is defined as the difference between 100% and the total of the calcium carbonate and the sand (Dufournier 1972). Although the granulometric analysis proposed by the author is very complete, there is a lot of criticism on the chemical analyses.

> As in the method of Jedrzejewska calcium carbonate is considered to be the only carbonate. In that respect the author suggests at least one complete mortar analysis for each building to be examined.

> The amount of carbon dioxide is measured in the fraction smaller than 2mm, while the sand and clay fraction are measured in a second sample. Due to the inhomogeneity of old mortars this procedure can cause important errors in the calculation of the different portions.

> The difference between 100% and the total of the calcium carbonate and the sand represents not only the clay fraction but also the soluble salts and the hydraulic silicoaluminates which are often found in more recent mortars.

A.E. Charola and M. Dupas worked out a method while they were studying the mortars from the archaeological excavation of the church at Theux. The oldest samples came from a Merovingian chapel and the most recent from a XIXth century restoration. The proposed method is derived from an analytical procedure that differentiates between the hydraulic and the non-hydraulic silicates (Dupas 1981).

A visual examination gives a rough classification of the samples, by means of the texture of the material and the nature and appearance of the aggregate. The use of X-ray diffraction, IR-spectrometry and scanning electron microscope gives additional information about the mineralogical composition. The investigation of the results obtained by chemical and physical examination of the samples leads to a system of equations that enables the analyst to calculate the composition of the mortar (Charola *et al.* 1984). The parameters required for this method are:

> the determination of the total silicon
> the amount of carbon dioxide
> the fraction insoluble in a 20% (vol.) HC1 solution
> the amount of Ca and Mg
> the amount of free lime (CaO)

The method has been tested on standardized mortars with a well known composition and is considered very reliable (Dupas and Charola 1986).

(SEE TABLES 1 AND 2)

Although the analytical methods give a good idea about the composition of a mortar, microscopic analyses should not be overlooked. Additional information can be obtained about, for instance, the presence of Pozzolana and tiledust which give the mortar a certain hydraulicity that could wrongly be appropriated to a hydraulic lime (Frizot 1981).

In the same group of methods another one should be mentioned. Ciach and Osler made different investigations on medieval mortars from Poland. They used macroscopic and microscopic analyses, chemical analyses, and also all kinds of methods to investigate the physical properties of the mortar such as its porosity, resistance, etc. It is a very complete method but very elaborate and not applicable on a great number of samples (Ciach and Osler 1972).

Among the great variety of methods to investigate mortar there is a special group oriented to the determination of the amount of cement in the mixture. They are applicable to modern materials and not very compatible with archaeological samples. To mention a few:

The technique used by the "American Society for Testing and Materials" that measures the quantity of cement in concrete. By gravimetric methods the content of soluble silicon is measured. Knowing that Portland cement contains 21% soluble silicon, the concentration of cement in the concrete can be calculated. This procedure has been tested on a series of synthetic mortars (Stewart and Moore 1981). The only good results were obtained when all the soluble silicon came from cement. Used in the study of old mortars, important deflections were noticed.

The procedure established by E. Dugniolle is based on the Belgian Standard for the analysis of hardened concrete. Considering that a cement P 300 contains about 20.5% of SiO_2 and 64% of CaO, the amount of cement is calculated by three parameters:

1. the amount of soluble silicon
2. the amount of CaO
3. the difference between 100% and the sum of the % of all the elements not belonging to the cement.

This method distinguishes itself primarily from the others by the conditions of the attack of the sample by the acid. The working conditions are very tight. The temperature must be maintained between 0 and 3°C. Although this method was originally not intended to serve the archaeologist, it seems to be very useful when some minor changes are made, especially in the way the results are presented.

RADIOCARBON DATING OF LIME MORTARS

PRINCIPAL OF LIME DATING.

The radiocarbon dating technique is based on the fact that a certain amount of radioactive carbon (^{14}C) is produced in the atmosphere. This radiocarbon reacts with atmospheric oxygen to form carbon dioxide (CO_2). Due to photosynthesis this radioactivity comes into the biosphere and enters the biological carbon cycle. This means that, in first approximation, all biologically produced carbon can be dated by radiocarbon (peat, bone, wood charcoal, textile, seeds, shells, etc.). In paragraph 3.1, it has been shown that fat lime hardens through the uptake of atmospheric carbon dioxide. Since, in this case, the carbon source is also the atmosphere, the radiocarbon content of lime mortar reflects the atmospheric concentration of the time at which the construction was made. A valid radiocarbon measurement can only be made if the absorption time of carbon dioxide (in other words the reaction time) is short compared with the radioactive decay of the radiocarbon (half life of 5730 years). This is true for most common organic materials such as wood, charcoal, seeds, etc. The reaction time for mortar is usually shorter than a decade.

CONTAMINATION

The first attempts to date lime by radiocarbon go back to the early sixties. Delibrias and Labeyrie obtained good results on mortar from the Château de la Madeleine and also from a Roman aqueduct. Their method was very simple: carbon dioxide was extracted from the mortar by heating the limecarbonate at 900°C. This gas was then used as a countergas in a proportional counter (Delibrias and Labeyrie 1965). The dating method was tested by Stuiver and Smith (Stuiver and Smith 1965) and Baxter and Walton (Baxter and Walton 1970). The release of the carbon dioxide gas was obtained by acid hydroloysis of the sample. They found dates that were far too old (e.g. Conway Town Wall: true age 665 years, radiocarbon age 2012 ± 53 BP).

This discrepancy between real age and radiocarbon age (even calibrated) can have many causes. First of all the limestone must be completely dead-burned before use; otherwise infinitely old carbonate from the bedrock will remain in the mortar. Although in the ancient lime kiln the temperature was high enough to degas the limestone completely, tests have shown that it takes about 15 hours to calcinate a 20cm carbonate lump. It was suggested that a previous microscopic examination for the presence of foraminifera could indicate whether the calcination was complete or not.

A second possible source of contamination is the sand. Sometimes calcareous sands were mixed with the lime. This carbonate also has an infinite old age and depletes the radiocarbon content of the mortar sample. The use of different types of sand is strongly related to the geological and economical situation which determines the nature and the origin of the sand. The contamination can also come from the aggregate. In most cases this contaminant can be separated from the mortar.

Walls can be either very porous or very dense. In some cases wind blows through the clefts of the walls, while other walls are completely impermeable. If the mortar is far inside a joint, it is possible that the lime never comes into contact with the atmosphere so that even after several centuries some lime is still present (Sonninen *et al.* 1985; Erämetsä, in prep.) This can only harm the radiocarbon dating if, in a later period, this lime comes into contact with the atmosphere due to the destruction of a part of the wall or during sampling.

Running water containing dissolved carbon dioxide can also cause a supplementary deposit on the mortar or an exchange in carbonate ions.

Examples of this contamination were also given by Willaime (Willaime *et al.* 1983) and Berger (Berger, in prep.).

SAMPLE PRETREATMENT

The aim of the pretreatment of the sample is to separate the lime carbonate from the pollutants as well as possible. First of all, care must be taken during sampling. The surface layer, continually exposed to the changing weather conditions, has to be removed. Also, one has to be sure that no restoration mortar is present.

THE VOLK AND VALSTRO METHOD

The method consists of a separation of mortar and aggregate by gently breaking the mortar lumps and rubbing the live white mortar powder from the aggregate. This powder is then poured through a series of sieves. The larger sand and aggregate grains will be separated from the mortar. This has to be checked by microscopic analysis. As an alternative the powder can be brought into a suspension which is passed through a 230 mesh screen. The fine mortar stays in the supernatant liquid which can be recuperated after decantation and will be dried before use (Folk and Valastro 1975, 1976 and 1979).

THE METHOD USED BY THE ROYAL INSTITUTE OF CULTURAL HERITAGE

This method is the same as the previous one, in so far that the mortar is gently broken into small pieces. All aggregate grains and doubtful materials are discarded. The powder that remains is ground and sieved through a 0.25mm sieve and dried. Each sample gets an "appearance parameter" (+ = favourable conditions, - = unfavourable conditions) on its homogeneity, solidity, amount of nodules and the possibility of separating the lime from the aggregate. A small part of the sample is chemically analysed to measure the CO_2 content of the sample and to know whether the carbonization is complete or not (Van Strydonck *et al.* 1983, 1983 and 1986).

For a conventional radiocarbon dating both methods need a lot of material. A normal sample size weighs at least 2kg. With this type of pretreatment it remains impossible to eliminate all of the pollution if the sample contains a very important fraction of fossil carbonate.

THE DATING OF DIFFERENT FRACTIONS

Baxter has already mentioned that there is a difference in appearance between the lime carbonate and the fossil rock carbonate. The former is fine-grained, powdery and porous and tends to react more quickly to the acid solution than the latter. By dating only the first part of the CO_2 that evolved by the reaction, the influence of the contaminating harder rock carbonate can be avoided. Valastro obtained very good results with this method (Table 3) (Malone *et al.* 1980). However, the procedure is questionable since he corrected the isotopic fractionation (see note 1) of the results to the wrong standard value (Evin 1983; Stuiver and Polach 1977). Also no good definition of the "first part" or "first fraction" was given.

(SEE TABLE 3)

To overcome this problem a method was designed by Van Strydonck *et al.* by which more fractions could be dated (fig. 3). Depending on the amount of samples available, four or more fractions are dated. The procedure is as follows: while constantly stirring, a HC1-solution is slowly added to the mortar powder, which is held in suspension in CO_2 free water. The amount of acid added to the mortar is just enough to release a known quantity of carbon dioxide (CO_2) from the mortar. There exist two alternative versions of the method (fig. 4). In the oldest version, the CO_2 was released completely from the first batch of the sample ($\eta=100\%$), from the second batch only the first 50% ($\eta=50\%$) was taken, from the next batch only the first 30% ($\eta=30$), etc. Instead of measuring fractions in an accumulated order in different batches, in the second version successive fractions are dated in one batch. So less material was needed and more fractions could be dated. With this second procedure the arbitrary choice of a fraction could be more or less overcome.

In Figures 5 and 6 two examples are given. One curve ($\delta^{13}C$) represent the isotopic fractionation of each fraction in function of the yield of the acid reaction (at the left the result for the first CO_2 released in the reaction at the right the result for the total sample = 100%). The other curve is the normalized sample radioactivity (the natural logarithm of this value multiplied by 8033 gives the radiocarbon age). The line representing the sample activity shows that the amount of fossil carbonate that reacted with the acid is more important near the end of the reaction, resulting in older fraction ages at higher yields of the reaction. The best radiocarbon date is obtained by extrapolating the activity line to $\eta=0$, because at that point the influence of the fossil carbonate will be minimum. The slope of the activity line gives an idea of the amount of fossil carbonate in the sample. If this amount is too important (more than a few %) the method will fail in eliminating the fossil carbonate completely. However, the method has the advantage that we can see, by means of the slope of the activity line, when the radiocarbon dates are questionable. In a sense the method is self-controlling. In the first example the slope is very weak, meaning that there is hardly any fossil carbonate present and the radiocarbon date should be good. In the second sample however, the slope indicates the presence of an important fraction of fossil carbonate.

The isotopic values occur in a very particular way, which could not be explained until very recently.

THE ABSORPTION OF ATMOSPHERIC CARBON DIOXIDE IN LIME DURING MORTAR FORMATION

From laboratory tests on small samples (Craig 1953; Ergin *et al.* 1970; Pachiaudi *et al.* 1986) it is known that during the absorption of carbon dioxide (CO_2) from the atmosphere, the $\delta^{13}C$

shifts from about -8°/oo in the atmosphere to about -21°/oo in the carbonate. This is a very important shift. In real mortars however all kinds of values have been measured from -22 up to about -5°/oo (Ambers 1987). This shift cannot be explained only by the presence of fossil carbonate. If this were true, then the isotopic curves in Figures 5 and 6 should have the same shape as the activity line. In figure 5 there is hardly any fossil carbonate present and still there is a shift in $\delta^{13}C$ through the fractions.

The problem was solved (Van Strydonck *et al.* in prep.) by measuring the absorption rate and isotopic fractionation in a mortar pillar, made from analytically pure $CaO + H_2O$ and SiO_2. Figure 7 shows the degree of carbonatisation in a 12cm pillar after being set in open air for about one year (in a rather unpolluted surrounding near the village of Vlimmeren, Belgium) and figure 8 shows the isotopic fractionation in the same pillar. The curves are drawn in the same way as the isotopic curves in figures 5 and 6. From these tests could be concluded that the absorption of CO_2 can be described as a first order reaction, during which the reaction kinetics are controlled by the exhaustion of one of the reagents (the CO_2). Here this exhaustion is not a function of time, but of depth. The rate controlling step cannot be the chemical reaction itself. Figure 9 shows all possible reactions that can take place, but since there is an excess of $Ca(OH)_2$ in the system the pH is maintained at approximately 11. As a consequence all CO_2 that goes into solution will precipitate immediately as $CaCO_3$. The only parameter left is the diffusion rate. This diffusion rate will be a function of the partial pressure of the CO_2 in the atmosphere, the permeability of the mortar and the amount of $Ca(OH)_2$ in the sample. The curve on figure 7 shows an inflexion at about 65 to 70% of Ca converted in carbonate, meaning a change in reaction rate. This is caused by a change in the diffusion of the CO_2 through the pillar because the mortar becomes more dense during the hardening process.

The isotopic variation through the pillar is explained as a Rayleigh-type diffusion, supposing a constant reequilibration between the relative concentration of the products in the liquid and in the gas phase. The dashed line in figure 9 gives the theoretical curve for Rayleigh diffusion in a closed system. However the mortar pillar is an open system which makes the values less outspoken. The fact that even in the completely carbonated mortars the shape of this isotopic

15

shift remains, means that the mortar inside the walls becomes isolated from the atmosphere and does not exchange carbon dioxide with the atmosphere.

To make the picture complete, we also have to mention a possible recarbonatisation. In normal mortar samples this does not occur since they are isolated from groundwater. In Mallorcan lime burials however this phenomenon has been noticed (Stuiver and Waldren 1975; Waldren 1982; Van Strydonck and Waldren in print). This recarbonatisation can make the first fraction younger or older depending on the source of the carbon dioxide in the water. In the case of the Mallorcan samples (fig. 10) the sample became younger. The Mallorcan samples showed also that the Rayleigh diffusion model is not valid on large pure lime lumps. This is confirmed by some absorption tests on pure lime.

The Mallorcan and Vlimmeren samples made it possible to draw a model for the carbon dioxide absorption. In figure 11 the age and the isotopic fractionation are given in function of the carbonatisation supposing that the mortar occurs as a spherical grain. Figure 11a gives a situation for a mortar grain that is completely free of fossil carbonate. In figure 11b some fossil carbonate is still present. In reality the mortar does not appear as a spherical grain. SEM pictures have shown that during mortar formation lime crystals ($Ca(OH)_2$) are glued together and form a more complex carbonate structure (Figure 12). The model however seems to be valid and can be adapted to special situations (very slow absorption of CO_2, recarbonatisation by younger CO_3^{--}, etc.).

CONCLUSION

The comparison of old mortars by means of chemical anaylses or radiocarbon dating is not a simple research due to the fact that mortar is a very complex and heterogeneous material even if only the two major components, binder and sand, are considered. Old mortars may contain all kinds of materials, which make the use of specific techniques necessary. It is obvious that there is no standard technique for the analysis of such type of material, even when all the samples come from the same building or site.

In most cases the constituents of the mortar come from the neighbourhood of the site. It is very well possible that, even within the same construction period, the origin of the constituents changes. So it is very incautious to draw conclusions from only this one parameter.

The heterogeneity of the mortar makes it very difficult to take a representative sample.

Upon the chemical and physical analyses, the visual analyses give a lot of information, microscopic as well as macroscopic. The macroscopic analyses give very important information about the general aspect and the form of the aggregate.

All the discussed methods have advantages and disadvantages, even gaps. It is the task of the chemist-archaeologist to choose a method appropriate to his needs. Still all results must be interpreted with care in close collaboration between the chemist and the archaeologist.

The radiocarbon dating technique of mortars is not yet a standard procedure. We only just know the different processes that are involved. The most important question is how to avoid fossil carbonate. Slightly or not contaminated samples can be dated without any problem if sufficient material is present. The future of mortar dating lies in the use of the Accelerated Mass Spectrometry (AMS) as a dating tool. With this machine milligram size samples can be dated which makes it possible to date only the pure mortar dust and avoid all contamination. It is expected that the first results of this AMS mortar dating will become available in 1989.

ACKNOWLEDGEMENTS

The authors wish to thank Dr. Wouters and Mr. Cillis (KBIN, Brussels) for the SEM pictures and Mrs. Theuns for the help in preparing this manuscript.

NOTE:

Isotope fractionation gives an expression of the ratio $^{13}C/^{12}C$. It is expressed as:

$$\delta^{13}C = \frac{(^{13}C/^{12}C)_{sample} - (^{13}C/^{12}C)_{standard}}{(^{13}C/^{12}C)_{standard}} \times 1000$$

This value can shift due to physical and chemical processes. In the atmosphere it is about -8⁰/oo, in oak about -25⁰/oo and in papyrus about -13⁰/oo.

The $\delta^{14}C$ is twice the $\delta^{13}C$. If samples are not corrected for isotope fractionation this means an error if age of: $(\delta^{13}C + 25) \times 16$.

BIBLIOGRAPHY

Ambers, J., 1987, Stable Carbon Isotope Ratios and Their Relevance to the Determination of Accurate Date for Lime Mortars. *Journal of Archaeological Science* 14:569-576.

Anstett, F.,1948, *Essai et Analyse des Matériaux de Construction et de Travaux Publics, Tome I, Matériaux de Maçonnerie,* 4e éd., Paris:Eyrolles. 243p.

Baxter, M.S., and Walton, A.,1970, Radiocarbon Datings of Mortars. *Nature* 225:937-938.

Berger, R. (in prep), Early Medieval Irish Buildings: Dating by Mortar. *^{14}C and Archaeology*, Conference Held at Groningen, 1987.

Charola, A.E., Dupas, M., Sheryll, R.P., and Freund, G.G.,1984, Characterization of Ancient Mortars: Chemical and Instrumental Methods. In *Scientific Methodologies Applied to Works of Art.* Proc. of the International Symposium, Florence, pp. 28-33.

Ciach, T.D., and Osler, S.,1972, Recherches sur les Mortiers de Haut Moyen Age Provenant des Pavements des Anciens Monuments de Wislica. *Momentum* VIII:55-69.

Cliver, E.B.,1974, Tests for analysis of Mortar Samples. *Bulletin of the Association of Preservation Technology* VI, 1:68-73.

Craig, H.,1953, The Geochemistry of the Stable Carbon Isotopes. *Geochim et Cosmochim Acta* 3:53.

de Bouard, M.,1975, Manuel d'Archéologie Médievale. *Société d'Édition d'Enseignement Supérieur*, pp.59-61. Paris.

de Henau, P., and Dupas, M.,1982, Contribution à l'Étude des Peintures Murales de la Villa Hadriana à Tivoli. In *Caractérisation, Datation, Technique de la Peinture Antique.* Proc. of the III Rencontres Internationales d'Archéologie et d'Histoire d'Antibes, pp. 99-107.

Delibrias, G., and Labeyrie, J.,1965, The Dating of Mortars by the Carbon-14 Method. In *Proc. of the 6th International Conference on ^{14}C and Tritium Dating,* edited by Chatters, R.M. and E.A. Olson. Washington, D.C., Clearinghouse for Fed. Sci. & Tech. Inf., Natural Bur. Standards, U.S. Dept. Commerce. pp. 344-347.

Dufournier, D.,1972, Sur le Méthode d'Analyse des Mortiers Anciens et son Application. *Archéologie Médiévale* II:325-345.

Dugniolle, E.,1975, L'Analyse des Mortiers de Maçonnerie. *Revue de Centre Scientifique et Technique de la Construction* 3, Sept.:26-30.

Dupas, M.,1981, L'Analyse des Mortiers et Enduits des Peintures Murales et des Bâtiments Anciens. In *Mortars, Cements and grouts Used in the Conservation of Historic Buildings*. Proc. of the Symposium, ICCROM, Rome. pp. 281-295.

Dupas, M.,1986, Analyse des Mortiers Prélevés dans l'Église de Theux. In L'Église-Halle des Saints Hermes et Alexandre à Theux, Histoire et Archéologie d'un Édifice Singulier, edited by Bertholet, P. and P. Hoffsummer. *Bulletin de la Société Verviétoise d'Archéologie et d'Histoire* LXV:266-273.

Dupas, M., and Charola, A.E.,1986, A Simplified Chemical Analysis System for the Characterization of Mortars. In *Materials Science and Restoration*. Proc. of the 2nd International Colloquium, Esslingen. pp. 309-312.

Erämetsä, P., Gustavsson, K., Sonninen, E., and Jungner, H., (in prep.) Radiocarbon Dating of Mortar and Thermoluminiscence Dating of Bricks from Aland. *^{14}C and Archaeology*. Conference held at Groningen. 1987.

Ergin, M., Harkness, D.D., and Walton, A.,1970, Glasgow University Radiocarbon Measurements II. *Radiocarbon* 12:486-495.

Evin, J., 1983, Materials of Terrestrial Origin, in Mook, W.G. and Waterbolk, H.T., eds, 14C and Archaeology, Pro: *PACT* 8, pp.235-276.

Folk, R.L. and Valastro, S., 1975, Radiocarbon Dating of Mortars at Stobi, in Studies in the Antiguities of Stobi, *Belgrade* 2, pp.29-412.

Folk, R.L. and Valastro, S., 1976, Successful Techniques for Dating of Lime Mortar by Carbon 14, *Journal of Field Archaeology* 3, pp.203-208.

Folk, R.L. and Valastro, S., 1979, Dating of Lime by 14C, in Berger, R. and Suess, H.E., eds, Radiocarbon Dating, *International 14C Conference, 9th Proceedings*, Berekly, University of California Oress, pp.721-732.

Frizot, M., 1977, Le Mortier Romain, Mystére ou Savaoir-Faire?, *Dossier de l'Archéologie* 25, pp.60-63.

Frizot, M., 1981, L'Analyse de Mortiers Antiques: Problémes et Résultats, in Mortars, Cements and Grouts Used in the Conservation of Historic Buildings, Proc. of the Symposium, *ICCROM* 2, pp.331-339.

Furlan, V. and Bissegger, P, 1975, Les Mortiers Anciens, Histoire et Essais d'Analyse Scientifique, *Revue Suisse d'Art et d'Archéologie* 32, pp.1-14.

Jedrzejewska, H., 1981, Ancient Mortars as Criterion in Analyses of Old Architecture, in Mortars, Cements and Grouts Used in Conservation of Historic Buildings, Proceedings of the Symposium, *ICCROM*, Rome, pp.311-329.

Jedrzejewska, H., 1960, Old Mortars in Poland, A New Method of Investigation: *Studies in Conservation* 5, 4, pp.132-138.

Jedrzejewska, H., 1967, New Methods in the Investigation of Ancient Mortars, Archaeological Chemistry, *University of Pennsylvania Press*, Philadelphia, pp.147-166.

Lafuma, H., 1952, Liants Hydrauliques, *Propriétés, Choix et Conditions d'Emploi*, eds Dunod, Paris.

Leduc, E. and Vhenu, G., 1912, Chaux, Ciments, Plâtres, eds Béranger, Paris-Liége.

Lucas, A., 1906, Ancient Egyptian Mortars, Annales du Service des Antiquités de l'Egpyte7,pp.4-8.

Malone, C.,m Valastro, S. and Vazela, A.G., 1980, Carbon 14 Chronology of Mortars from Excavations in the medieval Church of Saint Benigne, Dijon, France, *Journal of Field Archaeology* 7,pp.329-343.

Marien, G. and Pachiaudi, C., 1975, Les Isotopes Stables du Carbone et l' Oxygéne, in Maury, ed, Spelunca Mem. 8 Millau, France, pp.85-94.

Pachiaudi, C. Maréchal, J., Van Strydonck, M., Dupas, M. and Dauchot-Dehon, M., 1986, Isotopic Fractionation of Carbon during CO_2 Absorption by Mortar, in Stuiver, M. and Kra, R.S., eds, International 14C Conference, 12th Proceedings, *Radiocarbon* 28, 2A, pp.691-697.

Peroni, S., Tersigni, C. and Torraca, G., et al, 1981, Lime Based on Mortars for the Repair of Ancient Masonary and Possible Substitutes, in Mortars, Cements and grouts Used in the Conservation of Historic Buildings, Proceedings of the Symposium, *ICCROM*, Rome, pp.25-52.

Sickles, L.B., 1981, Organics vs Synthetics,: Their Use as Additives in Mortars, in Motars, Cements and Grouts Used in the Conservation of Historic Buildings, Proceedings of the Symposium, *ICCROM*, Rome, pp.25-52.

Sonninen, E., Erämetsä, P. and Jungner, H., 1985, Dating of Mortars and bricks from the Castle of Kastelholm, *Iskos* 5, pp.384-389.

Stewart, J. and Moore, J., 1981, Techniques of Historic Mortar Analyses, in Mortars, Cements and Grouts Used in the Conservation of Historic Buildings, Proceedings of the Symposium, *ICCROM*, Rome, pp.297-310.

Stuiver, M. and Smith, C.S., 1965, Radiocarbon Dating of Ancient Mortars and Plaster, in Chatters, R.M. and Olson, E.A., eds, International Conference on 14C and Tritium Dating, 6th Proceedings, Clearinghouse for Fed Sci and Tech Inf, Natl Bur Standards, U.S. Department of Commerce, Washington, D.C., pp.338-341.

Stuiver, M. and Waldren, W.H., 1975, 14C Carbonate Dating and the Age of the Post Talayotic Lime Burials in Mallorca, *Nature* 255, 5508, pp.475-476.

Van Strydonck, M., Dupas, M. and Dauchot-Dehon, M., 1983, Radiocarbon Dating of Old Mortars, in Mook, W.G. and Waterbolk, H.T., eds 14C and Archaeology, Prodeedings *PACT* 8, pp.337-343.

Van Strydonck, M., Dupas, M, Dauchot-Dehon, M., Pachiaudi, C. and Maréchal, J., 1983, A Further Step in the Radiocarbon Dating of Old Mortars, Bulletin Van Het Kon. Inst. voor het *Kunstpatrimonium* XIX, pp.155-171.

Van Strydonck, M., 1986, The Influence of Contaminating (fossil) Carbonate and the Variations of 13C in Mortar Dating, in Stuiver, M. and Kra, R.S., eds, International 14C Conference, 12th Proceedings, *Radiocarbon* 28, 2A, pp.702-710.

Van Strydonck, M. and Waldren, W.H., 1987, Radiocarbon Dating of Mallorcan Lime Burials, in preparation, *14C and Archaeology*, Conference held at Groningen.

Vionovitch, I.A., Debras-Guédon, J. and Louvrier, J., 1962, L'Analyse des Silicates, eds, Herman, Paris, pp.231-234.

Waldren, W.H., 1982, Radiocarbon Determination in the Balearic Islands, an Inventory 1962-1981, *Donald Baden-Powell Quaternary Research Centre*, Pitt Rivers Museum, University of Oxford.

Willaime, B, Coppens, R. and Jaegy, R., 1983, Datation des Mortiers du Château de Châtel-sur-Moselle par le Carbone 14, in Mook, W.G. and Waterbolk, H.T., Eds, 14C and Archaeology, Proceedings, *PACT* 8, pp.345-350.

TABLE 1: Stavelot (Belgium) Tower of old abbey. Typical analyses for restoration of buildings.

Sample 1: exterior of the tower
Sample 2: interior of the tower
Sample 3: small staircase tower

Analyses	Sample 1		Sample 2		Sample 3	
		*		*		*
insolub. in HCl	29.7	46.5	25.0	36.0	26.2	45.0
$CaCO_3$	47.9	36.5	56.9	48.5	63.6	47.4
$MgCO_3$	1.0	0.7	1.0	0.9	0.8	0.6
free lime	0	0	2.1	1.8	0	0
CaO (silic)	2.4	1.8	3.1	2.6	1.7	1.3
H_2O (silic) and organ. mat.	5.4	4.1	6.1	5.2	3.8	2.8
$CaSO_4 .2H_2O$	8.5	6.5	0.9	0.8	0	0
other SO_4^{--}	0.8	0.6	0.3	0.3	0	0
Na^+	0.2	0.1	0.2	0.1	0	0
K^+	0.3	0.2	0.2	0.2	0	0
Mg^{++}	traces	traces	0	0	0	0
Cl^-	0	0	0.2	0.2	0	0
not measured	3.8	3.0	4.0	3.4	3.9	2.9
(sol. SiO_2, R_2O_3) hydraulic index	0.13		0.11		0.10	

*: Visual analyses have shown that the aggregate in the 3 samples is not cal-careous. In this column the aggregate is included in the "insoluble" fraction. The aggregate respectively represents: 23.8%, 14.7%, 25.5% of the sample.

CONCLUSION: If the gypsum originates from a deterioration due to pollu-tion, the ratio CaO/MgO indicates that the lime of mortars 1 and 2 has the same origin. The 3rd one contains less Mg.

TABLE 2: Theux Belgium, Church of Saints Hermes and Alexandre: typical archaeological study analysis

Mortar ref.	%CaOfr	CaCO$_3$	%MgCO$_3$	%Q	%N-H	%H	Total
1042	0	38.7	2.37	22.1	26.2	5.20	94.6
1044	0	30.8	2.36	28.9	28.5	4.08	94.6
1049	0	62.9	1.91	14.1	13.1	3.32	95.3
1050	0	67.0	1.73	13.1	11.3	2.50	95.6
1009	0.005	39.1	1.78	42.4	11.9	3.12	98.3
1027	0.015	55.5	5.14	14.1	16.2	4.20	95.2
1029	0	43.5	2.78	29.3	15.2	6.18	97.0
1030	0.005	41.7	4.63	29.6	15.0	7.42	98.4
1038	2.060	8.1	1.97	46.8	20.9	18.30	98.1
1039	0.032	14.8	9.63	47.3	18.4	7.82	98.0
1041	0.017	37.1	2.67	38.5	14.4	5.02	97.7

Q: quartz, N-H: non-hydraulic silicate, H: hydraulic silicate, fr: free, Total: does not take into account the presence of organic material and soluble salts.
The ratio of CaCO$_3$/H gives an indication of the type of mortar. The highest values correspond to the Carolingian (1049 & 1050) mortars; the lowest to the nineteenth century restoration mortar (1038), which is a cement mortar.

TABLE 3: Mortars dated by the Valastro method

Ref.	$\delta^{13}C°/oo$	Calibrated date	Historical date
Tx-1941 Stobi, theatre	-9.32	260 ± 40 AD	Early 2nd century AD
Tx-1943 Stobi, Basilica	-19.21	400 ± 50 AD	385-410 AD
Tx-3443, Dijon St-Bénigne	-6.5	1605 ± 76 AD	Late 15th- early 16th AD

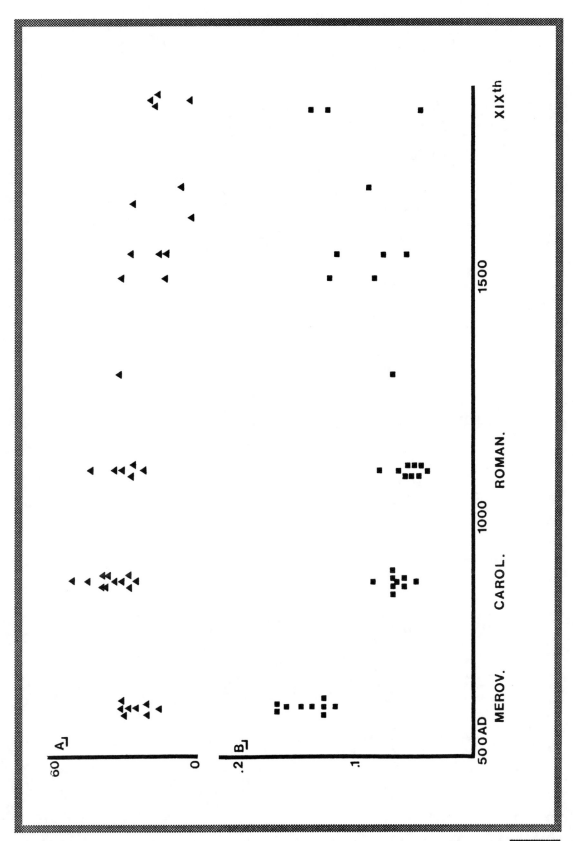

Figure 1

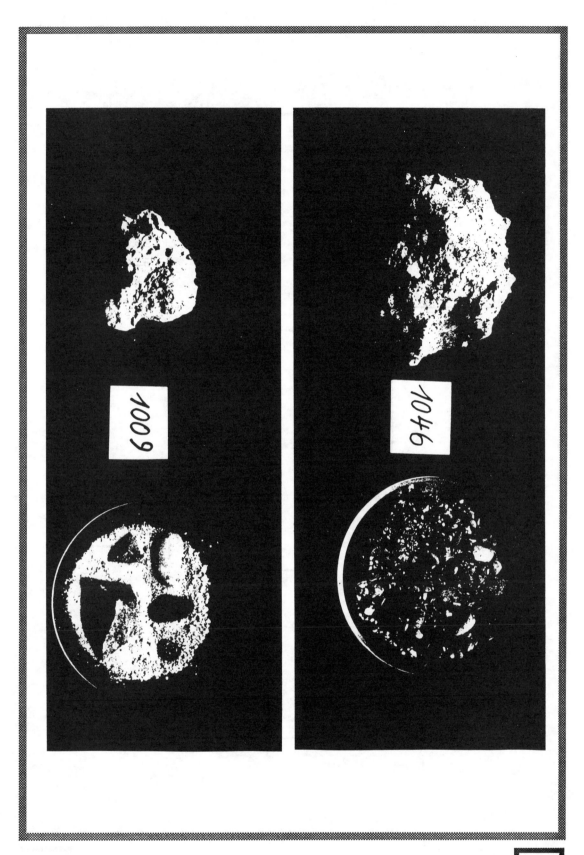

Figure 2

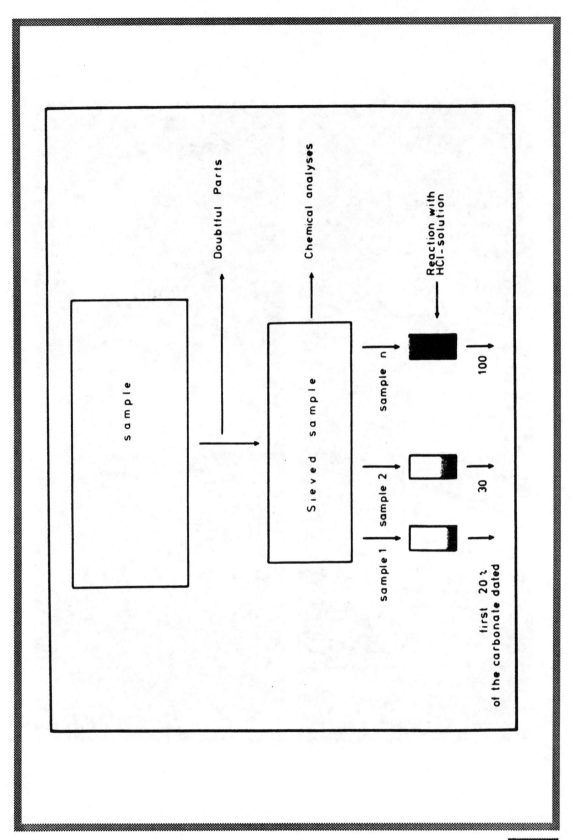

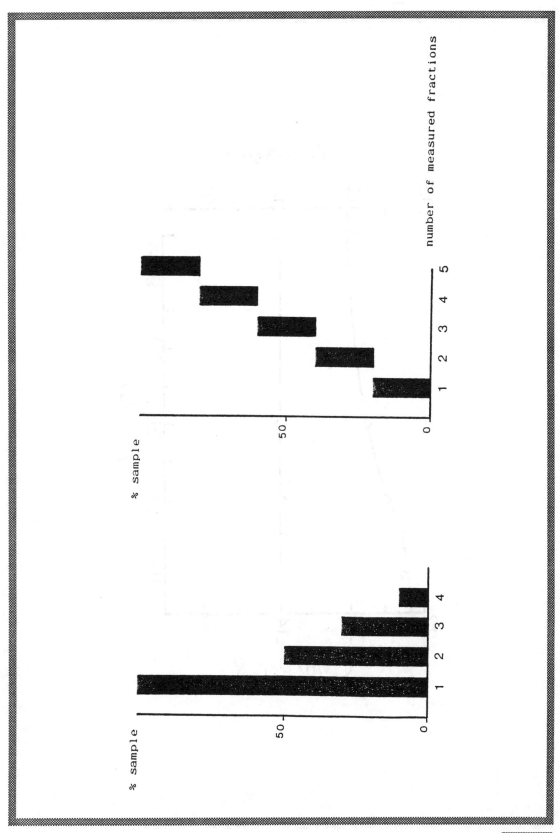

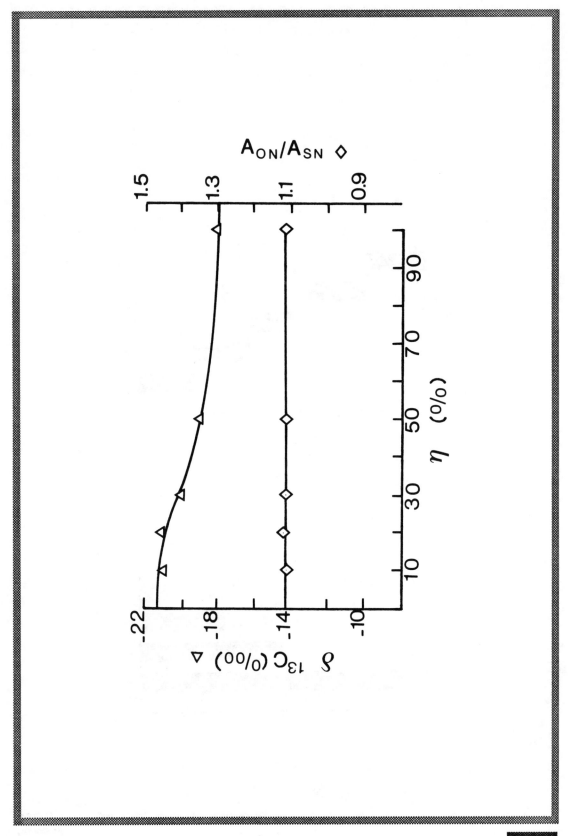

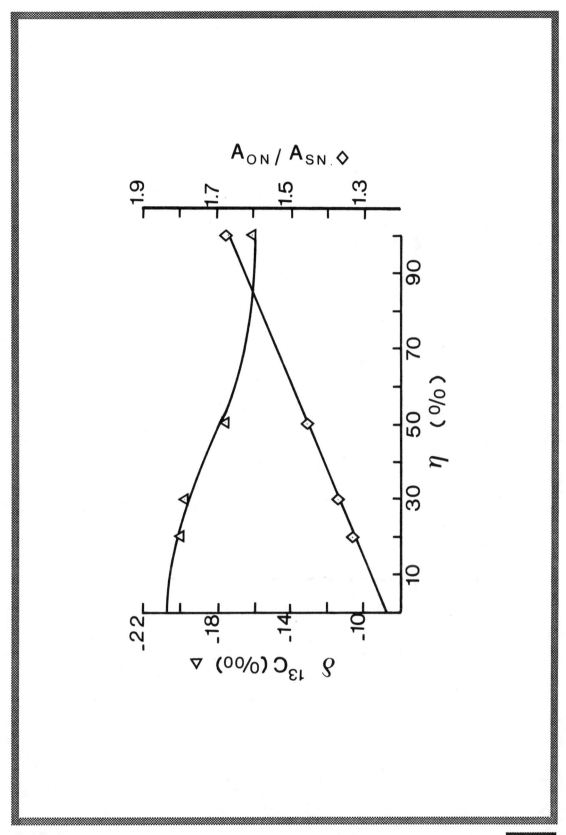

Figure 6

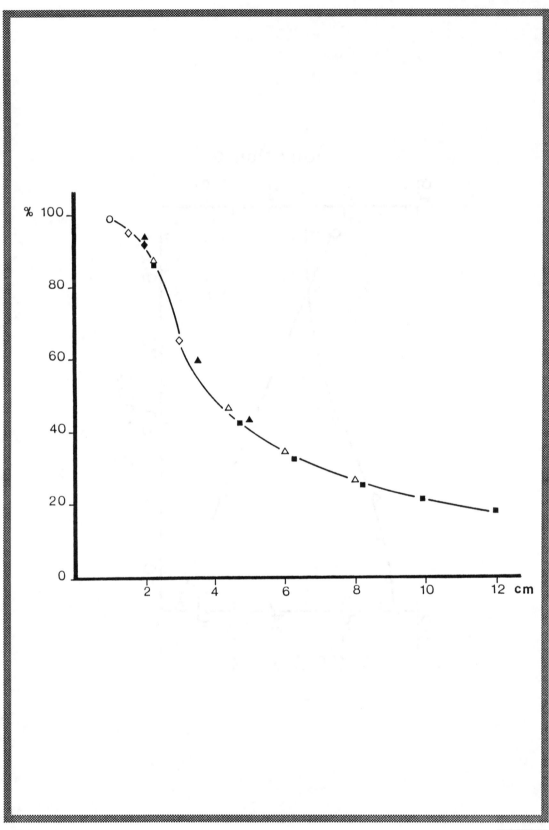

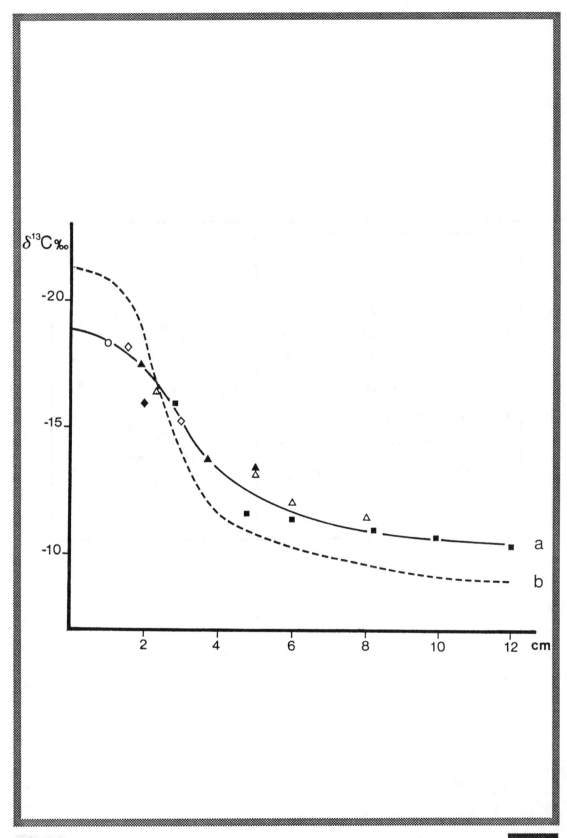

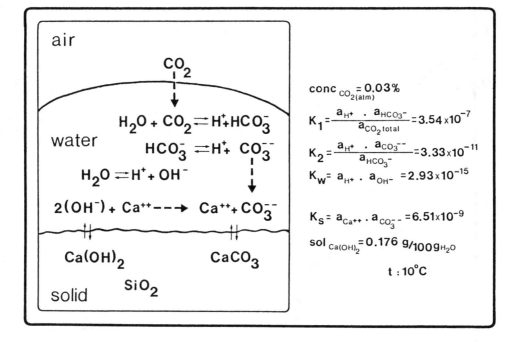

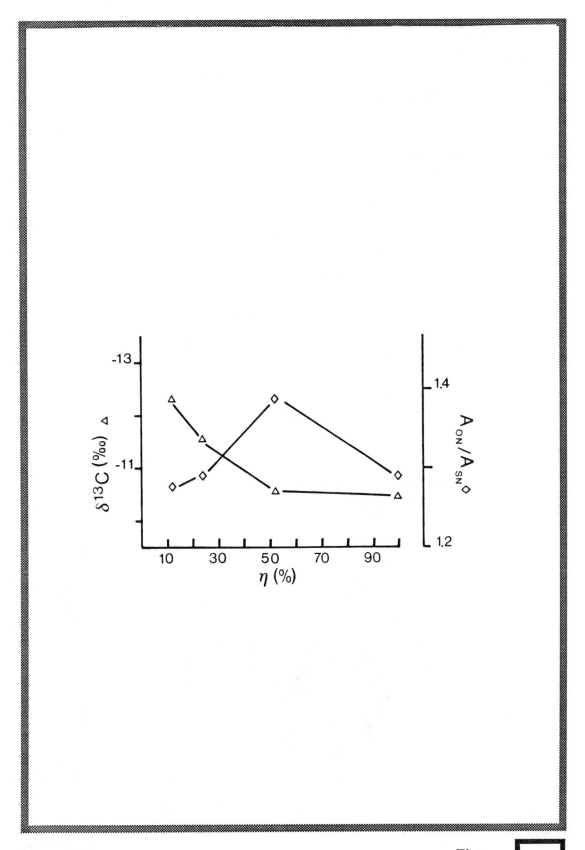

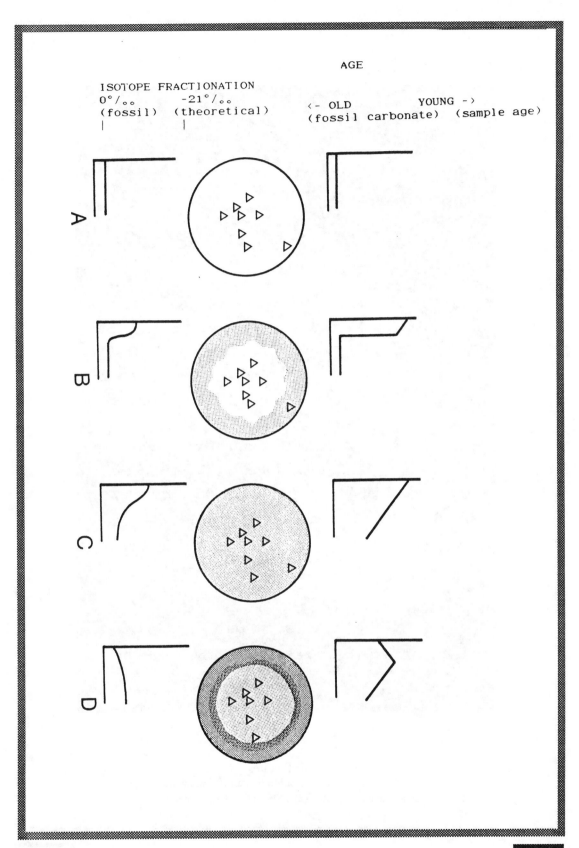

AGE

ISOTOPE FRACTIONATION
0°/₀₀   -21°/₀₀
(fossil)   (theoretical)

<- OLD   YOUNG ->
(fossil carbonate) (sample age)

A

B

C

D

DCATT&T

Figure 11:2

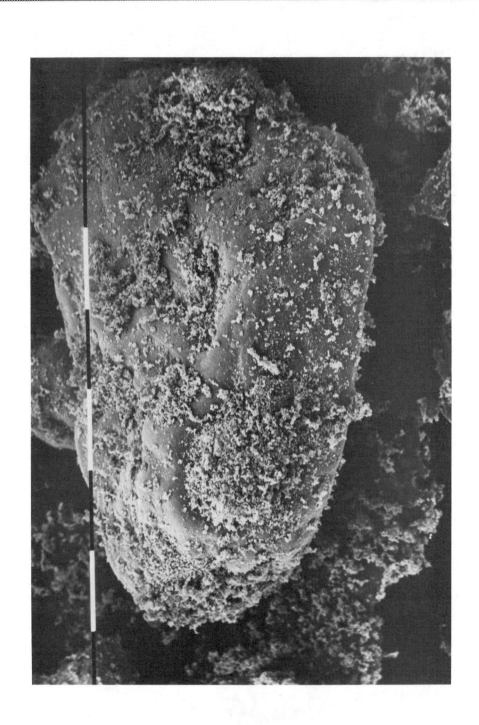

SEM- Pictures
SiO_2 Pellet with Lime (Not More Than 1% carbonate)
Enlargements (1) 150x: (2) 300x: (3) 2400x: (4) 20000x

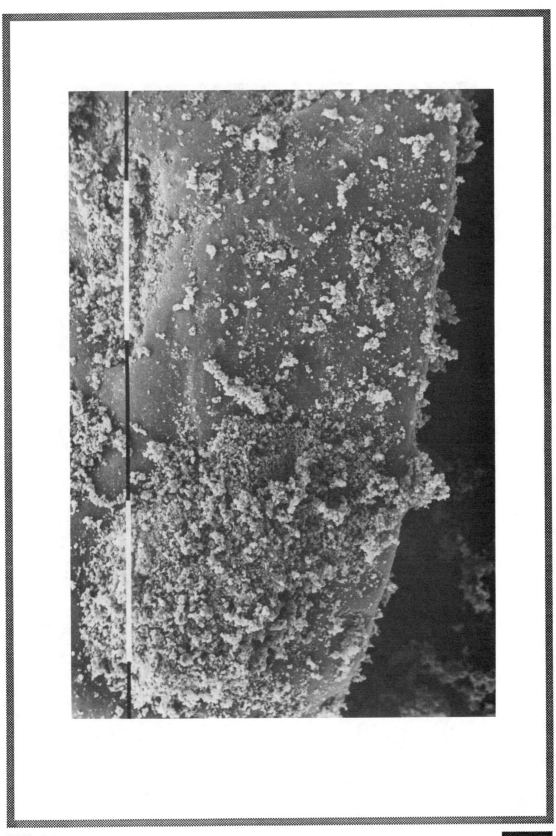

Figure 12:2

DCATT&T

Figure 12:4

SEM- Pictures
SiO$_2$ Pellet with Carbonated Lime (Detail)
Enlargements (5) 1200x: (2) 10000x

DCATT&T

Figure   **12:5**

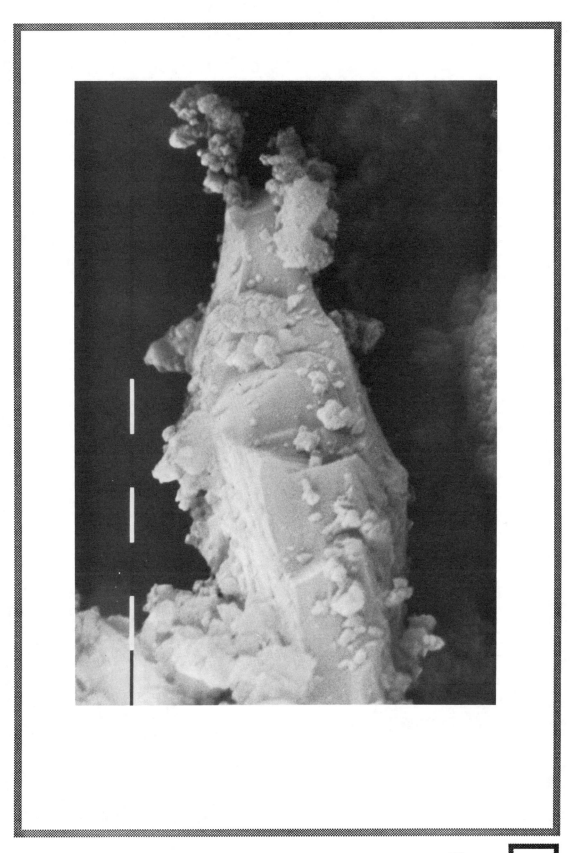

AGE DETERMINATION, CHRONOLOGY AND RADIOCARBON RECALIBRATION IN THE BALEARIC ISLANDS

WILLIAM H. WALDREN
Donald Baden Powell Quaternary Research Centre
Department of Ethnology and Prehistory
University of Oxford
Oxford OX2 6PN, England

RESUME

A long term and on-going dating survey programme has been in progress in the Balearic Islands since 1962. Several listings of chronometric results obtained from individual surveys carried out within the overall programme have been published periodically in a number of reports, including a recent comprehensive inventory of all Balearic dates available until 1986 (Waldren l986). At present survey readings have risen in number to over 225 chronometric analyses results, comprised of not only conventional radiocarbon method but other more esoteric methods: such as racemisation of aspartic acids and uranium thorium dating of bone, as well as calcium carbonate and palaeomagnetic dating (see Waldren, bibliographic listing).

These different dating techniques have been used basically in two types of physical situations: (1) in the closed environment of deep, vertical stratigraphy: characteristic of cave and rock shelter deposits, and (2) in the open environment of shallow, horizontal stratigraphy: characteristically representative of eroded open-air settlements.

From the outset of the dating surveys, the broader strategy behind the programme has been to use dating methods in large number in a few, selective, potentially informative- if somewhat geographically localised prehistoric sites- rather than establishing a greater number of isolated dates originating from widely dispersed geographical areas. Therefore, the resulting cluster of dates from the research sites is in the form of a nucleus centralised in the Northern Jurassic Sierras of Mallorca, rather than a more evenly distributed pattern . However over the years, the surveys have geographically widened their perspective, establishing major dating nuclei for other site locales, both elsewhere on Mallorca as well as on the sister island of Menorca; the latter of which at present has its own growing radiocarbon series (see distribution maps).

Approximately 145 of the total readings currently available for the different horizons relate to prehistoric contexts and radiocarbon documentation that come within the range of the last 8000 years. These form a closely knitted group of dates, as can be seen from the sample listings (Tables 1 and 2), falling well within the range of the latest Washington-Belfast Radiocarbon Recalibration Curve (Stuiver and Pearson 1986).

As a matter of introduction, the conference paper will include a brief historical background to the Balearic dating programme. It will describe and discuss the initial strategy and final objectives of the dating programme, as well as some of the results that have grown out of the findings . It will briefly examine the reasons for the choice of the site nuclei used in the dating programme. It will also briefly discuss the influence the findings have had on local chronological frameworks over the last twenty five years.

More importantly, it will go on to define, as suggested by the dating evidence (1) the large chronometric parameters for the author's pentapartite Balearic prehistoric sequence in general and possible influence recalibration may have on it. This is to say, there will be some discussion concerning the absolute chronological limits suggested by the use of radiocarbon method for the long period ranges attached to geological, palaeontological and cultural contexts. (2) It will further describe and define particular medial phase ranges within the larger periods. It will subdivide, where possible, these larger periods as well as signal important milestone events within the subdivisions, by suggesting dates for these (e.g. dates for the arrival of man, the introduction of various technologies, such as pottery and metal working, as well as earmarking outside cultural influences within the local sequence). In turn, (3) some definition is given the shorter activity ranges within the particular environments of the sites themselves; e.g. architectural (constructional) and utilisational (occupational) activities and their sequential character. And finally, (4) some attempt will be made to show the manner in which these findings relate to the wider perspective of mainland and European continental contexts. Finally, it will for those interested (5) present for their consideration and reference a first listing of the recalibrations of existing radiocarbon readings, falling within the Washington-Belfast Radiocarbon Recalibration Curve, with some observations on their possible interpretation.

Although the Balearic dates as they have been published so far in uncalibrated form are generally accepted, considerable local controversy still exists concerning chronological nomenclature (Waldren 1986; Topp 1986). Hence in view of the already existing contention dates derived from recalibration can well be predicted to cause additional inquietude. In fact, even under more favourable conditions recalibrations of the magnitude shown in the listings presented may well be expected to cause active response in many areas, regardless whether or not they break with the status quo of provincial attitudes and relative interpretations, in that they dramatically alter more soundly reasoned prehistoric chronological frameworks already based on radiocarbon dating. One need only compare the resulting newly calibrated versions alongside the conventional radiocarbon readings to become aware of the degree of difference between radiocarbon years and calendar years, as well as to establish a view of the general chronological areas they will most affect.

Undoubtedly, the research area where recalibration will have its greatest impact will fall on local chronological schemes; whether these be older relative chronological sequences or recent frameworks more firmly based on uncalibrated chronometric readings. While recalibration universally can be expected to affect questions of chronology, the subject of recalibration of Balearic dates it is feared will become particularly contentuous. Coupled with strong local tendencies toward insular thinking in general regarding the possible origins, influences and course of development of the islands' cultural, social and economic patterns in prehistory - as much as the strong penchant toward considering local prehistoric events as isolated phenomena and independent domain - the questions and problems arising, along with readjustments in thinking, can be expected to be present for some time to come. Under the circumstances, it is perhaps best in the long run to regard these problems philosophically and to accept that the process of recalibration of radiocarbon dating, sooner or later, is inevitable and eventually will become univerally acceptable and universally used.

While it is not the intent in this resumé to discuss in detail the different sequential frameworks that the dating surveys have supported over the years, some reference to the chronological nomenclature, as used by the present author, is given immediately below as it applies to the present subject of recalibration. For those caring to further their interest in the historical background to the research, other than what is offered in the text to come and separated from it, there is ample reading in the references suggested, as well as the more pertinent site reports themselves. These should fully equip readers with a substantial background and more details to the various hypotheses and chronological schemes currently in circulation than is possible to include in the present paper.

The paired uncalibrated radiocarbon and calendar year listings below are offered as immediately interesting examples of those found within the earlier Balearic cultural periods. While they are selected dates, part of a fuller and more extensive inventory and recalibration included in addendum to the text, they best illustrate the magnitude of change brought about by recalibration on conventional 14C readings, as well as their demonstrating the nature and character of the problems involved. In turn, they demonstrate in hard terms the chronometric ranges that recalibration will most affect here in the Balearic Islands.

As eventually will be discussed and demonstrated, both the methods and the strategy with which the programme surveys have been used have been particulary informative, not only locally but with implications reaching farther afield. In fact as pointed out (Almagro Gorbea 1978, Fernández-Miranda 1974), there are not many areas where it (radiocarbon) has been more successfully used as a dating tool than in the Balearic Islands.

There are 42 uncalibrated 14C dates available for the full range of the Early Settlement and Pretalayotic Periods, with 37 readings for the Pretalayotic Period proper. At the same time, the sites representing the Pretalayotic Period in terms of radiocarbon documentation are few in number, making them of special value as chronometric yardsticks. In these few, selective sites, the close sequence of dates is quite impressive, as can be seen for itself in the listings below.

The chronometric parameters and other evidence (artefacts etc.) define the overall chronological duration of the period and support in turn the subdivision of the Pretalayotic Period into three phases:

(1) the Neolithic Early Ceramic Phase (NECP), circa 3200 bc to circa 2000 bc.
(4000 BC to 2550 BC)
(2) the Early Beaker Phase (EBP), circa 2000 bc to circa 1700 bc.
(2550 BC to 2000 BC)
(3) the Late Beaker Phase (LBP), circa 1700 bc to circa 1300 bc.
(2000 BC to 1520 BC)

The framework of these three survey medial phase ranges are earmarked by a number of important prehistoric events which are well delineated by the radiocarbon dating documentation. For example (1) the introduction of pottery technology, (2) the introduction of domesticated animal species (circa 3200 bc: cal. 4000 BC) and (3) the extinction of the major endemic mammal, Myotragus balearicus (circa 2300 bc: cal. 2750 BC), within the NECP. As another example are found (4) the appearance of the first open-air settlements and (5) the first Beaker influences and (6) introduction of metal working technology (circa 2050 bc: cal. 2550 BC), within the EBP and (7)use of tin bronze (circa 1700 bc: cal. 2050 BC) in the LBP.

Other important events are also discernable in both the Early Settlement Period as well as the later Talayotic and Post Talayotic Periods of the Bronze and Iron Ages, similarly representing the surveys' medial phase ranges for those periods. These are also discussed in more detail in the subsequent text.

The same sort of sequential order of dates can be seen in the second example below (Table 2). In this case the surveys' shorter activity phase ranges are demonstrated in the individual architectural and habitational environments found within the contexts of a prehistoric open-air settlement complex. Here, radiocarbon method has been used to delineate not only the overall pattern of the open-air settlement, but equally the various individual activity sequences throughout.

In conclusion, it is logical to assume that here in the Balearics- as elsewhere- a transitional period of adjustment will be necessary; a period of getting used to and working with the new dimensions that recalibration attaches to all the local prehistoric divisions. The sooner we can make the necessary mental adjustments in our thinking the better it will be. In the interim, we simply have to live with the fact that recalibration is not a matter of archaeological fashion , subject to whimsical change, but that it is here to stay and can be expected to take a serious toll on the existing order of things; above all making its influence felt on the various local chronological schemes presently in circulation (the present author's included). This can therefore be said to be inevitables for the single reason that all serious local chronological frameworks are based, one way or another, on uncalibrated radiocarbon datings established during the last twenty five years. It is logical, therefore, to assume that if we want either to arrive at a sound interpertation of local prehistoric events or to place the Balearics in a wider perspective than one of insular phenomenon (an easy answer up until now), we must accept the important role that recalibration will play in all immediate or future attempts at local interpretation or correlations within those desired broader continental contexts.

Note* All recalibrated dates are average BC and BP age ranges. For one and two sigma calculations (age ranges obtained from intercepts (Method A)) consult conference paper tables in addendum.

INTRODUCTION

The 225 chronometric analyses results currently available for Balearic Prehistory have been compiled from a number of different dating techniques of which an inventory of 145 readings are conventional radiocarbon dates that fall within the calendar year ranges of the Washington-Belfast Radiocarbon Recalibration Curve (Stuiver and Pearson 1986). Other conventional radiocarbon dates outside the calendar year ranges also exist (Table 6) but are not immediately pertinent for this publication. Although the uncalibrated results of the current listings, as well as those outside the calibrated range, have been published periodically in a number of reports, including one recent comprehensive inventory of all Balearic dates available until 1986 (Waldren, BAR, International Series 282), no attempt hitherto has been made to recalibrate the readings falling within acceptable calendar year ranges.

Because of their number and nature, calendar year calibration in place of conventional 14C dates for Balearic sites falling within the last eight thousand years would be particularly useful in the consideration and eventual construction of a more accurate chronological, cultural framework for local prehistory. Now that the use in recent literature of calibrated dates for broad areas of Western Europe are becoming more frequent in place of conventional radiocarbon age results, recalibration into calendar years would serve also to put such a framework for the Balearic region into better perspective in regard to the larger contexts of mainland prehistory. In short, considerable value can be gained by the study, comparison and correlation of the existing Balearic chronometric data, including associated artefact and other evidence, with that of peripheral continental areas; as well as being of immediate value in localised and more specific chronological contexts. In fact, we need only consult, for example, the current literature for the Chalcolithic Period in the broader contexts (e.g. Harrison 1988 and others) to become aware that similar chronological difficulties and other problems of interpretation and questions of temporal duration prevail throughout most peripheral, mainland geographic areas. It seems to the author that any comprehensive listing in the form of a chronometric data bank for any geographic part of the western Mediterrranean, as limited in immediate geographic area as may be, would be of some general and positive use and contribution to the problems of chronological interpretation.

The present Balearic radiocabon inventory is also both interesting as well as informative from a methodological viewpoint, and is to some extent exemplary. The individual lists making up the larger inventory have been compiled using a general strategy of applying a large number of radiocarbon analyses to only a few, but, especially selected sites; sites with particularly rich, interesting and varied prehistoric environments and artefacts, in order to determine specific time ranges. This form of blanket coverage has consequently resulted in a number of sequential lists of uncalibrated dates from a group of different stratigraphical contexts, which combined and in themselves have produced an extensive chronometric data bank, as well as several smaller, individual, geographically and geologically varied series.

Indeed, it is a matter of fact that too few areas of Western Europe or the Western Mediterranean have equivalent concentrated radiocarbon series on which one can depend for a reliable basis of chronometrical measurement and interpretation. The few that have produced useful lists: for example Zambujal, Los Millares, Cerro de Virgen and Moncin in particular, these textbook sites do not have in their sum total as many readings as would be desired, and are for the most part widely dispersed geographically. At the same time, other less documented sites, that is to say with only single or a few radiocarbon dates, often present us with conflicting information; information which is too highly regional and fragmentary in character, and mainly applicable, only, in a relative way within their immediategeographical contexts; hence representing very broad, chronological polarity.

Apart from the different dating survey strategies and various interpretative methods used in the Balearic research sites, other interesting aspects are the highly, individual *physical environments* and the *strategraphical contexts* from which the representative evidence, data and other analytical results obtained from the research have emerged. In essence, the findings originate from two distinct types of *physical environment*:: (**1**) the *closed* contexts of deep,*vertical* stratigraphy; characteristic of cave and rock shelter deposits, and (**2**) in the *open* environment of shallow, *horizontal* stratigraphy; representative of eroded *open-air* settlements. Each of these quite different, physical environments present their particular, complex characters and natures; as well as their special shortcomings and problems.

Of the two types of stratigraphical conditions, as field archaeologists, it is the poor soil contexts found in badly eroded, open-air settlement environments that give us the most difficulty. Compared to the better known multi-sequencial soil conditions of deep *closed* environments, as found in caves and rock shelters, those sites with *open-air* contexts, especially in the Western Mediterranean Basin, where they are found more frequently than not, are the most problematic. While close and particular attention has to be paid at all times to the thin, vertical stratigraphical interfaces of the soil in both closed and open-air sites, it is the contexts of highly*eroded* stratigraphical conditions in which the tightest excavational controls possible on a horizontal meter to meter and linear distributional bases are most necessary. In such eroded environments, the potentials for good interpretation and the accurate dating of poor vertical stratigraphy, while not impossible, are under the best of conditions very difficult. Therefore, if any reliable results are to be expected in such cases, new ways as well as more environmentally suitable ones for tackling poor vertical stratigraphical situations become necessary.

ON THE RADIOCARBON SAMPLE COLLECTION METHODS USED IN THE RESEARCH

It is known that collection methods in radiocarbon dating are of great importance for reliability, and subsequently they are essential considerations in any question of contextual archaeological interpretation, as well as in the case of recalibration of conventional radiocarbon dates themselves. Such description and detail of collection methods are too often missing in the publication of radiocarbon dates.

The brief description of collection methods discussed below are given in order to better understand the individual environments and physical contexts from which they (the samples) originated, and to give some idea of the particular degree and level to which they have been used as interpretative tools in the sites studied. It is also done as a graphic demonstration of the individual techniques themselves; techniques some of which are largely innovative; the direct result of stratigraphical conditions and differential preservation. In short, the way in which they have been applied throughout the different physical environments and stratigraphical contexts, it is believed, are discriptively important and are directly responsible as well as related to their success.

To deal with the poor soil conditions found in the eroded sites examined, two direct types of dating *strategy* or *method* have been adopted (Figures 4a-b). These are referred to as *bracket* dating, mainly used in shallow, open-air stratigraphical environments, and *series* dating, mainly used in deep vertical stratigraphical conditions; although a combination of both types of dating strategy together have been frequently used just as effectively either in *deep* or *shallow* vertical soil conditions. They are in this respect interchangeable.

While essentially it is *series* dating used in the deep stratigraphies (e.g. Figure 6) that is most familiar- as this follows the principal of dating successive vertical strata- it is *bracket* dating which is normally the least used. The forms in which both *bracket* and *series* dating have been used in the different research sites under discussion consist of dating architectural features and stratigraphical contexts (Figures 4 and 5). Three of the examples used are from eroded open-air situations, where the stratigraphy of the site has been generally *shallow* and of a *linear* or *horizontal* nature. In one of the other examples used for demonstration, conditions are that of a *closed* situation where stratigraphy is that of conventional or *deep, vertical* deposition.

The method of *bracket* dating architectural features consists of establishing and radiocarbon dating (**1**) post constructional, (**2**) constructional and (**3**) preconstructional contexts directly associated with a site's different architectural features. This is done by carefully collecting datable organic materials and artefacts (**a**) from an activity zone adjacent to some architectural feature, (**b**) from within the wall fill of a particular architectural feature and (**c**) from bedrock fissures and bedding soils found beneath the wall fill and the architectural elements themselves (Figure 4a). Results of such bracketed as well as serial datings can, if carefully carried out, quite accurately date an architectural element, as well as aid interpretation in a significant way (Figures 4b and 5a).

Of the three open-air situations in which this method of bracket dating for interpreting age of levels, duration of occupation and building sequence has been used, it is the*Ferrandell-Oleza Chalcolithic Old Settlement* on Mallorca where it was first carried out (Waldren 1989). The other sites where it has also been used sucessfully are the *The Prehistoric Settlement Complex and Taula Sanctuary of Torrabla d'en Salort* on Menorca and the Mallorcan *Prehistoric Sanctuary of Son Mas*. These two sites and the use of the method are discussed in considerable detail in a separate paper found elsewhere in this publication. There, the use of bracket dating as a tool for chronological interpretation and of arcitectual and other contextual dating is well demonstrated.

THE LARGER DATING STRATEGY AND THE RESEACH SITES USED

From the outset of the Balearic dating survey, the main objective of the programme has been to use dating analyses in *large number*, forming extensive dating series in a few, selective, potentially informative- if somewhat geographically localised- prehistoric sites (Waldren 1986). This focus of geographic research area and limited number of research sites, rather than the documentation of a greater number of isolated dates originating from dispersed geographical areas has been carried with a number of motives in mind; equally administrative, equally financial, equally practical and methodological. Admittedly as a result of this selectiveness, the distributional cluster of dates from the research sites is in the form of a large series with nuclei for the most part centralised in the Northern Jurassic Sierras of Mallorca (Figure 3); rather than a more evenly distributed pattern more openly spread over the island. In the interim years since 1962, however, the survey has geographically widened its perspective, establishing major dating nuclei for other site locales, both elsewhere on Mallorca (e.g. Son Fornes, Gasull, P., Lull, V. and Sanahuja, C. 1984) as well as on the sister island of Menorca (Fernandez- Miranda and Waldren in preparation); where at present other radiocarbon series are in progress (also see Figure 3).

As is demonstrated by the total of 145 readings currently available for the different horizons of the Balearic chronometric cultural sequence, the radiocarbon documentation represents a span of the last 8000 years (see Table 3). The remaining 50 or so radiocarbon dates and other dating results are outside the limits of recalibration, dealing with the earlier periods of Balearic prehistory. A partial listing of these dates are included for reference and continuity (Table 6). As can be seen from the sample listings in Tables 1, 2, and 3, those within the limits of calibration individual listings form individual, closely knitted groups of dates falling well within the range of the latest Washington-Belfast Radiocarbon Recalibration Curve (Stuiver and Pearson 1986). With these groups of dates the full statistical effect of calibrated dates in the earlier age ranges can be graphically demonstrated (Figures 7). There are still other long listings available for the late age ranges not shown here where the differences between uncalibrated and calibrated dates are not so dramatic as the ones used for demonstration.

The first listing of dates (Table 1) is made up of a series of 35 dates obtained from both *bracket* and *series* dating as found in the Ferrandell-Oleza Chalcolithic Old Settlement and the nearby, contemporary, Prehistoric Sanctuary of Son Mas. It is both of these loci that are the principal site examples examined elsewhere in this publication. In both these sites, the use of *bracket* dating has been a contributing factor in establishing a *collective* series of individual analysis results from the sites' various and frequently different environmental conditions. Collectively, the individual *brackets* establish a *series* dating *pattern* or *format*, demonstrating the sites' duration of occupation during the local Pretalayotic period as circa 2080 bc to circa 1230 bc (cal 2550 BC to 1450 BC); as well as the ensuing Talayotic and Post Talayotic periods circa 1230 bc to 100 bc (cal 1450 BC to 100 BC). They have for the most part given us construction dates for individual architectural features, especially where *bracket* dating was used in attempting to establish construction dates for specific architectural elements .

In the second example listing illustrated, one of the two larger inventories of 42 readings (Table 2) illustrates the ranges of dates available exclusively for the local Early Settlement and Pretalayotic Periods and their various phases. They originate mainly from four sites (see table 4) with both *closed* and *open* environments and include cave, rock shelter and open-air settlement loci and demonstrate general the duration of the periods: circa 4730 bc to circa 1120 bc (cal 5589 BC to 1357 BC) .

The third listing (Table 3) consists of a second sequence of 42 dates exclusively from the *deep, vertical* stratigraphy of the Rock Shelter of Son Matge, Mallorca. It demonstrates *series* dating in the conventional sense of vertical deposition, showing a cultural succession of 23 strata spanning over five millennia, circa 4730 bc to 15bc (cal 5589 BC to 20 BC), covering all of the Balearic cultural prehistoric periods.

All in all, individual series like those found in the tables (1-3) along with the total inventory of approximately 145 dates available for the full range of the calibrated scale have made possible the *Pentapartite Division of Balearic Prehistory* as presented in Figure 2. How the calibration of conventional readings has altered the uncalibrated version of this framework can be seen by comparing the two versions illustrated (Figure 2 and 2a).

It is not my intention to discuss to any great extent the details, or argue the shortcomings or merits of this chronological scheme, or for that matter any of the others presented locally in this present publication, other than to refer to them in the most cursory manner as examples of what they are and the most likely areas where recalibration should and will have its greatest bearing in the future. It would take considerable space and time to discuss the merits and shortcomings of the other, often quite different chronological frameworks in circulation. This sort of discussion needs time and space and is best carried out in a separate paper to be prepared on that specific subject at a later date.

However, as a matter of continuity some brief reference to the chronological nomenclature and schemes used by other local investigators are illustrated as example (Figure 8), and the effects of recalibration on certain areas of these frameworks are examined by way of illustration to the question of recalibration of dates. At the same time, a few brief comments are also made on the general atmosphere of local thinking concerning chronological and archaeological nomenclature in general. For the time being, it will be enough to point out, for those caring to further their interest in the historical background to the research and details of the different chronological schemes in existence, that there will be ample reading in the references suggested in the final section of this paper. These should equip curious readers with a substantial background and considerably more detail than included here to the various hypotheses and chronological schemes currently in circulation.

To best emphasise the level of the discrepancies and the importance of those differences within a detailed divisional framework, two versions of the author's scheme are illustrated for comparative purposes (Figures 2 and 2a). It should also be understood that the frameworks illustrated here supercede all others priorly published. Changes can be expected from time to time in this schematic framework as important information and data grows and indicates a need for change.

In short, such a schematic framework represents a working hypothesis, not unlike a growing radiocarbon master listing itself (Waldren 1986); where frequent, new data gives a more detailed and broader perspective. In the author's thinking, no framework or chronological structure should ever be inflexible or reckoned permanent; a fault too often occurring in the past. Although, the lack of a steady flow of in-coming data held at a minimum from archaeological inactivity would not occasion frequent changes in many local schemes. Where there has been a steady flow of new data on a year to year basis as in the Balearics, frequent changes should be expected and considered a norm. It is a matter of keeping up with the literature.

One of the two schematics (Figure 2a) is the author's 1988 framework version using uncalibrated radiocarbon dates. The other (Figure 2) is the same framework illustrated with calibrated dates for 1990. As can be seen it is the *milestone* events, all of which fall within the recalibration parameters, such as (1) the suggested dates for the initial colonisation of the islands, circa 4730 bc: cal 5600 BC, (2) the extinction and introduction of indigenous and domesticate animals and pottery technology, circa 3000 bc: cal 3900 BC, (3) the introduction and establishment of open-air settlements and sanctuaries, circa 2100 bc: cal 2500 BC, (4) the introduction dates for metal working and other technology, circa 2000 bc: cal 2500 BC that are most effected by calibrated radiocarbon dates on divisional prehistoric frameworks like the ones shown here; where calibrated and uncalibrated versions can be compared.

Despite the apparent clear-cut and otherwise compartmentalised, detailed appearance of the two versions of the author's chronometric framework shown, it is the *longer and later ranged* parameters and interfaces of some of the earliest and late periods and their phasic divisions (Tables 1-3) which will be most effected by recalibration, and not the longer ranged ones outside the recalibration limit of 8000 years. These differences in the earliest and late periods within the range of recalibration can be seen by comparing the differences between uncalibrated and calibrated dates listings. They are also demonstrated graphically in chart form by the range of cultural dates from two of the listings (Figure 7).

At the same time, calibrated dates to a significant degree equally effect the various relationship with the *medial* and *short* ranged parameters and interfaces (Bronze and Iron Age). This general effect can be seen in the comparisons made and is applicable not only for the detailed framework illustrated, which is perhaps more detailed than most others in use, being based as it is on over 145 absolute readings, but will fall true for all the already existing chronological schemes, no matter how detailed or littled detailed they are at present. Besides most of the chronological schemes put forth so far have utilised to some degree radiocarbon dates available over the last 28 years. Hence, they cannot help but be significantly effected by recalibration of radiocarbon dates all the way down the line.

Although the Balearic radiocarbon dates as they have been published so far in uncalibrated form have been more or less generally accepted abroad, a great deal of local controversy still exists concerning what has been proper chronological nomenclature for some of the periods (e.g. Waldren 1986; Topp 1986). Hence, in the light of such contention, generally dates derived from recalibration can well be predicted to cause additional local inquietude.

Presented even under the most favourable conditions the recalibrations, especially of the magnitude shown in the listings can be expected to disturb the *status quo* of quite a few local hypotheses, in particular those uncalibrated radiocarbon dates circa 2000 bc to 1300 bc. In short, while world scale recalibration can be expected to have a strong impact on questions of chronology everywhere, the subject of recalibration of Balearic dates, I fear, will become particularly contentuous. Coupled with strong local tendencies toward *insular* thinking to begin with regarding possible influences or origins in Balearic prehistory itself, along with a natural *penchant* for considering local prehistoric events as *isolated* phenomena of *independent* invention, all of which has transpired on a *private* ground so to speak, the subject of calibrated dates can be expected to be present in the local literature for some time to come, or even in some cases to be unwisely and unscientifically completely ignored.

Under the circumstances, it becomes a matter of best regarding these local problems philosophically in accepting the inevitability of radiocarbon recalibration and its eventual universal application ....and to live with it.

To form a more detailed idea of the general chronological areas that will be most effected, we need only compare the calibrated versions for the local Pretalayotic Period alongside the conventional radiocarbon readings for any given period to become aware of the degree of difference between radiocarbon years and calendar years. This is especially so, for example, in the earlier ranges of the Pretalayotic period, as pointed out briefly above, where the differences are considerable; in some cases up to 500 years or more. With this example in degree of difference, under any circumstances, serious alterations in chronological thinking will have to take place and adjustments made in the construction of future schemes or other form of archaeological interpretation.

The paired uncalibrated radiocarbon and calendar year listings shown here (Tables 1-3) are offered as immediately interesting examples in particular of the temporal differences found within the earlier part of the Balearic cultural sequence. While they are selected dates, part of a fuller and more extensive inventory and recalibration of all existing dates, they best illustrate the magnitude of changes brought about by calibration of conventional ^{14}C readings, along with demonstrating the areas where serious change in thinking is most likely to be involved. As well as setting themselves up as a basis for general local reference, they also demonstrate and offer in hard terms the *chronometric ranges* and *differences* to be expected when compared to other such listings from the continental mainland.

In short, the implications are such that these analytical results viewed as a whole, calibrated or uncalibrated, are not only useful in suggesting the broader origin and date of prehistoric local events in the Balearic Islands, delineating and defining the actual chronometric sequence in which these took place, and perhaps more specifically even resolving serious controversial cultural issues, like the arrival or introduction of certain cultural influences as well as the introduction of various kinds of technology, but they can more importantly serve, possibly, as a guideline to similar problems of interpretation in adjacent mainland areas as well.

W. H. Waldren

MORE CONCERNING THE VARIOUS SURVEYS

Although there are very large statistical discrepancies in the radiocarbon dates outside the range of calibration, the existing readings (Table 6) (about which more is said below) are included here to exemplify the local Presettlement Period as part of the Balearic chronometric continuity. However, it is the contexts of the Early Settlement and the Pretalayotic Period, synonymous until recently with the *Culture of the Caves* (Colominas Roca 1915) and comparable to the European Upper Neolithic, Chalcolithic and Initial Bronze Age with which we are most concerned at present.

For the Balearics, there are 42 uncalibrated dates for the full range of the Early Settlement and Pretalayotic Periods combined with 38 of the readings for the Pretalayoic Period on its own. As we can see from the two detailed chronological schemes (Figure 2 and 2a), it has been possible to distinguish a number of *events* and *milestones* with the framework with some certitude, especially within the *early phase ranges*. For example (a) the introduction of pottery technology, (b) the introduction of domesticated animal species, both formerly indicated as circa 3000 bc: cal 3675 BC and (c) the extinction of the major endemic mammal, *Myotragus balearicus* dated circa 2300 bc: cal. 2735 BC, all within the NECP of the Pretalayotic. Other examples of particular milestones and the changes indicated by recalibration are (d) the appearance of the first Beaker influences and open-air settlement and (e) introduction of metal working technology dated circa 2000 bc: cal. 2548 BC, within the EBP and (f) use of tin bronze during the LBP, circa 1700 bc cal. 2040 BC. The calibrated dates listed and the differences will certainly require considerable getting use to as well some rethinking; especially with differences ranging as they do from 675 years in the lower dates to 340 years in the upper ones.

The first sequential order of dates can be seen in the example shown (Table 2), where 35 radiocarbon dates are available from the Ferrandell-Oleza-Mas Prehistoric Settlement Complex. This listing originates from an *architectural* and *open-air* environment. Here, radiocarbon dating has been not only used to date the duration of occupation of the settlement, but through the use of bracket dating (Figure 4) an attempt has been made equally to date the various architectural elements and building sequence itself. Considerable differences can be seen here between uncalibrated and calibrated dates, especially once again in the earliest ranges. For example, an approximate 900 year duration is suggested by the uncalibrated dates for the Complex's Old Settlement (Chalcolithic and Initial Bronze Age): 2080 bc for the intitial occupation with intermediary dates covering the period until the Old Settlement's abandonment circa 1130 bc. Calibration of those dates suggest a much longer duration of occupation of 2540 BC to 1360 BC, approximately 1200 years. As will be noted, there is much less discrepancy in the later ranges, where only 50 to 100 years separate uncalibrated from calibrated readings.

The second sequential order of dates originate from nine different sites all with largely different environments and with the inclusion of a few sites with only one or two dates; however, all covering the Pretalayotic Period from 4730 bc to 1120 bc: cal 5589 BC to 1357 BC. They represent the various phases of the Pretalayotic Period, forming the nucleus of the schematic frameworks illustrated (Figure 2 and 2a) for these ranges.

The third sequence of dates originate from the deep,*vertical* stratigraphy and *closed* environment of the Rock Shelter of Son Matge (Figure 6). Here, an occupation and use of the site suggests a range of approximately 4700 years, in uncalibrated terms 4730 bc to 15 bc: cal in a classical vertical stratigraphy from 5589 BC to 20 BC. In essence, on its own, it covers the entire cultural sequence for the Balearics and gives solid parameters for the sequence and further substantiation for the proposed pentapartite framework illustrasted in Figures 2 and 2a. It also

55

acts as a *yardstick* for the eroded, open-air stratigraphic environments examined here, as well as those elsewhere locally.

The last sequence (Table 6) originates from the Cave of Muleta and represents radiocarbon dates well outside conventional range of the method. As mentioned above, they are included here for continuity and reference.

Other tight sequences of radiocarbon dates exist for the Talayotic Period (Bronze Age) (20 readings), 1100 bc to 800 bc: cal 1350 BC to 1000 BC, as well as the Post Talayotic (Iron Age) (79 radiocarbon dates) 800 bc to 123 BC: cal 1000 BC to 123 BC, with late date listings up to 300 AD (Waldren 1990 in preparation). These are not included- as mentioned- for reasons of time and space.

CONCLUSIONS

Quite apart from filling in details concerning the ecological and cultural sequence, the method and the strategies used have other archaeological interests (although the former have been the main objective). In their broader application, they can be looked at in the light of a proving ground of sorts for the radiocarbon method and calibration itself. For as pointed out by Almagro Gorbea (1978) and Fernández-Miranda (1974), there are not many areas where radiocarbon dating has been more successfully used as a dating tool than in the Balearic Islands.

As discussed earlier, among the inconveniences of calibration will be the way in which it is bound to effect the various local schemes presently in circulation. This can be seen most dramatically in the listings and the detailed chronological scheme proposed by the author. In all events, changes in all the existing chronologies are inevitable, for the simple reason that data has been accumulating at an accelerated rate over the last twenty five years, and the only course forward is the utilisation of the existing data; otherwise we will have to return to the use of a relative chronology; a state of affairs that would put Balearic chronology back where it was at the turn of the century and a good 100 years behind the rest of European archaeology.

Nevertheless it is logical to assume that here in the Balearics- as elsewhere- a transitional period of mental adjustment will be necessary regarding recalibration; a period of *getting used to* and *working with* the new dimensions that calibrated dates attach to all the local prehistoric divisions and subdivisions. Meanwhile, we simply have to live with the fact that calibration is not a matter of archaeological fashion or something that will go away if we wait long enough, but that it is here to stay and can be expected to take a serious toll on the existing order of things.

If there is any one contribution the radiocarbon listings published here have made to the Balearic prehistoric sequence, apart from the proposed schematic framework offered as a working hypothesis, it is a demonstration of temporal continuity. This temporal continuity shows a tightly knitted time sequence which appears to emerge throughout the entire local prehistoric landscape. In this respect, it in some ways makes the conventional use of localised nomenclature for the various chronological periods somewhat arbitrary. After all, the more delineating features are the distinctive landmarks of the various periods and evidence supporting the occurrence of important temporal events, for example: the ecological environment before man, the first arrival of man, the extinction of endemic species and the introduction of new, domesticated species and agricultural practices such as land and animal management, the introduction and development of technologies such as metal working and ceramics and of course, evidence of demographic movement and cultural change and exchange throughout time etc. The definition and interpretation of which in the final analysis are the purposes of archaeological research ...and the result of individual interpretation.

57

ACKNOWLEDGEMENT

My deepest appreciation is extended to Dr Minze Stuiver, Chronological Laboratory Quaternary Research Center, University of Washington at Seattle, Washington for the majority of radiocarbon dates used in this the surveys as well as the use of the computer programme for the recalibrations. Appreciation must be extended to include Dr Mark van Strydonck of the Koninklijk Instituut voor het Kunstpatrimonium, Brussels, Belgium for the latest long series of radiocarbon dates. Further thanks are given to Dr Gerald Brush, Department of Biological Anthropology, University of Oxford, Oxford for using the calibration programme and the computerise print outs of the individual dates.

BIBLIOGRAPHY

Almagro Gorbea, M. 1978, C14 y Prehistoria de la Península Ibérica, *Seria Universitaria*, Fundación March, Madrid.

Bada, J.L. and Schroeder, R.A. 1973, Glacial-Postglacial Temperature Differences Deduced from Aspartic Acid Racemisation in Fossil Bones, *Science* 2, November, Vol. 182, pp. 479-482.

Baillie,M.G.L. and Pilcher, J.R. 1983, Archaeology Dendrochronology and the Radiocarbon Calibration Curve, editor, B.S. Ottaway, *University of Edinburgh*, Occasional Paper No.9, Edinburgh, pp. 51-63.

Burleigh, R. and Clutton-Brock, J. 19 80, The Survival of Myotragus balearicus Bate, 1909 in the Neolithic of Mallorca, *Journal of Archaeological Sciences* 7, pp. 285-288.

Clark, R.M.,1975, A Calibration Curve for Radiocarbon Dates, *Antiquity* XLIX, pp. 251-256.

Colominas, Roca, J. 1915. 'Sobre L'Edad de Bronce a Mallorca, *Anuari del'Institut d'Estudis Catalans* 5, Barcelona.

Damon, P.E., Long, A. and Wallick E.I., 1972, Dendrochronological Calibration of the Radiocarbon Time Scale, *Proceedings of the 8th Int'l Conference on Radiocarbon Dating*, Lower Hutt City, I, pp.45-59.

Fernandez Gomez, J., Plantalamor Massanet, L. and Topp, C. 1974, 'Excavaciones en el Sepulcor Megalitico de Ca Na Costa. Formentera, *Estudios de Prehistoria Balear* 1, Palma de Mallorca.

Fernandez, J., Plantalamor Massanet, L. and Topp, C., 1976, Excavaciones en el Sepulcor Megalitico de Ca Na Costa, Separata de Mayudga, 15, *Estudios de Prehistoria Balear*, Ministerior de Educación y Ciencia, Palma de Mallorca, pp. 109-138.

Fernandez Gomez, J. and Topp, C. 1984, Prehistoric Activity in the Pitiussae Islands, The Deya Conference of Prehistory ...Early Settlement in the Western Mediterranean Islands and their Peripheral Areas, *BAR International Series*, Oxford, vol. iii, pp.763-783.

Fernandez-Miranda, M. 1979, Secuencia Cultural de la Prehistoria de Mallorca, Biblioteca Prehistorica Hispana, Madrid.

Fernandez-Miranda, M. and Waldren, W.H., 1974, El Abrigo de Son Matge, (Valldemosa) y la Periodización de la Prehistoria Mallorquina Mediante las Análasis de Carbon 14, *Trabajos de Prehistoria* 31. Madrid, pp. 287-304.

Fernandez-Miranda, M. and Waldren, W.H., 1979, Periodificación Cultural y Cronológia Absoluta en la Prehistoria de Mallorca, *Trabajos de Prehistoria* 36, Madrid, pp. 349-377.

Gasull, P., Lull, V. and Sanahuja, C. 1984, Son Fornes I, la Fase Talayótica, Ensayo de reconstrucción Socio-Economica de una Comunidad Prehistórica de la Isla de Mallorca, *BAR. International Series* 209, Oxford..

Gasull, P., 1985. Arqueología, *Enciclopedia España-Calpe*, Suplemento 1983-1984, pp. 51-68.

Gottesfeld, M., Martin, P. and Waldren, W.H. 1968, Fossil Pollen Counts from the Cave of Muleta, Mallorca, *DAMARC Series* 5, Deya de Mallorca, Baleares, Spain.

Ivanovich, M. 1982. Spectroscopic Methods, in M. Ivanovich and R.S. Harmon (eds.) Uranium Series Disequilbrium Applications to Environmental Problems in the Earth Sciences, *Oxford University Press*, Oxford, pp. 107-144.

Morales, A. 1979, C14 y Prehistoria de la Peninsula Iberica, *Seria Universitaria*, Madrid, pp. 65-6.

Pericot, Garcia, L. 1973, The Balearic Islands, *Thames and Hudson*, London.

Ralph, E.K. and Michael, H.N., 1970, MASCA Radiocarbon Dates for Sequoia and Bristlecone Pine Samples, *Radiocarbon Variations and Absolute Chronology* (I.U. Olason, Ed.), pp. 100-138.

Renfrew, C., 1973, Before Civilisation: the Radiocarbon Revolution and Prehistoric Europe, *Jonathan Cape*, London.

Renfrew, C. and Clark, R.M., 1974, Problems of the Radiocarbon Calendar and Its Calibration, *Archaeometry* 16, pp. 5-18.

Rossello Bordoy, G., Kopper, J.S. and Waldren, W.H. 1967, Complejo Norde de Son Figueral de Son Real, Santa Margarita, Mallorca. *X Congreso Internacionale de Arqueologia*, Mahon y Saragosa, pp. 83-85.

Rossello Bordoy, G., 1973, La Cultura Talayotica en Mallorca: Bases para el Estudio de sus Fases Iniciales. *Caja de Ahorros y Monte de Piedad de las Baleares*, Palma de Mallorca.

Rossello Bordoy, G. and Waldren, W.H. 1973, Excavaciones en el Abrigo de Bosque de Son Matge, Valldemosa, *N.A.H. Prehistoria* 11, p. 1-86.

Schüle, W., 1981. 'El Cerro de la Virgen, Orce (Granada), *Excavaciones Arqueologicas en España* 46, Madrid

Schwarz, H.P. 1980, Uranium Series Dating of Archaeological Sites, *Archaeometry* 22, pp. 3-38.

Schwarz, H.P. 1982, Application of U-Series Dating to Archaeometry, in M. Ivanovich and R.S. Harmon (eds.) Uranium Series Disequilbrium Applications to Environmental Problems in the Earth Sciences, *Oxford University Press*, pp. 326-350.

Schwarz, H.P. , Gascoyne, M. and Harmon, R.S. 1982, Applications of U-Series Dating to Problems of Quaternary Climate, in M. Ivanovich and R.s. Harmon (eds.), Uranium Desies Disequilbrium Applications to Environmental Problems in the earth Sciences, *Oxford University Press*, pp.302-325.

Seitz, M.G. and Taylor, R.E., 1974, Uranium Variations in a Dated Fossil Bone Series from Olduvai Gorge, Tanzania, *Archaeometry* 16, pp. 129-135.

Stuiver, M. and Pearson, G.W., 1986, *Radiocarbon* 28, pp. 805-838 and 839-862.

Stuiver, M. and Waldren, W.H., 1974. 14C Carbonate Dating and the Age of Post Talayotic Lime Burials in Mallorca. *Nature*, Vol. 255, June, pp. 475-476.

Suess, H.E., 1970, Bristlecone Pine Calibration of the Radiocarbon Time Scale from 5400 b.c. to the Present, *Radiocarbon Variations and Absolute Chronology* (I.U. Olason, Ed.), pp. 303-312.

Switzur, J., 1973, in Clark's, A Calibration Curve for Radiocarbon Dates, *Antiquity* XLIX, pg. 251.

Szabo, B.J. and Collins, D., 1975, Ages of Fossil Bone from British Interglacial Sites, *Nature* 254, pp. 679-681.

Szabo, B.J., Malde, H.E. and Irwin-Williams, C., 1969. Dilemma Posed by Uranium Series Dates on Archaeologically Significant Bones from Valsequillo, Puebla, Mexico, Earth Plant. Sci. *Letters* 6, pp. 237-244.

Tarradell, M. and Woods, D., 1976, Excavaciones en la Necropolis de Son Real y Ille dels Porros. *Excavaciones Arqueologicas en Espana* 24, Madrid.

Van Strydonck, M. and Waldren, W.H., 1987, Radiocarbon Dating of Mallorcan Lime Burials, in preparation, *14C and Archaeology*, Conference held at Groningen.

Veny, C. 1968, Las Cuevas Sepulcrales del Bronce Antiguo de Mallorca. Consejo Superior de Investigaciones Cientificas, *Instituto de Prehistoria Espanol de Madrid*, Madrid.

Waldren, W.H. 1967, Informe Preliminar Sobre Analisis de Radiocarbono en Mallorca, *X Congreso Nacional de Arqueologia*, Mahon y Zaragossa, pp. 75-82.

Waldren, W.H. 1968, Mallorcan Chronology for Prehistory Based on Radiocarbon Method, *Pyrenae* 3, Barcelona, pp. 45-65.

Waldren, W.H. 1969. 'Beaker Ware from the Island of Mallorca, *DAMARC Series* No. 6, Deya de Mallorca, Baleares.

Waldren, W.H. 1972, Age Determination by Radiocarbon Method, *Sociedad de Historia Natural de las Baleares*, Palma de Mallorca, pp. 34-50.

Waldren, W.H. 1973, Excavations of the Rock Shelter of Son Matge, Valldemosa, *Prehistoria* II , Madrid.

Waldren, W.H. 1974, Prehistory and the Archaeology of the Balearic Islands, VI Symposium of Peninsular Prehistory, *University of Barcelona*, pp. 31-38.

Waldren, W.H. 1979, A Beaker Workshop Area in the Rock Shelter of Son Matge, Valldemosa, Mallorca, *World Archaeology*, Routledge and Kegan Paul, London, Vol 11, No. 1, pp. 43-67.

Waldren, W.H. 1980, Radiocarbon Determination in the Balearic Islands: an Inventory, *Donald Baden-Powell Quaternary Research Centre*, Oxford University, Oxford.

Waldren, W.H. 1980, The Settlement Complex of Ferrandell-Oleza, A Beaker Settlement from the Balearic Island of Mallorca, *Donald Baden Powell Quaternary Research Centre*, Oxford University, Oxford and DAMARC Series 8, Deya de Mallorca, Baleares, Spain.

Waldren, W.H. 1981, Preliminary Report on the Settlement Complex of Ferrandell-Oleza, Valldemosa, Mallorca. (in preparation) *DAMARC Series* 10, Deya de Mallorca, Baleares.

Waldren, W.H. 1982, Aspects of Balearic Prehistoric Ecology and Culture,. Oxford *Doctoral Thesis*, Oxford.

Waldren, W.H. 1982, Balearic Prehistoric Ecology and Culture: The Excavation and Study of Certain Caves, Rock Shelters and Settlements', *BAR International Series* 149 (ii) Appendix 3A, pp. 675-711. Oxford.

Waldren, W.H. 1983, Early Prehistoric Settlement in the Balearic Islands, *DAMARC Series* 13, Deya Archaeological Museum and Research Centre, Deya Mallorca.

Waldren, W.H. 1984, Chalcolithic Settlement and Beaker Connections in the Balearic Islands, The Deya Conference of Prehistory ...Early Settlement in the Western Mediterranean Islands and their Peripheral Areas. *BAR International Series* 229 , Oxford. vol. iii, pp.911-965.

Waldren, W.H. 1984, The Lithic Industry of the Balearic Islands....its Olezian Tradition of Tabular Flint Blades, The Deya Conference of Prehistory: Early Settlement in the Western Mediterranean Islands and their Peripheral Areas. *BAR International Series* 229 , Oxford. vol. iii, pp.859-909.

Waldren, W. H.,1985. 'A Rose by any other Name...A Question of Balearic Beakers...the Evidence', Oxford International Western Mediterranean Bell Beaker Conference, St. Catherines College, University of Oxford.

Waldren, W. H.,1985. 'The Pottery Distribution Statistics from Ferrandell-Oleza Copper Age Old Settlement' W. Waldren and J. Enseñat, *Oxford International Western Mediterranean Bell Beaker Conference*, St. Catherines College, University of Oxford.

Waldren, W.H.,1986. 'The Balearic Pentapartite Division of Prehistory in Radiocarbon and other Age Determination Inventories', *British Archaeological Reports* (B.A.R.) International Series 282.

Waldren, W. H.,1987. 'Bell Beakers in the Western Mediterranean', W. Waldren and R-C. Kennard (eds.), Oxford International Conference 1985, *British Archaeological Reports* (B.A.R.), Oxford, England.

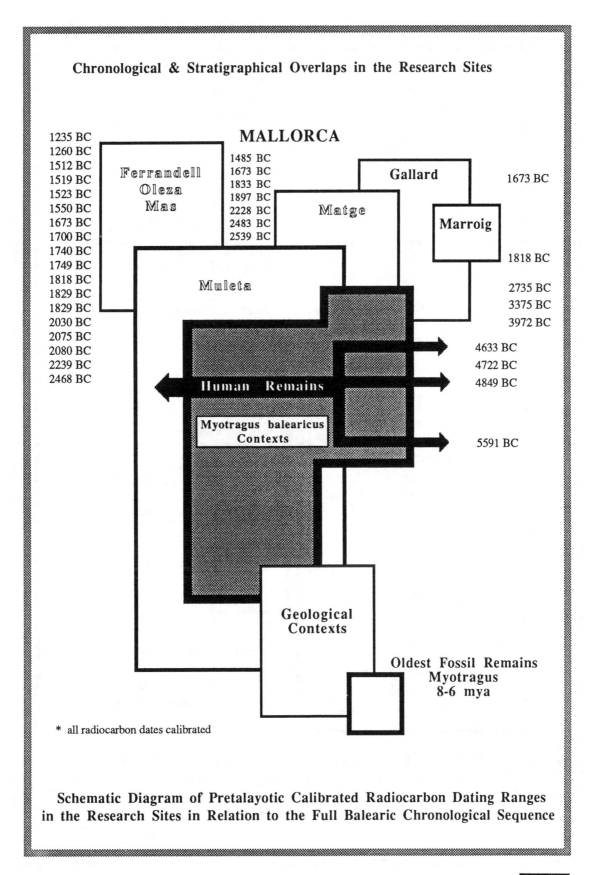

Chronological & Stratigraphical Overlaps in the Research Sites

MALLORCA

1235 BC
1260 BC
1512 BC
1519 BC
1523 BC
1550 BC
1673 BC
1700 BC
1740 BC
1749 BC
1818 BC
1829 BC
1829 BC
2030 BC
2075 BC
2080 BC
2239 BC
2468 BC

Ferrandell
Oleza
Mas

1485 BC
1673 BC
1833 BC
1897 BC
2228 BC
2483 BC
2539 BC

Gallard

Matge

Marroig

1673 BC

1818 BC

2735 BC

3375 BC

3972 BC

Muleta

4633 BC

4722 BC

4849 BC

Human Remains

Myotragus balearicus
Contexts

5591 BC

Geological
Contexts

Oldest Fossil Remains
Myotragus
8-6 mya

* all radiocarbon dates calibrated

Schematic Diagram of Pretalayotic Calibrated Radiocarbon Dating Ranges
in the Research Sites in Relation to the Full Balearic Chronological Sequence

DCATT&T

Figure 1

63

	ROMAN COLONISATION 123 BC	
V POST TALAYOTIC Iron Ages 1000 BC - 123 BC E M L 10-8 8-6 6-1	L	Varied Burial Techniques First Signs of Decline in Talayotic Architecture Military Involvements with Eastern Mediterranean Increase of Classical Trade
	M	First Roman Arriavals Decline in Pottery Technology Decline in Talayotic Architectural Techniques Continued Military Involvement
	E	Colonisation of Ibiza by Carthaginians in 654 BC Inhumation in Quicklime Introduction of Iron
IV TALAYOTIC Bronze Ages 1400 BC - 1000 BC E M L 14-12 12-11 11-10	L	Upper Interface for the Introductionof Iron Upper Interface of Classical Mediterranean Contacts North European (Hallstatt) Influences Continuation of Talayotic Building, Taulas etc.
	M	Apogee of Talayotic Architecture Population Growth Highly Structured Social Organisation New Pottery Technology and Forms
	E	Cremation Burials Common Use and Circulation of Bronze Lower Interface of Talayotic Culture Traditional Phase of Talayotic and Pretalayotic Periods

III
 	
PRETALAYOTIC
 	
Copper Age, Chalcolithic, Initial Bronze
 	
3900 BC - 1400 BC
 	
NECP EBP LBP N
39-25 25-18 18-14 E
                      C
                      P
	L
	B
	P
		Frequent Use of Tin Bronze
		Emergence of Surplus, Wealth and Status
		Social Differentiation
		First Use of Tin Bronze

	E B P	Early Metallurgical Techniques Introduction of Beaker Culture into the Balearics Earliest Open-Air Settlements and Sanctuaries First Quality Lithic Industry
	N E C P	SURVIVAL OF MYOTRAGUS Introduction of Domesticated Animals Introduction of Ceramic Technology
II EARLY SETTLEMENT Neolithic 5600 bc - 3900 bc		Incipient Agriculture Attempts at Domestication of Myotragus Coexistence of Man and Myotragus ARRIVAL OF MAN
I PRESETTLEMENT Paleo-Meso-Neolithic 8 - 6 million years ago - 5600 bc		Evolution of the Islands Endemic Species Myotragus (ruminant) Hypnomys (rodent) Nesiotites (insectivor)

PENTAPARTITE DIVISION OF BALEARIC PREHISTORY

the chronological, ecological and cultural sequence with uncalibrated radiocarbon dates

(after w. waldren)

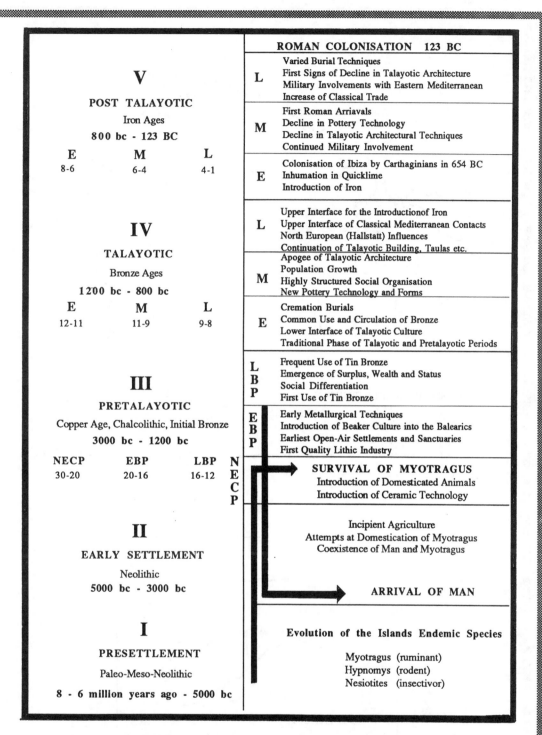

		ROMAN COLONISATION 123 BC
V **POST TALAYOTIC** Iron Ages **800 bc - 123 BC** E M L 8-6 6-4 4-1	**L**	Varied Burial Techniques First Signs of Decline in Talayotic Architecture Military Involvements with Eastern Mediterranean Increase of Classical Trade
	M	First Roman Arrivals Decline in Pottery Technology Decline in Talayotic Architectural Techniques Continued Military Involvement
	E	Colonisation of Ibiza by Carthaginians in 654 BC Inhumation in Quicklime Introduction of Iron
IV **TALAYOTIC** Bronze Ages **1200 bc - 800 bc** E M L 12-11 11-9 9-8	**L**	Upper Interface for the Introduction of Iron Upper Interface of Classical Mediterranean Contacts North European (Hallstatt) Influences Continuation of Talayotic Building, Taulas etc.
	M	Apogee of Talayotic Architecture Population Growth Highly Structured Social Organisation New Pottery Technology and Forms
	E	Cremation Burials Common Use and Circulation of Bronze Lower Interface of Talayotic Culture Traditional Phase of Talayotic and Pretalayotic Periods
III **PRETALAYOTIC** Copper Age, Chalcolithic, Initial Bronze **3000 bc - 1200 bc** NECP EBP LBP 30-20 20-16 16-12	**L B P**	Frequent Use of Tin Bronze Emergence of Surplus, Wealth and Status Social Differentiation First Use of Tin Bronze
	E B P	Early Metallurgical Techniques Introduction of Beaker Culture into the Balearics Earliest Open-Air Settlements and Sanctuaries First Quality Lithic Industry
	N E C P	**SURVIVAL OF MYOTRAGUS** Introduction of Domesticated Animals Introduction of Ceramic Technology
II **EARLY SETTLEMENT** Neolithic **5000 bc - 3000 bc**		Incipient Agriculture Attempts at Domestication of Myotragus Coexistence of Man and Myotragus
		ARRIVAL OF MAN
I **PRESETTLEMENT** Paleo-Meso-Neolithic **8 - 6 million years ago - 5000 bc**		**Evolution of the Islands Endemic Species** Myotragus (ruminant) Hypnomys (rodent) Nesiotites (insectivor)

PENTAPARTITE DIVISION OF BALEARIC PREHISTORY

the chronological, ecological and cultural sequence with uncalibrated radiocarbon dates

(after w. waldren)

The chronological framework illustrated here can be compared to that of Figure 2 on the preceding page. The sequence shown above demonstrates the parameters of the uncalibrated dates and the interfaces for the most important prehistoric events in the Balearics as found in the research sites examined.

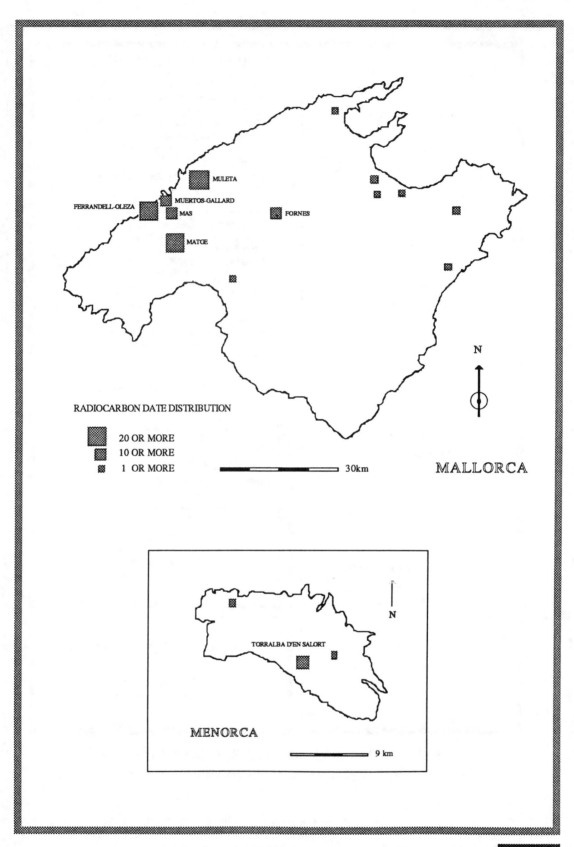

RADIOCARBON DATE DISTRIBUTION

20 OR MORE
10 OR MORE
1 OR MORE

30km

MALLORCA

MULETA
FERRANDELL-OLEZA
MUERTOS-GALLARD
MAS
FORNES
MATGE

N

MENORCA

TORRALBA D'EN SALORT

N

9 km

DCATT&T

Figure 3

Listing of Radiocarbon Results

Balearic Pretalayotic, Talayotic and Post Talayotic Periods

Ferrandell-Oleza, Valldemosa, Baleares, Mallorca, Spain

	Site Context	bc 14C	Date bp	Recalib BC/ Recalib BP		Lab. No
				Old Settlement		
1.	SFO-OS- EW	2080 ± 110 bc	4030 yrs	2548 BC	4497 BP	BM 1843R
2.	SFO-OS- NW	1840 ± 90 bc	3790 yrs	2239 BC	4188 BP	QL 1636
3.	SFO-WOS-W17	1750 ± 30 bc	3700 yrs	2090 BC	4039 BP	QL 1592
4.	SFO-WOS-W40	1690 ± 100 bc	3640 yrs	2030 BC	3979 BP	BM 1981R
5.	SFO-OS-CH1	1540 ± 80 bc	3490 yrs	1829 BC	3778 BP	QL 4042
6.	SFO-OS-AT1-2	1540 ± 30 bc	3490 yrs	1829 BC	3778 BP	QL 1859
7.	SFO-OS-SW	1520 ± 50 bc	3470 yrs	1819 BC	3768 BP	QL 4100
8.	SFO-OS-CH-1	1500 ± 110 bc	3450 yrs	1749 BC	3698 BP	QL 4043
9.	SFO-OS-WC	1440 ± 100 bc	3210 yrs	1713 BC	3760 BP	BM 2312R
10.	SFO-OS-EXW1	1400 ± 100 bc	3150 yrs	1673 BC	3620 BP	BM 1698R
11.	SFO-OS-WCS	1330 ± 120 bc	3280 yrs	1549 BC	3498 BP	QL 1896
12.	SFO-OS-WC	1290 ± 30 bc	3240 yrs	1519 BC	3468 BP	QL ?
13.	SFO-OS-SWF	1230 ± 80 bc	3180 yrs	1450 BC	3400 BP	QL-4191
			Old Settlement - Abandonment			
14.	SFO-O-C2	1120 ± 50 bc	3070 yrs	1357 BC	3306 BP	HAR 3490
15.	SFO-OS-CHS	1040 ± 160 bc	2990 yrs	1261 BC	3210 BP	QL 4044
16.	SFO-OS-SWS	800 ± 120 bc	2830 yrs	998 BC	2947 BP	QL 4041
			Younger Settlement			
17.	SFO-YS-T1	960 ± 100 bc	2910 yrs	1100 BC	3049 BP	HAR 3413
18.	SFO-YS-T1E	880 ± 100 bc	2830 yrs	998 BC	2947 BP	IRPA 782
19.	SFO-YS-T4	865 ± 60 bc	2815 yrs	975 BC	2969 BP	IRPA 907
20.	SFO-YS-T1	780 ± 30 bc	2730 yrs	897 BC	2847 BP	QL 4190
21.	SFO-YS-WT	750 ± 30 bc	2700 yrs	888 BC	2787 BP	QL 4074
22.	SFO-YS-T4	730 ± 60 bc	2680 yrs	868 BC	2770 BP	IRPA 880
23.	SFO-YS-HH1	710 ± 30 bc	2660 yrs	818 BC	2767 BP	QL 4075
24.	SFO-YS-T4	630 ± 60 bc	2580 yrs	793 BC	2745 BP	IRPA 881
25.	SFO-YS-T1	590 ± 60 bc	2540 yrs	786 BC	2735 BP	HAR 3458
26.	SFO-YS-T1	550 ± 40 bc	2500 yrs	685 BC	2693 BP	QL 1533
27.	SFO-YS-T2	510 ± 80 bc	2460 yrs A	646 BC	2595 BP	HAR 3459
28.	SFO-YS-T1	480 ± 230 bc	2430 yrs A	516 BC	2465 BP	BM 1842
29.	SFO-YS-T2	450 ± 60 bc	2400 yrs A	408 BC	2357 BP	I 5398
30.	SFO-YS-HHE	150 ± 60 bc	2150 yrs	200 BC	2200 BP	IRPA 885
			Son Mas Sanctuary			
31.	SFO-SMSS	1630 ± 70 bc	3590 yrs	2050 BC	4059 BP	IRPA 909
32.	SFO-SMSS	1620 ± 65 bc	3580 yrs	2050 BC	4059 BP	IRPA 908
33.	SFO-SMSS-PT	520 ± 25 bc	2470 yrs	650 BC	2600 BP	QL 4264
34.	SFO-SMSS-PT	260 ± 90 bc	2210 yrs	300 BC	2250 BP	QL 4200
35.	SFO-SMSS-PT	100 ± 150 bc	2050 yrs	100 BC	2050 BP	QL 4201

Reference for datasets (and intervals) used:
Stuiver, M. and Pearson, G.W. 1986, Radiocarbon 28, 805-838.
Pearson, G.W. and Stuiver, M. 1986, Radiocarbon 28, 839-862.
Comments:
A: This is Standard deviation (error) may include a lab error multiplier.
O: Represents a negative age BP
If so specify

DCATT&T   Table   1

Radiocarbon Results
Balearic Early Settlement and Pretalayotic Period
with Emphasis on Bell Beaker Contexts as of 1989

	Site	Context	bc 14C Date	bp Date	Recalib BC/Recalib BP		Lab. Date
				Early Settlement Period			
1.	ABSM	ESP	4730 ± 120 bc	6680 yrs	**5589 BC**	**7538 BP**	QL 29
2.	SM	ESP	3985 ± 110 bc	5935 yrs	**4848 BC**	**6798 BP**	KNB640
3.	ABSM	ESP	3870 ± 360 bc	5820 yrs	**4722 BC**	**6671 BP**	CSIC176
4.	ABSM	ESP	3800 ± 115 bc	5750 yrs	**4633 BC**	**6582 BP**	I 5516
				Pretalayotic Period			
				Neolithic Early Ceramic Phase (NECP)			
5.	AMG	PRT	3210 ± 100 bc	5160 yrs	**3972 BC**	**5920 BP**	BM 1994R
6.	ABSM	PRT	2700 ± 120 bc	4650 yrs	**3375 BC**	**5324 BP**	QL 988
7.	ABSM	PRT	2143 ± 398 bc	4093 yrs	**2735 BC**	**4701 BP**	BM 1408
				Early Beaker Phase (EBP)			
8.	SFO-OS	EBP	2080 ± 110 bc	3950 yrs	**2549 BC**	**4427 BP**	BM 1843R
9.	ABSM	EBP	2070 ± 50 bc	4020 yrs	**2539 BC**	**4488 BP**	QL 23
10.	ABSM	EBP	2030 ± 120 bc	3980 yrs	**2522 BC**	**4471 BP**	CSIC178
11.	ABSM	EBP	2020 ± 100 bc	3970 yrs	**2483 BC**	**4432 BP**	QL 5b
12.	SM	EBP	1960 ± 120 bc	3910 yrs	**2459 BC**	**4408 BP**	Y 2389
13.	ABSM	EBP	1870 ± 120 bc	3820 yrs	**2368 BC**	**4398 BP**	Y 2359
14.	SFO-OS	EBP	1840 ± 90 bc	3790 yrs	**2239 BC**	**4188 BP**	QL 1636
15.	AMG	EBP	1840 ± 80 bc	3790 yrs	**2239 BC**	**4188 BP**	Y 1789
16.	ABSM	LBP	1820 ± 100 bc	3770 yrs	**2214 BC**	**4165 BP**	BM 1995
17.	CX	EBP	1800 ± 115 bc	3750 yrs	**2168 BC**	**4117 BP**	I 5515
18.	SFO-OS	EBP	1750 ± 30 bc	3700 yrs	**2090 BC**	**4039 BP**	QL 1592
19.	ABSM	EBP	1750 ± 60 bc	3700 yrs	**2090 BC**	**4039 BP**	IRPA 835
				Late Beaker Phase (LBP)			
20.	ABSM	EBP	1720 ± 100 bc	3670 yrs	**2076 BC**	**4025 BP**	QL 24
21.	SFO-OS	EBP	1690 ± 100 bc	3640 yrs	**2046 BC**	**4055 BP**	BM 1981R
22.	SMSS	EBP	1630 ± 65 bc	3580 yrs	**2050 BC**	**4059 BP**	IRPA 909
23.	SMSS	EBP	1620 ± 70 bc	3570 yrs	**2050 BC**	**4059 BP**	IRPA 908
24.	ABSM	LBP	1620 ± 80 bc	3620 yrs	**1999 BC**	**3948 BP**	CSIC179
25.	SFO-OS	LBP	1540 ± 80 bc	3470 yrs	**1829 BC**	**3878 BP**	QL 4042
26.	SFO-OS	LBP	1540 ± 30 bc	3490 yrs	**1828 BC**	**3877 BP**	QL 1859
27.	ABSM	LBP	1530 ± 80 bc	3480 yrs	**1824 BC**	**3873 BP**	CSIC180
28.	SMRG	LBP	1520 ± 80 bc	3470 yrs	**1819 BC**	**3868 BP**	Y 1856
29.	SFO-OS	LBP	1520 ± 50 bc	3470 yrs	**1819 BC**	**3868 BP**	QL 4100
30.	SFO-OS	LBP	1500 ± 110 bc	3450 yrs	**1749 BC**	**3798 BP**	QL 4043
31.	ABSM	LBP	1470 ± 80 bc	3420 yrs	**1740 BC**	**3787 BP**	QL 5a
32.	SFO-OS	LBP	1440 ± 100 bc	3390 yrs	**1713 BC**	**3760 BP**	BM 2312R
33.	ABSM	LBP	1400 ± 60 bc	3350 yrs	**1673 BC**	**3620 BP**	QL 5
34.	SFO-OS	LBP	1400 ± 310 bc	3350 yrs	**1673 BC**	**3620 BP**	BM 1988R
35.	SFO-OS	LBP	1330 ± 120 bc	3280 yrs	**1549 BC**	**3498 BP**	QL 1896
36.	CNC	LBP	1320 ± 80bc	3270 yrs	**1526 BC**	**3475 BP**	BM 1667
37.	SFO-OS	LBP	1310 ± 100 bc	3260 yrs	**1523 BC**	**3472 BP**	QL 4040
38.	SFO-OS	LBP	1290 ± 30 bc	3230 yrs	**1516 BC**	**3465 BP**	BM ?
39.	ABSM	LBP	1250 ± 100 bc	3200 yrs	**1485 BC**	**3434 BP**	Y 2667
40.	SFO-OS	LBP	1230 ± 80 bc	3180 yrs	**1450 BC**	**3400 BP**	QL-4191
41.	SFO-OS	LBP	1140 ± 70 bc	3090 yrs	**1400 BC**	**3349 BP**	BM 1698
42.	SFO-OS	LBP	1120 ± 50 bc	3070 yrs	**1357 BC**	**3306 BP**	HAR 3490

DCATT&T　　　　　　　　　　　　　　　　　　　　　　　　Table　 2

	Site	Context	bc 14C Date	bp Date	Recalib BC/Recalib BP		Lab. Date
			Early Settlement Period				
1.	ABSM	ESP	4730 ± 120 bc	6680 yrs	5589 BC	7538 BP	QL 29
2.	ABSM	ESP	3870 ± 360 bc	5820 yrs	4722 BC	6671 BP	CSIC176
3.	ABSM	ESP	3800 ± 115 bc	5750 yrs	4633 BC	6582 BP	I 5516
			Pretalayotic Period				
			Neolithic Early Ceramic Phase (NECP)				
4.	ABSM	PRT	2700 ± 120 bc	4650 yrs	3375 BC	5324 BP	QL 988
5.	ABSM	PRT	2143 ± 398 bc	4093 yrs	2735 BC	4701 BP	BM 1408
			Early Beaker Phase (EBP)				
6.	ABSM	EBP	2070 ± 50 bc	4020 yrs	2539 BC	4488 BP	QL 23
7.	ABSM	EBP	2030 ± 120 bc	3980 yrs	2522 BC	4471 BP	CSIC178
8.	ABSM	EBP	2020 ± 100 bc	3970 yrs	2483 BC	4432 BP	QL 5b
9.	ABSM	EBP	1870 ± 120 bc	3820 yrs	2368 BC	4398 BP	Y 2359
10.	ABSM	EBP	1820 ± 100 bc	3770 yrs	2214 BC	4165 BP	BM 1995
11.	ABSM	EBP	1750 ± 60 bc	3700 yrs	2090 BC	4039 BP	IRPA 835
			Late Beaker Phase (LBP)				
12.	ABSM	EBP	1720 ± 100 bc	3670 yrs	2076 BC	4025 BP	QL 24
13.	ABSM	LBP	1620 ± 80 bc	3620 yrs	1999 BC	3948 BP	CSIC179
14.	ABSM	LBP	1530 ± 80 bc	3480 yrs	1824 BC	3873 BP	CSIC180
15.	ABSM	LBP	1470 ± 80 bc	3420 yrs	1740 BC	3787 BP	QL 5a
16.	ABSM	LBP	1400 ± 60 bc	3350 yrs	1673 BC	3620 BP	QL 5
17.	ABSM	LBP	1250 ± 100 bc	3200 yrs	1485 BC	3434 BP	Y 2667
			Talayotic Period- Post Talayotic Period				
			Middle Bronza Age (MBA), Early, Middle & LATE Iron Age (EIA)(MIA)(LIA)				
18.	ABSM	MBA	870 ± 50 bc	2820 yrs	943 BC	2942 BP	QL986
19.	ABSM	EIA	780 ± 100 bc	2730 yrs	897 BC	2846 BP	QL7
20.	ABSM	EIA	750 ± 170 bc	2700 yrs	838 BC	2787 BP	QL11
21.	ABSM	EIA	700 ± 60 bc	2650 yrs	815 BC	2765 BP	IRPA811
22.	ABSM	EIA	690 ± 100 bc	2640 yrs	809 BC	2758 BP	QL27
23.	ABSM	EIA	670 ± 160 bc	2620 yrs	800 BC	2750 BP	IRPA695
24.	ABSM	EIA	620 ± 100 bc	2570 yrs	795 BC	2744 BP	IRPA790
25.	ABSM	EIA	620 ± 100 bc	2570 yrs	795 BC	2744 BP	QL20
26.	ABSM	EIA	610 ± 60 bc	2560 yrs	800 BC	2760 BP	IRPA803
27.	ABSM	EIA	600 ± 60 bc	2550 yrs	791 BC	2740 BP	IRPA676
28.	ABSM	EIA	600 ± 60 bc	2550 yrs	791 BC	2740 BP	IRPA751
29.	ABSM	MIA	590 ± 80 bc	2540 yrs	786 BC	2735 BP	QL24
30.	ABSM	MIA	590 ± 80 bc	2540 yrs	786 BC	2735 BP	QL4
31.	ABSM	MIA	590 ± 60 bc	2540 yrs	786 BC	2735 BP	IRPA752
32.	ABSM	MIA	570 ± 80 bc	2520 yrs	770 BC	2719 BP	QL6
33.	ABSM	MIA	530 ± 70 bc	2480 yrs	655 BC	2630 BP	QL10
34.	ABSM	MIA	450 ± 80 bc	2400 yrs	408 BC	2357 BP	Y2669
35.	ABSM	MIA	400 ± 55 bc	2350 yrs	400 BC	2349 BP	IRPA710
36.	ABSM	LIA	340 ± 100 bc	2290 yrs	383 BC	2332 BP	QL5C
37.	ABSM	LIA	310 ± 60 bc	2260 yrs	379 BC	2328 BP	QL22
38.	ABSM	LIA	290 ± 70 bc	2240 yrs	370 BC	2319 BP	QL1A
39.	ABSM	LIA	250 ± 100 bc	2200 yrs	302 BC	2255 BP	QL9
40.	ABSM	LIA	130 ± 90 bc	2080 yrs	105 BC	2054 BP	QL8
41.	ABSM	LIA	120 ± 120 bc	2070 yrs	101 BC	2050 BP	QL7A
42.	ABSM	LIA	15 ± 55 bc	1965 yrs	20 BC	1970 BP	IRPA710

DCATT&T   Table   3

ABBREVIATIONS OF SITES AND SAMPLES ORIGINS

bp	Uncalibrated before the present dates
BP	Calibrated before the present dates
bc	Uncalibrated 14C dates
BC	Calibrated 14C dates
PSP	Presettlement Period
ESP	Early Settlement Period
PRT	Pretalayotic
T	Talayotic, Talayot
PT	Post Talayotic
NECP	Neolithic Early Ceramic Phase
EBP	Early Beaker Period
LBP	Late Beaker Phase
ABSM	Rock Shelter of Son Matge
AMG	Rock Shelter of Muertos Gallard
BCA	Talayot of Binicalf
CX	Ca Na Coxtera
SF	Son Fornes
SB	Son Baronat
SFO-YS	Ferrandell-Oleza Older Settlement
SFO-OS	Ferrandell-Oleza Younger Settlement
SILL	S'illot
SM	Cave of Son Muleta
SMAR	Son Marino
SMR	Naviforme of Son Morell
SMRG	Cave of Son Marroig
SO	Son Oms
SP	Son Severa-Pula
SPG	Cave of Son Puig
SRDC	Sa Regina dels Cans
SRF	Son Real Figureral
SRN	Son Real Necropolis
SSP	Ses Paisses
TT	Taula of Torralba den Salort
SMSS	Son Mas Sanctaury

LIST OF ABBREVIATIONS

Universities, Institutions and Laboratories

BM   British Museum, Radiocarbon Laboratory, London.

CSIC   University of Madrid, Centro Superior de Investigaciones Cientifica, Spain.

GIF   French Radiocarbon Laboratory.

HU   German Radiocarbon Laboratory.

I   Isotopes Incorporated, Englewood, New Jersey.

IRPA   Koninklijk Instituut voor het Kunstpatrimonium, Brussels, Belgium

KBN   Kaman Bio-Nuclear Inc., Colorado Springs, Colorado.

QL   Quaternary Research Centre, University of Washington Radiocarbon Laboratory, Seattle Washington.

SI   Smithsonian Institution, United States National Museum, Radiocarbon Laboratory, Washington, D.C.

SIO   Scripps Institute of Oceanography, University of California, La Jolla, California.

UCLA   University of California at Los Angeles, Radiocarbon Laboratory, Los Angeles, California.

UGRA   University of Granada, Granada, Spain.

UP   University of Pennsylvania, Museum School, Radiocarbon Laboratory, Philadelphia, Pennsylvania.

Y   Yale University, Peabody Museum, Radiocarbon Laboratory, New Haven, Connecticut.

Test Material Abbreviations

Ab.   Animal bone
Ca.   Carbonate
Cahl.   Carbonate from hearth levels
Cf.   Calcite floor
Cg.   Carbonised grain
Ch.   Charcoal
Ch.b.   Charred bone
Chhl.   Charcoal from hearth levels
Cps.   Coprolites
Gb.   Goat bone
Hb.   Human bone
Mb.   Myotragus bone
Mbhl.   Myotragus bone in hearth levels
Sc.   Stalactite core
Wd.   Wood

Radiocarbon Analysis Results Beyond the Range of Calibration
Cave of Muleta, Mallorca, Baleares, Spain

Early Settlement and Presettlement Period

	Site	Context	bc 14C date	bp Date	Lab. Number
1.	SM	ESP	3985 ± 110 bc	5935 yrs	KNB 640
2.	SM	PSP	5185 ± 80 bc	7135 yrs	KNB 640a
3.	SM	PSP	5350 ± 100 bc	7300 yrs	HAR 2968
4.	SM	PSP	5350 ± 100 bc	7300 yrs	HAR 2934
5.	SM	PSP	6498 ± 1180 bc	8448 yrs	KNB 640b
6.	SM	PSP	6620 ± 350 bc	8570 yrs	UCLA 1740c
7.	SM	PSP	6950 ± 400 bc	8800 yrs	HAR 2932
8.	SM	PSP	6950 ± 400	8800 yrs	HAR 2909
9.	SM	PSP	8735 ± 3517 bc	10,685 yrs	KNB 640c
10.	SM	PSP	12,050 ± 350 bc	14,000 yrs	SIO 1a RAA
11.	SM	PSP	12,515 ± 315 bc	14,465 yrs	SI 654
12.	SM	PSP	12,700 ± 850 bc	14,650 yrs	UCLA 1704b
13.	SM	PSP	13,395 ± 655 bc	15,885 yrs	SI 646
14.	SM	PSP	13,850 ± 600 bc	15,900 yrs	HAR 2933
15.	SM	PSP	14,385 ± 415 bc	16,335 yrs	SI 648
16.	SM	PSP	14,900 ± 200 bc	16,850 yrs	UCLA 1704d
17.	SM	PSP	14,950 ± 200 bc	16,900 yrs	HAR 2931
18.	SM	PSP	16,150 ± 600 bc	18,100 yrs	SI 649
19.	SM	PSP	16,785 ± 555 bc	18,735 yrs	SI 650
20.	SM	PSP	16,850 ± 500 bc	18,800 yrs	HAR 2971
21.	SM	PSP	17,030 ± 200 bc	18,980 yrs	UCLA 1704e
22.	SM	PSP	21,850 ± 480 bc	23,800 yrs	SI 647
23.	SM	PSP	21,850 ± 500 bc	23,800 yrs	HAR 2912
24.	SM	PSP	25,050 ± 600 bc	26,000 yrs	SIO 1cRAA
25.	SM	PSP	25,050 ± 600 bc	26,000 yrs	HAR 2910
26.	SM	PSP	26,650 ± 600 bc	28,600 yrs	UCLA 1704a
27.	SM	PSP	30,050 ± 715 bc	32,000 yrs	SIO 1g RAA
28.	SM	PSP	40,050 ± 1000 bc	42,000 yrs	HAR 2911
29.	SM	PSP	48,000 inf	48,000 yrs	QL 127
30.	SM	PSP	58,000 inf	58,000 yrs	QL 128
31.	SM	PSP	80,000 pm	80,000 yrs	Y 1cf

DCATT&T

Table 6

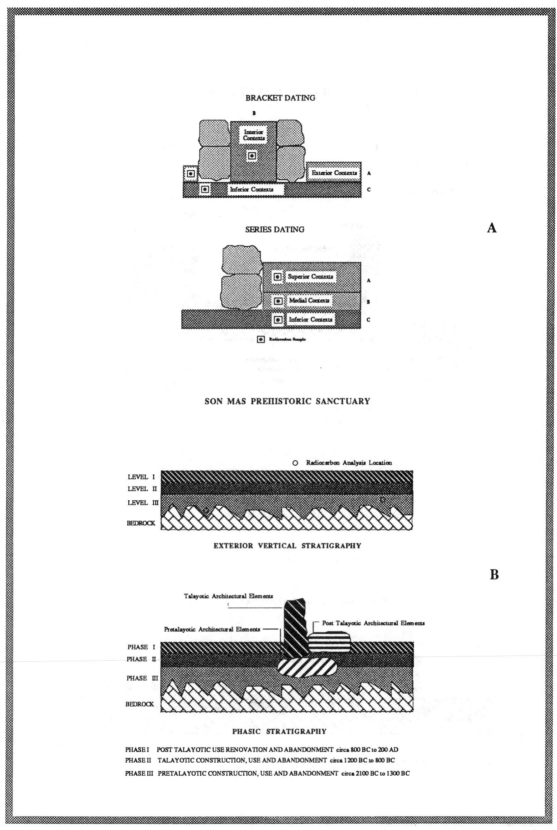

BRACKET DATING

SERIES DATING

A

SON MAS PREHISTORIC SANCTUARY

EXTERIOR VERTICAL STRATIGRAPHY

B

PHASIC STRATIGRAPHY

PHASE I   POST TALAYOTIC USE RENOVATION AND ABANDONMENT circa 800 BC to 200 AD
PHASE II   TALAYOTIC CONSTRUCTION, USE AND ABANDONMENT circa 1200 BC to 800 BC
PHASE III PRETALAYOTIC CONSTRUCTION, USE AND ABANDONMENT circa 2100 BC to 1300 BC

DCATT&T   Figure   4

73

TAULA OF TORRALBA BRACKET DATING

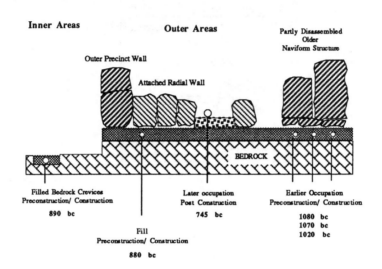

TAULA   **TALAYOT**

Inner Areas   Outer Areas   Partly Disassembled
                                                        Older
                                                  Naviform Structure

Outer Precinct Wall

Attached Radial Wall

BEDROCK

Filled Bedrock Crevices   Later occupation   Earlier Occupation
Preconstruction/ Construction   Post Construction   Preconstruction/ Construction

890 bc   745 bc   1080 bc
                                                       1070 bc
                                                       1020 bc

Fill
Preconstruction/ Construction

880 bc

PREHISTORIC SANCTUARY OF SON MAS

SANCTUARY INTERIOR

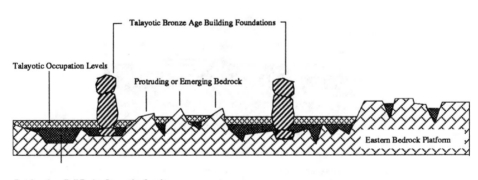

Talayotic Bronze Age Building Foundations

Talayotic Occupation Levels

Protruding or Emerging Bedrock

Eastern Bedrock Platform

Pretalayotic or Bell Beaker Occupation Levels

DCATT&T   **Figure**   5

74

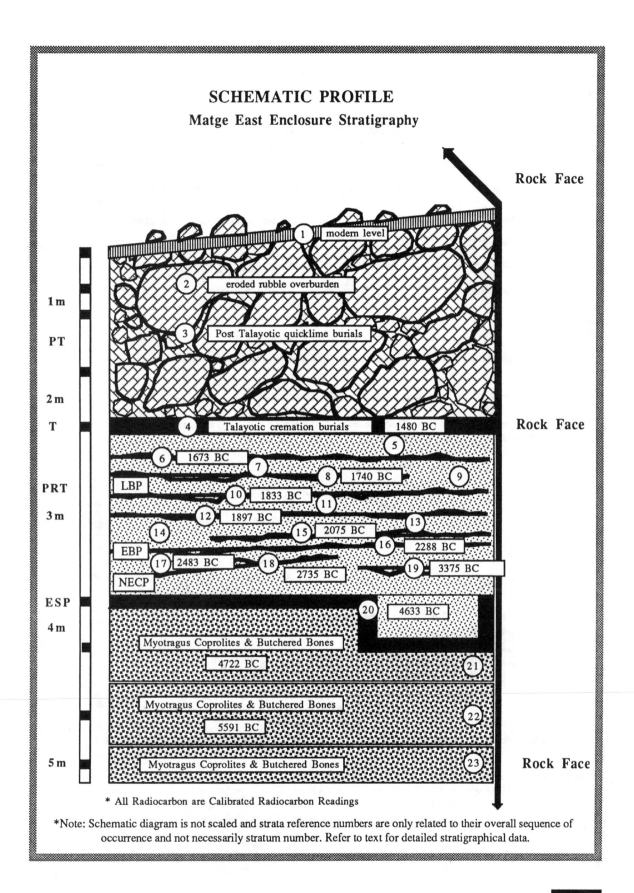

SCHEMATIC PROFILE

Matge East Enclosure Stratigraphy

Rock Face

(1) modern level

(2) eroded rubble overburden

1 m

PT

(3) Post Talayotic quicklime burials

2 m

T

(4) Talayotic cremation burials   1480 BC   Rock Face

(5)

(6) 1673 BC

(7)

(8) 1740 BC   (9)

PRT

LBP

(10) 1833 BC

(11)

3 m

(12) 1897 BC

(13)

(14)

(15) 2075 BC

(16) 2288 BC

EBP

(17) 2483 BC   (18)   (19) 3375 BC

NECP   2735 BC

ESP

(20) 4633 BC

4 m

Myotragus Coprolites & Butchered Bones

4722 BC   (21)

Myotragus Coprolites & Butchered Bones

5591 BC   (22)

5 m   Myotragus Coprolites & Butchered Bones   (23)   Rock Face

* All Radiocarbon are Calibrated Radiocarbon Readings

*Note: Schematic diagram is not scaled and strata reference numbers are only related to their overall sequence of occurrence and not necessarily stratum number. Refer to text for detailed stratigraphical data.

DCATT&T   Figure   6

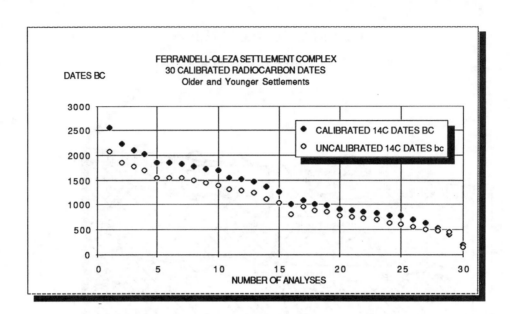

GRAPH A. Demonstrates the differences between uncalibrated and calibrated radiocarbon dates from the FERRANDELL-OLEZA OLD AND YOUNGER SETTLEMENTS on the island of Mallorca, according to the recent Washington-Belfast recalibration curve. These are the first 30 radiocarbon readings found in Table 2 available for the Balearic Pretalayotic Period and falling within the range of the last 8000 years.

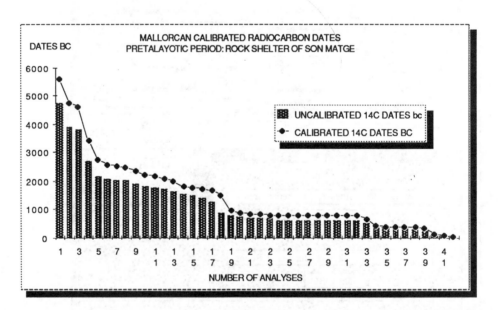

GRAPH B. Demonstrates the differences between the uncalibrated and calibrated radiocarbon dates from the Mallorca closed, deep stratigraphy of the ROCK SHELTER OF SON MATGE for all periods according to the latest Washington-Belfast recalibration curve. They represent 42 dates for the vertical deposition of the site found in Table 3, delineating the duration of occupation from the Neolithic through the following Copper, Bronze and Iron Ages.

DCATT & T

Figure 7

THE CHRONOLOGICAL SCHEME OF G. LILLIU

I.   **Talayótico I Casa 12** C14 950+110 a. de J.C. (nivel en lecho de roca)
     Casa 3 anterior al 800 a. de J.C. (nivel en lecho de roca)
II. **Talayótico II** 700 al 400 a. de J.C.
III. **Talayótico III** 400 al 200 a. de J.C.

THE CHRONOLOGICAL SCHEME OF G. ROSSELLO-BORDOY

I.	**Pretalayótico**	5000 al 1400 a. de J.C.
II.	**Talayótico I**	1400 al 1000 a. de J.C.
III.	**Talayótico II**	1000 al 800 a. de J.C.
IV.	**Talayótico III**	800 al 500 a. de J.C.
V.	**Talayótico IV**	500 hasta la Colonización Romana.

THE CHRONOLOGY OF M. FERNANDEZ-MIRANDA

I.	**Hombre Precerámico**	5000 al 2000 a. de J.C.
II.	**Horizonte de Cerámica Incisa**	2000 al 1700 a. de J.C.
III.	**Bronce Pretalayótico**	1700 al 1500 a. de J.C.
IV.	**Talayótico I**	1200 al 800 a. de J.C.
V.	**Talayótico II**	800 al 100 a. de J.C.

Shown above are the three most recognised and frequently used chronological schemes for the Balearic Islands, all of which are based on radiocarbon dating.

DCATT&T

Figure 8

CUEVAS SEPULCRALES PRETALAYOTICAS DE MALLORCA:
UN ENSAYO DE CLASIFICACION Y ANALISIS (*)

MARGARITA DIAZ-ANDREU
Departamento de Prehistoria
Universidad Complutense
Madrid, España

MANUEL FERNANDEZ-MIRANDA
Departamento de Prehistoria
Universidad Complutense
Madrid, España

RESUMEN

Las cuevas sepulcrales mallorquinas de época pretalayótica constituyen uno de los elementos arqueológicos más característicos de esa fase de la prehistoria de la isla, con casi centenar y medio de ejemplares localizados entre las naturales y las construidas artificialmente. Su cronología y tipología, así como los rituales funerarios o la forma de los objetos considerados característicos entre los ajuares que en ellas se depositaron, han servido para vincular estos monumentos con construcciones similares de áreas próximas del Mediterráneo occidental, sin considerar la existencia o no de relaciones entre ellas o la pertenencia de cada territorio de ámbitos culturales bien diferenciados. Cuevas similares, aunque un número muy reducido, han sido identificadas en la vecina isla de Menorca, donde las sucesivas fases de su prehistoria guardan evidente relación con Mallorca. Pero también se han vinculado con las cuevas sepulcrales colectivas de la Península Ibérica, sur de Francia e incluso Península Italiana e islas adyacentes.

La bibliografía sobre este tipo de yacimientos es larga y confusa. Tras las consabidas citas y hallazgos a lo largo del siglo XIX, e incluso antes, la primera exploración sistemática en estos sitios fue llevada a cabo por el Institut d' Estudis Catalans bajo la dirección de Josep Colominas, entre los años 1916 y 1919. Las similitudes entre sus ajuares cerámicos y algunos vasos de la cultura argárica del sureste peninsular hizo que este conjunto de monumentos mallorquines fuese considerado como un reflejo insular de aquella zona y su cronología situada dentro de la edad del bronce. Tal filiación será mantenida por la mayor parte de los arqueólogos que se ocuparon de ellas posteriormente. Una de las pocas excepciones la constituye W. Hemp, para quien los paralelos más evidentes a estas tumbas debían buscarse en Provenza, en particular en las cuevas artificiales de dominado grupo de Arlés. Por lo general los autores, a la relación de las cuevas sepulcrales mallorquinas con el llamado círculo de El Argar, añaden otras vinculaciones extendidas por toda la cuenca del mediterráneo occidentale. En la actualidad parece prevalecer la tesis que interpreta estas cuevas como una manifestación autóctona insular, aunque sin duda conectada con otros espacios mediterráneos occidentales próximos, que se desarrolla, según las dataciones C-14, a lo largo de los siglos XVII, XVI y XV a. C.

En 1968 se publicó una obra fundamental para el estudio de estos yacimientos. Se trata del libro de C. Veny Las Cuevas Sepulcrales de Bronce Antiguo de Mallorca, done se recogen todos las sitios conocidos hasta la fecha y se intenta su clasificación sistemática, tanto desde el punto de vista tipológico de construcciones y ajuares como desde las posibilidades que tales índices presentan para una posible ordenación cronológica del conjunto. Tras el trabajo de Veny la investigación se dividió entre quienes aceptaron su modelo y lo siguieron a pies juntillas y quienes lo pusieron en entredicho, total o parcialmente, por considerarlo excesivamente apriorístico. En todo este tiempo no se señalan innovaciones relevantes en el estudio de estos monumentos en lo que se refiere a nueva documentación aunque sí en el juicio que merecen a los investigadores.

El libro de Veny está concebido a modo de extenso catálogo al que se añade luego un estudio tipológico de cuevas y ajuares y unas conclusiones que tienen como finalidad primordial establecer, a partir de aquél, lo que el autor denomina las etapas culturales del complejo sepulcral mallorquín, concebido este como una manifestación más del megalitismo, aunque propia de la isla de Mallorca, fruto de la expansión de aquel por amplias zonas de Mediterráneo y el oeste europeo atlántico y nórdico. Se basa, por tanto, en una concepción marcadamente difusionista de la cultura, analizando después sus manifestaciones con criterios tipologistas excesivamente manejados desde una óptica evolucionista elemental. Así, la cultura en cuestión es presentada como una creación no generada en la isla, sino consecuencia de un eco que reproduce hechos llegados desde un centro extrabalear próximo o lejano, donde, sin embargo, se descarta prácticamente la filiación argárica o ibérica, muy al gusto de ciertas actitudes mentales baleares a las que no era ajeno el autor cuando escribió su obra, que se ve sustituida por una imprecisa referencia- imprecisa o deliberadamente confunsa, según las circunstancias- a la cuenca del Mediterráneo, con especial énfasis en la tierras que miran a oriente, como son las islas de Cerdeña, Sicilia o Malta. Esta es quizá la mayor diferenciación entre las tradición interpretiva de la escuela catalana, occidentalista en el desarallo de las culturas de la edad del bronce del oeste del Mediterráneo aunque se vuelva orientalista a la hora de explicar su génesis primigenia, frente al modelo reflejado en la obra de Veny, más en consonancia con un difusionismo orientalista ininterrumpido, aunque de intensidades variables, en el que, sin embargo, queda espacio para atisbar singularidades locales, y más en un espacio de carácter insular.

El análisis arqueológico de C. Veny se basa, en lo que respacta a los espacios funerarios estudiados, en realizar una primera discriminación entre cuevas naturales y artificiales, para luego, dentro de cada uno de esos grupos, distinguir entre yacimientos estrictamente funerarios, que son mayoría, y unos pocos de supuesto uso como habitación, lo que es discutible. En las cuevas artificiales distingue Veny tres tipos, con tres variantes a su vez para el tercero, que engloban a todas las construcciones, desde las más sencillas a las más complejas. El tipo I está formado por cuevas simples y pequeñas, de planta circular u ovalada y sin corredor. El tipo II se caracteriza por mantener esa clase de cámara pero precedida de un corto corredor de acceso. El tipo III se define por cámaras alargadas, rectangulares o elipsoidales, a las que se llega a través de un corredor largo y con añadidos, como por ejemplo los vestíbulos. Los tipos cobran valor cronológico a partir de formulaciones exclusivamente tipológico-evolutivas y difusionistas:

La forma de hipogeo simple...al ser el único que en su integridad reproduce la modalidad tumbal extranjera con capacidad para derivar de ella las demás formas, por fuerza tiene que representar la facies cultural más primitiva (Veny 1978, pág. 419).

Y ello resulta lógico porque:

el primer grupo humano al introducirse en la isla no podía inicialmente hacer otra cosa que explanar un cierto bagaje de formas importadas (Veny 1968, pág. 419)

El tipo II, aunque más evolucionado, podría ser sincrónico del I, según Veny, pues la diferencia que hay entre ambos no presupone necesariamente un cambio de mentalidad ni una evolución cultural propiamente dicha. Pero a ambos le sigue el grupo III, estadio final de la continuada línea evolutiva, presentado ya como una creación propia de la isla, cuando se alcanza la mayor perfección constructiva y los hipogeos de mayor tamaño y relevancia. Según vaya añadiendo atributos el grupo III conoce, a su vez, tres variantes, para las que también se insinúa un significado cronológico, ya que las tumbas más complejas, por ejemplo las de Cala Sant Vincenç, representan el último grado de evolución.

El otro criterio de clasificación de Veny se basa en los ajuares, particularmente los cerámicos. El hecho de que la mayor parte de estas cuevas estén exploradas y expoliadas desde antiguo llevó a Veny a sustentar sus observaciones en los restos exhumados en cuevas naturales, donde los depósitos arqueológicos no han tenido, por lo general, tan mala fortuna, aunque tampoco buena. Ello suscita, a simple vista, una polémica cuestión y es que por ese camino se mezclan los yacimientos campaniformes, entonces escasamente conocidos aún, con las cuevas sepulcrales pretalayóticas propiamente dichas, donde hasta ahora en ninguna ocasión han aparecido cerámicas u otros útiles de aquella filiación cultural. Distingue Veny entre yacimientos con cerámicas incisas caraterísticamente campaniformes, por lo que ahora sabemos y que carecen de conexión alguna con los hipogeos pretalayóticos, que constituyen la fase más antigua de su periodización, y otros con las llamadas cerámicas incisa B, que reflejan en decoraciones lineales de tal técnica una posible tradición campaniforme. Luego las estimaciones a partir de otros objetos se vuelven imprecisas conjeturas, pues como el propio autor señala en su obra en los ejemplos que integran los tres primeros tipos (se refiere a las cuevas artificiales tipos I, II y III... se aprecia una unidad sustancial...confirmada con la homogeneidad que se observa constantemente en el contenido de los ajuares (pág. 418). Sin embargo se mantiene el criterio tipológico-evolutivo a partir de la supuesta evolución de las construcciones de más sencillas a más complejas, con valor además cronológico. Una contradicción en las que sin duda tiene mucho que ver la filiación disciplinar del autor.

El trabajo que presentamos a esta reunión pretende sustituir los criterios anteriormente referidos por otros teóricamente más objetivos y, desde luego, perfectamente contrastados mediante el empleo de análisis matemáticos en computadora. Para ello se parte de la misma información que recogió y manejó Veny, con todo lo que ello significa de limitaciones según señalara él mismo en su libro. Los hallazgos posteriores o son muy fragmentarios o poco fiables, de manera que parece preferible mantener el nivel de información, y así facilitar la comparación, que añadir datos nuevos de dudoso valor. El trabajo tropieza con problemas evidentes, el principal el escaso número de yacimientos que presentan conjuntos arqueológicos amplios y por tanto significativos. Por ejemplo, en el caso de las cuevas artificiales, del total de 100 que Veny catalogó, 44 carecen de valor, debido a evidentes alteraciones por expolio o intrusión de materiales de época claramente posterior. De las 46 restantes sólo una decena registran conjuntos arqueológicos claros, y de otros cinco casos se pueden incorporar algunas piezas, casi con con toda seguridad precedentes de ajuares más amplios perdidos. Ni una sola cueva ha sido adecuadamente excavada y en ningún caso estamos seguros de manejar conjuntos arqueológicos completos. Estas dos últimas circunstancias son extensibles a las cuevas naturales, donde pese a que en muchos casos su descubrimiento se produjo en época relativamente reciente y sin remociones de importancia, no parece que cuantos trabajos se han llevado a cabo en ella sean acreedores a la mínima confianza que hace válida un excavación arqueológica.

De acuerdo con todo ello una primera observación parece evidente: este trabajo maneja una información parcial, alterada a causa de recuperaciones involuntariamente selectivas y carente de datos complementarios sobre los usos de los sitios. Tales limitaciones, en particular la segunda señalada, impide tener conocimiento sobre cuestiones tan fundamentales como si estos lugares funerarios se utilizaron en un solo momento o fueron usados a lo largo de una época larga de tiempo.

Partimos de la hipótesis de que las diferencias arquitectónicas entre hipogeos, a las que Veny y otros autores conceden especial relevancia, no tienen porque tener un valor evolutivo cronológico; tales variantes pueden perfectamente responder a otras causas, como el número de individuos que se preveía enterrar, la duración del uso del panteón, los distintos grados de concentración de la población, el status social de los enterrados...Igualmente consideramos que la diferenciación cuevas naturales/cuevas artificiales puede no tener más justificación que la posibilidad o imposibilidad de aprovechar lugares naturales, o igualmente estar en conexión con la mayor o menor densidad de población. Se parte, asimismo, de considerar que pueden existir variantes en las composición de algunas formas cerámicas, tal vez con valor cronológico o de otro tipo, por lo que su supuesta homogeneidad es un dato a comprobar o refutar. La finalidad del trabajo es demonstrar si el modelo de Veny es real o ficticio y si en su lugar es posible proponer otro alternativo de clasificación de estos monumentos y sus ajuares y con qué valores e interpretaciones culturales.

El estudio se plantea en tres fases, la primera relacionada con el estudio de los ajuares cerámicos, la segunda con el de las cuevas y la tercera y última con un análisis conjunto de cuevas y ajuares.

El primero paso para el estudio de los ajuares cerámicos de las cuevas ha sido decidir las variables a tener en cuenta, nominales (presencia o ausencia de carena, posición la carena en su caso, relación altura/anchura, forma, presencia o ausencia de cuello, en este último caso si se trata de una forma exvasada o no, volumen de la pieza en algún caso muy concreto, y decoración que presenta), o de intervalo (altura y anchura absolutas, díametro de la boca y del cuello y altura de la boca a la carena). La matriz de datos resultante consta de 325 individuos o formas cerámicas que se distribuyen en 38 cuevas diferentes, por las trece variables que se han enumerado. La toma de datos no se realizó sin problemas, ya que, aparte de la dificultad que suponen las distintas escalas y la especial técnica de dibujo en el libro de Veny para hallar las variables de intervalo, muchas forma encuentran incompletas y algunas de las construidas por el autor presentan perfiles dudosos. Asimismo en ciertos casos hay dificultad para relacionar la discripción con el dibujo de una misma vasija. Por último, bastantes cuevas quedan excluidas porque no se ha dibujado todo lo encontrado, los datos han quedado incompletos después de verificar que las atribuciones de tipos que da Veny no se corresponden con la tipología por él mismo definida (por ejemplo la vasija 29 de Na Fonda de Sa Vall).

Según el orden con el que se han enumerado las variables nominales, se ha clasificado el ajuar cerámico de las cuevas. También en este caso se han presentado algunos problemas, como el de establecer con rigurosidad la variable volumen. Esta variable se ha establecido para diferenciar dos tipos de vasos que, aun teniendo una forma similar, muestran un volumen claremente diferente, como son las formas 6c de Veny, o 2a y 2b de Fernández-Miranda. Para ello se ha realizado un análisis discriminante que proporciona las funciones frontera entre los dos conjuntos de vasos, sirviendo así como criterio de separación entre volumen pequeño y grande. Otro problema es la decisión de si tomar en cuenta todas las decoraciones (incisiones, impressiones, mamelones, etc.) o sólo considerar algunas de ellas. El criterio que se ha seguido ha consistido en no incluir como variables ni las impresiones ni las incisiones ya que éstas se presentan en diferentes vasijas con independencia de su forma. La clasificación resultante dintingue 23 grupos diferentes de vasijas, agrupados en 9 tipos subdivididos en variantes. Una vez clasificado el conjunto de ajuares cerámicos, se ha añadido a la matriz de datos el tipo o variante en la que se ha incluido cada vasija.

Como segundo paso en este estudio del ajuar cerámico, se investigan las relaciones entre los distintos tipos y variantes, con el fin de hallar algún tipo de estructuración en la distribución de los mismos. Para ello se ha realizado una matriz de contingencia, en la que se resalta qué grupos coinciden en una misma cueva en valor absoluto y otra matriz con valores porcentuales.

82

A partir de los porcentajes de cada tipo en cada cueva, se ha hallado la matriz de similaridad de Brainerd-Robinson, que muestra la similaridad existente entre cada par de cuevas según la semejanza de sus ajuares.

Como resultado del estudio de los ajuares cerámicos de las cuevas sepulcrales pretalayóticas, se establece en primer lugar una nueva tipología que sustituye a las anteriores, y se distinguen cuatro grupos diferentes de cuevas según en su ajuar sólo haya vasijas de forma globular (grupo que presenta problemas por ser vasijas que se encuentran en el resto de los grupos y quedar siempre la duda de si no nos encontramos ante cuevas con ajuares incompletos), o haya formas de carena baja, media o alta. En principio estos grupos no son excluyentes entre sí, y sólo se llegará a ordenarlos tras el estudio de cuevas y ajuares no cerámicos.

La segunda fase de este trabajo consiste en el estudio de las cuevas. Las variables que se han tomado en cuenta son de tipo nominal binario, de forma presencial/ausencia. El primer problema con el que hay que contar es que no se puede hacer una única matriz de datos, puesto que las cuevas de Mallorca, según el territorio geológico en el que se encuentren, son artificiales o naturales, y en cada uno de los casos las características que presentan son diferentes. Para las cuevas naturales se han tomado en cuenta la siguientes variables: situación (aislada, conjunto de dos o tres cuevas, conjunto de más cuevas), forma de cueva (retocada, acceso vertical u horizontal, nichos artificiales), ajuares no cerámicos de cobre (puñales triangulares, de hoja a bisel, puntas de flecha, punzones biapuntados sencillos o indeterminados), ajuares de huesos (botones en v, cónicos, troncocónicos, piramidales o semisféricos, botones de doble perforación), y ajuar lítico (brazales de arquero y sílex). La matriz resultante será por tanto de 37 cuevas por veinte variables.

Las variables que definen las cuevas artificiales son las siguientes: situación (aislada, conjunto de dos o tres cuevas o conjuntos de más cuevas), corredor (sin él, acceso en pozo, en escalera, en rampa u horizontal, tamaño corto o largo, con vestíbulo o cámara), cámara (de forma redonda u oval, o alargada, de tamaño pequeño, intermedio o grande, con foso central, con nicho absidal, lateral o a ambos lados, o sin ninguno), y ajuares no cerámicos con las mismas variables que en el caso anterior. La matriz en este caso tiene una dimensión de 56 cuevas por 24 variables.

Con estos datos aunque sin tomar en cuenta las variables del ajuar no cerámico, se ha realizado un análisis de correspondencias obtenidas en el mismo programa se ha realizado un cluster, para visualizar de otra manera las agrupaciones que muestran las cuevas según su forma.

La tercera y última fase de este estudio consiste en establecer si las distintas agrupaciones de formas cerámicas se corresponden con los grupos de cuevas y a su vez si el ajuar no cerámico se relaciona con una de las clasificaciones o con ambas.

El primer paso ha consistido en realizar una matriz de contingencia de los tipos, considerando en este caso como individuos a los distintos grupos de cuevas en la matriz de datos inicial, para averiguar si los datos muestran una esctructuración interna, y a partir de nuevo de los porcentajes de cada tipo cerámico, ahora en cada tipo de cueva, se ha construido la matriz de similaridad de Brainerd-Robinson.

Como último estudio se ha hecho un análisis de correspondencias entre las variables de las cuevas, añadiendo en este caso los ajuares no metálicos y la presencia o ausencia de vasijas globulares o con carenas bajas, medias y altas, para intentar descubrir de otra manera una posible relación entre tipos de cuevas y ajuares.

(*Nota)

Este trabajo tuvo su origen en un Seminario para alumnos postgraduados realizado durante el curso 1986-1987 en el Instituto Universitario Ortega y Gasset de la Universidad Complutense.

Cuevas Sepulcrales Pretalayoricas de Mallorca:
Un Ensayo de Classificacion y Analisis (*)
M. Diaz-Andreu y M. Fernandez-Miranda

Almost 150 burial caves belonging to the Pre-Talayotic period have been discovered in Mallorca. Both natural and artificial, they are the most abundant type of site of this period of the island's prehistory. A study of the chronology and typology of the caves, and of the funeral rites and of the types of objects found in them has linked them with similar constructions found in neighbouring regions of the Western Mediterranean. Similar caves, although fewer in number, have been found on the nearby island of Menorca, where connections have been found with Mallorca in other periods of prehistory. The Mallorcan caves have also been linked to the communal caves found on the Iberian Peninsula.

The published literature on the burial caves of Mallorca is long and unclear. Many caves were discovered in the XIXth century and even before. The first systematic excavation was carried out between 1916 and 1919 by the Institute for Catalan Studies under the direction of Josep Colominas. Because of similarities between the pottery found here and those of El Argar in the southeast of the Iberian Peninsula, this group of monuments was considered an island ramification of El Argar and was believed to belong to the Bronze Age. Most archaeologists who have examined the issue since have agreed with this. One of the few exceptions has been W. Hemp who found the nearest parallels of the so-called group of Arles. The authors link the burial caves of Mallorca not only to the so-called 'circle of El Argar' but also to other sites spread around the Western Mediterranean basin. The theory prevalent at the present time regards them as an indigenous insular product, no doubt related to other nearby Mediterranean areas, which evolved, according to C-14 dating, in the earlier second millennium BC.

In 1968, Cristobal Veny published the fundamental study of these sites. *The Burial Caves of the Early Bronze Age of Mallorca* describes all the sites known at that time and attempts to classify them systematically. Veny first studies the typology of their construction and their artefacts, and then, using this data, puts them into a possible chronological order. Research since Veny's publication has been divided between those who accept his model and follow it, and those who disagree totally or in part, considering it to be excessively reliant on *a priori* assumption.

Veny's book is an extensive catalogue to which he has added a typological study of the caves and artefacts, and conclusions which aim to establish what the author calls 'the cultural stages of the burial caves of Mallorca'. He sees them as another example of the Megalithic culture, native to the island of Mallorca but the result of the spread of the Megalithic culture through widespread areas of the Mediterranean, Atlantic and Northern coast of Western Europe. He bases his theory on the spread of culture, and analyses the concrete Mallorcan cases using simple typological-developmental criteria. As a result, he portrays the Pre-Talayot period as an echo of what was happening 'somewhere beyond the Balearic Islands', placing special emphasis on lands closer to the Eastern Mediterranean, such as the islands of Sardinia, Sicily and Malta, rather than seeing the caves as a product native to Mallorca.

Veny first differentiates between natural and artificial caves, and then within these two groups, he further distinguishes between burial sites, which account for the majority, and a few sites which appear to have been inhabited, although this itself is arguable. Veny divides the artificial caves into three groups, with the third group having three subdivisions. These groups encompass all the constructions, from the simplest to the most complex. The first group includes simple, small caves with circular or oval floors and no passageway. The second group has the same type of floor plan but also a short entrance gallery. The third group is composed of enlarged, rectangular or oval caves which are reached by a long passageway, with extra rooms such as entry chambers. The groups are put into chronological order using typological-developmental and diffusionist formulas:

> 'la forma de hipogeo simple... al ser el único que en su integridad reproduce la modalidad tumbal extranjera con capacidad para derivar de ella las demás formas, por fuerza tiene que representar la facies cultural más primitiva' (Veny 1968, p. 419)

and this is logical because:

> 'el primer grupo humano al introducirse en la isla no podía inicialmene hacer otra cosa que explanar un cierto bagaje de formas importadas' (Veny 1968, p. 419).

Although the caves in the second group are more complex, they could have been built at the same time as those of the first group, according to Veny, since the difference which exists between the two 'does not necessarily imply a change in mentality or a cultural development'. But both groups are followed by the third group, 'the final stage of a continuous, developmental sequence', which is seen as a creation indigenous to the island, when a better building technique is attained and the caves are larger and more impressive. The third group has three subdivisions, for which there also appears to be a chronological order, since the more complex caves, those of Cala Sant Vicenc, for example, represent the 'final stage of development'.

The other criterion used by Veny in his classification is based on the grave goods, in particular the pottery. The fact that most of these caves were discovered and ransacked a long time ago led Veny to base his observations on the pieces recovered from the natural caves where archeological contexts have generally suffered a slightly better fate. But by this method, inevitably, sites with Beaker ware, which were not well-known at the time, were combined with properly Pretalayotic burial caves, where until now neither pottery nor other items with Beaker characteristics have been found. Veny distinguishes between sites with characteristic incised Beaker ware (which we know have no connection with caves from the Pretalayotic period, and which he attributes to the oldest phase of his periodization), and other sites with the so-called incised ceramic B, which reflect a possible Beaker tradition (because their linear decoration).

Assessments based on other kinds of artefacts are very imprecise since, as the author himself points out 'in the cases which make up the first three groups' (he refers here to the artificial caves of groups I, II and III) ' a substantial unity can be seen ... confirmed in the homogeneity which is constantly observed in the content of the grave goods (Veny 1968, p. 418). However, contradictorily, he still uses a typological developmental criterion from the simplest constructions to the most complex, and gives that sequence chronological value.

The present work aims to substitute these criteria with theoretically more objective criteria tested using mathematical computer analysis. The study is based on the same information

Veny compiled and analysed, with all the limitations this includes, as he himself pointed out correctly in his book. Later findings are either incomplete, nor reliable, or remain unpublished. It therefore seems preferable to work with the same data, rather than referring to new data of doubtful value. In this way a comparison can be made between the two theoretical approaches that are tested here and their respective operational models. The present work faces some obvious problems. The main problem is the scarcity of sites that offer a wide and significant range of archaeological remains. For example, Veny counted and described 100 artificial caves. Of these, 44 cannot be used because they have been ransacked or materials from a clearly later period have been added. Of the 56 remaining sites, only about 10 contain complete archaeological assemblages. None of these sites has been excavated properly and we are not sure in any of them that we are dealing with a complete set of remains. These last two observations are equally true of the naturally-occurring caves. Although in many cases these caves have not been discovered until fairly recently and their contents have generally not been disturbed, it does not appear that the work carried out on them has reached the archeological standards necessary to make these excavations valid.

The present work is based on a theory which is radically different from the one Veny used in his day; namely that distinctions between types of burial chamber (natural vs. artificial, simple artificial vs. complex artificial) do not necessarily correspond to differences in the time of their initial use. His typological-chronological sequence is thus called into question. Instead, a study is made of the composition of the grave goods (in spite of the limitations already mentioned): the mutual associations between pottery vessel-form types, and the relationship between these types and the types of burial caves in which they were found. Our study is divided into four parts: the first studies the composition of ceramic assemblages; the second analyses the shape of the caves to verify the consistency of Veny's classification; the third studies the caves together with the artefacts, analysing the results to determine whether there is any regional patterning; and, finally, a more detailed analysis of the different locations of the caves is undertaken.

We do not use previous classifications of pottery (Veny 1968, pp. 411-416 and Fernández-Miranda 1978, pp. 159-166) because these overlooked certain kinds of vessels and in some instances used vague definitional criteria. Likewise, those items which are unique or are not found in more than one site are omitted since they are not significant in a study of this kind (an example of this is vessel 13 of Llucamet d'en Barraquer assemblage [Veny 1968, p. 256]). To carry out the systematic classification of these artefacts, a set of variables has been used which establish a typology necessary for the study of the Pre-Talayot burial sites of Mallorca.

The pottery shapes were studied using nominal and interval variables. The first set of variables, defined by numbers, are presence or absence of carinations, position of the carination when it exists, the relationship height/width, shape, presence or absence of neck, restricted or unrestricted form, the volume of the piece in cases where this variable appears significant, and the decoration. The measurement variables are absolute height and width, diameter of mouth, neck and height from the mouth to the carination. The resulting matrix consists of 325 entries and 13 variables, found in 38 different caves (2). The description of the pottery with respect to these variables was complicated in some cases by the fact that many pieces are incomplete and some may have been reconstructed inaccurately. In addition, Veny used different scales and drawing techniques. Finally, in other cases there is some difficulty in relating the description of the piece with its drawing and a number of caves are excluded because their contents are not known or because the data is incomplete.

Using the nominal variables (Figure 1), 23 different groups were identified. The volume variable was used in the case of flat-bottomed, slightly unrestricted vases. The problem was in drawing the line between the two groups. For this, a discriminating analysis (Sánchez Carrión (ed.) 1984, pp. 139-164; for specific applications to archeological data, Díaz-Andreu in press, and Wesse and Díaz-Andreu, in press) was done, that offered with a 96% probability of success, the following classificatory functions:

$$\text{Large vases} = (0.19511 * A) - 13.52588$$

$$\text{Small vases} = (0.06706 * A) - 2.20922$$

where A represents the total height of the piece in millimetres. The means obtained for these two groups are very different: 132 mm total height of vase and 220 mm diameter of mouth in the case of the large vases; 45 mm height and 77 mm mouth diameter in the small vases. This clearly shows the difference in volume between the two groups having distinguished the 23 shapes, these were used to make a contingency table which brought to light a number of correspondences. It was notable that vessels with low carinations were never found together with high-carinations. Medium-carinated vessels however, are accompanied by both high- and low-carinated vessels. Also, large flat-bottomed vessels with slightly subvertical walls are invariably found in the company of low- and medium-carinated though never high-carinated vessels. This contrasts with smaller but morphologically similar vessels that coincide with medium- and high carinated vessels. Both necked and neckless rounded shapes -independently of the presence of handles, lugs, etc.- seem to be associated with all the other vessel types and are therefore not significant. Finally, the vessels described by Veny as *tinajas* (large jars) are found in association with medium- and high-carinated vessels.

A hypothesis suggested by this set of observations is the existence of a seriation of pottery shapes. To facilitate comprehension of the resulting table, each vessel shape has been allotted a number and, where appropriate, a letter, designating types and variants. In this system the greatest significance, functional or chronological, is given to the types and not to the variants. The state of the research, however, leaves room for the possibility that systematic excavations in intact burial chambers could demonstrate that one or more of the variables presently considered as relatively insignificant, and so used for subdivision of types into variants, does in fact reflect time or functional differences between pieces. The resulting types and variants are (Figure 2):

TYPE 1. Neckless round-bottom shapes

       VAR. 1a. Restricted.
       VAR. 1b. Unrestricted.

TYPE 2. Necked round-bottom shapes.

       VAR. 2a. Plain.
       VAR. 2b. With lugs.
       VAR. 2c. With horizontal and/or vertical handles.
       VAR. 2d. With horn-shaped handles.

TYPE 3. Large, flat-bottom shapes.

TYPE 4. Small, flat-bottom shapes.

       VAR. 4a. Plain.
       VAR. 4b. With lugs.
       VAR. 4c. With horizontal handles.

TYPE 5. Large jars.

> VAR. 5a. Neckless.
> VAR. 5b. Necked.

TYPE 6. Cylindrical, flat-bottomed vessels.

TYPE 7. Low-carinated shapes.

> VAR. 7a. Wide, i. e. width greater than height, with concave-
convex carination.
> VAR. 7b. High, with concave-straight carination.

TYPE 8. Medium-carinated shapes.

> VAR. 8a. Wide, with concave-convex carination.
> VAR. 8b. Wide, with straight-straight carination.
> VAR. 8c. Wide, with concave-straight carination.
> VAR. 8d. High, with concave-straight carination.

TYPE 9. High-carinated shapes.

> VAR. 9a. Wide, with straight-concave carination.
> VAR. 9b. Wide, with concave-convex carination.
> VAR. 9c. Wide, with concave-straight carination.

For greater clarity, a further binary-type table (Figure 4) based on the contingency table in Figure 3 has been drawn up. It omits types 1 and 2 which show correlation with all others and therefore lack signicance.

The problem to be solved at this point of the analysis is the sequence and meaning of the pottery seriation. Certain pottery vessels offer some hints as to how they can be used as a tool for chronological sequencing. Thus, type 3 of the above classification, also occurs in contexts prior to the pre-talayotic phase, suggesting it belongs to an earlier time: e. g. at Son Gallard it is found together with strictly bell-beaker wares. Also, pottery with incised decoration, possibly of Bell-Beaker tradition, are found together with shapes 3, 7 and 8. In contrast, fully talayotic pottery is associated with types 4 and 9. These considerations lead us to hypothesise that the set of caves containing low-carinated ware (type 7) is older than the set of caves holding medium-carinated shapes (type 8), which is in turn earlier than the aggregate of caves with high-carinated shapes (type 9). Of course, low-, medium-, and high-carinated vessels are not found in mutually exclusive burial chambers; they are however, correlated with different types, as shown in Figure 5. The rounded shapes (types 1 and 2) create a problem because they turn up occasionally in caves in the absence of any other vessel shape. A double explanation can account for this. On the one hand, considering that this is the most frequent shape, its solitary presence in certain caves may indicate unrepresentative sampling of the total population of shapes duly deposited in the cave (it would not do to forget that very few items described by Veny come from archeological excavations). The second explanation, which does not exclude the first, may indicate the existence of a group of caves containing the more 'common' items that persisted throughout the whole pre-talayotic period. A convincing example of this latter hypothesis is the Son Mulet Cave, where 13 pots of type 1 and 96 of type 2 were found without the discovery of any other shape.

Veny proposed a chronological distinction based on cave form. According to his system, the earliest period was marked by the simpler caves and the caves became increasingly complex with time. The fact is that natural caves usually have a very simple ground plan, barely altered by man. This property thus automatically placed them among the oldest, but they would perhaps be better interpreted as representing an adaptation to the geological environment. To analyse Veny's hypothesis in greater depth, we looked into how to classify caves according to their floor plans. To this end two binary matrices were drawn up, one for natural caves and the other for artificial caves. Separate matrices were used because the two cave types have different characteristics and not all their variables are common to the two. The variables chosen for natural caves were position (isolated, in two- or three-cave group, in group of more than three caves) and cave form (presence or absence of human alterations, vertical or horizontal access, presence or absence of niches). For artificial caves the variables used were their position (isolated, in two-cave group, or in larger group), the characteristics of their passageway (present or absent, entry by shaft, stairs, ramp or horizontally; short or long' presence or absence of entrance hall or chamber) and characteristics of their chamber (round, oval or elongated; small, medium or large; presence or absence of central pit; apsidal niche, lateral niche or niche on both sides, or niche absent)

The main difficulty in the study of natural caves is their scarcity (3). For this analysis only eighteen caves, each with seven variables defining cave position and form were available. Since the caves, except for the Vernissa group and the Son Mas caves, occur as isolated structures, the inclusion of the position variables in the intended analysis would have meant giving excessive weight to exceptional attributes and consequent distortion of results. These variables were thus eliminated, leaving a matrix of eighteen by four. With the remaining data a correspondence analysis and a cluster analysis were carried out.

The correspondence analysis is a type of factor analysis in which individuals and variables are represented on axes (Lebart, Morineau and Fenelon 1974, p. 307-328; Lebart, Morineau and Warwick 1984, 1984; Fernández Martínez 1985; De Lagarde 1983). This analysis was carried out using an ADDAD programme package (Association pour le Développement et la Diffusion de l'Analyse des Donnés) (Jambu 1978; Jambu y Lebeaux 1978 and 1979), made available at the Data Processing Centre of the Universidad Complutense, Madrid. In the correspondence analysis carried out on natural caves (Figure 6), the first factor represents the type of entrance and the second represents whether caves have or have not been retouched. The factors derived from the correspondence analysis were used for a cluster analysis (Escudero 1975 and Sánchez Carrión (ed.) 1984, p. 165-191) which is shown in Figure 7. The cluster analysis allowed natural caves to be divided into four distinct groups. Following the top to bottom order in the figure, the first group comprises retouched caves with niches, i. e. the most complex ones architecturally speaking; the second group contains caves with a horizontal entrance; the third, caves with horizontal or vertical entrance. If one wished to classify the natural caves into types and variants, the above groups could be classified as variants 2b, 1a, 2a and 1b, respectively, that is to say, type 1 would consisted the simpler caves and type 2 of the more complex ones.

The results from the analysis of the correspondences in artificial caves (4) is shown graphically in Figure 8. The variables do not seem to permit us to distinguish clear groups among the caves. This is shown by the value of 35% for the cumulative percentage of eigenvalues with two axes, which ideally should be at least double this. In any event, it is observed that the first factor can be explained by the 'cave size' variable and the second factor by the 'location' variable (isolated, in twos or threes, or in larger groups, although the first category are not well sampled in the analysis). The cluster analysis carried out on the factors obtained from the analysis of correspondences (Figure 9) divides the artificial caves into four broad groups. The first is characterised by the simplest caves without passageway and normally having a horizontal entrance. The second cave group lacks passageways and is equipped with ramp or stairway. Third is a cave group showing ramps and chambers or halls, and the last group

90

similarly possesses chambers or halls although the passageway is lacking. A division into types and variants might classify them as types 1, 3 (variant 3a and 3b) and type 2, respectively.

To sum up then, the correspondence and cluster analyses seem to point to a working hypothesis that in the Mallorcan pre-talayotic Bronze-Age burial caves there are two types of natural cave and three types of artificial cave, the latter type being distinguished by the relative complexity of their floor plans.

The third phase of this study aims to determine whether there is a correspondence between the pottery shape clusters and cave groups and, furthermore, whether non-pottery item bear any relationship with either, or both, of the two classifications. Once again, the main problem is the paucity of caves offering the full set of data needed for an overall analysis. This is particularly so in artificial caves where only 11 of the 56 sites included in the cave form study contain pottery items, and of these, 6 have merely pottery shapes of types 1 and 2, and therefore cannot be dated so precisely.

To carry out an overall study of cave and item types, first a table was drawn up in which natural cave types were considered as statistical individuals and significant pottery types as variables (that is, types 1 and 2 were not taken into account). This table (Figure 10a) allows several conclusions to be drawn: the whole range of types of pottery items was found in caves of simpler form. This was not so, however, in modified natural caves or caves with niches of more complex plan. In these the absence of pottery types 3 and 7 points to more modern dates. The table of cave types and non-pottery item types (Figure 10b) indicates that the data can be explained by a single model, although the information in it shows excessive bias (it should not be overlooked that only a minimum of the caves catalogued by Veny were the subject of systematic excavation, so it can be assumed that in the rest of them the non-pottery items has 'disappeared' before the archeologist's arrival). The main feature of this table is the absence of flint flakes in caves of more complex ground plan, meaning that flint work had completely disappeared (except at Tolssals Verds, where a knife of this material was found). Pyramid-shaped buttons are another item perhaps belonging to more modern periods, as they always appear together with high-carinated pottery (Figure 10c).

As mentioned earlier, the problem arising in a study of artificial caves is the lack of data. The table of cave and item types (Figure 11a) shows two large gaps where cave types 1 and 3a should be, while the data for type 3b caves come from just three caves, two of which had few artefacts. For this reason, perhaps, no high-carinated shapes are found in the more complex caves with chamber, stairs and long passageway (type 3b), although their contents do include small vessels of shape 4 and medium-carinated shapes (Figure 11a). However, as was noted in natural caves, sites with simpler ground plans may possess both supposedly old and modern items. This may be seen in caves with stairs but without chambers (type 2) where finds have included type 3 shapes (from earlier periods) and type 4 and 9 vessels (later periods). The most significant correlation between cave types and non-pottery item types (Figure 11b) again seems to lie in the absence of certain items in the more complex type 3b caves. As in natural caves, artificial caves or a more complicated structure lack conical buttons and flint flakes. The correlation between pottery and non-pottery items (Figure 11c) corroborates the results of the above figure, although it was prepared from little data. The absence of pyramid-shaped buttons in caves with carinated pottery prevents us from confirming the hypothesis that these buttons are relative late.

In conclusion of this third part of the paper, we support the hypothesis that pre-talayotic burial caves can be arranged in a chronological seriation on the basis of their pottery. The oldest comprises low-carinated shapes and large flat-bottom shapes with slightly subvertical walls, which, moreover, are occasionally found together with pottery carrying the incised decoration habitual in the previous period. The more modern, comprises high-carinated shapes and small flat-bottomed vessels plus large jars and cylindrical, flat-bottomed vessels that are sometimes accompanied by talayotic pottery. This seriation does not show any correspondence with the different cave types except for certain absences suggesting that the more complex caves are in fact associated with the more recent items, although this does not deny the possibility of simpler caves containing high-carinated shapes. In addition, a study of both aspects -artefacts and cave types- this time focusing on non-pottery items, led to the conclusion that flint work flakes and conical buttons seem to be associated with older periods, while pyramid-shaped buttons seem to be found in later times.

Thus the sites belonging to the older period are the caves of Son Maiol, Llucamet d'en Barraquer, Sa Canova and Mulet. Attributable to an intermediate period conserving older features is the Son Marroig cave while more modern features are seen in the Ca S'Hereu, Bennoc, Son Mas, Son Sunyer IV and Sa Tanca caves, to which should be added, without the possibility of more accurate dating, the Trispolet, Son Primer, Montblanc, Ariant and Son Jaumell caves. Assigned to the most recent period are the Son Puig, Sa Mata, Cometa dels Morts, Tossals Verds, Son Sunyer XII, Son Toni Amer, Na Fonda de Sa Vall, Son Mesquida and Es Cabás de Santa Maria burial caves. With regard to the caves having pottery of type 1 and 2, those that can be considered relatively old are Son Vic de Superna, Son Bauca, Son Marroig, Son Sunyer IX and So N'Antelm, this conclusion being based on the presence of other items considered to be old (type 3 vessels, incised pottery pieces, etc.). Belonging to a later time are the Lledoner, Son Sunyer VII and VIII, Sa Tanca and perhaps the Rosells caves. Nothing can be said for the time being of the Fossaret the Son Fortuny, Marina, Son Vaquer, Sa Mola d'en Bordoi, Colonia de Sant Pere and Son Mulet caves, although we emphasis, as we have already done above, the great quantity of rounded vessels discovered in the latter cave, an occurrence whose explanation should perhaps be sought in other than chronological terms.

This demarcation of periods does not exclude the possibility of some caves being in continuous use. This is so in the Vernissa cave where old items such as pottery pieces with incised decoration and large vessels are found together with high carinated, cylindrical, and small, flat-bottomed vessels. Veny (1968, p. 287) explains that in this cave "this same arrangement [skeletons laid out lengthwise in the same direction, with neighbouring skulls having a small vessel between them] was repeated unchanged in three strata separated by layers of stone slabs" (our emphasis). Further, it is likely that the Son Jaumell cave was used for a long time because, even though it has a complex ground plan, its collection of items includes conical buttons which are considered to be of early fabrication.

Up to this point, we have considered the existence of archaeological periods as being the only explanation of the pottery seriation encountered. Other explanations are, however, conceivable, such as the possible existence of various contemporary cultural traditions, which would be reflected in different regional types. Figure 12 shows that no spatial pattern is identifiable in the distribution of caves containing low-, medium only-, and high-carinated shapes. Nor does the distribution of natural cave types (Figure 13) or artificial cave types (Figure 14) suggest a regional basis to the distinction of types, although a higher concentration of the former in the northwest of the island is clearly observed. This is due to the geological characteristics of the area which favour natural cave formation.

Other points to be considered are the fact that some rock cavities are isolated while others are members of groups, and the fact that burial sometimes make use of natural caves and other times employ hand excavated spaces. Numbers of these funerary sites were individually conceived, showing a variety of cave shapes and artifact assemblages. Single-tomb necropolises were usual throughout the pre-talayotic phase, demonstrating the constant presence of a population, either widely scattered or gathered into tiny units spread over the whole island. This dispersion is particularly characteristic of the mountainous part of the island, where almost all the cemeteries consist of natural, isolated tombs. Such an explanation is in agreement with the chronological hypothesis put forward in this work, and the agreement holds for both early and modern dates within the pre-talayotic phase. Therefore the assumption that a natural cave necessarily means an old site clearly lacks convincing support.

The differentiation between isolated caves and cave groups does not therefore seem to have a stable chronological basis, although maybe such a distinction could shed some light on differences in the settlements of the various areas on the island. It seems reasonable that burial groups, whether they be collective tombs in a single necropolis or several neighbouring necropolises, can be explained by the appearance of areas with higher population density. Since these burial groups are intermixed with isolated funerary caves in the flat part of the island, it seems that this plain was home to both larger population groups and others constituted by a few individuals. A different picture is seen in the mountainous part where such agglomerations must have been rare, as in the case of Cala Sant Vicenc which is, moreover, located near the valleys of Pollensa and the foothills. Another notable feature is the existence of a further cave 'group' near Arta formed by isolated sites in another moderately mountainous area. It is, thus, reasonable to suppose that throughout the pre-talayotic period the mountainous areas sheltered a population of isolated social units, each consisting of few individuals, while the plain held population units of clearly superior size.

The study of tomb types recorded in a single cemetery or in separate but nearby necropolises (such as the clusters recorded around Llucmajor or Campos). also has its points of interest. These associations are rarely formed by simple tombs: the two Na Tous de Son Suau tombs near Manacor, or the pair at Es Rafal Llinas, Campos, are the best known examples. Bellver Ric is the only site where various simple caves are associated with another of complex ground plan. There are no artefacts from any of these, making it impossible to situate these groups on the time scale. But the fact that larger ground plans predominate in associations of two, three or more caves suggests the existence of a link between these funerary agglomerations and a certain concentration of population.

Associations of simple and complex caves are fairly frequent. We know of six examples on the island: Son Sunyer, Son Antelm, Cas Perets, Sa Mola d'en Bordoi, Son Real and the group near the town of Alcudia. Only in the first have artefacts been documented. They were discovered in several of its tombs: number XII, of very simple ground plan, provided objects that, according to our chronological hypotheses, are from more recent times. Does this mean that synchronous tombs of differing size and type coexist in necropolises such as Son Sunyer? Above we pointed out that chronological spans of the pottery types indicate a diversity of dates in tombs of simple ground plan, this being so for both natural (as we noted for the Tramuntana Mountains area) and artificial tombs. If such chronological diversity is accepted, the association of tombs of varying size and markedly diverse ground plans has its explanation in non-chronological reasons, making it necessary to seek causes of another type.

The final case consists of necropolises formed by the association of two or more large tombs of complex ground plan. These are usually cemeteries made up of two or three caves, although at Son Toni Amer five have been identified and at Cala San Vicenc Hemp up to thirteen were observed. Where analysis was possible, their artefacts always belonged to the late pre-talayotic phase, as occurs in similar caves of the isolated sort of associated with others of simple ground plan and smaller dimensions.

To summarise the possible relationship that cave types may have with their items and chronology, geographic location, and occurrence in groups of singly, it should be pointed out that, due to the low quality and scarcity of available documentation, it is difficult to establish a firm, universal criterion for an overall analysis of the Mallorcan pretalayotic funerary complex. The information available does, however, seem sufficient to refute simplistic arguments frequently advanced on the possible evolution of cave types or the chronological succession of natural and artificial caves. Similarly, the data obtained allow the formulation of a hypothesis stating that initially the natural, isolated caves were more frequent than other kinds, both in the flat area and the Tramontana mountains area. This seems to be indicated by the Son Maiol and Mulet assemblages, in the mountains, and by the Llucamed and Sa Canova assemblages in the plain, in view of their classification in our older group, and also by Lledoner and Son Marroig, included in the second phase (but with archaic features). This second phase saw the appearance of the first burial groups, examples of which are Son Mas, Son Sunyer and the Alcudia group. The appearance of groups does not necessarily imply the disappearance of natural caves nor the end of the isolated distribution of natural or artificial caves. The last stage would be the coexistence of natural, isolated caves (Son Puig and Sa Mata in the plain, and Cometa dels Morts and Tossals Verds in the mountains) with simple (Son Sunyer XII) and complex (Na Fonda, Son Mesquida, Son Toni Amer, etc.) artificial caves found always in the plain and exhibiting both group and isolated arrangements.

This consideration of the characteristics of pre-talayotic necropolises allows us, in turn, to make suggestions of a more general nature as to the concomitant settlement and its probable evolution. To us, the pre-talayotic burial model suggests the existence of an initially dispersed population spread over the whole island, although it cannot be ruled out that from the beginning certain areas exerted a greater attraction. As this phase of Mallorcan prehistory progressed, it seems reasonable to assume the appearance of discrete population concentrations, never of great size but big enough to give rise to the first necropolis formed by various artificial tombs. Continued growth of population centres would generate a corresponding increase in cemetery size, a phenomenon that seems clearly marked in the final phase when there is a prevalence of collective graves of great size. This would occur independently of whether other causes, e. g. changes in funeral rites or the social representation of the tomb, had an influence on the transformation of the form of tombs. However, in conjunction with these tomb concentrations there was a continued use of isolated caves in both the plain and the mountains, while natural caves coexisted with artificial caves of smaller size or complex ground plan. There emerges a picture of a culture with an increasing tendency to aggregate in population units of variable size, in what is perhaps a prelude to the more complex talayotic society, and to construct and utilise funerary spaces that can be differentiated by their dimensions and other accessory architectural elements. Viewed in this light, it does not seem too farfetched to assume that the existence of different tomb types is a reflection of more complex causes that those deriving from their mere succession in time.

NOTES

(1) This work originated from a Seminar, entitled "Typology and Chronology in Prehistoric Archaeology", held for postgraduate students at the Instituto Universitario Ortega y Gasset, Universidad Complutense, during the 1986-87 academic year. The seminar aimed to analyse critically the typological-analytical method applied to practical example selected. By no means does it attempt to review or update the archaeological information contained in Veny's work *Mallorcan Burial Caves of the Late Bronze Age* which, in any case, continues being the major authoritative source published in this respect. We would like to thank Carmen Bravo, from the Data Processing Centre at the Universidad Complutense, Madrid, and Alfonso López for their technical assistance with the various programmes used in this work, and Antonio Gilman for his assistance with the translation into English.

(2) The data used in this study were obtained from the following caves: Fossaret de Son Fortuny, Son Vic de Superna, Son Bauca, Son Maiol, Son Puig, Ca S'Hereu, Bennoc, Llucamet d'en Barraquer, Rossells, Son Mas, Son Vaquer, Trispolet, Son Primer, Sa Canova, Montblanc, Vernissa, Sa Mata, Lledoner, Ariant, Cometa dels Morts, Tossals Verds, Mulet,

Son Marroig, Son Sunyer VII, VIII, IX and XII, So N'Antelm, Son Mulet, Son Toni Amer, Na Fonda de Sa Vall, Sa Mola d'en Bordoi, Son Mesquida, Son Jaumell, L'Hort dels Moros, Sa Tanca and Es Cabas de Santa Maria.

(3) The natural caves on which analysis was carried out are as follows: Son Puig, Ca S'Hereu, Bennoc, Llucamet d'en Barraquer, Rossells, Son Mas, Trispolet, Son Primer, Sa Canova, Montblanc, Vernissa, Sa Mata, Lledoner, Ariant, Cometa dels Morts, Tossals Verds, Mulet and Son Marroig.

(4) The artificial caves on which analysis was carried out are as follows: Son Sunyer IV, V, VI, VII, VIII, IX, X and XI, Son Antelm, Son Mulet, Son Toni Amer XXV, XXVII and XXIX, Na Fonda de Sa Vall, Sa Mola d'en Bordoi, Son Jaumell, Sa Tanca, Es Cabas, Son Caulelles, Ca Na Vidriera, Mandivia de Dalt, Son Cardell, Son Hereu XVI, XVII and XVIII, Son Gradana XIX and XX, Cugulutx, Son Fadrinet, Es Rafal Llinas, Ca's Perets, Mola d'en Bordoi, Cala Murada, Na Tous, Son Galiana, Son Ribot L and LII, Bellver Ric, Son Sureda, Colonia de Sant Pere, Son Real, L'Hort dels Moros, San Vicenc LXXIX, LXXX, LXXXI and LXXXII, Ses Coves, Ses Comunes, Son Bats LXXXVI and LXXXVII, Es Calderer, Pont d'en Cabrera, Gaieta Gran and En Rotget.

BIBLIOGRAPHY

Diaz-Andreu, (in press). "El análisis discriminante en la clasificación tipológica: aplicación a las hachas de talón de la Peninsula Ibérica". *Boletín del Seminario de Arte y Arqueología. Valladolid.*

Escudero, 1975. *Nuevos avances en las técnicas de análisis cluster.* Universidad Autónoma de Madrid. Centro de Investigación UAM-IBM. Madrid.

Fernandez Martinez, 1985. "La seriación automática en arqueología: introducción histórica y aplicaciones". *Trabajos de Prehistoria* 42, pp. 9-49.

Fernandez-Miranda, 1978. "Secuencia cultural de la prehistoria de Mallorca". *Biblioteca Praehistoria Hispana* XV. C.S.I.C. Madrid.

Jambu, 1978. *Classification automatique pour l'analyse des donées. 1. Méthodes et algorithmes.* Ed. Dunod. Paris.

Jambu and Lebeaux, 1978. *Classification automatique pour l'analyse des donées. 2. Logiciers.* Ed. Dunod. Paris.

Jambu and Lebeaux, 1979. "Aide-memoire pour l'utilisation des programmes de Calcul de l'analyse des donées (analyses factorielles, classifications automati-ques)". *Bulletin de l' ADDAD* nº. 3. January. Paris.

De Lagarde, 1983. *Initiation a l' analyse des donées.* Ed. Dunod. Paris.

Lebart, Morineau and Fenelon, 1978. *Tratamiento estadístico de datos.* Macombo Boixareu Ed. Barcelona.

Lebart, Morineau and Warwick, 1984. *Multivariate Descriptive Statistical Analysis, Correspndence Analysis and Related Technique for Large Matrices.* John Wiley. New York.

Sanchez Carrion (ed), 1984. *Introducción a las técnicas de análisis multivariable aplicadas a las ciencias sociales.* Centro de Investigacione Sociológicas. Madrid.

Siegel, 1980. *Estadística no paramétrica aplicada a las ciencias de la conducta.* Ed. Trillas. México.

Veny, 1968 "Las cuevas sepulcrales del Bronce antiguo en Mallorca". *Biblioteca Praehistorica Hispana* IX. C.S.I.C. Madrid.

Wesse and Diaz-Andreu (in press). "Die Aermchenbeile der Iberischen Halbinsel. Eine Gegenueberstellung verschiedener Typen-gliederungen". *Madrider Mitteilungen.*

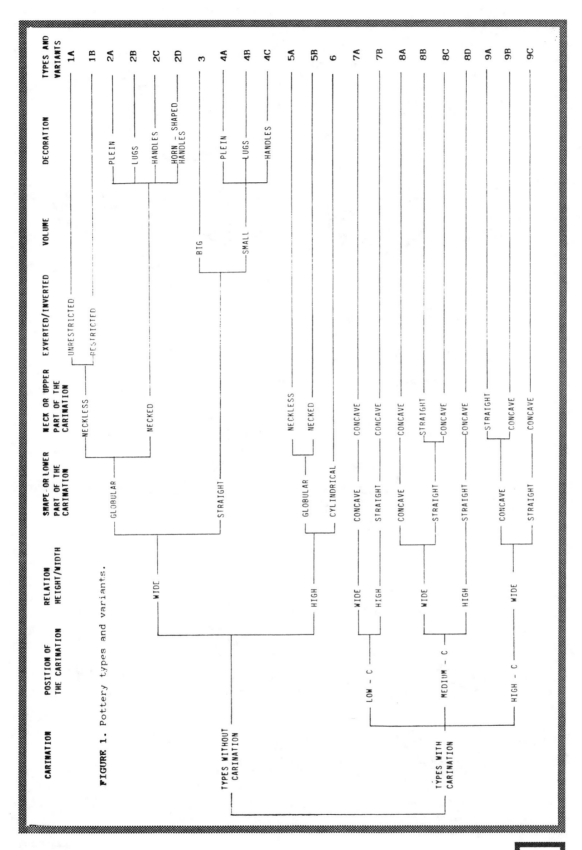

FIGURE 1. Pottery types and variants.

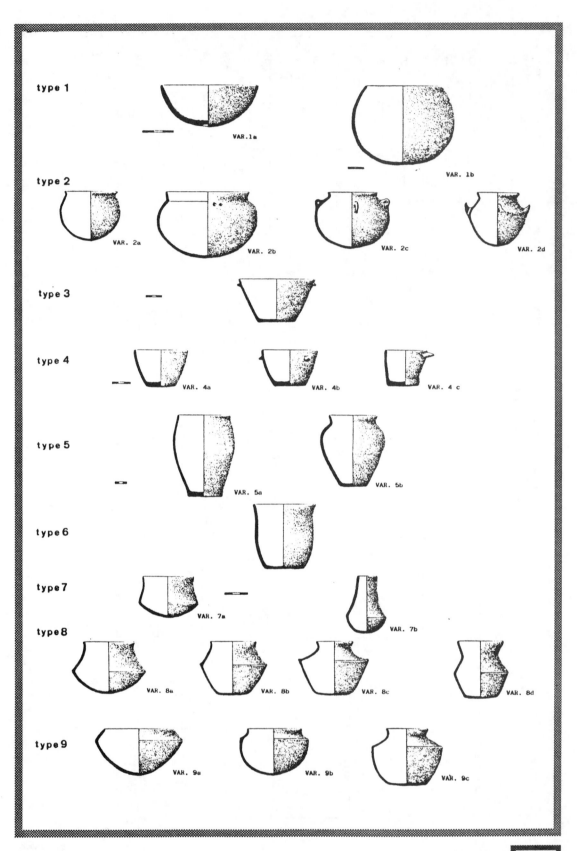

type 1   VAR. 1a   VAR. 1b

type 2   VAR. 2a   VAR. 2b   VAR. 2c   VAR. 2d

type 3

type 4   VAR. 4a   VAR. 4b   VAR. 4 c

type 5   VAR. 5a   VAR. 5b

type 6

type 7   VAR. 7a   VAR. 7b

type 8   VAR. 8a   VAR. 8b   VAR. 8c   VAR. 8d

type 9   VAR. 9a   VAR. 9b   VAR. 9c

DCATT&T   **Figure**   2

	1A	1B	2A	2B	2C	2D	3	4A	4B	4C	ME	5A	5B	6	7A	7B	8A	8B	8C	8D	9A	9B	9C
1A	14																						
1B	6	9																					
2A	9	7	14																				
2B	5	5	7	8																			
2C	5	4	5	6	7																		
2D	3	3	4	4	3	4																	
3	3	1	1	0	0	0	4																
4A	1	2	1	0	0	0	0	2															
4B	1	1	1	1	0	2	0	0	1														
4C	4	4	4	3	2	1	0	2	1	5													
ME	0	0	1	0	0	0	1	0	0	0	1												
5A	2	1	2	2	2	2	0	0	0	0	0	2											
5B	1	0	1	1	1	1	1	0	0	0	0	1	1										
6	1	1	2	1	0	0	0	0	0	1	0	0	0	2									
7A	3	1	0	0	0	0	3	0	0	1	0	0	0	0	3								
7B	0	0	1	1	0	0	1	0	0	0	0	0	0	0	0	1							
8A	8	5	6	3	2	2	3	1	1	1	1	1	1	1	3	0	9						
8B	1	1	1	1	0	1	0	0	0	1	0	0	0	0	0	0	0	1					
8C	2	2	4	2	1	1	2	0	0	0	1	0	0	1	1	0	1	1	5				
8D	0	0	1	1	0	0	0	0	0	0	0	0	0	0	0	0	1	0	1	1			
9A	1	1	1	0	0	0	0	0	1	1	0	1	1	1	1	0	0	0	0	0	1		
9B	5	3	3	4	4	2	0	2	0	3	0	1	0	1	0	0	1	0	0	0	0	7	
9C	1	1	2	1	1	0	0	1	0	1	1	0	0	0	0	0	0	0	0	0	0	1	2

Contingency table of pottery types and variants.

Table 3

3	7	8	5	6	4	9	
						1	9
					1	1	4
				1	1	1	6
			1	1	0	1	5
		1	1	1	1	1	8
	1	1	0	0	0	0	7
1	1	1	0	0	0	0	3

4. Presence/absence contingency table of ceramic types. (Vernissa cave is omitted for the reasons mentioned in the text).

Period A	-----------------------								
Period B	---								
Period C	------			-----------------------------					
Type	1	2	3	7	8	5	6	4	9

5. Proposed seration of pottery types.

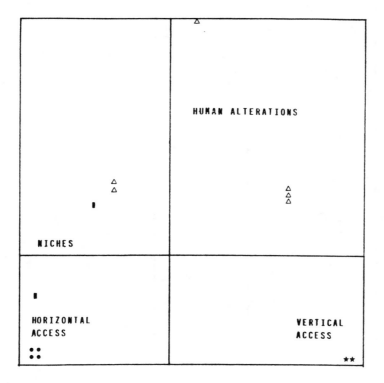

6. Correspondence analysis of the natural caves. The signs
   refer to types of caves (• type 1A, ★ type 1B, ∆ type 2A,
   ▮ type 2B).

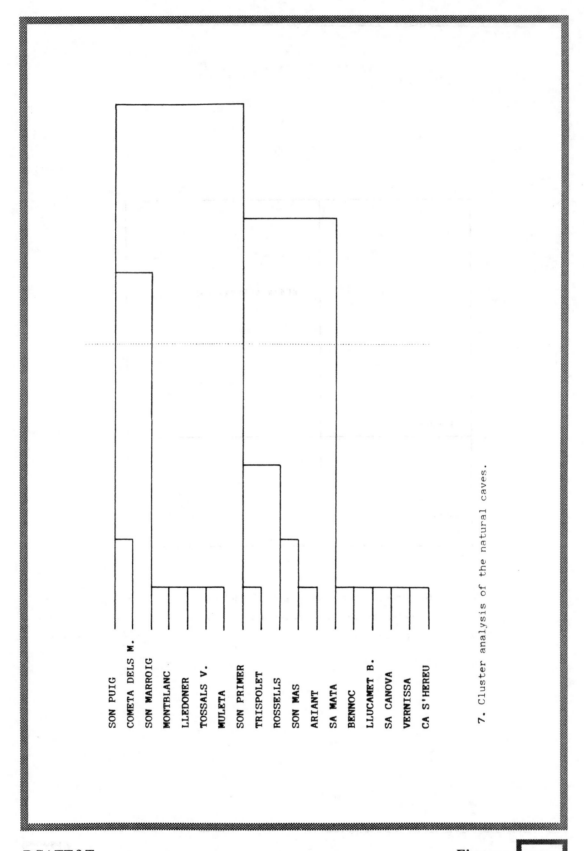

SON PUIG
COMETA DELS M.
SON MARROIG
MONTBLANC
LLEDONER
TOSSALS V.
MULETA
SON PRIMER
TRISPOLET
ROSSELLS
SON MAS
ARIANT
SA MATA
BENNOC
LLUCAMET B.
SA CANOVA
VERNISSA
CA S'HEREU

7. Cluster analysis of the natural caves.

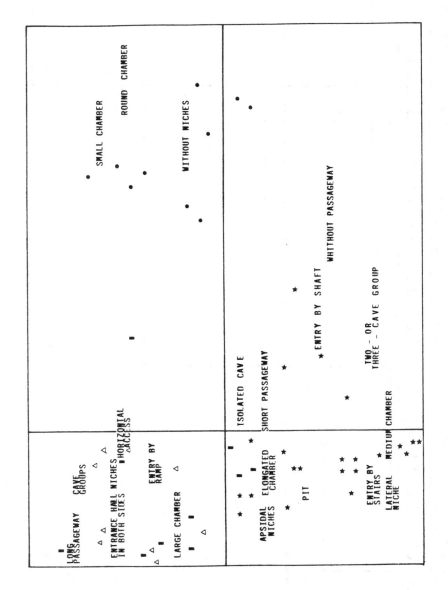

8. Correspondence analysis of the artificial caves. The signs refer to types of caves (● type 1, ★ type 2, ■ type 3A, △ type 3B).

Figure 8

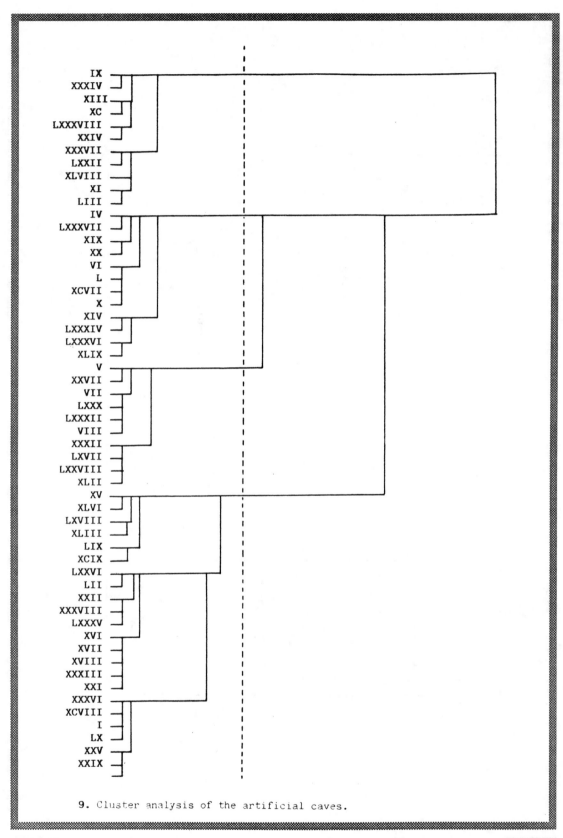

9. Cluster analysis of the artificial caves.

Figure 10.a)

Pottery types		3	7	8	5	6	4	9
Cave types	1a	1	1	1	0	0	0	1
	1b	1	1	1	1	1	1	1
	2a	0	0	1	0	1	0	0
	2b	0	0	0	0	0	1	1

Associations of natural cave types with grave goods.
Fig. 10a. Ceramic grave goods. Fig. 10b. Non-ceramic grave goods.
Fig. 10c. Associations of natural caves with low (b), medium (m), and high (a) carinated pottery with non-ceramic grave goods.

CAVE TYPE	1a	1b	2a	2b
NON – POTTERY ITEM TYPES				
TRIANGULAR DIGGER	1	1	1	1
BISELED BLADED DIGGER	0	1	1	0
ARROW HEADS	0	0	1	0
DOUBLE – ENDED AWL	0	1	0	1
SIMPLE AWL	0	1	0	1
INDETERMINATE AWL	0	1	0	0
CONICAL BUTTOMS	0	0	0	0
TRUNCONCATED BUTTOMS	0	0	0	0
PYRAMIDAL BUTTOMS	1	1	0	1
SEMI – SPHERICAL BUTTOMS	0	0	0	0
DOUBLE – PERFORATED BUTTOMS	0	1	1	1
ARCHER – WUSTGUARD	0	1	0	1
FLINT BLADES	1	0	0	0
FLINT FLAKES	0	1	0	0

10 b.

DCATT&T

Figure 10

CAVE WITH LOW, MEDIUM OR HIGH CARINATED TYPES	L	M	H
NON – POTTERY ITEM TYPES			
TRIANGULAR DIGGER	1	1	1
BISELED BLADED DIGGER	1	1	1
ARROW HEADS	0	1	1
DOUBLE – ENDED AWL	1	1	1
SIMPLE AWL	1	1	1
INDETERMINATE AWL	1	1	1
CONICAL BUTTOMS	0	0	0
TRUNCONCATED BUTTOMS	0	0	0
PYRAMIDAL BUTTOMS	0	0	1
SEMI – SPHERICAL BUTTOMS	0	0	0
DOUBLE – PERFORATED BUTTOMS	0	1	1
ARCHER – WUSTGUARD	0	0	1
FLINT BLADES	0	0	1
FLINT FLAKES	1	1	0*

* Except the Vernissa cave.

10 c.

Figure 11a)

Pottery types		3	ME	7	8	5	6	4	9
Cave types	1	?	?	?	?	?	?	?	?
	2	1	0	0	0	0	0	1	1
	3a	?	?	?	?	?	?	?	?
	3b	0	0	0	1	0	0	1	0

11. Associations of artificial cave types with grave goods.
Fig. 11a. Ceramic grave goods. Fig. 11b. Non-ceramic grave goods.
Fig. 11c. Associations of articial caves with low (b), medium (m),
and high (a) carinated pottery with non-ceramic grave goods.

CAVE TYPES	1	2	3a	3b
NON - POTTERY ITEM TYPES				
TRIANGULAR DIGGER	0	1	?	1
BISELED BLADED DIGGER	1	1	?	1
ARROW HEADS	1	0	?	1
DOUBLE - ENDED AWL	0	0	?	1
SIMPLE AWL	0	1	?	1
INDETERMINATE AWL	1	1	?	1
CONICAL BUTTOMS	1	1	?	0*
TRUNCONCATED BUTTOMS	0	1	?	1
PYRAMIDAL BUTTOMS	0	0	?	1
SEMI - SPHERICAL BUTTOMS	0	0	?	1
DOUBLE - PERFORATED BUTTOMS	1	0	?	1
ARCHER - WUSTGUARD	0	1	?	1
FLINT BLADES	0	0	?	0
FLINT FLAKES	1	0	?	0

* Except Son Jaumell Cave

11 b.

CAVE WITH LOW, MEDIUM OR HIGH CARINATED TYPES	L	M	H
NON – POTTERY ITEM TYPES			
TRIANGULAR DIGGER	?	1	1
BISELED BLADED DIGGER	?	1	1
ARROW HEADS	?	1	0
DOUBLE – ENDED AWL	?	0	0
SIMPLE AWL	?	1	0
INDETERMINATE AWL	?	0	1
CONICAL BUTTOMS	?	1	0
TRUNCONCATED BUTTOMS	?	0	0
PYRAMIDAL BUTTOMS	?	0	0
SEMI – SPHERICAL BUTTOMS	?	0	0
DOUBLE – PERFORATED BUTTOMS	?	1	0
ARCHER – WUSTGUARD	?	0	0
FLINT BLADES	?	0	0
FLINT FLAKES	?	0	0

11 c.

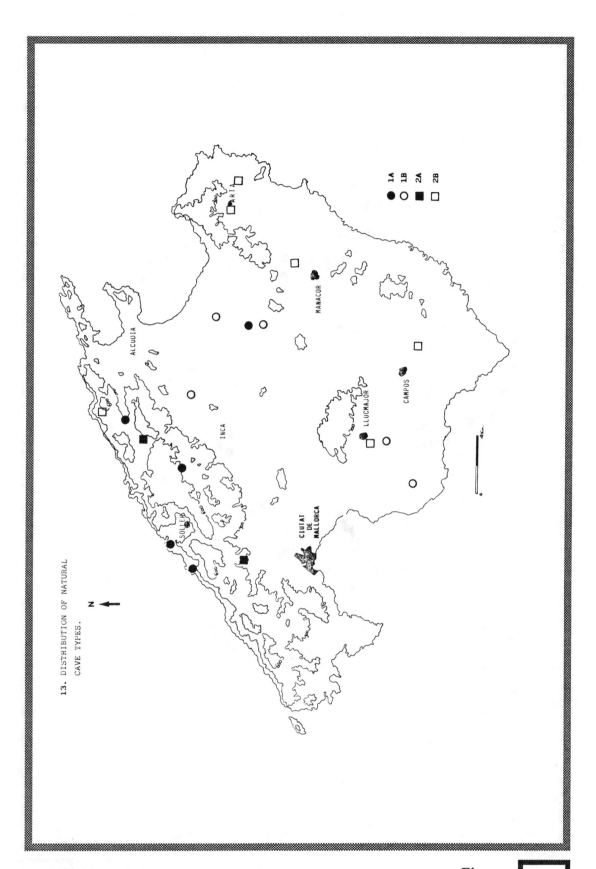

13. DISTRIBUTION OF NATURAL CAVE TYPES.

Figure 12

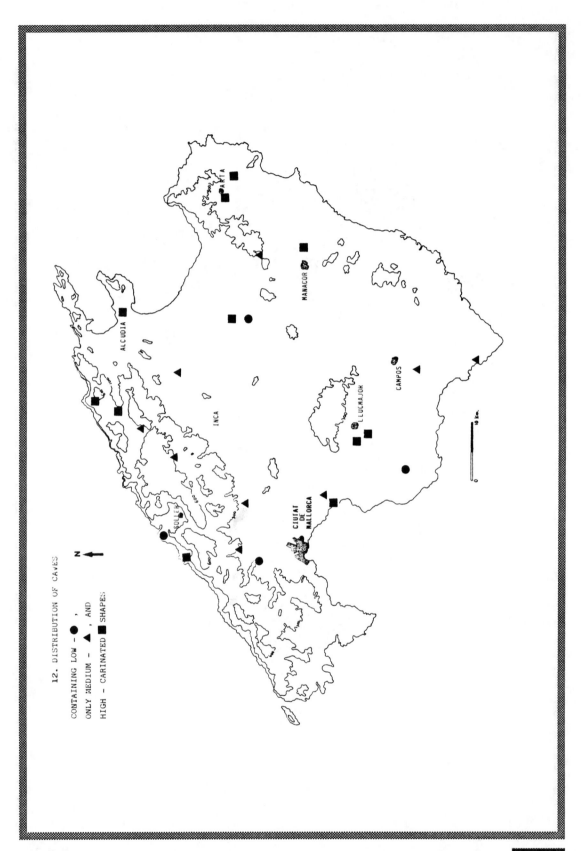

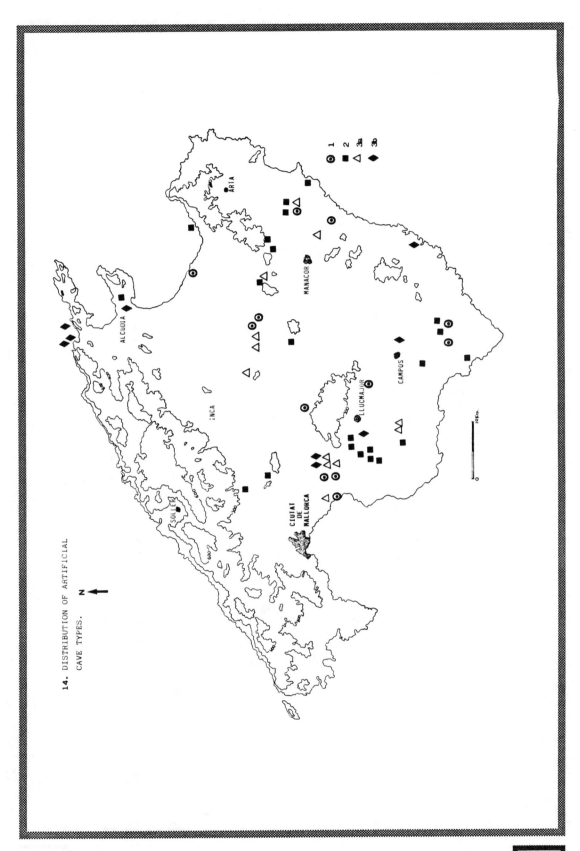

14. DISTRIBUTION OF ARTIFICIAL CAVE TYPES.

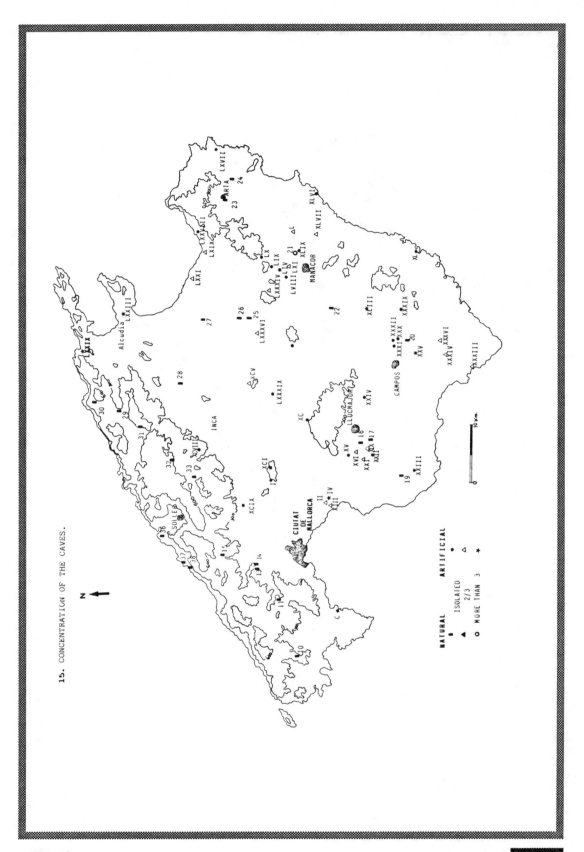

15. CONCENTRATION OF THE CAVES.

SIMPLE APPROACHES
TO THE ANALYSIS OF PREHISTORIC POTTERY

WILLIAM H. WALDREN
Research Associate
Department of Ethnology and Prehistory
University of Oxford
Oxford OX2 6PN, England

RESUME

The current paper outlines the methodology and presents a summary of preliminary results from a series of more in-depth studies initiated by the author during his Oxford doctoral research from 1978 to 1983, studies of which prior to this publication some interim reports have been published (Waldren 1981, 1982, 1983 and 1986).

The research deals principally with the techniques and findings obtained from the examination and physical analyses of prehistoric ceramics using the various simple approaches to pottery analysis outlined below and forms part of a long term, on-going project dedicated to the study of prehistoric pottery technology and other general problems in Balearic prehistory. The analysis and experiments are being carried out in two locations: the Donald Baden-Powell Quaternary Research Centre, Pitt Rivers Museum, University of Oxford, Oxford, England and the Deya Archaeological Museum and Research Centre, Deya, Mallorca, Baleares, Spain.

The scientific processes involved involve the physical examination, chemical quantitative analyses and practical experiments carried out on large series of prehistoric pottery samples. The test samples originate not only from the Spanish Balearic Islands but other immediately adjacent geographic area as well as, where experimental materials are available from stratigraphically and chronometrically documented caves, rock shelters and open-air settlements. The methods described and discussed in this paper, although dependent on criteria derived from long experience and familiarity with the materials in both the field and laboratory, are in some ways simplistic, being both uncomplicated and carried out relatively easily and inexpensively in great number.

The research is designed with a number of major aims in mind: (1) to ascertain if certain interrelated physical factors in the sample materials examined exist, (2) to quantify them, (3) to determine whether or not these can be said to relate to specific localised geographic zones (centres of distribution), (4) to determine whether or not they are characteristic of the different local chronological periods and (5) to determine, if possible, what compositional changes in the methods of manufacture occurred during each of those periods and (6) whether or not such changes may be taken as bi-products or indicators in time and space to social and economic changes and conditions.

This paper supports the premise that there is much to be learned from (1) simple chemical and quantitative analysis of idiosyncratic inclusion (temper) materials such as are found in local clays, (2) the use of thin and slab sectioning of sherd material for the identification and description of clay inclusions and other physical characteristics evident in the samples, (3) the use of refiring and duplication experiments for better understanding of the reaction of clay materials from firing, and some of the problems involved in the manufacturing techniques and (4) the use of statistical and computer-based studies in order to quantify these individual aspects. These four methods and the way they have been used locally in the Balearics are discussed at some length and certain results presented in this paper. However before this account takes place something should be addressed in this resumé concerning the overall analytical strategy used, and the general hypotheses involved.

The research contends that potters' clays are composed of a determinable number of mineral inclusions, some of which are idiosyncratic (diagnostic of the period or locale) and can be quantified. It contends that when optically examined and chemically tested the clays illustrate the types of atmospheric environment and other physical conditions present when first manufactured. It is further contended that such processes as clay composition and manufacturing practices can be to a reasonable degree reconstructed in duplication experiments, both in the field and in more controlled conditions of the laboratory.

It is assumed and generally accepted (1) that the mineral inclusions found in ancient pottery are traceable to two main agencies: (i) those found naturally in the clays chosen for manufacture and (ii) those introduced into a natural or prepared clay fabric by the potter himself. These two types of mineral inclusions are referred to in this research as: (a) natural inclusions (temper) and (b) artificial inclusions (temper); the latter which can consist of a wide variety of substances, ranging from hard minerals to vegetable and animal matter. It is assumed (2) that these inclusions are effected in varying degrees in a number of recordable ways by the type of kiln and the kiln's firing atmosphere present at the time of firing. It is further proposed (3) that a well recorded account of these properties and changes based on observations and practical tests, carried out on an extensive series of analytical materials can be of some positive contribution regarding our knowledge of the ancient techniques employed in the different chronological periods and geographic zones throughout local prehistory.

It is suggested (4) that the prehistoric potter, as in the case of the modern pottery technician and artisan (both primitive and sophisticated), had at his command formal and traditional recipes for the preparation of his clays for firing. It is thought that these methods - tantamount to formulae - were in most cases precisely adhered to in order to attain particular and desired results, which in themselves were either a question of tradition, technique or economy, or some combination of all three motives. It is also further suggested (5) that certain physical and chemical idiosyncracies exist which demonstrate the ancient methods of preparation as well as certain properties evident in the potter's choice of the clay itself as well as the temper reinforcement, which are by their particular (idiosyncratic) nature indicative and characteristic of (a) the geographic local and (b) the time framework in which they occurred, as well as (c) possibly being economical considerations.

This paper recognises that most ethnological information on primitive potters' techniques is generally poor in detail, especially concerning the contents and properties of the potter's clay as well as the manufacturing procedures themselves (Shepard 1965). In most ethnological reports concerning primitive pottery techniques, despite their frustrating lack of detail on other points, the technological observation frequently made by the ethnographers relates to the care and importance devoted to standards and requirements in the basic preparation of clay fabrics for pottery manufacture. Although this general care and importance given clay preparation, primitive potter's methods throughout the world do differ in matters of detail, for example in types of kiln or actual choice of raw materials used in the preparation; often showing distinctive and personalised methodology in the clay preparation and other firing procedures.

In the first section of this paper, for example, which deals with weights and percentages of natural and artificial mineral pottery inclusions found in the Balearic prehistoric pottery samples, analytical results are used to demonstrate characteristics diagnostic of particular pottery styles and chronological moments, and to some degree suggest the methods used and areas of manufacture. In the case of these analytical results from the Balearic sites, the use of these methods of analyses has been productive and the prospect of their continued successful use especially attractive. Here, a large number of test samples from a wide range of chronologically documented sites and varied stratigraphical contexts have been used (Waldren 1983 and 1986). While admittedly, these may only demonstrate and define prehistoric contexts within a yet limited insular territorial parameter, they do represent positive results regarding the question of simple approaches to the analyses of prehistoric pottery. In essence, although they have not as yet been tested elsewhere, similarly applied the simple approaches outlined above could, it is believed, make available a permanent tool in assessing not only pottery manufacturing processes but possibly patterns of interexchange in localised areas, and even interaction or demographic and trade movement on a wider scale.

One of the most common natural or artificial mineral inclusions found in potter's clay is calcium carbonate ($CaCO_3$), commonly found in the form of shell, limestone and calcite (Shepard 1965). This is particularly true for the prehistoric pottery of the Balearic Islands where the islands' geology is nearly entirely limestone. This geological factor, as will be shown presently, is the main contribution to the current research, forming the basis of most of the methods used and assessments made.

As a natural or artificial temper in pottery, calcium carbonate is one of the most unsuitable ingredients of the long list of clay binders used in pottery making (Shepard 1965). Seemingly unlikely ingredients such as feathers, grain and other organic materials, among more likely tempers such as quartz, hematite, feldspar, sand have been used successfully as prehistoric clay fillers.

It is proposed in this paper (6) that the prehistoric potters were well aware of its presence in clay, as well as its particular characteristics and limitations, (7) that its suitability, despite its instability, must have outweighed by far any inconvenience or limitation known to the prehistoric potter which might result from its use as a natural or artificial inclusion. It is also suggested (a) that the prehistoric ceramist exercised precise, probably even personalised recipes for its use as a binding medium and (b) that his measurements consisted of determinable quantity ranges, which as a result can be traced and interpreted as being idiosyncratic. Finally, it might be argued (c) that perhaps the pottery during certain periods was prepared by specialists and even circulated from a certain number of distribution centres, and (d) that the centres of manufacture and the resulting patterns of distribution, representing trade and other exchange may possibly be determined using the described methods of analysis.

ANALYTICAL METHODS

Each of the four analytical methods from which the present research is derived: (1) chemical analysis of the calcium carbonate content in the local pottery, (2) pottery sectioning, (3) refiring experiments and (4) duplication experiments, are briefly described in sections below. Although each of these is an analytical method in its own right, capable of providing independent results and deserving detailed individual study and publication, because of available publication space they will be reported on jointly in the eventual conference paper, where they generally demonstrate the manner in which they are interrelated. In due course each will require its own still more extensive individual report. The present resumé as well as the paper itself are by way of introduction to some of the questions asked and to offer the reader a concise outline of the overall research underway, along with a summary of the strategy and methods used.

It should be noted that whenever possible all four methods of analysis have been used on a single pottery sherd or two sherds related to one another. This is done in order to interrelate results and so attain a single body of information and data; although individual tests on individual sherds can be carried out effectively as well.

1.

CHEMICAL ANALYSIS FOR THE CONTENT OF CALCIUM CARBONATE

Chemical analysis for the quantitative calcium carbonate content (QACCCP) of selected pottery test samples consists of removing all calcium carbonate from a standard test sample by acid treatment, quantifying the measurement and statistically comparing the results with similarly collected samples analysed from centralised as well as widely geographically separated sites. This is done with a number of objectives in mind.

(1) To quantify the composition by simple chemical analysis an extensive series of pottery samples from different local prehistoric ages.

(2) To compare statistically the results of these chemical analysis from archaeological station to station to observe possible differences and similarities.

(3) To describe, if possible, these differences or similarities as they may apply in terms of age.

(4) To determine whether or not any of these differences or similarities may be indicative of or traceable to social and economic change.

(5) To determine (a) whether or not any of the technological differences can be traced to regional centres of manufacture and (b) if so whether these could be used to show local trade patterns.

(4) To assemble a reference collection of Munsell Colour samples of fired clay fabric samples from ground (pulverised) sherd materials for true colour identification, recording and evaluation.

2.

POTTERY SECTIONING

The thin and slab-sectioning research programme of pottery samples from the Balearic Islands was initiated by the author at Oxford in 1975. Preliminary reports are found in the appendices of his Oxford doctoral thesis (Waldren 1982: Appendix 3A). Pottery sectioning consists of the preparation of sherds as mounted slab-sections, along with conventional thin-sections, from a number of local prehistoric sites as well as those from several Mainland areas. These, once prepared, are destined for microscopic examination and photographing and other statistical recording.

The method of slab-sectioning used in the research as well as the conventional thin-sections were designed to achieve a number of specific objectives which are outlined below:

(1) To prepare a reference library of Balearic prehistoric pottery samples in the form of mounted slab-sections and, when thought significant, conventional thin-section. This is followed by the preparation of microphotographs (colour transparencies and black and white) taken at a standard magnification.

(2) To study and record the various 'features' and 'events' (as defined in the paper) brought about by the alteration of mineral inclusions or clay fabric itself; thus illustrating (a) the different physical properties of the various fabrics and (b) the changes and alterations resulting from the various idiosyncratic and technological processes used by their makers. Such a study, it is believed, can give clues to the firing processes and temperatures and other conditions involved in the manufacture of the individual vessels as well as the problems confronted by the potter.

(3) To build, if possible, a mineralogical thermo-scale, (a) deduced from the compositional, temperature and chemical changes of the mineral inclusions and clay fabrics themselves; and (b) to ascertain by experimental refiring of corresponding sherd samples, the stage and temperature at which the various actions (events) such as sintering, decomposition and incipient vitrification took place in the various clay mineral inclusions (e.g. limestone, quartz, feldspar and haematite etc).

(4) To study and record (a) any differences in the structure of the clay fabrics themselves and, eventually, (b) to determine by more quantitative methods the exact composition of the different clay fabric samples tested (this project is already underway in the QACCCP analyses outlined above).

(5) To determine optically whether or not any particular type of clay fabric may be ascribed consistently to a single chronological period. This is done on the basis of observational and quantitative comparison of prepared microscopic slides and chemical specimens, as well as from experimental methods, such as refiring and duplication trials.

(6) To determine (a) in statistical terms how reliable the physical and chemical differences between various clay fabrics samples from different geographic areas are and (b) whether or not they possibly may be ascribed either to changing idiosyncratic and technological skills as well as chronological age.

(7) To establish (a) whether or not any special type of pottery vessel clay fabric (e.g. Balearic Beaker ware) was locally manufactured or possibly imported into the indigenous pottery assemblages and (b) if so whether it can possibly be used to determine origin (unfortunately this project is not as yet advanced to any degree). While the first series of local Beaker ware sherds have been sectioned and prepared, very few Beaker sherd examples for sectioning are currently available; thus limiting possibilities for comparisons with those from mainland sites).

3.

POTTERY REFIRING EXPERIMENTS

This method consists of testing an off-cut of the sherd test sample selected previously (Figure 1) for use in sectioning studies for refiring experiments. The process of refiring pottery chips to interpret degrees of oxidation is known (Shepard 1965). While the method is recommended as a training procedure in Shepard's thesis for interpreting oxidation, the present author believes that more than interpreting rates of oxidation can be learned from controlled experiments in refiring ancient sherd samples; although this can be included also as one of the results from experimental refiring/ firing and duplication experimental firing.

The refiring and firing experiments have been done with several aims in mind. Listed, these are the following:

(1) To establish a criterion or scale for grading the degree of oxidation arrived at in the test samples as well as estimations of original firing temperatures.

(2) To observe and quantify colour changes in terms of Munsell colour scale in experimental fired and unfired clays, as well as from original sherd materials.

(3) To study and record changes in the character, nature or state of the original test sample's natural or artificial inclusions, or in the clay itself, brought about by reheating the test sample at increased, incremented temperatures and comparing these with an unaltered reference piece of the same sherd used for reference.

(4) To establish through experimental means (a) the types of kilns used (mound or pit kilns) and (b) details regarding the original firing conditions, as well as the original position of the pieces during firing (it has been observed that the colour of a pot is indicative of its position during firing in the kiln)

(5) To test samples of clays collected on-site for experimental firing in both field and laboratory conditions for subsequent comparison with those from ancient sherds.

4.

DUPLICATION EXPERIMENTS

The duplication experiments consist of making pottery from local on-site clays with various inclusion (natural)materials and admixtures (artifical) tempers and firing these in primitively constructed mound and pit kilns, designed after excavated kilns, using different fuels. This has been done with a number of objectives in mind:

(1) To determine (a) details of the types of kilns used for firing during the various prehistoric periods: mound or pit kilns and (b) to gain first hand information on the types of firing environments possible.

(2) To determine, if possible, whether or not on-site clays were used for production or possibly imported from elsewhere farther afield.

(3) To understand the local prehistoric pottery recipes for clay preparation, their firing properties and the firing procedures used in general.

(4) To duplicate as nearly as possible by experimental means prehistoric pottery, diagnostic of the various local prehistoric periods, as well as duplicating the conditions under which it was prepared and manufactured.

(5) To suggest possible reasons for the use of certain techniques and materials in the preparation and firing of the clay fabrics.

(6) To determine whether or not these methods of pottery preparation and other details of manufacture may possibly reflect local prehistoric social and economic conditions.

W.H. Waldren

It is recognised that these methods are basically experimental and basically simplistic and that results may eventually only be partly applicable elsewhere or only locally significant. Yet some of the information encountered, it is believed, has been both productive and informative and can only be obtained by using uncomplicated methods and techniques, such as those used here. It is at the same time the first attempt at an extensive descriptive analysis of local prehistoric pottery by a series of simplified experiments; although one other helpful attempt has been made recently on pottery from one local Talayotic settlement (Gasull, Sanahuija and Lull 1985) which although different in its approach has been equally valuable. and informative.

As the most common of all artefact material found on archaeological sites or in the warehouses of museums on which whole cultures, their social and economic structures have been assessed and described, the pottery sherd has not fully served it potential as sources of valuable information and data. If the current paper merely succeeds in stimulating a new interest or opens other avenues of thought in the simple forms of analysis of pottery, then it has served in one of the principal ways intended.

Primitive Pit Kiln Pottery

Primitive Mound Kiln Pottery

FRONTISPIECE

RESULTS OF TWO SIMULTANEOUS EXPERIMENTAL POTTERY KILN FIRINGS

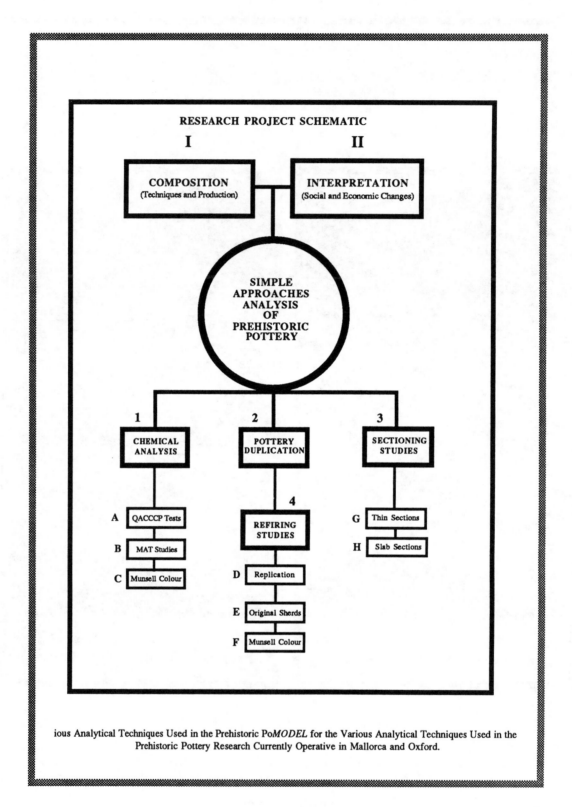

RESEARCH PROJECT SCHEMATIC

I

II

COMPOSITION
(Techniques and Production)

INTERPRETATION
(Social and Economic Changes)

SIMPLE
APPROACHES
ANALYSIS
OF
PREHISTORIC
POTTERY

1
CHEMICAL
ANALYSIS

2
POTTERY
DUPLICATION

3
SECTIONING
STUDIES

A QACCCP Tests

B MAT Studies

C Munsell Colour

4
REFIRING
STUDIES

D Replication

E Original Sherds

F Munsell Colour

G Thin Sections

H Slab Sections

ious Analytical Techniques Used in the Prehistoric Po*MODEL* for the Various Analytical Techniques Used in the Prehistoric Pottery Research Currently Operative in Mallorca and Oxford.

DCATT&T

Chart 1

INTRODUCTION

The scientific processes involved in the prehistoric pottery analysis deal with a number of different analytical methods, using the techniques of physical examination, chemical quantitative analyses and practical experiments. These have been carried out on prehistoric pottery samples from the Spanish Balearic Islands and other immediately adjacent geographic areas, where experimental materials are both available and plentiful from stratigraphically and chronometrically well documented caves, rock shelters and open-air settlements.

The research is basically designed to determine: (1) whether or not certain interrelated physical elements exist in the pottery sample materials examined and to what degree; (2) whether or not these can be accredited to specific geographic locales; (3) whether or not these are characteristic of the different local chronological periods; (4) what compositional changes in the methods of manufacture occurred; (5) whether such changes may or may not be indicators in time and space of particular social and economic changes and developments.

Simple and complicated petrographic analyses of both ancient and modern pottery are by no means new avenues of research. The beginning of petrographic analysis probably finds its roots, in one form or another, in the earliest domestic recipes for clay preparation; recipes certainly were in practice by the time the manufacture of early pottery was being carried out on a commercial basis. It is general knowledge, for example, that Greek and Roman pottery factories maintained high standards and precision of formulae for the preparation, finishing and firing of specialised clays which are precisely identifiable; some processes of which modern technology still has difficulty in fully understanding; e.g. the graphite-like, metalic finishes of Greek Attic and Roman Campanian wares.

In the last decade or so, sophisticated techniques of analyses, such as neutron activation analyses (Emeleus 1960), x-ray powder diffraction (Bimson 1969), thermoluminescence (Aitken 1974) and various types of computer-based analyses, as well as anthropologically oriented studies (e.g. Kempton 1981) for the physical examination of pottery, have become available to archaeologists. Certainly, much of what one would wish to know concerning the properties and composition of pottery can be gained from the use of most of these sophisticated techniques; techniques, for the better part, developed as the result of commercial enterprise, where they have been applied extensively and effectively to the analysis and manufacture of modern industrial ceramics. However, the use of all but a very few of these new methods require elaborate and expensive hardware, and in most cases the skill of specialists. Judging by the increasing rate of new developments and technology in these and other physical methods of examination (indeed, as in scientific fields in general), it would appear that, instead of becoming simpler and more readily available to the field archaeologist, analytical techniques are destined to become even more complicated, specialised and expensive.

As this paper will demonstrate, there are some relatively simple, efficient and inexpensive methods of analysing pottery sherd materials; methods that can be carried out both in the field and laboratory; methods by which reliable and highly informative analytical results can be attained. That is to say, analytical results that can provide us with clues concerning prehistoric pottery clay properties, ancient firing techniques, ancient pottery manufacturing processes, and analytical results which are capable of offering us insights into the more esoteric aspects of the social and economic environments of the times they represented.

In essence, it is the author's premise that utilising relatively simple and uncomplicated approaches to the analysis of prehistoric pottery clays, informative data and information can be procured that are otherwise unattainable from more sophisticated techniques. There is much to be learned, for example, from (1) simple chemical and quantitative analysis of particular inclusion (temper) materials, (2) thin and slab-sectioning of sherd material for the identification and description of clay inclusions and other physical characteristics evident in the samples, (3) the use of refiring and duplication experiments to better understand some of the problems involved in the manufacturing techniques, (4) statistical and computer based studiesthat quantify the results obtained. These four methods and the way they have been used locally in the Balearics are discussed at some length and certain results presented in this paper.

Before this account takes place something should be addressed concerning the overall analytical strategy used, and the general hypotheses involved. It is the author's premise that potters' clays are composed of a determinable number of mineral inclusions and that when examined and tested the clays show, after their original firing, the types of atmospheric and other physical environments present when they were first manufactured. It is assumed and generally accepted that (1) the mineral inclusions found in ancient pottery are traceable to two main agencies: (i) those found naturally in the clays chosen for manufacture and (ii) those introduced into a natural or prepared clay fabric by the potter himself. These two types of mineral inclusions are referred to in this research as: (a) natural inclusions and (b) artificial inclusions (tempers). These tempers can consist of a wide variety of substances, ranging from hard minerals to vegetable and animal matter and (2) that these inclusions are effected to different degrees in a number of recordable ways by the type of kiln used and the kiln's firing atmosphere. It is further proposed (3) that a well recorded account of these properties and changes based on observations and practical tests, carried out on an extensive series of analytical materials, can be of some positive contribution in understanding of the ancient techniques employed during the different local chronological periods throughout prehistory.

It is still further suggested (4) that the prehistoric potter, as in the case of the modern pottery technician and artisan (both primitive and sophisticated), had at his command formal and traditional *recipes* of sorts for the preparation of his clays for firing, and that these methods, tantamount to formulae, were in most cases precisely adhered to in order to attain particular and desired results. Results which in themselves were either a question of tradition, technique or economy, or some combination of all three incentives. It is further suggested (5) that certain physical and chemical idiosyncracies exist in the sherd materials which demonstrate the ancient methods of preparation as well as certain properties evident in the potter's choice of the clay itself. Properties which are by their particular nature indicative and characteristic of (a) the geographic locale and (b) the time framework in which it they occur.

In the first section of this paper which deals with weights and percentages of natural and artificial mineral inclusions found in the Balearic prehistoric pottery samples, analytical results are used to demonstrate characteristics diagnostic of particular pottery styles, chronological moments, methods used and areas of their manufacture. In the case of the Balearic sites, the use of these methods of analyses has been productive, and the prospect of their continued successful application especially attractive. Here, a large number of test samples have been available from a wide range of chronologically documented sites and varied stratigraphical contexts (Waldren 1983 and 1986). While admittedly these may only demonstrate and define prehistoric contexts within a yet limited insular territorial parameter, they do represent quite positive results regarding the question of simple approaches to the analyses of prehistoric pottery. In essence, although they have not as yet been tested elsewhere, the simple approaches outlined above could be similarly applied and would prove a permanent tool in assessing not only pottery manufacturing processes but patterns of exchange in localised areas, and possibly interaction or demographic and trade movement on a wider scale.

BACKGROUND TO THE PRESENT RESEARCH

While most ethnological information on primitive potters' techniques is generally very poor in detail, especially concerning the contents and properties of the potter's clay as well as the manufacturing procedures themselves (Shephard 1965), some ethnographers do comment briefly on the use of both residual and sedimentary clays in primitive pottery. For example, Rodgers (1936) reports the use of disintegrated granite containing 85% non-plastic material in the form of quartz, mica, limestone and partially altered feldspar by the Yuman tribes of Southern California. He also reports that the Indians of the Picuris and other Pueblo Indians of the Upper Rio Grande use highly micaceous residual clay for their cooking pots. Fewkes (1944) thinks that the Catawbas used residual pipe clay for their pottery.

In most ethnographic reports concerning primitive pottery techniques (despite their frustrating lack of detail on other points) the technological observation most frequently made by the ethnographers relates to the care and importance devoted to standards in the basic preparation of clay fabrics for pottery manufacture. Tschopik (1950) notes that the Aymara of Peru roll out balls of clay and flatten them in order to observe how soon they crack and in this way, they can evaluate a clay's consistency. Hill (1937) reports that the Navajos moisten their clay and further test its cohesiveness. As reported by Lothrop (1927), the potters of Guadajiagua of Salvador are especially careful in preparing their clay. In fact, they actually invite native visitors from surrounding areas who arrive during clay preparation time to test and comment on the clay's quality and consistency; for them, the clay is ready for use only when the clay fabric sticks to the fingers.

Almost inevitably, ethnographers emphasise the great care taken in clay preparation, standards of measurements and properties looked for and required in pottery manufacture and which are well known to the potters concerned; the recipe in most cases being traditional. Nevertheless it is, at the same time, a matter of record that particular care is rarely taken in firing or in the maintenance of even firing temperatures. In fact in known cases, the potters often rake aside the coals of still red hot kilns to remove pottery while it is still glowing. Whether this is done to achieve a desired affect or as a result of impatience and disregard are interesting questions. Then too, there are the problems of primitive and ancient kilns themselves, which because of their unsophisticated character (they are usually simple mound or pit kilns) offer commonly limited firing potentials.

Despite the fact that primitive potters' methods throughout the world do differ in matters of detail, for example in types of kiln, fuel or actual choice of raw materials, they nevertheless appear to show a common concern for distinctive and personalised methodology in preparation and to the importance of the clay chosen for pottery construction.

THE CURRENT RESEARCH

The current research report deals principally with the methodology and results obtained from Balearic prehistoric ceramics tests using the various simple approaches to pottery analysis outlined above. The analyses and experiments are being carried out in three locations: the Donald Baden-Powell Quaternary Research Centre, Pitt Rivers Museum, University of Oxford, Oxford, Churchill College, Cambridge, England and the Deya Archaeological Museum and Research Centre, Deya, Mallorca, Baleares, Spain. The research presented here forms part of a long term, on-going project dedicated generally to the study of Balearic ecology and prehistory.

While the methods discussed and described below are in some ways simplistic, being by nature uncomplicated, depending on criteria derived from long experience and familiarity with the local materials in both the field and laboratory, they are by this very nature of simplicity of particular value, in that they can be carried out in great number with readily, economically arrived at results. At the same time, as pointed out earlier, the results procured may be otherwise unobtainable by more sophisticated means.

It can be said that the research format and strategy, as it stands at present, have grown out of the author's field and laboratory familiarity with the test materials, as well as a natural curiousity to understand the material worked with. Their is a certain advantage and comfort in being familiar with one's materials, especially from the standpoint of field identification and other immediate assessments. However, regardless of how advantageous and important familiarity and experience or understanding are with field identification and assessment of one's materials, these are not enough and must be quantified and tested further; if any reliable interpretation or results are to be expected.

Apart from familiarity or experience there is another advantage- although some might say disadvantage- in the local materials, there exists a certain physical homogeneity in the pottery of the islands' different prehistoric periods; a homogeneity which may or may not be a product of an insular environment. This uniformity of nature in the Balearic prehistoric pottery of particular periods not only manifests itself in stylistic and traditionally similar pottery forms but, also, in their compositional nature. This homogeneity is found in the form of certain diagnostic characteristics that are present in the various pottery clay fabrics of the different periods that can be analytically quantified as well as relied on in identification. One of these diagnostic characteristics is the quantity and kinds of temper ingredient found in the different clay fabrics. In the case of the local wares, this appears in the form of a particular mineral inclusion: calcium carbonate (especially limestone); a single mineral ingredient which has become the basis for most of the current pottery fabric research and one that is present in all local prehistoric pottery.

At present more than 400 chemical analyses to determine calcium carbonate content (Tables 1-15) and 1800 pottery sherd sections and numerous refiring and duplication experiments have been carried out on Balearic pottery samples; detail interim reports of which can be found in the author's published doctoral thesis and elsewhere (Waldren 1981, 1982 and 1986).

DESCRIPTION OF THE ANALYTICAL METHODS

Each of the four analytical methods from which the present research is derived, (1) chemical analysis of the calcium carbonate content in the local pottery, (2) pottery sectioning, (3) refiring experiments and (4) duplication experiments, are described in the pertinent sections and in the organisational schematic (Chart 1) below. Although, each of these is an analytical method in its own right, capable of providing independent results and deserving individual study and publication, they are reported on jointly in the present paper to demonstrate the manner in which they are interrelated. In due course each will require its own more extensive individualistic report.

This present paper is by way of introduction to some of the results attained so far, and to offer the reader a concise account of the research along with some idea of the strategy and methods used. It is also a collaboration of a supportive nature, showing the evidence as it is related to the diagnostic and compositional characteristics of the local Balearic prehistoric pottery, in the hope that they may be applied elsewhere as successfully.

The most common object on any archaeological excavation is a pottery sherd, consequently the storage areas of museums and other storerooms of archaeological artefacts throughout the world contain and maintain tons of pottery fragments. In some case, crates of these materials excavated as long ago as the turn of the century are still packed in the very containers in which they were originally placed and shipped from excavations; a source of research materials which perhaps never will be tapped or studied.

As other sources of test materials, the plowed fields around known or potential archaeological sites contain abundant fragmentary pottery remains that are available for testing and experimentation. These sources of easily available test and experimental materials have until the present been sorely appreciated or completely neglected.

Another objective of the current research is to stimulate interest in the use of such reservoirs and materials for obtaining archeological data and information. Large series of test materials, using new and innovative techniques, should be encouraged. Such extensive programmes would, by and large, use only small percentages of the enormous stores of fragmentary pottery samples available. Or for that matter, if unavailable from museum collections, they could be collected in field surveys rather than retrieved from the storage areas of museums. Field collection surveys are excellent sources for all sorts of test and study materials.

In any event, when and if interests in prehistoric pottery analysis do increase (there are some recent signs of this occurring), extensive analytical series should be undertaken. Results from a few samples, while perhaps informative in some ways, are never as revealing as larger series: a general rule that pertains to other physical analytical research.

In three of the four analytical methods described here, testing has been carried out separately on different portions of the same ancient sherd sample. This has been done not so much as an economical gesture or reluctance to destroy a sherd, but rather to establish an unbiased testing and perhaps more accurate basis of interpretation and analysis. Besides, the choice of a large sherd or several belonging to the same vessel form in the end a better related series of results. Large series from one site locale also reflect any immediate continuity, discontinuity or general standardisation in the clay ingredients better than a few sherds from many locales; although testing of wide ranging collections are also essential. The ideal situation is to test large series from many areas. The division of the test sherd is illustrated in Figure 1.

1.
CHEMICAL ANALYSIS FOR THE CONTENT OF CALCIUM CARBONATE

One of the most common natural or artificial mineral inclusions found in potter's clay is calcium carbonate ($CaCO_3$), commonly found in the form of shell, limestone and calcite (Shepard 1965). This is particularly true for the prehistoric pottery of the Balearic Islands where the islands' geology is almost entirely limestone. This geological factor, as will be shown presently, is the main contribution to the current research, forming the basis of most of the methods used and assessments made.

As a natural or artificial temper in pottery, calcium carbonate is one of the most unsuitable ingredients of the long list of clay binders used in pottery making (Shepard 1965). Unlikely ingredients such as feathers, grain and other organic materials, among more likely tempers such as quartz, hematite, feldspar and sand have been used successfully as prehistoric clay fillers .

The reason for the unsuitability of limestone as a mineral temper is quite simple. It rests in the fact that most limestone decomposes when heated to temperatures of above 898° C, and in some forms of limestone such as sandstone slightly lower. Temperatures excessive to these convert limestone into calcium oxide (quicklime), which being hydroscopic is highly susceptable to moisture, causing an active reaction, a slaking of the calcium oxide on exposure to moisture. Pottery in which this happens quickly falls apart on contact with water; the calcium oxide particles rapidly slake and cause spalling. Experiments have shown this spalling can happen even during air-cooling of a heated pot fragment, where its calcium oxide particles draw moisture from the surrounding air during cooling. Should firing on the other hand exceed the conversion point of limestone, an incipient occurrence, the result is the complete decomposition of the limestone inclusions, leaving in some instances cavities. In such cases, the clay fabric is riddled with these degassing cavities, making the pot extremely porous.

Therefore, if limestone is used as a filler, the maintenance of firing temperatures less than 898° C are necessary for successful pottery manufacture. This firing factor was highly significant during at least one period of local prehistory, that of the local Bronze Age or Talayotic Period, circa 1200 bc to 800 bc and part of the Iron Age or Post Talayotic Period circa 800 bc to 400 bc, where abnormally large limestone fillers were used. After 400 bc increasingly high quantities of vegetal matter in the form of grain chaff admixtures were employed. Here, one is pressed to ask why extremely high quantities of limestone temper were employed and used successfully, or the later use of grain chaff?

Despite the known instability of calcium carbonate as a mineral inclusion (temper) in clay, along with its reputation of being one of the worst of possible binding mediums and greatly limiting the temperature firing range of such clays, and at times actually impairing the success of the firing itself, its use is frequent in pottery manufacture by primitive potters from nearly every geographic area and chronological period. Equally, modern potters are known frequently to use limestone temper as well as high content calcium carbonate clays; apparently as a matter of choice or lack of other resources.

As a result of the limitations in the use of limestone tempers and the natural content of calcium carbonate in local clays, certain assumptions are present in the current research. It is assumed (**6**) that the prehistoric potters were well aware of its natural presence in the clay, as well as its particular firing characteristics and limitations, and (**7**) that its suitability, despite its instability, must have outweighed by far any inconvenience or limitation known to the prehistoric potter, which might result from its having been used as a natural or artificial inclusion. It is also suggested (**a**) that the prehistoric ceramist exercised precise, probably even traditional or personalised recipes for its use as a binding medium and (**b**) that their measurements consisted of determinable quantity ranges, which as a result can be traced and interpreted as being idiosyncratic. Finally, it might be argued (**c**) that perhaps the pottery during certain periods was prepared by specialists and even circulated from a certain number of distribution centres, and (**d**) that the centres of manufacture and the resulting patterns of distribution, representing trade and other exchange may possibly be determined using the described methods of analysis. Finally, (**e**) it is argued that the use of of such high calcium carbonate pottery techniques in Talayotic and Post Talayotic times were carried out for strong economic issues

Chemical analysis for the quantitative calcium carbonate content (QACCCP) of the selected pottery test sample (Figure 1) consists of cutting the test sample in half (Figures 1A and 1D),using part of the first half of the original, large specimen pottery sherd sample (1D) for the chemical analysis. The remaining second half of the sherd is cut in half in turn and put aside for use in subsequent slab/ thin sectioning (Figure 1C and B), refiring experiments (Figure 1F and G) and as a reference sherd, if required for duplication tests (Figure 1A). Eventually, each individual sherd test sample should provide at least four relatively large parts, each carefully classified and catalogued.

Preparation of the test sample for the QACCCP (Quantitative Analysis of Calcium Carbonate Content of Prehistoric Pottery) is carried out by grinding a portion of the pottery test sample (Figure 1D) to a fine powder in a mortar and pestle (Plate 5). The Munsell colour of the ground powder is then recorded (Plate 6). The author considers this to be the best procedure for noting any meaningful colour identification of prehistoric pottery, the wide variation of pot's surface colour, hue and tone, makes any true colour identification impossible to determine, while the ground up sherd gives the fired clay's true colour. Experiments have also shown that there is some relationship between heat and the colour of the finished clay product, similar to the preparation of artist's earth colour pigments. From a basic yellow ochre ground pigment a full range of artist's earth colours can be attained by heating the pigment in increased stages. The sample hue and chroma can be regulated by temperature stages.

The resulting pulverised sherd sample should weigh 10 grams or more, to provide ample testing material, as well as a pulverised reference sample to be kept. It is essential that an established or standard weight measurement should be maintained for all subsequent QACCCP sherd test samples; although this is not absolutely necessary as recent test have shown (Table 15). Half of the pulverised sherd sample is then precisely weighed and recorded and used for chemical treatment (5 grms) (Plate 6). More than this cannot be successfully treated for complete removal of the sample's calcium carbonate content in a standard 100 ml test tube. If a larger amount be desireous, two 5 grm treatments of the same sherds test sample should be tested in two separate test tubes, and results compared and averaged.

For the weighing of all samples, an electronic or mechanical precision pharmaceutical scale with the capacity of registering 3 or 4 points below zero (0.989 or 0.9889) should be used. The weighed pulverised sherd sample is fed after weighing into the 100 ml test tube containing a 10% solution of hydrochloric acid (38% by concentration), agitated slightly and treated overnight, to remove most of the test sample's calcium carbonate content (Plate 7). The pulverised test sample remaining settled at the bottom of the test tube after the overnight acid treatment is then centrifuged and the acid solution poured off. The remaining residue from the test sample is then washed in distilled water and centrifuged. This washing and pouring off of the distilled water after centrifuging is done three times, to ensure the removal of possible soluble bicarbonates.

The remaining residue of the pulverised test sample is finally poured off after the last washing and centrifuging, (Plate 8) and is then fully dried in a low temperature oven in less than 20° C (Plate 9). This low temperature insures that drying does not alter any of the sample's oxides, should further analysis or colour coding be desired. After drying, the remaining sherd sample residue is then weighed again on the electronic scale. The difference in the weight, between the untreated pulverised sherd test sample and the acid treated, washed and dried residue sherd test sample, represents the calcium carbonate content of the sample in quantitative terms of weight and percentage (see sample recording sheets).

In the enclosed tables (1-10), the results of 400 QACCCP analyses are presented; two hundred from the Pretalayotic Period (Chalcolithic and Initial Bronze Age), circa 2100 bc to circa 1300 bc and the Talayotic Period (Bronze Age), circa 1200 bc to circa 800 bc. The result of these tests show an additional (additive) use of limestone temper of approximately 17% more in Talayotic times than found in the earlier Pretalayotic Period.

The results show averages of 34.33% calcium carbonate content for Pretalayotic pottery (Table 1) and 51.78% calcium carbonate for Talayotic wares (Table 2). This includes test ranges as low as 25.10% to a high of 47.60% in Pretalayoic Chalcolithic and Initial Bronze Age pottery and test ranges as low as 38.85% to a high of 65.39% in Talayotic Bronze Age wares. These percentage results are arrived at from test sample series of 10 samples randomly selected sherds in each major series (series of 10). Individual test results percentages for each of the major test series can be seen in Tables 3 to 15.

Similar analyses of clays collected on site from several different zones indicate ranges similar to those found naturally in the Pretalayotic calcium carbonate ranges above (20% to 35%). In checking individual calcium carbonate percentage ranges and averages in Tables 3-15, in each series of 10 samples for the Pretalayotic wares there are nearly always one abnormally high percentage result. It has been noted that this occurred frequently when a sherd from an extra large pot with extra large natural limestone inclusions was used for testing and would account for the abnormally high percentages in testing. Large utilitarian vessels require larger temper inclusions for strength; a normal procedure in pottery construction. The clays collected on site occasionally contained large natural inclusions, although normally clay was collected for replication experiments for the construction of smaller vessels and not large ones; thus resulting in some bias in the clay collected on site. Further tests of on site clays will have to include fabrics selected for heavier inclusion properties in order to test a fuller range of raw material.

The overall percentages of the prehistoric test samples clearly quantify and delineate the differences in calcium carbonate content for the two periods as present in several local sites. When linked with other results from the other analytical methods used and discussed below, these differences in calcium carbonate contents take on additional significance. The quantification experiments strongly suggest that despite very broad differences of content the Talayotic potters were purposely adding additional limestone temper to the already heavy content naturally found in the local clays. For what reasons?

As slab-sectioning shows in the following research section, the limestone inclusions of the Pretalayotic Period can be seen to have been natural to the clays selected (Plate 1A). This is illustrated under magnification by the rounded inclusions, a signal of long term erosion of the particles, such as would occur naturally in the clays over a long period of weathering. Whereas, inclusions or temper in the Talayotic examples show sharply angled edges, indicative of newly broken or artificial temper (Plate 1B). The particularly high percentage of limestone temper also strongly suggest conscious application and reinforcement of the clays before pot manufacture.

Still other results from duplication experiments strongly suggest legitimite reasons for the large quantities of limestone added to the clay fabrics. These are demonstrated and discussed in the appropriate section below. It will suffice to say here that the reasons for adding what could be considered an undesireable element to the naturally heavy percentage of calcium carbonate already found in the local clays are mainly sound and practical reasons with considerable economic advantages. It demonstrating a completely conscious application of limestone temper and even what is tantamount to formulae in clay preparation; creating in its wake a homogeneous quality to the Talayotic wares in general; a similar homogeneity which is equally evident in the wares of the Pretalayotic Period; a homogeneous quality on the part of the pottery of both periods that is demonstrated in the statistical percentages (Tables 1 and 2) .

Together, the different analytical methods used in the analyses, at least with the Balearic pottery materials, seem to work in an interdisciplinary manner, providing interrelated data and information traceable equally culture and tradition as well as to having economic considerations and social application.

2.
POTTERY SECTIONING

The thin and slab-sectioning research programme of pottery samples from the Balearic Islands was initiated by the author at Oxford in 1975. Until that time, no work of this kind had been attempted on Balearic pottery, apart from a minor study by M. Murray (1938). Since 1975, a field and laboratory sampling programme has been in progress, and while that programme here in 1987 is still in its intitial stages, a substantial collection of reference slides and other material are available for study, as well as the results at present .

Pottery sectioning consists of the preparation of sherds as mounted slab-sections and (optionally) conventional thin-sections. These are destined for study and photographing, eventually forming part of an extensive library reference collection. For this the second half of original sherd test sample (Figure 1) is used. Cut in two pieces, each of these remaining sherd test samples (Figures 1B and 1C) should be large enough to accommodate the mounted slide samples, refiring sample (Figures 1F and 1G) and reference sample (Figure 1A).

Apart from the identification of rare mineral elements possible in conventional geological thin-sectioning, well prepared (cut and polished) slab-sections are equally valuable in identifying a prehistoric sherd sample's mineral content and, indeed, in some respects even more informative. What the author refers to as features and events are more discernible. In the author's glossary of terms (Waldren 1982) a *feature* is an individual characteristic, such as a pit or cavity, mineral grains, special temper particle, degassing channel, shrinkage or stretch lines, etc.; while an *event* is an alteration or apparent change in the physical or chemical appearance of the clay fabric or inclusion particle: such as sintering, incipient vitrification, etc.

The method of slab-sectioning used in the research as well as the conventional thin-sections was designed to achieve a number of objectives which are outlined below:

(1) To prepare a reference library of Balearic prehistoric pottery samples in the form of mounted slab-sections and, when thought significant, conventional thin-section. This is followed by the preparation of microphotographs (colour transparencies and black and white) taken at a standard magnification.

(2) To study and record the various 'features' and 'events' (as defined in the paper) brought about by the alteration of mineral inclusions or clay fabric itself; thus illustrating (a) the different physical properties of the various fabrics and (b) the changes and alterations resulting from the various idiosyncratic and technological processes used by their makers. Such a study, it is believed, can give clues to the firing processes and temperatures and other conditions involved in the manufacture of the individual vessels as well as the problems confronted by the potter.

(3) To build, if possible, a mineralogical thermo-scale, (a) deduced from the compositional, temperature and chemical changes of the mineral inclusions and clay fabrics themselves; and (b) to ascertain by experimental refiring of corresponding sherd samples, the stage and temperature at which the various actions (events) such as sintering, decomposition and incipient vitrification took place in the various clay mineral inclusions (e.g. limestone, quartz, feldspar and haematite etc).

(4) To study and record (a) any differences in the structure of the clay fabrics themselves and, eventually, (b) to determine by more quantitative methods the exact composition of the different clay fabric samples tested (this project is already underway in the QACCCP analyses outlined above).

(5) To determine optically whether or not any particular type of clay fabric may be ascribed consistently to a single chronological period. This is done on the basis of observational and quantitative comparison of prepared microscopic slides and chemical specimens, as well as from experimental methods, such as refiring and duplication trials.

(6) To determine (a) in statistical terms how reliable the physical and chemical differences between various clay fabrics samples from different geographic areas are and (b) whether or not they possibly may be ascribed either to changing idiosyncratic and technological skills as well as chronological age.

(7) To establish (a) whether or not any special type of pottery vessel clay fabric (e.g. Balearic Beaker ware) was locally manufactured or possibly imported into the indigenous pottery assemblages and (b) if so whether it can possibly be used to determine origin (unfortunately this project is not as yet advanced to any degree). While the first series of local Beaker ware sherds have been sectioned and prepared, very few Beaker sherd examples for sectioning are currently available; thus limiting possibilities for comparisons with those from mainland sites).

While one of the longer ranged objectives of this slab and thin-section research is gradually to build up an extensive reference library of pottery sections and other data sources, the most immediate project has been to prepare a sound *preliminary* set of reference slide sections along with corresponding photographs (both black and white and colour transparencies); a preliminary set of sherds from good stratigraphic contexts and varied age, which are radiocarbon dated in as many cases as possible; a preliminary set of sherd samples that forms a representative cross-section of the various *features* and *events* found in the pottery of the Balearics (Waldren 1982, vol 2, p. 658).

Along with the preparartion of this preliminary set of reference slide sections, an illustrative glossary as well as an inventory of analytical results of the samples' clay ingredients are other objectives of the pottery sectioning project. In turn, all three of these objectives are interrelated, forming part of the longer list of aims outlined in the discription of each of the techniques used. This long term strategy of designing what amounts to an interrelated programme of analyses has been to bring out, if possible, the supportive nature of each of the methods; thus, in a sense testing one against the other.

Here in 1987, the collection of slab and thin-sections, sherd materials for simple analyses and the results derived from them are much more extensive than as first published in 1982. New collections have been made and reference slides prepared, in the five year interim, from a large number of sites locally and elsewhere in the Balearics (e.g.Menorca), as well as from a number of sites from continental areas (e.g. Northern Italy, etc.) (although their processing is far from complete). It should be emphasised that while the preparation of slide section and other test samples is uncomplicated and quite fast, to prepare them in large number is all the same somewhat time consuming.

The process for the preparation of these slide sections for the reference collection are described in some detail in the appendices of the author' thesis (Waldren 1982, vol ii, Appendix 3a). Several sample slide microphotgraphs are found below (Plates 10 and 11 of the slab-sections). These demonstrate the visual differences typical of finished slide samples from each of the recognised Balearic chronological periods.

There is little need to describe the process of mounting pottery slab or thin-sections here, as they are quite conventional and can be successfully done by almost anyone with a little bit of patience and practice. It will suffice to say that the slab-section takes considerably less time for preparation than thin-sectioning and are quite easy to do, with the minimum of equipment; the most complicated of which is a basic lapidary or geological rock cutting set up.

The slab-section for the study of *features* and *events* is better suited for viewing pottery inclusions etc, and in some ways more informative than thin-sectioning, which is designed for the finer task of identifying rare minerals. At the same time, the slab-sections make it possible to accually take statistical count of qauntity in numbers of the temper particles showing on the surface of the slide slab-section.

The most labour intensive task in the preparation of the slab-section slides is the actual mounting and polishing of the surface of the mounted section. Once this is done, it is only a matter of identification and labelling the sample and subsequent microscopic study. Storage is no problem and the finished reference slides can be kept in standard microscopic slide boxes.

3.
POTTERY REFIRING EXPERIMENTS

This method consists of using the last portion (Figure 1F and 1G) of the sherd test sample for refiring experiments. The process of refiring pottery chips to interpret degrees of oxidation is known (Shephard 1965). While the method is recommended as a training procedure in Shepard's thesis for interpreting oxidation, the present author believes that more can be learned from controlled experiments in refiring ancient sherd samples in a controlled environment than only determining degrees of oxidation, although this is one of the reasons for experimental firing.

The recent experiments in refiring a sample collection of pottery sherds were carried out on a selected number of test materials from the same collection used for slab-sectioning. The refiring as described here was done with several aims in mind which can be listed:

(1) To establish a criterion or scale for grading the degree of oxidation or reduction arrived at in the test samples.

(2) To study and record any colour change in terms of the Munsell colour scale: the technique to accurately grade colour in pottery.

(3) To study and record any change in the character or appearance of the test sample's natural or artificial inclusions, or in the clay fabric itself; changes brought about by reheating the test sample at different temperatures, and comparing these with a non-refired reference piece of the same sherd. It is proposed that in time a form of thermal scale might possibly be arrived at, based on the degree of alteration of the limestone inclusions as well as alteration of colour in the corresponding pulverised sample. Experiments of the same sort can be made on especially prepared samples of modern on-site clay mixtures, both fired and unfired, which have been fired at controlled temperatures in the laboratory in the same way as ancient pieces.

(4) To determine kiln environments through experimental firings and in order to collect data concerning the firing conditions originally carried out in them.

A small compact commercial electric oven with an inner-oven chamber (10cms x 10cms x 6.5cms) is used for refiring purposes, although this size is not significant in itself. The kiln used has a cover door aperture for inserting a pyrometer graded from $0°$ to $1200°$ C. (the author

used a Hydebourne enameling kiln and pyrometer, however any professional mark of kiln with a reliable pyrometer would be as effective). The test sherds used for reheating are placed on a block made of a composition of firebrick of the kind used by jewellers to place metal jewellery on for brazing or soldering. The composite block should be capable of withstanding very high temperatures and numerous refirings, although any fire-brick composition for this pad will due as well, as long as it is small enough to fit in the kiln chamber. Neither of these pads will effect the process during refiring and at the same time permit the easy removal and insertion of the test sherds in and out of the kiln, whenever several sherds are fired at the same time. It will also ensure uniform heating and cooling of the sherds, as well as keeping them centred in the chamber of the kiln. Usually four sherds can be heated at any one time, they need not be of the same chronological age or archaeological context or same ceramic vessel, since exposure to one another in the kiln does not affect the results obtained for individual sherds. As far as the author has been able to observe, preheating of the kiln from 200° to 400° C before inserting the sherds does not affect the results of refiring, and it certainly saves time. However removing the heated test samples from the kiln too soon after firing can cause cracking of the surface or clay wall of the sherds; although experience has showed that removing the sherds from the kiln should not be done, for purposes of control, before
the temperature has fallen to 200° C. Temperature curves for all firings should be kept as part of the record of refiring experiments.

As suggested earlier, similar firings of specially prepared experimental sherd samples, made from on site clays into test clay slabs of various temper mixtures, can reveal a great deal concerning firing and general clay reaction. Besides such modern test samples can be used as comparative specimens with refiring experiments of ancient test samples. It is best to use clays prepared both with and without artificial temper to observe changes in drying and firing. Forming these clay experimental samples into recorded strip-plaques and firing part of these to observe structural similarities or differences are part of the routine procedure. Similar test clay slabs or plaques prepared in this way also serve as test samples for firing in primitive replica kiln duplication experiments described below, as well as laboratory kiln firing. The more diverse and supportive the test series are of one another the more useful and informative they become.

The results of the first series of refiring experiments have been published in the author's doctoral thesis (Waldren 1982, vol ii, Appendix 3A, pp. 694-712). The reader is recommended to seek out description and results found there. Details of the results and other observations are presented and discussed and while some details will be included in the final edition of this present publication, along with others, space at present does not allow them to be justly or adequately detailed and included here.

4.
DUPLICATION EXPERIMENTS

The duplication experiments are quite straightforward and consist of making pottery from local on-site clays tempered with different inclusion mixtures, mainly those tempers and amounts known to be found in local prehistoric wares as determined through sectioning and chemical analysis and other experimental methods. The pottery made in this manner is fired in duplicated, primitively constructed mound and pit kilns, using different fuels and in different climatic conditions. This is done with a number of objectives in mind:

(1) To duplicate as nearly as possible, through data collected from experimention, prehistoric pottery from the various local prehistoric periods.

(2) To determine whether or not on-site clays were used for production or imported from elsewhere.

(3) To understand the local prehistoric pottery recipes for clay preparation in general.

(4) To ascertain the types of kilns used for firing during the various prehistoric periods.

(5) To study and record firing environments and conditions from the replica kilns.

(6) To attempt to reproduce the surface appearance (colours and surface finishes etc) in replicas for comparative purposes.

These five objectives are simple enough and are capable of reproducing by experimentation many of the conditions, effects present in prehistoric kiln prototypes and other results arrived at by ancient potters. The findings here are the data collected and some of the results obtained from many open-air firings in replica kilns of replica ceramics in which local clays have been used and clay tempera admixtures prepared, according to analytical results from chemical and other experiments reported on in the sections above.

Having had, personally, an early ceramic education in the form of what are considered proper procedures for successful firing, and having graduated in the accepted techniques of modern pottery making, the author has found that many of the recognised correct, modern procedures and techniques are of little use in the actual act of reproducing modern day prehistoric replica ceramics, nor were they the methods of the ancients. Although in all fairness, a knowledge of good ceramic procedures and techniques are worthwhile if only as a field of reference. With the author, the process has been one of putting aside most of what was learned; a process in a sense like the realist painter turning to abstract painting, where an awareness of the abstract has always been present in realist art and is at hand but not in the practice. The conceptions of modern pottery technology and primitive pottery manufacture are that far apart.

From the technological standpoint, the utter simplicity of primative kilns is upsetting to those concerned with proper preparation and firing. According to reports by ethnographers (e.g A. Osborn 1979), in some cases, they consist of simply placing the air dried vessel to be fired on an ordinary cooking fire. In a slightly more sophisticated form, as found in prehistory locally, they are nothing more than a ring of stones and a mound or bondfire of wood or, perhaps, a little more sophisticated, a hole dug in the ground in the form of a pit kiln with a ramp-like draught in one end. Each of these are problematic even in their simplicity and as experience has taught highly unpredictable, being very susceptable to all forms of interior and exterior environmental conditions and mishaps; for example wind velocity and direction as well as other climatic conditions.

The so called closed chamber kiln is of relatively uncertain age and probably its first use by potters varied from geographic area to geographic area. In the Baleares, there is absolutely no evidence to conclude that the closed chamber kiln (apart from the pit kiln in which there is evidence of its use prior to 2500 bc) was never used until long after the first indigenous contact with the classical world (circa 200 to 300 AD). Until that time the indigenous wares were made by the ancient and traditional methods of hand turned, coil or strip constructed wares, fired in mound or pit kilns.

There is also evidence from the badly constructed Balearic indigenous pottery of the Late Iron Age from about 200 bc forward that the local wares underwent a severe degeneration of techniques, ending in what are known from Southern French IIIrd century BC counterparts as *poterie grossiere*; a style of unprecedented ugliness and lack of skill which seems to be geographically, widely distributed throughout Northeastern Spain and Southern France and associated with the Iron Age. In these wares organic temper in the form of grain chaff has been used in an attempt to bring about vitrification in the pottery. The end result is a burning out of the chaff, leaving degassing channels or charred particles and a highly porous as well as fragile product.

It is generally accepted that the presence of this type of low quality pottery, at least in the Balearic Islands, was probably due to the great surge and easy availability of imported classical wares in these areas during the IIIrd to IInd centuries BC, and beginning as early as the Vth and IVth centuries, although at this time some of the earlier quality from the Talayotic Bronze Age is still present in the use of limestone and sand tempers. In the Balearics, its presences coincides with these dates from about the IIIth century BC (the Roman Colonisation of the islands in 123 BC) to the IInd century AD.

BALEARIC PREHISTORIC KILNS

The author has had the good fortune of having excavated samples of both mound and pit kilns (Waldren 1978 and 1982). These have consisted of two mound kilns (dated circa 860 bc from the charcoal) and a pit kiln (dated 450 bc from the charcoal). In both case, the kiln area had copious pottery sherds, the result of unsuccessful firings and evidently left in the kiln as refractory material or general rubbish. From these a great deal of reconstructable and experimental materials are available to study.

The experiments in pottery duplication have been carried out in mound and pit replica kilns (Frontisepiece) (Plates 3a to 3c), similar to the ancient prototypes excavated. In both types of firing, the experiments have had excellent success rates and ended in strikingly similar results as those found in the ancient pottery. Firing ranges as high as 850º C to 1000º C (the latter height briefly arrived at in a mound kiln on a breezy day) were attained and it was found with the use of the right fuels, like cow or horse dung, even temperatures over reasonable long periods could be maintained without refueling.

EXPERIMENTAL OBSERVATIONS AND RESULTS

A number of experimental observations and results have been obtained during the course of the experimental research so far. These are best listed according to each type of experiment. Many of the observations and results overlap one another as the experiments themselves do, and coincide in a general and parallel direction with one another in a still further supportive context.

POTTERY CHEMICAL ANALYSIS

Chemical Analysis for the Content of Calcium Carbonate of Prehistoric Pottery (QACCCP) as the first analytical example have produced the following observations and results:

1. The method in the case of the local prehistoric wares examined has quantified, not only, the differences in the percentage content of calcium carbonate present in the various wares of the different periods, but has demonstrted a general homogeneity in the pottery fabrics of these periods (Tables 1-15). The approximately 500 quantitative analyses currently available illustrate, not only, the homogeneity on different levels, but the differences themselves, between stations and between chronological periods in regards to their calcium carbonate contents.

2. The analysis results suggest that the changes in the preparation of the clays from the use of naturally reinforced clay fabrics to artificially reinforcement may well have been the result of

one or two origins: (a) a necessity for change in the traditional processes of clay preparation to supply increasing demographic demands and increased demand or (b) the arrival of other cultural influences, replacing the old with new and hence different technology. A third possibility (c) consists of a combination of the two. As shown by evidence from the other experiments, the former of these two origins is strongly suggested and may have been the main influences and most likely origin of change: that of demographic change and need for faster and more economical production methods .

3. The test results show that there were at least two and possibly three different qualities of clay used for the Pretalayotic or earlier wares: a fine, medium and rough grade of clay fabric by calcium carbonate percentages, probably related to size, use and fundtion of the pieces themselves. Talayotic wares show less variation in percentages in the clay preparation with a standardisation of additive temper; probably also related to size and function of the vessels.

4. It is suggested that whatever the actual cause of the change in techniques and composition that it was a conscious and premeditated one on the part of the potters from the two different periods. It is also suggested that the earlier, older Pretalayotic traditional preparations of clay were carried out probably on a home-industry basis, according to traditional recipes, using natural clay sources, fundamentally untreated and containing natural inclusions; apart from finewares which show careful preparation of the clays, or a search for clays with particularly fine properties.

5. There are indications that the QACCCP method, on the basis of its successful use locally in the differentiation of the different clay fabrics, may well be useful in other areas outside the insular limits of the Balearics in the analysis of the clay fabrics of high percentage calcium carbonate content. There is good indication at the same time that the results apply just as successfully to the prehistoric wares from the sister Island of Menorca, which bear great similarity in calcium carbonate content ranges. Although the geology issomewhat different on Menorca, the traditional clay preparations compare favourably. This of course leads to the future possibilitiy that analysis series from other geographic areas farther afield than the Balearics may be equally helpful.

6. There are strong indications that on-site clays were used in the fabrication of all local wares, or at least where they were eassily available. Ancient clays have been collected from bedrock crevices within the sites for this purpose and used with and without treatment or augmented with inclusive materials or used directly with natural inclusions. When tested these fell well withing the calcium carbonate ranges established from the analysis of ancient sherd material. When correlated with duplication experiments results from modern clay preparation, firing and refiring, the properties of these clays prove substantially similar.

POTTERY SECTIONING

1. Slab-sectioning has shown the particular properties (e.g. minerals, types of clays) of the local clay fabrics during the different prehistorical periods. An excellent reference study collection of about 2000 sherd sample slides are available from the technique and have given a useful glossary of identifiable *events* and *features* found in the local wares. This includes an evergrowing collection from outside the geographic limits of the Baleares and includes three series from Northern and Central Italy as well as Sardinia.

2. The method has successfully demonstrated the differences in clacium carbonate content of the different wares and their periods, quantifying them visually and assisting in the identification and duplication processes.

3. It has also assisted in the better understanding of ancient kiln conditions and environments as reflected in the test samples and what conditions and environments that were possible aa well as those that can be expected from prehistoric pottery from the use of the two kinds of primitive kilns.

4. It has further led to the possibility of establishing a termal scale to quantify the alteration of mineral inclusions during ancient firing and modern experimental firings, based on the degree of visual alterations of particular inclusions, such as calcium carbonate. Observed changes in the surface and shape of limestone particles in slab-sections are visible with refiring of ancient sectioned test samples or modern prepared ones (next section).

POTTERY REFIRING EXPERIMENTS

1. Refiring has been helful in giving us details as to the original firing temperatures of the pieces examined and studied. Temperatures of 750 to 800 degrees centigrade are indicated for high percentage limestone tempered clays (Talayotic). Temperatures of 800 to 850 degrees centigrade are suggested for low percentage clays for Pretalayoic fine wares. Above these temperatures the pottery is susceptable to spalding and breaking up. These observations have been arrived at by incremented temperature rises on test samples, both ancient and modern, in a controlled kiln situation and comparison with the corresponding faces or surfaces of the refired and and unfired halves of the same experimental sherd samples.

2. It is also the method from which a workable thermal scale for mineral alteration may be eventually derived.

3. The refiring has been helpful in understanding the firing and other limitations of the various ancient clay fabrics ofrom the different periods in the assessment of original firing temperatures, drying, shrinking, cracking and other alterations to minerals like calcium carbonate brought about by high temperatures.

4. These experiments too have help the understanding of the ancient pottery techniques used and the kiln conditions as well as those of modern replica experiments, acting as a cross-check with the other methods of analysis.

DUPLICATION EXPERIMENTS

These experiments provide the bulk of the practical information for which the other methods have given us constructional data and details. The experiments also vary in that they provide us with a number clues to the different stages in the process of manufacture present locally from which reliable applicable understanding, observations and results can be directly derived; stages of manufacture that have not greatly varied or radically changed from ancient times, and which in themselves to a high degree still exist in primitive modern pottery in many parts of the world at present. It is also the basis for most of the study and understanding of the other elements of techniques, technology and and other thinking related to these topics as demonstrated in the clay fabrics and different kinds of kilns by the local potters in ancient times.

Experiments have taught us much about the ancient kilns used, the clays fabrics, their mixtures and as we will see in the final conclusions, conjointly tell us something about the possible reasons for these. For purposes of continuity and the actual manufacturing sequence, four principal stages are recognised: (a) the preparation of the clays for manufacture, (b) the construction of the vessels, (c) the drying stage and (d) the firing stage. Using this order of process, a list of the results and observations can be summed up in the following.

The clays used for experimental purposes most likely have their sources within the research sites where the ancient experimental sherd test materials originate. They probably come from bedrock crevices or other source of filtering water where they have collected over time as in the case of the the inner lining of a water catch basin and a water channell on-site in the Ferrandell-Oleza Chalcolithic Old Settlement; where the catch basin and water channel may have served a secondary purpose for clay accumulation. Otherwise the clays appear to have been collected randomly spread over the sites, wherever sufficiently available.

In these experiments in pottery construction as in all pottery making, whether modern or ancient, the most critical and important stage in the manufacturing process is the air drying of the clay fabrics after the vessel is formed. That is to say, the stage that exists between the preparation of the clays, the formation of the vessel and its consignment to the kiln. Apart from its importance as a critical stage in all of pottery manufacture; it is one which has to be universally respected if any success is to be expected with any certainty at all, and one that was certainly recogonised as essential by both ancient and modern ceramist. The length of this most critical of all stages varies in time according to clay properties, pot thickness, ambient temperatures and other environmental conditions. These too have to do with the essential character of all clays no matter where they are found throughout the world.

Water must evaporate from the pot including all inter-molecular moisture if success is to be expected. This inter-moleculer moisture is trapped deep down between the plates of which clays are formed and is not always apparent in a pot's surface appearance. If any inter-moleculer moisture remains in the vessel when consigned to the kiln, this moisture trapped between the clay plates turns upon firing to steam and results in the explosion of the vessel in the kiln. So all moisture must be air dried out. Forced drying usually results in shrinkage in the clay fabrics, as well as a cause of warping and cracking. The importance of a proper drying out period for pottery is well known and recognised unviersally by potters of the present and the past. It is, in short, a time stage which is both critical and essential to success and unavoidable; although as shown by direct experiment and practical experience, one which can be considerably reduced under certain conditions.

CONCERNING EXPERIMENTAL CLAY FABRICS AND AIR DRYING

(1) When left unmixed or mixed with similar percentages of limestone temper as found in Pretalayotic and Talayotic (Copper and Bronze Age) pottery, the replicas clay fabrics made from the on-site clays bear remarkably similar characteristics to the clay fabrics of the ancient wares when fired.

(2) When tabular test samples or vessels are made from these replica clay fabrics, certain properties have been displayed that were probably well known and taken into account by the ancient potters in the use of their clay preparation recipes. It has been noted that when compared to untempered clays or clays with less temper than those reinforced with limestone temper, for example, the heavily tempered clays have certain advantages:

(a) Heavy limestone tempered clay fabrics, as shown by practical experiments, air dry up to 5 times faster than less highly tempered ones; e.g. depending on quantity, temporal conditions and considerations like pot wall thicknesses .

(b) Heavy limestone tempered clays, as shown by practical experiments, do not shrink, warp or crack as frequently or severely as less tempered ones. This can be tested by placing tabular test samples made of different limestone temper mixtures on nonporous and pourous drying surfaces. There, these properties and advantages become clearly evident.

(c) Heavy limestone tempered clays are stronger and stand up to shock and general use better, as long as not fired to the conversion temperature of limestone or calcium carbonate. They would also fair better during shipment or storage. The principle of mixing limestone tempers is parallel to amalgamation of sand and gravel in cement and concrete. Cement on its own is not strong and suject to cracking and warping if used too pure. Once mixed with ideal percentags of sand, a durable strong product is attained, when further mixed with gravel a concretion (concrete) is arrived at; one that is essentially stronger than either pure cement or sand mixture cement. The admixture of high quantity limestone acts on the same binding principles.

(d) While there are limiting factors in the firing temperature of heavy limestone tempered clays because of inherent properties, and lower temperature must be assured for successful firing, there are also advantages: (i) less firing time is needed and (ii) less fuel to achieve higher temperatures.

POTTERY CONSTRUCTION AND KILN DUPLICATION FIRINGS

A group of observations and results are outlined here.

(1) Pottery duplication carried out both in coil and pinch pot methods have been successfully fired both in mound and pit kilns (frontisepiece and Plates 12a to 12c). Vessels made using both these techniques have been remarkably successful in the duplication, not only, the ancient forms but, also, the surface textures and colours.

(2) Experimental kiln firings have also duplicated and recorded temperature ranges and firing times and as well, it is believed, similar conditions to those undergone in the authentic vessels.

(3) Based on attributes like colour and surface details from experimental replicas (e.g. both on the pot's inside and outside surfaces), it has been possible to ascertain with probability the positions of pottery within the ancient kilns when originally fired (e.g. whether the vessel has been rightside up or inverted; whether fired in an oxidised or reduced atmosphere).

(4) Time investment estimates for construction of tdifferent kinds of vessels have been possible through duplication (e.g. time investment necessary for highly decorated wares as well major large storage vessels) in order to understand ancient pottery making techniques.

While there are undoubtedly many improvements still to be made in the development of most of these simple analytical techniques (this is after all the nature of such uncomplicated test methods), on the whole, some interesting and informative results have been obtained. A data base for the limestone composition of the local wares and other attributes have been made available, as well as reference pottery slide study collections; both of which are nuclear beginnings of an extension to the current research and perhaps of some use elsewhere.

CONCLUSIONS

In the current research (QACCCP) the centre of focus has been on the high percentage of limestone or calcium carbonate use in the local wares, especially during the Talayotic Period or Balearic Bronze and Iron Ages, where it was deliberately used as an artificial inclusion or temper.

The disadvantages and inherent dangers of such heavy limestone tempered pottery have been discussed at some length. The obvious disadvantages and inherent dangers of its extensive use have from the beginning been the main catalyst to its quantitative analysis in the indigenous pottery of the balearic Islands.

The identification in the field of such limestone tempered wares and the questioning concerning the temper's extensive use in Talayotic times has not been in the long run motive enough. Nor has it been the quantification in statistical terms of the amounts present in the clay fabrics been the sole objective. A closer line of questioning has been:"Why the potters of this particular period used high percentages of limestone or calcium carbonate in their clays and what could it extensive use possibly imply?".

More than any single answer or response to the first of these two questions of why it was used so extensively centres on the advantages its use had and which are demonstrated in the research. Namely, those (**a**) of speeding up of the essential and necessary pottery drying stage, (**b**) the prevention or lowering of shrinkage, cracking and warping during drying, (**c**) the resulting superior strength and wear in transport and (**d**) lower firing requirement. These certainly are advantages of some import and value. However, another question arises: "What do each of these advantages really imply or possibly represent?" If we examine them closely, we see that each in its own right is an economic factor. Therefore, here, the what they imply and possibly represent can be regarded as essentially and collectively a strong economic consideration on the part of the potters of the time.

These economic considerations would be of particular importance when viewed conjointly with demographic factors during the time they were practised. The Talayotic wares were in use at a time when population over the former Pretalayotic communities was on the increase; as is shown by the large number of Talayotic communities, some of them quite extensive, and the relatively few smaller Pretalayotic settlements throughout the Balearics.

Certainly a demand for pottery at this time during the Talayotic Period would have been greater than in former Pretalayotic times. This would generate demand for the manufacture of more wares and in the event of specialist manufacture cheaper ways of doing so. If centres of manufacture existed and trade between settlements were in progress, pottery that was easier to make and that traveled better would be in demand, if not by the populace, as strong incentives by those that made them.

Any treatment or preparation of clay that would increase drying rates (one that is unavoidable), and that would do so up to 5 times as fast, would be an important factor in the manufacting process (one of time); hence, economic in the manufacturing rate and process.

Any treatment or preparation of clay that would measureably avoid shrinking, cracking and warping would be equally an important factor (a success rate factor, one again of time); hence, economic in the manufacturing process.

Any treatment or preparation of clay that would produce a stronger, more durable product would be also another important factor (a success factor and one concerning time); hence, further economic in the manufacturing process.

Any treatment or preparation of clay that would require less firing without endangering the product would in its right be an important factor (one of time); hence, economic in the manufacturing process.

Any treatment or preparation of clay that would require less firing would require less fuel and would be still another important factor (one of cost effectiveness); hence, economic in the manufacturing process. It would also be economical in the long run regarding the limited wood supply one would expect to find on an island.

Each of these factors on their own are strong economic considerations which are reflected in the compositional makeup of the clay fabrics of the Talayotic Period. Combined they demonstrate considerations that may well have been (and were it is argued) in the minds of the potters of the Talayotic Period, when population was on the increase and the demand of pottery certainly growing hand in hand with it. Whether or not the wares were actually distributed from centres of manufacture is not as yet known and is an area of research to be considered. It may well be that each village made their own or that pottery was still done at this time from the home, as seems may have been the case during the Pretalayotic Period. These are other possibilities for which no really direct evidence is found, although the latter, that of home manufacture has been suggested and argued (Gassull, Sanahuija and Lull 1985).

Finally, what is hopefully shown in this publication is that there are some relatively simple and economical methods which are both effective and informative and that some insights into the ancient pottery manufacturing processes from the Balearics have emerged, insights and details which in turn can be useful elsewhere.

BIBLIOGRAPHY

Fiegl, F., 1937, Quantiative Analysis by Spot Tests, New York.

Fewkes, V.J.,1944, Catawba Pottery Making, with Notes on Pamunkey Pottery Making, Cherokee Pottery Making and Coiling, *Proceedings American Philosophic Society*, 88 pp. 69-125, Philadelphia.

Gasull, P., Lull, V. and Sanahuja, C. 1984, Son Fornes I, la Fase Talayótica, Ensayo de Reconstrucción Socio-Economica de una Comunidad Prehistórica de la Isla de Mallorca, B.A.R. International Series 209, Oxford.

Hill, W.W., 1937, Navajo Pottery Manufacture, *University of New Mexico Bulletin, Anthropological Series*, No.31, pp 731-754, Menasha.

Lothrop, S.K., 1927, The Potters of Guatajiagua, Salvadore, *Indian Notes, Museum of the American Indian*,Vol 4,No.2, New York.

Osborn, A.,1979, La Ceramica de los Tunebos: un Estudio Etnografico, *Fundación de Invesigaciones Arqueològicas Nacionales*, Banco de la Republica, Bogatà

Rodgers, M.J., 1936, Yuma Pottery Making, *San Diego Museum Papers 2*,San Diego.

Shepard, A.O., 1965, Ceramics for the Archaeologist, Publication 609, *Carnegie Institution*, Washington.

Tschopik, H.,1950, An Andean Ceramic Tradition in Historic Perspective, *American Antiquity 15*, pp. 196218, Menasha

Waldren, W.H. 1982. Aspects of Balearic Prehistoric Ecology and Culture, *Oxford Doctoral Thesis*, University of Oxford, Oxford.

Waldren, W.H. 1982. 'Balearic Prehistoric Ecology and Culture: The Excavation and Study of Certain Caves, Rock Shelters and Settlements', British Archaeological Reports *BAR International Series 149* (ii) Appendix 3A, pp. 675-711. Oxford.

Waldren, W.H. 1983. 'Early Prehistoric Settlement in the Balearic Islands', *DAMARC Series 13*, Deya Archaeological Museum and Research Centre, Deya Mallorca.

Waldren, W.H. 1984. ' Chalcolithic Settlement and Beaker Connections in the Balearic Islands', The Deya Conference of Prehistory ...Early Settlement in the Western Mediterranean Islands and their Peripheral Areas, W.H. Waldren, R.W. Chapman, J.G. Lewthwaite and R.C. Kennard (eds), British Archaeological Reports, *BAR International Series 229* , Oxford. vol. iii, pp.911-965.

Waldren, W. H. 1983. 'Prehistoric Pottery...Simple Approaches to Analysis, *Deya Archaeological Museum and Researh Centre*, Deya, Mallorca, Spain, DAMARC Series No. 14.

Waldren, W. H.,1985. 'A Rose by any other Name...A Question of Balearic Beakers...the Evidence', *Oxford International Western Mediterranean Bell Beaker Conference*, St. Catherines College, University of Oxford.

Waldren, W. H.,1985. 'The Pottery Distribution Statistics from Ferrandell-Oleza Copper Age Old Settlement', W. Waldren and J. Enseñat, *Oxford International Western Mediterranean Bell Beaker Conference*, St. Catherines College, University of Oxford.

Waldren, W.H.,1986. 'The Balearic Pentapartite Division of Prehistory in Radiocarbon and other Age Determination Inventories', *British Archaeological Reports (B.A.R.)* International Series 282).

Waldren, W. H.,1987. 'Bell Beakers in the Western Mediterranean', W. Waldren and R-C. Kennard (eds.), Oxford International Conference 1985, *British Archaeological Reports (B.A.R.)*, Oxford, England.

SIMPLE APPROACHES TO THE ANALYSES OF PREHISTORIC POTTERY

Selected Pottery Fragment

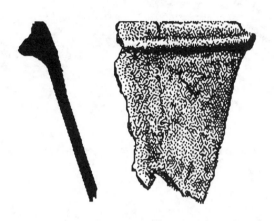

Sectioned Pottery Fragment

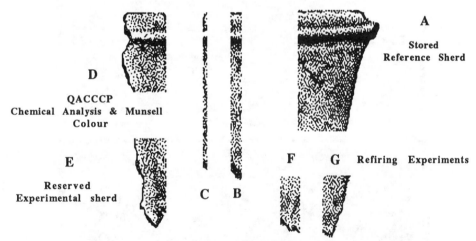

A

Stored Reference Sherd

D

QACCCP Chemical Analysis & Munsell Colour

E

Reserved Experimental sherd

C　**B**

F　**G**　**Refiring Experiments**

Thin and Slab Sections

Illustration Shows the Division of an Experimental Pottery Fragment for Analytical Study in the Series of Simple Analyses of Prehistoric Pottery Used in the DAMARC-OXFORD Research Project.

cms

DCATT&T

Figure 1

EXPERIMENTAL POTTERY MOUND KILN FIRING

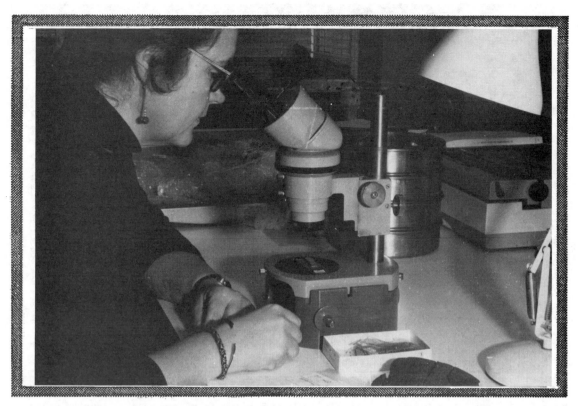

Plate 4. The photograph shows the standard procedure in the preparation of a test sample for calcium carbonate analysis. The pottery slab-section slide corresponding to the pottery sherd test sample for acid treatment is first examined under the microscope for particular characteristics. Any special sherd features or events are recorded and sample coding is carried out.

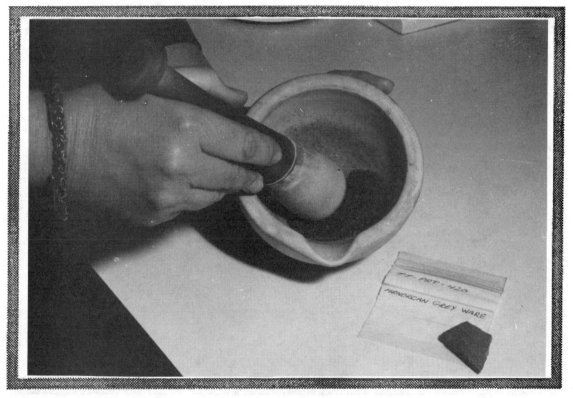

Plate 5. Part of the pottery sherd selected and recorded for quantitative analysis of CaCo3 content is placed in a mortar and ground to a fine powder to facilitate the acid treatment of the sample's limestone content. When the sample is ground fine enough, it is placed in a plastic bag with its designation for storing along with the remaining part of the sherd test sample, seen in the plastic bag below

Plate 6. The ground pottery sherd test sample is selectd from the stored samples, then weighed and recorded. The standard QACCCP test sample (5 grms) is then weighed out of the bulk of the ground pottery sherd test sample. These weights are recorded and the QACCCP test sample is immediately ready for its acid treatment, as seen in the following photograph.

Plate 7. The weighed QACCCP test sample is then poured into a numbered test tube (100ml) containing a 15% solution of hydrochloric acid (HCl) (38% by concentration). The test sample is then stirred frequently to assure that all the ground powder's particles are exposed to the acid's action. This solution is then left over night in order to make sure that all the test sample's solid $CaCO_3$ content is desolved

Plate 8. After acid treatment the QACCCP test sample is centrifuged to settle remaining clay particles to the bottom of the test tube. The acid solution is then poured off and remaining test sample washed and centrifuged three times in distilled water to remove any remaining soluable bicarbonates. After the last centrifuging, the water is then finally drained off and remaining test sample dried.

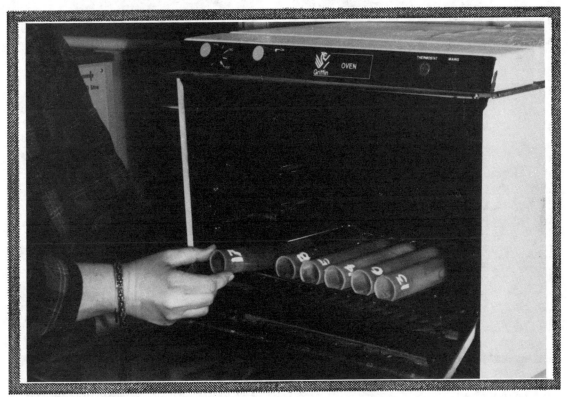

Plate 9. The QACCCP test samples are then dried at a low temperature in an oven at 20 gegrees C. This is done in order not to change the composition or alter delicate minerals such as iron oxides left in the pottery fabric of the test sample. Once the sample is fully dried, they are weighed and recorded again to determine the difference in weight between an untreated and treated sample. The difference between the two represents the original CaCO3 content of the test sample, both in weight and percentage.

POTTERY SLAB-SECTIONS

 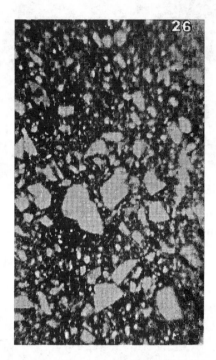

A   B

PRETALAYOTIC SHERD   TALAYOTIC SHERD

Microphotographs show two examples of slab-section slides. Plate A is a section of a
Pretalayotic sherd showing natural inclusions. The rounded edges and general weathered
appearance is typical of inclusions found naturally in the clays. Plate B is a section of a
Talayotic sherd in which heavy limestone temper has been used. The sharp edges of the
inclusion particles are diagnostic of especially prepared artificial temper.

DCATT&T   Plate   10

POTTERY SLAB-SECTIONS

A

BELL BEAKER SHERD

B

POST TALAYOTIC SHERD

Microphotographs show two examples of slab-section slides. Plate A is a section of a Pretalayotic sherd showing natural inclusions. The rounded edges and general weathered appearance is typical of inclusions found naturally in the clays. Plate B is a section of a Post Talayotic sherd in which vegetal temper has been used. The de-gassing channels sre diagnostic of a burning out of the organic vegetal material. Sectioning and microscopic examination of similar sherds has shown that the chaff of grain was used and is in some cases preserved as charred fragments of the chaff.

DCATT&T

Plate 11

	A	B	C	D	E	F	G
1							
2							
3							
4	CACO3 CONTENT FOR PRETALAYOTIC PERIOD ALL RESEARCH SITES						
5							
6	SITE	SERIES	NO.SAMPLES				CACO3 %
7							
8	SM-VAR	1A	10				37.20
9	SM-VAR	1B	10				44.50
10	SM-VAR	1C	10				38.70
11	SM-VAR	2A	10				42.90
12	SM-VAR	2B	10	39.66			35.00
13	SFO-OS-H3-W2	3A	10				30.70
14	SFO-OS-H3-W2	3B	10				32.20
15	SFO-OS-H3-W2	3C	10				28.00
16	SFO-OS-H4-X3	4A	10				37.20
17	SFO-OS-C2-EXN	4B	10				33.00
18	SFO-OS-SW-VAR	4C	10				38.40
19	SFO-OS-CSS-SW	5A	10	32.79			30.00
20	SFO-OS-CSS-SW	5B	10				35.00
21	SFO-OS-CSS-EXW	5C	10				25.10
22	SFO-OS-CSS-EXW	5D	10				29.00
23	SFO-OS-WCS	6A	10				35.30
24	SFO-OS-WCS	6B	10				27.30
25	SFO-OS-EX	6C	10				25.20
26	SFO-OS-H4-X1	6D	10	32.07			47.60
27							
28							
29							
30							
31							
32							
33							
34							
35		TOTAL AVERAGE		34.33			

	A	B	C	D	E	F	G	H	I
1									
2									
3									
4			CACO3 CONTENT FOR TALAYOTIC PERIOD ALL RESEARCH SITES						
5									
6	SITE	SERIES	NO.SAMPLES				CACO3 %		
7									
8	SFO-YS-T1-L5	1A	10				57.38		
9	SFO-YS-T1-L5	1B	10				59.65		
10	SFO-YS-T1-L5	1C	10				59.01		
11	SFO-YS-T1-L5	1D	10				51.93		
12	SFO-YS-H1	2A	10				40.98		
13	SFO-YS-T1-L5	2B	10	53.40			51.44		
14	SF0-YS-T2-1A	3A	10				55.15		
15	SFO-YS-T2-2B	3B	10				52.32		
16	SFO-YS-T2-2B	3C	10	51.44			46.85		
17	ABSM-CA-VAR	1A	10				53.18		
18	ABSM-CA-VAR	1B	10				56.16		
19	ABSM-CA-VAR	1C	10	58.24	54.12		65.39		
20	TT-0T-R3-L3	1A	10				54.75		
21	TT-OT-VAR	1B	10				52.55		
22	TT-OT-VAR	1C	10				56.88		
23	TT-OT-T	1D	10				52.55		
24	TT-WCE-L3	2A	10				45.41		
25	TT-WCE-L4	2B	10				38.85		
26	TT-WCE-L4	2C	10				41.81		
27	TT-OT-L2	2D	10		48.28		43.41		
28									
29									
30									
31									
32									
33									
34									
35		TOTAL AVERAGE		51.78					

	A	B	C	D	E	F	G	H	I
1	Quantitative Analysis of Ca CO3 Content of Pottery					OLD SETTLEMENT			
2									
3	No	Serie	Site Inv. No.	Period	Comments	WGT/BAT	WGT/AAT	WGT/LOSS	%CaCo3
4	1	4a	SFO-OS-H4-X3	PRT		4	2.62	1.38	34.50%
5	2	4a	SFO-OS-H4-X3	PRT		4	2.09	1.91	47.75%
6	3	4a	SFO-OS-H4-X3	PRT		4	2.58	1.42	35.50%
7	4	4a	SFO-OS-H4-X3	PRT		4	3.16	0.84	21.00%
8	5	4a	SFO-OS-H4-X3	PRT		4	2.37	1.63	40.75%
9	6	4a	SFO-OS-H4-X3	PRT		4	2.26	1.74	43.50%
10	7	4a	SFO-OS-H4-X3	PRT		4	1.9	2.1	52.50%
11	8	4a	SFO-OS-H4-X3	PRT		4	2.71	1.29	32.25%
12	9	4a	SFO-OS-H4-X3	PRT		4	2.64	1.36	34.00%
13	10	4a	SFO-OS-H4-X3	PRT		4	2.78	1.22	30.50%
14			37.23%		Mean % of CaCO3 Content in Series of 10 Analyses				
15									
16	1	4b	SFO-OS-C2-EXN	PRT		4	1.11	2.89	72.25%
17	2	4b	SFO-OS-C2-EXN	PRT		4	2.94	1.06	26.50%
18	3	4b	SFO-OS-C2-EXN	PRT		4	3.18	0.82	20.50%
19	4	4b	SFO-OS-C2-EXN	PRT		4	3.26	0.74	18.50%
20	5	4b	SFO-OS-C2-EXN	PRT		4	2.85	1.15	28.75%
21	6	4b	SFO-OS-C2-EXN	PRT		4	3.31	0.69	17.25%
22	7	4b	SFO-OS-C2-EXN	PRT		4	2.82	1.18	29.50%
23	8	4b	SFO-OS-C2-EXN	PRT		4	3.26	0.74	18.50%
24	9	4b	SFO-OS-C2-EXN	PRT		4	2.12	1.88	47.00%
25	10	4b	SFO-OS-C2-EXN	PRT		4	1.94	2.06	51.50%
26			33.03%		Mean % of CaCO3 Content in Series of 10 Analyses				
27									
28	1	4c	SFO-OS-SW-V	PRT		4	2.81	1.19	29.75%
29	2	4c	SFO-OS-SW-V	PRT		4	1.96	2.04	51.00%
30	3	4c	SFO-OS-SW-V	PRT		4	2.99	1.01	25.25%
31	4	4c	SFO-OS-SW-V	PRT		4	2.19	1.81	45.25%
32	5	4c	SFO-OS-AT2-7	PRT		4	2.88	1.12	28.00%
33	6	4c	SFO-OS-C2-XN	PRT		4	2.12	1.88	47.00%
34	7	4c	SFO-OS-CS-XN	PRT		4	2.17	1.83	45.75%
35	8	4c	SFO-OS-AT2-7	PRT		4	2.72	1.28	32.00%
36	9	4c	SFO-OS-H4-X3	PRT		4	2.37	1.63	40.75%
37	10	4c	SFO-OS-C2-XN	PRT		4	2.45	1.55	38.75%
38			38.35%		Mean % of CaCO3 Content in Series of 10 Analyses				

	A	B	C	D	E	F	G	H	I
1	Quantitative Analysis of Ca CO3 Content of Pottery					OLD SETTLEMENT			
2									
3	No	Series	Site Inv. No.	Period	Comments	WGT/BAT	WGT/AAT	WGT/LOSS	%CaCo3
4	1	5a	SFO-OS-CSS-SW	PRT		4	2.64	1.36	34.00%
5	2	5a	SFO-OS-CSS-SW	PRT		4	2.61	1.39	34.75%
6	3	5a	SFO-OS-CSS-SW	PRT		4	3.14	0.86	21.50%
7	4	5a	SFO-OS-CSS-SW	PRT		4	2.83	1.17	29.25%
8	5	5a	SFO-OS-CSS-SW	PRT		4	2.81	1.19	29.75%
9	6	5a	SFO-OS-CSS-SW	PRT		4	2.96	1.04	26.00%
10	7	5a	SFO-OS-CSS-SW	PRT		4	3.04	0.96	24.00%
11	8	5a	SFO-OS-CSS-SW	PRT		4	2.74	1.26	31.50%
12	9	5a	SFO-OS-CSS-SW	PRT		4	2.73	1.27	31.75%
13	10	5a	SFO-OS-CSS-SW	PRT		4	2.58	1.42	35.50%
14			29.80%		Mean % of CaCO3 Content in Series of 10 Analyses				
15									
16	1	5b	SFO-OS-CSS-SW	PRT		4	2.64	1.36	34.00%
17	2	5b	SFO-OS-CSS-SW	PRT		4	3.11	0.89	22.25%
18	3	5b	SFO-OS-CSS-SW	PRT		4	2.86	1.14	28.50%
19	4	5b	SFO-OS-CSS-SW	PRT		4	2.69	1.31	32.75%
20	5	5b	SFO-OS-CSS-SW	PRT		4	2.85	1.15	28.75%
21	6	5b	SFO-OS-CSS-SW	PRT		4	2.85	1.15	28.75%
22	7	5b	SFO-OS-CSS-EX	PRT		4	2.75	1.25	31.25%
23	8	5b	SFO-OS-CSS-EX	PRT		4	2.21	1.79	44.75%
24	9	5b	SFO-OS-CSS-EX	PRT		4	2.16	1.84	46.00%
25	10	5b	SFO-OS-CSS-EX	PRT		4	1.99	2.01	50.25%
26			34.73%		Mean % of CaCO3 Content in Series of 10 Analyses				
27									
28	1	5c	SFO-OS-CSS-EXW	PRT		4	2.71	1.29	32.25%
29	2	5c	SFO-OS-CSS-EXW	PRT		4	2.99	1.01	25.25%
30	3	5c	SFO-OS-CSS-EXW	PRT		4	2.94	1.06	26.50%
31	4	5c	SFO-OS-CSS-EXW	PRT		4	2.86	1.14	28.50%
32	5	5c	SFO-OS-CSS-EXW	PRT		4	3.25	0.75	18.75%
33	6	5c	SFO-OS-CSS-EXW	PRT		4	3.46	0.54	13.50%
34	7	5c	SFO-OS-CSS-EXW	PRT		4	2.91	1.09	27.25%
35	8	5c	SFO-OS-CSS-EXW	PRT		4	3.2	0.8	20.00%
36	9	5c	SFO-OS-CSS-EXW	PRT		4	2.36	1.64	41.00%
37	10	5c	SFO-OS-CSS-EXW	PRT		4	3.29	0.71	17.75%
38			25.08%		Mean % of CaCO3 Content in Series of 10 Analyses				
39									
40	1	5d	SFO-OS-CSS-EXW	PRT		4	2.89	1.11	27.75%
41	2	5d	SFO-OS-CSS-EXW	PRT		4	3.02	0.98	24.50%
42	3	5d	SFO-OS-CSS-EXW	PRT		4	3.24	0.76	19.00%
43	4	5d	SFO-OS-CSS-EXW	PRT		4	3.05	0.95	23.75%
44	5	5d	SFO-OS-CSS-EXW	PRT		4	3.07	0.93	23.25%
45	6	5d	SFO-OS-CSS-EXW	PRT		4	2.44	1.56	39.00%
46	7	5d	SFO-OS-CSS-EXW	PRT		4	2.9	1.1	27.50%
47	8	5d	SFO-OS-CSS-EXW	PRT		4	2.42	1.58	39.50%
48	9	5d	SFO-OS-CSS-EXW	PRT		4	3.28	0.72	18.00%
49	10	5d	SFO-OS-CSS-EXW	PRT		4	2.24	1.76	44.00%
50			28.63%		Mean % of CaCO3 Content in Series of 10 Analyses				

	A	B	C	D	E	F	G	H	I
1	Quantitative Analysis of Ca CO3 Content of Pottery				OLD SETTLEMENT				
2									
3	No	Series	Site Inv. No.	Period	Comments	WGT/BAT	WGT/AAT	WGT/LOSS	%CaCo3
4	1	6a	SFO-OS-WCS	PRT		4	2.21	1.79	44.75%
5	2	6a	SFO-OS-WCS	PRT		4	2.3	1.7	42.50%
6	3	6a	SFO-OS-WCS	PRT		4	2.81	1.19	29.75%
7	4	6a	SFO-OS-WCS	PRT		4	3.16	0.84	21.00%
8	5	6a	SFO-OS-WCS	PRT		4	2.97	1.03	25.75%
9	6	6a	SFO-OS-WCS	PRT		4	2.4	1.6	40.00%
10	7	6a	SFO-OS-WCS	PRT		4	3.21	0.79	19.75%
11	8	6a	SFO-OS-WCS	PRT		4	2.12	1.88	47.00%
12	9	6a	SFO-OS-WCS	PRT		4	2.39	1.61	40.25%
13	10	6a	SFO-OS-WCS	PRT		4	2.31	1.69	42.25%
14			35.30%		Mean % of CaCO3 Content in Series of 10 Analyses				
15									
16	1	6b	SFO-OS-WCS	PRT		4	2.91	1.09	27.25%
17	2	6b	SFO-OS-WCS	PRT		4	2.49	1.51	37.75%
18	3	6b	SFO-OS-WCS	PRT		4	3.08	0.92	23.00%
19	4	6b	SFO-OS-WCS	PRT		4	3.57	0.43	10.75%
20	5	6b	SFO-OS-WCS	PRT		4	3.07	0.93	23.25%
21	6	6b	SFO-OS-WCS	PRT		4	2.41	1.59	39.75%
22	7	6b	SFO-OS-WCS	PRT		4	3.04	0.96	24.00%
23	8	6b	SFO-OS-WCS	PRT		4	3.08	0.92	23.00%
24	9	6b	SFO-OS-WCS	PRT		4	3.19	0.81	20.25%
25	10	6b	SFO-OS-WCS	PRT		4	2.24	1.76	44.00%
26			27.30%		Mean % of CaCO3 Content in Series of 10 Analyses				
27									
28	1	6c	SFO-OS-WCS	PRT		4	2.66	1.34	33.50%
29	2	6c	SFO-OS-WCS	PRT		4	2.37	1.63	40.75%
30	3	6c	SFO-OS-WCS	PRT		4	2.51	1.49	37.25%
31	4	6c	SFO-OS-CSS-EX	PRT		4	3.22	0.78	19.50%
32	5	6c	SFO-OS-CSS-EX	PRT		4	3.3	0.7	17.50%
33	6	6c	SFO-OS-CSS-EX	PRT		4	3.16	0.84	21.00%
34	7	6c	SFO-OS-CSS-EX	PRT		4	3.17	0.83	20.75%
35	8	6c	SFO-OS-CSS-EX	PRT		4	3.22	0.78	19.50%
36	9	6c	SFO-OS-CSS-EX	PRT		4	3.3	0.7	17.50%
37	10	6c	SFO-OS-CSS-EX	PRT		4			
38			25.25%		Mean % of CaCO3 Content in Series of 10 Analyses				
39									
40	1	6d	SFO-OS-H4-X1	PRT		4	1.68	2.32	58.00%
41	2	6d	SFO-OS-H4-X1	PRT		4	2.69	1.31	32.75%
42	3	6d	SFO-OS-H4-X1	PRT		4	2.2	1.8	45.00%
43	4	6d	SFO-OS-H4-X1	PRT		4	2.53	1.47	36.75%
44	5	6d	SFO-OS-H4-X1	PRT		4	2.02	1.98	49.50%
45	6	6d	SFO-OS-H4-X1	PRT		4	2.01	1.99	49.75%
46	7	6d	SFO-OS-H4-X1	PRT		4	1.91	2.09	52.25%
47	8	6d	SFO-OS-H4-X1	PRT		4	1.37	2.63	65.75%
48	9	6d	SFO-OS-H4-X1	PRT		4	2.51	1.49	37.25%
49	10	6d	SFO-OS-H4-X1	PRT		4	2.06	1.94	48.50%
50			47.55%		Mean % of CaCO3 Content in Series of 10 Analyses				

	A	B	C	D	E	F	G	H	I
1	Quantitative Analysis of Ca CO3 Content of Pottery					OLD SETTLEMENT			
2									
3	No	Series	Site Inv. No.	Perio	Comments	WGT/BAT	WGT/AAT	WGT/LOSS	%CaCo3
4	1	3a	SFO-OS-H3-W2	PRT		3.36	2.61	0.75	22.32%
5	2	3a	SFO-OS-H3-W2	PRT		3.36	2.44	0.92	27.38%
6	3	3a	SFO-OS-H3-W2	PRT		3.36	2.44	0.92	27.38%
7	4	3a	SFO-OS-H3-W2	PRT		3.36	1.75	1.61	47.92%
8	5	3a	SFO-OS-H3-W2	PRT		3.36	1.91	1.45	43.15%
9	6	3a	SFO-OS-H3-W2	PRT		3.36	2.4	0.96	28.57%
10	7	3a	SFO-OS-H3-W2	PRT		3.36	2.25	1.11	33.04%
11	8	3a	SFO-OS-H3-W2	PRT		3.36	2.42	0.94	27.98%
12	9	3a	SFO-OS-H3-W2	PRT		3.36	2.59	0.77	22.92%
13	10	3a	SFO-OS-H3-W2	PRT		3.36	2.46	0.9	26.79%
14			30.74%		Mean % of CaCO3 Content in Series of 10 Analyses				
15									
16	1	3b	SFO-OS-H3-W2	PRT		3.36	2.66	0.7	20.83%
17	2	3b	SFO-OS-H3-W2	PRT		3.36	2.4	0.96	28.57%
18	3	3b	SFO-OS-H3-W2	PRT		3.36	2.52	0.84	25.00%
19	4	3b	SFO-OS-H3-W2	PRT		3.36	2.43	0.93	27.68%
20	5	3b	SFO-OS-H3-W2	PRT		3.36	2.01	1.35	40.18%
21	6	3b	SFO-OS-H3-W2	PRT		3.36	2.48	0.88	26.19%
22	7	3b	SFO-OS-H3-W2	PRT		3.36	2.47	0.89	26.49%
23	8	3b	SFO-OS-H3-W2	PRT		3.36	2.42	0.94	27.98%
24	9	3b	SFO-OS-H3-W2	PRT		3.36	1.24	2.12	63.10%
25	10	3b	SFO-OS-H3-W2	PRT		3.36	2.15	1.21	36.01%
26			32.20%		Mean % of CaCO3 Content in Series of 10 Analyses				
27									
28	1	3c	SFO-OS-H3-W2	PRT		3.36	2.61	0.75	22.32%
29	2	3c	SFO-OS-H3-W2	PRT		3.36	2.06	1.3	38.69%
30	3	3c	SFO-OS-H3-W2	PRT		3.36	2.59	0.77	22.92%
31	4	3c		PRT		3.36			
32	5	3c		PRT		3.36			
33	6	3c		PRT		3.36			
34	7	3c		PRT		3.36			
35	8	3c		PRT		3.36			
36	9	3c		PRT		3.36			
37	10	3c		PRT		3.36			
38			27.98%		Mean % of CaCO3 Content in Series of 10 Analyses				

DC ATT&T

Table 6

	A	B	C	D	E	F	G	H	I
1	Quantitative Analysis of Ca CO3 Content of Pottery					SON MULETA CAVE			
2									
3	No	Serie	Site Inv. No.	Period	Comments	WGT/BAT	WGT/AAT	WGT/LOSS	%CaCo3
4	1	2a	SM-8-18B	PRT		4	0.8113	3.1887	79.72%
5	2	2a	SM-22-14E	PRT		4	2.44	1.56	39.00%
6	3	2a	SM-25-12C	PRT		4	3.16	0.84	21.00%
7	4	2a	SM-33-15C	PRT		4	1.61	2.39	59.75%
8	5	2a	SM-12-1C	PRT		4	3.23	0.77	19.25%
9	6	2a	SM-5-13C	PRT		4	1.59	2.41	60.25%
10	7	2a	SM-27-2C	PRT		4	2.03	1.97	49.25%
11	8	2a	SM-28-7D	PRT		4	1.9	2.1	52.50%
12	9	2a	SM-20-3C	PRT		4	3.26	0.74	18.50%
13	10	2a	SM-21-11C	PRT		4	2.82	1.18	29.50%
14			42.87%		Mean % of CaCO3 Content in Series of 10 Analyses				
15									
16	1	2b	SM-6-17	PRT		4	3.31	0.69	17.25%
17	2	2b	SM-2-4C	PRT		4	3.38	0.62	15.50%
18	3	2b	SM-12-8C	PRT		4	1.46	2.54	63.50%
19	4	2b	SM-25-5C	PRT		4	2.56	1.44	36.00%
20	5	2b	SM-11-7C	PRT		4	1.59	2.41	60.25%
21	6	2b	SM-22-9C	PRT		4	1.93	2.07	51.75%
22	7	2b	SM-16-16C	PRT		4	2.45	1.55	38.75%
23	8	2b	SM-15C-10D	PRT		4	3.21	0.79	19.75%
24	9	2b	SM-3-9D	PRT		4	1.57	2.43	60.75%
25	10	2b	SM-9-5D	PRT		4	2.56	1.44	36.00%
26			39.95%		Mean % of CaCO3 Content in Series of 10 Analyses				
27									
28	1	2c	ABSM-507-16D	PRT		4	2.82	1.18	29.50%
29	2	2c	ABSM-602-6D	PRT		4	2.28	1.72	43.00%
30	3	2c	ABSM-505-2D	PRT		4	2.74	1.26	31.50%
31	4	2c	ABSM-503-1D	PRT		4	2.85	1.15	28.75%
32	5	2c	ABSM-501-3D	PRT		4	2.56	1.44	36.00%
33	6	2c	ABSM-503-10D	PRT		4	1.96	2.04	51.00%
34	7	2c				4			
35	8	2c				4			
36	9	2c				4			
37	10	2c				4			
38			36.60%		Mean % of CaCO3 Content in Series of 10 Analyses				

DC ATT&T   Table   7

	A	B	C	D	E	F	G	H	I
1	Quantitative Analysis of Ca CO3 Content of Pottery					SON MULETA CAVE MALLORCA			
2									
3	No	Series	Site Inv. No.	Period	Comments	WGT/BAT	WGT/AAT	WGT/LOSS	%CaCo3
4	1	1a	SM- VAR	PRT		3.36	2.27	1.09	32.44%
5	2	1a	SM- VAR	PRT		3.36	1.89	1.47	43.75%
6	3	1a	SM- VAR	PRT		3.36	1.91	1.45	43.15%
7	4	1a	SM- VAR	PRT		3.36	1.56	1.8	53.57%
8	5	1a	SM- VAR	PRT		3.36	2.69	0.67	19.94%
9	6	1a	SM- VAR	PRT		3.36	1.73	1.63	48.51%
10	7	1a	SM- VAR	PRT		3.36	2.71	0.65	19.35%
11	8	1a	SM- VAR	PRT		3.36	2.81	0.55	16.37%
12	9	1a	SM- VAR	PRT		3.36	2.14	1.22	36.31%
13	10	1a	SM- VAR	PRT		3.36	1.45	1.91	56.85%
14			37.02%		Mean % of CaCO3 Content in Series of 10 Analyses				
15									
16	1	1b	SM- VAR	PRT		3.36	1.33	2.03	60.42%
17	2	1b	SM- VAR	PRT		3.36	1.18	2.18	64.88%
18	3	1b	SM- VAR	PRT		3.36	1.67	1.69	50.30%
19	4	1b	SM- VAR	PRT		3.36	2.05	1.31	38.99%
20	5	1b	SM- VAR	PRT		3.36	2.36	1	29.76%
21	6	1b	SM- VAR	PRT		3.36	2.63	0.73	21.73%
22	7	1b	SM- VAR	PRT		3.36	1.4	1.96	58.33%
23	8	1b	SM- VAR	PRT		3.36	2.67	0.69	20.54%
24	9	1b	SM- VAR	PRT		3.36	1.38	1.98	58.93%
25	10	1b	SM- VAR	PRT		3.36	2.05	1.31	38.99%
26			44.29%		Mean % of CaCO3 Content in Series of 10 Analyses				
27									
28	1	1c	SM- VAR	PRT		3.36	2.73	0.63	18.75%
29	2	1c	SM- VAR	PRT		3.36	2.93	0.43	12.80%
30	3	1c	SM- VAR	PRT		3.36	2.1	1.26	37.50%
31	4	1c	SM- VAR	PRT		3.36	1.51	1.85	55.06%
32	5	1c	SM- VAR	PRT		3.36	1.27	2.09	62.20%
33	6	1c	SM- VAR	PRT		3.36	1.99	1.37	40.77%
34	7	1c	SM- VAR	PRT		3.36	1.89	1.47	43.75%
35	8	1c		PRT		3.36			
36	9	1c		PRT		3.36			
37	10	1c		PRT		3.36			
38			38.69%		Mean % of CaCO3 Content in Series of 10 Analyses				

	A	B	C	D	E	F	G	H	I
1	Quantitative Analysis of Ca CO3 Content of Pottery					YOUNGER SETTLEMENT			
2									
3	No	Series	Site Inv. No.	Period	Comments	WGT/BAT	WGT/AAT	WGT/LOSS	%CaCo3
4	1	1a	SFO-YS-T1-L5	T		4	1.84	2.16	54.00%
5	2	1a	SFO-YS-T1-L5	T		4	1.43	2.57	64.25%
6	3	1a	SFO-YS-T1-L5	T		4	1.58	2.42	60.50%
7	4	1a	SFO-YS-T1-L5	T		4	1.85	2.15	53.75%
8	5	1a	SFO-YS-T1-L5	T		4	2.59	1.41	35.25%
9	6	1a	SFO-YS-T1-L5	T		4	1.59	2.41	60.25%
10	7	1a	SFO-YS-T1-L5	T		4	1.61	2.39	59.75%
11	8	1a	SFO-YS-T1-L5	T		4	1.58	2.42	60.50%
12	9	1a	SFO-YS-T1-L5	T		4	1.56	2.44	61.00%
13	10	1a	SFO-YS-T1-L5	T		4	1.42	2.58	64.50%
14			57.38%		Mean % of CaCO3 Content in Series of 10 Analyses				
15									
16	1	1b	SFO-YS-T1-L5	T		4	1.88	2.12	53.00%
17	2	1b	SFO-YS-T1-L5	T		4	1.57	2.43	60.75%
18	3	1b	SFO-YS-T1-L5	T		4	1.77	2.23	55.75%
19	4	1b	SFO-YS-T1-L5	T		4	0.93	3.07	76.75%
20	5	1b	SFO-YS-T1-L5	T		4	1.95	2.05	51.25%
21	6	1b	SFO-YS-T1-L5	T		4	1.79	2.21	55.25%
22	7	1b	SFO-YS-T1-L5	T		4	1.02	2.98	74.50%
23	8	1b	SFO-YS-T1-L5	T		4	1.66	2.34	58.50%
24	9	1b	SFO-YS-T1-L5	T		4	2.24	1.76	44.00%
25	10	1b	SFO-YS-T1-L5	T		4	1.33	2.67	66.75%
26			59.65%		Mean % of CaCO3 Content in Series of 10 Analyses				
27									
28	1	1c	SFO-YS-T1-L5	T		4	2.28	1.72	43.00%
29	2	1c	SFO-YS-T1-L5	T		4	1.59	2.41	60.25%
30	3	1c	SFO-YS-T1-L5	T		4	1.15	2.85	71.25%
31	4	1c	SFO-YS-T1-L5	T		4	1.4	2.6	65.00%
32	5	1c	SFO-YS-T1-L5	T		4	1.58	2.42	60.50%
33	6	1c	SFO-YS-T1-L5	T		4	1.76	2.24	56.00%
34	7	1c	SFO-YS-T1-L5	T		4	1.64	2.36	59.00%
35	8	1c	SFO-YS-T1-L5	T		4	1.72	2.28	57.00%
36	9	1c	SFO-YS-T1-L5	T		4	1.85	2.15	53.75%
37	10	1c	SFO-YS-T1-L5	T		4	1.43	2.57	64.25%
38			59.00%		Mean % of CaCO3 Content in Series of 10 Analyses				
39									
40	1	1d	SFO-YS-T1-L5	T		4	2.87	1.13	28.25%
41	2	1d	SFO-YS-T1-L5	T		4	1.26	2.74	68.50%
42	3	1d	SFO-YS-T1-L5	T		4	1.26	2.74	68.50%
43	4	1d	SFO-YS-T1-L5	T		4	2.85	1.15	28.75%
44	5	1d	SFO-YS-T1-L5	T		4	1.11	2.89	72.25%
45	6	1d	SFO-YS-T1-L5	T		4	2.88	1.12	28.00%
46	7	1d	SFO-YS-T1-L5	T		4	1.18	2.82	70.50%
47	8	1d	SFO-YS-T1-L5	T		4	2.76	1.24	31.00%
48	9	1d	SFO-YS-T1-L5	T		4	1.37	2.63	65.75%
49	10	1d	SFO-YS-T1-L5	T		4	1.69	2.31	57.75%
50			51.93%		Mean % of CaCO3 Content in Series of 10 Analyses				

	A	B	C	D	E	F	G	H	I
1	Quantitative Analysis of Ca CO3 Content of Pottery					YOUNGER SETTLEMENT			
2									
3	No	Series	Site Inv. No.	Period	Comments	WGT/BAT	WGT/AAT	WGT/LOSS	%CaCo3
4	1	3a	SFO-YS-T2-IA	T		3.36	1.15	2.21	65.77%
5	2	3a	SFO-YS-T2-IA	T		3.36	1.77	1.59	47.32%
6	3	3a	SFO-YS-T2-IA	T		3.36	1.6	1.76	52.38%
7	4	3a	SFO-YS-T2-IA	T		3.36	1.71	1.65	49.11%
8	5	3a	SFO-YS-T2-IA	T		3.36	1.43	1.93	57.44%
9	6	3a	SFO-YS-T2-IA	T		3.36	1.58	1.78	52.98%
10	7	3a	SFO-YS-T2-IA	T		3.36	1.01	2.35	69.94%
11	8	3a	SFO-YS-T2-IA	T		3.36	1.57	1.79	53.27%
12	9	3a	SFO-YS-T2-IA	T		3.36	1.64	1.72	51.19%
13	10	3a	SFO-YS-T2-IA	T		3.36	1.61	1.75	52.08%
14			55.15%		Mean % of CaCO3 Content in Series of 10 Analyses				
15									
16	1	3b	SFO-YS-T2-2B	T		3.36	1.12	2.24	66.67%
17	2	3b	SFO-YS-T2-2B	T		3.36	1.65	1.71	50.89%
18	3	3b	SFO-YS-T2-2B	T		3.36	1.71	1.65	49.11%
19	4	3b	SFO-YS-T2-2B	T		3.36	1.57	1.79	53.27%
20	5	3b	SFO-YS-T2-2B	T		3.36	1.49	1.87	55.65%
21	6	3b	SFO-YS-T2-2B	T		3.36	1.89	1.47	43.75%
22	7	3b	SFO-YS-T2-2B	T		3.36	1.52	1.84	54.76%
23	8	3b	SFO-YS-T2-2B	T		3.36	1.79	1.57	46.73%
24	9	3b	SFO-YS-T2-2B	T		3.36	1.44	1.92	57.14%
25	10	3b	SFO-YS-T2-2B	T		3.36	1.84	1.52	45.24%
26			52.32%		Mean % of CaCO3 Content in Series of 10 Analyses				
27									
28	1	3c	SFO-YS-T2-2B	T		3.36	1.52	1.84	54.76%
29	2	3c	SFO-YS-T2-2B	T		3.36	1.59	1.77	52.68%
30	3	3c	SFO-YS-T2-2B	T		3.36	1.52	1.84	54.76%
31	4	3c	SFO-YS-T2-2B	T		3.36	2.41	0.95	28.27%
32	5	3c	SFO-YS-T2-2B	T		3.36	1.82	1.54	45.83%
33	6	3c	SFO-YS-T2-2B	T		3.36	1.79	1.57	46.73%
34	7	3c	SFO-YS-T2-2B	T		3.36	1.86	1.5	44.64%
35	8	3c	SFO-YS-T2-2B	T		3.36	1.81	1.55	46.13%
36	9	3c	SFO-YS-T2-2B	T		3.36	1.66	1.7	50.60%
37	10	3c	SFO-YS-T2-1B	T		3.36	1.89	1.47	43.75%
38			46.82%		Mean % of CaCO3 Content in Series of 10 Analyses				
39									
40	1	3d	SFO-YS-T2-1B	T		4	1.91	2.09	52.25%
41	2	3d	SFO-YS-T2-1B	T		4	2.02	1.98	49.50%
42	3	3d	SFO-YS-T2-1B	T		4	1.81	2.19	54.75%
43	4	3d	SFO-YS-T2-1B	T		4	1.82	2.18	54.50%
44	5	3d	SFO-YS-T2-1B	T		4	2.03	1.97	49.25%
45	6	3d	SFO-YS-T2-1B	T		4	1.81	2.19	54.75%
46	7	3d	SFO-YS-T2-1B	T		4	1.72	2.28	57.00%
47	8	3d	ABSM-CA38-5	T		4	1.34	2.66	66.50%
48	9	3d	ABSM-CA38-5	T		4	1.54	2.46	61.50%
49	10	3d	ABSM-CA38-2	T		4	1.83	2.17	54.25%
50			55.43%		Mean % of CaCO3 Content in Series of 10 Analyses				

	A	B	C	D	E	F	G	H	I
1	Quantitative Analysis of Ca CO3 Content of Pottery					YOUNGER SETTLEMENT			
2									
3	No	Series	Site Inv. No.	Period	Comments	WGT/BAT	WGT/AAT	WGT/LOSS	%CaCo3
4	1	2a	SFO-YS-H1	T		4	2.02	1.98	49.50%
5	2	2a	SFO-YS-H1	T		4	2.36	1.64	41.00%
6	3	2a	SFO-YS-H1	T		4	2.39	1.61	40.25%
7	4	2a	SFO-YS-H1	T		4	2.31	1.69	42.25%
8	5	2a	SFO-YS-H1	T		4	2.71	1.29	32.25%
9	6	2a	SFO-YS-H1	T		4	2.41	1.59	39.75%
10	7	2a	SFO-YS-H1	T		4	2.38	1.62	40.50%
11	8	2a	SFO-YS-H1	T		4	2.21	1.79	44.75%
12	9	2a	SFO-YS-H1	T		4	2.35	1.65	41.25%
13	10	2a	SFO-YS-H1	T		4	2.47	1.53	38.25%
14			40.98%		Mean % of CaCO3 Content in Series of 10 Analyses				
15									
16	1	2b	SFO-YS-H1	T		4	2.56	1.44	36.00%
17	2	2b	SFO-YS-T1-L5	T		4	1.35	2.65	66.25%
18	3	2b	SFO-YS-T1-L5	T		4	1.57	2.43	60.75%
19	4	2b	SFO-YS-T1-L5	T		4	1.19	2.81	70.25%
20	5	2b	SFO-YS-T1-L5	T		4	1.45	2.55	63.75%
21	6	2b	SFO-YS-T1-L5	T		4	1.74	2.26	56.50%
22	7	2b	SFO-YS-T1-L5	T		4	2.1	1.9	47.50%
23	8	2b	SFO-YS-H1	T		4	2.48	1.52	38.00%
24	9	2b	SFO-YS-T1-L5	T		4	3.04	0.96	24.00%
25	10	2b		T		4			
26			51.44%		Mean % of CaCO3 Content in Series of 10 Analyses				

	A	B	C	D	E	F	G	H	I
2									
3	No	Series	Site Inv. No.	Period	Comments	WGT/BAT	WGT/AAT	WGT/LOSS	%CaCo3
4	1	1a	ABSM-CA-VAR	T		3.36	1.63	1.73	51.49%
5	2	1a	ABSM-CA-VAR	T		3.36	1.68	1.68	50.00%
6	3	1a	ABSM-CA-VAR	T		3.36	1.21	2.15	63.99%
7	4	1a	ABSM-CA-VAR	T		3.36	1.63	1.73	51.49%
8	5	1a	ABSM-CA-VAR	T		3.36	1.47	1.89	56.25%
9	6	1a	ABSM-CA-VAR	T		3.36	1.72	1.64	48.81%
10	7	1a	ABSM-CA-VAR	T		3.36	1.46	1.9	56.55%
11	8	1a	ABSM-CA-VAR	T		3.36	1.46	1.9	56.55%
12	9	1a	ABSM-CA-VAR	T		3.36	1.76	1.6	47.62%
13	10	1a	ABSM-CA-VAR	T		3.36	1.71	1.65	49.11%
14			53.18%		Mean % of CaCO3 Content in Series of 10 Analyses				
15									
16	1	1b	ABSM-CA-VAR	T		3.36	1.75	1.61	47.92%
17	2	1b	ABSM-CA-VAR	T		3.36	1.56	1.8	53.57%
18	3	1b	ABSM-CA-VAR	T		3.36	1.35	2.01	59.82%
19	4	1b	ABSM-CA-VAR	T		3.36	1.5	1.86	55.36%
20	5	1b	ABSM-CA-VAR	T		3.36	1.51	1.85	55.06%
21	6	1b	ABSM-CA-VAR	T		3.36	1.25	2.11	62.80%
22	7	1b	ABSM-CA-VAR	T		3.36	1.4	1.96	58.33%
23	8	1b	ABSM-CA-VAR	T		3.36	1.57	1.79	53.27%
24	9	1b	ABSM-CA-VAR	T		3.36	1.34	2.02	60.12%
25	10	1b	ABSM-CA-VAR	T		3.36	1.5	1.86	55.36%
26			56.16%		Mean % of CaCO3 Content in Series of 10 Analyses				
27									
28	1	1c	ABSM-CA-VAR	T		3.36	1.46	1.9	56.55%
29	2	1c	ABSM-CA-VAR	T		3.36	1.2	2.16	64.29%
30	3	1c	ABSM-CA-VAR	T		3.36	1.14	2.22	66.07%
31	4	1c	ABSM-CA-VAR	T		3.36	1.47	1.89	56.25%
32	5	1c	ABSM-CA-VAR	T		3.36	0.78	2.58	76.79%
33	6	1c	ABSM-CA-VAR	T		3.36	0.58	2.78	82.74%
34	7	1c	ABSM-CA-VAR	T		3.36	1.19	2.17	64.58%
35	8	1c	ABSM-CA-VAR	T		3.36	1.05	2.31	68.75%
36	9	1c	ABSM-CA-VAR	T		3.36	1.21	2.15	63.99%
37	10	1c	ABSM-CA-VAR	T		3.36	1.55	1.81	53.87%
38			65.39%		Mean % of CaCO3 Content in Series of 10 Analyses				
39									

	A	B	C	D	E	F	G	H	I
1	Quantitative Analysis of Ca CO3 Content of Pottery					TAULA TORRALBA DEN SALORT MENORC			
2									
3	No	Series	Site Inv. No.	Period	Comments	WGT/BAT	WGT/AAT	WGT/LOSS	%CaCo3
4	1	1a	TT-OT-R3-L3	T	MENORCAN SERIES	4	1.66	2.34	58.50%
5	2	1a	TT-OT-R3-L3	T		4	1.7	2.3	57.50%
6	3	1a	TT-OT-R3-L3	T		4	1.8	2.2	55.00%
7	4	1a	TT-OT-R3-L3	T		4	1.27	2.73	68.25%
8	5	1a	TT-OT-R3-L3	T		4	2.12	1.88	47.00%
9	6	1a	TT-OT-R3-L3	T		4	1.87	2.13	53.25%
10	7	1a	TT-OT-R3-L3	T		4	1.69	2.31	57.75%
11	8	1a	TT-OT-R3-L3	T		4	1.98	2.02	50.50%
12	9	1a	TT-OT-R3-L3	T		4	2.17	1.83	45.75%
13	10	1a	TT-OT-R3-L3	T		4	1.84	2.16	54.00%
14			54.75%		Mean % of CaCO3 Content in Series of 10 Analyses				
15									
16	1	1b	TT-ECE-L4	T	MENORCAN SERIES	4	2.14	1.86	46.50%
17	2	1b	TT-ECE-L4	T		4	2.88	1.12	28.00%
18	3	1b	TT-ECE-L4	T		4	1.94	2.06	51.50%
19	4	1b	TT-ECE-L4	T		4	1.77	2.23	55.75%
20	5	1b	TT-OT-S1-5	T		4	1.53	2.47	61.75%
21	6	1b	TT-OT-S1-5	T		4	1.47	2.53	63.25%
22	7	1b	TT-OT-S1-5	T		4	1.51	2.49	62.25%
23	8	1b	TT-0T-S1-5	T		4	2.32	1.68	42.00%
24	9	1b	TT-OT-S1-5	T		4	1.98	2.02	50.50%
25	10	1b	TT-OT-L4	T		4	1.44	2.56	64.00%
26			52.55%		Mean % of CaCO3 Content in Series of 10 Analyses				
27									
28	1	1c	TT-OT-L1	T	MENORCAN SERIES	4	1.74	2.26	56.50%
29	2	1c	TT-OT-L1	T		4	1.64	2.36	59.00%
30	3	1c	TT-OT-L1	T		4	1.52	2.48	62.00%
31	4	1c	TT-OT-L2	T		4	2.3	1.7	42.50%
32	5	1c	TT-OT-L2	T		4	1.96	2.04	51.00%
33	6	1c	TT-0T-L4	T		4	1.63	2.37	59.25%
34	7	1c	TT-OT-L4	T		4	1.53	2.47	61.75%
35	8	1c	TT-OT-L3	T		4	1.86	2.14	53.50%
36	9	1c	TT-OT-T	T		4	1.61	2.39	59.75%
37	10	1c	TT-OT-T	T		4	1.46	2.54	63.50%
38			56.88%		Mean % of CaCO3 Content in Series of 10 Analyses				
39									
40	1	1d	TT-OT-T	T	MENORCAN SERIES	4	1.68	2.32	58.00%
41	2	1d	TT-OT-T	T		4	1.69	2.31	57.75%
42	3	1d	TT-OT-T	T		4	1.65	2.35	58.75%
43	4	1d	TT-OT-T	T		4	1.91	2.09	52.25%
44	5	1d	TT-OT-T	T		4	1.86	2.14	53.50%
45	6	1d	TT-OT-T	T		4	1.58	2.42	60.50%
46	7	1d	TT-OT-T	T		4	1.85	2.15	53.75%
47	8	1d	TT-OT-T	T		4	3.18	0.82	20.50%
48	9	1d	TT-OT-T	T		4	1.55	2.45	61.25%
49	10	1d	TT-OT-T	T		4	2.03	1.97	49.25%
50			52.55%		Mean % of CaCO3 Content in Series of 10 Analyses				
51									

	A	B	C	D	E	F	G	H	I
1	Quantitative Analysis of Ca CO3 Content of Pottery					TAULA TORRALBA DEN SALORT MENORCA			
2									
3	No	Series	Site Inv. No.	Period	Comments	WGT/BAT	WGT/AAT	WGT/LOSS	%CaCo3
4	1	2a	TT-WCE-L3	T	MENORCAN SERIES	4	1.25	2.75	68.75%
5	2	2a	TT-WCE-L3	T		4	2.21	1.79	44.75%
6	3	2a	TT-WCE-L3	T		4	2.13	1.87	46.75%
7	4	2a	TT-WCE-L3	T		4	2.61	1.39	34.75%
8	5	2a	TT-WCE-L3	T		4	2.81	1.19	29.75%
9	6	2a	TT-WCE-L3	T		4	1.84	2.16	54.00%
10	7	2a	TT-WCE-L3	T		4	2.19	1.81	45.25%
11	8	2a	TT-WCE-L3	T		4	1.85	2.15	53.75%
12	9	2a	TT-WCE-L3	T		4	2.55	1.45	36.25%
13	10	2a	TT-WCE-L3	T		4	2.4	1.6	40.00%
14			45.40%		Mean % of CaCO3 Content in Series of 10 Analyses				
15									
16	1	2b	TT-WCE-L3	T	MENORCAN SERIES	4	1.65	2.35	58.75%
17	2	2b	TT-WCE-L3	T		4	2.16	1.84	46.00%
18	3	2b	TT-WCE-L4	T		4	3.65	0.35	8.75%
19	4	2b	TT-WCE-L4	T		4	2.06	1.94	48.50%
20	5	2b	TT-WCE-L4	T		4	3.44	0.56	14.00%
21	6	2b	TT-WCE-L4	T		4	2.78	1.22	30.50%
22	7	2b	TT-WCE-L4	T		4	2.78	1.22	30.50%
23	8	2b	TT-WCE-L4	T		4	2.47	1.53	38.25%
24	9	2b	TT-WCE-L4	T		4	2.41	1.59	39.75%
25	10	2b	TT-WCE-L4	T		4	1.06	2.94	73.50%
26			38.85%		Mean % of CaCO3 Content in Series of 10 Analyses				
27									
28	1	2c	TT-WCE-L4	T	MENORCAN SERIES	4	1.74	2.26	56.50%
29	2	2c	TT-WCE-L4	T		4	2.14	1.86	46.50%
30	3	2c	TT-WCE-L4	T		4	2.99	1.01	25.25%
31	4	2c	TT-WCE-L4	T		4	2.58	1.42	35.50%
32	5	2c	TT-WCE-L4	T		4	2.54	1.46	36.50%
33	6	2c	TT-WCE-L4	T		4	1.21	2.79	69.75%
34	7	2c	TT-WCE-L4	T		4	2.61	1.39	34.75%
35	8	2c	TT-ECE-L4	T		4	3.02	0.98	24.50%
36	9	2c	TT-ECE-L4	T		4	2.24	1.76	44.00%
37	10	2c	TT-ECE-L4	T		4	2.21	1.79	44.75%
38			41.80%		Mean % of CaCO3 Content in Series of 10 Analyses				
39									
40	1	2d	TT-ECE-L4	T	MENORCAN SERIES	4	1.87	2.13	53.25%
41	2	2d	TT-OT-L2	T		4	3.88	1.23	30.75%
42	3	2d	TT-OT-L2	T		4	2.68	1.32	33.00%
43	4	2d	TT-OT-L2	T		4	2.83	1.17	29.25%
44	5	2d	TT-OT-L2	T		4	1.98	2.02	50.50%
45	6	2d	TT-OT-L2	T		4	1.95	2.05	51.25%
46	7	2d	TT-INT-L2	T		4	2.81	1.19	29.75%
47	8	2d	TT-INT-L2	T		4	1.98	2.02	50.50%
48	9	2d	TT-OT-L2	T		4	1.95	2.05	51.25%
49	10	2d	TT-OT-L2	T		4	1.82	2.18	54.50%
50			43.40%		Mean % of CaCO3 Content in Series of 10 Analyses				
51									

	A	B	C	D	E	F	G	H	I	J
1										
2										
3		QACCCP MAT ANALYSIS SPREADSHEET TRIAL 1								
4										
5		POTTERY FRAGMENT: SFO OLD SETTLEMENT								
6										
7	No.	MX/L	MX/W	AREA	MX/TH	LXWXTH VOL	WGT/BAT	WGT/AAT	WGT LOSS	%CACO3
8	1	3.53	3.07	10.837	0.6	6.50226	6.26	3.76	2.5	39.94%
9	2	3.61	3.81	13.754	0.58	7.977378	12.88	4.71	8.17	63.43%
10	3	2.67	4.23	11.294	0.67	7.567047	8.23	6.21	2.02	24.54%
11	4	4.51	3.74	16.867	1.07	18.048118	14.06	10.75	3.31	23.54%
12	5	3.86	2.59	9.9974	0.75	7.49805	6.66	4.71	1.95	29.28%
13	6	3.93	3.58	14.069	1.01	14.210094	6.63	4.74	1.89	28.51%
14	7	3.45	5.11	17.63	0.75	13.222125	8.84	6.21	2.63	29.75%
15	8	2.85	3.34	9.519	0.83	7.90077	5.61	3.27	2.34	41.71%
16	9	3.04	4.02	12.221	1.08	13.198464	10.43	8.51	1.92	18.41%
17	0	4.06	4.29	17.417	0.92	16.024008	15.03	10.02	5.01	33.33%
18	1	2.75	2.87	7.8925	1.9	14.99575	5.86	3.31	2.55	43.52%
19	2	3.78	3.02	11.416	1.06	12.100536	12.07	8.85	3.22	26.68%
20	3	3.25	2.21	7.1825	0.71	5.099575	3.81	2.11	1.7	44.62%
21	4	3.61	2.06	7.4366	1.11	8.254626	7.01	5.19	1.82	25.96%
22	5	3.03	3.12	9.4536	0.81	7.657416	6.64	5.08	1.56	23.49%
23	6	3.38	3.19	10.782	0.71	7.655362	6.18	3.34	2.84	45.95%
24	7	3.03	1.87	5.6661	0.61	3.456321	3.64	1.31	2.33	64.01%
25	8	3.31	2.53	8.3743	0.61	5.108323	4.81	2.85	1.96	40.75%
26	9	2.55	1.31	3.3405	0.41	1.369605	1.28	0.6967	0.5833	45.57%
27	0	3.71	3.51	13.022	0.71	9.245691	10.66	8.72	1.94	18.20%
28	1	1.57	2.51	3.9407	0.51	2.009757	1.97	1.03	0.94	47.72%
29	2	2.81	2.87	8.0647	0.58	4.677526	4.26	2.16	2.1	49.30%
30	3	2.11	1.46	3.0806	0.51	1.571106	1.56	1.13	0.43	27.56%
31	4	2.31	1.82	4.2042	0.51	2.144142	1.91	1.41	0.5	26.18%
32	5	2.73	1.85	5.0505	0.71	3.585855	3.84	2.53	1.31	34.11%
33	6	2.53	2.69	6.8057	0.51	3.470907	2.51	1.87	0.64	25.50%
34	7	2.13	2.54	5.4102	0.41	2.218182	2.2	1.22	0.98	44.55%
35	8	3.47	2.38	8.2586	0.78	6.441708	4.3	2.78	1.52	35.35%
36	9	3.17	2.56	8.1152	0.61	4.950272	4.3	2.56	1.74	40.47%
37	0	3.21	2.92	9.3732	0.61	5.717652	4.75	2.21	2.54	53.47%
38	1	2.03	3.51	7.1253	0.71	5.058963	4.34	3.42	0.92	21.20%
39	2	2.81	2.07	5.8167	0.61	3.548187	3.54	2.15	1.39	39.27%
40										
41								MEAN %		36.12%

ARCHAEOLOGICAL TECHNIQUES, TECHNOLOGY AND THEORY

THE METALS OF SON MATGE, MALLORCA, SPAIN
TECHNOLOGY AS CULTURAL ACTIVITY AND BEHAVIOUR

CHRISTOPHER R. HOFFMAN
Department of Anthropology
University of California, Berkeley
Berkeley, Ca., 94720, U.S.A.

RESUME

In this paper, an assemblage of over four hundred metal artifacts from the rock shelter site of Son Matge, Mallorca, Spain will serve as the focus for a discussion of technological behavior, which can be broadly defined here as human cultural behavior as it relates to technical or technological systems. Although technological behavior can be studied in any cultural context, past or present, in this archaeological case, the evidence is limited to material culture. Of course, the material culture of a technological system is not limited to its final products, such as a bronze axe or an iron dagger. It also included the furnaces, crucibles, molds, and even ores and fluxes that are part of the whole production process.

In order to avoid a sort of technological determinism, archaeologists and anthropologists must begin to examine the human relationship and activities that are involved in the making of things, realizing that the activities and the material culture play an active role in the negotiation of meaning within an individual and cultural context. In the metallurgical example, this refers to the ways humans relate to each other and to their material world when mining ores out of the earth, processing and smelting them into molten metal which can be poured into a variety of shapes, finished with a variety of techniques, and finally, by any number of means, distributed into a cultural context where they are used and consumed.

A number of factors make the metals of Son Matge an interesting opportunity to investigate these issues. First, these objects are located in a variety of contexts suggesting domestic, production and burial activities. Second, they cover a time period of nearly two thousand years, from the initial appearance of metallurgy on Mallorca, c. 2000 bc., to the appearance of the Romans in 123 BC. Third, these archaeological contexts were well excavated and dated by a series of over fifty radiocarbon dates in the 1970's by William Waldren and the Deiá Archaeological Museum and Research Centre (Waldren 1979, 1982).

TECHNOLOGY, TECHNIQUES OF PRODUCTION AND STYLE IN TECHNOLOGY

In the first section of this paper, this perspective on technology and its potential for the discussion of cultural activity and behavior will be expanded. An approach that emphasizes the techniques for producing items as well as the items themselves is well suited to a number of archaeological and anthropological questions. In addition to traditional questions of typology and cultural history, technical activities can provide another source of information for the reconstruction of the economics and social organization of procurement, production and distribution across a cultural landscape. However, by realizing that encoded within each artifact is a history of human behavior in the individual and cultural sense, archaeologists can begin to discuss technological behavior. And as is being emphasized here, even those 'pragmatic' aspects of human activities, such as the production of a functional axe, are embedded in cultural behavior and a process of cultural beings relating to themselves, to others and to their material word.

Of course, this is no simple task, even if all the spatial and economic aspects of a production system were known. The difficulty of accessing the ideational realm via material culture in ethnographic and ethnoarchaeological work has made this quite clear (e.g., Wiessner 1985 and Sackett 1985). How then do archaeologists, particularly those working in prehistoric contexts, begin to frame their questions? A number of approaches do seem to have potential. Heather Lechtman and a number of colleagues and students have developed an approach called style in technology (Lechtman and Merrill 1977, Lechtman 1977, 1984). For Lechtman, style is the "formal, extrinsic manifestation of intrinsic pattern" (1977:4). She emphasized that technological behavior is stylistic in its own right. That is, technological activities are nonrandomly organized according to cultural patterns and rules and are not completely dependent upon such cross-cultural notions as efficiency and functionability. However, although the notion might be acceptable that technological activities and behavior are 'stylistic' in a cultural and ideational sense, the formulation of this relationship, the bridge-building between one level of analysis and the other, is problematic.

In summary, techniques of production are not simply functional ways of doing things but are choices made by people and have their own stylistic and aesthetic dimensions which have cultural and behavioral bases. Therefore, archaeologists can look for assemblages of techniques, at levels both specific and more general (for instance, the production of a specific item such as a copper awl, to metallurgy, and to pyrotechnology and total technological systems) and their distribution across a cultural landscape. It will be up to archaeologists and anthropologists to examine the ways in which these assemblages of techniques are related to each other and to other aspects of human cultural behavior.

METHODOLOGY

Basically this research is an attempt to examine technological behavior in a series of particular contexts over approximately two thousand years. Although this study is limited by the lack of ethnohistoric evidence, the techniques used to produce objects of metal can be assessed and questions posed in the appropriate directions. For instance, in the Early Iron Age levels of the site of Son Matge, a number of objects are based on the spiral but are made in different sizes or made of either bronze or iron. The techniques used to produce such a spiral are certainly related but not identical. Therefore, there seems to be a variety of ways to satisfy the production of a certain form which were considered suitable to the producer and the consumer of the object. In this approach, then, the range of techniques employed by makers of things will be discussed, emphasizing their relationship to a number of contexts - contexts of production, distribution, use and discard or consumption.

During the summers of 1987 and 1988, the metal objects were recorded, drawn and catalogued at the Deià Archaeological Museum and Research Centre in Deià, Mallorca, Spain. Dr. Peter Northover of Oxford University provided analyses of 45 samples for the compositions of twelve elements (Cu, Sn, Sb, Pb, Co, Ni, Fe, Ag, Au, Zn, Bi, As) (Waldren 1986, Table 19). In addition approximate concentrations and grain structures of five artifacts were determined with the use of the electronic microscope (Northover in Waldren 1979).

A major part of this project was the creation of a database, basically a problem-oriented typology of the assemblages in an attempt to code the basic series of steps involved in the manufacture of the object. Contextual information on the provenience and general typology was also included. Note that this is not intended to replace traditional typologies for European metallurgy but to investigate a variety of questions about 2000 years of metal artifacts from a single site. The assessment of techniques included a number of assumptions, not all of which are completely secure, resulting from the fact that each artifact was not sampled and subjected to metallographic examination.

THE METALS OF SON MATGE

In this section of the paper, the metals of Son Matge will be discussed in detail and placed in their archaeological context. The goals of this discussion will be to (1) reconstruct the the assemblages of techniques involved in the production of various types of metals during the various periods represented at the site (the Pretalayotic, Chalcolithic, the Talayotic Bronze Age and the Post Talayotic Iron Age); (2) discuss patterns of procurement, production and distribution across a cultural landscape; and (3) interpret the objects and the assemblages of techniques used to produce them within a cultural context. Continual reference to the specific contextual associations will be made at the specific level of the site of Son Matge and on larger geographical scales as well.

The Metals of Son Matge, Mallorca, Spain
Technology as Cultural Activity and Behavior
Christopher Hoffman

INTRODUCTION

In this paper, over five hundred metal artifacts and objects associated with the production of metals are the focus for a discussion of metal production, use and deposition. These objects come from a single site -- the rock shelter of Son Matge (Mallorca, Baleares, Spain) -- and were excavated from Copper Age, Bronze Age and Iron Age contexts. Such an investigation can help answer and even reframe not only our questions about the culture history of particular areas, but also the nature of technology as cultural behavior and the ways that metals operate as material culture. Technology, the making of material culture, is inherently cultural.

It is argued here that the investigation of archaeological metals has become too engrossed in technological and provenance questions. Technological answers should not be the final goal of analysis but the springboard for other questions of a more anthropological, historical and archaeological nature. We have yet to systematically ask how innovations are accepted, and how and by what mechanisms specific techniques are transmitted in specific contact situations. It is time now to begin framing our questions about metals and metal technology in terms of people and to investigate (and if need be, to dismiss) the assumptions that have characterized so much work. These assumptions cover a wide range of very important issues including the nature of innovation and invention and the spread of technologically superior items.

A number of factors make the metals of Son Matge an interesting opportunity to investigate these issues. First, these objects cover a time period of over 2000 years. The rock shelter site of Son Matge has a well-stratified sequence with metals in levels dating to 1) the Copper Age Pretalayotic levels, 2) the Bronze Age Talayotic levels, and 3) the Iron Age Post Talayotic levels. Second, these metals appear in an interesting set of domestic, production and burial contexts. Third, these archaeological contexts were well excavated between 1968 and 1976 and dated by a sequence of thirty two radiocarbon dates (Waldren 1982; Fernández-Miranda and Waldren 1974, 1979; Rosselló Bordóy and Waldren 1973). Such an assemblage of metal artifacts provides a unique opportunity to examine and discuss a wide variety of issues.

In the first section of this paper, the potential of technology -- or more appropriately, techniques, the ways things are made -- for the interpretation of cultural behavior and activity will be discussed. Second, the methodology and approach employed here will be made explicit. Finally, an analysis of the metals of Son Matge in their archaeological and cultural contexts will follow.

"TECHNOLOGY", TECHNIQUES OF PRODUCTION, AND STYLE IN TECHNOLOGY

One of the primary vehicles for this investigation is the ways in which the metals were produced. Here, the label "technology" can be examined more closely. The people using the rock shelter of Son Matge were making things, procuring them from other groups, using them, and eventually, after any number of cycles of reworking and melting, depositing or discarding them in the contexts of what later would become an archaeological site. The label "technology" can not objectively provide a title for a certain repertoire of objects and may be particularly inappropriate for any prehistoric contexts. It is embedded in Western culture with particular meanings and reified in ways that affect our interpretation of human cultural activity and behavior -- past, present, and future -- in ways both subtle and overt.

An approach that emphasizes the techniques for producing items of material culture as well as the objects themselves is well suited to a number of anthropological and archaeological questions. First, traditional questions of typology and culture history can be addressed. At a larger level, the economics and social organization of procurement, production and distribution across a cultural landscape can be discussed more fully. In addition, archaeologists must realize that encoded within each object is a history of human behavior, in both the individual and collective senses. Each artifact is literally packed with time, from the procurement of the raw material, in this case the mining of the metalliferous ores, to the final deposition of the object in a particular context. All of these activities involve people, as individuals and as members of larger groupings that are traditionally called "cultures", in the process of doing, making, and relating.

Of course, identifying these deeper aspects of material culture is no simple task, even if all the spatial and economic aspects of a production system were known. Recent ethnographic and ethnoarchaeological work has demonstrated the difficulty of accessing the ideational realm via material culture (e.g., Wiessner 1985 and Sackett 1985). How then do archaeologists, particularly those working in prehistoric contexts, begin to frame their questions? A number of approaches do seem to have potential. Heather Lechtman and a number of colleagues and students have developed an approach called style in technology (Lechtman and Merrill 1977, Lechtman 1977, 1984). For Lechtman, style is the "formal, extrinsic manifestation of intrinsic pattern" (1977:4). She emphasizes that technological behavior is stylistic in its own right. That is, technological activities are organized according to cultural patterns and rules and can not be reduced to value-laden measures of efficiency and utility. However, although it might be acceptable that technological activities and behavior are "stylistic" in a cultural and ideational sense, the formulation of this relationship, the bridge-building between one level of analysis and the other, is problematic.

In summary, techniques of production are not simply functional ways of doing things but are choices made by people, and they have their own stylistic and aesthetic dimensions that have cultural and behavioral bases. Therefore, archaeologists can look for assemblages of techniques, at levels both specific and more general (for instance, the production of a specific item such as a copper awl, metallurgy, pyrotechnology and total technological systems) and their distribution across a cultural landscape. It will be the task of archaeologists and anthropologists to examine the ways in which these assemblages of techniques are related to each other and to other aspects of human cultural behavior.

METALLURGICAL TRADITIONS

As stated above, many treatments of archaeological metals are fetishized discussions of typology or technology. Implicit assumptions about the social organization and practice of metallurgical production almost inevitably rely on models of itinerant metalsmiths and the historical image of the medieval blacksmith. It is at this level of interpretation that archaeologists must begin to direct their attention. In order to bring the objects back to social forces and actors, the approach advocated here will take a more holistic look at metals. All objects of material culture can be viewed at one level in terms of the stages that people put them through. For metal objects, this includes the mining or procurement of metal ores and other necessary raw materials, the production of ingots or finished items, their use and reuse, eventual discard or deposition into the ground, and the relationships that people enter into while carrying out these activities. Such a "metallurgical tradition" can be defined broadly here as the technical and social aspects of metal production for a particular regional and cultural context. Within this framework, a large range of interrelated activities can be considered together. Identifying and mapping the distribution of these activities across a natural and social landscape and observing the changes in such networks through time are difficult but archaeologically feasible goals, and they provide an excellent opportunity to address questions about the social organization of production and the historical and cultural dimensions of material culture.

From such a perspective, this research examines the social manipulation of metals in a series of particular contexts covering approximately two thousand years. One of the greatest problems with this particular case study at this point is the lack of control over the location of production. That is, many of the artifacts were not manufactured on the island of Mallorca but were brought there by a variety of means from a variety of places. Obviously, this is a vital point when discussing the different types of objects produced and the different types of techniques employed. The usual archaeological tool for such problems is typology. Similarities between objects from different places are used to draw arrows from one place to another. This is a technique that is extensively used to trace the development of metallurgical assemblages throughout prehistoric Europe. This information is then taken to indicate relationships of one sort or another -- connections, influences, and colonizations. Typology plays an important role in this investigation as well. However, its limitations must be noted. The process of design innovation and acceptance is very complex. In most cases, typology can only provide information that can be used to support other lines of evidence. Used alone, similarities between objects from different areas can be used to draw arrows from any one place to any other, no matter how distant spatially or culturally. In addition, the reading of these arrows imposes an interpretation on the societies that can be very misleading.

During the summers of 1987 and 1988, the metals of Son Matge were recorded, drawn, and catalogued at the Deya Archaeological Museum and Research Centre in Deya, Mallorca, Spain. A database was created in an attempt to code the basic series of steps taken to manufacture each object as well as general information about typology and provenance. This problem-oriented typology is not intended to replace traditional typologies for European metallurgy but to investigate a variety of questions about 2000 years worth of metal objects from a single site. Dr. Peter Northover of Oxford University analyzed 45 samples using Neutron Activation Analysis to determine the concentrations of twelve elements (Cu, Sn, Sb, Pb, Co, Ni, Fe, Ag, Au, Zn, Bi, As) (Waldren 1986, Table 19). In addition, electron microscope analysis, a semi-quantitative technique, was used to determine approximate concentrations and the grain structure of five more objects.

For photographs and drawings of the objects and maps of the site itself, please refer to the various site reports (Waldren 1979, 1982; Fernández-Miranda and Waldren 1974, 1979; Rosselló Bordóy and Waldren 1973).

THE SITE OF SON MATGE AND THE PREHISTORY OF MALLORCA

The rock shelter of Son Matge is a very important site for Balearic prehistory. The well-excavated cultural contexts date from the earliest human presence on the island of Mallorca, c. 5000 b.c., through to the presence of the Romans, who founded Pollentia in 123 B.C. A series of thirty-two radiocarbon dates provide a solid chronological framework.

The chronological scheme for Mallorca and the Balearics is still being developed. Although rigorous excavations in the last 25 years have greatly increased the understanding of Balearic prehistory, a great amount of culture history remains to be done. The Balearic chronology developed by Waldren (1982, 1986) is used here because it was developed partly from the Son Matge sequence. However, a number of other chronologies do exist (Mascaro Pasarius 1978, Pericot Garcia 1972, Fernández-Miranda 1979, Veny 1984).

The location of the Son Matge rock shelter is particularly interesting. Situated at the narrowest juncture of one of the few passes linking the coastal areas beyond the northern sierras with the central plain, Son Matge would provide an ideal location for controlling or gaining access to interregional communication and exchange. In addition, there are arable lands and water sources near to the site. Certainly the density of settlement in this region of the island suggests its ability to sustain population (Waldren 1982). This control of access to the pass would have been very important when Son Matge was used for human occupation. Later, when it was turned into a cemetery, the location would have taken on different meanings to the people burying their dead there.

At this point, the metals of the Son Matge rock shelter will be discussed and placed in their archaeological context. The goals of this discussion will be to 1) reconstruct the assemblages of techniques involved in the production of various objects during the various periods represented at this single site, 2) discuss patterns of procurement, production and distribution across a landscape, and 3) interpret the objects and the assemblages of techniques used to produce them within a cultural context. A number of problems exist that make this attempt difficult. First, it is difficult to reconstruct the techniques used to produce items with any certainty at the level of analysis presented here. Only a limited amount of technical information is available from elemental characterization and metallographic analyses (Waldren 1986, table 19). More extensive work will be reported in a related thesis project. Second, the chronological associations of these objects, at Son Matge itself and at other sites, is complicated by site formation processes and excavation strategies.

Very little work has been done on Balearic metallurgy (Rosselló-Bordóy 1974, 1987; Waldren 1979; Delibes de Castro and Fernández-Miranda 1984) although a recent publication does much to improve the situation (Delibes de Castro and Fernández-Miranda 1988). As is the case with the majority of prehistoric European metallurgy, it has been used to define culture chronologies and culture contact using morphological attributes. This approach ignores other technical features of the object as well as its total context. A further complicating problem with this approach is the lack of any explicit idea about what stylistic similarity and variability mean. There is a hidden assumption that similarity and variability reflect group identity and culture, but there is no formulation about how this is accomplished.

PRETALAYOTIC PERIOD

Metals first appear in the Son Matge levels during the Balearic Chalcolithic or Pretalayotic period. Habitation in caves and rock shelters, such as Son Matge, is relatively well documented as is habitation and collective inhumation in artificially enlarged caves and megalithic structures called navetiformes or navetas (Veny 1968, 1984). At this time, similar developments are taking place on Menorca. Although this period was previously referred to as the "cultura de las cuevas", a large open-air site, the Son Ferrandell-Oleza Old Settlement, located less than five kilometers from Son Matge is currently being investigated (Waldren 1984, 1986, 1987). An interesting feature of this time period is the appearance of a burnished and incised fine ceramic ware. Waldren (1982, 1987) refers to this material as "Beaker" or "Beaker-related", linking the sequences in Mallorca with those in mainland Europe, while others prefer to retain the local terminology of "Incisa tipos A y B" (Topp 1984, Veny 1984).

At Son Matge, eight radiocarbon dates place the fifteen levels (strata 23 through 9) of the eastern sector (the Eastern Enclosure) between 2030 ± 170 b.c. and 1400 ± 40 b.c. The four levels (strata 12 through 9) of the central sector (the Central Enclosure) do not have radiocarbon dated materials but can be stratigraphically related to those from the eastern sector. These Pretalayotic levels are alternating charcoal and ash levels.

Excavations in the central sector of the site recovered a range of important metal items and objects related to metallurgical production. In stratum 11, several sherds of a small bowl crucible were found. The insides of the vessel were heavily fired, and small patches of green copper oxide slags were adhering in spots. Unfortunately only the upper walls of this piece were recovered. If it is indeed a crucible, the base would most likely have a larger amount of slag. As it is, the small size of the slag hinders analysis. However, when viewed under a low-power microscope, a thin section of one of these sherds demonstrates that the slag had diffused into the ceramic material. This fact renders unacceptable the suggestion by Delibes de Castro and Fernández-Miranda that the presence of copper oxides on the bowls could be the result of weathering (1988, p.7). Importantly this vessel was decorated on the outside with incisions of a type that relate it directly to Beaker ceramics. In another part of this level, two distinctive objects were unearthed: a flat cast bronze spearhead and a bone comb incised with geometric designs similar to those found on Beaker ceramics.

In a crevice which has been linked stratigraphically to stratum 10, a "hoard" of 114 awls, 39 of them complete, was discovered. The awls are normally square or rectangular in section, rounding to a point at one end and flattening out at the other. However, some are pointed at both ends. They vary in length from fragments less than one centimeter long to complete awls up to seven centimeters long. Eight of these were hafted into either the distal or proximal end of the metatarsal or metacarpal of an ovicaprid. One awl was set into a "sheath-like" object that Waldren (1979) interprets to be a mold for awl production. If this object was indeed used as a mold, a great deal of hammering and probably annealing under considerable heat would be required to reach the final shape. Qualitative (electronic microscope analysis) and quantitative (neutron activation analysis) analyses indicate that the awls are of a true tin bronze (5 to 10% tin) and that they were annealed (Waldren 1979, 1986 table 19). Also found in conjunction with this group of objects was a bone awl and a number of bone and shell beads.

Elsewhere on the island of Mallorca during the Pretalayotic period, metals are not frequent finds. Awls similar to those found in the Son Matge levels are known in several contexts. A smaller number of flat cast projectile points have also been reported. An item which is often reported in burials is the triangular "laurel-leaf" dagger. No daggers of this type were found in Son Matge. In terms of production, evidence is more restricted. Crucible sherds and an ingot of pure copper (Waldren 1987) are known from the contemporary open-air site of the Son Ferrandell-Oleza Old Settlement. Two molds for the production of flat spearheads are known from the site of Can Roig Nou located on the northern coast of the island (Rosselló-Bordóy 1974). Although more research on the regional aspects of metallurgical production is needed, the fact that two contemporary sites within five kilometers of each other (Son Matge and Son Ferrandell-Oleza) have evidence for production suggests a decentralized structure of regional production.

From this evidence, the range of techniques, as well as the range of forms produced, is quite limited. Among the 116 Pretalayotic metals of Son Matge, all but two are awls from a presumably single depositional event. Although the number of analyses performed is very small, all objects were probably made in one-piece flat molds followed by annealing and cold-working. An interesting point is the early date (i.e. 1800 b.c.) for the use of a true tin bronze in this part of Mediterranean Europe. Tin bronzes are not common in mainland Spain until c. 1300 b.c. (Harrison and Craddock 1981, Hook et al 1987). Prior to this date, the great majority of metal objects in Spain are arsenical bronzes. A limited number of objects from Pretalayotic contexts do have a significant percentage of arsenic (0.4-1.3%), but this amount could be attributed to the use of arsenical ores.

There are a number of copper ore sources located on the island of Mallorca, primarily in the northern sierras (IGME 1973). At least one of these is reported to have arsenical copper associations. There is no evidence for mining during this time period on Mallorca. However, there has been little survey in the appropriate regions and no work focused directly on this problem. Geologically the majority of these ores occur in stratified deposits in relatively soft sandstones. Such ore could be easily mined.

An interpretation of the Pretalayotic levels of Son Matge must consider the activities represented. First, the hearths and kitchen debris from the eastern sector suggest a range of domestic activitie s. The total assemblage of materials from the central sector indicate that a different set of tasks was taking place. First, no kitchen debris are reported. The presence of crucible sherds, the mold and the hoard of awls suggests strongly that they were being produced there. Eight of these items were further modified by being hafted into bone handles. Waldren (1979) has noted that the copper awls are in varying stages of production, citing the mold, the varying lengths, and the hafted and unhafted awls.

Two points are relevant here to a discussion of the evidence for copper production. First, the "Beaker" incised crucible raises some interesting questions. Ceramics with Beaker geometric incisions are normally assumed to have some sort of special significance due to their fine production and generally widespread distribution. Although the incisions on the Beaker crucible are somewhat more roughly and irregularly applied, the fact that a crucible for the production of metal objects was incised with the same designs may indicate that metal production was also allied with the Beaker phenomenon, whether it was based in ritual, authority or just "nicely made" objects. Second, judging from the small size of the crucible and the number of awls found in this single context (114), it is likely that they were made in a large number of smelting or melting events. If the "sheath-like" mold was typical for awl production then a large number of such molds would be required. Alternatively, a large number of flat molds would also be required to produce this number of awls in one event. This is of course all conjecture at this point. However, the evidence points to a large number of production events.

Two lines of evidence can be used to suggest that some of these items were also being used in the central sector of Son Matge. First, the awls are of varying sizes. Depending on the material the awl was used on and the composition of the tool, the sharp end would need occasional reworking to form a point. This would reduce the length of the awl until it would have to be discarded or melted down. Second, the presence of the bone awl found in conjunction with the bronze awls can be explained if the objects are assumed to be "in use" as well as "in production". Such sharp objects could be employed in a variety of tasks -- textile production, hide preparation, ceramic decoration, or bone and shell button manufacture. Needless to say, more direct evidence for the use of these objects would be helpful.

The associated objects found in the central sector also provide useful information. There are a large number of objects that are normally considered to be ornamental and/or related to the Beaker phenomenon -- Beaker incised ceramics, bone and shell beads, the incised bone comb, and the hard stone "archer's wristguard". This all suggests that the production and use of bronze awls at Son Matge was associated with the display and use of Beaker mat erial culture. Furthermore, the discreet spatial association of these activities, separated from the domestic activities of the eastern sector, indicates that the occupants of Son Matge had conceptually divided the rock shelter prior to the construction of a stone wall during the Talayotic Bronze Age.

TALAYOTIC EARLY BRONZE AGE OR TALAYOTIC I

The Bronze Age of the Balearics is traditionally known as the Talayotic period because of the construction of stone built towers with circular floor plans. During this period, Talayots and other stone structures normally occured as isolated features on the landscape. They were utilized well into the first millenium b.c., and eventually, rectangular house blocks were added adjacent to an individual or pair of Talayots and enclosed within a low wall (Gasull et al 1984a, 1984b). Again, natural and artificial caves were still used, though increasingly for burial. Many archaeologists have used the structure of the Talayots and Talayotic settlements to argue for commerce with and population movement between other islands in the Mediterranean, particularly Corsica and Sardinia (Pericot Garcia 1972).

Although open-air settlements are known during the Pretalayotic Copper Age (e.g. Son Ferrandell-Oleza Old Settlement, Waldren 1984, 1986, 1987), there is a significant move to settlements on the level plains and valley floors at the beginning of the Talayotic Bronze Age, circa 1300 b.c. This represents a different conceptual use of the landscape. The caves and rock shelters are still used but for purposes other than occupation, as cemeteries and probably as seasonal and temporary shelters related to herd movement. The discovery of a ceramic kiln dated to 870 ± 40 b.c. in the Late Bronze Age levels of Son Matge suggests that specialized production may have also been a feature of this exploitation of the highlands. Interestingly, until recently there was a tradition on Mallorca of seasonal specialized production of charcoal and ice in the mountainous areas. Whether or not this tradition goes back as far as the beginnings of the Talayotic Bronze Age is a matter of future research. However, the special character and distinctive use of highland regions is a notable feature of many Mediterranean cultures (Braudel 1966).

At Son Matge, a series of stone walls were constructed at the beginning of this time period. These building activities partly used rock fall from the shelter overhang to define the East Enclosure and Central Enclosure. The total area of the Central Enclosure is substantially smaller than that of the East Enclosure. Also, the walls of the Central Enclosure are thicker. At this point, these two areas are used as a burial cemetery for partial cremations, a practice which is prevalent during this time period in Mallorca. Although it appears that the dead were originally laid out articulated and in an extended position, the later activities of the Post Talayotic period disturbed their orientation and associations considerably. A large number of grave goods, including hundreds of whole pots, were also deposited. The top and therefore latest level in this sequence in the East Enclosure is dated to 1250 ± 100 b.c. placing this toward the end of the Son Ferrandell-Oleza Old Settlement occupation but before the construction of the Talayotic structures of the Son Ferrandell-Oleza Young Settlement.

A number of bronze items were deposited in these burial levels. In addition, many were found in relatively discreet groups or "caches". One group of items consisted of a heavy cast sword with a cast hilt, a dagger, a heavy cast bracelet, a cast pin, and several brooches. Two unusual pots were found associated with these items. A second group of items contained a triangular bladed object with a central rib and a heavy cast hilt, several triangular or semi-circular bladed objects with tangs, and two awls with spherical handles of bronze cast over a clay core. Other bronze items found in these contexts include flat cast projectile points, awls of a type very similar to those from the Pretalayotic levels, and a number of fragments of wire or of flat or slightly curved sheet.

This range of items is relatively standard for the Early and Middle Bronze Age Talayotic period of Mallorca. Other objects found in Talayotic I contexts include chisels, flat and tubular axes, and pectorals formed of curved tubular units. These objects are known from both burial and occupation contexts. Unfortunately, it is difficult to chronologically separate the majority of the finds from those of the Iron Age since most of those objects that have provenance information do not have reliable dating. However, the metal objects do display a vastly increased variety of forms or types relative to the Pretalayotic period. Many of these forms are quite unique in Europe, and a great amount of energy has been expended trying to find typological associations (Almagro Basch 1940; Bosch Gimpera 1954; Almagro Gorbea 1977). The general consensus today (Delibes de Castro and Fernández-Miranda 1988) emphasizes the singularity of the pieces but suggests that the inspiration for certain aspects of the assemblage came from other areas. It is important to note that these large distinctive items have received the most attention. From these items, it is obvious that heavier objects were emphasized. These may or may not have been related to an ideology of an offensive/defensive or warrior nature. Those items which are smaller, and probably more common, such as the flat projectile points and awls, have been ignored.

Just as the range of forms is increased, the range of techniques used is also much larger in this time period. First, many of these items are much larger, demonstrating that a larger smelt was involved. Second, the swords, daggers and triangular items were undoubtedly made in two-piece molds. Third, the massive hilts on the sword and the tria ngular bladed object with a central rib were produced forming a hollow socket necessitating the use of a cored mold. A similar technology is represented by the spherical handles attached to the awls. These are of bronze cast over a fine clay core. Fourth, the hilts of these objects exhibit a technique called "casting on" (Delibes de Castro and Fernández-Miranda 1988). Fifth, the analyses performed so far show that these items are of a higher and more regular tin content. From this it can be inferred that the alloying techniques had been refined.

Although most authors suggest that these are locally produced items, evidence for the production of these items on Mallorca is very limited. There are isolated reports of molds (e.g. Hospitalet Vell, Rosselló-Bordóy 1987), but these are flat molds which appear to have been designed for the manufacture of awls. Either the larger more complicated items were imported, or the production centers have not been located. The possibility that these sites might be located in areas that have not received systematic investigation has already been discussed.

In these Early Bronze Age contexts, metals played a very different role relative to earlier times, both in the specific contexts of this rock shelter and on the island as a whole. At Son Matge, a heavy and distinctive assemblage of metal objects was deposited with the dead. Although later activities disturbed the spatial orientation of the bodies and the funerary items, groups of metal objects appear to have been deposited together in association with specific individuals. Large amounts of ceramics were also deposited in these burial levels. The types and techniques represented by the metal objects are substantially more varied and more complex relative to the metals of the Copper Age levels. Unfortunately, we have little or no understanding of the organization or economy of metal production during this time.

THE TALAYOTIC LATE BRONZE AGE

During this phase of activities at Son Matge, a stone wall was built in the western sector, defining the Western Enclosure. A kiln for the production of ceramics was constructed and used in this sector, and charcoal from a level (stratum 8) containing ash and over fifty kilograms of sherds gives a date of 860 ± 50 b.c. No metals are known from this level.

The chronological associations of the rock shelter become quite confused at this point. The date from stratum 8 places the kiln at the end of the Talayotic Bronze Age of Waldren (1982) and the Talayotica I period of Fernández-Miranda (1979). A number of iron objects were found in a later level dated by two radiocarbon samples to 780 ± 100 and 750 ± 100 b.c. This level lies below the limestone burials in the levels of the Iron Age Post Talayotic (or Talayotica II) period. The question then becomes: Are these iron objects of the West Enclosure part of the Bronze Age sequence or of the Iron Age? In part this is not a legitimate question. The mere presence of iron can not be used to define these levels as Iron Age.

Although undated, a number of typologically Late Bronze Age objects have been located in crevices of the wall that defines the Central Enclosure. These materials could date to the beginning of the Early Iron Age however. These objects which have been assigned to the Late Bronze Age on typological grounds are the socketed spearheads that are common in Europe at this time. The production of such items does involve another type of mold, one that can allow the use of a core (which could have been of a sand-clay mixture) for the formation of a hollow or socket. There is no evidence for the production of these objects in the Balearics, but they are common throughout Europe at this time. Hoards of such items are known in many contexts and molds are known in Sardinia and elsewhere (Tylecote 1987). During this period, commerce and contact throughout the Mediterranean and into the Atlantic and onto the European mainland was undoubtedly increasing.

THE POST TALAYOTIC IRON AGE OR TALAYOTIC II

The Post Talayotic Iron Age is normally considered to begin c. 700 bc with the appearance of iron and to end with the initial Roman settlement of the city of Pollentia in 123 BC. The variety of site types and material culture during this period points to a complicated picture of interaction within the context of the Balearics and with groups from elsewhere. According to historical sources, Carthaginians established a factory site and then a city on the southern coast of Ibiza in 654 BC. At a later date, the Punic-Ebusitano groups of Ibiza established factory sites on small islands off the coast of Mallorca (e.g. Na Guardis, Guerreros Ayuso 1984) and intensified the introduction of such items as iron antenna-hilted swords and daggers, vitreous paste beads, and wheel-turned ceramics (Mayoral Franco 1984). This process presents an excellent opportunity to investigate a situation that is normally called "colonization". Like "technology", this is a value-laden term that should be applied with discretion only. Future investigations should focus on the ways that indigenous communities reacted to the increasing presence of foreign peoples and foreign material culture. Early in the first millenium B.C., Iron Age Urnfield cemeteries and settlements were appearing in Catalonian Spain, and this may have had some impact on the material culture and population of Mallorca. From the fifth millenium B.C., Mallorquin mercenaries were recruited by Carthaginians, and their ability with the sling was well known.

Between c. 700 b.c. and c. 100 a.d., the entire site of Son Matge was used as a cemetery. The burial tradition used was inhumation in quicklime, a process that seems to have been restricted to the Balearics. Quickliming also bends the bones considerably, making any kind of osteological determination difficult. Later burials involved digging pits in the lime/bone matrix to bury more individuals and to recycle the quicklime, complicating the stratigraphy more. Obviously it is important to know how metal artifacts are affected by these processes. Lead, for instance, has a melting point of 327 degrees celsius. In some levels, all that remained of bronze objects was a green stain.

The most noticeable characteristic of the Post Talayotic metal assemblage is the increased number of objects and the increased variety of types, materials and techniques. Even when adjusted to take into account the time span covered by the different levels, metals are nearly twice as common in this period compared to previous periods. Half of the objects are now ornamental in character, but the number of raw types has increased considerably. The ability to combine individual pieces with other objects of a variety of materials is also marked.

In terms of the techniques used to produce these items, a greater variety and complexity is demonstrated. Delibes de Castro and Fernández-Miranda have demonstrated the coexistence of different alloys at this time, including ternary copper-tin-lead alloys. Iron appears first in a level dated to 780 ± 100 b.c. and becomes very common in the Post Talayotic quicklime inhumation levels. Fully two thirds (215/338) of the metal artifacts are of iron. Lead, which appears at a later date, is smelted to make a particular kind of pectoral or plaquette. Unfortunately, the confusing stratigraphy of the quicklime inhumations does not allow any further chronological subdivisions of the burials and the associated metals.

In bronze, common items include beads, rings, bracelets, spirals, and tintinabulums. It is significant that weapons such as swords and daggers are no longer made of bronze. A hoard of nearly 200 beads was discovered. Though nearly identical in basic form, the beads were not of the same size, fluctuating between 0.25 centimeters and 0.65 centimeters in length. Thin wire can be seen in several of the beads, suggesting that they were strung together. Most of these beads are very corroded and their method of manufacture could not be determined. Their importance may be overstated, however, since they are probably associated with a single burial. The rings come in a variety of types and sizes, some with with faces, and of various cross-sections. The bronze spirals are formed by twisting a strand of plano-convex wire into spirals of diameters ranging between under a centimeter to three centimeters.

A tintinabulum is a rod or bar connected by a chain to a flat disc that is normally decorated with a series of concentric ridges produced in the mold. These three elements of the tintinabulum are connected via a variety of mechanisms, including eyelets and hooks. It appears that the eyelets were not formed at the same time as the disc, but were soldered on later. However, it is difficult to determine this at this scale of analysis. Regardless, a variety of techniques went into t he production of these items. They have often been interpreted as symbols of authority or prestige and are found throughout Mallorca. Similar objects are known in the Punic settlement of Ibiza and in Carthage. In other Mallorcan burial sites, bells of a conical form with concentric incisions are known. These are common in the necropolis of Ibiza and in other Carthaginian contexts, and the bells may have been an important item in funerary rituals. Ensenat (1981) has suggested that the tintinabulums might have served a similar role although the tonal qualities of such a disc have not been investigated.

Objects in iron include bracelets, spirals, wire, rings, nails or stakes, daggers, knives, and a spear. These objects have not been analyzed but are presumably not carburized. Cast iron had not yet been developed in western Europe, and these objects would require a great deal of forging in order to form these shapes. The spirals are particularly interesting, often being shaped into the form of an ellipsoid. Some of the wire used to form these objects is hollow in cross-section, a very strange structure considering that these piece were hammered into shape from large blooms of iron metal and slag. Other ellipsoid and wire forms show a variety of structures visible to the naked eye suggesting that a variety of techniques were used to form similar objects. In addition, ellipsoids nearly identical to these iron ones are known in bronze from other sites in Mallorca. The swords and daggers are of two types, the centrally ribbed antenna-hilted sword and the single edge or afalcatada knife. The interpretation of these phenomenon is limited by the lack of knowledge about the location of production.

The lead pectorals or plaquettes of Mallorca and Menorca are very common in burial contexts and are apparently unique to the Balearics. They are flat with geometric motifs formed on the face and hooks or eyelets on the reverse that would allow them to be attached to thread, string or wire. Ensenat (1981) suggests that these objects were formed in simple bivalve molds with negative engraving. A number of flat molds with the face motifs are known, but the reverse sides which would be used to produce the eyelets have not been found. Instead, it appears from visual inspection that the plaquette itself was formed in a flat mold and the eyelet attached after the object had cooled. Again, this is just a hypothesis at this point. It is important to note that the pectorals are known from burial contexts only while the three molds that are known come from settlement contexts. A source of lead is known on the island of Mallorca. However, there has been no systematic survey of the area for evidence of mining or smelting. Droplets of lead from Son Matge may be evidence for production or the results of direct contact with the process of quicklime inhumation.

Although it is not completely clear which of these objects were produced in Mallorca and which were introduced from either Ibiza or other external regions, it is evident that the diversity of materials, techniques, and products is very high in this period. The increasing interaction of communities throughout the Mediterranean, in this case particularly among groups on Mallorca and the Punic-Ebusitano communities of Ibiza, stimulated this production and exchange. One strategy of the Phoenician and Carthaginian communities was the linking up of distinct production systems and the procurement of raw materials and finished goods (Frankenstein 1978). Tarradell (1974) suggests that indigenous communities in the Balearics were supplying foodstuffs to the Carthaginians. What was the Mallorquin response to the increased presence of foreign peoples and foreign material culture? One alternative is that people in Mallorca developed new traditions and techniques, such as lead smelting and quicklime inhumation. These were not for export, nor were they simply for maintaining group boundaries relative to the Carthaginians and Punic-Ebusitanos. Instead, they became part of Mallorcan life, particularly in funerary ritual. Other items, such as tintinabulums, were assimilated and developed and made suitable to the Mallorcan context.

CONCLUSIONS

In some ways, the changes in metallurgy demonstrated by the materials from Son Matge are typical, even exemplary, of sequences in much of Europe. For instance, from the Copper Age to the Bronze Age and from the Bronze Age to the Iron Age, there is an increasing sophistication of metallurgical technology and possibly an increasing specialization of production. Although such trends "make sense" given our understanding and assumptions about technological and cultural evolution, the conditions in which these processes occur and the specific details of their development are rarely considered. When the specific process of, for example, the gradual replacement of bronze by iron in the early first millenium B.C. in Mallorca is compared to that of mainland Spain, a number of substantial differences are likely to appear. These differences will show how different communities negotiated changes in their metallurgical traditions in different ways. This will provide a richer and more dynamic picture of prehistoric Europe. In addition, such an investigation can show how people define and redefine the cultural place and meaning of technology and production and the role of material items in their social contexts.

BIBLIOGRAPHY

Almagro Basch, M. 1940. El hallazgo de la Ria de Huelva y el final de la Edad del Bronce en el Occidente de Europa. *Ampurias* II, pp. 85-143.

Almagro Gorbea, M. 1977. El Bronce Final y el Periodo Orientalizante en Extremadura. *Biblioteca Praehistórica Hispana* XIV. Madrid.

Bosch Gimpera, P. 1954. La Edad del Bronce en la Península Iberica. *Archivo Español de Arqueología* XXVII: pp. 45-92.

Braudel, Fernand. 1972. *The Mediterranean and the Mediterranean World in the Age of Philip II, volume I.* New York: Harper and Row.

Chapman, R. W. 1984. Early Metallurgy in Iberia and the Western Mediterranean: Innovation, Adoption and Production. In *The Deyá Conference of Prehistory*. Edited by William Waldren, et al., pp. 1139-1165. Oxford: B.A.R.

Delibes de Castro, German and Manuel Fernández-Miranda. 1984. Metalurgia Balear de la Edad del Bronce: Hachas de Cubo, de Talon y de Apendices Laterales. In *The Deyá Conference of Prehistory*, edited by William Waldren et al, pp. 998-1026. Oxford: B.A.R.

Delibes de Castro, German and Manuel Fernández-Miranda. 1988. *Armas y utensilios de bronce en la Prehistoria de las Baleares.* Studia Archaeologica 78. Valladolid: Universidad de Valladolid.

Enseñat Enseñat, Catalina. 1981. Las Cuevas Sepulcrales Mallorquines de la Edad del Hierro. *Excavaciones Arqueologicas en España* 117. Madrid: Ministerio de Cultura.

Fernández-Miranda, Manuel. 1978. *Secuencia Cultural de la Prehistoria de Mallorca.* Biblioteca Praehistorica Hispana vol. XV. Madrid.

Fernández-Miranda, Manuel and William H. Waldren. 1974. El abrigo de Son Matge (Valldemosa) y la periodización de la perhistoria mallorquina mediante los analisis de carbono-14. *Trabajos de Prehistoria* 31:297-304.

Fernández-Miranda, Manuel and William H. Waldren. 1979. Periodificación cultural y cronología absoluta en la Prehistoria de Mallorca. *Trabajos de Prehistoria* 36:349-378.

Frankenstein, Susan. 1978. The Phoenicians in the far West: a function of Assyrian imperialism. In *Power and Propaganda*. Edited by M.T. Larsen, pp. 263-94. Copenhagen.

Gasull, Pepa, Vicente Lull and Maria Encarna Sanahuja. 1984a. Estudio Comparativo de los Talaiots no. 1 y 2 de Son Fornés (Montuiri-Mallorca). In *The Deyá Conference of Prehistory*, pp. 1239-68. Oxford: B.A.R.

Gasull, Pepa, Vicente Lull, and Ma. Encarna Sanahuja. 1984b. *Son Fornés I: La Fase Talayotica.* Oxford: B.A.R.

Guerrero Ayuso, Victor M. 1984. *Asentamiento Punico de Na Guardis*. Excavaciones Arqueologicas en España. Madrid.

Harrison, Richard J. 1974b. A Reconsideration of the Iberian Background to Beaker Metallurgy. *Palaeohistoria* 16:64-106.

Harrison, R.J. and P.T. Craddock. 1981. A Study of the Bronze Age Metalwork from the Iberian Peninsula in the British Musuem. *Ampurias* LXIV:113-79. Barcelona.

Hook, D.R., A. Arribas Palau, P.T. Craddock, F. Molina and B. Rothenberg. 1987. Copper and Silver in Bronze Age Spain. In *Bell Beakers of the Western Mediterranean*. Edited by W. Waldren and R.C. Kennard, pp. 147-72. Oxford: B.A.R.

Instituto Geologico y Minero de España. 1973. *Mallorca-Cabrera, Mapa Metalogenetico de España*, Escala 1:200.000.

Lechtman, Heather. 1977. Style in Technology -- Some Early Thoughts. In *Material Culture: Styles, Organization, and Dynamics of Technology*. Edited by Heather Lechtman and Robert S. Merrill, pp. 3-20. St. Paul, Minn: West Publishing Co.

Lechtman, Heather. 1984. Andean Value Systems and the Development of Prehistoric Metallurgy. *Technology and Culture* 25(1):1-36.

Lechtman, Heather and Robert S. Merrill. Editors. 1977. *Material Culture: Styles, Organization, and Dynamics of Technology*. St. Paul, Minn: West Publishing Co.

Lemonnier, Pierre. 1986. The Study of Material Culture Today: Toward an Anthropology of Technical Systems. *Journal of Anthropological Archaeology* 5:147-86.

Mascaró Pasarius, J. Editor. 1978. *Historia de Mallorca*. Palma de Mallorca.

Mayoral Franco, Florencio. 1984. La Fase Postalayotica Mallorquina: Periodización y Dinámica Económico-Sociál. In *The Deyá Conference of Prehistory*, pp. 1299-314. Oxford: B.A.R.

Monteagudo, L. 1977. *Die Beile auf der Iberischen Halbinsel*. Prehistorische Bronzefunde IX, 6. Munich.

Pericot Garcia, L. 1972. *The Balearic Islands*. London: Thames & Hudson.

Rosselló-Bordóy, G. 1974. Los ajuares metálicos mallorquines como elemento cronológico. *In Prehistoria y Arquelogía de las Islas Baleares*, VI Symposium de Prehistoria Peninsular, pp. 115-28. Publicaciones Eventuales, 24. Barcelona: Universidad de Barcelona.

Rosselló-Bordóy, G. 1987. Metalurgia en el Pretalayótico Final de Mallorca. *Archivo Prehistoria Levantina* XVIII. pp. 147.

Rosselló-Bordóy, G. and William H. Waldren. 1973. Excavaciones en el abrigo del Bosque de Son Matge (Valldemosa, Mallorca). *Noticiario de Arqueologico Hispánico* 2: pp. 211.

Sackett, James R. 1985. Style and Ethnicity in the Kalahari: A Reply to Wiessner. *American Antiquity* 50(1): 154-59.

Tarradell, M. 1974. Ibiza púnica: algunos problemas actuales. *Prehistoria y Arqueología de las Islas Baleares*, Publicaciones Eventuales 24:243-268.

Topp, Celia. 1987. Further Considerations of the Beaker Phenomenon. In *Bell Beakers of the Western Mediterranean*. Edited by W. Waldren and R.C. Kennard, pp. 19-22. Oxford: B.A.R.

Tylecote, R. F. 1987. *The early history of metallurgy in Europe*. London: Longman.

Veny, Cristobal. 1968. *Las cuevas sepulcrales del Bronce Antiguo en Mallorca*. Biblioteca Praehistorica Hispaña IX. Madrid.

Veny, Cristobal. 1984. Cuatro hipogeos naviformes del Bronce antiguo balear. *Trabajos de Prehistoria* 41:209-36.

Waldren, W. 1979. A Beaker Workshop Area in the Rock Shelter of Son Matge, Valldemosa, Mallorca. *World Archaeology* 11(1):43-67.

Waldren, W. 1982. *Balearic Prehistoric Ecology and Culture: The Excavation and Study of Certain Caves, Rock Shelters and Settlements*. Oxford: B.A.R. 149.

Waldren, W. 1984. Chalcolithic Settlement and Beaker Connections in the Balearic Islands. In *The Deyá Conference of Prehistory:*, edited by William Waldren et al, pp. 911-966. Oxford: B.A.R.

Waldren, W. 1986. *The Balearic Pentapartite Division of Prehistory*. Oxford: B.A.R.

Waldren, William H. 1987. A Balearic Beaker Model: Ferrandéll-Oleza, Valldemosa, Mallorca, Spain. In *Bell Beakers of the Western Mediterranean*. Edited by W. Waldren and R.C. Kennard, pp. 207-66. Oxford: B.A.R.

Wiessner, Polly. 1985. Style or Isochrestic Variation? A Reply to Sackett. *American Antiquity* 50(1):160-66.

ARCHAEOLOGICAL TECHNIQUES, TECHNOLOGY AND THEORY

OBSERVACIONES SOBRE LOS SANTUARIOS TALAYOTICOS MALLORQUINES

VICTOR M. GUERRERO AYUSO
Palma de Mallorca
Baleares, España.

RESUMEN

Revisión actualizada de los santurarios Talayóticos como uno de los principales lugares de culto, aunque no los únicos, cuya aparación coincide con todo un complejo de aculturación.

Intento de interpretación funcional, tanto del recinto sacro como de sus áreas complementarias en el exterior de los mismos (zonas de sacrificios, pozos, cisternas, estanques, etc.).

Sus paralelos dentro de la cultura fenicio/púnica, tanto en lo que se refiere a sus aspectos estructurales como funcionales y rituales.

Observaciones Sobre Los Santuarios Talayóticos Mallorquines
Victor M. Guerrero Ayuso

Una de las cuestiones que parece fuera de discusión entre los investigadores dedicados al estudio de la cultura talayótica de Mallorca es el carácter de recinto sacro de algunas construcciones indígenas cuyas cararacterísticas arquitectónicas comentaremos más adelante. En principio es obligado señalar que en ningún caso constituye el unico lugar sagrado adoptado por los indígenas mallorquines del Talayótico III-IV (Rosselló, 1972; 1979), antes al contrario, con toda seguridad los lugares de culto presentan una multiforme pluralidad de ambientes (Guerrero, 1985:126-132; 1986:370-374), entre los que tienen no poca importancia los espacios naturales que, sin aditamentos antrópicos, debían tener una especial significación religiosa para la comunidad indígena. Ello es una constante en todas las religiones mediterráneas y nada tiene de original su existencia en la cultura talayótica, por mucho que la documentación arqueológica tenga dificultades en evidenciarlos, dada la falta de estructuras arquitectónicas que puedan identificar con claridad este tipo de yacimientos de carácter cultural.

El santuario talayótico, es pues uno más de los lugares de culto en la sociedad talayótica, sin embargo no tiene precedentes, desde un punto de vista formal, en la arquitectura talayótica de las fases iniciales. Esta situación nos lleva a pensar que su aparición no tuvo lugar por generación espontánea, ni fruto de la evolución de estructuras anteriores, sino que nuevas necesidades de culto estimularon la creación de un recinto sagrado con características propias. En el estado actual de nuestros conocimientos, no es posible discernir si se debe a la introducción de un culto totalmente nuevo adoptado de una mitología extranjera o si es consecuencia de la evolución sincrética de un sustrato mitológico indígena, motivada, no obstante, por los contactos con los pueblos colonizadores preromanos del Mediterráneo Occidental. Ambas posiciones nos llevan a un mismo punto de partida, que la aparición del santuario talayótico se inscribe en un complejo proceso de aculturación que afecta a todos los aspectos de la formación social talayótica.

El factor clave de este proceso de aculturación, aunque seguramente no el único, es la aparición de asentamientos púnicos en la costa (Guerrero, 1948a; 1984b; 1985), expresión material evidente de una colonización que, teniendo características peculiares (Guerrero, 1987b), necesariamente actúa como motor principal de este proceso histórico. La salida al exterior de importantes contingentes mercenarios indígenas y la posible presencia de guarniciones militares cartaginesas en la isla (Guerrero, 1988) son factores nada despreciables a tener en cuenta como elementos dinamizadores de la aculturación indígena, que se inscribe, no obstante, dentro de una "koiné" claramente púnica centromediterránea.

El sustrato cultural talayótico y su capacidad de asimilación de nuevas pautas culturales, es un elemento que siempre hemos considerado sustancial en el proceso de aculturación, en consecuencia, a los efectos que aquí nos interesa, damos por sabido que no es aceptable interpretar los cambios habidos en la mitología talayótica y en sus manifestaciones litúrgicas, como una aceptación pura y simple de mitos y rituales extranjeros, sino la evolución sincrética de unas creencias indígenas que, sin duda, tenían en sus orígenes muchos elementos comunes con las religiones agrarias y pastoriles del Próximo Oriente y el Egeo, entre ellas, por ejemplo, la simbología taurolátrica.

LA ARQUITECTURA SACRA

Una de las características comunes a todos los edificios talayóticos, hasta ahora identificados como santuarios, es que se trata de construcciones exentas, aparecen aisladas y sin adosamientos dentro del poblado, seguramente porque los exteriores y principalmente la fachada eran utilizados en celebraciones litúrgicas. Existen en la cultura talayótica otro tipo de recintos que con toda seguridad tenían también una finalidad sacra, los cuales aparecen adosados o formando parte de otras estructuras arquitectónicas y en esencia no presentan ninguna característica formal que los diferencie de las edificaciones con función de hábitat; sólo la naturaleza de los hallazgos nos permite asegurar que estamos ante un recinto sacro, el ejemplo mas elocuente es el de Son Favar (Amorós y García Bellido, 1974) y es posible que también sea el caso de Son Carrió (Amorós, 1944-46).

El número de santuarios por poblado no sigue una regla fija, aunque de todas formas es una cuestión difícil de tratar debido al escaso número de poblados que han sido exhaustivamente explorados en su integridad. En muchos poblados no ha sido posible constatar su existencia pero, por la razón antes expuesta, este dato no puede tenerse por definitivo; en otros casos, como Ses Antigors (Colominas, 1915-20:725-726), Son Oms (Rosselló, 1984) o Es Fornets (Guerrero, 1982:161-166), está plenamente confirmada la existencia, al menos, de un santuario. En el poblado de S'Illot se ha identificado la existencia de dos construcctiones, aún por excavar, con sus fachadas enfrentadas, que responden perfectamente a la estructura arquitectónica del santuario talayótico (Rosselló y Frey, 1966), pero el caso más singular de todos lo constituye el poblado de Almallutx que dispone de tres santuarios idénticos entre sí, aunque con notas peculiares que los diferencian de los hasta ahora conocidos en el resto de la isla (Fernández-Miranda, Ensenyat y Ensenyat, 1971). El hecho tiene, a nuestro juicio, una importancia notable, pues se hace muy difícil pensar que respondan a las necesidades de culto de una comunidad extremadamente pobre; a no ser que admitamos que todo el yacimiento de Almallutx cumpliese funciones de lugar sacro colectivo para diferentes comunidades indígenes de la isla. El paraje de alta montaña, donde se sitúan estos tres santuarios, pudo tener, ya de forma natural, una cierta significación mitológica, en la línea de los "altos lugares" de las religiones semitas y especialmente la fenicia.

En sociedades contemporáneas a la talayótica y con similares influencias culturales, es un fenómeno bastante extendido la existencia de lugares sagrados utilizados por diferentes comunidades indígenas, seguramente con celebraciones litúrgicas conjuntas. En Ibiza podría ser el caso del santuario rupestre de Es Cuieram (Aubet, 1982; Ramón 1982; 1985), o Grotta Regina en Sicilia (Bisi, Guzzo y Tusa, 1969); en cierto modo paralelos a los santuarios rurales ibéricos (Blázquez, 1983), cretenses (Foure, 1967) o chipriotas (Karageorghis, 1970; 1973), que también están presentes en la religión púnica (Grottanelli, 1981:109-133). El yacimiento menorquín de So Na Caçana, con varios recintos de taula, de los que L. Plantalamor ha excavado algunos, es también un buen ejemplo de "territorio sagrado" utilizado conjuntamente por diversas comunidades indígenas.

El santuario talayótico mallorquín es una edificación de planta cuadrada o rectangular con los ejes poco diferenciados; sin subdivisiones internas. Este simple esquema arquitectónico presenta modificaciones que afectan sobre todo a la fachada posterior, unas veces marcadamente absidial, como el de Son Marí (Guerrero, 1983) o Son Mas, en vias de excavación por el equipo de W. Waldren; otras totalmente rectas, como en los casos de Almallutx. Entre estos dos extremos se dan también los ejemplares con planta absidial atenuada, como los de S'Illot, o simplemente con las esquinas posteriores romas, como los casos de Ses Antigors o Es Fornets de Santa Ponsa.

El portal se abre siempre en la fachada opuesta al abside, en ocasiones de forma excéntrica como ocurre en Almallutx y en Es Fornets. La entrada se marca siempre con unas losas a modo de umbral o varios escalones descendentes como en Son Marí (Guerrero, 1983: lam. XXXIV-XXXV).

La construcción misma del santuario, así como de sus elementos, en apariencia, más insignificantes, están sujetos en todas las religiones antiguas a prescripciones muy rigurosas y tienen un alto valor mítico. Así, el umbral tiene una gran importancia simbólica en su función separadora entre lo profano, al exterior y lo sagrado, delimitado por el muro o vallado del santuario, en el interior. Es proverbial en las religiones semitas el complicado ritual y las estrictas normas relativas a la entrada en los templos (Eliade, 1981:370 y sig.).

Algunos santuarios, como el de Son Mas y el de Pla de Ses Arenes de Formentor (Encinas, 1981:129), tienen la fachada principal cóncava, detalle arquitectónico que los aproxima a las taulas menorquinas.

Este esquema arquitectónico se rompe con el santuario de Son Oms (Rosselló, 1984) cuya planta tiene forma rectangular irregular y el portal se abre en uno de los lados mayores del edificio.

Ningún santuario talayótico ha conservado elementos estructurales que nos permitan aventurar una hipótesis fundada sobre el tipo de cubierta. Las columnas, por las razones que luego expondremos, no son por sí solas un dato suficiente para presuponer la existencia de una cubierta. A nuestro juicio, los santuarios talayóticos debieron constituir, en origen, recintos a cielo abierto (Guerrero, 1983,:326), que constituye una tradición genuina de los recintos sacros semitas (Moscati, 1960:117) esta tradición se extiende posteriormente a todas las zonas de influencia fenicia y púnica (Barreca, 1987:249 y sig.); la estructura arquitectónica de estos recintos es sumamente sencilla, en esencia un muro de altura variable que delimita el lugar sacro y en cuyo interior se instala un ara y varios betilos en forma de tambores de columna. Dentro de este recinto se realizan las ofrendas, libaciones y sacrificios de animales, en cuya litúrgia está siempre presente el fuego, necesario para la incineración de las ofrendas animales o la cocción de los mismos que luego serán consumidos en el "refrigerium" sacro, según unas reglas canónicas muy rigurosas.

Seguramente el santuario talayótico obedece a este esquema, que en realidad es la arquitectura sacra más elemental y antigua que se conoce, aunque naturalmente la religión fenicio/púnica cuenta también con otro tipo de santuarios arquitectónicamente más complejos, con disposición tripartita y cubierta, que en época helenística, sobre todo, incorporarán elementos típicos de la arquitectura griega. Este otro tipo de santuario se extiende también de Oriente a Occidente, donde el Herakleion gaditano constituiría uno de los ejemplos más afamados (García Bellido, 1958; Blázquez, 1977), pero otros más anónimos están también presentes en el área de dominio cultural púnico y, desde luego, en las islas próximas de Sicilia (Fiorentini, 1980), y Córcega (Acquaro, 1983:629). Pero aún así, la combinación de estructuras con cubiertas y áreas a cielo abierto es una constante en los santuarios donde se celebraban ofrendas de animales en cuyo ritual debían de ser quemados o cocinados; en los dos santuarios siciliotas de Adranone esta situación es bien patente (Fiorentini, 1980), la gran nave central del templo de la acrópoli es una estancia rectangular a cielo descubierto con grandes pilastras rituales en el centro, por el contrario, las salas anexas, donde no se celebraban sacrificios, tenían una cubierta a doble vertiente, como lo indica el hallazgo de tégulas, un fragmento de tímpano y un elemento de gola egípcia. El segundo complejo sacro de esta misma ciudad púnica siciliota estaba también compuesto por un templo con una gran nave rectangular a cielo descubierto, de igual forma estaba provista de dos betilos en forma de pilastra sobre base cuadrada de arenisca y un ara (Fiorentini, 1980:913, Figura 16).

En cualquier caso esta arquitectura sacra más compleja no parece que tuvo ninguna influencia en la cultura talayótica, por lo tanto es necesario reconducir el tema hacia los recintos sacros de estructura simple.

En todos los santuarios talayóticos, que han podido ser excavados con rigurosidad metodológica, están bien documentados los restos de cremaciones rituales que se extienden a todo el ámbito del recinto sacro; por ello la naturaleza de edificio a cielo descubierto del santuario no obedece sólo a tradiciones de índole mitológica, sino, y muy especialmente, a cuestiones de necesidad física, que hacen muy difícil o imposible, sin peligro para los oficiantes, verificar cremaciones en el interior de un espacio reducido y cerrado.

En relación directa con el problema de la existencia o no de la cubierta están las columnas. En la mayor parte de los santuarios es muy dudoso que tengan una función arquitectónica de sosten de la cubierta; salvo excepciones sólo se ha podido documentar la existencia del tambor inferior. En muchos santuarios la disposición y número de las supuestas columnas indican claramente que no constituían un elemento arquitectónico, así, por ejemplo, en Costitx disponía de trece, de las cuales once se sitúan en la mitad Oeste del recinto (Ferrá, 1895-1896:85-89). En Son Marí y en Ses Antigors algunos de estos tambores de columna aparecen adosados a los muros, con lo que su funcionalidad arquitectónica es nula. Para el santuario de Son Oms se ha planteado la hipótesis de una cubierta arquitrabada con losas planas sostenidas por muros y columnas (Rosselló, 1984:8-10), pero no es en absoluto seguro que las losas pertenezcan a la cubierta y si, tal vez, a un enlosado procedente de algunas de las readaptaciones que sufrió el monumento (Rosselló, 1984:8). De las columnas documentadas en Son Oms, seis en total, una sóla era monolítica con una altura de 2,30 m., de las otras cinco sólo se ha documentado la existencia de un tambor, con dimensiones muy discretas como para aguantar una cubierta de losas. En torno a estos tambores aparecieron numerosas ofrendas de cuernos de cápridos (Rosselló y Camps, 1971:302), lo que, a nuestro juicio, acentúa claramente el carácter de elemento ritual y no arquitectónico de las mismas.

Un caso excepcional viene representado por los santuarios de Almallutx, los tres disponían de una sola columna central trilítica, dos grandes tambores y un tercer bloque a modo de rústico capitel, en los tres santuarios sobrepasan de los tres metros de altura. La excavación no proporcionó ningún rastro de cubierta y los autores de la misma mantienen la hipótesis de que se trata de un elemento de culto y no arquitectónico (Fernández-Miranda, Ensenyat y Ensenyat, 1971:110-111) con la que estamos plenamente de acuerdo.

La columna, como es bien sabido, tiene en las religiones orientales un significado mitológico bien determinado que arrancaría del "Djed" o columna sagrada egípcia, adoptada por los fenicios, su simbolismo mitológico se extendió hasta el Extremo Occidente. A nuestro juicio, los tambores de columna que frecuentemente aparecen en los santuarios indígenas estarían más próximas a la idea del betilo fenicio que de ninguna otra. Columnas con función ritual están documentadas por las fuentes escritas en el Herakleion gaditano (García Bellido, 1958) y se conocen ejemplares aislados que se han interpretado como aras (Blázquez, 1975:lam. 156b; Cintas, 1976:lam XC, 10-11). También en Ibiza existen pequeños monolitos de arenisca en forma de columnas o aras rituales (Fernandez, 1983:lam. IV). Los dos edificios sacros de Monte Adranone disponían en la sala de los sacrificios de sendas parejas de "tambores de columnas" con señales de cremación en el plano superior de las mismas (Fiorentini, 1980:910) lo que indica claramente su función de elemento litúrgico y no estructural. En la iconografía religiosa púnica, manifestada en las estelas, es frecuentísimo el tema de la tríada de betilos en forma de pilastras.

La litúrgia sacra no se celebraba exclusivamente en el interior del santuario, sino que con toda seguridad los exteriores del mismo cumplían un papel importante. Desgraciadamente son muy escasos los santuarios excavados y nada sabemos de los hallazgos en el exterior. En el estudio de Almallutx, ya citado, no se menciona nada referente a la excavación del área externa, todo parece indicar que no se llegó a excavar. El estudio completo de Son Oms permanece aún inédito. El resto de los santuarios conocidos, o no han sido excavados, o lo fueron en épocas en las que el rigor metodológico, tanto en la excavación como en la publicación de los resultados, no era precisamente la nota característica de la actividad arqueológica. Por ello todas las esperanzas están centradas ahora en los resultados de la excavación del santuario de Son Mas por el equipo de W. Waldren que, con buen criterio, ha prestado igual interés al interior del recinto y a su área circundante. La excavación no está concluida y es prematuro opinar sobre los hallazgos, pero por lo que amablemente nos ha podido mostrar sobre el terreno W. Waldren, parece fuera de toda duda que los sacrificios de animales, con ritual de fuego, se celebraban igualmente en el área externa de la fachada. Varios grandes bloques de roca natural, en torno a los cuales se acumulaban ofrendas y señales de fuego intenso, debieron tener un claro simbolismo sacro.

La inclusión de bloques de roca natural sin retocar entre los elementos rituales del recinto sacro es una nota frecuente en los santuarios púnicos, está muy bien documentado en las estructuras sacras de la acrópolis de Adranone (Fiorentini, 1980), su valor simbólico puede ser equivalente a los betilos. Al igual que en Adranone, en Son Mas, varias de estas rocas naturales están unidas por muretes que delimitan un espacio de utilización sacra.

Entre los elementos auxiliares de culto, que suelen aparecer en el área externa de los santuarios púnicos, no falta la cisterna, cada santuario disponía, al menos, de una, normalmente de forma rectangular poco profunda, la tienen los dos recintos sacros de Adranone, ya citados, e igualmente la tenía el santuario rupestre púnico ebusitano de Es Cuieram (Ramón, 1982; 1985), el agua y el fuego constituyen dos de los factores más constantes de la litúrgia púnica.

Los pozos sagrados o fosas rituales constituyen junto con la cisterna otros elementos frecuentes entre las estructuras complementarias de los recintos sacros, por el momento no sabemos si los santuarios talayóticos se dotaron de ellos, pero entra dentro de los muy posible.

LA LITURGIA

Uno de los elementos comunes en todos los santuarios talayóticos es el sacrificio de animales con la presencia de fuego en el ritual. En Ses Antigors los restos de sacrificios correspondían exclusivamente a mandíbulas de verracos y machos cabríos (Colominas, 1915-1920:725), las mismas especies fueron sacrificadas en Son Marí (Guerrero, 1983), en Son Oms se ofrendaron básicamente cuernos de machos cabríos, entre otras especies que restan por analizar (Rosselló y Camps, 1971:302). En Almallutx son también los restos de cápridos los más abundantes, algunos de los cuales aparecieron en el interior de vasijas indígenas. Del santuario-1 de Almallutx disponemos del único estudio estadístico realizado hasta el presente, que arroja los siguientes datos:

Los fragmentos identificables son:

> Cabeza de fémur de cerdo.
> Fragmento de mandíbula inferior de oveja con cuatro piezas dentarias.
> Gran número de incisivos de oveja y cabra.

Molares de cerdo.
Fémur de roedor.
Cinco costillas de oveja.
Ocho vértebras dorsales de oveja.
Grand abundancia de huesos pertenecientes a las extremidades de ovejas y cabras.
Varios fragmentos indeterminables de bóvido.

Porcentaje del edificio:

67,5% de oveja.
14,2% de cabra.
17,1% de cerdo.
2,5% de bóvidos.

El estudio de los restos de sacrificios de Son Mas arrojará, sin duda, datos muy reveladores, aunque en líneas generales parece seguir la misma tónica ya expuesta para otros santuarios en cuanto a especies sacrificadas. Convendrá prestar mucha atención a la estadística relacionada con las partes de los animales que aparecen en mayor porcentaje, pues todos los datos apuntan a que, entre las especies más aptas para los sacrificios, -cápridos, óvidos, verracos y bóvidos-, algunas porciones del animal revestían especial importancia en el ritual. Sin duda los cráneos, mandíbulas inferiores de verracos y cuernos, son los restos más frecuentes y los que aparecen depositados con más esmero en torno a las supuestas bases de columnas, en el interior de vasos y en las aras de piedra.

En el ritual, como ya se ha dicho, intervenía el uso del fuego, así lo indican las potentes señales de cremación que aparecen en el interior de todos los recintos sacros talayóticos hasta ahora excavados y, a juzgar por lo que ocurre en Son Mas, este ritual se celebraba también en la esplanada que se extiende en la fachada del santuario.

Todo parece indicar que estamos ante un ritual relacionado con la fertilidad de los ganados y de las personas, a juzgar por las especies sacrificadas. Este hecho es común a diversas culturas mediterráneas y sin duda los fenicios actuaron de agente catalizador de este tipo de litúrgia; sin perjuicio de que determinados ritos de fertilidad, con sacrificio de toros y otros animales machos, estuviesen ya enraizados en los cultos indígenas anteriores al proceso de aculturación colonial más tardío.

Por lo que respecta a dos de las especies más significativas sacrificadas en los santuarios talayóticos, ovejas y cabras, vale la pena constatar su permanente presencia en el rito fenicio-cartaginés del "mlk", celebrado en los tofets, bien sea companãndo a los neonatos humanos o como elemento sustitutorio de los mismos. Decisivos análisis realizados recientemente en Cartago y Tharros (Fedele y Foster, 1988) ponen en evidencia varias cuestiones a destacar: en primer lugar que los animales sacrificados son siempre, salvo rarísima excepción, un ovicaprino o un cordero (Ovis Aries L.) neonatos (de 0 a más o menos 6 meses). Otra cuestión remarcable es el carácter estacional de los ritos, en concreto primaveral, el 91% de los sacrificios se celebraron en torno a 50 días tomando como centro el uno de marzo. Parece imponerse la idea de una celebración anual regida por el calendario lunar, sin duda en estrecha relación con el carácter astral de la divinidad y sus atributos referidos al ciclo vital de la vegetación y de la fecundidad.

El idéntico ritual empleado en el sacrificio, tanto si se trata de neonato humano como animal, aboga en favor del carácter de lugar sacro del tofet y no funerario (Fedele y Foster, 1988). Algún autor ha señalado también que el "mlk" debía de ser una celebración nocturna (Barreca, 1987:158), lo que en cierta forma enlazaría con la celebración periódica según el calendario lunar y tendría su reflejo iconográfico o simbólico en la proliferación sobre las estelas de los tofets del creciente lunar.

Un poema ugarítico nos refiere como el rey Kéret ofrece al Dios un sacrificio propiciatorio "...Tomo un cordero de sacrificio en una mano, /un cabrito en entrambas, /todo el resto del pan; /tomó las vísceras de un pájaro de sacrificio, /en una taza de plata derramó vino, /en una copa de oro miel; /...levantó sus manos al cielo /y sacrificó al toro..." (Pritchard, 1955:144).

En esencia todos los elementos ofrendados al dios, incluida la libación de vino y miel, se repiten, juntos o por separado, en muchos pasajes bíblicos, en uno de ellos se relata un sacrificio relacionado con la fertilidad de la mujer, en agradecimiento por la concepción de un hijo, se sacrifica un toro de tres años acompañado de una ofrenda de harina y vino (I Samuel, 1, 20-28). En los santuarios chipriotas son frecuentes los sacrificios de animales con cuerno, como en Ayia Irini y Enkomi, igual ocurre en los santuarios rurales cretenses, como Dreros con depósito de cuernos de cabra. En Occidente se documenta una litúrgia muy similar en el santuario de Cástulo, con toda seguridad introducida por los finicios (Blázquez, 1986:57-61). El mismo ritual a base de uso intenso de fuego y numerosas ofrendas animales, aunque desconocemos las especies concretas sacrificadas, se observa en los dos santuarios púnicos siciliotas de Adranone (Fiorentini, 1980). También el santuario rupestre púnico ebusitano de Es Cuieram registró una gruesa capa de cenizas y carbones con restos de animales procedentes de sacrificios, mezclados con las conocidas terracotas propias de este santuario (Aubet, 1982:47).

Parece claro que el ritual sacro celebrado en los santuarios talayóticos, al igual que ocurre en otras religiones contemporáneas del Mediterráneo, estaba sujeto a unas reglas muy precisas cuyos detalles se nos escapan, aunque, con muchas reservas, se puede recurrir a ciertos paralelos para ilustrarlo. Desde un punto de vista gráfico, resulta interesantísima la escena reproducida en la terracota chipriota de Vounous, que representa un recinto sacro a cielo descubierto donde varios oficiantes se disponen a sacrificar dos toros (Karageorghis, 1978:35, Figura 23). Otra terracota, también chipriota, procedente de la necrópolis de Kotchati, reproduce una escena ritual en la que aparecen tres pilastras (o tríada de betilos) coronadas por cabezas de toros, entre ellas y sobre la pared del santuario, se sitúan dos cuernos sueltos de toro. A los pies del betilo central, un oficiante efectúa libaciones en una gran vasija (Karageorghis, 1978:35, Figura 22). No es posible dejar de recordar aquí los hallazgos de las tres cabezas de Costitx, acompañadas también de cuernos sueltos, cuya disposición y uso en el santuario talayótico pudo ser efectivamente similar. Esta tríada taurolátrica se repite también en un carro votivo cretense de terracota (Andronicos, 1978:55, Figura 56). Otra ilustración gráfica interesante está reflejada en el "pinax" votivo de la gruta corintia de Pitsa, con una escena en la que se va a sacrificar un cordero mientras se efectuan libaciones sobre un ara y se tocan instrumentos musicales (Karouzou, 1980:135).

Entre los abundantes pasajes bíblicos que relatan escenas de sacrificios, merece la pena recordar las reglas del sacrificio eucarístico (Levítico 3, 1-17), según las cuales las reses a sacrificar son degolladas a la entrada del tabernáculo, la sangre se derrama en torno al altar. El sebo, junto con los riñones y el lomo se incineran en honor a Yavé; si el animal sacrificado es un cordero, a ello se añadirá el rabo. En otras celebraciones en las que se sacrifica un novillo se sigue básicamente el mismo ritual, pero la piel, las carnes, la cabeza, las piernas, las entrañas y los excrementos se quemarán fuera "en el lugar donde se tiran las cenizas" (Levítico, 4, 3-12). El relato, que es muy minucioso y contempla sacrificios por diferentes causas, nos pone en guardia sobre la necesidad de investigar detenidamente las partes de animales sacrificadas en el interior de los recintos sacros talayóticos y su distribución microespacial, si es posible; igualmente convendrá saber si los restos de sacrificios en el exterior del santuario coinciden o complementan las porciones del animal sacrificado en el interior. Por desgracia estos datos se han perdido en las excavaciones antiguas, pero afortunadamente podrá documentarse en la excavación de Son Mas.

La cocción de animales para el consumo en el ágape ritual por los oficiantes y fieles está también documentado en el santuario de Cástulo (Blázquez, 1986:56-62), e igualmente pudo ser el origen de las señales de cremación que aparecen en los santuarios talayóticos, donde seguramente no todo el animal era incinerado, pues los restos de sacrificios que hemos podido estudiar en Son Marí no presentan señales de incineracióon, aunque tal vez pudieron ser cocinados y consumidos in situ. Los cuchillos de hierro que aparecen en este santuario, entre el ajuar litúrgico, pudieron usarse efectivamente en el despiece de las reses sacrificadas (Guerrero, 1983:303, Figura 20).

Es seguro que junto con el sacrificio de animales se hacían también ofrendas de alimentos vegetales y líquidos. La libación es un acto litúrgico igualmente universalizado de Oriente a Occidente, que consiste en la ofrenda de líquidos mediante su vertido sobre el ara, betilo, etc., procediéndose después a romper intencionadamente los vasos usados en la libación, arrojándolos contra el suelo. Es posible que el vaso talayótico empleado en este ritual sea la copa crestada, que constituye el recipiente más característico y abundante de los santuarios, apenas aparece en los lugares de habitat y en proporción más discreta se encuentra en algunas necrópolis.

Relacionados con este tipo de ritual deben estar los hallazgos de aras de arenisca como la de Son Oms, o las once que aparecieron en Ses Antigors, seguramente urnas de arenisca idénticas a las de la necrópolis infantil de Cas Santamarier (Rosselló y Guerrero, 1983). También la sala contigua a la de los sacrificios en el santuario de Adranone disponía de una series de urnas de arenisca (Fiorentini, 1980:Figura 12-14). La posibilidad de que las urnas de Ses Antigors contuviesen restos de niños de muy corta edad, como ocurre en Cas Santamarier, no se ha podido comprobar, pero en el santuario-1 de Almallutx se localizó una mandíbula infantil en el interior de un vaso. La ofrenda de los despojos de niños muertos prematuramente a la divinidad entra dentro también de los esquemas rituales propiciatorios de la fecundidad, probablemente uno de los aspectos de la religión fenicia más conocidos y extendidos.

La inhumaciones, tal vez rituales, en recintos sacros está también documentada en el mundo ibérico; el ejemplo más claro lo tenemos en el recinto rectangular de La Escudilla (Gusi, 1970), que dispone de un hogar central cuadrado delimitado por losas, donde seguramente se preparaban las ofrendas y un betilo situado delante de este hogar sacrificial. Las inhumaciones se habían efectuado en urnas que contenían entre dos y cinco neonatos cuya edad oscilaba entre escasa horas y los tres meses, no sobrepasando en ningún caso la edad de un año (Gusi, 1970), lo que coincide plenamente con los datos de los neonatos de Tarros y Cartago ya citados.

En Thysdrus, un recinto funerario estaba reservado a los niños, los cuales eran inhumados bajo la advocación de una diosa protectora que podría identificarse con una Tanit romanizada (Slim, 1982).

Tiene interés señalar el hallazgo de un crisol en el santuario-1 de Almallutx, pues las actividades metalúrgicas tienen también su reflejo en el plano mitológico con la aparición de una sacralidad telúrica con divinidades protectoras de las minas y de los procesos de fundición (Eliade, 1974) que revisten un profundo carácter esotérico. Esta relación de ritos de la fertilidad con otros propiciatorios de la metalurgia están bien documentados en el santuario de Cástulo, donde se han hallado tortas de fundición e instrumentos mineros (Blázquez ,1986:60). Tiene paralelos en los santuarios chipriotas, como Enkomi con ofrendas de pequeños lingotes de carácter votivo y representaciones de divinidades protectoras de la metalurgia (Karageorghis, 1976).

ENCUADRE CRONOLOGICO

La aparición de las estructuras arquitectónicas que hemos identificado como santuarios talayóticos es un fenómeno tardío en la prehistoria insular, ya señalamos al principio que con toda seguridad constituye la fase culminante de un proceso de sincretismo, en el que se funden sustratos mitológicos ancestrales, propios de una formación social agrícola-pastoril, con formas religiosas más elaboradas, aunque en absoluto contradictorias, aportadas por la colonización prerromana de la isla.

Un proceso paralelo se produce en la cultura nurágica, constatado en los reacondicionamientos de algunos santuarios, como en Santa Vittoria di Serri, cuya fase final, coincidente con los inicios de la colonización fenicia, acusa la presencia de protomos taurinos, columnas-betilo, etc. (Santoni, 1977), lo cual denota claramente cambios sustanciales, no sólo en la arquitectura edilicia, sino también y sobre todo en el orden ideológico-cultural, con la adquisición de contenidos claramente emparentados con la religión fenicia, entrando en retroceso el componente animista y megalítico.

Es necesario señalar la más que posible perduración de lugares sacros, cuya frecuentación con fines rituales puede remontarse a fases muy arcáicas de la prehistoria isleña, en este sentido, tienen un interés extraordinario las últimas revelaciones proporcionadas por la excavación de santuario de Son Mas (Waldren, Ensenyat y Cubí, en prensa), según las cuales, la frecuentación del lugar sacro parece iniciarse en la fase pretalayótica (2.000-1.700 a. C.) con una extraordinaria abundancia y calidad de cerámicas incisas, las cuales pueden denotar un uso no doméstico, sino precisamente ritual del lugar. Queda por el momento más oscura la frecuentación en época talayótica inicial, aunque algunas formas cerámicas pueden ciertamente corresponder a las fases Talayótica I y II. No sabemos si podrán documentarse fases de inutilización, abandono o cambio de función del lugar sobre el que, en una fase ya tardía, se erigirá el santuario. El fenómeno no tiene nada de extraordinario en otros lugares, así, por ejemplo, en Tas Silg, santuario maltés prehistórico, es reocupado y adaptado al culto fenicio (Busuttil et al., 1969; Cagiano de Azevedo et al. 1972). También el templo sardo de Antas pasa de una advocación púnica a Sid en los siglos IV-III a.C. a un culto latinizado dedicado al Sardus Pater (Barreca, 1974:1-13).

No es tarea fácil precisar una fecha para la aparición de este tipo de santuarios. Por procedimiento indirecto y admitiendo que su aparición obedece a nuevas exigencias de culto generadas en el proceso de aculturación prerromana, cabe señalar, en base a los datos que de la colonización púnica de Mallorca tenemos en la actualidad, que la aparición generalizada de santuarios no iría más allá del siglo V a. C.

Las manifestaciones de cultura material más arcáicas introducidas en la isla por el comercio colonial arrancan de mediados del siglo VI a. C.; algún hallazgo esporádico, como un ánfora fenicia occidental del tipo R-1 tardío, encontrada en la factoría de Na Guardis, podría remontarse a la primera mitad de siglo VI a. C. Antes de estas fechas es ciertamente difícil, hoy por hoy, documentar algún tipo de relación entre los indígenas de Mallorca y los comerciantes fenicios ya asentados en Ibiza desde la primera mitad del siglo VII a. C.

El siglo V a. C. verá radicalmente cambiar las cosas y el proceso de aculturación entra en una fase de acelerado dinamismo por las razones ya expuestas al principio y que hemos desarrollado con más detalle en otros trabajos.

La aparición de un fondo de pátera ática en el recinto sacro de Son Carrió, aunque no constituye el modelo arquitectónico ortodoxo de santuario que estudiamos aquí, es un dato objetivo importante que nos señalaría el siglo IV a. C. como un momento seguro en el que este tipo de santuarios podía ya estar en uso.

En las fechas de la conquista romana, de forma generalizada, todos estos santuarios y otros recintos sacros están en uso. La conquista de la isla por las tropas de Q. Cecilio Metelo y el asentamiento posterior del poder romano, supone el abandono, cuando no la destrucción violenta y seguramente intencionada, de algunos de ellos. Los ajuares litúrgicos del momento de abandono de Son Favar, Son Carrió y Roca Rotja se fechan sin dificultad en la segunda mitad del siglo II a. C. (Guerrero, 1987a).

Otros santuarios como Ses Antigors y Son Marí siguen en uso hasta la primera mitad del siglo I a. C. (Guerrero, 1983); mientras que el santuario de Son Oms llegaría en uso como recinto sacro hasta época augústea, abandonándose hacia la primera mitad del siglo I de la Era (Rosselló y Camps, 1971:302).

En esta línea de recintos sacros extraurbanos situados en "lugares altos", con estructuras sin cubrir y en los que suele aparecer como elemento importante la cisterna, cabe señalar la existencia de una serie de interesantes yacimientos en Ibiza que reunen estas características. Uno de ellos está en curso de excavación (Ramón, 1987-88) y aunque es prematuro extraer conclusiones, conviene constatar que su construcción y uso se desarrolla con una cronología estrictamente paralela a la época álgida del los santuarios talayóticos (s. II a. C.), el lugar sacro ebusitano sufre un reacondicionamiento hacia época augústea que no parece cambiar su función como lugar sacro, la frecuentación del lugar, ya en ruinas, con deposición de lucernas como ofrendas se prolongará a lo largo de toda la época imperial romana (100-400/450 d. C.). Cuestión que coincide, hasta época augústea, con las fases de utilización de Son Oms.

A partir del cambio de Era se inicia un periodo realmente oscuro en lo que respecta a la documentación arqueológica relacionada con la mitología indígena, seguramente el peso de la cultura romana se ha dejado ya notar sobre la población autóctona. Entraríamos en un nuevo capítulo de la historia antigua isleña.

BIBLIOGRAFIA

Acquaro, E., 1983. *Nuove ricerche a Tharros.* I Congresso Internazionale di Studi Fenici e Punici, Roma (1979). p. 623-631.

Andronicos, M., 1978. *Musée d'Hérakleion et sites archéologiques de la Crète.* Athènes.

Aubet, Mª. E., 1982. 'El santuario de Es Cuieram'. *Trabajos del Museo Arqueológico de Ibiza* 8.

Amorós, L., 1944-46. 'Nuevos hallazgos en Son Carrió'. *Boletín de la Soc. Arq. Luliana* XXIX:359-364.

Amorós, L. y A. García Bellido, 1947. 'Los hallazgos arqueológicos de Son Favar (Capdepera-Mallorca)'. *Archivo Esp. de Arqueología* XX (66):3-27.

Barreca, F., 1987. *La Sardegna fenicia e punica.* Sassari.

Bisi, A. Mª., Guzzo, Mª G. y V. Tusa, 1969. *Grotta Regina*-I. Roma.

Blázquez J. Mª., 1975. *Tartessos y los orígenes de la colonización fenicia en Occidente.* Salamanca.

Blázquez J. Mª., 1977. 'El Hérakleion gaditano. Un templo semita en Occidente'. En *Imagen y Mito.* Madrid.

Blázquez J. Mª., 1983. *Primitivas religones ibéricas.* Madrid.

Blázquez J. Mª., 1986. 'La colonización fenicia en la Alta Andalucía (Oretania). s. VIII-VI a.C.'. *Rivista di Studi Fenici,* XIV,(1):53-80.

Cintas, P., 1976. *Manuel d'archéologie punique,* vol. II. Paris.

Colominas, J., 1915-20. 'Habitació romana dels Antigors a les Salines de Santanyí'. *Anuari Institut d'Estudis Catalans* VI.

Eliade, M., 1974. *Herreros y alquimistas.* Madrid.

Eliade, M., 1981. *Tratado de historia de las religiones. Morfología y dinámica de sagrado.* Madrid.

Encinas, J. A., 1981. *Pollença.* Semblança d'un poble. Palma.

Fedele, F. y G. V. Foster, 1988. 'Tharros: ovicaprini sacrificali e rituale del tofet'. *Riv. di Studi Fenici* XVI (1):29-46.

Fernández, J. H., 1983. *Guia del Puig des Molins.* Ibiza.

Fernández Miranda, M., Ensenyat, C. y B. Ensenyat, 1971. El poblado de Almallutx (Escorca, Baleares). Madrid:*Excavaciones Arqueológicas en España,* 73.

Ferrá, B., 1895-96. 'Hallazgos arqueológicos en Costitx'. *Boletín de la Sociedad Arqueológica Luliana* :85-89.

Fiorentini, G., 1980. 'Santuari punici a Monte Adranone di Sambuca di Sicilia'. En *Miscellanea di Studi Classici in onore de E. Manni*, tomo III:906-915. Roma.

Foure, P., 1967. 'Nouvelles recherches sur trois sortes de sanctuaires crétois'. *Bulletin de Correspondance Hellénique* 91.

García Bellido, A., 1958. 'Hercules Gaditanus'. *Archivo Esp. de Arqueología* 36:70-153.

Grottanelli, C., 1981. 'Santuari e divinità delle Colonie d'Occidente'. *En La Religione Fenicia. Matrici Orientale e Sviluppi Occidentali*, p. 109-133. Roma (1979).

Guerrero, V. M., 1982. *Los núcleos arqueológicos de Calvià*. Palma.

Guerrero, V. M., 1983. 'El santuario talayótico de "Son Marí" (Mallorca)'. *Boletín de la Soc. Arq. Luliana* 39:293-336.

Guerrero, V. M., 1984a. La colonización púnico ebusitana de Mallorca. *Estado de la cuestión. Ibiza:Trabajos del Museo Arqueológico de Ibiza* 11.

Guerrero, V. M., 1984b. El asentamiento púnico de Na Guardis. Madrid: *Excavaciones Arqueológicas en España* 133.

Guerrero, V. M., 1985. *Indigenisme i colonització púnica a Mallorca*. Palma.

Guerrero, V. M., 1986. 'El impacto de la colonización púnica en la cultura talayótica de Mallorca'. En Los fenicios en la Península Ibérica., *Aula Orientalis* 4:339-375.

Guerrero, V. M., 1987a. 'Problemas en torno al inicio de la romanización de Mallorca'. Én *Actas de Jornades Internacionals d'Arqueología Romana*. Granollers.

Guerrero, V. M., 1987b. 'Naturaleza y función de los asentamientos púnicos en Mallorca'. En Actas del IIº Cong. *Int. di Studi Fenici e Punic.*, Roma.

Guerrero, V.M., 1988. 'Mallorca durante las guerras púnicas. Algunas evidencias arqueológicas'. En *Actas del VIII International Colloquium, Punic Wars, Background, Evidences, Consequences*. Antwerp.

Gusi, F., 1970. 'Enterramientos infantiles ibéricos en vivienda'. *Pyrenae* 6:66-70.

Karageorghis, V., 1970. 'Two religious documents of the Early Cypriot Bronze Age'. En *Report of the Department of Antiquities of Cyprus*.

Karageorghis, V., 1973. 'Contribution to the Religion of Cyprus in the 13th and 12th Centuries, B.C.'. En *The Mycenæans in the Eastern Mediterrranean* p. 105 y sig.

Karageorghis, V., 1976. *Kition. Mycenæan Phoenician discoveries in Cyprus*. London.

Karageorghis, V., 1978. *Musée de Chypre et sites archéologiques de Chypre*. Athènes.

Karouzou, S., 1980. *Musée National. Guide illustré du musée.* Athènes.

Moscati, S., 1960. *Las antiguas civilizaciones semíticas.* Barcelona.

Pritchard, J. B., 1955. *Ancient Near Eastern texts relating to the Old Testament.* Princeton.

Ramón, J., 1982. *Es Cuieram* 1907-1982: 75 años de investigación. Eivissa

Ramón, J., 1985. *Es Cuieram* 1981'. Noticiario Arqueológico Hispánico 20:227-253.

Ramón, J., 1987-88. 'El recinto púnico del Cap des Llibrell (Ibiza)'. *Saguntum* 21:267-293.

Rosselló, G., 1972. 'La prehistoria de Mallorca. Rectificaciones y nuevos enfoques al problema'. *Mayurqa* VII:115-156.

Rosselló, G., 1979. *La cultura talayótica en Mallorca.* Palma

Rosselló, G., 1984. 'Son Oms: El santuario talayótico, su traslado y reposición'. *Mayurqa* 20:3-32.

Rosselló, G. y J. Camps, 1971. 'Las excavaciones de Son Oms (Mallorca), 1969-1971'. En *XII Cong. Nacional de Arqueología,* Jaèn, p. 301-306.

Rosselló, G. y Frey, O. H., 1966. Levantamiento planimétrico de "S'Illot" (San Lorenzo, Mallorca). Madrid: *Excavaciones Arqueológicas en España* 48.

Rosselló, G. y V. M. Guerrero, 1983. 'La necrópolis infantil de Cas Santamarier (Son Oms)'. *Noticiario Arqueológico Hispánico* 15:407-448.

Santoni, V., 1977. 'Osservazioni sulla protostoria della Sardegna'. *Melanges de l'Ecole Française de Rome* 89:447-470

Slim, L., 1982. 'L'Univers des morts à Thysdrus'. *Histoire et Archeologie* 69:74-85.

Waldren, W., Ensenyat, J. y C. Cubí, 1989. 'Son Mas: A New Mallorcan Prehistoric Sanctuary'. En II Deià Conference of Prehistory. Edited by W. Waldren et alii. Oxford: *British Archaeological Reports. International Series.*

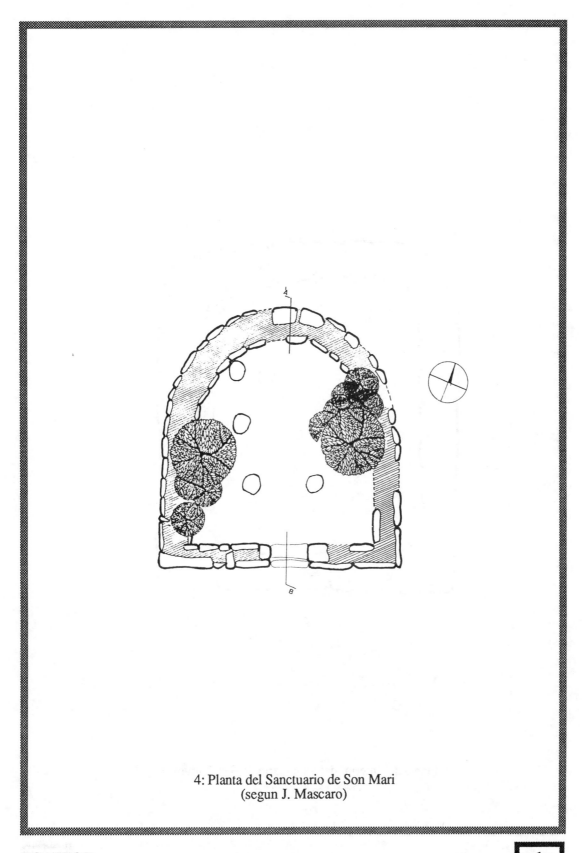

4: Planta del Sanctuario de Son Mari
(segun J. Mascaro)

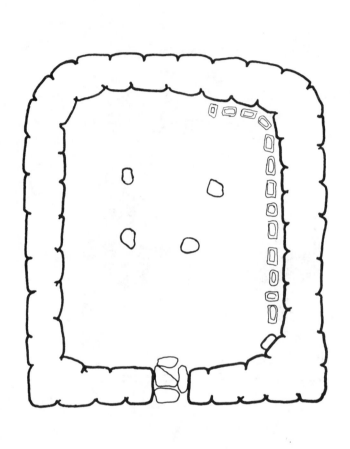

2: Planta del Interior del Sanctuario de Ses Antigors
(segun Colominas)

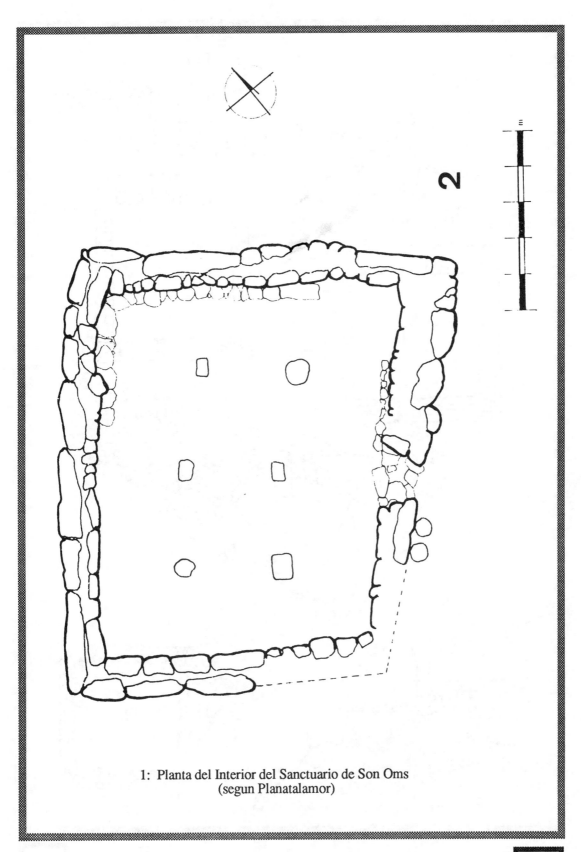

1: Planta del Interior del Sanctuario de Son Oms
(segun Planatalamor)

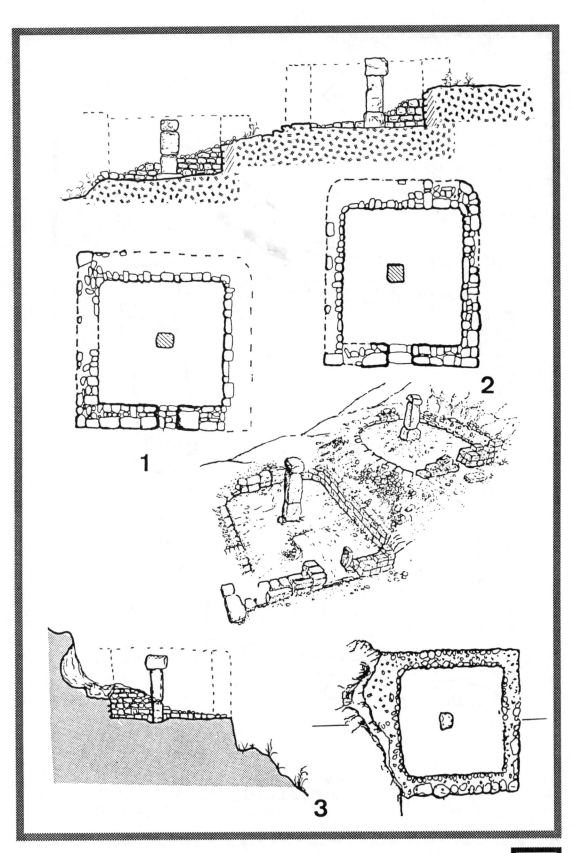

1

2

3

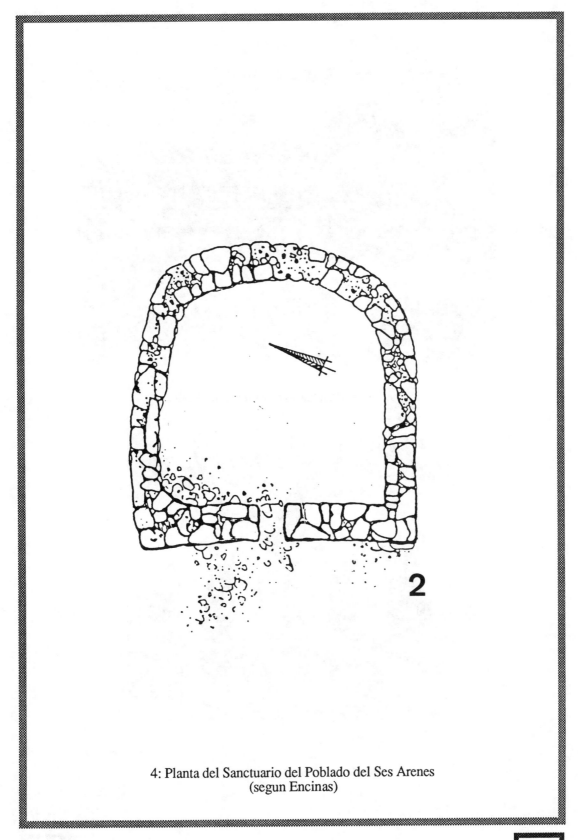

2

4: Planta del Sanctuario del Poblado del Ses Arenes
(segun Encinas)

2: Interior del Sanctuario de Son Mari: Detalle

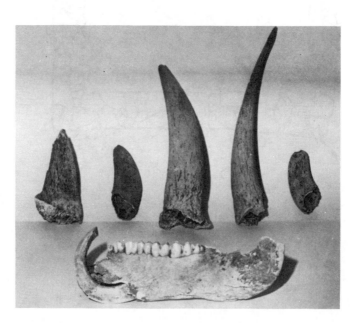

3: Restos de Animales Sacrificados

I: Interior del Sanctuario de Ses Antigors
(segun Colominas)

1: Interior del Sanctuario de Son Oms (Figura 3) Planta del Mismo Sanctuario
(segun Planatalamor)

1: Columna del Sanctuario Almallutx-1

3: Terracota de Karalis, Cerdiña.

1: Terracota Chipriota de Vounous

2: Terracota Chipriota de Necropolis de Kotchati

3: Carro Votivo Cretense de Terracota

THE TAULAS OF MENORCA

MICHAEL HOSKIN
Churchill College
University of Cambridge
Cambridge, England

RESUME

Archaeoastronomy has the outward marks of an established discipline, with two specialist journals and regular conferences; but there is not yet agreement as to its subject matter. Those working on early civilisation in the New World can often supplement the archaeological record with written documents and even with an oral tradition that survives to this day. They therefore see archaeoastronomy as the interdisciplinary study of astronomical aspects of early civilisation.

If this definition is translated into the European context, one finds the astronomy of Ptolemy-- even of Copernicus-- consigned to archaeoastronomy, although the historian of European astronomy is hard put to see any purpose in this: whether he is studying the second or the twentieth century AD, the great bulk of his sources are written and call for much the same approach. On the other hand, in areas of the history of astronomy where the source material is wholly or largely in the form of physical remains, quite a different methodology is necessary and it makes sense to see here a new discipline. In Europe, therefore, archaeoastronomy bears much the same relation to history of astronomy that archaeology does to history.

European-style archaeoastronomy comes into its own as a technique for investigating the attitude of prehistoric societies to the heavens above them. This attitude can have various aspects. The most obvious one is the practical: knowledge of the seasonal year, of the time for planting, of navigation, or whatever. Another is religious or symbolic: a modern counterpart would be the Moslem's interest in the direction of Mecca. An unlikely, but nevertheless possible, aspect, is scientific: it has been maintained with great vigour in recent decades that in Britain and elsewhere prehistoric man observed the moon with sufficient precision to predict the occurrence of eclipses; and whatever his motive in doing this, predictions of this kind can reasonably be termed scientific.

If any clues have come down to us that will shed light on these problems, they are likely to be in the form of orientations, either of stand-alone man-made structures that have a defined axis, or of the lines joining one such structure to another or to a natural feature such as a distant mountain peak. To take a simple example: on Menorca a taula precinct has a well defined direction, the one in which you face when you stand with your back against the taula, looking out through the entrance of the precinct. All such taulas always face the southern half of the horizon, and we ask, is this fact significant; and if so, why is it that they do this?

At first sight, a claim that taulas always face south "plus or minus ninety degrees" seems so inexact as not to be worth making. But it is in fact a very significant claim indeed. To see this we have to do a little statistics. Suppose, knowing nothing of the orientations of taulas, we visit our first taula and ask ourselves whether it faces the northern or the southern half of the horizon. It faces the southern half, so we write S in our notebook. The second taula also calls for a S. So far, of the equally-likely possibilities NN,NS,SN,SS, it is the SS that has actually occurred--a chance of 1 in 4. Our third taula is also S, so the odds are now 1 in 8; the fourth taula makes it 1 in 16; and by the time we visit our tenth taula, it is virtually certain that the taulas face the southern half of the sky, not as random chance but for a reason.

It may be that in the end we shall be able to offer no better explanation than the speculation that the prevailing winds blow from the north and a south-facing taula was pleasantly sheltered. But supposing (though this is not in fact the case) every taula faced south, not plus-or-minus ninety degrees, but plus-or-minus one degree. This precision would not be explained by the speculation, for any southerly direction would give shelter; nor is such precision likely to be explained by the lie of the land or any other local circumstance. We would have to take seriously the possibility that the direction was deliberately chosen for reasons involving astronomy.

If we could have claimed that all taulas face precisely south, an astronomical explanation would be difficult to resist. But, as Plato would have reminded us, such perfection of measurement is not to be found in this world. Any measurement we make in the field is subject to instrumental error; the vertical face of a taula was never perfectly flat and we cannot be certain of the precise direction it was intended to face; and the passage of time may have tilted or eroded the monuments and introduced further uncertainty.

It will be necessary for the archaeoastronomer to establish as objectively as possible what these errors are. He must in particular avoid the danger of making a measurement with the knowledge of what it ought to be if it is to confirm his hypothesis, for he may then suspend his critical faculties and find what he wants to find. Many of the claims that prehistoric man in Britain used distant horizon features to track the motions of the moon have been attacked on the ground that the modern investigator singled out those horizon features that fitted his requirements.

Because these errors of measurement are inevitable, we are always in the realm of mere probability, never certainty; and the archaeologist may be tempted to turn away in despair. But this would be a mistake, for we know that primitive peoples living today often make sophisticated applications of astronomical knowledge, for example in their calendar or for navigation; and if the prehistoric people we are studying did the same, we must be alert to clues that may have come down to us.

Suppose for example that we find the taulas do not all face (almost) exactly south, but that they face various directions, none of them more than a few degrees from south-east. It occurs to an astronomer among us that the directions involved are not far from the place on the theoretical horizon where the mid-winter sun rises at the latitude of Menorca. Unfortunately there is a complication. In Menorca the sun never rises vertically, but follows a slanting path. If from each of our taulas the line of sight to the horizon in the south-east was itself horizontal, this would not matter: the sun would rise in the same direction as seen from each taula. But on land the horizon in any direction is usually elevated, especially so if there are nearby hills. As a result, the compass direction to the point on the horizon where the sun on a given day appears to rise will vary somewhat from taula to taula, the actual direction in a *particular case depending on where in its slanting path the sun appears above the skyline; and at each site our astronomer must do some measurements and some calculations. This done, let us imagine that he finds to his delight that in every case-- to the limits of available accuracy-- the taula faces the observed direction of the sun on the horizon at midwinter sunrise. He naturally believes that he has uncovered the reason for the orientations of taulas.*

If the measurements were exempt from the errors we have described (and if we knew which part of the disk of the rising sun interested the prehistoric Menorcans), it would be hard to resist his conclusion. As it is, his conclusion will be at best probable, and open to debate. But he could well be right, and if an archaeologist's mind is closed to the possibility of an astronomical explanation, that archaeologist is limiting his capacity to understand the prehistoric people he is studying.

As we see, archaeoastronomy demands a (very elementary) knowledge of astronomical matters, and a sensitivity to statistical considerations. Astronomy and statistics have not normally formed part of the education of archaeologists, and so most contributors to European archaeoastronomy have had a background in science. This has sometimes caused them to make elementary mistakes in archaeology, and given archaeologists an excuse to disregard their message--to the impoverishment of archaeology. I hope in my paper to contribute to the building of bridges between the two groups of co-workers, by showing archaeologists that the science they need to master is well within their grasp.

The Taulas of Menorca
M. Hoskin

The 'talayotic' civilization of the Balearic Islands of Mallorca and Menorca reached its zenith around the year 1000 B.C.; and although it later declined in response to outside influences, it survived in attentuated form until the occupation of the island by the Romans in 123 B.C. The civilization takes its name from the Arabic word for the stone towers that are its most prominent monuments. But although the civilization was widespread on both islands, only on Menorca do we find the *taulas* that have provoked so much controversy (1). In this paper I discuss the orientations of the known taulas, and offer a possible explanation for them.

A taula (from the Catalan for 'table') is a monument consisting of two stones, one on top of the other. The lower stone is a vertical slab with straight sides, typically tall, wide and slim, with its base set into a slot cut into the bedrock. The upper stone is a horizontal slab that rested on (or is slotted onto) the lower, so that the two together have the form of a letter T. Not surprisingly, in the majority of cases the upper stone has since fallen, or has disappeared entirely (though this will not affect what follows provided we can be sure that the remaining component is indeed the remnant of a taula).

A taula was surrounded by a horseshoe-shaped precinct wall with an entrance, and around the interior of the precinct wall were pilasters and other features that do not concern us here. What is important to us is that of the two principal faces of the lower (vertical) stone of the taula, one faced the entrance to the precinct. This, the 'front' face of the taula, was always flat; the other face was sometimes similarly fashioned, sometimes left rough.

Most major settlements on Menorca had one or more talayots and a single taula. There would also be other substantial buildings, often formed of a surrounding wall, one or more central columns made of stones that increased in width towards the top, and a roof made of large flat stones that extended from the top of one of the columns to the surrounding wall or from one column to another. Such buildings have a superficial similarity to taula precincts, in that both had a surrounding wall and a central feature made of stones that increase in width towards the top. This similarity led earlier this century to two controversies. The first was as to whether a taula together with its precinct wall formed a *secular* building no different in kind from those just described, or whether the precinct had by contrast a *religious* significance. This question was finally resolved by excavations, at Torre d'en Gaumes, where a statue of Imhotep, the Egyptian god of medicine, was found with an inscription (2), and at Torralba d'en Salort, where the statues recovered included a bronze bull. Clearly, a taula precinct was a religious sanctuary. The second controversy was less fundamental: were taula precincts roofed with flat stones? Most, but not all, archaeologists believe that the centre of the precinct (if not the whole) was that rose between (say) south-east and south would have already moved a considerable way south of their rising position on the (near-horizontal) skyline. Furthermore, it is difficult to believe that any but the very brightest of all would be the individual objects of religious worship -- although *constellations* had long been the object of worship in, for example, Egypt (6).

In today's southerly Menorcan skies, no stars of note are to be seen; the brightest star that rises to the south of south-east is Shaula, which is less than one-twentieth the brightness of Sirius. Whether any bright stars were to be seen near the south in talayotic times I did not know but thought unlikely: I had intentionally left myself in ignorance of how the sky looked in Antiquity, for I was anxious to escape the criticism made of Thom -- that he often carried out his fieldwork knowing in advance the results that would support his claims, and found what he wanted to find. As the significance of constellations (rather than individual stars) had not then ocurred to me, my fieldwork was carried out in the belief that an astronomical explanation was well-nigh impossible.

In the study of orientations it is of course essential for the investigators to establish objective standards of measurement. With the vertical faces of taulas this is not easy, because the stones were never perfectly flat, and have since weathered; in a few cases they are now very irregular. More secure measurements will be possible as and when excavation of a taula precinct exposes the slot in the bedrock which was cut out to receive the taula, thereby revealing the orientation intended by the builders. But this is for the future. The present investigation is restricted to measurements of the orientations of the stones themselves, and the figures cited are therefore subject to later refinement.

This brings us to the problem of deciding the direction in which the vertical taula stone faces today, when uneven weathering has compounded whatever irregularities there were in the stone when first erected. My solution was to observe the stone by looking from one side along the face (and then adding or subtracting 90º), in order to estimate limits *within which* the desired direction must surely lie. I would do this from both sides (ideally, the results would be the same) and, when possible, on different days; and I had my companions do the same. From a consideration of all the measurements, I hoped to establish a form of consensus.

Occasionally, the limits I arrived at were only one degree apart. More usually, they differed by several degrees. At two sites (Binimassó and Es Tudons) the stones were exceptionally irregular and it proved impossible to proceed by the method of limits. At a third site, Torre d'en Gaumes, where the precinct entrance survives, the stone is irregular and one of the limits far exceeded the view through the entrance and was reduced accordingly. But otherwise the method of limits was to work well.

The measurements themselves were nornally taken by mariner's compass. I had planned to use a theodolite to establish true north; but the terrain is often so rough that it would have been difficult to transport such heavy equipment, and the investigation would have been delayed with little prospect of a compensating gain in accuracy. This is because geologists assure me that Menorca is formed of sedimentary rocks, none of which is of a composition that might give rise to anomalous compass bearings (7). The reliability of the compass was confirmed at the three sites where independent measurements could be made by sextant observations of known landmarks. Here again, however, there is scope for future refinement of our results.

At two sites measurements by magnetic compass were excluded by the presence of electricity cables supplying nearby farms. At one, Binimassó, where we have remarked that the stone is so rough that it defeats the method of limits, one can say little more than that the taula faces southerly. At the other, Torralba, the situation is fortunately very different. The huge upright is superbly fashioned and wonderfully flat from side to side. The orientation of the stone near uncovered, and this for a variety of reasons. In particular, the quantity of stone found today in the ruins of a precinct seems insufficient to represent the remains of a roof.

A taula precinct, then, was certainly a religious monument and its centre was probably open to the sky. It also had a clear, if not precisely defined, orientation: the direction in which the flat 'front' face of the taula looked out through the entrance. The catalogue of taulas published in 1958 by J. Mascaró Pasarius gives rough orientations in terms of the cardinal points of the compass (3); and it is very remarkable that (with one possible exception (4)) all the orientations are towards the southern half of the horizon. Mathematically the significance of this is easy to see. If it is equally likely that a taula will face either the northern or the southern half of the horizon, then the chances of one taula facing the southern half is 1 in 2; the chances of two doing so, 1 in 4; the chances of three doing so, 1 in 8; of four, 1 in 16; and so on. If two dozen taulas all face the southern half of the horizon, it is quite certain that this cannot be by accident.

Mascaró's orientations do not aspire to precision, and as his catalogue aims at completeness it includes taulas of doubtful authenticity. Yet the questions it raises are clear and dramatic: did the taula builders indeed erect their monuments to face directions in the arc east-south-west, and if so, why? Accordingly, in June and July 1988, I set out to remeasure as carefully as possible the orientations of those taulas whose authenticity is certain (or at least very probable), in order to establish the facts and perhaps offer an explanation.

I have come to archaeology out of a interest in what is now called archaeoastronomy, the study of the role of astronomy in early civilizations, and I cannot deny that I was alert to a possible astronomical explanation of the taula orientations. An astronomical explanation may be scientific or symbolic (or a combination of the two). The orientations of mosques towards Mecca, or of Christian churches towards east, are purely symbolic: no *use* is made of this layout. By contrast, an alignment used (say) to pinpoint the summer solstice and so regulate the calendar may be said to be scientific. Now in Old World archaeoastronomy the most innovative and controversial investigator has been the late Alexander Thom, who argued that in Britain and elsewhere stones were carefully lined up with natural features among distant mountains, in such a way that the stones and the distant mountain features together formed observing instruments many kilometres in size and of great accuracy (5). These, according to Thom, were then used to monitor with precision the cycles of the sun and moon. Would similar alignments exist in Menorca? The answer was negative: I found that the taulas, far from looking up and away to distant mountains, were themselves located on prominent ground; and the skyline they faced was always featureless and sometimes merely the meeting-place of sea and sky.

It was then clear that the taula orientations were always roughly defined and so any *astronomical* explanation of them would be symbolic -- as indeed would befit religious monuments. Yet it was also clear, from Mascaró's catalogue, that even a symbolic astronomical explanation was highly improbable, because most of his orientations are too far south to involve the sun, moon and planets -- which of course rise and set throughout the year within limited distances of east and west. On the other hand, a number of the orientations were too far from *due* south for them to be explained away as incompetent attempts at a south-facing orientation; in particular the magnificent taula of Torralba, oriented ESE according to Mascaró, does indeed face -- exceptionally but inescapably -- not far from east.

If taulas do not face the rising or setting of sun, moon and planets, and do not face due south, there are few (if any) remaining astronomical targets save the rising and setting of stars; and although there are innumerable stars, only the brightest have light enough to be seen near the horizon, before they have climbed above the earth's atmosphere. By that time most stars would already be hidden from an observer at the taula by the lintel of the precinct entrance, and those the base can be determined within a dozen minutes or so of arc; and the angle between this face and a distant pylon can be measured by sextant to a similar accuracy. The pylon in turn can be located on the 1:25,000 maps of the Cartografía Militar de España, and as a result the orientation of the taula can be established within limits of about one degree.

In June and July 1988 I visited and measured 13 taula sites. This sounds simpler than it is, for although some of the sites are well known and easily reached, an increasing number are difficult to locate. Monuments of stone are obstacles to cultivation and often neglected by farmers, but before the arrival of bottled gas one could hope that the trees growing on them would have been cut down for use as firewood. Today this is seldom done, and indeed many of the farms themselves are abandoned to nature. One taula precinct, fortunately not of immediate concern in that it lacked both taula stones, proved literally impenetrable. Another taula, located on one visit, was not to be found two days later. Archaeology on Menorca is becoming more, not less difficult.

On my return to England, I gave my data to an astronomer friend who generously undertook to compute the relevant *declinations*. As the sky (apparently) spins, each star moves round us daily on a circle whose angular distance north of the equator is the star's declination (stars south of the equator have negative declinations). Where the star's circular path meets the skyline in a given locality is the place on the skyline where the star appears to rise and set. So, if one wishes to consult a star catalogue to see whether a monument is oriented towards the rising or setting of a star, one must first convert into declination the orientation (which is expressed as a compass bearing, or more exactly, in angle of *azimuth* measured clockwise from true north), taking into account the latitude of the site and the altitude of the skyline.

Because the earth is not a perfect sphere, it wobbles slowly like a top. In consequence the North Pole steadily moves position among the stars, as therefore does the celestial equator from which we measure declinations. In other words, declinations vary with time (hence star catalogues must always be drawn up for a given date, their *epoch*); and the position where we see a star today may be some distance from where it was to be seen by the talayotic Menorcans. Fortunately a list of star positions in past centuries was published in 1967 (8), and from it I found, to my great surprise, that in talayotic times the southern skies appeared dramatically different from what we see today. Nowadays the Southern Cross and the stars in Centaurus known as Alpha Cen and Beta Cen are invisible from anywhere in Europe. But the talayotic observer would have seen the Southern Cross rise some way east of south, and curve across the southern horizon before setting a similar distance to the west; it would have been followed by the bright star Beta Cen, and this in turn by the brilliant Alpha Cen, the second brightest star in the whole of the Menorcan sky. Friends at the Washington Air and Space Museum were later to use their sophisticated planetarium to reproduce for me this dramatic procession of stars, and they did so for a range of dates in talayotic times. It was especially helpful to witness how the procession of stars altered appearance as the centuries passed because it so happened that in Antiquity precession produced striking changes in the location of Centaurus (which in classical astronomy included the Southern Cross). In effect the southern horizon appeared to rise, century by century. To observers looking out to sea in 1400 B.C., Alpha Cen rose 26 degrees east of due south and set 26 degrees west of south -- a total arc of 52 degrees. When it culminated, it was more than six degrees above the horizon. By 600 B.C., this arc had reduced to some 30 degrees, and for much of it the star was lost in the atmosphere of the earth, for it climbed little more than 2 degrees above the horizon: Alpha Cen was fast disappearing from sight. By the time the Romans arrived, this had indeed happened. Of this, more anon.

Disappointingly, the declinations derived by my friend from the measured taula orientations were very different from those of the bright stars we have just mentioned, and I concluded that hopes of an astronomical explanation for taula orientations, always slim, had now totally vanished. Archaeoastronorers are sometimes accused of preferring torture and death to the abandonment of an astronomical explanation for prehistoric alignments, but to this I plead not guilty, and quote what I wrote at the time about taula orientations: "Esto no puede ser por casualidad, pero yo todavía no tengo una explicación astronómica que ofrecer, no siguiera otra explicación gue dar.... Por el momento no soy capaz de explicar porque las taulas miran aproximadamente hacia el sur, pero de hecho es así."

Further examination of the declinations, however, suggested that the figures might be flawed, and on investigation a defect was discovered in the computer programme. The corrected results were exciting indeed, for they showed that most of the 13 taulas would have faced the rising or setting of Alpha Cen (or, more generally, of the procession of stars of Centaurus), *provided* suitable dates could be assigned for their construction.

It is important at this stage of our discussion that we appreciate the strictness or otherwise of the astronomical tests we are applying. The strictest test will be at a taula site where (i) the orientation of the taula is accurately known, (ii) the date of construction of the taula is known (from radiocarbon dating), and (iii) the proposed target is a single bright star. From (i) we derive one declination, and from (ii) and (iii) another (that of the star at the date of construction), and the test is whether these two values are (nearly) the same.

At the other extreme will be a test where none of these conditions is satisfied: where the orientation of the taula is poorly defined, the date of construction uncertain, and the proposed target a whole constellation. Each of the two derived declinations will then have considerable uncertainty and a match between the two will be less convincing.

In brief, the results from the 13 taulas were as follows. Torralba satisfied the strictest test by accurately facing the rising of Sirius, the brightest star in the whole sky, at the known date of construction. Sa Torreta was problematic. Most of the others faced the rising or setting of Alpha Cen, the second brightest star in the sky, with varying accuracy in the determination of their orientations and for plausible (but unconfirmed) dates of construction. The remainder also fitted the Centaurus hypothesis, but only if uncomfortably early dates of construction were postulated, or if other stars of the constellation were included in the target.

Since all but two of the taulas fitted one or other form of the Centaurus hypothesis (that is, with Alpha Cen as the well-defined target and with plausible construction dates, or in the vaguer formulation), I was eager to test this hypothesis by further fieldwork. And so, in September, I set out to locate and measure six further taulas, and was fortunate to find them all. All six conformed to the stricter form of the Centaurus hypothesis, *with Alpha Cen as the (well-defined) target and construction dates no eartlier than that of Torralba*. Specifically, all six face between SSE and SSW, a mere one-eighth of the total horizon, which cannot be by chance; yet four (if not five) of the six taulas point a minimum of 13 degrees from due south, which is therefore unlikely to have been their target. It is not easy to imagine any alternative hypothesis that will accommodate both these facts.

The data for all 19 taulas are set out in Table 1. Leaving aside for the present the anomalous site of *Sa Torreta*, we begin our discussion of these data with *Torralba*, which is of the greatest interest, for many reasons. The site has been fully excavated, and we know that it was settled long before the year 1400 B.C. when it happened that Sirius and Rigel, the sixth brightest star in the Menorcan sky, had identical declinations and so rose in exactly the same position on the horizon. In contrast to Centaurus, Rigel was affected little by precession and Sirius even less: in 1000 B.C., the radiocarbon date for the construction of the taula, they still rose within a degree of each other. Our limits for the orientation of the superb taula stone, arrived at in advance of any astronomical considerations, are but one degree apart; yet these limits actually include the rising point of Rigel in 1000 B.C., and are less than a degree from the rising point of Sirius. We are fortunate to have a site where the data are so precisely defined.

Sirius is incomparably the brightest star in the sky, and was worshipped as Isis in Egypt, where its *heliacal rising* marked the beginning of the calendar year and heralded the flooding of the Nile. The heliacal rising of a star occurs when the star reappears briefly in the dawn sky after several weeks of invisibility following its disappearance in the glare of the sun, and it is much the most striking phenomenon associated with the star. Now Mr. Edward Sanders, the specialist in bones in the team from the Deya Archaeological Museum and Research Centre that played a major role in the excavation of Torralba, remarked to me that the animals sacrificed at Torralba seemed all to be in the second half of the first year of life, or the second half of the second year. The peak month for the birth of the animals in question would have been November, and the heliacal rising of Sirius took place in the third week after midsummer (9), so that the animals would indeed have had the appropriate age if they were then sacrificed to mark the reappearance of the star.

It may seem rash to mention Egyptian mythology in the context of the eastern Mediterranean, but it is well known that worship of Isis was widespread in Greece and Rome in the last centuries before Christ, and we have already mentioned the discovery at Torre d'en Gaumes of a statue of Imhotep, the Egyptian god of medicine, together with an inscription in hieroglyphics. It is indeed entirely possible that Egyptian religious beliefs were brought to Menorca at the very beginning of the talayotic period, through the mysterious Sea Peoples that we know about from Egyptian sources.

The *Cambridge Ancient History* speaks of them as follows:

> Among the 'peoples of the sea' who made raids on the coasts of the Mediterranean and against Egypt in the period 1400 to 1190 B.C. and who were employed as mercenaries in the Egyptian army soon after the middle of the second millenium B.C, were a people calling themselves Sherden. There are two main views about the origin of these people. One is that they came from Sardinia itself, in a word that they are Nuraghic heroes campaigning in the east Mediterranean, already well known to them by trade. The other view is that they came ... from Sardis and the Sardinian plain. This second view would appear to be the more likely.

> We can then see in the period 1400-1190 B.C. groups of people led by warlike chieftains, themselves expert sailors and with a knowledge of the routes between the east Mediterranean and the west, setting out from some such area as Sardis and, after periods of harassing Egypt, ending up in the island of the west Mediterranean which was eventually called after them, Sardinia (10).

If therefore there was intense Egyptian influence on the culture of Sardinia at this time, it is far from impossible that this influence extended to Menorca, at the time when taula construction began.

The complexities of Egyptian and Greek mythology are endless, but they may nevertheless shed light on our taulas. Although the statues found in taula precincts are much later than the taulas themselves, they give an indication of contemporary practices, which must surely have evolved from the rituals conducted when the taulas were first built.

Although Sirius/Isis was used in Egypt to mark the beginning of the year, this was only one of many star-constellations used in the control of time. The other constellation south of the ecliptic that we can indentify with certainty is Orion, the brightest star of which is none other than Rigel (Beta Orionis). In Egypt Orion was routinely identified with Osiris, and Orion rose shortly before Sirius. That Torralba is a religious monument that faced with great precision the rising of the brightest star in the sky is a fact; we speculate that -- either at the time of construction, or in later centuries -- Egyptian influences led Torralba to be associated not only with Sirius/Isis, but also with Orion/Osiris.

Now in Egypt, when the Apis bull died in the temple of Ptah near Memphis, the corpse of the animal was mummified and identified with Osiris; and it was at Torralba that excavations produced the statue of a bronze bull. It is therefore not impossible that the bronze bull of Torralba (tentatively dated to the fourth century B.C. (11)) represented Osiris.

Although the Torralba bronze is usually supposed to be of a bull, the sex of the animal is in fact uncertain. If it is in fact a cow, it happens that this would likewise support the Sirius/Orion hypothesis, for cows were sacred to Isis, who is often represented with some of the attributes of a cow. By the last centuries B.C., Isis had become not only the universal mother-goddess (whose statues are strongly reminiscent of the later Christian Virgin and Child), but also goddess of the earth and its fruits. As such her counterpart in Punic mythology would have been the fertility goddess Tanit, figurines of whom were also found at Torralba (12).

The remaining religious artefact found at Torralba was the bronze feet of a horse (the rest of the statue having been broken off). Before we can offer a speculative explanation for these horse's hooves, we need to discuss the remaining 17 taulas. My suggestion is that these may have been directed towards the very bright star Alpha Cen, or more generally to the procession of bright stars of the Southern Cross followed by Beta Cen and Alpha Cen, or more generally still to the constellation Centaurus. Because of the dramatic impact of precession on the rising and setting points of the stars of Centaurus in these centuries (as we have seen, the rising and setting points converged towards south as time went on), dating will be crucial in our discussion, especially if the single star Alpha Cen is taken as the target. It is the *beginning* date for the period of taula construction that is important, as this date controls the *maximum* angular distance from south that a Centaurus-directed taula could be intended to face. On the other hand, if a taula faced east of south towards a skyline encumbered with trees (for example), the star or stars towards which the taula was directed would become visible at the sanctuary only when it/they had climbed above the trees and in the process had already moved some way towards the south; and the same is true of a taula facing west of south, towards the setting stars. A taula may therefore face further south than its construction date would otherwise imply; and conversely its orientation places an *earlier* limit to the date of its construction.

Note that *every* horizon was encumbered by the earth's atmosphere, so that even Alpha Cen would have to climb a degree or so above the horizon (and move thereby a little to the south) before it became visible. As with the passage of centuries the curve traced out by the star became more and more shallow, so its actual first appearance would occur increasingly southerly of its theoretical rising point on the horizon, and its last appearance increasingly southerly of its setting point.

Let us see how far we can press the strictest hypothesis, that the target was the rising or setting of the single bright star Alpha Cen. We know from radiocarbon dating that the taula of Torralba was constructed around 1000 B.C. (13) Of the 17 taula orientations that remain to be discussed, 13 point in directions where Alpha Cen rose or set no earlier than this date, and so readily fit into our hypothesis (for there is no reason whatever for thinking that taula construction ended with Torralba).

Nor is construction likely to have begun with Torralba, for Torralba is the finest of the taulas, the high point of taula construction. Of the remaining four taulas, *Talatí* faced the rising of Alpha Cen if it was constructed in the thirteenth century B.C., which is not impossible. *Torre d'en Gaumes* and *Na Comerma* are more difficult. These neighbouring taulas may possibly have symmetric orientations, one facing the rising of a star or constellation and the other its setting. Torre d'en Gaumes is the largest settlement in the Balearics and grew out of pre-talayotic origins, so the taula there may be unusually early. Similarly, the small settlement of Na Comerma, only a few hundred metres from Torre d'en Gaumes, is itself within a stone's throw of a megalithic (that is, pre-talayotic) sepulchre and so may also have pre-talayotic origins. If we take for each orientation the middle value between our limits, and assume the taulas faced Alpha Cen, we get an unacceptably early date for construction -- around 1600 B.C. for Torre d'en Gaumes, and earlier still for Na Comerma. But it happens that both taulas were difficult to measure. That at Torre d'en Gaumes is exceptionally irregular, so much so that the southerly of our two limits is directed to the setting of Alpha Cen as late as 1000 B.C. At Na Comerma the taula is buried deep in rubble and protected by thorns, so that only a single rough measurement was possible, that of the top edge of the vertical stone; if the same had been the case at Torralba our measurements would have been in error by two degrees, for the Torralba taula has a 'twist' from top to bottom of this magnitude, and it may be that when Na Comerma is excavated and the base of the taula uncovered, we shall need to make an adjustment to the south that would give a later date at which the taula would have faced Alpha Cen.

It is not therefore impossible that 16 of these 17 taulas faced the rising or setting of the single star Alpha Cen at the date of their construction, and from this hypothesis provisional dates of construction could be estimated.

There remains however *Torre Trencada*, a famous taula of unusual construction. Our best estimate of the orientation of the upright (one corner of which is excessively weathered) is 146 degrees. This is too far east for Alpha Cen, and if we wish to maintain the strictest form of our hypothesis, that Alpha Cen alone was the target, we must assume a modest error on the part of the erectors of Torre Trencada.

The cumulative effect of these last-named taulas, and of Torre Trencada in particular, is to suggest that the target of the southerly taulas was not the single star Alpha Cen, but rather the striking procession of the Southern Cross followed by Beta Cen and Alpha Cen. Torre d'en Gaumes and Na Comerma then no longer present any difficulty, and Torre Trencada would have faced the rising of the most northerly star of the Southern Cross late in the twelfth century B.C.

The stars we have so far considered form part of the extensive constellation of Centaurus in the star-catalogue of the great Alexandrian astronomer of the second century A.D., Claudius Ptolemy, and all 17 of our southerly taulas could easily be taken as facing the rising or setting of this constellation. We of course do not know if the Menorcans saw a comparable image in the sky, but in the context of Centaurus the statue of Imhotep found at Torre d'en Gaumes may contain a clue to later thinking. In Greek mythology the centaur of Centaurus was the benign Chiron, skilled in medicine, whose greatest pupil was Asclepius, the Greek counterpart to Imhotep (14). Asclepius himself is commemorated in the constellation Ophiuchus, but this was circumpolar in Menorca. Of the constellations that rose and set, therefore, that most closely associated with Asclepius/Imhotep was Centaurus.

If we venture to speculate further, we note that at Torralba the excavation team also found embedded in rock, three hooves of a bronze horse. If, at the period the statue was erected, the great majority of Menorcan taula precincts were indeed dedicated to Centaurus, who had the body of a horse but the head and trunk of a man, perhaps the hooves belonged to a statue of Centaurus.

Lastly, a word about Sa Torreta. This is a remote site on the north-east coast at some distance from any other settlement, and it was excavated in the 1930s by the Cambridge Egyptologist

Margaret Murray (15). The taula faces a little south of the winter solstice of the Sun. It could be directed to the region of the skyline where the Moon reaches its most southerly declination, the exact position of which varies from year to year; or it could have similarly faced one of the planets. We do not have enough information on which to suggest an intended target.

In summary, then, we can say that Sa Torreta is exceptional, but may have been directed to the southerly winter moonrise. The Torralba taula faced with great precision the rising points of Sirius and Rigel around 1000 B.C, the time of its construction. Thirteen taulas were oriented to points where Alpha Cen rose or set no earlier than 1000 B.C.; the remaining four were oriented more generally to the rising or setting of the Southern Cross and the two bright stars of Centaurus for construction dates no earlier than the twelfth century B.C., or to the rising of a more extensive constellation for later construction dates.

These hypotheses can be tested in several ways. First, we hope to measure the very few remaining taulas, though these are remote and difficult to locate. Second, we invite other investigators to repeat our measurements and correct them where necessary. Third, a more refined analysis will be possible when precincts are excavated in sufficient numbers and the orientations of the slots prepared for their taulas can be measured. Fourth, it is implied by our Centaurus hypothesis *in the strictest form where Alpha Cen alone is the target,* that in general, though not invariably, the earliest of the 17 southerly taulas are the ones that face furthest from true south; this can be checked against construction dates when these are available from radiocarbon dating or otherwise.

In conclusion, we note that our hypothesis that taulas are directed to horizon phenomena provides an explanation for the presence of taula sanctuaries on Menorca and their absence on Mallorca. Menorca is mostly flat, especially in the southern limestone outcrops where the great majority of the settlements are to be found, and the settlements are normally located on whatever high ground was available; it is not surprising that their southerly skyline was rarely above the horizontal, or that the inhabitants should have been aware of what was to be seen on that skyline. By contrast, major areas of Mallorca are mountainous with the settlements located in the plains below. The presence of nearby mountains would then, in many cases, totally obstruct the southerly skyline, and render impossible any religion involving horizon phenonmena.

ACKNOWLEDGEMENTS

For information on the excavation at Torralba, I am indebted to my mentor in Balearic archaeology, William H. Waldren, who was one of the principal investigators at the site. His colleague Edward Sanders kindly provided information on the animals sacrificed at Torralba. I am much obliged to David DeVorkin and colleagues at the National Air and Space Museum in Washington for using their planetarium to reproduce some of the phenomena discussed in this paper. J.A. Bennett, T.R.E. Owen and Colin Shell generously provided eguipment for the fieldwork. I am grateful to N.H. Woodcock and H.B. Whittington for advice on the geology of Menorca, and to D. Gubbins for advice on magnetic variation. C.L.N. Ruggles kindly converted my azimuths into declinations. Those who helped with the fieldwork were Clare Dorrell, Elaine Genders, D.A.J. Hoskin, Sarah Law, and Margarita Orfila-Pons.

REFERENCES

1. A simple introduction to the talayotic civilization of Menorca is contained in *Taulas and Talayots* by Michael Hoskin and William Waldren (Cambridge, 1988, obtainable from the present author).

2. The excavation at Torre d'en Gaumes in general and the discovery of the statue of Imhotep in particular are described by G. Rosselló-Bordoy in *El Poblado Prehistórico de Torre d'en Gaumes (Alaior)* (Palma de Mallorca, 1986).

3. J. Mascaró Pasarius, "Las Taulas", *Revista de Menorca*, special number (Mahon, 1968), pp. 213-330.

4. The entry for Alfurinet, which I have not yet visited, is garbled. In the table the orientation is given (in the wrong column) as NE, and in the text as ENW!

5. For example, in A. Thom, *Megalithic Sites in Britain* (Oxford, 1967).

6. The standard authority on Egyptian astronomy is O. Neugebauer and R.A. Parker, *Egyptian Astronomical Texts* (3 vols., Providence, R.I., 1960-69).

7. Dr N.H. Woodcock and Professor H.B. Whittington of the Department of Earth Sciences at Cambridge write in a private communication: "Miocene limestones crop out in the southern half of the island, the sedimentary rocks of the northern half are older and more varied in nature and construction. None of these rocks is of a composition that might give rise to anomalous compass bearings."

8. Gerald S. Hawkins and Shoshana K. Rosenthal, "5,000- and 10,000-year star catalogs", *Smithsonian Contributions to Astrophysics*, x/2 (1967).

9. According to Richard A. Parker ("Egyptian Astronomy, Astrology, and Calendrical Reckoning", *Dictionary of Scientific Biography*, xv, 706-27, p. 707), the heliacal rising of Sirius fell around 17/19 July in the Julian calendar throughout Egyptian history.

10. *The Cambridge Ancient History*, ii/2, 3rd edn (Cambridge, 1975), pp. 741-2.

11. W.H. Waldren, private communication.

12. W.H. Waldren, private communication.

13. William H. Waldren, Josep Ensenyat Alcover and Carlos Morell Orlandis, "Son Mas Balearic Prehistoric Sanctuary; Preliminary Report" (Deya Archaeological Museum and Research Centre, 1988).

14. Ian Ridpath, *Star Tales* (Cambridge, 1988), pp. 47-48.

15. Margaret A. Murray, *Cambridge Excavations in Menorca: Sa Torreta* (Cambridge, 1934).

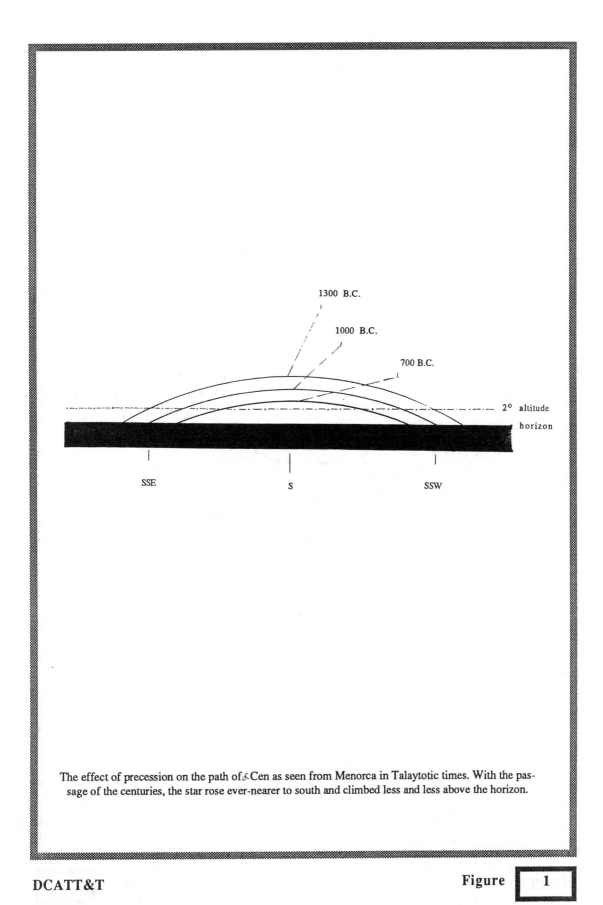

1300 B.C.

1000 B.C.

700 B.C.

2° altitude

horizon

SSE

S

SSW

The effect of precession on the path of ♌Cen as seen from Menorca in Talaytotic times. With the passage of the centuries, the star rose ever-nearer to south and climbed less and less above the horizon.

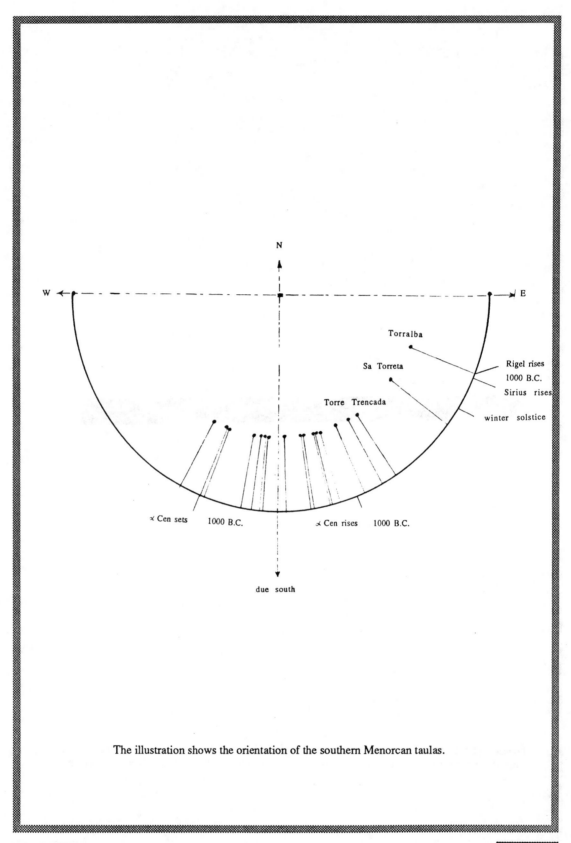

The illustration shows the orientation of the southern Menorcan taulas.

Figure 2

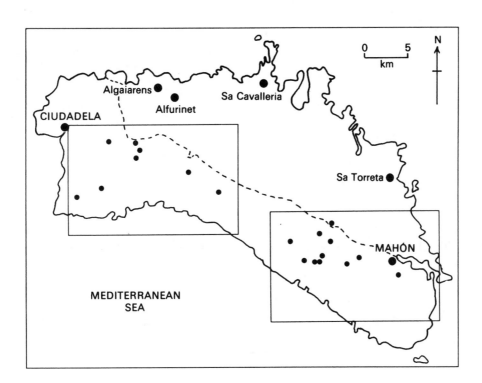

The island of Menorca. The broken line shows the geological division between north and south; the southern region with its limestone caves was densely covered with settlements, often as little as one kilometre from one another, and any of these settlements must have been grouped in larger social units and have shared a common culture. The four isolated settlements in the northern region where taulas have been identified are shown. The rectangles show the location of the more detailed maps in the following figure

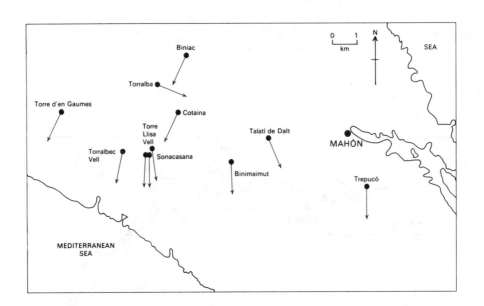

The illustration shows the surviving taulas of south-east Menorca, with their orientations.

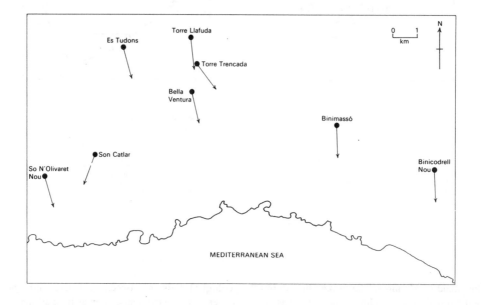

The illustration shows the surviving taulas of south-west Menorca, with their orientations.

..

THE DEVELOPMENT OF COMPLEX SOCIETIES IN S.E. SPAIN:
THE GATAS PROJECT

ROBERT W. CHAPMAN
Department of Archaeology
University of Reading
Whiteknights
Reading RG6 2AA, England

M. PICAZO
Universitat de Barcelona
Barcelona, España

VINCENTE LULL
Universitat Autónoma de Barcelona
Barcelona (Bellaterra) España

M. ENCARNA SANAHUJA
Universitat de Barcelona
Barcelona, España

RESUME

The prehistoric cultures of S.E. Spain have been known to archaeologists since the pioneering fieldwork of the Siret brothers, beginning in 1880. In the modern provinces of Almería, southern Murcia and eastern Granada, they discovered evidence for Copper and Bronze Age cultures which appeared as complex as any others in Europe outside of the Aegean. The emergence of this complexity was attributed to diffusion from the east Mediterranean, and this interpretation was closely followed by the majority of prehistorians until the last two decades. The abandonment of diffusionism has led to the proposal of very different models for the emergence of complexity in S.E. Spain. At the same time, excavations since 1960 have aimed to improve our knowledge of the chronology of local Copper and Bronze Age cultures. Important sites excavated include Cerro de la Virgen, Cerro del Real, Cuesta del Negro, Cerro de la Encina, El Malagón, Los Millares and Fuente Alamo. Much new data has been collected, mainly of a stratigraphic and chronological kind. The problem which lies at the centre of this paper is the degree to which such field research is being designed to test the various theoretical models proposed in recent years by the Spanish archaeologists Lull and Ramos, and by the foreign scholars Chapman, Mathers and Gilman.

These models derive from different bodies of theory and make different assumptions about cultural change. For example there are differences of opinion as to the degree to which intensification of production can be attributed to population growth and pressure. The scale of intensification is rarely specified. There are differences of opinion as to the actual changes which took place (e.g. climatic change, vegetational change, the nature of intensification, the complexity and integration of cultures and the degree of mutual interaction). Thus there are not only differences of theory, but also differences in the meaning given to the archaeological record.

The multi-disciplinary Gatas project has been designed with these problems at its centre. In this paper we will outline the aims of the project, the logical structure which underlies its planning, the results of fieldwork from 1985-88, our plans for future fieldwork, and our conception of the role of the Gatas project in the development of research into the later prehistory of S.E. Spain.

The Development of Complex Societies in S.E.Spain: the Gatas Project
R.W.Chapman, V.Lull, M.Picazo and Ma.E.Sanahuja

THE ARCHAEOLOGICAL RECORD OF S.E.SPAIN AND ITS STUDY

The prehistoric cultures of S.E.Spain have been known to archaeologists since the pioneering fieldwork of Louis and Henri Siret, beginning in 1880 (Siret and Siret 1887). In the modern provinces of Almería, southern Murcia and eastern Granada, they discovered evidence for Copper and Bronze Age societies which appeared as complex as any others in Europe outside of the Aegean. The emergence of this complexity was attributed to diffusion from the east Mediterranean, and this interpretation was followed closely by the majority of prehistorians until the last two decades (for a critical review, see Renfrew 1967; Chapman, in press). The abandonment of diffusionism has led to the proposal of very different models for the emergence of complexity in S.E.Spain. At the same time, excavations since 1960 have aimed to improve our knowledge of the chronology of local Copper and Bronze Age cultures: important sites excavated include Cerro de la Virgen (Schüle 1980), Cerro del Real (Pellicer and Schüle 1962, 1966), Cuesta del Negro (Molina and Pareja 1975), Cerro de la Encina (Arribas et al 1974), El Malagón (Arribas et al 1979a; Torre et al.1984; Torre and Sáez 1986), Los Millares (Arribas et al 1979b, 1983; Arribas and Molina 1982, 1984, 1987) and Fuente Alamo (Arteaga and Schubart 1981; Schubart and Arteaga 1986). Much new data has been collected (although the record of publication of this data is uneven), but in the main this data has been of stratigraphic and chronological kind. There has been less concern with general socioeconomic processes and with the explicit models by which field research must be structured. Thus we see a disparity between the models proposed to account for the origins of complexity, and the data which is available to test these models. In this paper we will show how the Gatas project aims to contribute to the debate over the origins of complexity in S.E.Spain by creating a more interactive relationship between models and data. We will describe briefly the archaeological record of S.E.Spain and the models currently competing to explain that record, before summarising the aims of the Gatas project, and the results of our fieldwork in the years 1985-87.

According to the current archaeological evidence, the agricultural colonisation of lowland S.E.Spain begins in the early third millennium bc, with the appearance of (poorly defined) Final Neolithic occupation on such sites as Terrera Ventura (Gusi 1986), Peñon de la Reina (Martínez and Botella 1980) and Ciavieja (Suárez et al 1986). Much better data comes from the copper-using culture of Los Millares which extends over lowland Almería, southern Murcia and eastern Granada by the middle of the third millennium bc. The defining characteristics of this culture include copper-working, fortified settlements, false-vaulted megalithic tombs, bifacially-worked flint projectiles and daggers, painted, incised, symbol-decorated and Beaker pottery (e.g.Leisner and Leisner 1943; Martín and Camalich 1982; Martín, Camalich and Tarquis 1983; Arribas and Molina 1987). Metal production may have involved part-time specialisation, but in any case the scale of production was small (Chapman 1984), and there is still debate as to whether metal artefacts should be understood within an economic or an exclusively social and ideological context . Variations in the types, sizes and contents of the megalithic tombs have been interpreted in terms of the beginnings of ranking of corporate groups (Chapman 1981). Analysis of site sizes suggests the existence of, at best, a two level settlement hierarchy (Chapman, in press; c.f. Copper Age sites in the province of Jaén, Nocete 1984). The largest settlement is Los Millares, with its complex, multi-phase fortifications, its associated cemetery of megalithic tombs, and the 'forts' located on adjacent ridge tops. Regional patterns of settlement are still poorly understood, as is the internal organisation of such settlements.

Succeeding the Copper Age of Los Millares is the culture of El Argar, which is defined mainly by its metallurgy, settlements, burials and pottery (Lull 1983). The metals used include arsenical copper (in the majority), bronze, gold and silver, with the last two being reserved for the production of personal ornaments and items demarcating social differences. The range of tools and weapons produced increased, and there is debate over the degree of specialisation in their production. The most distinctive settlements are easily defended, terraced into hillsides at middle altitudes, and often dominate important communication routes. Site sizes again indicate at most a two-level hierarchy (Chapman, in press). Burial now occurred for individuals within these settlements, in urns, cists, pits or artificial caves, which are located under house floors or behind their walls. The pottery associated with domestic and funerary contexts is predominantly undecorated. Analysis of the burials suggests to some the existence of different social classes characteristic of an emerging state society (Lull and Estévez 1986). Radiocarbon dating spans the period c.1900/1800 - 1300 bc, with a period of expansion from lowland Almería into upland Almería, eastern Granada and Jaén c.1650-1550 bc.

The full recognition and periodisation of the Later Bronze Age is a product of research since 1962, principally on settlements within Granada (Molina 1978). First there is a period called Bronce Tardío, c.1300-1100bc, based upon sites such as Cerro de la Encina and Fuente Alamo, in which burial is no longer found inside settlements, characteristic Argaric metalwork and some pottery (e.g.copas) disappear, and new pottery types (e.g. of the Cogotas 1 horizon) appear. These new types have been attributed by some (e.g. Molina 1978) to the results of cultural expansion by transhumance from the northern Meseta. Succeeding Bronce Tardío is Bronce Final (c.1100bc-600BC), subdivided by Molina into three periods, the last of which is contemporary with the first Phoenician colonies in southern Spain. One of the problems involved in the study of this Later Bronze Age is the poor and limited quality of much of the data.

Five models which attempt to explain these changes in the archaeological record of S.E.Spain have been published within the last ten years. Chapman (1978) argued that the arid climate of the south-east led to population aggregation around areas of effective water control, thus making an intensification of production, through irrigation, the key to successful cereal cultivation. Population aggregation in turn necessitated new arrangements for land tenure, inheritance, access to vital resources and leadership. He reconstructed the beginnings of social ranking in the Copper Age, and his arguments were limited essentially to this period. Gilman (1976, 1981; Gilman and Thornes 1985) also concerned himself with the emergence of social inequality, but followed social change through into the Bronze Age. He argued that the use of intensified production as a means of coping with an arid environment required new social relations of production. Capital investment would require defence. It would also counter social fission and enable elites to establish control over local populations. Thus hereditary leadership emerged. Ramos and Lull took different approaches, but both argued for a more humid, woodland-covered landscape in the Copper and Bronze Ages. Ramos (1981) argued that population pressure in the early Copper Age resulted in competition for resources, settlement expansion, fortified settlements, the beginnings of social ranking and intensification of production. Lull (1983, 1984) focussed on the Argaric culture, and an increase in production which promoted inter-regional diversification through differences in economic yields. This led to a marked division in society and in the organisation of labour, including the removal of metallurgy from the domestic sphere. At the same time, the expansion of metal production acted as a 'dynamizer', breaking down local self-sufficiency and leading to complementary production within local ecosystems. This ought to have been produced in the context of a territorial organisation which made possible stable communication routes through the circulation of products over large distances. A major consequence of agricultural and metallurgical intensification was environmental degradation by the end of the Argaric culture. Lastly Mathers (1984a, 1984b)returned to the environmental reconstruction adopted by Chapman and Gilman, and argued for the emergence of social differentiation, institutionalised leadership and labour intensive 'buffering mechanisms' as a means of coping with unpredictable water supplies. Extensive alliance networks were also necessary, giving variations in agricultural production between regions. With the development of the Argaric culture, southern Almería (the most vulnerable area for agriculture) was depopulated, but in other areas (e.g.eastern Almería), social differentiation was expressed more openly, especially through control over a prestige goods economy.

These models derive from different bodies of theory and make different assumptions about cultural change. For example, there are differences of opinion as to the degree to which intensification of production can be attributed to population growth and pressure.Also the question of scale is little discussed in relation to cultural change. To take the case of intensification, we should note that it operates at different scales (Carlstein 1982) . At the largest scale, there may be intensification in the region as a whole. Within the region there may be intensification at the level of some, but by no means all local communities. At the lowest scale, there may exist imbalances in production and the organisation of labour between individual production units within settlements.

Equally important to us is the lack of agreement as to the actual changes in culture and environment which took place in prehistoric S.E.Spain. How arid or humid was the climate, and were there fluctuations through time? What was the vegetational cover and what effects did human settlement have on it? What forms did intensification of production take (e.g. when and where did animal traction and carriage, water control, crop rotation, polyculture, appear) and when did it occur in each area? What were the forms and scales of production during the Later Bronze Age? What were the sizes and scales of different socio-economic formations ? What was the scale of interaction within and between regions, and how far was there political integration? All these questions require that we collect data relevant to the variables of interest to us, rather than continue to populate prehistoric south-east Spain with cultural traits. This is the vital process of giving meaning to the archaeological record, without which any empirical evaluation of the hypotheses about cultural change in S.E.Spain cannot be attempted. In addition, the measurement of cultural change requires refinement, rather than continuing dependence upon outmoded typologies or limited, qualitative analyses from the poorly published excavations of only a few sites. The techniques for data collection must be appropriate for the variables under study.

THE GATAS PROJECT

It was the need for a better, empirical evaluation of competing hypotheses about cultural change in prehistoric S.E.Spain which led us to design the Gatas project. The project centres upon the excavation of the settlement of Gatas,near Turre, in the south of the basin of Vera in eastern Almería. The site is located in what might be called the 'heartland' of the Argaric culture, as the type-site of El Argar lies 12kms to the north, while Fuente Alamo (currently under excavation by Schubart and Arteaga) lies a further 10kms to the north, on the edge of the basin. Excavations at Gatas by the Siret brothers in 1886 (Siret and Siret 1887, pp.209-225), produced cultural material suggestive of occupation in the Copper Age and throughout the

Bronze Age. Argaric structures were excavated on the top of the hill and burials were found within these structures. The richest burial was in grave 2, which contained a female associated with a silver diadem, bracelets, pendants and beads of silver and copper, and a copper awl with a wooden haft covered in silver plate, among other grave goods. Evidence for all stages of metal production was found. Below the hill, to the east, were found two structures called 'galleries', which the Sirets thought were used for water storage.

Since 1886 there have been no further excavations at Gatas. Given the potential of the site for studying cultural change over at least one and a half millennia, we planned the Gatas project in three phases, each concerned with different questions, and each developing in a logical order. Phase 1 aimed to collate the evidence for cultural, environmental and economic change in S.E.Spain, to present a critical view of different hypotheses about such change (which would enable us to frame specific questions for the project), and to undertake a survey of the site of Gatas in its contemporary environmental and economic context. Phase 2 was planned to test the nature of preserved stratigraphic deposits, as well as cultural, economic and environmental data, in different parts of the settlement. With this information in mind, we planned Phase 3 as one of extensive excavation to study the internal organisation of the settlement during its successive phases of occupation, and the relationship between this organisation (as seen, for example in the spatial patterning of structural, cultural, funerary, and economic data) and the political, social and economic organisation of the later prehistoric populations living at Gatas. In each phase of the project, an understanding of the dynamics of he settlement's occupation cannot be obtained solely with reference to the site of Gatas. For example, the organisation of technological production cannot be understood without reference to the sources of raw materials such as metals, while evidence for the demography, disease and diet of the inhabitants of Gatas must be placed within the context of population dynamics in south-east Spain as a whole.

In order to accomplish the aims of the project, and to pursue both on-site and off-site analyses, we have assembled a multi-disciplinary team, including a botanist (Dr.Martin Jones), a faunal analyst (Annie Grant), a physical anthropologist (Dr.Jane Buikstra), a geologist (Narcís Carulla) , two metallurgists (Drs. Noel Gale and Sofie Stos-Gale) and a geomorphologist (Dr.Marie-Agnes Courti).

THE GATAS PROJECT-PHASE 1

Phase 1 of the project was undertaken in 1985, and the results published as a monograph in 1987 (Chapman, Lull, Picazo and Sanahuja 1987), to which reference should be made for more details than are given here. The survey of the location of Gatas in its local context included studies of the modern vegetation and land use, as well as the geology, hydrology and geomorphology, within an area of c.2 x 2km. These studies have yielded data of importance for comparison with data to be collected from archaeological contexts at Gatas. For example, the survey of modern vegetation revealed a frequency of endemic species which suggested that the climax vegetation would have been transitional between thorny scrub and Mediterranean woodland, with the former dominant in the lowest and hottest areas, and the latter increasing with altitude and deeper soils. Such a reconstruction agrees with that proposed on the basis of the fauna and wood charcoals from Fuente Alamo (Schoch and Schweingruber 1982). A second example of the value of the survey may be taken from the analysis of the geological sources of construction materials and material culture items found on the surface of Gatas.Thus, for the construction materials, the majority had sources within 300m of the site, and the furthest away were only at a distance of 1km. In contrast to the ease with which such materials could be obtained, only small, derivative samples of copper (within a matrix of chloritic schist) of little potential for sustained exploitation were located within the survey area, suggesting reliance upon more distant sources (an observation to be tested by lead isotope analyses).

With regard to Gatas, the 1985 season saw the mapping of the site, its division into topographic zones (for example, the Meseta Superior, on the top of the hill, where evidence of the Sirets' excavations can still be seen, and the Ladera Este where the 'galleries' in 1886 are still preserved for study), and geophysical survey in all zones to assess the potential for excavation of occupation deposits. Surface cultural material, primarily pottery, but also including lithics, shell, bone and metal, was analysed according to its morphology and production, its dating and its distribution among the different topographic zones. The dating of the materials supported our expectation that occupation began in the Copper Age and continued until the Bronce Final period, while the distribution of materials according to zones suggested the possibility of differences in either their use or in the spatial extent of settlement at different periods.

THE GATAS PROJECT-PHASE 2

Using the results of the survey, for example the surface distribution of cultural materials and the geophysical analysis, we were able to undertake the stratigraphic excavations of phase 2 of the Gatas project in 1986-87. Four trenches (sondeos 1-4), each 4 x 4m in area, were exavated, in the following zones of the site: Ladera Sur (S2, S4), Ladera Media 1 (S1) and Ladera Media II (S3). Of the other zones in the site, it is important to note that we did not include excavation of the Meseta Superior in this phase, as the activities of the Sirets in this zone have made extensive excavation a more appropriate method of study during phase 3 of the project.

Differences in stratigraphy and in cultural materials were observed between the different sondeos, especially between S2 / S4 at the southern foot of the hill and S1 and S3 on northern slopes of the hill.

No pre-Argaric occupation was found at the southern foot of the hill. In contrast, on the northern side of the hill, in S1 the pre-Argaric material occurred in a red, fine grained deposit, which may be the result of oxidisation of the natural limestone by water action (although this requires further study by soil micromorphology). Among the materials from this deposit were blades, cores and worked flakes, produced on a variety of types of flint(the sources of these flints have still to be identified). The pottery from S1 , although very worn and fragmented, was clearly distinct from other pottery at Gatas, with yellowish and pinkish fabrics and forms such as deep bowls.

Argaric Bronze Age occupation has been identified in all four sondeos, though only in S3 are there stratified floor levels, walls of structures, the range of material culture items, evidence of food consumption and storage and three urn burials (graves 19-21). In contrast, the Argaric levels in S1 were not in structural contexts, and in S2 and S4 were traces of disturbed floors and other structural evidence.

Of special importance is the quantity of Later Bronze Age material excavated in S2, in a sequence of deposits without any structural evidence, but consisting of fine, dark sediments which are provisionally interpreted as forming part of a cultivation terrace. Such an interpretation is still to be tested by analysis of soil micromorphology. If supported, this interpretation is of great importance for our currently limited knowledge of subsistence practices during the Later Bronze Age in S.E.Spain.

Subsequent to the Later Bronze Age, the only occupation deposits revealed by the 1986-87 excavations were of Arab date, and these were most clearly represented in S3 in a re-use of Argaric structures. This re-use dates probably to the tenth to twelfth centuries A.D., along with the construction of terracing on adjacent northern slopes of the sierra Cabrera.

During the course of the phase 2 excavations, sampling was undertaken for a variety of purposes, both environmental and economic. Many of these samples are still under study, but it is interesting to note that the seeds from the upper Argaric contexts in S3 suggest the storage and consumption of barley (with crop cleaning having taken place elsewhere), in contrast to the concentration upon legumes in the lower layers of this sondeo. Whether this is part of a real economic change, or whether it relates to differences in the spatial location of storage/consumption of different crops within the settlement, will have to be studied during more extensive excavations in phase 3 of the project. The botanical evidence from S2 has also yielded interesting provisional results, with the presence in the proposed terrace deposits of large numbers of mineralised seeds of Lithospermum arvense, which are suggested to be the remnants of a rich arable seed bank in once cultivated soils (Martin Jones, pers.comm).Thus the botanical evidence provides some initial support for the inference we have made on the basis of the Later Bronze Age deposits in S2.

CONCLUSIONS AND PROSPECTS

By way of conclusions to this paper, we would like to summarise some of the empirical and theoretical points which we think are central to the Gatas project. A good starting point is to note that for all the fieldwork which has been undertaken in the last two decades in S.E.Spain, there have been few major advances in our understanding of the dynamics of cultural change. The reason for this, we think, is the absence of research designs which have been constructed in the light of theoretical problems, and which aim to contribute to the empirical evaluation of different models for the origins of complexity during the Copper and Bronze Ages. The models which have been proposed (as outlined above) have been based on essentially the same data base, which in turn has been compiled, since the 1880s, with questions of culture and chronology in mind. Clearly some evaluation of these models is required, using a new methodology for confirmation or falsification by empirical data , or there will continue to be a disparity between models and fieldwork.

Given that empirical evaluation of these models is thought desirable, how do we go about this process? In general terms the answer to this question could be debated for an entire Congress, especially if we were philosophers of science and not archaeologists, but for now we restrict ourselves to some particular observations. First, we have emphasised the need to design the evaluation process in the light of existing models, and in the light of the variables which play important parts in such models. Thus our interest is in, for example, intensification of production as a variable, how it changes through time and space, and specifically how we can measure it with archaeological data. Our concern is not with cultural traits in their own right and for their own sake.

Secondly, our concern is with one site, Gatas, albeit in its regional context, and it would be foolish for us to claim that we could 'test' all the existing models for cultural change by using the data from this one settlement. For example, using the example of intensification of production again, this could vary in both form and scale within a region, so that some communities intensify more, and in different directions, than others. We might find differences between the degree of intensification at Gatas and, say, Fuente Alamo. But the data from Gatas would still be a contribution towards an empirical evaluation of the role of intensification of production in cultural change in S.E.Spain, and it would hopefully encourage other projects to contribute further to this evaluation.

Thirdly, such projects need to be designed with a logical structure, moving from survey to small-scale, and then large-scale excavations, with each stage yielding observations which can be fed into the design of the next stage. At each stage, the problems under study will change, as ours have done from phases 1-2 of the Gatas project.

245

On a particular level, the results so far from the 1985-87 seasons of the Gatas project have enabled us to test the preservation of deposits for large-scale excavation, to establish the duration of occupation of the settlement and give us a sequence of occupation on one site which is without parallel in lowland S.E.Spain , to show that evidence for metallurgy and for subsistence activities is preserved, to raise the possibility that we have new evidence on subsistence production in the later Bronze Age, and to reveal the potential for analysis of intra-site variation in relation to the social and economic organisation of the communities which inhabited Gatas in the Copper and Bronze Ages. These results are now being prepared for publication in a further monograph, and will be integrated in our plans for the large-scale excavations of phase 3 of the project.

ACKNOWLEDGEMENTS

The Gatas project has been carried out with the financial support of the Consejería de Cultura of the Junta de Andalucía (who have given permits for fieldwork), the National Geographic Society, the British Academy, the Society of Antiquaries, the Prehistoric Society, the Mediterranean Archaeological Trust and the University of Reading.

BIBLIOGRAPHY

Arribas, A. and F. Molina, 1982. 'Los Millares. Neue Ausgrabungen in der Kupferzeitlichen Siedlung (1978-81)', *Madrider Mitteilungen* 23, pp.9-32.

Arribas, A. and F.Molina, 1984. 'The latest excavations of the Copper Age settlement at Los Millares, Almería, Spain, in W.H.Waldren, R.Chapman, J.Lewthwaite and R.C.Kennard (eds), *The Deyá Conference of Prehistory*, pp.1029-1050, B.A.R. Int. Series 229, Oxford.

Arribas, A. and F.Molina, 1987. 'New Bell Beaker discoveries in the South-east Iberian peninsula', in W.H.Waldren and R.C.Kennard (eds), *Bell Beakers of the Western Mediterranean*. pp.129-46, B.A.R.Int. Series 331, Oxford.

Arribas, A., E.Pareja, F.Molina, O.Arteaga and F.Molina, 1974. *Excavaciones en el poblado de la Edad del Bronce "Cerro de la Encina". Monachil (Granada). El corte estratigráfico num.3*, Excavaciones Arqueológicas en España 81, Madrid.

Arribas, A., F.Molina, F. de la Torre, T.Najera and L.Saez, 1979a. 'El poblado de la Edad del Cobre de "El Malagón" (Cúllar-Baza, Granada). Campaña de 1975', *Cuadernos de Prehistoria de la Universidad de Granada* 3, pp. 67-116.

Arribas, A., F.Molina, L.Sáez, F.de la Torre, P.Aguayo and T. Nájera, 1979b. 'Excavaciones en Los Millares (Santa Fe de Mondújar, Almería). Campañas de 1978 y 1979', *Cuadernos de Prehistoria de la Universidad de Granada* 4, pp. 61-110.

Arribas, A., F.Molina, L.Sáez, F.de la Torre, P.Aguayo, A.Bravo and A.Suárez, 1983. 'Excavaciones en Los Millares (Santa Fe de Mondújar, Almería). Campañas de 1982 y 1983', *Cuadernos de Prehistoria de la Universidad de Granada* 8, pp. 123-47.

Arteaga, O. and H.Schubart, 1981. 'Fuente Alamo 1979', *Noticiario Arqueológico Hispánico. Prehistoria* 11, pp. 9-22.

Carlstein, T., 1982. *Time, Resources, Society and Ecology*, Lund Studies in Geography 49.

Chapman, R.W., 1978. 'The evidence for prehistoric water control in south-east Spain', *Journal of Arid Environments* 1, pp. 261-74.

Chapman, R.W., 1981. 'Archaeological theory and communal burial in prehistoric Europe', in I.Hodder, G.Isaac and N.Hammond (eds), *Pattern of the Past; studies in honour of David L. Clarke*, pp .387-411, Cambridge.

Chapman, R.W., 1984. 'Early metallulrgy in Iberia and the West Mediteranean: innovation, adoption and production', in W.H.Waldren, R.Chapman, J.Lewthwaite and R.C.Kennard (eds), *The Deyá Conference of Prehistory*, pp. 1139-1165, B.A.R. Int. Series 229, Oxford.

Chapman, R.W., in press. *Emerging Complexity: prehistoric south-east Spain, lberia and the West Mediterranean*, Cambridge.

Chapman, R.W., V.Lull, M.Picazo and Ma.E.Sanahuja, 1987. *Proyecto Gatas. Sociedad y Economía en el Sudeste de España c.2500-800 a.n.e. 1. La Prsopección Arqueoecológica*, B.A.R.Int.Series 348, Oxford.

Gilman, A., 1976. 'Bronze Age dynamics in southeast Spain', *Dialectical Anthropology* l, pp. 307-19.

Gilman, A., 1981. 'The development of social stratification in Bronze Age Europe', *Current Anthropology* 22, pp.1-23.

Gilman, A. and J.Thornes, 1985. *Land-use and Prehistory in south-east Spain*, Allen and Unwin, London.

Gusi, F., 1986. 'El yacimiento de Terrera Ventura (Tabernas) y su relación con la cultura de Almería', in *Homenaje a Luis Siret 1934-84*, pp. 192-95.

Leisner, G. and V.Leisner, 1943. *Die Megalithgräber der Iberischen Halbinseli: Der Süden*, Walter de Gruyter, Berlin.

Lull, V., 1983. La "cultura" de El Argar. *Un modelo para el estudio de las formaciones economico-sociales prehistóricas*, Akal, Madrid.

Lull, V., 1984. 'A new assessment of Argaric society and economy', in W.H.Waldren, R.Chapman, J.Lewthwaite and R.C.Kennard (eds), *The Deyá Conference of Prehistory*, pp. 1197-1238, B.A.R.Int.Series 229, Oxford.

Lull, V. and J.Estévez, 1986. 'Propuesta metodológica para el estudio de las necrópolis argáricas', in *Homenaje a Luis Siret 1934-84*, pp. 441-452.

Martín, D. and M.D.Camalich, 1982. 'La "cerámica simbólica" y su problemática (aproximación a través de los materiales de la colección L.Siret)', *Cuadernos de Prehistoria de la Universidad de Granada* 7, pp. 267-306.

Martín, D., M.D.Camalich and E.Tarquis, 1983. 'La cerámica con decoración pintada del Eneolitico en Andalucía Oriental', *Tabona* 4, pp.95-130.

Martínez, C. and M.C.Botella, 1980. *El Peñón de la Reina (Alboloduy, Almería)*. Excavaciones Arqueológicas en Espana 112, Madrid.

Mathers, C., 1984a. 'Beyond the grave: the context and wider implications of mortuary practices in south-east Spain', in T.F.C.Blagg, R.F.J.Jones and S.T.Keay (eds) Papers in Iberian Archaeology. pp. 13-46, B.A.R.Int. Series 193, Oxford.

Mathers, C., 1984b. "Linear Regression", inflation and prestige competition: second millennium transformations in southeast Spain', in W.H.Waldren, R.Chapman, J.Lewthwaite and R.C.Kennard (eds), *The Deyá Conference of Prehistory*, pp. 1167-1196, B.A.R.Int. Series 229, Oxford.

Molina, F., 1978. 'Definición y sistematización del Bronce Tardío y Final en el Sudeste de la Peninsula Iborica', *Cuadernos de Prehistoria de la niversidad de Granada* 3, pp.159-232.

Molina, F. and E.Pareja, 1975. *Excavaciones en la Cuesta del Negro (Purullena, Granada),* Excavaciones Arqueológicas en Espana 86, Madrid.

Nocete, F., 1984. 'Elementos para un estudio del patrón de asentamiento en las campiñas occidentales del Alto Guadalquivir durante la Edad del Cobre', in *Arqueología Espacial* 3, pp. 91-102.

Pellicer, M. and W.Schüle, 1962. *Cerro del Real, Galera (Granada)* I, Excavaciones Arqueológicas en España 12, Madrid.

Pellicer, M. and W. Schüle, 1966. *El Cerro del Real. Galera (Granada) II*, Excavaciones Arqueológicas en España 52, Madrid.

Ramos, A., 1981. 'Interpretaciones secuenciales y culturales de la Edad del Cobre en la zona meridional de la Peninsula Iberica. La alternativa de materialismo cultural',*Cuadernos de Prehistoria de la Universidad de Granada*, 6, pp. 242-56.

Renfrew, C., 1967. 'Colonialism and megalithismus'. *Antiquity* 41, pp.276-88.

Schoch, W. and F.Schweingruber, 1982. 'Holzkohlenanalytische Ergebnisse aus der Bronzezeitlichen Siedlung Fuente Alamo, Prov. Almería, Spanien', *Archäologisches Korrerpondenzblatt* 12, pp. 451-55.

Schubart, H., 1976. 'Relaciones mediterráneas de la cultura de El Argar', *Zephyrus* 26-27, pp. 331-42.

Schubart, H. and O.Arteaga, 1986. 'Fundamentos arqueológicos para el estudio socio-económico y cultural del area de El Argar', in *Homenaje a Luis Siret 1934-84*, pp. 289-307.

Schüle, W., 1980. *Orce und Galera. Zwei Siedlungen aus dem 3 bis I Jahrtausend v.Chr. im Südosten der Iberischen Halbinsel l*, Philipp von Zabern, Mainz am Rhein.

Siret, H. and L.Siret, 1887. *Les Premiers Ages du Métal dans le Sud-Est de l'Espagne*, Anvers.

Suárez, A., M.Carrilero, A.Bravo and J.L.Garcia, 1986. *Excavaciones arqueológicas en Ciavieja, El Ejido (Almería). Primeros resultados*, Cuadernos Ejidenses 2.

Torre, F. de la, F.Molina, F.Contreras, I.Blanco, M.A.Moreno, A.Ramos and M.P. de la Torre 1984. 'Segunda Campaña de Excavaciones (983) en el poblado de la Edad del Cobre de El Malagón (Cúllar-Baza, Granada)', *Cuadernos de Prehistoria de la Universidad de Granada* 9, pp.131-46.

Torre, F.de la and L.Sáez, 1986. 'Nuevas excavaciones en el yacimiento de la Edad del Cobre de "El Malagon" (Cúllar-Baza, Granada)', in *Homenaje a Luis Siret 1934-84*, pp. 221-26.

ISLAND COLONISATION IN THE WESTERN MEDITERRANEAN:
THE BALEARIC ISLANDS

JOSEP F. ENSENYAT ALCOVER
Department of Ethnology and Prehistory
University of Oxford
Oxford OX2 6PN, England.

RESUME

This paper will deal with the question of colonization of islands in the West Mediterranean, and particularly focusing the attention on the case of the Balears. The principles of island biogeography, as suggested by Cherry (1981), provide a valid pattern for the human colonization of islands, when studied as a whole. All islands share two features that are implicit to insularity: limited size and isolation. However we must be aware of the different characteristics of each island, that is, size, topography, natural resources, an so on.

Island ecosystems have reached a very vulnerable dynamic equilibrium before the arrival of man (Fosberg, 1963). When human populations enter island ecosystems they do so together with a range of species associated with them -plants and animals- that provokes instability in the ecosystem. This will be the immediate indirect cause for the extinction, due to competition, of many species already present in the island (Simberloff, 1974; Rappaport, 1963). Man's direct effect on the island's ecosystem may also be the elimination or drastic reduction of certain species (Williamson, 1981) by over-exploitating them during the adaptation phase after the arrival of a human group to the island, as well as the effect of land-use over the landscape through deforestation, cultivation, drainage, irrigation, terracing. In the case of the Balears the introduction of domesticated animals along with what so far appears to be the earliest pottery technology are dated circa 2700 b.c. (Waldren, 1982:253) and the extinction of the endemic Myotragus Balearicus circa 2100 b.c. (Burleigh & Clutton-Brock, 1980).

The first problem that must be taken into account is the interpretation that is given to the first evidence of human presence in the islands. Quite often archaeologists tend to concentrate their work in the islands towards the finding of the oldest remains, and even more often they identify these remains as being the proof of human colonization or permanent habitation of the island.The colonization of an island by human populations is the result of planned migrations, usually through intensification and prolongation of their visits. We should try to reconstruct in fully the process from the first arrival of man to the island (or even the first occupation) to the moment in which the island becomes the main residence throughout the year and supplies most of their subsistence, that is, when there is a permanent settlement of the island, making a clear distinction between exploitation and Colonization of the island (Cherry, 1981).

In the process of Colonization of islands there are two areas involved: the island itself and the mainland, whether the continent or another island, which provides the colonizer population. What I am presenting in this paper is a series of queries that will help to clarify the possible connections between the mainland and the island, in order to determine the origins of the parental population.

When studying the island colonization we ought to pay attention to the differences between the mainland conditions and the island environment. The first step would be the delineation of areas of study on both the island and the mainland. The selection of the mainland areas is dependent upon the distance between the island and the mainland -to minimize the distance effect (MacArthur & Wilson, 1967)- and also on the sailing conditions, to show which crossings are easier to illustrate how the first knowledge of the island was acquired and even reveal the possibility of a stochastic colonization of the island. The biogeographical study of these areas -highlands, lowlands, coastal and inner areas- in terms of geology (soil composition, relief), climate (rainfall pattern, seasonality, temperatures, winds, humidity), water resources, flora, fauna, agricultural potential, pasture lands, forest will determine the habitat diversity of the chosen areas, presenting which areas on the mainland are best and least suited for the colonization of the island, on the one hand, and to predict which areas on the island are most likely to be Colonized first, on the other.

The pioneer human group will find an environment somewhat different from that of the mainland. Hence, in order to take the maximum economic advantages from the new environmental conditions, the colonist community will have to adapt their cultural traits to the new situation. The contrast between mainland and island conditions gives us a reference on the amount of change in the agricultural and pastoral practices that might have been necessary when colonizing the island. This cultural change will be aimed at a short term efficiency (Gumerman, 1986), these representing the major problem that the new group will have to face. Consequently, the closer both environments are the easier and faster the adaptation will be and the advantages of a new habitat free of competitors will be greater. This leads to the suggestion that the parental population will have its origins in an area ecologically similar to the island.

The events that are taking place on the mainland is another aspect to look at. Specially those referring to demographic pressure that can be interpreted in the archaeological record in the form of increase in the number of open-air settlements, intensified exploitation of resources, exploitation of less desirable goods to complement the diet, and expansion to other areas. As long as the mainland can support the population increase the islands will remain under-exploited, but when the pressure of population on resources in an adjacent mainland zone surpassed the threshold set by this barrier, colonization occurred (Lewthwaite, 1985:220). The colonization of the Balears could be considered as part of a series of waves of colonization in the mainland's closest areas during the Chalcolithic period (Lewthwaite, 1985).

The adaptation to less productive island environments favours the dispersion of small populations. The founder group is normally formed by a small number of individuals from a larger community. This group will not bring to the island all the cultural traits of the source area, founder principle (MacArthur & Wilson,1967). The differentiation of the island's culture from that of the mainland will be dependent upon the ability to reproduce in full the parent culture (Vayda & Rappaport, 1963). The analysis of the archaeological record -chronology, sites, settlement pattern, social organization, subsistence patterns, economy, metallurgy, burial rituals, pottery (range of forms, fabrics, and decoration), lithic industry, prestige goods, etc.- of both relevant areas, the mainland and the islands, will verify the consequence of the founder effect on the Colonization of the Balears. The evaluation of artifacts and assemblages similarities will assist the understanding of interaction between both areas (Chapman, 1985).

Island Colonization in the Western Mediterranean:
The Balearic Islands.
Josep F. Ensenyat Alcover

THE PROCESS OF ISLAND COLONIZATION

The aeon old colonization of islands by flora and fauna seems to have followed a pattern. However, one that could arguably be applied to every island. Since, when we study the islands throughout the world, we realize how different they are from each other. They differ in size, remoteness, topography, natural resources, and so on. Some have very much to offer, others almost nothing and still all of them suit some living species. Despite these differences all islands share two features that are implicit to insularity: limited size and isolation. From the study of the colonization process of islands MacArthur and Wilson (1967) set the basic principles that are common to all the islands.

The immediate cause of islands colonization is generally the pressure that mainland populations have to resist. If island colonization is a stochastic process, it will be affected by the distance between the mainland and the island and its area. Large islands close to the mainland will be colonized at a faster rate than small islands further away. The number of species present in the island is a dynamic equilibrium between the immigration of new species and the extinction of the ones already there.

The differences between islands and mainland, and among islands themselves, in terms of biota, are due to the small population that migrates to the islands. There it becomes isolated and has to adapt to a new environment through major changes that immediately make distinct from other populations.
When it comes to man, the same principle of island colonization should be applied. In this case, changes will be cultural rather than genetic.

THE ISLAND ENVIRONMENT

The essential characteristic of an island is a dry-land area surrounded by water. This water barrier isolates islands from other land. It ranges from 3,800 Km. down to a very narrow channel. The larger is the gap, the more isolated is the island. Islands vary in size, from New Guinea or Greenland, having many of the insularity features, to tiny rocks that can hardly support temporary or microscopic biota (Fosberg, 1963). This limitation in size and isolation determines the basic feature of insularity. Consequently, island environment is limited in size-space resources (Fosberg, 1963), limited habitat diversity, limited availability, or even absence, of other resources such as water, minerals (Evans, 1973). Island environment have a very poor temporal autocorrelation of habitat rank, meaning that an habitat which is currently very good is likely not to be so a few years hence (Diamond, 1977), therefore they are expected to have a very high variable productivity of land. Isolation and limited size make islands very vulnerable to environmental disaster: drought, cyclone, volcanic eruptions (Terrel, 1984). These perturbations or environmental hazards have longer lasting effects in an island situation (Cox & Moore, 1980). Even small changes are capable of profound general effects (Fosberg, 1963).

Islands are very affected by topographic diversity. High islands usually have a greater variety of habitats (Bates,1963; Terrell, 1984). However, due to their effect on air movements, they have a heavy rainfall although the rainshadows can also have extensive dry areas. Low islands are drier, and therefore have impoverished biota (Fosberg, 1976, in Williamson, 1981).

Another special characteristic of islands is their high proportion of coastal conditions (Bates, 1963). This leads to a tendency toward climatic equitability. The climate of an island is more temperate than that of the nearest mainland, but it is also more humid and windier (Williamson, 1981).

These features, limited area, and consequently, limitation in the range of habitat types, and isolation mark the island environment as being a very impoverished as well as a fragile and vulnerable one.

THE COLONIZATION OF ISLANDS

As seen above, islands do not offer a very attractive environment to settle down. On the contrary, they are secondary, marginal environments, imposing constraints on any group that chooses to inhabit them (Evans, 1977). So then, we may not expect the island environment to be the first choice for a taxon to live in. We have to seek the causes that lead a propagule to colonize an island, in the mainland or another island acting as such.

The origin of the colonization cycle lies in the changes that occur in the source area. These modifications of the ecosystem are in terms of climatic change, habitat, food supply, change in the population composition and change in competitors or predators. Consequently affecting the availability, whether increase, whether decrease, of resources for a species. In the case of an increase in resources a species iniciates a process of silmultaneous changes that will lead to the colonization of the newly available resources. This process includes selection for better dispersal ability, so the taxon will reach the resources more easily, and selection for higher reproductive rate, in order to dispose of enough individuals able to rapidly arrive to the resource before a competitor (Diamond, 1977). In the event of a resource shortage caused by the depletion of mainland resources, the consequent struggle for survival incites the population to disperse in search of available resources elsewhere. Species occupying coastal or secondary habitats will be most affected by the deficiency of means and therefore more predisposed for colonization.

When it comes to move, not all the species or populations within the species have the same dispersal ability. It depends on the number of individuals and the distance that they are able to disperse. This diversity is essentially due to anatomical, or cultural, in the case of man, reasons (Diamond, 1977). The main barrier that plants or animals have to cope with when dispersing is the ocean. Thus, those that can disperse by wind, by floating, flying or carried by any other agent have good dispersal strategies; they are more likely to reach the islands (Williamson, 1981). But animals, apart from those that can fly, can reach the island only by swimming or on a raft of vegetation, with its consequent risks, are bad dispersers (Gorman, 1977). We can see then, that the colonization process is a passive one which is subject to the principles of immigration and extinction (MacArthur & Wilson, 1967). Dispersal involves costs and potential benefits. The costs are the energy expenditures and the risk of death in their attempt (Diamond, 1977). Therefore upon their arrival to an island there is a large element of chance that will increase according to the remoteness of the island (Dobzhansky, 1963; Gorman,

1979). The potential benefits are the possibility of improving their living conditions in the new habitat (Diamond, 1977).

If migration to islands is a stochastic process then islands closer to the mainland will have a faster immigration rate than islands further off. But the presence of stepping-stone islands, there are islands between the source area and the outer islands reduces the distance effect and speeds the immigration rate (MacArthur & Wilson, 1963).

However, getting to an island is not the hardest part of the process. Island environment imposes many constraints to the newcomer and its chances to succed in colonizing it are still very low. Once they have survived the journey, the taxon will have to respond to the challenges presented by the environment, which will not always be suitable, free of competitors. If the colonizer group is small, as usually happens, even after becoming established they will be subjected to random situations that can have fatal consequences to small populations (Gorman, 1979). In order to prevent this precarious state, the colonizing species needs a minimum number of individuals - propagules - capable of procreation and population increase that is achieving colonization (MacArthur & Wilson, 1963; Simberloff, 1976 in Williamson, 1981).

The colonist population begins to adapt to the new environment. Even if this environment is similar to that of the source area, there will still be a readaptation process because the size of the immigrant population is generally very small. Then, there will be an internal unbalance in the gene pool (Dobzhansky, 1963). This adaptation phase will be aimed at a rapid population increase, expanding the population size. The survival of the immigrants and, therefore, the accomplishment of the colonization goal will depend almost entirely on their ability to reproduce. The expected life of the population will be related to its size (MacArthur & Wilson, 1967).

The adaptation phase involves biological as well as behavioural responses of the individual to the new environment. It is likely to be some mismatch between the island habitat and that which the colonies occupied in their source area. There is, then, a niche shift (Diamond, 1977). The adaptation responses will implicate habitat, foraging, and dietary shifts (Gorman, 1979).

After the pioneer community has succeeded in its adaptation to the island's environment and as the reproductive rate is still very high, the newly established population expands its niches to take advantage of available resources that would probably have been exploited by other species in their source area (Diamond, 1977). Since islands are limited in size, thus limited in habitat availability, the expansion phase will eventually spread throughout the available new territory, hence increasing the popul;ation density. Once the colonies have reached the maximun size permited by the environment - carrying capacity - in the expansion phase, the colonization strategy will shift towards a greater selection in policy. This implies a decreasing dispersal to the necessary level to replace death and extinctions, a similar decline in the reproductive rate, and regulation in the utilization of resources. Saturated habitats enhace competition either by increasing the productive efficiency, specialization and intensification of production, or by agression to potential competitors (Diamond, 1977).

When colonization pressure is maintained or even increased by the arrival of new colonizers - invaders - from other populations or species, then other colonies are forced to specialize ecologically and to reduce their niches. During the retreating phase (Diamond, 1977) they occupy more stable or extensible habitats, or easily defensible areas. The main consequence of the habitat regression is a reduction in the population size and subsequently an increase in the chace of extinction (Gorman, 1979). The retreat progresses until the original taxon or the descendents become extinct (Diamond, 1977). At this state the colonization process shows two main strategies. Species with less dispersal ability become restricted to stable habitats where extinction is rare, yet possible in the long term. Species with high dispersal ability will initiate another colonization process.

ISLAND BIOGEOGRAPHY

The biota of islands is not only formed by the first species that arrives. It is composed by the combination of the species selected from the total species pool aiming to form a stable community in which their exploitation of resources counterparts the total production of the island (Gorman, 1979). Biota composition varies with the arrival of a new species but the total production of the island remains the same. Consequently, in order to maintain the stability of the environment, these arrivals need to be compensated for by the extinction of the former species. Islands communities are a dynamic equilibrium between immigration of new taxa and the extinction of those already present (MacArthur & Wilson, 1967). Flora and fauna of islands have particular characteristics that differentiate them from those of continents (Williamson, 1981). Species colonizing islands show a high overwater dispersal ability and a considerable ecological flexibility. They are able to change their way of life for the purpose of survival on islands (Simberloff, 1974).

The variety of species on an island depends, in the short term, upon the size of the island, its topography and, especially, the immigration rate. This is strongly affected by the degree of isolation of the island and the richness of the source area (Cox & Moore, 1980). The size of the island determines its ecological variability, habitat diversity and richness of resources. Since each habitat contains its own assembly of plants and animals, large islands support more species than smaller ones - area effect. A reduction in the size could lead to a reduction in the species number (MacArthur & Wilson, 1967).

Equal areas hold approximately equal number of individuals. If the number of species increases then the average population size of each species will decrease (Williamson, 1981). However, an area in the mainland will usually contain more species than will a comparable island of the same size because continents have a greater degree of floods with organisms moving easily from area to area. The composition of a species on an island is a dynamic equilibrium resulting from a continuous immigration of a species to the island and the extinction of a species already there. Once the equilibrium has been reached, the number of species remain relatively constant, although the composition of the species pool will change (MacArthur & Wilson, 1967). The number of species on an island can only increase by a species disappearance from an island, i.e., extinction. Immigration is explicitly affected by distance. If colonization is a pasive process then islands closer to the mainland will receive new arrivals at a faster rate than islands at some distance - distance effect - (MacArthur & Wilson, 1967). It will also depend on the population size of potential colonies on the mainland which is always varying and so are the probabilities of immigration (Williamson, 1981).

Extinction, on the other hand, is liable to the area effect. Small islands will normally support small populations, therefore they will be more exposed to the risk of extinction (Gorman, 1979).

The disposition of islands in clusters - archipelagos - and the presence of stepping-islands increases the area and reduces the distance between the island and the source area thus mitigating the area and distance effect. The source area for an archipelago will be a continent. While the pool for the individual islands on the archipelago will be other islands in the archipelago itself (Williamson, 1981).

The founder population of a species - propagule - is usually formed by a small number of individuals and will bring only a segment of the gene pool (Dobzhansky, 1963). This will lead to genetic readaptation because the new genetic pool will be unbalanced - founder effect (MacArthur & Wilson, 1967). This population will be affected by evolutionary developments which are caused by the need to adapt to the environment. Consequently, this will lead to a genetically distinct population. When this population becomes reproductively isolated, the final effect of evolution will eventually be the splitting of one species in two, i.e., speciation (MacArthur & Wilson, 1967). If the populations are maintained continuously long enough in their islands, an endemic species will be formed, i.e., forms that are found nowhere else (Williamson, 1981).

Islands compared to continents tend to be conservative (Bates, 1963). The major evolutionary events take place on continents. Evolution generally progresses more rapidly in larger continental areas than in smaller ones (Williamson, 1981). Continental populations, especially of abundant and mobile species, are subject to migration and gene diffusion between numerous groups (Dobzhansky, 1963). Islands being isolated do not participate in this process. They are protected by the water barrier from the external events.

As opposed to extinction, islands shelter relincts, that is, species that have survived on certain islands but have become extinct elsewhere (Williamson, 1981).

The number of species on an island is limited. The reasons why a particular species may be absent from a particular island are that (a) it has been unable to reach it; (b) it may have reached it but has been unable to colonize it; (c) it may have colonized it but has become extinct; (d) it may not have reached the island yet (Cox & Moore, 1980).

MAN AS COLONIST

Man's movements in search of better environments that satisfy his needs have been a constant feature in human evolution. When studying human migration we should be able to compare it to any other animal population. In that case we must be aware that man's behaviour responses to the environment are faster than those which are genetic (Diamond, 1977). Humans rely mainly upon cultural means rather than on biological evolution (Rappaport, 1963).

The migration of man to islands is a late phenomenon of hominid evolution (Cherry, 1981). The high population growth of sedentary, food producing communities on the mainland let the coastal groups increase the exploitation of marine resources. The result of this was the development of the appropiate technology, that is, watercraft, navigational skills, and preparation of food for long journeys (Diamond, 1977). Seafaring gave the coastal communities the actual knowledge of the islands themselves (Cherry, 1984) as well as the ability to disperse on water. But the adquisition of the idoneous technology, or what Evans called "adequate means of transport" (1977:14), does not necessarily mean that they rush out to colonize islands. As Cherry points out: "... to agree that they could put to sea in boats is not to say that they did so, with colonization in mind." (1984:12). At this point we must distinguish between exploitation and colonization of an island. Seasonals visits to an island for the exploitation of its resources or in the course of fishing expeditions are simply utilization of the island by a group living elsewhere. But when the island becomes the main residence throughout the year and supplies most of their subsistence then we can talk about colonization in a proper sense. The archaeological evidence for year round occupation will be the presence of clusters of burials and architectural features in association with artefacts related to the procurement and preparation of food (Cherry, 1981). As long as the mainland can support the increase of population the islands will remain underexploited, as mere complementary area. The effective colonization of the island generally occurs when the resources in the mainland cannot support the demographic pressure.(Lewthwaite, 1985). The demographic expansion in the mainland is shown in the archaeological record in the form of increase in the number of open-air settlements, intensified exploitation of resources, exploitation of less desirable goods to complement the diet, and expansion to other areas.

Although the discovery of islands is a matter of chance, their colonization is the result of planned migrations usually through intensification and prolongation of their visits. Passive colonization of islands by man is very unlikely to succeed because the possibility of finding a mate will be very slight and the awkward conditions of island life will be practically insuperables. When the pioneer human group reaches an island they find ecological vaccuum (Rappaport, 1963), free of competitors. However, they will find an impoverished environment which is less variable ecologically, i.e., it has less species than the mainland, and not all the species that are present on the island will be be known by the colonist group - cognized environment (Rappaport, 1963). Islands' environments are somewhat different from those of the mainland. In order to take the maximum economic advantages of the islands environmental conditions, the colonist community will have to adapt their cultural traits to the new situation. The cultural changes will be aimed at a short term efficiency to maximize their reproductive capability (Gumerman, 1986), and therefore, reduce the risk of extinction. The effect of nature on man will differ according to the stage and type of culture that he carried to the island (Bates, 1963).

The process of colonization of islands involves two areas: the island itself and the mainland, whether the continent or another island acting as such. In order to determine the origins of the parental population, we should clarify the possible conections between the island and the mainland. The first step would be the comparison of both the mainland and the island, to establish the similarities and differences in their environment. The selection of the areas in the mainland will be dependent upon the distance between the island and the mainland - to minimize the distance effect (MacArthur and Wilson, 1967) - and also on the sailing conditions, to show which crossings are easier to illustrate how the first knowledge of the island was adquired and even reveal the possibility of a stochastic colonization of the island. The biogeographical study of these areas - highlands, lowlands, coastal, and inner areas - in terms of geology (soil composition, relief), climate (rainfall pattern, seasonality, temperatures, winds, humidity), water resources, flora, fauna, agricultural potential, pasture lands, forest, etc., will determine the habitat diversity of the chosen areas, presenting which areas on the mainland are best and least suited for the colonization of the island, on the one hand, and to predict which areas on the island are most likely to be colonized first, on the other. The contrast between mainland and island conditions gives us a reference on the amount of change in the subsistence practices (agricultural and pastoral) that might have been necessary when colonizing the island. Consequently, the closer both environments are the easier and faster the adaptation phase will be and the advantages of a new habitat free of competitors will be greater. This leads to the suggestion that the parental population will have its origins in an area ecologically similar to the island.

The adaptation to less productive island environments favours the dispersal of small populations. The founder group is normally formed by a small number of individuals from a larger community in the mainland. This group will not bring to the island all the cultural traits of the source area. If the founder population is "unable to reproduce in full the parent culture then the culture in the new place will be immediately different from the culture in the mainland" (Vayda & Rappaport, 1963:134-135). The new culture will differ from the mainlad's depending on the capability of the migrants to reproduce it (Vayda & Rappaport, 1963). The evolution and differentiation of the island's cultures will be highly influenced by the limited area and the degree of isolation of the island. Large islands will present a richer environment, closer to that of the mainland, thus requiring less cultural change and being more attractive to colonists than small areas. Islands at greater distance from the mainland will require a higher technology to be reached and will involve a higher risk and will be less exposed to outside contact than islands closer to the mainland. The presence of stepping-stone islands will contribute on the one hand to reduce the distance and therefore isolation, and will decrease the area effect on the other. The analysis of the archaeological record - chronology, sites, settlement pattern, social organization, subsistence patterns, economy, metallurgy, burial rituals, pottery (range of forms, fabrics, and decoration), lithic industry, prestige goods, etc. - of the mainland and the island, will verify the consequences of the founder effect on the colonization of the island.

Isolation takes a major account for cultural differentiation because it involves an obstacle to the flow of goods and ideas. Not all the changes achieved by one isolated group may be expected to have been independently achieved by another (Vayda & Rappaport, 1963). Isolation will be relative when there is an interaction between islands and mainland or among islands themselves. Islands lack many needed or desirable items to a human population that may try to satisfy by bringing them from elsewhere. In exchange islands have particular items that are in demand in other areas (Evans, 1973). By establishing contacts with other areas, island communities will break isolation down and, therefore, will be exposed to other cultures that, with little doubt, will influence them. The evaluation of artefacts and assemblages similarities will assist the undereastanding of interaction between the islands and other areas (Chapman, 1985).

Islands ecosystems have reached a dynamic equilibrium before the arrival of man that made them very vulnerable when isolation is broken down (Fosberg, 1963). When human populations enter island ecosystems they do so together with the range of species associated to them, i.e., animals and plants. The sudden introduction of a fairly large number of species provokes instability in the ecosystem. This will be the immediate indirect cause for the extinction of many species already present (Simberloff, 1974; Rappaport, 1963), for these species will now have to face competition from the species introduced by man and the possibility of the introduction of new diseases against which they do not have any immunity. Man's direct effect on extinction may also be by eliminating or drastically reducing certain species (Williamson, 1981) during the adaptation phase, because they were pests, were overexploited or, simply, because they "were in the way" (Rappaport, 1963), as well as the effect of land-use over the landscape through deforestation, cultivation, drainage, irrigation, terracing, etc., thus altering the island's ecosystem.

The adaptation phase after the arrival of a human group to the island is characterized by an intensive exploitation of the natural resources while the adaptive changes are taking place (Kirch, 1984). During this stage, population will grow at a very fast rate with the consequent increase of the demand of supplies that will eventually lead to the overexploitation and final extinction of many local species. As demographic growth is maintained at a high rate, population begins to expand - expansion phase - throughout the available island area. At this stage the whole island ecosystem will be affected by the human action with the virtual extinction of the majority of the local species and their replacement with the species grown by man which produces a modification of the landscape (Kirch, 1984).

When demographic pressure is reaching its limits in an island community, there will be a tendency to fully exploit the available resources within the limited territory (Vayda & Rappaport, 1963). The agricultural development will increasingly intensify - intensification phase - (Kirch, 1984) in order to maximize the productivity of the resources available. This will affect the technology and organization of food production in terms of increased labour per unit area, decrease of fallow periods, development of irrigation, exploitation of marginal areas, assignment of production quotas, storage facilities, and craft specialization (Vayda & Rappaport, 1963; Kirch, 1984). The social organization will evolve towards complex forms reflecting an increased competition over the resources as a result of population pressure (Gumerman, 1986). The final stage of the intensification phase would be the development of certain usages for delemiting population growth such as abortion, infanticide, celibacy, coitus interruptus, the often fatal seafaring, and warfare (Vayda & Rappaport, 1963). At this point another colonization wave is ready to start the process again. In this case islands will act as mainlands.

THE BALEARIC ISLANDS.

The early prehistory of the Balearic Islands was thought to have begun around 2000 b.c. (Rosselló-Bordoy, 1963; Enseñat, 1971) until the discovery in the Cova de Muleta of human bones associated with Myotragus balearicus that were radiocarbon dated at 3985 ± 110 b.c. (KBN-640d) (Rosselló-Bordoy et alii., 1967). The new discovery effectively raised the established chronology of the earliest evidence for human occupation on Mallorca by almost 2000 years. However, the Muleta date also produced a gap which could not be filled by the existing evidence. The next radiocarbon date in the Muleta sequence - Y-2359, 960 ± 120 b.c. - (Stuiver, 1969:637) corresponds to the pre-Talaiotic level. Although this date has been quoted as 1960 ± 120 b.c. (e.g. Fernández-Miranda and Waldren, 1979; Rosselló-Bordoy and Waldren, 1975; Waldren, 1981; 1982), it has been confirmed as it was originally published in Radiocarbon at 960 ± 120 b.c. (Reimer, personal correspondence).

The discovery and excavation of the rock shelter of Son Matge revealed a very deep stratigraphy that covers the whole Balearic prehistoric sequence. This deep stratigraphy and its large corpus of radiocarbon dates have made Son Matge the key stratified site on which Balearic chronology and cultural history rests (Lewthwaite, 1985). The lowest levels at Son Matge are a series of layers that contained Myotragus balearicus coprolites and bones that were radiocarbon dated at 4730 ± 120 b.c. (QL-29) , 3870 ± 380 b.c. (CSIC-177), and 3800 ± 115 b.c. (I-5516) (Fernández-Miranda and Waldren, 1974; 1979; Waldren, 1981; 1982). However no direct evidence of human activity associated with radiocarbon dating is recorded until 2140 ± 390 b.c. (BM-1408) (Burleigh and Clutton-Brock, 1981). The evidence for the introduction of pottery technology in the island at 2700 ± 120 b.c. (QL-998) (Fernández-Miranda and Waldren, 1979; Waldren, 1982) is highly controversial as it is the result of the relocation and reinterpretation of evidence previously reported to have been found in a different, younger level (Rosselló-Bordoy and Waldren, 1973).

Despite the nature and scarcity of the Muleta and Son Matge evidence, the current interpretations of early Balearic prehistory (e.g. Rosselló-Bordoy, 1972; Pericot, 1975; Fernández-Miranda, 1978; Waldren, 1982) state that the human colonization of Mallorca took place in the fifth millennium b.c. with a permanent occupation of the island since then, and even an earlier human presence in the island, based on the Canet cave finds, has been suggested (Kopper, 1984; Pons and Coll, 1984). These finds are interpreted as prove of human colonization or permanent habitation of the island. However, the chronological gap between the early dates and the evidence for the permanent settlement of the island remains unexplained.

Island biogeography provides a valid framework to explain the initial process of colonization of the Balearic Islands which are the westernmost and most isolated islands of the Western Mediterranean. The archaeological record shows that Mallorca was the first Balearic island to have been colonized. Mallorca is the largest island of the archipelago and thefore it has more habitat diversity, with three major geomorphological units: the Serra de Tramuntana or northern ranges, the Pla or central plain, and the Serres de Llevant or the low lying mountain range along the southeastern coast of the island (Riba et alii, 1980). Although Mallorca is not the closest island to the mainland, the distance effect could have been reduced by the presence of Eivissa, midway from the Iberian Peninsula and Mallorca. The earliest archaeological evidence for human presence in the island is found in the Serra de Tramuntana which also corresponds to the area that offers the best conditions for the adaptation phase during the colonization process. The geomorphological characteristics of this humid and subhumid area, rich in natural resources, availability of water resources, arable land in the alluvial intermontane valleys, rainfall pattern that allows agriculture without irrigation technology, good pasture land, forests, offer optimal conditions for a mix economy. It is also in the Serra de Tramuntana where the earliest archaeologicals indicators of a permanent settlement of the island are located.

The archaeological record shows a large chronological difference between the earliest evidence for the human presence and the evidence for permanent settlement in the island that does not reflect a continuous occupation of the island. The events that are taking place in the mainland during the third millennium b.c. would indicate that the conditions in which the mainland was would favour the colonization of the islands.

In conclusion, according to the current available data, the Muleta and Matge early evidence suggests that this area was the object of the first visits to the island by a human group. These visits would correspond to the utilization stage of the island that would eventually lead to the proper colonization of Mallorca during the third millennium b.c. Beaker horizon as evidenced in Son Torrella (Enseñat, 1971), Son Ferrandell-Oleza (Waldren, 1984), Son Gallard (Waldren, 1982), Son Matge (Rosselló-Bordoy and Waldren, 1973; Waldren, 1982), Son Mas (Waldren et al ii., this volume) and Ca Na Cotxera (Cantarellas, 1972), among others.

BIBLIOGRAPHY

Alcover, J. A., Moyá, S. and J. Pons, 1981. Les Quimeres del Passat. Palma de Mallorca: Moll.

Bates, M., 1963. 'Nature's Effect on and Control of Man'. In *Man's Place in the Island Ecosystem: A Symposium*. Edited by F. R.

Fosberg. Honolulu. pp. 101-113.

Barker, G. et al. (eds.), 1985. Beyond Domestication in Prehistoric Europe. *Academic Press*, London.

Bernabeu, J., 1984. El Vaso Campaniforme en el Pais Valenciano. Valencia:Servicio de Investigación Prehistórica. *Trabajos Varios* n° 80.

Burleigh, R. and J. Clutton-Brock, 1980. 'The Survival of Myotragus Balearicus Bate, 1909, into the Neolithic on Mallorca'. *Journal of Archaeological Science* 7:385-388.

Cantarellas, C., 1972. 'Excavaciones en Ca Na Cotxera (Muro, Mallorca)'. Noticiario Arqueológico Hispánico. *Prehistoria* I:179-228.

Chapman, R. W., 1985. 'The Later Prehistory of Western Mediterranean: Recent Advances'. Advances in *World Archaeology* 4:115-187.

Cherry, J. F., 1981. 'Pattern and Process in the Earliest Colonization of the Mediterranean Islands'. *Proceedings of the Prehistoric Society* 47:41-68.

Cherry, J. F., 1984. 'The Initial Colonization of the West Mediterranean Islands in the Light of Island Biogeography and Paleogeography'. In *The Deià Conference of Prehistory*. Edited by

Waldren, W., Chapman, R., Lewthwaite, J. and R. Kennard 1986, Ist Deìa Conference of Prehistory, Early Settlement in the Western Mediterranean Islands and their Peripheral Areas, *B.A.R.*, Oxford, pp. 7-27.

Cox, C. and P. Moore, 1980. Biogeography, an Ecological and Evolutionary Approach. *Blackwells*, Oxford.

Cura, M., 1987. 'L'Horitzó Campaniforme Antic als Països Catalans'. *Fonaments* 6:97-128.

Diamond, J. M., 1977. 'Colonization Cycles in Man and Beast'. *World Archaeology* 8:249-261.

Dobzhansky, T., 1963. 'Biological Evolutions in Island Populations'. In Man's Place in the Island Ecosystem: A Symposium. Edited by F.

Fosberg, R. Honolulu. pp. 65-74.

Enseñat, B., 1971. 'Historia Primitiva de Mallorca'. In *Historia de Mallorca*. Edited by J. Mascaró Pasarius. Palma de Mallorca. pp. 289-352.

Evans, J. D., 1973. 'Islands as Laboratories for the Study of Culture Change'. In The Explanation of Culture Change. *Models in Prehistory*. Edited by C. Renfrew. London:Duckworth.

Evans, J. D., 1977. 'Islands Archaeology in the Mediterranean:Problems and Opportunities'. *World Archaeology* 9:12-26.

Fosberg, F. R., (Ed.), 1963. Man's Place in the Island Ecosystem: A Symposium. Honolulu.

Fosberg, F. R., 1963. 'The Island Ecosystem'. In *Man's Place in the Island Ecosystem: A Symposium*. Edited by F. R. Fosberg. Honolulu. pp. 1-6.

Fernández-Miranda, M., 1978. Secuencia Cultural de la Prehistoria de Mallorca. Madrid:Biblioteca Praehistórica Hispana XV.

Fernández-Miranda, M. and W. Waldren, 1974. 'El Abrigo de Son Matge (Valldemossa) y la Periodización de la Prehistoria Mallorquina mediante los Análisis de Carbono-14'. *Trabajos de Prehistoria* 31:297-304.

Fernández-Miranda, M. and W. Waldren, 1979. 'Periodificación Cultural y Cronología Absoluta en la Prehistoria de Mallorca'. *Trabajos de Prehistoria* 36:349-377.

Gorman, M., 1979. Island Ecology. London:Methuen.

Gumerman, G., 1986. 'The Role of Competition and Cooperation in the Evolution of Island Societies'. In Islands Societies: Archaeological Approaches to Evolution and Transformation. Edited by P. V. Kirch. University Press, *Cambridge*. pp. 42-49.

Hallam, S., 1977. 'The Relevance of Old World Archaeology to the First Entry of Man into New Worlds: Colonization seen from the Antipodes'. *Quaternary Research* 8:128-148.

Houston, J. M., 1964. The Western Mediterranean World. *Longmans*, London.

Kirch, P. V., 1984. The Evolution of Polynesian Chiefdoms. *University Press*, Cambridge.

Kirch, P. V., (Ed),1986. Islands Societies: Archaeological Approaches to Evolution and Transformation. *University Press*, Cambridge.

Kopper, J. S., 1984. 'Canet Cave, Esporles, Mallorca'. In The Deià Conference of Prehistory, Early Settlement in the Western Mediterranean Islands and their Peripheral Areas. Edited by Waldren, W., Chapman, R., *B.A.R*, Oxford.

Lewthwaite, J. and R. Kennard. B.A.R., Oxford, pp. 61-69.

Lewthwaite, J., 1985. 'Social Factors and Economic Change in Balearic Prehistory, 3000-1000 b.c.' In Beyond Domestication in Prehistoric Europe, edited by G. Barker et al. *Academic Press*, London, pp. 205-231.

MacArthur, R. H. & E. O. Wilson, 1967. The Theory of Island Biogeography. *Princeton University Press*, Princeton.

Mills, N., 1983. 'The Neolithic of Southern France'. In Ancient France. Neolithic Societies and Their Landscape. 6000-2000 B.C., edited by C. Scarre. *University Press*, Edinburgh, pp. 91-145.

Pericot, L., 1975. Las Islas Baleares en los Tiempos Prehistóricos. *Destino*, Barcelona.

Pons-Moyá, J. and J. Coll, 1984. 'Les Industries Lítiques dels Jaciments a l'Aire Lliure de la Zona de Santanyí (Mallorca)'. In The Deià Conference of Prehistory, Early Settlement in the Western Mediterranean Islands and their Peripheral Areas. Edited by Waldren, W., Chapman, R., *B.A.R.*, Oxford.

Lewthwaite, J. and R. Kennard. *B.A.R.*, Oxford, pp. 841-858.

Rappaport, R. A., 1963. 'Aspects of Man's Influence upon Islands Ecosystems: Alteration and Control'. In Man's Place in the Island Ecosystem: A Symposium. Edited by F. R. Fosberg. Honolulu. pp. 155-170.

Renfrew, C., 1973. The Explanation of Culture Change. Models in Prehistory. London:Duckworth.

Riba, O. et al., 1980. Geografia Física dels Països Catalans. *Ketres*, Barcelona.

Rosselló-Bordoy, G., 1963. Una Aproximación a la Prehistoria de Mallorca. Barcelona:Instituto de Prehistoria y Arqueología. Monografías 23.

Rosselló-Bordoy, G., 1972. 'La Prehistoria de Mallorca'. Trabajos del Museo de Mallorca 11. Also *Mayurqa* 7:115-156.

Rosselló-Bordoy, G. and W. Waldren, 1973. 'Excavaciones en el Abrigo del Bosque de Son Matge (Valldemossa, Mallorca)'. Noticiario Arqueológico Hispánico. *Prehistoria* II:1-86.

Rosselló-Bordoy, G. and W. Waldren, 1975. 'Excavaciones en la Cueva de Muleta (Sóller, Mallorca)'. Noticiario Arqueológico Hispánico. *Prehistoria* 3:73-108.

Rosselló-Bordoy, G., Waldren, W. and J. Kopper, 1967. 'Análisis de Radiocarbono en Mallorca'. *Trabajos del Museo de Mallorca* 1, Palma.

Sauer, J. D., 1977. 'Biogreographical Theory and Cultural Analogies'. World Archaeology 8:320-331.

Scarre, C., (Ed.), 1983. Ancient France. Neolithic Societies and Their Landscape. 6000-2000 B.C. The University Press, Edinburgh.

Simberloff, D. S., 1974. 'Equilibrium Theory of Island Biogeography and Ecology'. *Annual Review of Ecology and Systematics* 5:161-182.

Stuiver, M., 1969. 'Yale Natural Radiocarbon Measurements IX'. *Radiocarbon* 11:545-658.

Terán, M. de, 1977. Geografía General de España I. *Ariel*, Barcelona.

Terrell, J., 1977. 'Biology, Biogeography and Man'. *World Archaeology* 8:237-247.

Terrell, J., 1986. Prehistory of the Pacific Islands. University Press, Cambridge.

Vayda, A. P. and R. A. Rappaport, 1963. 'Islands Cultures'. In Man's Place in the Island Ecosystem: A Symposium. Edited by F. R. Fosberg. Honolulu, pp. 133-142.

Waldren, W. H., 1982. Balearic Prehistoric Ecology and Culture. The Excavation of Certain Caves, Rock Shelters and Settlements. *British Archaeological Reports International Series* 149, Oxford.

Waldren, W., 1984. 'Chalcolithic Settlement and Beaker Connections in the Balearic Islands'. In The Deià Conference of Prehistory. Edited by Waldren, W., Chapman, R., Lewthwaite, J. and R. Kennard. Oxford:B.A.R. Pp. 911-966.

Waldren, W., Chapman, R., Lewthwaite, J. and R. Kennard, (Eds.). 1984. The Deià Conference of Prehistory. Early Settlement in the Western Mediterranean Islands and Their Peripheral Areas. British Archaeological Reports International Series 229, Oxford.

Waldren, W., Ensenyat, J. and C. Cubí, 1990. 'Son Mas: Balearic Prehistoric Sanctuary'. In The IInd Deià Conference of Prehistory. Edited by W. Waldren, J. Ensenyat and R. Kennard. B.A.R., Oxford.

Waldren, W., Ensenyat, J. and R. Kennard, (Eds.), 1990. The IInd Deià Conference of Prehistory. Archaeological Techniques, Technology and Theory. *British Archaeological Reports International Series*, Oxford.

Williamson, M., 1981. Islands Populations. University Press, Oxford.

SOME THEORETICAL CONSEQUENCES OF THE USE
OF ADVANCED STATISTICS IN ARCHAEOLOGY

JUAN A. BARCELO
University of Madrid,
Madrid, Spain

RESUME

"For this is the thing the priests do not know, with their One God and One Truth: that there is no such thing as a true tale. Truth has many faces and the truth is like to the old road to Avalon; it depends on your own will, and your own thoughts, whither the road will take you, and whether at the end, you arrive in the Holy Isle of Eternity or among the priests with their bells and their death and their Satan and Hell and damnation".

Marion Bradley, The Mists of Avalon

The year 1987 was a very good year for Theoretical Archaeology. Very interesting and important books and articles were published: Binford (1987), Gaffney and Gaffney (1987), Leone et al. (1987), Earle and among others Preucel (1987), Shanks and Tilley (1987a and 1987b), Hodder (1987a and 1987b), Aldenderfer (1987), Lagrange (1987), etc. If we add other interesting publications in the recent years: Carr (1985), Gardin et al. (1986), Hodder (1986), The World Archaeological Congress Proceedings,... we shall discover a new and influential period for all those subjects related to Theoretical Archaeology.

However, we are not experiencing a new paradigmatic revolution in Kuhn's sense. We can not see any real advance in Archaeology; all these publications are a new development of ideas coming from the beginnings of the seventies. But they show something new: a deeper understanding of the epistemology and the limits of archaeological constructs.

"The discipline is at present theoretically rich, with approaches ranging from system analysis through marxist and structural archaeology to the post processualists. Such theoretical diversity is healthy but cannot help to describe and explain past cultural developments until there is an equally strong set of methodological tools to infer past behaviour from the materials of the archaeological record. Only then can competing

theoretical approaches be evaluated and progress in understanding the past made" *(Mithen 1988).*

In this paper I will discuss only some reflections related to the role of Statistics in Archaeology. It is an important topic of our discipline, because there is no standard theory in order to help the archaeologist with the use of mathematical techniques. There is also some confusion in the goals of a Statistical Archaeology. For instance, two recently published books show a very different view of statistics. Shanks and Tilley write:

> *"Quantification, motivated by a belief in the objectivity of exactness and calculability, leads eventually to mathematization -the conception of the archaeological record in terms of neutral patterns and relations capable of precise definition and expression in terms of formulae... In the end, we are left with the impression that idyosyncratic and irrational human subjectivity opposes regular, precise and predictable objectivity. It is only in so far as humans can be transformed into regular and predictable objects that they are important...This goal (objectivity), when reached, destroys Archaeology because it is not ultimately the data that matter any more but the internal coherence of the statistics to which they are fitted" (Shanks and Tilley 1987a).*

And M. Aldenderfer answers:

> *"What is overlooked, however, is the appearance of a quantitative idiom as a major conceptual approach to archaeological thinking. Simply put, a quantitative idiom is one in which measurements and their manipulation are seen as significant ways in which to gain insight into some phenomenon of interest. The idiom, however, does not simply consist of the use of some statistical or quantitative procedure but is instead a way of thinking about things; a quantitative idiom attempts to express a problem in quantitative terms and seeks solutions through the application of appropriate quantitative methods" (Aldenderfer 1987a).*

I intend to discuss these two approaches to Archaeology, the first negative and the second positive to the existence of a Statistical Archaeology -or Mathematical Archaeology, the name is not important-; one prefers a Subjective Archaeology, while the other deals with objective procedures.

ARCHAEOLOGICAL TECHNIQUES, TECHNOLOGY AND THEORY

Some Theoretical Consequences of the Use of Advanced Statistics in Archaeology
J.A.Barcelo

STATISTICS. FOR WHAT?

We have heard many times that the use of Mathematics in Social Sciences is the use of a neutral technique. Statistics or Mathematics do not build Theories, but take part in the verification. We can deduce from this statement:

-Statistics belongs to Experimental Sciences
-Scientific inferences have to be compatible with Statistical Theory (Bunge 1983).

Statistics is, then, a methodological discipline and a dialectical juxtaposition of quality (object, data) and quantity (method). Statistics as a Science looks like a procedure of first verifying construction materials (data) and then constructing a building (statistical model) (Schvyrkov and Davis 1987). This is the starting point of most researchers.

However, some scientists think of the difference between Statistics, as an auxiliary tool for a Logic of Discovering, and Statistics as an auxiliary tool for a Logic of Justification (Tuckey 1984). Statistics is not limited to giving criteria to the likelihood of an inference. It is used in order to detect non random patterns which need an interpretation.

Phelps and Musgrove (1986) draw attention to the existence of three ways to do such statistical interpretations:

Descriptive Statistics - the use of group processing to produce displays of data that can be easily processed to bring out of the structure inherent in the data.

Exploratory Statistics - more complex and sophisticated techniques used on data where the structure that perhaps exists is unknown or only vaguely appreciated. Again the aim is to find a structure in the data which is comprehensible to the human brain.

Inferential Statistics - the basic aim is finding a mapping from the input (evidence) onto the output (validity scores for the hypotheses, based on posterior probabilities). This is essentially a "black box" process since no internal model of the problem domain is constructed: the essential structure which humans use to think about the problem is missing.

In the end, the goal of many of the statistical techniques is to describe the pattern found in data through a model, a representation of what the scientist sees in the population which is being studied (Cox and Hinkley 1974, Everitt and Dunn 1983). This mathematical model is a set of equations which summarizes a population of multivariate data. Such a model is seen as an abstraction of the real world, in which relationships among real elements are replaced by relationships among mathematical objects: a simplification of the original structure in data. Therefore, the aim of building a statistical model of a population of objects is to obtain a simpler description to be consistent with data (Daniel and Wood 1980; Everitt and Dunn 1983; Aivazian et al. 1983; Hinkley 1984).

Is Statistics used as a Logic of Discovering contradictory with Statistics used as a Logic of Justification? Some statisticians, like Thisted (1986), think that because of its emphasis in searching latent structures, Data Analysis (Logic of Discovering) is different to Statistical Decision-making (Logic of Justification). They are, nevertheless, two complementary aspects of analysis: Statistics is concerned, simultaneously, with specific and particularistic features of the set of data and to the fact that this set of data is typical of the general run of things (Finch 1981). In other words, Statistics deals with the coincidences and contradictions existing between particular subjects and general theories.

From this second aspect we can deduce one of the most important concepts of Mathematical Statistics: Probabilities. Probability Theory is a mathematical discipline which defines the laws which rules the interaction of a big quantity of random factors (Aivazian et al. 1983). Those factors will be random if we cannot find a regularity to predict the scores (Kolmogorov 1983). Randomness means lack of regularity: if a statistical model is significantly different from a random process, the regularity mathematically defined in data set will be interpretable.

Probability Theory studies the properties of mathematical models which simulate the mechanisms of real processes or systems which are affected by random factors. One of the main objectives of Statistics will be the selection made between different mathematical models in order to find the model with a better fit in the real world. On the other hand, it will be necessary, to verify that the relationships defined between objects, between variables or between objects and variables are significant. For verification of such models, statisticians use another "aspect" of Statistics: Hypotheses Testing (Domenech et al. 1985).

A statistical hypothesis is a statement about the scores of one or more of the parameters of a distribution, or the shape of this distribution. A statistical hypothesis is a statement about the population (the data set) described by this distribution (the mathematical model) (Hacking 1965; Afifi and Azen 1979). The distribution or probabilistic law has two main functions:

- to describe the mechanism of the real process by induction from the general population statistically analyzed.
- to be used as auxiliary techniques of Statistical Analysis.

Statistical Analysis is a way of subsuming an event or particular population in a more general way: a statistical regularity is explained, whenever possible, to see how it is subsumed in a more general model of regularities. (M. Salmon 1982; W. Salmon 1984).

Here we are at the crossroads of an important contradiction. Data have no meaning in themselves, they are meaningful only in relation to a conceptual model of the phenomenon studied (Box et al. 1978). If this conceptual model was produced by the Statistical Analysis, mathematical methods would then be criteria for the Truth of the Scientific Theory. Simultaneously, Statistics would be the Logic of Discovering and the Logic of Justification. What Statistics did discover in this case would be justified by Statistics.

Are all statistical models Scientific Theories? Most statisticians describe the process of building a model in this way:

a.- research of systematic structures in the data set
b.- generalization of these structures
c.- description of the model (cf. Ehrenberg 1984)

We can ask ourselves if it is enough to estimate the parameters of a model, by verifying its fit through tests and the examination of residuals (the part of the mathematical model which does not fit the data). Is this mathematical construction a Scientific Theory? I do not think so. Mathematics (or Statistics) is the means of making Scientific Theories, but is not at all a Scientific Theory in itself (Rashed 1972). All explanation is a cognitive process, and not only one of verification (Bailyn 1977). Verification is affected by the particular limits of Social Sciences:

- possible uniqueness of social-level events
- an infinite a priori set of relevant social-level variables
- constraints on social-level experimentation
- assumptions about the underlying distribution in social statistical inference (Neuberg 1977).

The risk in such a point of view is that we may see Statistics as an accessory matematization, foreign to the object studied: statistic procedures would not be able to give meaning. Even when Statistical Analysis shows relationships which direct observation has not discovered, the need of interpretation remains. In this sense, Statistics would show only the need of introducing the elements which describe the variability in data set in the Scientific Theory of the domain studied (Bresson 1972).

D. Baird (1987) proposes a more suggestive way of using Statistical Analysis, by making a comparison with the concept of "information-transformation". Statistical techniques transform and extract the information from the real world in the same way as they would do it an "instrument". Statistical Analysis for Social Sciences is like a microscope used for Biology (cf. also Hacking 1983).

I consider Statistics as a language, a way of transforming observable reality in order to show the complexities. As a language, Statistics gives scientists a means of communication: objective simply means that the rules for observation are made explicit, so that another observer using the same rules would see, if given the opportunity the same fact (Binford 1987), therefore, Statistics has to be the way of objectivating the reasoning.

But in using such a point of view there are also many important problems. First is the concept of transformational language: Statistics expresses an unobservable reality in another way. However, how can we perceive reality? Is Statistics a language for creating and for simultaneously describing the structure of relationships among variables and objects? In fact, a statistical model would be a Scientific Theory only if we knew all the relevant factors and if the same multivariate statement was a deterministic explanation. There are as a result always other factors which affect any observed relationship (Przeworski and Teune 1970). It is impossible to introduce "Reality" in the computer and think that the machine gives us a definitive interpretation. It is the scientist who imposes a system of variables constraining all the study. We "observe" reality according to these constraints, according to a series of appropriate criteria. I accept the fundamental statement of P.K. Feyerabend: we do not have to choose among theories, we have to study reality with a great quantity of different theories, even those that are contradictory.

If Statistics is a set of rules which allow us to transform initial data in an isomorphic set, there will be an infinite number of possible transformations (Thisted 1986); each one of which will be used in order to solve a certain kind of problem. For instance:

"Principal component analysis describes the variation of the n-individuals in a p-dimensional space in terms of a set of uncorrelated variables which are linear combinations of the original variables. The new variables are derived in decreasing order of importance so that, for example, the first principal component accounts for as much as possible of the variation in the original data. The usual objective of this type of analysis is to see whether the first few components account for most of the variation in the original data (...).

In geometrical terms it is easy to show that the first principal component defines the line of best fit (in the least squares sense) to the n p-dimensional observations in the sample" (Everitt and Dunn 1983).

We can compare this definition with the Scientific Strategy proposed by M. Bunge (1983):

Description of Phenomenon

What is it? (Reference)
How is it? (Properties, Variables, Attributes)
Where is it? (Place)
When is it? (Time)
Of what is it made? (Composition)
How interrelated are its parts? (Configuration)
How much? (Quantity)

Interpretation of Phenomenon

What are the relevant variables? (Factors)
What are the determinant factors? (Causes)
Which relationships have relevant variables? (Laws)

The Explanation of a Phenomenon comes after its Description. Once we know the properties and the configuration of the Phenomenon, we seek the relevant variables and deterministic factors of this configuration (statistical model). Factorial Analysis is a mathematical model of relationships among variables; through it we differentiate between observed variables (Description) and latent ones (Explanation). Each observed variable is considered as the linear function of latent variables or factors. Is the meaning of these factors exhausted by its relation with the observable variables that define the factors? S.A. Mulaik (1987a) asserts the non causal nature of latent factors, and I agree.

Following D. Baird (1987), I have categorized Statistics as an Instrument for the Science; if microscopes are the instrument to discover what is little, Principal Components Analysis (PCA) will be the instrument to discover sets. As a consequence the output of such an analysis will not be an hypothesis but a particular ordering of data:

"Factor Analysis does identify real patterns in a correlation matrix. These patterns may not persist in the correlation matrix of replications of the test or if the patterns do persist, they may be artefacts of the correlational summarising of the test data and the factor-analytic summarising of the correlations. The patterns are real enough, even if they do not correspond to a natural piece of the real world. Further substantive theoretical and empirical investigation is necessary to determine if these real patterns connect with some specific part of the real world" (Baird 1987, italics added).

However, I think that the process of interpretation of the factors produced by PCA has not to be entirely extrinsic to analysis. According to A.S.C. Ehrenberg (1975) -although I do not agree with his conception of Statistics as a technique for reducing dimensionality of data set- the descriptive use of probabilities (Multivariable Normal Distribution, Wilk's lambda) does not imply that the phenomena really occur by chance, but only that they appear so irregular that they can be satisfactorily described as if they were random. That is to say, Multivariate Analysis gives "form" to a data set, a geometrical model, in order to see unobservable relationships (Aivazian et al. 1983; Phelps and Musgrove 1986). The same structure between form and substance in a linguistic communication exists between Statistical Models and Scientific Theories (Tonnelat 1972).

Factorial structure allows us to use statistical relationships between several lower-level variables as empirical evidence for or against the establishment of a semantic relationship of indication between these variables and an abstract concept which may be measured and transformed into a variable with a high semantic extension and theoretical importance (Marradi 1981). This semantic structure is imposed by the scientist: the resulting factorial structure is to a certain extension predetermined (Suarez 1981; Blalock 1982). In this way, any relations that we may discover are partly a function of our own conceptualization and measurement process. It is nonsense to ask whether the relationship discovered is linear or not, unless the concept has been given an operational meaning.

How can we represent such conceptualization in a Factorial structure?

"Let us imagine the concept as the center of a semantic space, and its indicators (or attributes) as points scattered around that center at distances inversely proportional to their validity. We want to infer the distances between the points to the center (which we cannot measure) from the distances between any couple of points (which we can measure because they are the inverse of the correlations between the corresponding indicators). If a point is located near the center, its average distance from other points will be smaller (i.e., its average correlation higher). Therefore, close correlations with other indicators is the best evidence available of small distance from the concept (...) In Factor Analysis, it is precisely the separate empirical existence and adequate means of measurement of certain concepts -not their mutual relationship- that is in question" (Marradi 1981).

In the end, Factor-analytic results are useful to study the researcher's hypotheses about the conceptual structure of the world. The danger of imposing dimensions on the statistical groupings is the same as imposing conceptualizations on reality: whatever labels we attach to the continua that are created, they are likely to be confounded with other closely correlated dimensions that, in fact, may suggest very different theoretical interpretations (Blalock 1982).

Nevertheless, it is important to realise that in any given situation there are numerous possible ways we might interpret or respond to what is before us (Mulaik 1987b), we can use very different ways of transformation of data to express a conceptual structure. Nobody has enough with only a concept to explain the world.

THE LOGIC OF REASONING IN STATISTICAL ARCHAEOLOGY

At the beginning of the seventies, innovations in Archaeological Theory produced a new definition of the role of Statistics in this discipline. In this chapter I not only explain the historical development of this subject, but I will develop different aspects of statistical reasoning applied to Archaeological Inferences in order to arrive at a description of the philosophy underlying the approach.

Statistics as a language:

> "The kind of reasoning involved in statistical inference is required whether we make any formal computations or not, whenever we wish to assess the evidence relevant for any statement which asserts more than is asserted by sheer description of observations. This is so whether or not we have made all the relevant observations that could conceivably be made" (Cowgill 1977).

Analysis is seen as a process of searching for and discovering order or structure in a set of data (Whallon 1982). The primary task of Archaeology is to discover and describe whatever structure, order or pattern of predictability there may be in archaeological data.

According to Doran and Hodson, some essentially archaeological concepts can be formulated and manipulated mathematically in order to transform "the unmanageable mass of individual units that form the basic archaeological record into a coherent body of information"; statistical procedures can be used to describe and summarise data and to suggest hypotheses, but not to estimate parameters. By conceptualizing Statistics as a "technique" and by limiting its domain to "Quantifiable Archaeology", Doran and Hodson (1975) do not need to transform archaeological analytical philosophy.

I do not agree. The quantitative structure of relationships measured in the archaeological record must be interpreted. If we explain it with the help of a model built from another discipline (Anthropology, Geography, Economics, History), Statistics will be only a technique for making comparisons; but if we consider that the statistical structure discovered in data is meaningful, then we will accept that statistics is a language meant to express certain kind of ideas:

> "Nor does the 'methodology' such as it is stem from considerations of the linkage between behavior and, say, morphological and any other distinguishing characteristics of artefacts but is justified only on the grounds that nonrandom patterning must to some degree, reflect patterned behavior. If our methodology is to create units that are measures of behavior, then there must be a direct connection between the distinctions we make and aspects of behavior." (Read 1982).

D. Clarke (1978) defined Archaeology as a mathematical discipline. According to him, Archaeology has three fundamental aims:

> 1) The definition of the fundamental entities that pervade the diverse material, their elements, structures and patterns, the process which operates on them, and the effects of the processes on the entities in the dimensions of space and time. A study in statistics and dynamics going beyond particular instances.

> 2) The search for repeated similarities or regularities in form, function, association or developmental sequence among the particular entities from every area, period and environment.

> 3) The development of higher category knowledge or principles that synthesize and correlate the material at hand whilst possessing a high comprehensive and informative general models and hypotheses.

Clarke "translated "empirical observations into a mathematical language in order to build models analogous to reality. Clarke started his analysis locating the variables which define the problem; he studied the dependence among these variables (through covariance, regression, correlation) and their nature (through Factorial Analysis); he built a model organizing the results of such experiments in order to draw attention to the chosen problems; he designed new experiments to verify the model or the hypotheses which have the function of relationing observed properties through a structural concept: a hypothesis or a hypothetical model is formulated in order to predict certain correlated regularities.

Clarke constructed a hierarchical system of "Concepts" which function as syntactical rules of a carnapian system (1). The result has the form of a taxonomic tree but the different archaeological entities have been ordered hierarchically. The formation rule of this taxonomic unit is the correlation of lower-level units. In order to give meaning to this unit statistically obtained, Clarke made comparisons with other sociocultural dimensions: levels of kinship, linguistic hierarchies, genetic taxonomies. He tried to give meaning to the observed variability in the archaeological record using statistical procedures. He superimposed different isomorphic taxonomies.

In this approach, the described statistical regularities are significant in themselves; therefore, the archaeologist must try to express it in a comprehensible way (a system or a model). Statistical Archaeology will be the discipline which studies these regularities. This study is not just limited to subsume measured regularity in a general aprioristic theory, but in the progressive decoding of underlying structures. In other words, the "treatment of information" is more important than the validation of hypotheses (Borillo and Virbel 1978; Borillo et al. 1977).

The philosophy proposed by Clarke to "read" the underlying structures in the archaeological record has been only partially developed. For instance, Doran and Hodson think that Statistics is the method to obtain interpretative conclusions from the archaeological record. In order to obtain such an interpretation of quantitative structures they develop the hierarchical conceptual system proposed by Clarke, but without his analytical depth.

In fact, Clarke and Doran and Hodson built a conceptual clustering. This is a process of inference defined by Michalski (1980), which addresses the problem of determining conceptual representations from object clusters. In this process, the similarity between two objects is dependent on the quality of concepts used to describe the two objects. That is to say, the quality of an object cluster depends on the quality of concepts that describe the cluster. In conceptual clustering the researcher is interested in identifying higher level characterizations (conceptual descriptions) of object groups and using these caracterizations to guide the search for a set of best object groups (Bietti et al. 1985; Fisher and Langley 1986; Read 1987).

The approach by Clarke, Doran and Hodson and others is, then, a conceptual clustering avant la letre. This kind of statistical reasoning should be related to the predominant paradigm in the Scientific Community of those years: the concept of Culture was in the center of discussion. Archaeologists tried to give a not ambiguous definition, statistically founded, of Culture. From this definition they derived a system of conceptual clustering in which the similarity among attributes was in the lower hierarchical level, and the concept of Culture, defined through the similarity among attributes was at the top.

In an earlier section I gave a view of Statistics as a language, a way of speaking about things and their relationships. Statistical methodology is, then, fundamentally a means to think logically about data. It is by providing a language through which one can reason logically with quantitative data, that the statistical framework is given its analytical power (Read 1987). In a certain sense, it is the same view as that of Clarke: the pattern discovered by statistical procedures was form without substance. To express this content, the archaeologist developed a complex hierarchical conceptual system in which Statistics serves the role of formation rules for the different concepts at different levels.

This approach has been more or less adopted by many archaeologists. For instance, Newell and Dekin (1978) ask for the existence in the archaeological record of discrete clusters of artefacts and whether or not these clusters are the result of different behavioral process. They separate empirical clusters of artefacts from that of the output of behavioral actions. The formation rule for this last taxonomic unit is not correlation in Clarke´s sense, but the more salient presence of certain attributes with implicit cultural meaning: spatial, morphological or chronological association.

In a similar way, I. Airvaux (1984) asserts that certain morphological attributes are the only features which define clusters of objects. What he names morphological ruptures are the first units of analysis. Each association of artefacts has certain morphotechnical elements that justify the morphological rupture. In a different way to Clarke, Airvaux joins his statistical analysis with a hypothetico-deductive inference: it has to do with the study of statistical homogeneity (alternative hypothesis); if this were to be the case, it would start the statistical analysis of associations in the morphological features previously defined. Each of the morphotechnical subsets identified, if the nule hypothesis is rejected, are studied tipometrically and morphologically in order to define the morphological stability of the associations among taxonomic units.

In this approach, there is a great disparity in the statistical procedures used (Regnier 1966; Sneath and Sokal 1973; Bietti 1979, 1982; Whiteley 1983). For instance, A.C. Spaulding rejects the utility of Multivariate Analysis. He accepts only the analysis of full contingency tables by means of hierarchical and log-linear models. For Spaulding, the archaeologist should be concerned only with nominal variables and their interrelationships. The reasons for this concern are:

- many of our observations are inescapably in the nominal mode.
- there is a fair inference that the makers and users of the archaeological artefacts characteristically operated in the nominal mode.

In Spaulding's own words, the statistical structure discovered by Multivariate Analysis is not an Archaeological one, it is uninterpretable (Spaulding 1982).

I do not agree with this last idea. Like Charles Redman I think the archaeologist ought to seek a Multivariable structure that explains the micropatterns of variation for understanding data:

"To describe or to explain the archaeological record we must categorize it into classes in order to recognize the empirical patterns that are reflections of past behavior. Categorization is a complex process that is influenced by a variety of learned and physiological factors. Any attempt to propose simple procedures or solutions to the problems of archaeological classifications is unrealistic and destined to be inadequate...

Culture is a complex multidimensional phenomenon... For an analytical system to take the incredibly complex data of ceramic variability and simply represent it along a single axis of variation does not do justice to our potential for documenting complex organizational patterns. Accepting this position, the real challenge becomes the development of methods for both maintaining this complexity of information and deriving understandable behavioral patterns from it." (Redman 1978).

After formulating a Model of Attributes expected to be relevant to study, Redman tries to study the nature of attributes with the aid of simple descriptive statistics (histograms, cross-tabulations). Cluster Analysis, Multidimensional Scaling and Factor Analysis are the mathematical tools he uses for:

- discovering nonrandom associations of more than two variables at a time: If on the same artifact, this defines a type; if only in the same site units this defines an activity set.
- discovering groups of similar units
- determining distributional grouping of similar units
- delineating distributional patterns of attributes identified by Factor Analysis.

In the end of the analysis he can identify various organizational structures on the basis of the distributional patterns of the data variability.

According to F. Djindjian, this kind of analysis is only a stricto sensu patterning construction showing the intrinsic meaning of physical finds. However, archaeologists need an Explanation construction based on this intrinsic description. In other words, the aims of a Statistical Archaeology would be:

- to show a patterning with archaeological meaning in a data set (Patterning)
- to explain the observed differences among material culture with another set of information (Explanation)
- to assign an object or a site to an explanation construction.

For the second kind of statistical goal, Djindjian uses contextual information. He has used a set of attributes measured on the object in order to find the statistical patterning behind the attributes, but to understand this pattern he needs to analyse the information obtained at the archaeological excavation: the context of the object. Quantitative techniques let him to discover the interaction between:

- intrinsic information (measured on the elements of the system). A classification or typology of physical features, geographic or chronological phases, seriation schemes, distribution of artefacts,...
- extrinsic information affecting the elements of the system: stratigraphic sequence, activity areas in the site, marketing patterns of the distribution of certain artefacts.

This formalism ends with the definition of the empirical level of the system: a site, a cultural or chronological phase, a region,... (Djindjian 1981, 1985a).

This approach has a considerable success nowadays. For instance, Ch. Chataigner and M. Plateaux define two aspects of a spatial analysis:

- the study of archaeological artefacts through its quantitative distribution to discover the clusters and relationships with different meaningful areas in the site.
- The study of these relationships among archaeological areas in order to identify significative differences which can be interpreted as behavioral ones (Chataigner and Plateaux 1986).

Nevertheless, we should not follow this way of doing Statistics for archaeological purposes without an analytical philosophy that allows us to identify the possible existence of contradictions between statistical patterns and real-world phenomena. In the last chapter we have seen the danger of confusing Logic of Discovering and Logic of Justification. If Statistics is a language to expressing certain behaviors in the real world which cannot be expressed in another language (for instance, natural language), what epistemological level will have Statistical Archaeology within a General Explanatory System? Is Statistical Archaeology a discipline closed in itself or is it a part of a Scientific Archaeology?

STATISTICS AS A METHOD

As a methodological tool, Statistics is not a kind of Theory; according to Cowgill (1977), statistical results cannot be directly converted into probabilities or warranted degrees of belief in, hypotheses or explanations. Statistics is then a way of helping us to see more clearly which is the evidence, relevant to various alternative hypotheses or possible explanations.

Mathematics or mathematical thinking may imply to bear a deeper understanding of relationships, of forms and process; but mathematics are not any magic wand:

> "The mathematical expressions are simply being used as an aid to clarity of thought. I am not claiming to have applied topological ideas or the theory of groups to archaeological problems, but merely suggesting that the approach may be fruitful" (Renfrew 1979).

> "Statistics is a quantitative tool that cannot provide qualitative judgements. Such judgements can only be rendered by those familiar with the corpus of relevant anthropological method and theory (...) Whether a mathematical difference has any anthropological significance can only be determined by anthropological arguments" (Scheps 1982).

Typically, archaeologists approach their data by having in mind some rather ill-defined problems or questions, such as the identification and understanding of settlement pattern changes, the determination of activity areas on living floors or the understanding of intrasite deposits in a village or urban site. Of course, in order to approach these problems analytically, whether quantitatively or not, archaeologists usually formulate a representation of the data as a set of measures on relevant variables and they must figure out which methods may be applied using this representation of data to address the question of interest (Kintigh 1987).

The starting point of Binford is related to these considerations. He seeks new facts as well as new ways to discover properties of the archaeological record. He seeks ways of evaluating the interpretative principles in use to convert contemporary observations into accurate statements about the past. The use of new techniques in both data recovery and analysis resulted in so many new types of facts that the inadequacy of the traditional interpretative principles became obvious for him, even without formal testing (Binford 1983); his use of Statistics must be seen in this context. As he wrote in 1966:

> "Our analytical methods must allow us to determine (a) when variability does in fact reflect past behavior and is not simply the product of sampling error; and (b) what differences and similarities in archaeological assemblages signify in terms of past behavior. The first problem can be solved by the use of research designs planned to control sampling error and by the use of standard statistical tests. It is toward the solution of the second problem that the methods developed here have been directed" (Binford and Binford 1966).

However, according to Binford, Statistics has no function in the development of a Theory or an Explanation:

> "Statistical or probability statements as relationships among things are simply complex empirical facts. The only assumption one needs to make in order to project from such facts is that the system will remain unchanged, that things will stay as they are. They are projections, not predictions... Statistical summaries and probabilistic statements about the patterning do not explain, they simply describe" (Binford 1977).

According to Binford, one does not build a theory by accumulating universal facts or empirical generalizations. Getting to the past is then a process in which the archaeologist gives meaning to static phenomena in dynamic terms (Binford 1975, 1983); the archaeologist must develop ideas and theories regarding the formation process of the archaeological record (a middle-range Theory). Only through an accurate understanding of such a process can the archaeologist reliably give meaning to the facts that appear from the past in the contemporary era (Binford 1977, 1982):

> "Archaeological knowledge of the past is totally dependent upon the meaning which archaeologists give to observations on the archaeological record. Thus, archaeologically justified views of the past are dependent upon paradigmatic views regarding the significance of archaeological observations" (Binford and Sabloff 1982).

Binford makes a clear distinction between Theory and Method: they are different concepts, but related because the validity of a theory is a direct function of the character of reasoning and methodology. Middle-range Theory and Statistical Analysis are not the same thing. Statistical procedures are tools, methods:

> "...dependence of our knowledge of the past and inference rather than direct observation. It is this condition that renders the imperative that our methods for constructing the past be intellectually independent of our theories for explaining the past. That is, that theories explaining the archaeological record, the work that provides our observational language and conveys meaning to archaeological phenomena, must be intellectually independent of our a priori ideas of the past, or our Theories regarding the process responsible for past events, patterns of change or stability" (Binford 1981).

G.A.Clark arrives to similar conclusions: "statistics is simply a tool... but an extremely useful one" (1982). His approach is one of the most complete and interesting of the Statistical Archaeology. He tries to find the balance between Induction and Deduction, then he asserts the existence of a Descriptive Mode and a Confirmatory Mode related to the descriptive and inferential functions of Statistics.

He starts with the fact that behavioral hypotheses cannot be evaluated directly, so it is necessary to transform them into statistical hypotheses, that is to say, substantive research propositions must be translated into unequivocal statements of relationships between or among variables; data are defined in terms of hypotheses, and not exist in any formal sense apart from them. All data are regarded, in this formal theory, as comprised of two components: the smooth and the rough:

$$DATA = SMOOTH + ROUGH$$

The smooth is the underlying simplified structure of a set of observations -the general shape of a distribution of relationship usually summarized by the standard measures of central tendency, regression lines and the like. The rough constitutes the residuals -what is left behind after the smooth has been extracted. The quest for this structure is facilitated by reexpression, transformations (e.g. roots, logs, cf. Hoaglin, Mosteller and Tuckey 1983; Barceló 1987a). In this way, the analysis proceeds from the examination of single variables to examination of relationships between two or more variables, to Multivariate Analysis. The rationale behind this incremental approach is to allow for as complete an understanding as possible of the structure of each variable as an entity, to understand pairs of variables as relationships and, finally, understand groups of variables as models.

F. Djindjian defines this structure in the archaeological record as a construct which shows an ordering in data or a pattern with "archaeological" meaning. This structure may have very diverse natures: a taxonomy, a set of geographical locations, chronological phases, schemes of seriation, schemes of distribution. This structure is described by the use of different algorithms:

QUANTIFYING.- simultaneous treatment of discrete and continuous attributes and the appropriate metric choice.

REDUCTION.- obtained by factorization and selection of pertinent factors.

COMPREHENSION.- obtained by both simultaneous projections of elements and variables in factors.

PATTERNING.- is seen here as the quest of the characteristic geometrical configuration on reduced space (clusters, serial polynomial curves, spatial distributions) by an interactive process in making supplementary an element or an attribute (by which is meant a simple projection in factor space). A pattern is, then, a point configuration in reduced space.

MODELISATION.- patterning more again may be modelised by an adjustment of the reduced configuration (Djindjian 1981, 1983, 1985b, 1986; Djindjian and Leredde1980).

With such an approach we have the risk of accept data as necessarily meaningful. Without a concordance between the technical assumptions of statistical methods and the behaviorally relevant aspects of a data structure, those patterns quantitatively found within an artifact distribution may be distorted representations of behaviorally significant patterns or may reflect other irrelevant sources of variation. C. Carr (1985a) gives this proposal for an spatial archaeology:

- do not accept data as necessarily meaningful as given
- dissect the density distribution
- assign meaning to each density component
- delete irrelevant components
- Multiple, fine-grained analyses

It is necessary that the archaeologist considers the distribution of each artifact type, that is fairly numerous and widely distributed, as the composite result of multiple behavioral and natural formation and disturbance processes that overlap spatially, that have operated at different scales and that have occurred in only segments of a site. The point-location distribution is transformed into a density distribution and dissected into component density distributions having scales of density variation of two general kinds: relevant and irrelevant. The first set should include components that encompasses density variations of different geographic scales consistent with the expected, inductively suggested or documented scales of those process that are of interest (depending on the source of general knowledge). The second set should include other components that encompasses residual density variations of scales consistent with those of processes not of interest and to be removed from analysis. As a third step, it is necessary to interpret each density component in terms of the behavioral, geological, agricultural or other formation or disturbance process responsible for it. This can be done:

- deductively - by comparing the scale of variation of the component and its spatial distribution to the expectable scales and distributions of formation process thought likely to have generated the palimpsest, as argued from contextual information.

- inductively - by comparing the spatial distribution of the component to the spatial distribution of various indicators of formation process (the dip and orientation of artefacts, patterns of refit among dispersed pieces of broken artefacts, etc.)

Components that do not reflect those behavioral process or whatever kind of process that are of interest should be deleted from the data to be analyzed later with the fine-grained methods performing a separate analysis for each set of relevant density components that pertain to different artifact classes but with the same scale of variability (Carr 1985a).

In conclusion, inferential methods, or those that seek structure must not be allowed to influence the analysis and creation of relational structure:

"the concepts, from empirical to theoretical, have logical priority. It is at this point that we decide whether or not numbers have meaning or not and whether they are appropriate to the study of the problem at hand" (Aldenderfer 1987b, italics added).

In the Confirmatory Mode of statistical reasoning (Clark 1982), the design is based on classic Neyman-Pearson inference and assumes that the generation of hypotheses and the evaluation of these in probabilistic terms is a legitimate perspective to assume in the conduct of scientific research. To be viable, a Confirmatory Research Design should be based on statistical inference and should specify how one goes from a general proposition of anthropological interest

- to a series of hypotheses meaningful in behavioral terms
- to propositions amenable to statistical testing with empirical data
- to a procedure that defines how those data have to be acquired and manipulated and in which decision-making criteria have been made explicit
- to a reassessment of the behavioral implications of decisions based on statistical conclusions.

In this general research design proposed by G.A. Clark statistical techniques enter only:

- at the analysis stage of a project, after all data have been collected.
- near the beginnings of the research process, when initial plans for analysis are being formulated.
- whenever a sample has to be drawn and evaluated.

According to this view of Statistical Archaeology, the statistical pattern in data is not directly significant. It must be compared with a model in which anthropological or sociological or any other nature theories adopt a statistical form. The lack of conformity between the pattern described in data through statistical analysis and such theoretical baselines is what becomes significant: it is there that we will be getting at individual phenomena. In other words, the archaeologist tries to answer the question: "how deviations from the statistical model which are to be encountered in the real world can be expressed in significant terms?" (see the discussion in van der Leeuw 1981; especially Johnson 1981; Voorrips 1981; van der Leeuw 1981a; cf. also Hietala 1984).

An example of this approach is the Law of Monotonic Decrement (Hodder 1974, 1977; Renfrew 1977). This statistical law is a mathematical statement which asserts the existence of invariant relationships among three indigenous variables (Stylistic Variability, Interaction and Cultural Similarity) and one exogenous variable (Distance). This mathematical statement is described under the form of a Multiple Regression Model.

This mathematical model is the mathematical expression of a geographical theory, that is to say, it has form and substance. Most models that apply mathematics and statistics to archaeological problems are a formal representation of a piece of empirical reality:

> "These models belong to 'lower level' of archaeological theory and are initially descriptive. The latter does not concern similarity between the elements of reality and the elements of the model, but rather analogy between the relationships among the modeled entities and the relationships among the formal entities in the model" (Voorrips 1987).

If the statistical pattern described by the archaeologist in his data has only form without substance it will be necessary, in order to obtain "meaning", to compare the particular pattern with the theoretical model. If the fit between the archaeological record and the theory was exact, then this particular archaeological case would be interpretable as a subsummation of the general theory. Statistics is the method that allows this kind of comparison between the particular and the general, between the observable and the theoretical.

The archaeologist's prior knowledge is presented under the form of a statistical model. The particular archaeological record is statistically compared with a geographical, anthropological or sociological set of ideas expressed in mathematical terms (Hodder and Orton 1976; Hodson and Orton 1981; Cannon 1983; Barceló, in press). Nevertheless, we should not limit us to prior existing knowledge. It is necessary also to formalize the patterns observed in the data which do not support any initially stated hypotheses, but from which contestable hypotheses may be derived. According to Fletcher and Lock (1985) such an approach would be much more flexible that any other based in the Principle: the choice of what to measure and how to measure it must affect the nature of the patterns observed. This kind of sets of ideas mathematically presented is then a statistical hypothesis that can be a very simple one or a very complex one, it depends on the social process described or on the kind of mathematical methods used.

A special case of statistical hypothesis is, for example, classification. A classification is an obligatory auxiliary hypothesis of an explanation. Such precise definition consists in two parts. The first part is the set of logically possible classes; the second part is the definition of our expectations in which real world phenomena are identified as members of different classes.

The prediction of class frequencies is thus the set of rules that in fact assign an empirical content to the abstract calculus. According to A. Voorrips (1982), when the results of the identification of real world phenomena into our classes are known, we can perform the appropriate statistical tests to see if the observed frequencies in the various classes differ significantly from the frequencies that were expected in the light of the explanation being tested.

Then, if we agree that hypotheses are statements of relationship between two or more variables and that the testing of such relationships is necessary to evaluate the utility of our ideas and assertions, we must develop appropriate instruments to doing the test. This testing requires that the relationship must be measured in some way. With this purpose in mind, classifications can be constructed as instruments for measurement (Vierra 1982).

THE CHARACTER OF STATISTICAL ARCHAEOLOGY

Archaeological data have no meaning in themselves; it is the archaeologist who gives them meaning by building a conceptual model of the phenomenon studied. Statistical reasoning is the inferential method which allows the inclusion of quantitative patterns in conceptual schemes. Statistics gives the means to translate archaeological observations into a language in which it is possible to describe a wide range of relationships among different artefacts and attributes. Nevertheless, are the interpretative concepts in which we have subsumed the quantitative pattern of a statistical nature?

The output of a Statistical Analysis is not an hypothesis, but the same observational fact seen in a different way. If Statistics is the scientific instrument that allows us to see special cases of phenomena, all essay of giving them meaning must have a statistical nature. The criteria of existence (not of truth or verisimilitude) is the Statistical procedure used. Then, it is necessary to consider it as a formation rule for interpretative concepts: the statistical procedure will be the formation rule for the archaeological fact and for its interpretative concept.

We have three components of a system:

-real world phenomena
-theoretic conceptual system
-statistical regularities among observational facts

The problem is to know if statistical facts are also real world phenomena.

To do research is to decode Reality by coding it in an artificial language in order to be able to understand what is it and how is it. I want to discover what is there under the real appearance of things. I search the same goal as the structuralists: the few elements which I can observe are particular realizations of basic relational constants, realizations which are governed by combinational and transformational rules. We do not perceive external objects directly and intuitively in themselves, but rather in the form of a text of statistical or mathematical nature elaborated by the joint action of the sensory and intellectual apparatus. Structuralist anthropologists discover the unity and coherence behind cultural phenomena by studying the relationships among phenomena rather than the phenomena themselves, which are more complex and difficult to penetrate than their reciprocal relationships (Rossi 1982).

We can apply these intellectual principles to archaeological research: a single population of archaeological observations (a phenomenon of interest) can have any of several organizations and can be represented by any of several relevant data structures, that is to say, those aspects of a data set that reflect single phenomenon of interest and its nature of organization. A data set's relevant structure includes only those variables and observations that pertain to a single process or parallel, continuous process that define a homogenous population. This relevant relational structure in data is comprised of those particular relationships among variables and observations that are of a kind that reflect the organizational nature of the single phenomena of interest (Carr 1987).

We transform observations from real world phenomena into data, and these into a conceptual system assigning meaning to them (Aldenderfer 1987b). But that translation from real world observations into a mathematical language is difficult when a separation is made between problem formation and application of statistical methods. This separation of goal and method leads to a disjunction between concept (meaning) and data, hence to obfuscation of the meaning that can be derived from the statistical analysis of data brought forward to study. The disjunction is not of the archaeologist's making but a consequence of the framework used for the application of statistical theory (Read 1987).

Meaning is only a set of contextual relationships; a meaning is not a thing, it is not expressed by the object, but it is a cluster of semantic components (Coseriu 1977; Nida 1975; Eco 1971, 1977; Wotjak 1977). We must clarify the contextual relationships that are expected to hold between the observations; and we attempt to anticipate the types, range and content of the patterns we expect to discover when we finally begin to analyze our data:

> "Numbers take on meaning within the context of concept formation. Concepts serve to mark the categories which will tell us more about our subject matter than any other categorical sets. The content of a concept ranges across a continuum of the empirical or observational to the theoretical. The former are simple, direct statements or descriptions of what can actually be seen or observed... Indirect observables are concepts in which inference plays a role; many of the things we observe as archaeologists are this type of concept" (Aldenderfer 1987b, italics added).

I do not agree with archaeologists who think that:

> "standard quantitative techniques are incapable of using any knowledge that we as anthropologists have learned about human behavior or the formation of the archaeological record in general. Nor are these methods able to make use of any specific knowledge that we may have about the classes of material being analyzed or the specific archaeological context. All any statistical analysis can do is deal with numbers." (Kintigh 1987, italics added).

Statistical reasoning is the form of archaeological concepts; therefore, these techniques are not neutral procedures without relation with meaning. All interpretative system must be isomorphic to structural pattern. An interpretation will be significative only if there is an isomorphism between the cluster of semantic concepts and the regularities observed in the real-world through statistical procedures (Hofstader 1979).

I have argued that Statistics are like microscopes, an instrument to transform and summarize the real world observations (Baird 1987; Hacking 1983). Indeed, it is possible to say that Statistical Analyses are like the Experiments of "Hard" Sciences: according to D.W. Read, a real world process that leads to the production of phenomena can be seen as an experiment (the process) with outcomes (the phenomena or classes produced by the process). Each instance of the production of phenomena via the process can be interpreted as one repetition of the experiment. Parameters in a statistical model are properties of the process, not of entities; a statistical model is a means to characterize directly the process and the real world population indirectly:

> "The Experiment=Process is not just the translation of the ideational structure into the phenomenological domain... but is also, through the probabilities associated with the outcomes, the translation of the material conditions into the ideational domain where in these material conditions affect and constrain the frequency with which certain outcomes are selected by artisans" (Read 1987).

TRUTH, EMPIRICISM AND RELATIVISM

> "There can be no completely objective account of the Past. The truth of the Past can never be known for certain... Archaeologists can draw increasingly close but never quite get there because of subjectivity belonging to the Present...

We would strongly criticize the view that there is a mechanical, albeit indirect, relation between material culture and the contexts of its production. The aim of a science of material culture, a science of the archaeological record, is a mistaken one, a futile search for scientific objectivity... There can be no objective link between patterning perceived in material culture and process which produced that patterning" (Shanks and Tilley 1987a).

I do not think so. I have asserted that Statistics is the way to reach objectivity. I think that objectivity is the main goal for all Hard and Soft Sciences. Without objectivity we have not communication among scientists.

It is wrong to say that it is not possible to judge between competing theories and statements because different observers cannot agree on what they actually see as a result of the theory-laden nature of observational statements (Shanks and Tilley 1987a). The impossibility to judge between competing theories is a typical feature of the followers of the Radical Critique: Shanks and Tilley affirm that there is no way to choose between alternative pasts except on essentially political grounds, in terms of a definite value system or a morality (Shanks and Tilley 1987b). Therefore, their view of Statistics -full of misconceptions- is negative:

"Statistical practice is conceived as a technical and therefore neutral practice, including the collection, processing, assessment and presentation of facts. It meets the need for generalization based on objective data, controlling for subjective bias, and meets the requirement for practical rules for deciding when generalization is justified or when data are inadequate. These needs accompany the conception of reality as the observable, of theory being brought into agreement with and affirming reality, of the facts being theory-neutral and intersubjectively acceptable" (Shanks and Tilley 1987a).

We are again in front of the contradiction between Logic of Discovering and Logic of Justification. This is not the only critique of Shanks and Tilley against Statistics -however, I think it is the cleverest-: they do not understand the concept of meaning. To say that "for mathematization meaning is a meaningless question" and that "this is the inevitable conclusion to a belief in the objectivity of precision and calculability" is ridiculous.

The main misconception of Shanks and Tilley is their concept of objectivity:

"Objectivity is abstract, uniform, neutral, because it exists separately from the archaeologist, the observing subject. Objective facts count and archaeological knowledge is thought to be entirely dependent on them" (Shanks and Tilley 1987b).

I can find such concept not even in Carnap nor in the first Wittgestein (the nucleus of positivism): facts do not determine if the use of a proposition is right or wrong, but only how many times the phenomenon studied will be produced (Carnap 1939, 1966); according to Wittgestein, a word cannot be true or false in the sense of not coinciding with reality (Wittgestein 1914-1916). (2)

This is a very important problem in Archaeology. Perhaps the mistake was the conception of Statistics as a way of contrasting hypotheses, which was defended at the beginnings of the New Archaeology (Watson, LeBlanc and Redman 1971; Cannon 1983). I agree with Shanks and Tilley and with Hodder (1986) with the fact that there is no definitive testing of a hypothesis:

"The material formations observed and recorded by field archaeologists are not directly perceived phenomena but classes of criteria constructs. Concepts like context and association are used so frequently that there is a tendency to forget their theoretical nature. The object of analysis and policy, as represented in archaeological records, is therefore theory-laden as a result of processes of definition, convention and abstraction" (Reilly 1985).

"We test our hypotheses not against any solid bedrock of fact but in terms of basic theory-laden terms and observations we have supposedly been trained to know. If theory is involved in the very act of observation then testing cannot be a rational procedure" (Shanks and Tilley 1987a).

However, scientists need this rationality for communication. All facts need propositions in wittgesteinian sense; statistical observations are then a kind of propositions which are not true nor wrong. It has important consequences for a conceptualization of Statistics: it is not a criteria of truth or verisimilitude but a language for expressing special kind of ideas unexpressable in other languages. Therefore I prefer do not speak about Truth but about well-formulated theories, that is to say, theories that can be expressed and understood because they are not arbitrary nor ambiguous.

According to C. Carr (1985b) it is impossible to speak in absolute terms about the accuracy, appropriateness or relevance of a theoretical construct, analytic technique or data structure in relation to the real world or a portion of the real world. However, it is possible to speak in relative terms about the accuracy, appropriateness or relevance of a theoretical construct, analytic technique or data structure in relation to a phenomenon of interest as a selected but actual facet of a portion of the real world. In consequence, Statistics is not the procedure to compare theoretic statements to evidence in real world. I want to study only a facet of complexity with the help of a theory expressed in statistical language. Statistics is, I would say, a language that allow to transform observables according to a theory. This theory is a set of concepts, variables of a conceptual system, that is to say, the meaning structure of the archaeological record. I am not only interested in the discovering of latent structures in a data set but also in the particular ordering of this conceptual system in the underlying structures of a particular archaeological record.

With a theory, with a Conceptual system I have only series of unstructured ideas; Substance without Form. Only when I apply these concepts to different data sets I can obtain a structured meaning expressed in mathematical terms in order to assure the objectivity of the interpretation. According to Feyerabend (1970) we ought to understand the world with the help of very different theories. If I use different conceptual systems, I will obtain different meanings, different ways of understanding the particular archaeological record.

Form versus Substance; Discovering versus Justification. These two contradictions are the nucleus of all discussions about the epistemological role of Statistics. Regularities in real world have many substances, many meanings. Scientists have to study all these meanings describing their particular form. Science is not a search of Truth in the sense of Carnap or Popper but a way of speaking about the things in the world. Statistics is a language that allows it.

I do not pretend an irrationalist analytical philosophy but I am not either a positivist scientist. I prefer a Semantics of Science based on these principles:

  - there is a world which existence does not depend on my mind
  - that world can only be partially known
  - knowledge of world come from Theory; anyone can give a final truth to it
  - knowledge is always indirect and symbolic

(synthesis of the realist philosophy by Popper, Tuomela, Bunge and Hacking, cf. Rivadulla 1986). Statistics as a language and a method must be understood within this epistemological reference. Working with mathematics we will obtain only an indirect and symbolic knowledge of the archaeological record. I do not agree with the principle of empiricism: "only experience can decide about the truth or falsity of a factual statement". Therefore, I do not agree either with the popperian principle of closer-to-the-truth because, for me, it is a nonsense to speak about a measure of truth.

Chi square, Fishers's test, Student's test, or whatsoever measure based upon probabilities are not a measure of Truth. They are only linguistic rules in order to allow the non-ambiguity of an inference process.

I do not agree with Shafer's Theory of Evidence (1976): the existence of a weight of evidence scale, which is only a development of the concept closer-to-the-truth . Data can be uncertain, facts can be unreliable; only rules (Statistical techniques) ought to be not ambiguous and logically consistent. Interpretations are always a conceptual system, external to the observed record but expressed in the same statistical language. These Interpretations are never true nor false; they can be only possible (Fox 1986; López de Mántaras 1985).

RECAPITULATION

It would be a nonsense to propose some conclusions to the ideas and concepts expressed in this paper. Therefore I have preferred to give a recapitulation of the key sentences I have used:

> Analysis is seen as a process of searching for and discovering order or structure in a set of data. The primary task of Archaeology is to discover and to describe whatever structure, order or pattern of predictability may there be in archaeological data.

> A Theory is a set of concepts, variables of a conceptual system, that is to say, the meaning structure of the archaeological record. I am not interested in the discovering of latent structures in a data set but in the particular structuration of this conceptual system in a particular archaeological record.

Behavioral hypotheses cannot be evaluated directly, so it is necessary to transform them into statistical hypotheses, that is to say, substantive research propositions must be translated into unequivocal statements of relationships between or among hypotheses, and not exist in any formal sense apart from them.

To research is to decode Reality by coding it in an artificial language in order to be able to understand what is it and what is it.

> Statistics deals with coincidences and contradictions between particular subjects and general theories.

> Statistics is the method which allows a comparison between the particular and the general, between the observable and the theoretic.

> Statistical Analysis is a way of subsuming an event or particular population in other more general: a statistical regularity is explained when it is possible to see how it is subsumed in a more general model of regularities.

> Statistical reasoning is the inferential method which allows the inclusion of quantitative patterns in conceptual schemes.

Statistical techniques transform and resume the social information from the real world in the same way as microscopes do it with biological information.

The goal of many of the statistical techniques is to describe the pattern found in data through a model, a representation of what the scientist sees in the population which is being studied... Such a model is seen as an abstraction of the real world, in which relationships among real elements are replaced by relationships among mathematical objects.

Statistics is not limited to give criteria for likelihood of an inference. It is used to detect non random patterns which need an interpretation.

Mathematics (or Statistics) is the means to make a Scientific Theory but it is not at all a Scientific Theory in itself... All explanation is a cognitive process, and not only of verification... Even when statistical analysis shows relationships which direct observation has not discovered, the need of interpretation remains.

The described statistical regularity is significative in itself; therefore, the archaeologist tries to express it in a comprehensible way. Statistical Archaeology will be the discipline which studies such regularities. This study is not limited to subsume measured regularity in a general appropriate theory, but in the progressive decoding of underlying structures.

The archaeologist ought to seek a Multivariable structure which explain the micro-patterns of variation for understanding data.

Statistics is a language, a way of transforming observable reality in order to show the complexity. As a language, Statistics give scientists a means of communication.

Statistics has to be the way of objectivating the reasoning.

If we consider that statistical structure discovered in data is meaningful, then we will accept that statistics is a language to express certain kind of ideas.

The same structure between Form and Substance in a linguistic communication exists between statistical models and scientific theories.

Statistics gives the means to translate archaeological observations into a language in which it is possible to describe a wide range of relationships among different artefacts and attributes

The pattern discovered by statistical procedures is Form without Substance. To express this content the archaeologist develops a complex hierarchical conceptual system in which Statistics has the role of formation rules for the different concepts at different levels.

Statistical reasoning is the Form of Archaeological Concepts; therefore, these techniques are not neutral procedures without relation to the meaning. All interpretative system must be isomorphic to structural pattern. An interpretation will be significative only if there is an isomorphism between the cluster of semantic concepts and the regularities observed in real-world through statistical procedures

If the statistical pattern described by the archaeologist in his data has only Form without substance it will be necessary, in order to obtain meaning, to compare the particular pattern with a theoretical model.

Data have no meaning in themselves, they are meaningful only in relation to a conceptual model of the phenomenon studied.

The descriptive use of probabilities does not imply that the phenomena really occur by chance, but that they appear so irregular that they can be successful described as if they were random.

The statistical pattern in data is not directly significant. It must be compared with a model in which anthropological or sociological or any other nature theories adopt a statistical form. The lack of conformity between the pattern described in data through statistical analysis and such theoretical baselines is what becomes significant.

Statistical methodology is fundamentally a means to think logically about data. It is impossible to introduce Reality in the computer and to think that the machine gives us a definitive interpretation. The scientist imposes a system of variables constraining all the study. We observe reality according to these constraints, according to a series of appropriate criteria.

We can use very different ways of transformation of data in order to express a conceptual structure. Nobody has enough with just a concept to explain the world.

Interpretations are always a conceptual system, external to the observed record but expressed in the same statistical language. These interpretations are never true nor false; they can only be possible.

Statistical observations are a kind of propositions which are not true not wrong.

Statistics are not a criteria of truth or verisimilitude but a language to express a special kind of unexpressable ideas in other languages.

Science is not a search of truth in the sense of Carnap or Popper, but a way to speak about the things in the world. Statistics is the way which allows it.

NOTES

(1) Quotations of Carnap works and even citation are not significant in *Analytical Archaeology*. However all the proposal is inspired in positivist inductivism.

(2) Nevertheless, this is an ambiguous concept in the first Wittgestein: "um sagen zu koennen *p* ist wahr (oder falsch), muss ich bestimmt haben, unter welchen Umstaenden ich *p* wahr nenne, und damit bestimme ich den Sinn des Satzes" (*Tractatus...* 4.063)

BIBLIOGRAPHY*

Afifi, A.A. and Azen, S.P., 1979. *Statistical Analysis. A computer oriented approach*. New York: Academic Press.

Airvaux, I., 1984. "Methodologie systematique en typologie analytique". *Dialektike*.

Aivazian, S., Enukov, I. and Mechalkin, L., 1983. *Elements de Modelisation et Traitement Primaire des Donées*. (Traduction française). Moscow: MIR.

Aldenderfer, M.S., (ed.) 1987. *Quantitative research in Archaeology*. Progress and Prospects. Newbury Park (California): SAGE Publications.

Aldenderfer, M.S., 1987a. "Assessing the Impact of Quantitative Thinking on Archaeological Research". In *Quantitative research in Archaeology. Progress and Prospects*. Edited by M.S. Aldenderfer. Newbury Park (California): SAGE Publications.

Aldenderfer, M.S., 1987b. "On the Structure of Archaeological Data". In *Quantitative research in Archaeology. Progress and Prospects*. Edited by M.S. Aldenderfer. Newbury Park (California): SAGE Publications.

Bailyn, L., 1977. "Research as a cognitive process: Implications for Data Analysis". *Quality and Quantity* 11,2:97-117.

Baird, D., 1987. "Exploratory Factor Analysis, Instruments and the Logic of Discovery". *British Journal for the Philosophy of Science*. 38,3: 319-337.

Barceló, J.A., 1987. "La Arqueología y el estudio de los ritos funerarios: métodos matemáticos de análisis". I *Coloquio Internacional Sobre Religiones Prehistóricas de la Península Ibérica*. Salamanca-Cáceres

Barceló, J.A., 1988 "La Prehistoria y la Sociología matemática: algunos avances recientes". *Butlletí de l'Associació Arqueológica de Castelló*. IX,5: 9-14.

Barceló, J.A., 1988a. "Introducción al Razonamiento estadístico aplicado a la Arqueologia: un análisis de las estelas Antropomorfas de la Península Ibérica. *Trabajos de Prehistoria*. 45: 51-86.

Barceló, J.A., in press. "La Ley del Decrecimiento Monotónico y la Arqueología Espacial". *Estudios de la Antiguedad*.

Bietti, A., 1979. "Metodi Matemaci e statistici applicati all'archeologia e alla paletnologia". *Contributi del Centro Linceo interdisciplinare di Scienze Matematiche e loro applicazioni* nº 47. Roma: Accademia Nazionale dei Lincei.

Bietti, A., 1982. "Tecniche Matematiche nell'Analisi dei dati Archeologici". *Contributi del Centro Linceo interdisciplinare di Scienze Matematiche e loro applicazioni* nº 61. Roma: Accademia Nazionale dei Lincei.

Bietti, A., Burani, A., and Zanello, L., 1985. "Interactive pattern recognition in prehistoric archaeology: some applications". In *To pattern the past*. Proceedings of the Symposium on Mathematical Methods in Archaeology, Amsterdam, 1984. Edited by A.Voorrips, S.H.Loving, PACT 11: 205-228.

Binford,L.R.,1975. "Sampling, Judgement and the Archaeological record". In *Sampling in Archaeology*. Edited by J.W. Mueller. pp. 251-257, Tucson: University of Arizona Press.

Binford,L.R., 1977. "General Introduction". In *For theory building in Archaeology*. Edited by L.R. Binford, New York: Academic Press.

Binford,L.R., 1981. *Bones: Ancient Men and Modern Myths*. New York: Academic Press.

Binford,L.R., 1982. "Objectivity-Explanation-Archaeology". In *Theory and Explanation in Archaeology*. Edited by C.Renfrew, M.J. Rowlands, B.A. Segraves. New York: Academic Press.

Binford,L.R., 1983. *Working at Archaeology*. New York: Academic Press.

Binford,L.R., 1987. "Data, Relativism and Archaeological Science". *Man* (N.S.)22:391-404

Binford,L.R. and Binford,S., 1966, "A preliminary analysis of functional variability in the Mousterian of Levallois facies. *American Anthropologist* 68: 238-295.

Binford,L.R. and Sabloff,J.A., 1982. "Paradigms, systematics and archaeology" *Journal of Anthropological Research* 38 (2): 137-153.

Blalock, H.M., 1982, Conceptualization and Measurement in the Social Sciences. Beverly Hills: SAGE Publications.

Borillo,A, Borillo,M. and Virbel,J., 1977. "Proprietés remarcables d'un systeme de representation et de traitement por l'Analyse du discours relatif a un domaine scientifique determiné". In *Analyse et validation dans l'étude des données textuelles*. Edited by M, Borillo, J. Virbel. Paris: Editions du CNRS.

Borillo,M. and Virbel,J., 1978. "Statut scientifique de l'Archéologie et formalisation de l'analyse des textes". In *Archéologie et calcul*. Edited by M. Borillo, Paris: Union Generale d'Editions.

Box, G.P., Hunter, W.G. and Hunter, J.S., 1978. *Statistics for experimenters*. New York: John Wiley and Sons.

Bresson,F., 1972. "Problemes de la Mathematisation en Psychologie". In *La Mathematisation des doctrines informes*. Edited by C. Canguilhem, Paris: Hermann ed.

Bunge,M., 1959. Causality. In *The place of causal principle in modern science*. Cambridge (Massachussets): Harvard University Press (Traducción castellana Buenos Aires: EUDEBA).

Bunge,M., 1972. *Teoría y Realidad*. Barcelona: Editorial Ariel.

Bunge,M., 1983. *La investigación científica* (2º ed). Barcelona: Ariel.

Bunge,M., 1985. *Racionalidad y Realismo*. Madrid: Alianza Editorial.

Cannon,A., 1983. "The quantification of artifactual assemblages: Some implications for behavioral inferences" *American Antiquity* 48, 4: 785-792.

Carnap,R., 1939. "Foundations of Logic and Mathematics". In *International Encyclopedia of Unified Sciences*, Chicago: The University Press (traducción castellana Madrid: Taller de Edicjones JB).

Carnap,R., 1966. *Philosophical foundations of Physics* (traducción castellana Barcelona: Editorial Orbis).

Carr,C. (ed.), 1985. *For concordance in Archaeological Analysis. Bridging Data structure, quantitative technique, and Theory*. Kansas City: Westport Publishers.

Carr,C., 1985a. "Screening intrasite artifact distributions with Fourier and filtering methods" In *To pattern the past*. Proceedings of the Symposium on Mathematical Methods in Archaeology, Amsterdam, 1984. Edited by A.Voorrips, S.H.Loving, PACT 11: 249-286.

Carr,C., 1985b. "Getting into Data: Philosophy and Tactics for the Analysis of Complex Data Structures". In *For concordance in Archaeological Analysis. Bridging Data structure, quantitative technique, and Theory*. Edited by C.Carr, Kansas City: Westport Publishers.

Carr,C., 1987. "Removing discordance from Quantitative Analysis". In *Quantitative research in Archaeology. Progress and Prospects*. Edited by M.S Aldenderfer, Newbury Park (California): SAGE Publications.

Chataigner,Ch. and Plateaux,M., 1986. "Analyse spatiale des habitats rubanés et informatique" *Bulletin de la Societé Prehistorique Française*. 83, 10: 319-324.

Clark,G., 1982. "Quantifying archaeological research". In *Advances in Archaeological Method and Theory*. Edited by M. Schiffer, pp. 217-273 New York: Academic Press.

Clarke,D., 1978. *Analytical Archaeology* (2º ed.). London: Methuen & Co.

Coseriu,E., 1977. *Principios de Semántica Estructural* (traducción castellana Madrid: Gredos).

Cowgill,G.C., 1977. "The trouble with significance tests and what we can do about it". *American Antiquity* 33: 367-375.

Cox,D.R. and Hinkley,D.V., 1974. *Theoretical Statistics*. London: Chapman and Hall.

Daniel,C. and Wood,F.S., 1980. *Fitting Equations to Data* (2º ed.). New York: John Wiley and Sons.

Djindjian,F., 1981. "Knowledge building interactive system in Archaeology: patterning and assigment". In *Manejo de datos y métodos matemáticos en Arqueología*. IUPPS. X Congreso, IV Comisión. México.

Djindjian,F., 1983. "Mathematiques et Informatique appliées a l'Archeologie Prehistorique" *Informatique et Sciences Humaines* 14e. année, nº 59-60: 95-107.

Djindjian,F., 1985a. "Typologie et culture. L'exemple de l'Aurignacien" In *La signification culturelle des industries lithiques*. Actes du Colloque de Liege. (ed. M. Otte) Studia Praehistorica Belgica 4. Oxford: British Archaeological Reports (International Series 239).

Djindjian,F., 1985b. "Seriation and toposeriation by correspondence analysis". In *To pattern the past*. Proceedings of the Symposium on Mathematical Methods in Archaeology, Amsterdam, 1984. Edited by A. Voorrips, S.H.Loving, PACT 11:119-136.

Djindjian,F., 1986. "Apport des techniques statistiques et informatiques aux méthodes et aux theories de l'Archeologie" *Bulletin de la Societé Prehistorique Française* 83,10: 372-377.

Djindjian,F. and Leredde,H., 1980. "Traitement automatique des données en Archeologie" *Dossiers de l'Archaeologie*, 42: 52-69.

Domenech,J.M., Riba,M.D. and Viladrich,M.C., 1985. *Manipulación de la matriz de datos para investigar relaciones entre variables*. Bellaterra: Universidad Autónoma de Barcelona Press.

Doran,J. and Hodson, F.R., 1975. *Mathematics and computers in Archaeology*. Cambridge (MA): Harvard University Press.

Earle,T.K. and Preucel,R.W., 1987. "Processual Archaeology and the radical critique" *Current Anthropology*. 28,4: 501-538.

Eco,U., 1971. *La forma del contenido* (traducción castellana, Barcelona: Lumen).

Eco,U., 1977. *Tratado de Semiótica General* (traducción castellana, Barcelona: Lumen).

Ehrenberg,A.S.C., 1975. *Data Reduction. Analysing and interpreting statistical data*. London: John Wiley and Sons.

Ehrenberg,A.S.C., 1984. "Data Analysis with Prior Knowledge" In *Statistics: an appraisal* eds. H.A.David and H.T. David. Awes: The Iowa State University Press.

Everitt,B.S., Dunn,G., 1983. *Advanced methods of data exploration and modeling*. London: Heinemann Educational Books.

Feyerabend,P.K., 1970. *Against method: outline of an anarchistic theory of knowledge*. Minnesota Studies in Philosophy of Science, vol. IV (traducción castellana, Barcelona: Ariel).

Finch,P.D., 1981. "On the role of description in statistical enquiry" *British Journal for the Philosophy of Science* 32, 2: 127-144.

Fisher,D. and Langley,P.,1986 "Conceptual clustering and its relation to Numerical Taxonomy". In *Artificial Intelligence & Statistics* ed. by W.A. Gale. Reading (MA): Addison-Wesley.

Fletcher,M. and Lock,G.,1985. "Investigating relationships within large-scale data sets as a precursor to the application of Multivariable techniques". In *To pattern the past*. Proceedings of the symposium on Mathematical Methods in Archaeology, Amsterdam, 1984. Edited by A.Voorrips, S.H Loving. PACT 11:169-180.

Fox,J., 1986. "Knowledge, Decision Making and Uncertainty" In *Artificial Intelligence & Statistics* ed. by W.A. Gale. Reading (MA): Addison-Wesley.

Gaffney,C.F. and Gaffney,V.L., (eds.), 1987. *Pragmatic Archaeology: Theory in crisis?* Oxford: British Archaeological Reports (British Series 167).

Gardin,J.C.,Guillaume,O.,Herman,P.O.,Hesnard,A.,Lagrange,M.S.,Renaud, M. and Zadora-Rio,E., 1986. Systèmes Experts et Sciences Humaines: le cas de l'Archéologie. Paris: Eyrolles.

Hacking,I., 1965. *Logic of Statistical Inference*. Cambridge: The University Press.

Hacking,I, 1983. *Representing and intervening*. Cambridge: The University Press.

Hietala,H. (ed.), 1984. *Intrasite spatial Analysis in Archaeology*. Cambridge: The University Press.

Hinkley,D.V., 1984. "A Hitchhiker's Guide to the Galaxy of Theoretical Statistics". In *Statistics: an appraisal* eds. H.A.David and H.T. David. Awes: The Iowa State University Press.

Hoaglin,D.C., Mosteller,F. and Tukey,J.W., 1983. *Understanding robust and Exploratory Data Analysis* . London: John Wiley and Sons.

Hodder,I., 1974. "Regression analysis of some trade and marketing patterns", *World Archaelogy*, 6.

Hodder,I, 1977. "Some new directions in the spatial analysis of archaeological data at the regional scale". In *Spatial Archaelogy*. Edited by D.Clarke. London: Academic Press.

Hodder,I. 1986, *Reading the Past. Current approaches to interpretation in Archaeology*. Cambridge: The University Press (Traducción castellana, Barcelona: Editorial Crítica).

Hodder,I., (ed.), 1987a. *The archaeology of contextual meanings*. Cambridge: The University Press.

Hodder,I.,(ed.), 1987b. *Archaeology as long-term history*. Cambridge: The University Press.

Hodder,I and Orton,C., 1976. *Spatial Analysis in Archaeology. Cambridge*: The University Press.

Hodson,F.R. and Orton,C., 1981. "Rank and class: interpretation of the evidence from prehistoric cemeteries". In *Mortality and Immortality: the Anthropology and Archaeology of death*. Edited by Humphreys,S.C., King, H. London.

Hofstadter,D.R., 1979. *Goedel, Escher, Bach: an Eternal Golden Braid*. New York: Basic Books (traducción castellana, Barcelona: Tusquets).

Johnson,G.A., 1981. "Monitoring complex system integration and boundary phenomena with settlement size data". In *Archaeological Approaches to the study of complexity*. Edited by S.E. van der Leeuw, CINGULA VI. Amsterdam: The University Press.

Kintigh,K.W., 1987. "Quantitative methods designed for archaeological problems". In *Quantitative research in Archaeology. Progress and Prospects*. Edited by M.S. Aldenderfer. Newbury Park (California): SAGE Publications.

Kolmogorov,A.N., 1983. "On logical foundations of Probability Theory". In *Probability Theory and Mathematical Statistics*. Edited by K.Ito and J.V. Prokhorov. Lecture Notes in Mathematics nº 1021, Berlin: Springer Verlag.

Kuipers,T.A.F., (ed.), 1987. *What is Closer-to-the-Truth. A parade of approaches to Truthlikenes*. Poznan Studies in the Philosophy of the Sciences and the Humanities, vol. 10, Amsterdam: Editions Rodopi B.V.

Kyburg,H., 1985. "Logic of statistical reasoning". In *Encyclopedia of Statistical Sciences* vol.5 Edited by S.Kotz and N.L. Johnson. New York: John Wiley and Sons.

Lagrange,M.S., 1987. "La sistematisation du discours archéologique". In *La logique du Plausible* Edited by J.C. Gardin (2ºed.) Paris: Editions de la Maison des Sciences de l'Homme.

Leone,M.P., Potter,P.B. and Shackel,P.A., 1987. "Toward a Critical Archaeology" *Current Anthropology*, 28, 3: 283-302.

López de Mántaras,R., 1985. "Técnicas de representación del conocimiento aproximado". In *Inteligencia Artificial: Sistemas Expertos*. Edited by J. Cuena, pp.69-110. Madrid: Alianza Editorial.

Marradi, A., 1981. "Factor Analysis as an aid in the formation and refinement of empirically useful concepts". In *Factor Analysis and Measurement in sociological research. A multidimensional perspective*. Edited by D.J. Jackson and E.F. Borgatta., London: SAGE Publications.

Michalski,R., 1980. "Knowledge acquisition through conceptual clustering: a theoretical framework and Algorithm for partitioning data into conjunctive concepts." *International Journal of Policy Analysis and Information Systems* 4, 3: 219-243.

Mithen,S.J., 1988. "Simulation as a methodological tool". In *Computer and Quantitative Methods in Archaeology*. Edited by C.L.N. Ruggles and S.P.Q. Rahtz. Oxford: British Archaeological Reports (International Series 393).

Mulaik,S.A., 1987a. "A brief history of the Philosophical Foundations of Exploratory Factor Analysis" *Multivariate Behavioral Research* 22: 267-305.

Mulaik,S.A., 1987b. "Toward a conception of Causality applicable to experimentation and Causal Modeling" *Child Development*, 58: 18-32.

Neuberg,L.G., 1977. "The limits of Statistics in Planning Analysis" *Quality and Quantity* 11,1: 1-26.

Newell,R.R. and Dekin,A.A., 1978. "An integrative strategy for the definition of behaviorally meaningful archaeological units" *Palaeohistoria* XX.

Nida,E., 1975. *Componential Analysis of Meaning*. The Hague: Mouton.

Phelps,R.I. and Musgrove,P.B. "Artificial Intelligence Approaches in Statistics". In *Artificial Intelligence & Statistics* ed. by W.A. Gale. Reading (MA): Addison-Wesley.

Przeworsky,A. and Teune,H., 1970. *The logic of comparative social inquiry*. New York: John Wiley.

Rashed,R., 1972. "La mathematisation de l'informe dans la science sociale: la conduite de l'homme bernoullien". In *La Mathematisation des doctrines informes*. Edited by C .Canguilhem, Paris: Hermann ed.

Read,D.W., 1982. "Toward a theory of archaeological classification". In *Essays on Archaeological Typology* Edited by R. Whallon and J.A. Brown Evanston: Center for American Archaeology Press.

Read,D.W., 1985. "The substance of archaeological analysis and the mold of statistical method: enlightenment out of discordance?". In *For concordance in Archaeological Analysis. Bridging Data structure, quantitative technique, and Theory*. Edited by C .Carr, Kansas City: Westport Publishers.

Read,D.W., 1987. "Archaeological Theory and statistical methods: Discordance, Resolution and New Directions". In *Quantitative research in Archaeology. Progress and Prospects*. Edited by M.S. Aldenderfer. Newbury Park (California): SAGE Publications.

Redman,C.L., 1978. "Multivariable artifact analysis: a basis for multidimensional interpretations". In *Social Archaeology. Beyond subsistence and dating*. Edited by C.L. Redman et allii New York: Academic Press.

Regnier,S., 1966. "Classification et analyse des expressions plastiques non-figuratives des malades mentaux" (reprinted in *Mathematiques et Sciences Humaines* 82, 1983).

Reilly,P., 1985. "Computers in field archaeology: agents of change?". In *Current Issues in Archaeological Computing*. Edited by M.A. Cooper and J.D. Richards. Oxford: British Archaeological Reports (International Series 271).

Renfrew,C., 1977. "Alternative models for exchange and spatial distribution" In *Exchange Systems in Prehistory*. Edited by T.K. Earle and J.E. Ericson. New York: Academic Press.

Renfrew,C., 1979. "Transformations". In *Transformations. Mathematical approaches to Culture Change*. Edited by C. Renfrew and K.L. Cooke, New York: Academic Press.

Rivadulla,A., 1986, *Filosofía actual de la Ciencia.* Madrid: Tecnos.

Rossi,I., 1982. "On the assumptions of Structural analysis: revisiting its linguistic and episemological premises" In *The logic of Culture. Advances in Structural Therory and Methods.* Edited by I. Rossi. London: Tavistock.

Salmon,M., 1982. *Philosophy and Archaeology.* New York: Academic Press.

Salmon,W., 1984, *Scientific Explanation and the Causal structure of the world.* Princeton: The University Press.

Scheps,S., 1982. "Statistical blight" *American Antiquity* 47,4: 836-851

Schvyrkov,V.V., Davis III, Arch. C., 1987. "The homogeneity problem in Statistics" *Quality and Quantity* 21,1: 21-36.

Shafer,G., 1976. *A mathematical theory of Evidence.* Princeton: The University Press.

Shanks,M., Tilley,C., 1987a, *Reconstructing Archaeology. Theory and Practice.* Cambridge: The University Press.

Shanks,M. and Tilley,C., 1987b. *Social Theory and Archaeology.* London: Polity Press

Sneath,P.H.A. and Sokal,R.S., 1973, *Numerical Taxonomy,* San Francisco: W.H. Freeman & Co.

Spaulding,A.C., 1982. "Structure in Archaeological data: Nominal Variables". In *Essays on Archaeological Typology* Edited by R. Whallon and J.A. Brown Evanston: Center for American Archaeology Press.

Suarez,P., 1981. "Alternative coding procedures and factorial structure of attitude and belief systems". In *Factor Analysis and Measurement in sociological research. A multidimensional perspective.* Edited by D.J. Jackson and E.F. Borgatta., London: SAGE Publications.

Thisted,R.A., 1986. "Representing statistical knowledge for Expert Data Analysis Systems". In *Artificial Intelligence & Statistics* ed. by W.A. Gale. Reading (MA): Addison-Wesley.

Tonnelat,M.A., 1972. "Limites d´extension du concept de doctrine informe". In *La Mathematisation des doctrines informes.* Edited by C.Canguilhem, Paris: Hermann ed.

Tukey,J.W., 1984. "Data Analysis: History and Prospects" In *Statistics: an appraisal* eds. H.A.David and H.T. David. Awes: The Iowa State University Press.

van der Leeuw,S.E., (ed.), 1981. *Archaeological Approaches to the study of complexity.* CINGULA VI. Amsterdam: The University Press.

IInd Deya Conference of Prehistory: Archaeological Techniqies, Technology and Theory

van der Leeuw,S.E., 1981a. "Information flows, flow structures and the explanation of change in human institutions". In *Archaeological Approaches to the study of complexity*. Edited by S.E. van der Leeuw CINGULA VI. Amsterdam: The University Press.

Vierra,R.K., 1982. "Typology, Classification and Theory building". In *Essays on Archaeological Typology* Edited by R. Whallon and J.A. Brown Evanston: Center for American Archaeology Press.

Voorrips,A., 1981. "To tailor the infected tail: reflections on rank-size relationships". In *Archaeological Approaches to the study of complexity*. Edited by S.E. van der Leeuw CINGULA VI. Amsterdam: The University Press.

Voorrips,A., 1982. "Mambrino´s helmet: a framework for structuring archaeological data". In *Essays on Archaeological Typology* Edited by R. Whallon and J.A. Brown Evanston: Center for American Archaeology Press.

Voorrips,A., 1987. "Formal and Statistical Models in Archaeology". In *Quantitative research in Archaeology. Progress and Prospects*. Edited by M.S. Aldenderfer. Newbury Park (California): SAGE Publications.

Watson,P.J., LeBlanc,S.A. and Redman,C.L., 1971. *Explanation in Archaeology. An explicitly scientific approach*. Columbia University Press (Traducción castellana, Madrid: Alianza Editorial).

Whallon,R., 1982. "Variables and Dimensions: The critical step in Quantitative Typology". In *Essays on Archaeological Typology* Edited by R. Whallon and J.A. Brown Evanston: Center for American Archaeology Press.

Whiteley,P., 1983. "The Analysis of Contingence Tables". In *Data Analysis and the Social Sciences*. Edited by D. McKay, N. Schofield, P. Whiteley. London: Frances Pinter.

Wittgestein,L., 1914-1916. *Notebooks*. Oxford: Basil Blakwell (1961) (Traducción castellana, Barcelona: Ariel).

Wittgestein,L., *Tractatus logico-philosophicus* (Edition in Castellano-Deutsch, Madrid: Alianza Editorial.

Wotjak,G., 1977. *Untersuchungen zur Struktur der Bedeutung. Ein Beitrag zu Gegestand und Methode der modernen Bedeutungsforschung unter besonderer Beruecksichtigung der semantischen Konstituenten-Analyse*. Berlin: Akademie Verlag. (Traducción castellana, Madrid: Gredos).

World Archaeological Congress, 1986. *Archaeological 'objectivity' in Interpretation*. Edited by P. Ucko. Southampton: Allen & Unwin.

* When it has been impossible to find the original version, I have used its Spanish translation (traducción castellana)

ARCHAEOLOGICAL TECHNIQUES, TECHNOLOGY AND THEORY

L'EVOLUTION TECHNOLOGIQUE DU BIGE AU QUADRIGE EN MEDITERRANEE ORIENTALE, AU MAGHREB ET AU SAHARA: QUAND ET PORQUOI?

ALFRED MUZZOLINI
7 Rue J. de Resseguier
Toulouse, 31000, France

RESUME

Les premiers quadriges sont connus très anciennement : en pays sumérien, ce sont les chars de combat, tels que ceux du fameux Etendard d'Ur. Mais il ne s'agit alors que de chars lourds à roues pleines attelés à des onagres, probablement d'engins lents, peu maniables. Ils sont, il est vrai, figurés dans des contextes militaires, avec des personnages armés comme passagers, mais on ne saisit guère leurs possibilités au cours de la bataille. S'ils ne reflétaient pas déjà un simple stéréotype héroïque, ils pouvaient tout au plus servir au transport, soit de la troupe, soit plus probablement des seuls officiers. Dès l'époque sargonide, vers 2400 BC, ils sont abandonnés pour les usages militaires, et relégués à des fonctions culturelles (transport des statues lors de cérémonies) (Littauer-Crouwel, 1979).

Les biges, connus eux aussi dès l'époque sumérienne, deviennent alors l'équipement exclusif des armées asiatiques, et deux inventions technologiques les rendent enfin beaucoup plus légers et manoeuvrables : la roue à rayons et le mors, qui apparaissent dans la première moitié du IIème millénaire BC. En outre l'attelage est maintenant constitué par des chevaux. L'arme de la charrerie est alors adoptée dans toute l'Asie du Sud-Ouest, en Anatolie, à Mycènes, et, pour la première fois, en Egypte dès les débuts du Nouvel Empire. Ce type de bige léger, utilisé à l'exclusion absolue de tout trige et quadrige, correspond à un modèle très bien standardisé à travers toutes ces contrées, au cours du IIème millénaire.

Pour la même periode, les figurations rupestres sahariennes, et les documents de fouille, ne révèlent aucune trace de char en Afrique au-delà de l'Egypte, ni en Europe méditerranéenne au-delà du Péloponèse ou de la Crète.

Les premiers attelages de triges et quadriges, tractant d'abord le même modèle de char léger, apparaissent, d'une façon très précise, au cours du IXᵉ-VIIIème siècles, en Assyrie et dans le royaume d'Urartu (Arménie) (Piggott, 1983), et, en même temps ou très peu après, en pays néo-hittite, au Levant, à Chypre. L'épopée homérique, qui se forme alors, les mentionne également. Les documents manquent pour l'Egypte de cette époque (la première figuration de quadrige n'y date que de l'époque de la conquête assyrienne, vers le VIIème siècle BC) (Littauer-Crouwel, 1979).

Très rapidement, le quadrige devient en Assyrie l'équipement standard, et les autres contrées l'imitent. Mais les chevaux sont maintenant attelés, dès le règne de Tiglat-Pileser III (vers 750 BC), à un char lourd, équipé de grosses roues, et capable de porter trois ou quatre hommes. La Perse achéménide conservera ce char lourd, et les textes nous assurent qu'il était effectivement uitilisé à des fins militaires, mais presque uniquement au sein des armées asiatiques. Il y resta en usage jusqu'à la bataille d'Arbèles (331 BC) qui démontra définitivement l'inefficacité des charges de quadriges, si lourds soient-ils, contre une armée ordonnée suivant le modèle de la phalange et bien commandée.

Après les campagnes d'Alexandre, on signale encore quelques rare utilisations sporadiques de chars de combat, parfois des quadriges (comme dans les "guerres hellénistiques" mettant aux prises les Grecs de Sicile et Carthage, ou dans les guerres marmariques livrées par Cyrène), parfois des biges (comme les biges des Bretons, qui étonnèrent César). Mais, pour l'essentiel, les chars n'étaient plus utilisés que dans les courses.

La vogue des courses de chars remonte très probablement à l'empire hittite et à Mycènes. Cet usage se généralisa dans les terre égéennes au début du 1er millénaire mais resta inconnu en Assyrie, au Levant, à Carthage, en Egypte. Vers 650-600 bc, la vague orientalisante le diffusa à Cyrène - d'où il gagna le Sahara central (c'est la période des chars, notamment des chars au galop volant), l'Atlas saharien et l'Atlas marocain. Des quadriges sont repérés au sein des ensembles rupestres du Sahara et du Maghreb (Muzzolini, 1986). Le char de course gagne également l'Etrurie, où les courses deviennent très populaires. En Andalousie, des biges du type étrusque ou grec, de fonction inconnue, sont figurés sur les stèles du Sud-Ouest.

A l'époque classique, dans les cités grecques comme à Rome, les courses deviennent le sport favori, elles continuent à mettre en compétition, jusqu'en basse époque, biges et quadriges.

CAUSES DE L'ADOPTION DU QUADRIGE DE COMBAT

L'évolution technologique des types de chars de combat correspond évidemment à des modifications dans les conceptions ou les possibilités tactiques des armées. Les textes s'avèrent peu prolixes là-dessus ou, comme dans l'Iliade, suspects d'archaîsation et héroîzation (Greenhalgh, 1973). Les figurations sont souvent, elles aussi, héroîsées, ou biaisées pour magnifier l'ordonnance superbe du camp ami et le désordre ou l'inexpérience du camp ennemi. Néanmoins, quelques déductions restent possibles.

Jusqu'au début du Ier millénaire BC, et malgré les figurations comme celles de Medinet Habou, qui prétendent illustrer le choc frontal des charreries hittite et égyptienne à la bataille de Kadesh, les chars légers ne servent en fait qu'à transporter les archers égyptiens et mésopotamiens ou les fantassins hittites au plus près de l'ennemi (c'est la fonction dite parfois usage homérique, c'est-à-dire, ironise Greenhalgh, le taxi-service). Sans doute aussi tournoyaient-ils autour ou au sein des formations ennemies, en voltigeurs, dans des batailles fluides.

Mais des innovations décisives dans la tactique, peu après 1000 BC, amènent à reconsidérer ce rôle:

> *(1) Les premiers corps de cavalerie apparaissent alors, d'abord constitués d'archers montés. Or les cavaliers assurent l'approche ou le harcèlement avec plus de facilité et plus de fluidité que le char, leur rapidité de manoeuvre les rend moins vulnérables que le char, qu'ils vont donc rapidement remplacer à cet effet.*

(2) Les armures (cuirasses en fer, etc.) se généralisent et deviennent efficaces contre les flèches que les archers, portés par les chars, tirent de trop loin; l'arme efficace contre ces armures, c'est désormais le javelot, qu'il faut il est vrai lancer de plus près, mais il est plus meurtrier. On ne peut guère le lancer qu'a pied, un char est trop secoué pour permettre de bien équilibrer son lancement.

(3) Contre les premières formations en phalanges, qui apparaissent alors, les chars légers en voltigeurs sont totalement impuissants.

Il vient à l'esprit que, sauf à s'en remettre au choc frontal phalange contre phalange, ce qu'on ne peut accepter que si l'on dispose d'une armée aussi disciplinée que celle de son adversaire (or les armées asiatiques, mêmes l'armee assyrienne, comptaient sur le nombre plus que sur l'organisation de leurs effectifs), le seul moyen de rompre la phalange adverse reste la charge de rupture. Tentation de toujours, dans l'usage militaire des chars! La force vive constituée par un cavalier et son cheval ne suffisait pas, en effet, pour emporter plusieurs piques pointées contre eux. Par contre, les chars, si on les adapte non plus pour rapprocher des archers, mais pour foncer, en masse, peuvent tout balayer sur leur lancée. Opération dangereuse, et même désepérée, mais la seule qui restât possible contre une phalange cohérente.

Le char léger du type classique du IIème millénaire n'était évidemment pas conçu pour la charge. Malgré un entraxe vraiment très large (1,50 à 1,80 m), sa stabilité en tous terrains à grande vitesse restait problématique, elle reposait essentiellement sur les dons d'équilibristes de ses passagers. Mais dans l'usage en voltigeurs, la vitesse était rarement indispensable. Par contre, pour la charge, il faut nécessairement lancer les chevaux au galop. Les Assyriens augmentèrent la largeur et le poids de la plateforme, ajoutèrent des blindages aux parois, ce qui abaissait le centre de gravité, ils augmentèrent le diamètre, l'épaisseur et le poids des roues, mais surtout on ajouta un et même deux chevaux, en bricolliers, de part et d'autre des deux chevaux timoniers.

Pourquoi? Non point parce que quatre chevaux tirent deux fois plus que deux chevaux : au contraire, eu égard au poids relativement faible des ciasses tractées, ils se contrarient, et la vitesse résultante ne peut qu'en être diminuée. Mais parce que, d'une part, la force vive de la charge de l'ensemble ainsi lancé est, à vitesse égale, multipliée presque par deux. Et surtout parce que les deux chevaux "bricolliers" empêchent absolument le renversement, pour peu qu'on attache leur trait directement à la caisse, sur le bord extérieur de la plateforme et au point le plus bas. On peut alors lancer l'attelage à toute allure, même en "tous terrains", sans être à la merci d'un ressaut de terrain ou d'une grosse pierre venant buter contre une roue. Or la force vive est proportionnelle au carré de la vitesse : le facteur décisif dans une charge, c'est bien la vitesse atteinte au moment du choc avec la phalange adverse.

Le retour à l'emploi du quadrige, au 8ème siècle BC, correspond à ces nouvelle exigences tactiques.

LA QUADRIGE DE COURSE

Pour les attelages de course, le motif de l'adoption du trige et du quadrige est également - et ici, uniquement - l'améloration de la stabilité.

En ligne droite, et sur terrain plat, les deux chevaux timoniers exercent leur force de traction (le tirage), presque horizontale, sur la plateforme extrêmement légère, augmentée du poids de l'aurige : c'est-à-dire que les chevaux n'ont pratiquement à vaincre que les forces de frottement de la roue au moyeu et sur le sol, forces insignifiantes par rapport à leur puissance de traction.

Plus que du poids réellement tracté, les limitations proviennent des pertes d'énergie dues à la gêne causée par le timon, le joug, les traits, la présence de l'autre cheval etc. C'est dire qu'un troisième ou un quatrième cheval n'ont certainement pas pour effet de soulager l'effort minime exercé par les deux premiers pour la seule traction de la caisse. Sil'on se bornait à ce point de vue, cette addition de chevaux serait non seulement inutile, mais plutôt nuisible, par la gêne supplémentaire que leur proximité et leur liberté de mouvement risquent d'occasionner aux deux chevaux timoniers.

Par contre, le rôle de ces chevaux supplémentaires apparaît primordial pour la stabilité de la plateforme, toujours à condition que leur trait soit lié à la base et à l'extérieur de celle-ci. En ligne droite, si une roue rencontre un obstacle ou un creux, compromettant l'horizonalité de la plateforme, l'un des traits des deux chevaux extérieurs sera sollicité, et ramènera brutalement la plateforme à l'horizontale. Dans une courbe - par exemple, dans les stades antiques, lors du passage de la borne - si l'aurige ne diminue pas la vitesse, un bige verra inévitablement la roue externe déraper et se soulever...peut-être au-delà du point d'équilibre, et surviendra alors la rupture du timon et le renersement du véhicule (pour l'éviter, nos routes modernes ménagent un devers, c'est-à-dire présentent un bord externe plus haut que le bord interne de la courbe ; les stades antiques l'ignoraient). Dans un trige avec cheval extérieur en bricollier, la plateforme sera ramenée plus ou moins brutalement au sol. Dans un quadrige, le cheval extérieur acomplira la même fonction ; le bricollier intérieur semble, lui, inutile (c'est peut-être la raison pour laquelle les Etrusques pratiquaient surtout les courses de triges). Sans doute ne servait-il qu'à entraîner les autres car, n'étant, lui, gêné par rien, il pouvait maintenir son allure, excitant la compétition. Tout l'art de l'aurige consiste, en portant son poids plutôt vers l'extérieur au moment voulu, et en jouant de l'aiguillon pour écarter à distance voulue le cheval extérieur, à faire en sorte que le trait liant ce bricollier extérieur à la plateforme reste bien tendu, et pas trop. Ainsi, le rappel à l'horizontale ne sera pas trop brutal, et le retour à la pleine vitesse, une fois la borne passée, s'effectuera plus vite et san à-coups : quelques dixièmes de seconde qui feront la différence à l'arrivée.

On notera que l'aurige du char de course, c'est-à-dire essentiellement du char de type grec d'âge géométrique puis classique (type qui sera adopté par les Etrusques et les Romains), dispose encore d'un autre élément concourant à la stabilité de l'engin : sa propre position, à l'avant ou à l'arrière de la plateforme. En effet, celle-ci est, au repos, dans les chars de course, équilibrée par rapport à la position de l'essieu (l'essieu est dit en position centrale). Au contraire, dans les chars de guerre (assyriens, égyptiens, phéniciens, hittites, chypriotes), l'essieu est presque toujours en position arrière, c'est-à-dire que la plateforme se situe toute entière en avant de l'essieu (1). Cette différence de position de la plateforme, souvent présentée comme résultant de traditions technologiques locales (le type grec opposé par exemple au type égyptien), reflète seulement une fonction différente. Dans le char de guerre, en effet, on ne peut prendre aucun risque quant à la stabilité : l'archer transporté par le char doit pouvoir viser sans être trop cahoté, et surtout un renversement de l'engin mettrait les passagers, non armés pour le combat rapproché, à la merci des ennemis. La plateforme à l'avant appuie sur le timon et sur le joug - et donc charge un peu les chevaux - quelle que soit la position du conducteur et de l'archer, on ne laisse pas jouer cette variable.

Dans le char de course, au contraire, on accepte de prendre des risques sportifs : au pire, si le char se renverse, l'aurige aura généralement le temps de sauter à bas, sans craindre des piques ou des épées hostiles. On peut donc lui laisser le choix, grâce à la "position centrale" de l'essieu sous la plateforme, entre deux possibilités. Soit, dans les moments difficiles, par exemple au passage de la borne, porter son poids vers l'avant : ce qui reproduit le diagramme des forces des chars de combat, amène le centre de gravité de l'ensemble char-aurige en avant de l'essieu, et diminue le rayon de courbure décrit par ce centre (et diminue donc la force centrifuge), la stabilité est donc augmentée. Soit, sur la ligne droite, porter son poids vers l'arrière de la plateforme, libérant ainsi le poids du joug sur les chevaux timoniers, et leur permettant de donner toute leur mesure, mais la stabilité de la plateforme devient alors plus précaire. L'aurige devra savoir composer à tout moment ces équilibres délicats entre vitesse et stabilié.

En conclusion : pour le char de guerre comme pour le char de course, l'adoption du trige ou du quadrige, à la place du bige, vise essentiellement à assurer la stabilité de la plateforme. Une fois celle-ci assurée, on peut se permettre la vitesse : nécessaire pour la charge de rupture contre les phalanges nouvellement apparues, et nécessaire à Delphes ou Olympie pour remporter les trophées.

NOTE

(1) On relève parfois un mélange des deux types dans les contrées et les époques qui à la fois utilisent le char de guerre et pratiquent les courses de char (pays hittite, Mycènes, Chypre, Cyrène). Sur les figurations rupestres du Sahara, les chars au galop volant sont essentiellement des chars de course, la plateforme à l'avant y est néanmoins habituelle, vraisemblablement parce qu'elle est la plus simple à construire, sur ces engins très fruste, réduits à l'essentiel.

The Technological Evolution From Biga to Quadriga
In the Eastern Mediterranean, the Maghreb and the Sahara:
When and Why?
Alfred Muzzolini

INTRODUCTION

W heeled vehicles from the Mediterranean and Danubian areas during Antiquity may be divided into two main groups :

> 1. Those from the great empires and cities around the Eastern Mediterranean: Mycenae, Hittite Empire, Sumer, Assyria, pharaonic Egypt, Cyprus, along with Greek chariots from the Geometric Period and the classical age, from which the Etruscan and Iberian chariots and also the chariots on the rock-drawings from the Sahara and the Maghreb derive. Within this group the chariot is firstly a war-chariot, later on a racing chariot.

> 2. Those from the Danubian world and Western Europe: during the Bronze Age and the Hallstatt Period these vehicles are nearly always equipped with four wheels (we are dealing with "wagons" rather than "chariots"), then in La Tène Period with two wheels. Their function is for prestige and mainly for funeral use. Only some later Celtic groups retain the two wheel war-chariot. Racing is unknown in these countries, at least until the Roman conquest.

The present article deals with the first group. We intend to give a general outline of its technological evolution. Starting from the crude Sumerian quadrigae, which were soon given up, this evolution resulted in a type of light biga which was adopted by all the armies around the Eastern Mediterranean towards the middle and the end of the 2d millennium BC. However, as soon as the beginning of the 1st millennium BC, some countries, mainly Greece, abandon the use of chariots for war, because such chariots turn out to be inefficient against the phalanx formations which now appear. These countries only use racing chariots, but now with four horses, the classical Greek racing quadrigae. Other countries - Assyria, the Levant, Cyprus - also give up the biga, but then reinvent the war-quadriga.

Why this late evolution from the biga to the quadriga, for racing as for war? We first give a succinct historical account of the diverse types of chariots (the literature we have used for it is mainly: Vigneron 1968; Garelli 1968; Cassin 1968; Greenhalgh 1973; Harmand 1973; Littauer and Crouwel 1979a, 1980; Farber 1980; Crouwel 1981 and Piggott 1983). Then we will analyse the causes of this evolution.

I. THE WAR-VEHICLE UNTIL 1000 BC:
HEAVY QUADRIGAE, THEN LIGHT BIGAE

The first wheeled vehicles are attested from a very early date: they are the heavy *battle-wagons* from Sumer. The earliest date back to around 3000 BC. They are four-wheelers, on solid disk or tripartite wheels, drawn by four equines, probably onagers (it is difficult to identify the species). The represented contexts are military. These wagons usually carry the driver and a soldier armed with a short thrusting spear or an axe. The "Standard of Ur" is a well-known example of them (Parrot 1960, p. 146). The reins go to a simple nose ring. It is not easy to understand what so heavy and so little manoeuvrable vehicles could be used for in battle. Maybe they already represented a mere artistic stereotype, "heroized" and not realistic? An alternative explanation is that their use could be solely for the transport of the troops, or more likely of the officers.

These vehicles were slightly modified : from the beginning of the 3d millennium BC we see two-wheelers, the *straddle-cars* (Lefebvre des Noëttes' *chars-chevalets*, 1931, I, p. 28). They are still drawn by four equines but the driver is now sitting astride on a very thick pole (e.g. the Tell Agrab quadriga, s. Parrot 1960, p. 152). True platforms are also attested. But all these kinds of quadrigae apparently remain as slow and little manoeuvrable as before. From the Sargonid epoch (around 2400 BC) on, all these types are abandoned for war. Henceforth they are restricted to cult ceremonies (for the transport of statues, as in the Danubian world). For this usage they will remain in operation until very late.

Since this period bigae are now currently attested in the Middle East. The earliest ones, still equipped with disk or tripartite wheels, are as heavy as the Sumerian vehicles. But two decisive technological inventions soon make them light and manoeuvrable : the spoked wheel and the bit, the use of which is spreading mainly from the first centuries of the 2d millennium BC. Moreover this new type is from now on always drawn by horses.

This type of Mesopotamian light biga is quickly adopted by all the armies in the Middle East and around the Eastern Mediterranean, among others by the Hittites and the Mycenaeans. Also Egypt, which until now had never used chariots, adopts it from the beginning of the New Kingdom, towards 1600 BC. What is now emerging from the representations, in spite of some local features, is that this type of light biga becomes a standard one throughout all countries of the Near East and at Mycenae, during the 2d half of the 2d millennium BC. We must emphasize that the civil dignitaries as well as the armies used it to the complete exclusion of any triga or quadriga.

Was this type of chariot known more westwards? During the episode of the "Peoples of the Sea" around 1200-1300 BC in the Egyptian Delta, chariots of this light type were brought into battle - if we can give credence to the chronicles from the scribes - both by the Egyptians and the "*Libyans*". But figurations of "Libyans" on chariots are practically unknown and such "Libyans" cannot be other than the immediate neighbours of pharaonic Egypt - indeed even, according to some egyptologists, mere rebels from the Delta. We shall contest below the traditional thesis which maintains that the origin of the Saharan chariots would be linked with the "Peoples of the Sea" or with these "Eastern Libyans". In actual fact no trace of such vehicles has ever been found for this period west of the Nile Valley, either on rock-drawings or in excavations (Muzzolini 1986 and 1988). The same holds true for the countries along the European front of the Mediterranean : except in Peloponnesus and Crete, there is no mention of either war or racing chariots throughout the 2d millennium BC.

II. EARLY FIRST MILLENNIUM BC:
THE WAR-QUADRIGA

Major changes occur in warfare during the early centuries of the 1st millennium BC. The establishment has now become important - especially in the Assyrian army - men are brought into battle in tens of thousands, chariots in thousands. Hence a more rigorous command is required. The discipline in the many corps is from now on more necessary than individual prowess. Above all the first phalanges appear, organised in dense squares of spearmen; the bow is given up or restricted to mobile forces: chariots and shortly afterwards cavalry.

As a matter of fact the light chariot had become inefficient against a disciplined, well-commanded square of soldiers, able to aim their spears all at the same time on one or other of the four sides. It could do no more than approach a bowman to shoot his arrow - from quite a distance - then come back to his own camp. But restricted to this function only, the chariot turned out to be a sophisticated device, expensive (the upkeep of the horses!), slow and vulnerable. A better way out was now available: cavalry.

Riding had been practiced long since and in many countries: the representations of Elamite, Sumerian, Hittite, Mycenaean or Egyptian riders previous to 1000 BC are few but unequivocal. However riders of the 2d millennium BC were used in warfare just for auxiliary functions (messengers, scouts), also eventually for the pursuit of the vanquished. Inscriptions as representations illustrate these various uses. But cavalry constituted as a corps appears nowhere before the 1st millennium BC. Indeed we know from an often-quoted letter addressed to the king of Mari (Powell 1971, p. 2) how reluctant to riding nobles, dignitaries and officers were. Riding was everywhere considered a breach of good manners, something as out of place and unacceptable, in a word, as a city gentleman or an officer who would today ride a bicycle. Meanwhile toward 1000-800 BC, chiefly through the great Assyrian campaigns, war is becoming too serious a thing, calling up to battle masses of troops from various origins, and the concern for efficiency sweeps away these yesteryear social conventions. The first cavalry corps appear at this time: because riders take charge of the approach and the harassment more easily and flexibly and their quick manoeuvring makes them less vulnerable than the chariot. Therefore they will rapidly supersede it for these purposes.

Assyrian riders first faithfully reproduce the chariot's team. They appear in curious pairs: a squire and a bowman. The former controls both horses while the latter shoots his arrow (Littauer-Crouwel 1979a, fig. 76). Then pairs of riders can be seen, each of them armed with a spear (thrusting spear or lance); eventually isolated mounted archers are brought into action. The evolution is somewhat different in Greece, where mounted archers appear very rarely (e.g. Greenhalgh 1973, fig. 76).

Concurrently leather then metal armours (corselets, helmets, etc.) which had been spreading towards the end of the 2d millennium BC are improving and become efficient against the arrows that chariot-carried bowmen shoot from too long a distance. The only efficient weapon against corselets is from now on the throwing-spear or javelin. It precisely becomes widespread towards the very end of the 2d millennium and chiefly in the beginning of the 1st millennium BC (Greenhalgh 1973, p. 170). Its weight gives it a force on impact and a penetration power greater than that of an arrow (Bergman *et al* 1988, p. 666). It admittedly must be thrown from much closer as its maximum throwing range is in the region of 30-35 m., whereas the draw length of a bow ranges in the 160-175 m. (Harmand 1973, p. 149). But it is finally more deadly. Now, in order to hurl it accurately against a target, it must first be poised with precision. A chariot in motion is jolted too much as to allow such a delicate adjustment (some passages from the Iliad and a very few vase-paintings from the Geometric Period suggest spears thrown from a chariot, but we are dealing here with mere poetic or artistic imaginings (s. Greenhalgh 1973 p. 9-13, 41).

The consequences of these new warfare conditions were varied:

1. In Greece and in the islands or the coasts of the Aegean sea the war chariot was simply and solely given up. The fact and even more the date of this abandonment are somewhat controversial but it seems very likely that after the collapse of the Mycenaean world around 1200 BC Greek cities could not afford any more the expenses of the upkeep of a chariotry. Anyway during the Geometric Period (900-700 BC) i.e. when the bulk of the Homeric epics was composed, there remained just a faint "heroised" recollection of these ancient war chariots (Greenhalgh 1973).

2. In Assyria - and consequently among her enemies, in the Levant, the Phoenician cities, the neo-Hittite land, Cyprus - it was considered that the new state of affairs could be faced by launching at full speed a new, heavy type of chariot, heavy enough to crush the enemy phalanx. The *war-quadriga* is the result of such a decision.

Indeed some three-horse teams, then soon afterwards four-horse teams appear, firstly in the Assyrian armies. The earliest quadrigae still draw a light chariot of the traditional type. These quadrigae are precisely found from the 9th-8th cent. BC on, in Assyria (Littauer-Crouwel 1979a, p. 113) and in the kingdom of Urartu (Armenia) (Piggott 1983, p. 136). The same evolution can even be seen in China who also replaces the biga by the quadriga around the same time (Zhou Period) (Gernet 1968). Not long after, quadrigae appear in the neo-Hittite land, in the Levant and in Cyprus as well. There are mentions of them in the Homeric poems, they must likely be understood as a feature from the centuries where the poems were composed i.e. around the 9th-8th century BC and not from the time of the Trojan War.

Quadrigae soon become in Assyria the standard vehicle and the other Asiatic countries imitate her. But since Tiglat-Pileser IIIs reign (around 750 BC) the four horses are harnessed to a heavy two-wheel chariot, equipped with thick wheels and able to carry three men: the driver, the archer, and a shield bearer entrusted with protecting them from arrows. Sometimes four men are shown on the platform (with a second shield bearer), especially on the king's chariot. We probably may interpret it as an unrealistic conventional magnification or a mere prestige vehicle. Scale armours occur commonly; also horses are protected by metal breast-plates or gorgets and trappers on their flanks.

The Achaemenid Persia maintained this heavy chariot. We know by many texts that it was really used in warfare, but mainly in the Asiatic armies. Evidence is almost completely lacking for Egypt between the 13th and the 7th century BC. The earliest representation of an Egyptian quadriga dates back only from the time of the Assyrian conquest around the 7th century. Moreover its type and some features in the equipment suggest an influence of oriental models (Littauer-Crouwel 1979b).

In the Middle East the heavy chariot became heavier and heavier, with the armours of the crew and the horses becoming larger and larger. Eventually the box was arranged as an armour-plated turret. It remained in use until the battle of Arbella (331 BC), in which it was definitively shown how inefficient mass charges of quadrigae, even the heaviest ones, were against an army extended according to the phalanx pattern and well-commanded.

However, after Alexander's campaigns, some sporadic occurrences of war-chariots are still mentioned. They are sometimes quadrigae - as those of Antiochus II at Magnesia (190 BC) or of Mithridates at Chaeronea and Orchomenus (86 and 84 BC) - sometimes bigae - as the British bigae which were a surprise for Caesar. Another survival of the war-chariot, reported as an anomaly by the ancient historians themselves, is that of bigae and quadrigae (both are recorded) used during the "Hellenistic wars" of the 4th century BC, in which Greeks from Sicily and

Carthage were fighting, or during the "Marmaric wars" fought by Cyrene against the Libyans from the desert. It seems likely that Carthaginians still brought into battle, for mass charging, heavy quadrigae of the Asiatic type, whereas Cyrenaean chariots were now only used for the transport of a "carried infantry" in order to pursue the Bedouins (s. discussion *in* Anderson 1965 and Greenhalgh 1973, p. 16). But for the most part, in this late period, chariots were used only for racing.

III. THE RACING CHARIOT

The practice of chariot-racing spread among the Indo-European groups - and only among them - since the middle of the 2d millennium BC: among the Hittites (Littauer-Crouwel 1979a, p. 95), among the Mitannians (Culican 1967, p. 38) and also in Mycenae (Crouwel 1981). We note that this practice, originally linked with cult or funeral ritual, came into general use throughout the Aegean world towards the beginning of the 1st millennium BC. The vase-paintings from the Geometric Age and the Homeric epics abundantly illustrate it. The first Olympic Games (since 776 BC) ran bigae. Quadriga-racing was introduced in the 25th Olympiad, in 680 BC (Pausanias, *Descr. Greece*, V. 8). Racing chariot remains unknown in Assyria, the Levant, Carthage, and also in Egypt, at least until the Ptolemaic Period.

Towards 700-600 BC the "orientalizing wave" spreads throughout the Mediterranean, and in Africa the racing chariot is no more confined within the only Greek city of Cyrene (founded in 630 BC). From Cyrene it reaches the central Sahara - then we have there the "chariot period" of the Saharan rock art - the Saharan Atlas and the Moroccan Atlas (Muzzolini 1982b, 1988). Also quadrigae can be seen within the compositions of rock pictures in the Sahara as well as in the Maghreb, and more particularly among the famous "flying gallop" painted chariots in Tassili. The latter represent in the central Sahara a group of chariots, either the earliest, or among the earliest. These Tassilian quadrigae provide the sure proof that - in opposition to the traditional theories - the Saharan chariots can only be more recent than the 9th-8th cent. BC, since we have shown that quadrigae reappear around the Eastern Mediterranean no sooner than this date (Muzzolini 1987). Therefore the Saharan chariots have nothing to do with the Egyptians or the "Libyans" from the Egyptian chronicles of the 2d millennium BC, to which traditional theories link them (Lhote 1982; Camps 1974, 1982). These theories only represent a residue of a romantic thesis from the 30's, which maintained that the origin of Saharan chariots was to be found in the "Peoples of the Sea"'s chariots of the 13th cent. BC. In all probability Saharan chariots - mainly bigae, and also some trigae in addition to the few quadrigae mentioned above - merely reflect, after 630 BC, the vogue of the chariot races in Cyrene, a city famous for her aurigas (Muzzolini 1982b, 1986).

The racing chariot is also introduced around 600-650 BC by the "orientalizing wave" into Etruria (Bronson 1965; Stary 1979): here it is the triga-racing which becomes popular. In Andalusia and Portugal, bigae of the Etruscan or Greek type are engraved on the stelae of the South-West of the Peninsula, their function is unknown (Muzzolini 1988).

During the classical age, in the Greek cities as in Rome, races become the favourite games. They still run firstly bigae and quadrigae, later on only quadrigae.

We intend to demonstrate that although the two usages, war and racing, are quite different, both war-quadriga and racing-quadriga were adopted, towards the beginning of the 1st millennium BC, as a consequence of the concern for the necessary stability of the vehicles.

IV. WHY THE WAR-QUADRIGA WAS ADOPTED

The technological evolution of the types of war-chariots evidently mirrors what the armies think, need or can do in the field of tactics. On these topics texts do not give many details, or they may be suspected of "archaization" and "heroization", as with the *Iliad* (Greenhalgh 1973). The representations on the monuments, on the portable objects or on the documents are often "heroized" as well, or they are distorted in order to magnify the superb order in one's own camp and the inexperience or disorder in the enemy's camp. Meanwhile some inferences prove possible.

What were the light bigae of the 3d and 2d millennia, until the earlier first millennium BC, used for? It is likely that these chariots, which then were the only ones in operation, were mainly used to carry the Egyptian and Mesopotamian bowmen or the Hittite spearmen as close as possible to the enemy. This function is often called the "Homeric usage", for in the *Iliad*, except for one ambiguous passage (Nestor's harangue) and in spite of many mentions of chariots, neither a breakthrough charge nor even a clash between chariotries are described anywhere. On the other hand the noble warriors frequently use the chariots to go to meet their opponents. Greenhalgh (1973, p. 2) speaks ironically of this "Homeric usage" as a "taxi-service" to and from the battlefield. However the Homeric chariots went into the heart of the battle but for the sole function - of primary importance in the eyes of the Greeks - of carrying back the dead in order to pay them the necessary funeral honours. But which epoch is really reflected by these Homeric war chariots? that of Mycenae? The Dark Age? The Geometric Period? Or none, according to Greenhalgh, who asserts they only represent a deliberate poetic invention and cannot be taken at face value? The issue is much debated.

Anyway the use of such light bigae for the mass charge at speed is very unlikely (Braunstein-Silvestre 1982, p. 40). In spite of the representations of chariotry charges magnified on the walls of Abydos, Abou Simbel or the Ramesseum in Thebes, one can reasonably doubt that such chariots were really used for charging at speed. The battles of this time, very loose, did not absolutely call for such charges. Moreover they seem to have been impractical, if we consider the type of chariots which have been actually found in Egyptian tombs (admittedly we are dealing with prestige items, meanwhile they have been built in the same manner as those really in operation for war, except for some gold sheathing and other embellishments of that sort).

First the weight of these chariots is no more than in the order of 30-40 kg (Spruytte, 1977, p. 39). So small a weight adds little or nothing to the kinetic energy, which essentially derives from the weight of the horses and the crew. Besides the dimensions of the wooden pieces - even from the best species of trees - are obviously too weak (e.g. the diameters of the axles are in the order of 5 cm) (Littauer-Crouwel 1979a, p. 78). They cannot absorb the stresses which result from uneven ground or from stones abruptly knocked by the wheels when charging at speed.

Above all the stability of the whole set (box and crew) when running on natural ground and at full speed was hazardous. It was increased by way of a huge base between the two wheels: 1.50 to 1.80 m in Egypt (and 1.80 to 2.50 m in China!) (Littauer-Crouwel 1979a, p. 78; Gernet 1968, p. 311). Such wide bases certainly were a nuisance for manoeuvring. Nonetheless stability had essentially to rely on the talent of the crew as equilibrists. Hence the too beautiful representations of the battle of Kadesh, alleged to illustrate the clash between Egyptian and Hittite chariotries, seem no more reliable than the superb representations of the Pharaoh charging, alone, the enemy ranks with his reins daringly tied around the hips.

It seems likely that these light chariots of the 2d millenium BC turned around and around on the flanks and the weak points of the enemy lines, handling the harassment. They also were used for quickly transporting fresh troops in given time and place. A new "reading" of the tactics used in the battle of Kadesh suggests that the chariots have not been used there for other purposes than this transport, in order to take the Egyptian flank by surprise. Later on the Egyptian chariotry arrived for a counterattack (Littauer-Crouwel 1979a, p. 93). The main function of these light chariots was to provide a firing platform for the bowmen, slightly elevated above the battlefield, not very mobile, however ready for pursuing the vanquished... or for one's own flight. In these diverse ways of using the chariot maximum speed is seldom required and stability was not generally a serious problem.

But the innovations we have described in warfare soon after 1000 BC provoked a reappraisal of the part these light chariots played in the battle. Superseded by cavalry for the function of harassment and pursuit, almost useless for the spearmen, restricted to carrying the bowmen, what can this vehicle still be used for? The close phalanx formations which are now to be faced mean the end of loose battles. Light mobile chariots as well as cavalry turn out to be completely powerless against them. This is the major change.

Two alternatives are offered. The first one is to constitute one's own phalanx, then to leave it to the frontal clash phalanx against phalanx. One can make up one's mind to accept it only if one has at one's command troops as disciplined as those of the enemy. For an absolute discipline is the main requirement to provide impenetrability and mobility which are the only but decisive assets of a phalanx. But the Asiatic armies, even the Assyrian one, included ill-assorted contingents. This fact appears obvious when we read for instance in Herodotus (History, VII, 54-88) the incredible description of the Great King's army crossing the Hellespont: e.g.: preceding the elite corps of the Immortals, "Libyans armed with fire-hardened woodenspears were marching". Such armies rely on numbers more than on the organization of the troops.

A second alternative consisted, before anything else, of dislocating the enemy phalanx. And the only means for this dislocation is the mass breakthrough charge at full speed. A temptation always too strong to be resisted, when using war chariots, this breakthrough charge! How to achieve it?

The kinetic energy (= $1/2$ m v^2) first is proportional to m, the mass launched against the enemy's phalanx. But the kinetic energy represented by one rider and his horse was not enough to crush several spears aimed at them. Asiatic armies preferred to stick to the chariot. However the Assyrians increased the width and the weight of the platform, added metal sheathing on the panels, reinforced the pole and all fastening pieces, mainly increased the diameter, thickness and weight of the wheels, put on a three-man instead of a two-man crew. Above all they added one, then very quickly two horses to the team. The mass of the whole was now becoming considerable : the weight of the horses was contributing for the main part, indeed it clearly appears that, for the same speed, the kinetic energy of a quadriga is almost twice that of a biga.

Meanwhile it remained a chief requirement : not to diminish v - velocity - a squared factor. This means necessarily launching the team at full gallop. Its tractive power is anyway by far greater than the total drawn weight - the box plus the team - hence the increase of the drawn weight by no means hinders the horses. But the problem of the stability at full speed is met here again. Chariots adapted in view, not of approaching bowmen, but of charging in a body, can sweep everything away under their impetus, provided that they do not overturn on the way or, still worse, among the enemy's ranks. In the latter case the crew, which is not equipped for close combat, is immediately killed. We know that this danger of overturning was rightly perceived as the main one, thanks to a detail reported by Arrian. The day before the battle of Arbella, Darius prepared the battlefield through which he intended to launch his chariotry against Alexander's phalanges : he carefully smoothed out the dangerous bumps of the ground.

By increasing the weight of the box and crew, the centre of gravity was already slightly lowered, hence the stability was increased. But the decisive invention consisted of the way of harnessing the two extra horses. Contrary to a Herodotus' statement, this new way of harnessing was not shown to the Greeks by the "Libyans"; it appears in Asia before Cyrene's foundation in 630 BC. The early quadrigas in the beginning of the 1st millennium BC show that it was not immediately discovered : some representations and some finds of chariots from excavations (chariots in Salamina tombs, bas-reliefs of Sargon II and Sennacherib's epochs, Oxus treasure, etc. - s. Littauer-Crouwel 1976, e.g. figs. 21 and 22) indicate that the four horses were first put

> - either to chariots of the previous type, equipped with one pole, but with an astonishing yoke designed for the four horses together
> - or, since 700 BC, to chariots equipped with two poles, each of them drawing a two-horse yoke.

Such methods of harnessing, in which each of the four horses is drawing, and must draw in keeping with the others, are almost unmanoeuvrable. Imitations of such crude early quadrigas are to be found even in the Sahara (e.g. at Oued Zigza, Fezzan - s. Graziosi 1942, Tav. 38 and p. 96) and two-pole chariots also appear then among the Tassilian "flying gallop" chariots (which gives a confirmation of their "low" dating, anyway after 700 BC).

But as soon as the 8th-7th cent. BC, in Assyria, Asia Minor (e.g. the votive model from Gordion, Littauer 1976, fig. 24) as in Greece, a new method of harnessing is emerging and it will become the classic and exclusive one : the one-pole quadriga with only two "pole-horses" under the yoke, and two extra horses harnessed as "out riggers". The latter are attached by a trace *only to the box*, thus they are independent from the pole (fig. 1).

Why this return to the quadriga?

The present author's purpose is to sustain the following thesis : around the 8th c. BC the quadriga is adopted everywhere again, but not because one thinks that four horses should draw two times more than two horses. Owing to the comparatively light weight of the box drawn, the reverse is true, they hinder one another and the resulting speed can only be reduced. The real reason was that, besides the nearly doubling of the total mass, the two side horses prevent, or at least considerably impede, the upset. A necessary condition however is that these side horses must be harnessed as "outriggers" i.e. with the trace directly linked to the box on the external edge of the platform (fig. 1).

Why this? Because when the chariot is launched in the straight line, if one of the wheels is raised after hitting an obstacle, in such a way that the platform is too far from the horizontal line, the trace of the outrigger put on the same side will be pulled upon, and it will brutally bring the platform back to the horizontal level. It is therefore possible to launch the team at full speed, even on irregular ground, without depending from the shock of a wheel against a bump or a big stone. Thus the decisive factor in a charge, the speed reached when the clash with the enemy phalanx happens, can be controlled.

The return to using quadriga in the 8th c. BC reflects the adaptation to these new tactical requirements. However history tells us that in spite of these modifications the Assyrian or Persian breakthrough quadriga was efficient against the ill-commanded armies of the Asiatic or Egyptian powers, but proved helpless against a well-trained Macedonian phalanx. At Arbella (331 BC) Alexander merely arranged an extended line of foot soldiers some distance in front of his troops. The spears they threw on the chariots already slowed down the impetus of the horses. Then he ordered that the Persian chariots be allowed to enter into the Greek ranks. When they were surrounded they became an easy prey, quickly disarmed and exterminated.

V. WHY THE RACING-QUADRIGA WAS ADOPTED

As for the racing chariots, trigae and quadrigae were adopted for the same reason - and in this case the only reason - of getting a better stability. In a straight line and on an even terrain, the tractive power is exerting an almost horizontal direction; it pulls the extremely light platform and the weight of the driver. The horses of a biga have just to overcome the forces of friction of the axle against the nave of the wheel and the ground, which are quite unimportant forces when one compares them to their tractive power. Limitations are not really due to the weight drawn, but energy loss rather proceeds from inconvenience created by the pole, the yoke, the traces, the presence of the other horse etc. This means that a third or a fourth horse cannot be considered in order to lighten the tiny stress put on the first two horses by the only traction of the box. If we look only at this aspect, these two extra horses, also in this case, not only would be useless but rather mean a nuisance, on account of the increased constraint they cause to the two pole-horses.

On the other hand these two outriggers, independent from the pole and the yoke, are of prime importance as far as platform stability is concerned - always keeping in mind that their traces must be connected to the external sides of the box (fig. 1).

In a straight line, as we have already explained for the war quadriga, if it happens that one wheel is suddenly raised when hitting a stone or a bump in the ground, the trace of one of the outriggers will brutally pull back the platform to the horizontal position. In a curve - for instance in the ancient stadia when passing the turning-post - the wheels of a biga, if the driver does not reduce the speed, will inescapably skid and rise... maybe beyond the point of equilibrium. In this case either the pole breaks or the vehicle is upset (it is in order to prevent this that our modern roads provide a "banking" i.e. an external border higher than the internal one; but the ancient stadia did not). On the contrary, in a triga with an external horse as an outrigger the platform will be more or less brutally pulled back to the ground. In a quadriga, one of the external horses will function likewise whereas the outrigger on the other side will not intervene in these events. But although the latter does not contribute for the time being to regaining stability, he is not altogether useless: as he is hindered by nothing he can keep his speed and stimulates the others. The prowess of a driver will consist of distributing his own weight rather outwards at the given moment, then using his goad to slightly move aside the outrigger in order that the trace connecting this outrigger to the platform would remain properly tightened, but not too much. Thus the return to the horizontal position will not be too brutal and the full speed, after passing the turning-post, will be regained more quickly and without jolting : some fractions of a second which will differentiate the competitors at the arrival.

Note that when dealing with a very pronounced curve, as around the turning-post, the danger of upset is greater if the desequilibrated wheel is the external one (the farthest one from the centre of the curve). For the reason that the centrifugal force (mw^2R, where w = angular velocity, R = radius) is stronger on this wheel. When it happens that the horizontal component of the frictional force is suddenly lacking (this component was exactly compensating for the centrifugal force), the danger for the chariot is greater. This is the reason why the Etruscans mainly ran trigae, with only one outrigger put on the side farthest from the centre. They accepted the risk of being upset from the interior wheel, because such risk was weaker on this side. The horses of a triga were less hindered than those of a quadriga, therefore they could run faster, but the resulting stability was more risky, albeit judged sufficient.

Moreover the driver of a racing chariot (i.e. mainly of the Greek type of chariot during the Geometric then the Classic period, a type subsequently adopted by the Etruscans and the

Romans) has another means at his disposal in order to achieve a better stability of the chariot : his position at the front or at the rear of the platform. For the platform, in a racing chariot at rest, is just balanced on the axle (the axle is said to be in "central position"). On the contrary, on war chariots (either Assyrian, Egyptian, Phoenician, Hittite or Cypriot), the axle is almost always in the "rear position", i.e. the entire platform is in front of the axle (figs. 2 and 3).

These different positions are often said to result from different technological traditions (for instance the "Greek type" is opposed to the "Egyptian type"). Indeed they are only an indication of a different function. As a matter of fact no risk can be accepted in the war chariot as far as stability is concerned : the bowman on the chariot must not be shaken too much, so that he can take aim. Above all, an overturning of the chariot would place the crew in the enemy's power. The "front platform" leans on the pole and the yoke - therefore it slightly burdens the horses - whatever the position of the driver or of the bowman is : this variable is not allowed to be operative. Consequently the equilibrium of the crew is less hazardous.

On the contrary, in a racing chariot, "sporting" risks are consciously taken : at worst, if the chariot is upset, in most cases the driver can jump down, without any fear of hostile spears or swords. Therefore he can be allowed to choose for himself, thanks to the "central position" of the axle, between two alternatives. Either, when in difficult stretches, e.g. when passing by the turning-post, to bring his own weight forwards : which reproduces the same force diagram as for the war chariot, moves the centre of gravity of the whole vehicle (chariot and driver) well before the axle, slightly diminishes the radius of the curvature which this centre is describing (hence the centrifugal force is reduced), consequently stability is increased. Or, when in a straight line, to bring his own weight backwards : which alleviates the weight of the yoke on the pole-horses so as to allow them to run at their full speed, but in this case the platform stability is less sure. As the balance of the whole vehicle is always kept close to the danger point (the limit where the ground friction forces do not compensate for the centrifugal force any more), even very light modifications of the operating conditions of this balance have immediate important consequences on stability and speed.

In conclusion, for the war chariot as for the racing chariot, the replacement of the biga by the triga or the quadriga was essentially for the purpose of increasing the platform stability. As soon as the latter is achieved, speed becomes possible. It was required in order to try, against the newly appeared phalanges, the breakthrough charge - a dangerous, desperate, and eventually disastrous alternative - and it was required also at Delphi or Olympia for winning the trophies.

NOTE

(1) Both types can sometimes be observed in the regions or the periods in which both war and racing chariots were used (e.g. Hittite land, Mycenae, Cyprus). On the Saharan rock drawings, the so-called "flying gallop" chariots are mostly racing chariots, however their platform is usually a "front platform". Probably because it was more easily built, on these very crude vehicles restricted to the essential parts, and also because they reproduced Cyrenaeans racing chariots, which show, as an exceptional feature among the Greek cities, this "front platform" ("two-pole and crossbar" type of chariots - e.g. Muzzolini 1988, figs. 8 and 10)

BIBLIOGRAPHY

Anderson, J.K., 1965. Homeric, British and Cyrenaic Chariots. *Am. Jal Arch.* 69, 4, pp. 349-352.

Bergman, C.A., MacEwen, E. and Miller, R., 1988. Experimental archery: projectile velocities and comparison of bow performances. *Antiquity*, 62, 237, pp. 658-670.

Braunstein-Silvestre, F., 1982. Coup d'oeil sur le cheval et le char dans l'Egypte du Nouvel Empire. Actes Coll. "*Les chars préhistoriques du Sahara*", Senanque (mars 1981), G. Camps et M. Gast éds, pp. 35-44.

Bronson, R.C. 1965., Chariot racing in Etruria. *Studi in Onore L. Banti*, Rome, pp. 89-106.

Camps, G. 1974., Les civilisations préhistoriques de l'Afrique du Nord et du Sahara. Paris, Doin, 374 p.

Camps, G. 1982., Le cheval et le char dans la préhistoire nord-africaine et saharienne. Actes Colloque Sénanque "*Les chars préhistoriques du Sahara*", G. Camps et M. Gast éds, pp. 9-22.

Cassin, E. 1968., A propos du char de guerre en Mésopotamie. In "*Problèmes de la guerre en Grèce ancienne*", J.P. Vernant éd., EHES, Paris, pp. 297-308.

Crouwel, J.H., 1981. Chariots and other means of land transport in Bronze Age Greece. Allard Pierson, Amsterdam, 215 p.

Culican, W., 1967. Le Levant et la Mer. Histoire et Commerce (éd. franç.). Sequoia-Elsevier, Bruxelles, 144 p.

Farber, W., 1980. Kampfwagen (Streitwagen). A. Philologisch. *Reallexikon der Assyr. und vorderasiat. Archäologie*, O.E. Edzard herausg., pp. 336-344.

Garelli, P., 1968. Note sur l'évolution du char de guerre en Mésopotamie jusqu'à la fin de l'empire assyrien. In "*Problèmes de la guerre en Grèce ancienne*", J.P. Vernant éd., EHES, Paris, pp. 291-295.

Gernet, J., 1968. Note sur le char en Chine. In "*Problèmes de la guerre en Grèce ancienne*", "J.P. Vernant éd., EHES, Paris, pp. 309-312

Graziosi, P., 1942. L'arte rupestre della Libia. Napoli, 2 vol., 326 p.

Greenhalgh, P.A.L., 1973. Early Greek warfare. Cambridge, Univ. Press, 212 p.

Harmand, J., 1973. La guerre antique, de Sumer à Rome. P.U.F., Paris.

Lefebvre des Noettes, R., 1931. L'attelage, le cheval de selle à travers les âges. Picard, Paris, 2 vol.

Lhote, H., 1982. Les chars rupestres sahariens. Des Syrtes au Niger, par le pays des Garamantes et des Atlantes. Ed. des Hespérides, Toulouse, 288 p.

Littauer, M.A., 1976. New Light on the Assyrian Chariot. *Orientalia*, NS, 45, pp. 217-226

Littauer, M.A. and Crouwel, J.H., 1979a. Wheeled vehicles and ridden animals in the ancient Near East. Leiden, Brill, 185 p. 85 fig.

Littauer, M.A. and Crouwel, J.H., 1979b. An Egyptian wheel in Brooklyn. *Jal Egypt. Arch.*, 65, pp. 107-120

Littauer, M.A. et Crouwel, J.H., 1980. Kampfwagen (Streitwagen). B. Archeologisch. *Reallexikon der Assyr. und vorderasiat. Archäologie*, O.E. Edzard herausg:, pp. 344-351

Muzzolini, A.. 1982a. La période des chars au Sahara. L'hypothèse de l'origine egyptienne du cheval et du char. Actes Coll. *"Les chars prehistoriques du Sahara"*, Sénanque, mars l981, G. Camps et M. Gast éds, pp. 45-56

Muzzolini, A., 1982b. Sur un quadrige "grec", de style Iheren-Tahilahi, au Tassili du N.-O. *Ars Praehistorica*, I, pp. 189-197

Muzzolini, A., 1986. L'art rupestre préhistorique des massifs centraux sahariens. British Arch. Reports, Cambridge Monogr. Afric. Arch. 16, *B.A.R. Internat. Ser.* 318, Oxford, 355 p.

Muzzolini, A., 1987. La datation des plus anciens chars sahariens. Cyrène et la 'vague orientalisante" en Afrique. *Actes 11e Congrès U.I.S.P.P.*, Mainz, Août 1987 (in press).

Muzzolini, A., 1988. Les chars des stèles du Sud-Ouest de la péninsule ibérique, les chars des gravures rupestres du Maroc et la datation des chars sahariens. Actes Congreso Internac. *"El Estrecho de Gibraltar"*, Ceuta (Nov. 1987), I, pp. 361-389.

Parrot, A., 1960. Sumer. Gallimard, Paris, 399 p.

Piggot, S., 1983. The Earliest Wheeled Transport. Thames and Hudson, 272 p.

Powell, T.G.E., 1971. The Introduction of Horse-Riding to Temperate Europe : A Contributory Note. *Proc. Preh. Soc.* 37, 2, pp. l-14.

Spruytte, J., 1977. Etudes expérimentales sur l'attelage. Crépin-Leblond, Paris, 143 p.

Stary, P.F., 1979. Foreign Elements in Etruscan Arms and Armour : 8th to 3d centuries B.C. *Proc. Preh. Soc.*, 45, pp. 179-206

Vigneron, P., 1968. Le cheval dans l'antiquite gréco-romaine. 2 t., *Annales de l'Est*, Nancy, 338 p., 105 pl.

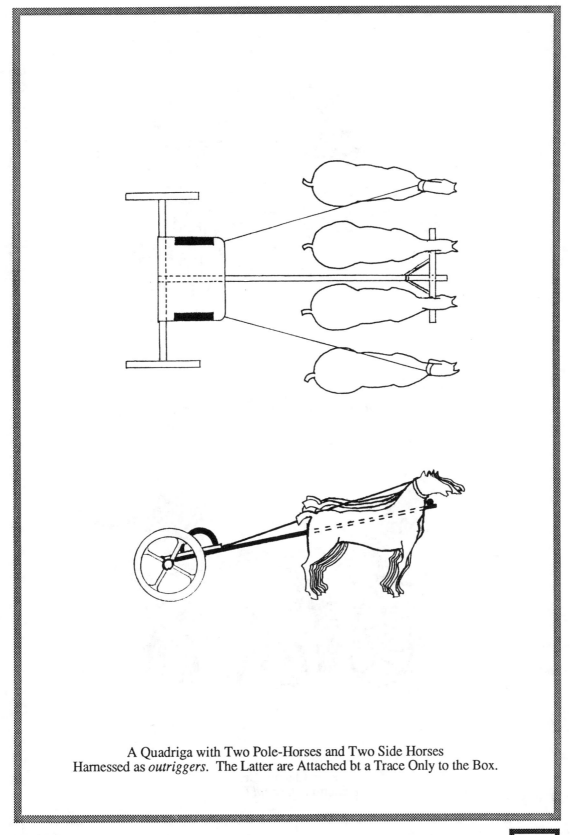

A Quadriga with Two Pole-Horses and Two Side Horses
Harnessed as *outriggers*. The Latter are Attached bt a Trace Only to the Box.

2

War- Chariot (Egypt)
Axle in *Rear Position* (the Whole Platform is in Front of the Axle

3

Racing Chariot (Greece)
Platform in *Central Position*

ARCHAEOLOGICAL TECHNIQUES, TECHNOLOGY AND THEORY

LH SOCIO-POLITICAL AND ECONOMIC ACTIVITY IN CENTRAL AND
EASTERN PELOPONNESE - WITH SPECIAL EMPHASIS ON ARCADIA
(AN IN-DEPTH STUDY)

E.J. KRIGAS
Cambridge University
15 Stretten Avenue
Cambridge CB4 3ES, England.

RESUME

Central and especially East Arcadia has been left in darkness for most part of the up-to-date recorded Prehistoric research. One of the reasons may be the absence of what archaeology has traditionally characterised monumental structures (or architecture). By this term archaeologists used to refer mainly to palaces or royal buildings which could give rise to theories of magnificent civilizations, of royal life and remarkable activity, of slavery and ill-fated subjects, who were the ones leading the royal chariot to success and in some instances were rewarded. In other cases, their fate might be death, because we could not expect autarchic rulers to exercise a completely fair justice judging by our own standards (as dangerous or daring that might be). Meanwhile, it has been very recently supported that the Maya were only conscripting builders and generally workforce very occasionally, thus, as it is being estimated, it would take each worker only three times in his lifetime to work for the elite ruling class (cf. American Antiquity, vol. 52, p. 485) Why not suppose the same for Pylos or Knossos, or, even Mycenae?

Arcadia has not been directly mentioned in the Pylos tablets... or elsewhere and that linguistic lack has also contributed a lot to the emergence of conclusions and theories which contradict each other. Are we then researching in vain, or do we try to conceal facts which help constituting a link among the then known Mycenaean cultures?

Evidence in the Pylian Linear B tablets has been summarised in two Mycenaean Greek words (i.e., i-wa-so and i-wa-si-jo-ta) which analysed may include more than what we can try to transcribe linguistically. For, they refer to a place-name (the former) and an ethnic name (the latter) both of which originate from the East Arcadian site which is currently known under the classical name of IASOS, (cf. E.J. Krigas, Polisma Iason, Athens 1984, Ph.D.), or, modern Greek, ANALEPSIS.

The archaeology from the area has been rich in Mycenaean finds which include mainly a Mycenaean (beehive type) tholos tomb and a few cist cut-in-the-rock smaller tombs. They seem to constitute a different tomb-group, i.e. different from the three small tholos-like tombs near the main Mycenaean tholos. That difference may characterise another phase in the prehistory of the area, but certainly has contributed much to the noticeable gap between the set chronological time limits for the contemporary areas. What does that gap mean? A lack of resources? A state of emergency? A change of sites?

The topography of a site plays much more importance for the general activity it portrays than the site itself many times. That is correct for most sites in prehistoric and later times and in the case of IASOS we can say that it par excellence dominates the rest of the active during Mycenaean times areas. Another place-name with equally active Mycenaean background is that of HELLENIKON. There are many parallels between the two sites in many respects but especially in the case of wheel-ruts which presuppose the use of chariots and which seem to be inter-connected. The extensive obsidian found in the area on the other hand gives rise to a hypothesis of extensive communication practices in the form of exchange of goods. The Iasos ceramics has parallels in Pylos and Crete even in Ras-Shamra. The group arrangement of the small tholos-like Mycenaean type tombs is not unknown to the Hettite cultures, in Ugarit and Tell-Fara. But the fact that we can find parallels with Anatolian cultures originating from a place which has but only little been mentioned might have given the opportunity to B. Sergent (in Minos, 1977) to suppose a reference to Arcadia in the Kom-el-Hetan list.

We do not know whether it is the same mistake (if it is a mistake) that Homer had made by refering to an Arcadian Kingdom in the Catalogue of Ships. Many Linear B linguists would be very happy with the idea of that mistake. They would be very happy with the theory of Homer, the Mythologist.. But they would not at all seem to consider that if it was not for the archaeology of Pylos for example they would not be able to connect their transcriptions with the facts.

We would be content to show that two theories might be true for the case of Iasos. That either it existed as part of the Pylian Further District (pe-ra-a₂-ko-ra-i-ja, the references to i-wa-so are mentioned in the offering tablets, i.e. An and Cn and the chances are that it contained non - Greek tribal elements conscripted under the Pylian oligarchy for border duties, just like the o-ka units mainly of the defensive type) or, that at about the end of the Pylian domination various classes of the population, feeling rather dissatisfied or underprivileged moved out of the Pylian influence and created their own small states in places as far as Arcadia and Laconia. The character of the finds and the general social activity of the Arcadian mainland is rather local and lacking wealth. The Iasos ware during the last part of the LHIIIB-C is rather imitating foreign prototypes than creating new styles. It is the widespread sign of decline that has almost at the same time overwhelmed the Mycenaean cultures. And its peak is tragically ironic, too. The fire which destroyed all the sites (and almost paradoxically the Iasos one) has helped much in the preservation of the written documents (Pylian and Knossian Linear B archives) refering to the past year in such a bureaucratic detail that could very appropriately mirror the effort of the Mycenaeans in record-keeping. Records which unavoidably had included references to Arcadia in the two aenigmatic rubrics: i-wa-so and i-wa-si-jo-ta (see, further Z.A. 1985).

THE EMERGENCE OF THE BRONZE AGE: THE THEORY

We would like to start the discussion of our project in this summary in what may be characterised an unorthodox, or, rather conflicting approach, that is, the chronological one. Because we believe that chronology does not matter a lot dealing with the continuity in time of obscure periods especially in Pre- and Protohistory. Whether a few thousand years before or after a set time-limit could change our view of studying the environment into which a civilisation started developing or peaked is not certain. What is certain is the existence of the civilisation and more definitely its connections with similar ones which might have coexisted....that is the point where we need the time and it would be proper to say an acceptable or reasonable time limit into which we could fit our guesswork.

Following a generally accepted system of chronology (which by no means could claim to be accurate) we could distinguish sub-periods in the Bronze Age (Early: Br1A-A2; Middle: Br B-C; Late: BrD) with its peak at about the last stage when the main use of the metal (bronze) seems prevailing as a general characteristic. It is mainly at about that stage when the two terms governing the whole era (namely, Mycenaean and Minoan) run parallel with respective periods in the Anatolia and are spreading to other places of the Western World leaving traces in Europe. The question prevailing is rather who did something first than who was first and studying the two civilisations in their context we will try to trace their enactments and be closer to the answer ofwho influenced whom regarding their connections with Mesopotamian and Babylonian cultures.

It can be thus shown that in dealing with the Mycenaeans as a spreading common culture dominating the last phase of the Bronze Age we are at the same time dealing with a culture that communicates common code-language (i.e. Mycenaean Linear B) which transcribed has given to be Greek. In its variant form (as Linear A) it is also found in tablets in Crete. But that linguistic variation portrays the cultural variation met in Mainland Greece at various subperiods of the LH. From Mycenae and Lerna to Pylos, Kakovatos, Midea, Dendra and Sparta and from Tiryns to the northern Mainland and the Aegean. And the extent of the Mycenaean world can still be traced in the Near Eastern cultures even in Europe. It is a miraculous spread which took some years to form, in contrast with the abrupt end, somewhere in the LHIIIC which is important and monumental just for the dramatic end of a civilisation ending in fire and destruction leaving behind the mystery of the unexpected force of catastrophe. If only somebody could recall to his mind that it is the same period which at the beginning marks a whole range of innovations, from weapons to means of transport, from new artistic motives to new types of tombs and rather symbolically from the burial of the dead to the cremation.

THE DATA

But it is time now to concentrate on our subject which deals specifically with the activity in Central and Eastern Peloponnese with special emphasis on Arcadia. It would not be too preposterous I suppose to suggest Arcadian periods for the duration of the cultural activity there and we would be rather tempted to use the Minoan example as a prototype. We are well aware of course that the absence of what archaeologically has been characterised as monumental evidence, i.e. a palace or a complex of buildings acting as a neuralgic point of central authority (whether that could take the form of a king/ queen/ deity is still uncertain and we could expect various explanations/ guesses from the Linear B archive at Pylos) makes us cautious as to how we could venture mentioning Arcadian culture as parallel to Pylian, for example. Our own view on this point based on facts drawn by the existence of vast Mycenaean type tomb-groups mainly in areas such as ANALEPSIS and HELLENIKON in Kynouria, S.E. Arcadia is that the Arcadian periods can be placed roughly at about the middle of the LHIIIA1 and LHIIIA2 periods. Then the development runs as follows:

CRETE	MAINLAND GREECE	ARCADIA	NEAR EAST
LMIIIA1	LHIIIA1	ARCADIAN I	MIDDLE BABYLONIAN MIDDLE ASSYRIAN
LMIIIA2	LHIIIA2	ARCADIAN I	NEW BABYLONIAN NEW ASSYRIAN
LMIIIB	LHIIIB	ARCADIAN II	NEW BABYLONIAN NEW ASSYRIAN
LMIIIC	LHIIIC	ARCADIAN III	LATE BABYLONIAN LATE ASSYRIAN (?)

The above mentioned chronological diagram could be used only as a guide for the activity in the years following the monumental and mainly of Mycenaean origin tholos tomb in ANALEPSIS, which can be taken as one of (if not the only one in the area) characteristic Mycenaean construction.

The existing gaps in the data collected from various sites in central and east Peloponnese may verify the hypothesis of a discontinued settlement in the area due to a continuous evolution which implied a considerable movement of sites from one place to another, not necessarily contemporarily. It has been supported some time ago that Arcadia used to be the in-between stage of Mycenae and Pylos or Sparta. That was a theory based mainly on the Homeric description in the Catalogue of Ships, where there is a reference to an Arcadian Kingdom. Meanwhile lack of supportive linguistic evidence contributed much to a very obscure and almost non-existent presentation of facts. We shall try to show, however, that during the late stages of the main Pylian domination in Messenia (SW Peloponnese) there happened a highly remarkable movement of tribal populations to areas as far as Arcadia where existing evidence could support a theory of continuation of the Mycenaean (of Pylian or Myceaean type) culture. The similarity of these facts along with ones from LHIIIC areas outside the main area of Pylian influence (N. Messenia) could give rise to a possible hypothesis of a late renaissance of the Mycenaean spirit just before its final dive into the vastness of the Dark Ages.

LH Socio-Political and Economic Activity in Central and Eastern
Peloponnese- With Special Emphasis on Arcadia (an In-Depth Study)
E.J.Krigas

INTRODUCTION

Central and especially East Arcadia has been left in darkness for most part of the up-to-date "recorded" Prehistoric research. One of the reasons may be the absence of what archaeology has traditionally characterised "monumental structure" (or, architecture). By this term archaeologists used to refer mainly to palaces or royal buildings which could give rise to theories of magnificent civilizations, of royal life and remarkable activity of slavery and ill-fated "subjects'", who were the ones leading the royal chariot to success and in some instances were rewarded. In other cases, their fate might be death, because we could not expect autarchic rulers to exercise a completely fair justice judging by our own standards (as dangerous or daring that might be). Meanwhile, it has been recently supported that the Maya were only conscripting builders and generally workforce very occasionally, thus, as it is being estimated, it would take each worker only three times in his lifetime to work for the elite ruling class (c.f. *American Antiquity*, vol. 52). Why not suppose the same for Pylos or Knossos, or even Mycenae?

Arcadia has not been directly mentioned in the Pylos tablets -- or elsewhere and that linguistic lack has also contributed a lot to the emergence of conclusions and theories which contradict each other. Are we than researching in vain, or do we try to conceal facts which help constituting a link among the then known Mycenaean cultures?

Evidence in the Pylian Linear-B tablets has been summarised in two Mycenaean Greek words (i.e., *i-wa-so* and *i-wa-si-jo-ta*) which analysed may include more than what we can try to transcribe linguistically. For, they refer to a place-name (the former) and an ethnic name (the latter) both of which originate from the East Arcadian site which is currently known under the classical name of *Iasos*. (c.f. E.J. Krigas, *Polisma Iason*, Athens 1984, Ph.D)

The archaeology from the area has been rich in Mycenaean finds which include mainly a Mycenaean (beehive type) tholos tomb and a few cist cut-in-the-rock smaller tombs. They seem to constitute a different tomb-group, i.e. different from the three small tholos-like tombs near the main Mycenaean tholos. That difference may characterise another phase in the prehistory of the area, but certainly has contributed much to the noticeable gap between the set chronological time limits for the contemporary areas. What does that gap mean? A lack of resources? A state of emergency? A change of sites?

The topography of a site plays much more importance for the general activity it portrays than the site itself many times. That is correct for most sites in prehistoric and later times and in the case of Iasos we can say that it *par excellence* dominates the rest of the active during Mycenaean times areas. Another place-name with equally active Mycenaean background is that of Hellenikon. There are many parallels between the two sites in many respects but especially in the case of wheel ruts which presuppose the use of chariots and which seem to be interconnected. The extensive obsidian found in the area on the other hand gives rise to a hypothesis of extensive communication practices in the form of exchange of goods. The Iasos ceramics has parallels in Pylos and Crete even in Ras-Shamra. The groups arrangement of the small tholos-like Mycenaean type tombs is not unknown to the Hettite cultures, in Ugarit and Tell-Fara. But the fact that we can find parallels with Anatolilan cultures originating from a place which has but only little been mentioned might have given the opportunity to B. Sergent (in Minos, 1977) to suppose a reference to Arcadia in the Kom-el-Hetan list.

We do no know whether it is the same mistake (if it is a mistake) that Homer had made by referring to an "Arcadian kingdom" in the "Catalogue of Ships". Many Linear-B linguists would be very happy with the idea of that mistake. They would be very happy with the theory of "Homer, the mythologist". But they would not at all seem to consider that if it was not for the archaeology of Pylos for example they would not be able to connect their transcriptions with the facts.

We would be content to show that two theories might be true for the case of Iasos. That either it existed as part of the Pylian Farther District (pe-ra-a2-ko-ra-i-ja, the references to i-wa-so are mentioned in the "offering" tablets, i.e. An and Cn and the chances are that it contained non-Greek tribal elements conscripted under the Pylian oligarchy for border duties, just like the o-ka units mainly of defensive type) or, that at about the end of the Pylian domination, various classes of the population, feeling rather dissatisfied or underprivileged moved out of the Pylian influence and created their own small states in places as far as Arcadia and Laconia. The character of the finds and the general social activity of the Arcadian mainland is rather "local" and lacking in wealth. The Iasos ware during the last part of the LHIII bc is rather imitating foreign prototypes than creating new styles. It is the widespread sign of decline that has almost at the same time overwhelmed the Mycenaean cultures. And its peak is tragically ironic, too. The fire which destroyed all the sites (and almost paradoxically the Iasos one) has helped much in the preservation of the written documents (Pylian and Knossian Linear-B archives) referring to the "past" year in such a bureaucratic detail that could very appropriately mirror the effort of the Mycenaeans in record keeping. Records which unavoidably had included references to Arcadia in the two enigmatic rubrics: i-wa-so and i-wa-si-jo-ta (see further Z.A. 1985).

A. THE EMERGENCE OF THE BRONZE AGE - THE THEORY

We would like to start the discussion of our subject in this paper in what may be characterised as an unorthodox, or rather conflicting approach; that is, the *chronological* one. Because we believe that chronology does not matter a lot when dealing with the continuity in time of obscure periods especially in Pre- and Proto-history. Whether a few thousand years before or after a set time limit could change our view of studying the environment into which a civilisation started developing or peaked is not certain. What is certain is the existence of the civilisation and more definitely its connections with similar ones which *might* have co-existed --- that is the point where we need the time and it would be proper to say an "acceptable" or "reasonable" time limit into which we could fit our guesswork.

Following a generally accepted system of chronology (after, A.F. Harding, *The Mycenaeans and Europe*, [London 1981] and H.G. Buchholtz, *Ägaische Bronzezeit* [1987]), which by no means could claim to be accurate, we could distinguish sub-periods in the Bronze Age (Early: B_rA_1-A_2; Middle: B_rB-C; Late B_rD) with its peak at about the last stage when the main use of the metal (bronze) seems prevailing as a general characteristic. It is mainly at about that stage when the two terms governing the whole area (namely, Mycenaean and Minoan) run in parallel with respective periods in the Anatolia and are spreading to other places of the Western world leaving traces in Europe. The question prevailing is rather, "Who did something first?" rather than, "Who was first?"; and studying the two civilisations in their context we will try to trace their enactments and be closer to the answer of "who influenced whom" regarding their connections with Mesopotamian and Babylonian cultures.

It can be thus shown that in dealing the Mycenaeans as a spreading common culture dominating the last phases of the Bronze Age, we are at the same time dealing with a culture that communicates common code-language (i.e. Mycenaean Linear-B) which transcribed has been proven to be Greek. In its variant form (as Linear A) it is also found in tablets in Crete. But that linguistic variation portrays the cultural variation met in mainland Greece at various sub-periods of the LH. From Mycenae and Lerna to Pylos, Kakovatos, Midea, Dendra and Sparta and from Tiryns to the northern Mainland and the Aegean. And the extent of the Mycenaean world can still be traced in the Near Eastern cultures even in Europe. It is a miraculous spread which took years to form, in contrast with the abrupt end, somewhere in the LHIII century which is important and monumental just for the dramatic end of a civilisation ending in fire and destruction leaving behind the mystery of the unexpected force of castrophy. If only somebody could recall to his mind that it is the same period which at the beginning marks a whole range of innovations, from weapons to means of transport, from new artistic motives to new types of tombs and rather symbolically from the burial of the dead to the cremation.

B. THE DATA

But it is time now to concentrate on our subject which deals specifically with the activity in Central and East Peloponnese with special emphasis on Arcadia. It would not be too preposterous I suppose to suggest "Arcadian" periods for the duration of the cultural activity there and we would be rather tempted to use the Minoan example as a prototype. We are well aware of course that the absence of what archaeologically has been characterised as "monumental evidence", i.e., a place or a complex of buildings acting as a neuralgic point of central authority (whether that could take the form of a king/queen/deity is still uncertain and we could expect various explanations/guesses from the Linear-B archive at Pylos) makes us cautious as to how we could venture mentioning "Arcadian" culture as parallel to Pylian, for example. Our own view on this point based on facts drawn by the existence of vast "Mycenaean" type tomb-groups mainly in areas such as Analepsis and Hellenikon in Kynouria, S.E. Arcadia is that the beginning of Arcadian periods can be placed roughly at about the middle of the LHIIIA$_1$ and LHIIIA$_2$ periods. Then the development runs as follows:

CRETE	MAINLAND GREECE	ARCADIA	NEAR EAST
LMIIIA1	LHIIIA1	Arcadian I	Middle Babylonian Middle Assyrian
LMIIIA2	LHIIIA2	Arcadian I	New Babylonian New Assyrian
LMIIIB	LHIIIB	Arcadian II	New Babylonian New Assyrian
LMIIIC	LHIIIC	Arcadian III	Late Babylonian Late Assyrian (?)

The above mentioned chronological diagram could be used only as a guide for the activity in the years following the monumental and mainly of Mycenaean origin tholos tomb in Analepsis, which can be taken as one of (if not the only one in the area) characteristic Mycenaean construction.

The existing gaps in the data collected from various sites in central and east Peloponnese may verify the hypothesis of a discontinued settlement in the area due to a continuous evolution which implied a considerable movement of sites from one place to another, not necessarily contemporarily. It has been supported some time ago that Arcadia used to be the in-between stage of Mycenae and Pylos or Sparta. That was a theory based mainly on the Homeric description in the Catalogue of Ships, where there is a reference to an "Arcadian Kingdom". Meanwhile lack of supportive linguistic evidence contributed much to a very obscure and almost nonexistent presentation of facts. We shall try to show, however, that during the late stages of the main Pylian domination in Messenia (SW Peloponnese) there happened a highly remarkable movement of tribal populations to areas as far as Arcadia where the existing evidence could support a theory of continuation of the "Mycenaean" (of Pylian or Mycenaean type) culture. The similarity of those facts along with the ones for LHIIIB-C areas outside the main area of Pylian influence (N. Messenia) could give rise to a possible hypothesis of a late renaissance of the Mycenaean spirit just before its final dive into the vastness of the Dark Ages.

C. THE FACTS: ADMINISTRATION AND ECONOMY

From the Pylian and Knossian archives of Linear-B we get a thorough glimpse of the way the ruling class (there may certainly be more than one ruling body in Pylos from the data we get from the tablets, but all under a high authority: *king* or *god*) used to keep track of their subjects' activities. Even though what we have refers to one year and specifically the "past" year (cf. Ma 378.2 pe-ru-si-nu-wo) the archives seem to have been filed in such a detailed and bureaucratic system that obviously presupposes a certain knowledge of dealing with entries in a complicated code-language. But what amazes us most is the urgency in which those archives were composed. The reference to large areas of cultivated land (ko-to-na) and their distribution to people belonging to classes (te-re-ta) and individuals through a land-occupied unit, the *da-mo*, the noticeable lack of bronze (which must have been imported) namely the terms ta-ra-si-ja (in the Jn tablets >TALANSIA , the epithet a-ta-ra-si-jo > ATALANSIOS (referring to the ka-ke-we > KHALKEIS in the same (Jn) group of tablets as well as the entries in the Ma tablets probably the most important ones since they contain negative facts underlined by the continuous use of the 3rd person plural verb o-u-di-do-si and the totals in the Ng tablets (referring to both the Pylian districts and stating the amounts of not collected a-pu-do-si > APODOSIS of an o-pe-ro > OFELOS actually a source of questions. What was the reason, for example for the cultivation of only a limited amount of land? Why was there a lack of bronze? Can we infer a kind of bad season for the palace which might have caused unemployment to certain types of vocations, like the ka-ke-we who (though they might have been among the well-to-do classes) could not pay back last year's taxes/debts (cf. Ma 378.2)? What is the difference between do-so-mo > DOSMOS (usually reserved for the god) and a-pu-do-si? Finally, is there a certain economic crisis for one year or the prerequisite of an oncoming catastrophe? And if so, are we right in our hypothesis of a violent internal discord and dissatisfaction which led to the tribal elements to other areas after having uprooted the status quo in Pylos? And is that dissatisfaction linked with the dispute in Ep 704.5?

The remarkable vastness of the palaces could easily raise the question of the reason why the emphasis was on the big and complicated side. There have been a lot of explanations offered but comparisons with the Mesopotamian or Babylonian edifices makes us consider a two-fold reason. Firstly, that of a royal "show-off", which could be translated as overall power in those times and could inspire awe and respect; and secondly, for practical reasons merely one of them being the housing of so many administrative assistants as well as domestic palatial staff, let alone for those cases in which certain social classes might have been gathering in feasts or banquets.

D. THE ARTEFACTS

Activity is not only the construction plans or the arrangement of the tombs or the palaces in an area. It is also the content of the tomb, the various small surface finds, the everyday used objects which speak of themselves. Here again in Central and East Peloponnese and especially in Arcadia the chances are that we can discern Anatolian influence.

There is a large number of small objects found in the East Arcadian areas which have shown themselves descendants of Hittite or Akkadian legend. Does that actually mean a transition to Mycenaean through Anatolian prototypes? Or, even a certain degree of influence? And if so, who influenced whom? Here again the chances are that we have to do with a strong Mycenaean influence. Many comparative studies (see Harding, *The Mycenaens and Europe*, 230) mention various numbers of Mycenaean type pottery found in as many as 60 sites in Anatolia, 80 in the Levant and 28 in Egypt. The Arcadian pottery is mainly local but it seems to have to some extent at least used Anatolian prototypes. Those mainly have come through contacts with Crete or even Cyprus, which because of its in between placement seems to have benefited most of such a type of contact or "exchange of goods'", by keeping "the cream" of the pottery crossing through the land (see Hankey 1967, p. 146).

The character of the Arcadian pottery is purely domestic. The character of the sherds is primarily ritual and there is an equally substantial number of votive and ornamental type beads which exist in the tholos tombs of the area. The golden pendant from Analepsis, found in the large tholes tomb and currently in the Berlin Museum is one of the few examples of votive artefacts in the Mycenaean times. This as well as the collected pieces of a comb, made of elephant tusks constitute the proof of the special care taken for female burials. The quality of the construction as well as the materials are in great contrast with the generally cheap and local character of the rest of the finds. The general notion of the use of such objects and probably their own reason for placement in the tombs could be both votive and ritual, their votive role referring to the goddess worshipped in the area.

Among the other important artefacts from the tombs in Analepsis are the boar's tusk helmet, the daggers and spearheads. They clearly portray their functional character as well as the different status of the buried underlined by the variation in the construction materials. The dates provided for those (mainly by H.G. Buchholz) are late LHII to early LHIII and they seem to have a common spread and use throughout the known Mycenaean centres. They clearly belong to local warriors but also skilled hunters. It is meanwhile significant to notice this interaction in the construction technique which could presuppose a degree of communication.

But how and where from do we expect or discern influences? Are they clearly of local character or did they imitate foreign prototypes? What is the relevant situation in the Hittite and Akkadian cultures and how could we probably label Stonehenge for example as Mycenaean Greek?

Meanwhile, we have already understood that the importance of the subject is not simply whether we could discern a Mycenaean spread in Europe or the East but what the actual impact of such a spread has been in socio-economic terms. Linguistically, we are somewhat led to a very hypothetical communication network which could include names such as Nauplion, Kythera or even Troy, with the possible course coming through the Aegean and possibly along the Syrian coast (cf. K.A. Kitchen, BASOR, No. 181, Feb. 1966, 23-24). Such a route could probably explain or at least emphasize the fact that we can discern Mycenaean names in the Kom-el-Hetan list (and probably that of Tegea in Arcadia) which could in turn give rise to a remark that somehow there had been an established communication practice with the East and the South --- and that probably Arcadia might have its share in that communication link.

Where could we then expect the influence to stem from? Obviously from both ends (Mycenaean and Near Eastern) starting probably with the established ceramic ware exchanges in the Aegean where the culture of the Ahhijawa seems to have located itself. Following the lists of names of two places of the Near East under the names of *Ka-f-tu* and *Ta-na-ju* (as mentioned in Egyptian texts), the location of which can only be guessed and placed roughly within the Aegean "frontier" we are tempted to accept that some names mentioned therein could have Peloponnesian or Cretan derivation, namely:

AKKADIAN	LINEAR-B	TRANSCRIPTION
à-m-ni-sa	a-mi-ni-so	Amnisos
ku-tu-na-ja	ku-do-ni-ja	Kydonia
ku-nu-sa	ko-no-so	Knossos
mu-k-a-nu		Mykenai (?)
r/li-ka-ta	ru-ki-to	Lyktos
sa-ja-ta-ja	se-to-i-ja	Seteia (?)
di-ga-e-z		Tegea (?)

In the Annals of Totmes III both the above mentioned regions of Ta-na-ju (or Ta-na-ja) and Ka-f-tu seem to be very near each other while in some cases Ka-f-tu seems to have been more involved with the islands in the Aegean particularly Miletos (which was considered to have been a "colony" of the Ahhijawa) and Lesbos. In another case, in the inscriptions from the temple of Amenophis III there is an attempted link between Ta-na-ja and the Peloponnese and Ka-f-tu with Crete. But we will examine this linguistic subject a little later.

E. THE TOMBS

i. Archetypes and construction characteristics.

The types of the tombs and the elements which characterise their importance are closely linked with the various phases in the development of the Bronze Age. The type of the tombs has given its name to the relevant chronological space in which it was for the first time constructed and used.

The LHI-II period is clearly characterised by a common technique in tomb building which has borrowed the construction plan from those very studious and fastidious insects, the bees, hence beehive or tholos tombs. There is a remarkable spread of the technique from Thorikos in Attica to Messenia, marked by in between "stops" in Arcadia. The emphasis was mainly on the large and impressive, something that brings back to mind the real purpose of the construction of the Anatolian and Near Eastern Palaces (in Alalakh, Ugarit, Zinnçirli, Beyçesultan and Mari, among others) and their opposite numbers in Pylos and Knossos, namely to show off and impress the faithful subjects. One could venture the same thought for the tombs as well --- and doubts still torment the minds and the opinions of those dealing with Prehistory as to what they were principally meant to be for --- deities or people? And was it Crete, Pylos, Mycenae, or Ugarit, Alalakh, Mari first? Meanwhile, in LHII Mainland Greece because they were found near palatial sites they were very inadvertently called "Royal" or at least belonging to princes or other royal persons. And why should it be a certain factor the fact that whatever exists in a tomb can safely (?) characterise or even date the whole structure or even the era in which it was built or functioned? And why should we always suppose that the "Agamemnon" mask could be the one portraying the mythical hero "in honour"? Would it not be equally plausible to suppose that it could belong to some person of still unknown identity, imported and deposited in the tomb after its initial purpose (equally doubtful) had been fulfilled? Why should we be so keen on the "traditionally accepted" method of putting identity tags on objects of doubtful origin while just neglecting the theory of similarities? How safe and sure can we be in our conclusions? After all, the Mycenaean dagger found in Stonehenge would not be enough to label the whole construction Mycenaean, let alone Greek....

But if tradition and mythos have much contributed to the creation of whatever kind of impressions and for whatever reasons in the LHII, things may not be the same in the main Mycenaean Era of the LHIII and its subsequent stages. The Shaft Graves Era, having mainly peaked in Mycenae, though not safely the only place of origin with the subsequent stage of the chamber and its descendant and cist type of tomb-technique seem to be more practical both in their construction and function. For they (luckily or not) do not seem to be so distant from the previous category of the tholos tombs. Their abundance and spread could probably herald the beginning (or, correctly, the end) of an epoch not no much full of pompous and wealth, great "tomb feasts" (: nekrika deipna) and golden swords, kings, queens or princes. Symbolically we are tempted to see the tomb construction peak, decline and fall as parallel to the relevant activity of the persons connected with and in a more general sense the whole socio-political system: from the tholos (and the royals?) to the shaft and chamber tombs (the middle class, still in power) and from there to the cist or plain-cut-in-the-rock types (reserved for the "Third

World type" (see, H.J. Gehrke, *Jenseits von Athen und Sparta. Das dritte Griechenland und seine Staatenwelt*, Munich, Beck 1986) of citizens of the "Third World type" of states) of the last stages of the LHIIIb-c.

The above diversion was only intended to mark the periphery of the framework into which the area we are concerned with (i.e. Analepsis) managed to contain all three successive chronological periods and the subsequent activity they entailed. Because it is one of the few areas and probably the only one in that part of NE Peloponnese where the LH stages have left considerable traces, with reasonable lapses occasionally as it so often happens when dealing with Bronze Age settlements.

ii. The Analepsis Tombs: influences and inferences

If we were to use modern terminology regarding the finds and the activity of the Bronze Age settlements we could say that we could discern a Third World type of activity in the Bronze Age, as it has been pointed out recently. And it is this kind of activity that we are constantly reminded of when we deal with settlements like the Analepsis one. Its importance lies in the fact that locality is the prevailing feature in the area, but a special kind of locality stemming from the grandeur of the impressive Palace-style amphorae and the golden swords or daggers. The arrowheads in Analepsis are made of stone and iron and the daggers are not gold-inlaid. They show exactly what they were made for --- everyday use, and that is why they are important.

The necropolis in Analepsis is not vast. It could not have been even if we accept the theory of geological evolutions. In such a peaceful environment (about half-distance from both Sparta in the South and Tripolis in the North) the ground is so steep and harsh that could be only suitable for the building of a castle or a fort. Its natural protection is underlined by the gorge --- Sarantapotamos --- full of history and local mythology just like the water it brings down from the steep, rocky mountain mass of Parnon in the winter. The soil particularly of the interzonal limestone type has been ideal for the cultivation of potatoes, apple trees and pears but it can also show the variation one meets in the Greek landscape where fertile or semi-fertile soils can be found near non-fertile ones. Just opposite the main settlement area and towards the South, the soil sharply changes to the porous calcic limestone type affected by the rocky environment of the area called Tournou. The very rare grass springing through the calcic rocks is promptly devoured by the sheep whose owners come from the nearby village of Vourvoura, lost among the green slopes of Parnon.

The settlement lies on a hill of about 300m. in diameter and was protected by a fortification wall in the Neolithic times. The Mycenaean necropolis (cemetery) lies outside the perimeter of the fortification wall (cf. the respective Mycenaean settlements of Chandrinou and Chora [in Messenia] where the site lies outside the Neolithic walls) and consists of a large tholos tomb and a few (about six still identifiable) of various type tombs, two of which may belong to the shaft-grave type of the Mycenaean prototype. The construction of the large tholos tomb follows the technique of the tholos-building in Attica (Thorikos, tholos B) and Thessaly (Pteleon, tholos E). In Mycenae the closest parallel would be the Aigisthos tomb as well as the Epano and Kato Phournos tholoi. In Messenia, there are plenty of examples in Kakovatos and the Pylos area (Peristeria). In Lakonia the most striking contemporary structure is that of the Vapheio tholos. In Arcadia itself, the Alea tholos, a contemporary find.

But if we interpret that spread of the tholos structure as a common technique of a common culture then one would expect common artefacts from the tholoi, or at least of common nature. This could be the case for Mycenæ, Kakovatos, Vapheio and a few palatial or non-palatial sites in Crete (Knossos, Zakros, Pseira) where the finds --- not necessarily coming from the tombs --- seem to share the decorative motifs. In Analepsis, as in most other Arcadian sites the craftsmen or even the builders look eager and very keen on copying subjects which undoubtedly they had seen elsewhere. How can we explain the marine-style motives on the Analepsis amphorae, for example? Could it be artists from the same 'school' or imported ware having an Egyptian origin? As A.F. Harding explains the problem exists "...because the connections exist" (*The Mycenaeans and Europe*, pg. 8) and in some cases those "connections" could simply be coincidences.

Meanwhile, there is no coincidence the fact that Arcadia has been widely characterised by a lack of wealth and impressive artefacts. That is once more proved by the finds in the tholos tomb in Analepsis which of course, despite the fact that they might not be of the same finesse as their Mycenaean or Cretan opposite numbers, have contributed much to the preservation of this link among the Mycenaean centres of the LHII and III. They prove once more that Analepsis had been a local Mycenaean centre (*Tholoi* were mentioned in Alea-Palaiochori as well. *Chamber* tombs at Palaiokastro-Palaiopyrgos [probably at Kallianion as well] while *cist* tombs were found in *Analepsis* and Asea) and that the lack of lustre or of a palace is not a reason to be denied its share in the cohesion in the Mycenaean times. But its main role as we shall see was played somewhere in the LHIII when all the states were in turmoil and just a few, in places naturally protected by their remote vastness could still have the chance of preserving the Mycenaean culture. Because that was the role of Arcadia in Mycenaean times. Protective of the style (be it Mycenaean or Pylian) of both the decorative and ritual element in the Mycenaean art, protective of a system of socio-political values as it has stemmed out of the Pylian Linear-B tablets where the distinction between the rulers and the subjects could only be expressed in terms of the wealth and/or size of the tombs. There are no tholoi in Pylos --- but there is a whole range of small tombs/tumuli in the outskirts and in places such as Voidokoilia and Gouvalari. Their meaning could be controversial, but in essence they are not very far from their counterparts in Arcadia.

The Mycenaean cemetery in Analepsis (as in the site of Hellenikon, in Kynouria, Arcadia) is characterised by a sparseness, something that we can find in modern times, too when villages were created mainly near rivers and on fertile slopes of mountainous areas. The variation in the shape of the tombs (all of which can be dated in the last phase of the LHIIIc stage, by the kylix stems prevailing as a common characteristic of that chronological period) could most probably proclaim a variation in the burial customs dictated either by a necessity or a change in the accepted beliefs, a novice or a rebellious (?) mood pushing towards novelties. The small tholos-like tumuli in Gouvalari (constantly reminding us of the largesse of the great tholos age) have clear similarities with at least two graves of the Analepsis small tomb-group and also with a few in Hellenikon. The finds are mostly of the everyday type ones, characterised by the poverty one can still detect in those small villages today. The importance of the finds from the small tombs in Analepsis is that they seem to have been copies of metal prototypes which the local craftsmen had as a guide. The "Vapheio-type" of cup (in the tumulus I) had the golden original as a pattern and the small of the "impressed type" technique globular jug may belong to a MH stage which in turn could safely date that tomb in the Shaft Grave age. The rest of the ceramic finds have got parallels in Argolis (Berbati, Mycenæ, Zygouries) Messenia (Pylos, Peristeria, Gouvalari) and Laconia (Agios Ioannis Monemvasias, Vapheio), and their use was mainly domestic and votive. Obviously, the local craftsmen lacking the abundance of metal used what was more available to them. Warfare weapons completing the picture of the artefacts found in those small graves include bronze daggers and bronze arrowheads which have parallels in Mycenæ, Dendra, Asine, Gouvalari (Koukounara, Messenia) and Isopata (Crete). Their spread denotes active "exchange" among the Greek "types" of warfare and those of the "barbarian" cultures in such a way that their origin still remains unknown.

The continuous or non-use of the tombs could mean a new chronological era developing somewhere between the last use in the latest detectable chronological stratum and the one following it though one can not claim accuracy at this point. An absence of continuity in the use or structure, or even, a multiple use could mean another probably new or unique course through the time. The following diagrammes will help towards the understanding of the multiple (and sometimes no) use of the tholos and shaft-grave like tombs in Analepsis during the various stages of the Bronze Age (See Tables 1, 2 &3).

Stratigraphically, we can distinguish a gap in the habitation and the subsequent activity in the area after the end of the Neolithic Age. Early Helladic signs are only few and probably that underlines the scarcity of any kind of remarkable finds of that period not only in Analepsis but in Arcadia (mainly at Asea [with Urfirnis-ware] and Ayioryitika but also in smaller sites: Levidhi-Panayia, Merkovouni-Ayiolias, Stadhion, Khotoussa, Vlacherna, Thanas, Garea and Kamari) as well. The Middle Helladic shaft-grave like tombs are the main surviving clues of the period while the Late Helladic is abundantly represented by a lot of either grave or surface (settlement) finds. In Analepsis the multiple sex burials (in the large tholos A and the tumuli) (see Table 1) show the progressive course of the tomb use and the variety in the shape (towards the typification of a cut-in-the slope, slab-strengthened type of grave, of the cist archetype) could subsequently mean the abolition of a type of grave-building and the adoption of a more practical type responding to the needs of the time. That should be in reasonable connection with the decreasing number of remarkable finds and the increasing paucity of the LHIIIc finds (see Tables 2&3). The sub-Mycenaean (protogeometric) finds are just a few. The most remarkable is a lekythos with a stem which carries a wavy line style of pattern and belongs to the matt-painted ware. We shall see later on whether we can discern a "transfer" from the Mycenaean to the sub-Mycenaean stage. But for the time being we are tempted to return to the importance of the connections or communication practices among the Mycenaean settlements and the elements that could define such a communication.

During the years archaeologists, topographers, tourists and geographers have been keen on identifying any kind of what they could term "track lines" of whatever nature with the possibility of communication among the settlements in the Bronze Age by means of vehicles led by either horses or pack animals. In Analepsis and not only in one site but in at least three more areas in Arcadia (Pegadakia, Hellenicon and the toponym "Agioi Deka" near the Argolid border) the chances are that we can have serious evidence of communication by means of wheel-carrying vehicles (it could be chariots or carts). The characteristics of those "wheel ruts" which make them special in their kind and provide us with the certainty of abolishing any other type of explanation due to geological/natural phenomena (corrosion, etc.) are the following:

   a. steady width between the wheel ruts (gauge) measured to 1.60m.
   b. steady wheel width (measured to 0.10m.)
   c. continuous track-line on both steep and "easy" ground

They seem to form a crossroads just behind the hill of the Analepsis site. Generally, they follow a straight course which southbound leads to the Tournou hill (just opposite the Analepsis hill) and from then on to the village of Karyai (Arachova) and northbound goes parallel to the river bed of Sarantapotamos, through the modern village of Pegadakia, following on to the ancient site of Tegea. Similar wheelruts have been found (and up to a point, followed) in the Arcadian village of Sellasia, Anemodhouri (probably on the same route as the Analepsis ones, just like the Mycenaean traces in the area and the habitation evidence going parallel to the Analepsis one), Hellenikon (the wheelruts are showing a direction towards the Argolid) and Oion. Wheelruts have been mentioned in the Argolid (especially near the Arcadian border) and in Messenia (on a pass of the Aigaleon mountain).

The nature of the wheelruts (forming a track-line) makes us think of sizeable wheeled vehicles used for the transport of both goods and people. Such a type of vehicle could be the so-called rail-chariot (see J.H. Crouwel, *Chariots and other means of land transport in Bronze Age Greece*, Amsterdam 1981) initially designed for the transport of army and military equipment (13th century BC). If it could be used on the carriageable routes of Argolis and Messenia, why not in Analepsis? And is Analepsis (and to an extent, Arcadia) the in-between stage of the Mycenaean and Pylian cultures?

Evidence from the Pylos Linear-B tablets has been connected with two dubious rubrics, namely i-wa-so (PY An 519.8, 654.17, 661.3 PY Cn 655.6) and i-wa-si-jo-ta (PY Cn 3.5) both in connection with the o-ka ideogramme. Excluding coincidences, preposterous conclusions and immature thoughts we may be tempted to see them as defining ethnic minorities residing in rural areas within or probably a little outside the vicinity of the Pylos domination.

The allegation that we have got to do with ethnic names defining place-names (cf. the variety of place names after personal names [mainly ethnic such as a-ma-ru-ta-o [Eo 224 > Amarynthios] e-wi-ri-po [An 610, Euripos] etc.) supports the view that the o-ka units might not be composed entirely by local inhabitants. Those residing in the areas of the seemingly Arcadian i-wa-so/i-wa-si-jo-ta were called to Pylos to join their forces and it seems that they contributed in kind as well (except manpower, see PY An 519.8, 654.17, 661.3 and Cn 655.6). After all, it is highly important that in Classical times this rural corner of Eastern Arcadia has been given the name of Iasos and has been very active during the years, as it constituted a vital fortress changing hands between the Spartans and the Arcadians. Its "use" has been continuous ever since and especially during periods of occupation in Greece, and that despite the changes in the geological landscape. And if it is true that certain connections could establish the activity of a site over the centuries, then in the case of Iasos the connections or consecutive stages through which it has made its presence quite outstanding have started quite early in Prehistory, leaving the Classical element just as a natural outcome.

It has been customary after the relation of facts and the definition of documents for one to seek similarities and influences from places and cultures lying outside the frontiers of the site one is mainly dealing with. Though it is not always important, it is immensely valuable for the ethnological, socio-economic and political aspect of a study, because, in the final analysis, this *is* the object of archaeological study --- a look back to those roots out of which what we consider new or modern, has simply been contemporary with something else elsewhere at a given time. In the case of Arcadia and especially Analepsis there have been similar examples from the Near East (not to mention the North) with the Lachish tombs and MBII Tell-Fara, which in turn have been compared to the Mycenaean chamber tombs. The Gouvalari-Koukounara tumulus-like 'tholoi' (showing the imitation of the tholos structure) in Pylos seem to be nearer to the ones in Analepsis, both in structure and burial customs. It remains to be seen whether chronology could probably help at this point.

F. THE BURIAL CUSTOMS

In sites where the lack of a palace has been the main obstacles in the "safe" as much as possible interpretation of the activity of the area the only remaining elements from which we expect to extract the data for such an activity are the graves. In the case of Arcadia, we can say that we can discern the usual practice of typified burials as they progressed stage-by-stage throughout the Bronze Age. There occurs again the distinction of "here" and "there". Here, just a few coarsely made household-use wares, deposited in the graves after their use. There (in the rest of the Mycenaean centres and Crete) the magnitude of the wealth, the lustre of the amphorae and the ornaments. Here the numbered stone and bronze arrowheads, stilettoes and daggers, beads and the rest ornaments of the burial. There (and in Anatolia and the Near East) the ivories and the alabaster and faience vases. Common here and there: the burial of the dead, in a contracted position and facing the West. There has been a common (as it seems) reduction in the deposition of grave materials starting gradually in the first LHIII stages, denoting, as A.F. Harding notes, a change in cultural/socio-economic terms (*The Mycenaeans and Europe*, 226), most probably due to economic difficulties we might say, a prerequisite to an oncoming period of decline. Which when it occurs, somewhere in the LHIII, it brings with it the new element of the era, that of the cremation burial. The amazing weight and size of the burial objects of the large tholoi (were they actually made to be deposited to the tombs, or were they made on the spot, "on custom order"? Were they the result of some kind of trade practice, then used and deposited as debris?) has gradually given its place to more conveniently carried smaller vessels and finally to no vessels at all (cf. the underground pit-graves in Tiryns, dated only by context!) in the LHIIIc, coinciding with the arrival of the invaders and general climate of decline and fall as it is clearly represented by both the tomb building technique and the decreasing number of artefacts.

But as regards Arcadia and the Mycenaean cemetery in Analepsis it becomes evident that we are dealing with a society keeping an "organised" burial system of multiple use in the tombs. The fact that we can discern male, female and child burials (separate, in a small pit) could probably support the claim of a family burial, or, at least kin-related individuals in the large Tholos A. The small graves lying further apart and suggesting use at a different chronological period seem to form a cluster of graves probably of kin-related individuals from various households, but linked by some type of social proximity, judging by the group-arrangements of their burial. *Group arrangement* of Bronze Age graves is not unknown in the Pylos district where the cluster of graves in the area of Koukounara-Gouvalari may be parallel to the ones in Hellenikon or Analepsis. The MBII tombs in Tell Fara (probably parallel to the chamber tombs in Mycenæ) could give us another aspect of what was happening in the Near East.

G. ARKADIA IN AKKADIAN TEXTS?

Maurice Pope in his informative book "The Story of Decipherment" quotes the following about the decipherment of the cuneiform scriptures, ".....the decipherment of Late Babylonian; this was a true decipherment in which hitherto unknown characters had to be allocated values....." (pg. 113) thus giving an indirect definition of the word decipherment, in contrast to interpretation, when he speaks about the scripts. Today we can marvel at the feats of the Linear-B decipherment and transcription: but it was not the only one. Archives of various types of scripts mainly cuneiform had been kept in the Hittite, Elamite and Semitic kingdoms and as Maurice Pope mentions, ".....The Middle Babylonian or Akkadian script had international status and the Assyrian and Hettite scribes adopted many of its practices.....". But what are the factors that may have contributed to the reference of Mycenaean names in Akkadian texts?

In the Hittite and Akkadian kingdoms the archives were closely related with the royal authority, in the form of letters or "epistles" sent from the one to the other, thus keeping in touch, between themselves. Those epistles are usually written by a king and are addressed to another king. That is one of the differences between the Pylos and Knossos Mycenaean Greek archives, the nature of which is simply informative, i.e. a stock of information for the use of the palace about the activities of its subjects. Meanwhile the Hittite epistles mentioned simply by the name of the king who wrote them or to whom they were addressed seem to be a valuable source of information concerning the order of things as they were happening in the Near East and the South (Egypt). From the information we get from the list of names of the Amenophis III temple in West Thebes (Egypt) there are two place names (Ka-f-tu, Ta-na-ju) which, in turn, "contain" *per se* place names (see, above Part D) which have tempted from time to time various researchers as to the extent at which we can link them to Arcadian, Pylian and

Cretan toponyms. Particularly the *d -q -j -s* (*de/di-gha-j-s*, Tegeais (?) or Diktais(?) rubric has been quite puzzling in its assumed transcription which could give an Arcadian or Cretan place name, especially when the odds are that both may be somehow linked geographically (cf. Tegea in East Crete). Excluding coincidences and misspellings we are tempted to see the place name of *de/di-gha-j-s* having something in common with other neighbouring place names (cf. *mu-ka-n*[W] (Mykenæ, Mycenae (?), *nu/nau-pi-r/l-yi* Naupliii, Nauplia (?) and *mi-da-na* Messana, Messene (?)) by their proximity in the tablet with names implying Cretan toponyms (cf. Amnisos, Knossos, Kydonia). Assuming that *ta-na-ju/ja* (da-na-ju) could imply the Peloponnese and *ka-f-tu* a more sea oriented district, based in Crete and including the islands of Lesbos and Rhodes (cf. H.G. Bucholtz, Ägaische Bronzezeit, 1987 and F. Schachermeyer, Griechische Frühgeschichte 1984) supposedly of the Achiava culture, could we then infer something about the Seapeoples? Could it be then that their starting point was somewhere in the Aegean, from where they overwhelmed the Mycenaean culture?

It is amazing that the place names contained in the ta-na-ju- sense seem to form a cluster of the most important Mycenaean centres in the Peloponnese. As it is equally amazing that the cluster of finds in areas not far from the Arcadian Tegea (and plausibly contained in the Tegea-sense, namely, Asea, Iasos [Analepsis], Hellenikon and a lot of small villages represented by surface finds [sherds] mainly) includes the large and miniature-type tholos tombs and shows the continuation of the Bronze Age stages (esp. in Iasos) in close parallel to Mycenae and to such an extent that the French archaeologist B. Sergent thought that we might have to deal with an alternative for Mycenae, after its destruction (Minos 1977, 143).

Even if we think that the various opinions expressed at times by various scholars may not be quite reliable by the fact that we can not witness palatial structure in Arcadia (and therefore we may have limited sight as regards the extent of the influences it might have exercised on the nearby cultures) we can not ignore the importance of both linguistic and archaeological evidence and regard Arcadia as an in-between inland stage between the Mycenaean and Pylian cultures. That there were connections with the East and the South is evident (we shall talk about them in the final chapter). That we can discern influences from the East and South is equally evident, as is the fact that we can discern periods of development in a culture which has been the aftermath of an illustrious past and one with a clear intention of preserving the styles of that illustrious past. It is of paramount importance that the so-called "Arcadian" periods as we have seen them tabulated in the first chapters of this paper run in parallel up to a point with the relevant Cretan and Mainland Greek ones but mostly in accordance with the relevant Assyrian and Babylonian stages of development and it is not left to chance that the final Arcadian III period has been continuing just from the point where the last LHIII century part seems to have elapsed for most of the Mainland Greece sites.

As it is not by chance that the data from the Akkadian and Egyptian texts have included the di/de-gha-j-s dubious toponym in parallel to the rest and conveniently transcribed toponyms of mu-ka-n[W] and mi-da-na.

The list of names contained in the tablets from the temple of Amenophis III constitutes a significant document in the sense that it portrays the extent of knowledge the neighbouring to the Mycenaean cultures had for the then activity in the Mediterranean basin and might have been used as a guide by those referred to as "Seapeoples" for the commencement of their conquering trips.

H. SOCIO-POLITICAL AND ECONOMIC FRAMEWORK:
A GLIMPSE OF A SOCIETY DESTROYED IN ITS BIRTH

The archaeological finds of a site are in most cases closely related to the social background of it. Even in these cases where the finds could be branded as "imported" or "foreign". In the case of Iasos and in most areas around it (Asea, Hellenikon, Pegadakia, Tegea etc.) we can discern a constant reminder that tells us of the need for something new, something that may have copied its prototype from somewhere else but has been full of urgency to protect it from the oncoming fire, to preserve it from the overwhelming destruction. The character of most of the finds in all areas in Arcadia is included in the sense of one word --- provincial. It could be better defined as "local" in the sense that the materials used were local. But it is significant that just at the time when that process of preservation had begun there suddenly came the end that left everything in a state of turmoil, a state of confusion as it is underlined by the variety of the tomb types and the burial customs. They are the tell-tale signs of a disintegrating economy and in a broader sense, a disintegrating society.

What are those common facts about the Mycenaean societies as we have been trying to interpret them based on the tablets? Continuous communication, an exchange of goods (probably the first aspect of trade, but not in its modern meaning) based on non-market and non-profit terms (see J. Killen, *The Linear-B: a survey* 1984). The repetition of artistic motifs could probably explain something more than what we understand by saying "copying". It could mean an act of goodwill, a recognition of a set type of art which has gained ground because it has appealed to the craftsmen and might have probably been the motive for a further extensive exchange between the various society groups. The marine-style decorated amphorae (of Egyptian or Cretan origin) might have been very much "in fashion" during their time, and might have facilitated the trading practices of those social groups that were exchanging them for, say, wheat or any other cereals or even metals. But this homogeneity in styles might probably be explained as one of a 'standardised' production made especially to fulfil local needs, or at least "directed" towards that purpose by some higher standing authority, such as the palace. Because it should be remembered that although pottery (mass) production could be on a village workshop level, trade or any type of exchange of goods as such was definitely "organised" and probably "streamlined" by the palaces.

Evidence from both archaeology and the tablets (including the Linear-B and the Near East documents of Ugarit and Akkad) suggests an extensive and plausibly thriving "trade" by sea, mainly exercised by the East Mediterranean cultures through "state/palace-controlled" ships via Crete and Cyprus. (*Cyprus and the Aegean: A Spatial Analysis, 1985*). But there are examples of individual sea-traders, or entrepreneur merchants as well as of pirates (see above reference). Generally, it seems that there were all the ingredients from the creation of what we could call "a large scale interaction" among the Bronze Age cultures in both East and West. Can we then speak of a thriving economy, too?

In a society in which money is not the means of trading exchanges, such as the Mycenaean, it seems that we can not speak of thriving economy, even less by our standards. On the contrary we can speak of a "controlled" economy, chiefly "state/palace-controlled" and responsible for decision making regarding serious projects such as the building of a palace or other premises, the despatch of trading ships, the organisation of land transport and regarding Egypt or Mesopotamia, the hydraulic projects on the rivers (The distribution of lands and commodities to the working class was another concern of the decision-making collective administrative bodies). The formation of clusters of tombs, like the Shaft Graves in Mycenae, full of wealth gives rise to the hypothesis of ruling elite groups who could plausibly be the only responsible for the exploitation of the accumulated wealth. In Pylos, there is evidence in the tablets of great plots of land, only a few cultivated and yielding a limited harvest of crops, probably less than needed for the Pylos population. The same seems to be true for the bronze industry. In

Arcadia, where the lack of a controlling body, such as a palace could not overshadow the importance of the lesser extent wealth accumulated in the graves (esp. tholos A) it looks as if the local economy was mainly based on cattle rearing, and up to a point, on land cultivation. When i-wa-so were asked to offer they contributed both manpower and cattle. (PY An 519.8, 654.17, 661.3 and Cn 655.6). And that brings us to the subject of offering/contributing. Could it be another form of "exchange" and how far was it related to the status of those offering? How could it be related to the accumulation of goods?

Until now scholars are of the opinion that there might be two forms of exchange: one, related to gift-offering and very much related to religious persons (cf. the Mycenaean Greek *do-so-mo, o-na-to, e-to-ni-yo and* o-pe-ro exchange units as in P. de Fidio, *I dosmoi Pilioi a Poseidon*) and another of a reciprocal nature, i.e., "obligatory gift-and-counter-gift giving between persons who stand in some socially defined relationship to one another" (M. Sahlins, *Stone Age Economics*, London 1972) which could include all types of hospitality, ceremonial gift exchange, marriage transactions etc. as A.F. Harding points out (*The Mycenaeans and Europe*, London 1984). A third form of exchange and more likely to be the one proper for the primitive type of societies like the Mycenaean is that of redistribution, favoured by the majority of Mycenaeologists. According to G. Dalton (Tribal and Peasant Economies, in *Readings in Economic Anthropology*, Univ. of Texas Press, Austin 1967) by redistribution we mean..."*obligatory payments of material items.....*or *labour services* to some socially recognised centre, usually, *king, chief or priest*, who *reallocates* portions of what he receives to provide *community services*...and to reward specific persons..." (my italics). Goods accumulated in large quantities formed "surpluses" in Pylos and the rest primitive type societies in Mycenaean times and it is remarkable that the study of those surpluses leads to the conclusion that they were meant for the use of those elite classes on the one hand (in order to consolidate their status by the accumulated wealth) and partly for collective interest enactments on the other. We can not be sure whether the allocation of portions to the subjects (a product of tribute or taxing procedures gained mainly after the exchange/trade practices from imports or exports) through the redistribution system were fair or not. But facts from the Pylos tablets (cf. the Ep 704.5 "dispute" not unknown in Ugarit as well and the very important Jn and Ma series of tablets about the situation in the bronzesmiths' class) for the *past* year may be a guide to a better understanding of the development of things very shortly before the catastrophe.

The data from Iasos in Eastern Arcadia seem to to have a few common points with the rest of the development in the Peloponnese. That is underlined especially by the reference of the two important Mycenaean Greek rubrics i-wa-so and i-wa-si-jo-ta in the o-ka series of Pylos Linear-B tablets. If we view the o-ka tablets as a military document, containing the contributions of areas within or outside the Pylos influence area for defensive purposes then we have a strong hint that those areas were not unknown to the Pylos archivist who dutifully noted the numbers of their contribution. That the names looked "non-Greek" or, rather "tribal" (see Sainer, *SMEA* 1976) may account for the fact that we cannot exclude 'imported' population in Pylos in the form of either slaves or workers. But the numbers of their "contribution" (was it a regular one based on the principle of offering in order that they remained "independent" or, a response to an urgent "call" from the collective powerful body in Pylos?), namely about 90 men and if we consider i-wa-si-jo-ta a variant of i-wa-so, about 70 male sheep (Cn 656.6) make us think of a well-organised community, of rural origin and of a thriving cattle-rearing economy, such as the ones somebody can still find in the rural central Peloponnese. Meanwhile, it is still unclear why there are three separate entries for the same subject (i-wa-so) in the An series while there is only one in the Cn series referring to the contribution of the i-wa-si-jo-ta. The factor of an emergency situation should not be excluded here as well as in other cases which could presuppose the urgency in which the archivist had been trying to list as much information as possible.

The fire in Iasos (just as in Pylos, and a common denouement to the majority of Bronze Age settlements) has been responsible for two subsequent results. Firstly, the demolition of the elite classes and their pompous systems of self-sustained economies, of state-controlled trade and fascinating or even exotic imports for the sake of supporting their own regime of sometimes unidentifiable or imaginary ritualistic processes (cf. to-ro-no-e-ke-ti-ri-jo); of unevenly distributed land and allotments (necessary for the sustaining of vocations such as the bronzesmiths) of the highly impressionistic element and the step-by-step deregulation of a system based not on the exploitation of manpower values but rather on the accumulated wealth (mainly by the few). Secondly, the rise of small states, of "third world type" economies, which having "defected" from the system they had been incorporated into, tried to form their own way, unavoidably following the principles they had been affected by, up to a point. The lack of wealth (as proven in both central Arcadia (Iasos, Hellenikon, Asea and Gouvalari-Koukounara outside Pylos), the separate placement of the tomb-groups (farther from the original Mycenaean clusters), the very practical grave plans, but more important, the "kinship" factor, a remnant from the old system, are a few of the points which until now can not persuade us for sure whether they succeeded or not in that effort of theirs. And it might not be by chance that the Dark Ages helped in their seclusion into darkness, leaving nothing but graves behind them through which we are expected to trail their course. And a few well-used wheel-ruts, definitely showing the way through the vastness of the wild nature, inherently reminding us of their (and could it be our?) course through the centuries.

APPENDIX: THE ECONOMY IN PYLOS AND KNOSSOS

Similarities and Differences:

Generally, there is the same way of controlling the subject, though not entirely *under* the king. It seems that the system of collective authority (exercised rather by ruling classes instead of a ruling person) is common in both cultures. The production, receipt, storage of goods and commodities as well as the organisation system of workers at different tasks are common practice in both states as it is the supervision of cult activity.

In particular differences include:

In Knossos: The economy is based on wool production or sheep.

In Pylos: There are references to land-holders and the upkeep of sacral lands (along with their personnel) was very close to the interest of the ruling dynasty. There are two provinces in Pylos while there is no mention in Knossos.

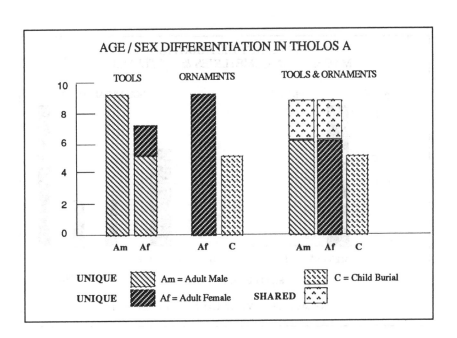

A

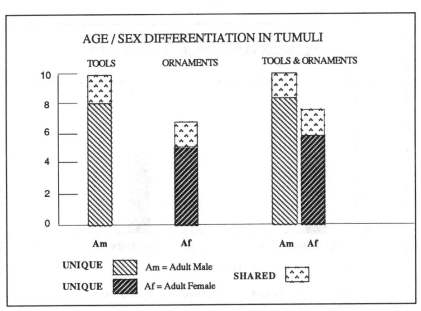

B

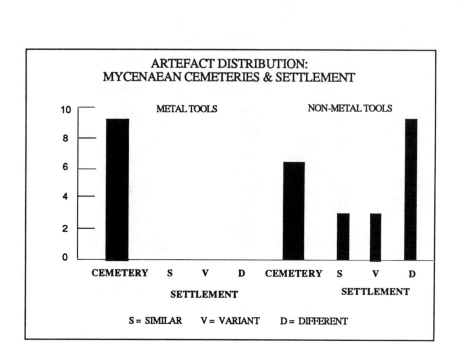

A

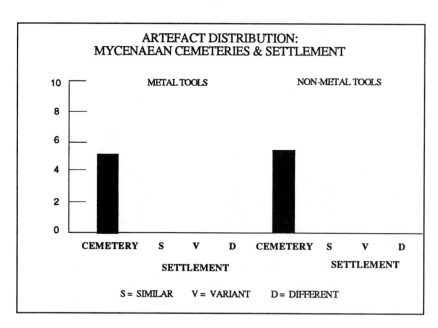

B

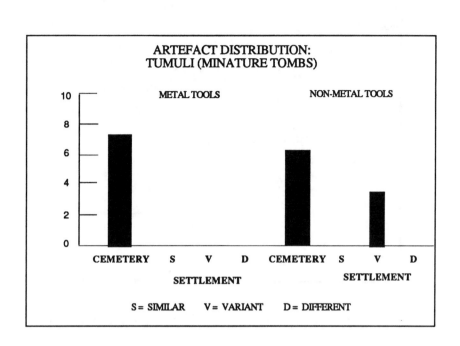

A

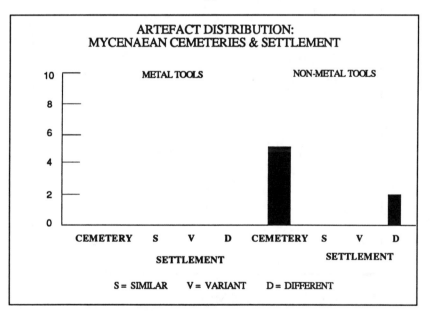

B

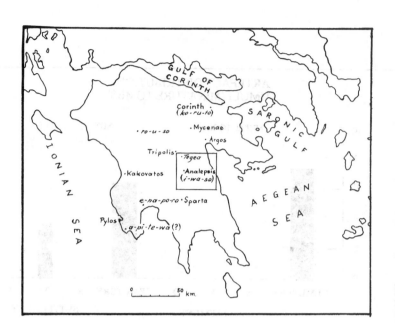

A. Map: Topography of Eastern Arcadia and Traces of Ancient
Roads

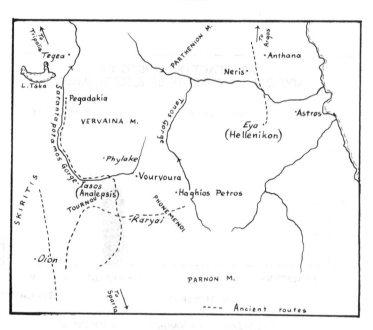

B. Detail of Topographical Map

Photograph Shows Details of the Wheel-Base of the Wagon-Ruts (1.60 m) at
Analepsis

AN ANALOGIC ARGUMENT FOR A PREHISTORIC WHALING TRADITION AMONG THE
HAIDA

STEVEN ACHESON
Department of Ethnology and Prehistory
University of Oxford
Oxford OX2 6PN, England

RESUME

The large quantity of whalebone recovered from a selection of archaeological sites on the southern Queen Charlotte Islands raises the possibility of a prehistoric whaling tradition among the Haida. To explore this interpretation the faunal assemblage is compared with neighbouring Nootka sites such as Ozette and Hesquiat where whaling was known to have occurred. Archival sources reviewed for references to hunting and the use of whales by the Haida, using techniques described as analogic and ethnohistorical, tend to support the idea that they indeed hunted whales. The evidence for whaling and its possible role among the Haida challenges our understanding of subsistence behaviour for this lesser known Pacific Northwest Canadian coastal group.

An Analogic Argument for a Prehistoric
Whaling Tradition Among the Haida
Steven Acheson

INTRODUCTION

Haida subsistence pursuits differed somewhat from other Pacific Northwest coast groups at the time of European contact, given their much greater emphasis on the halibut fishery than on salmon. Subsistence activities generally were more diversified and largely directed to offshore resources. These activities, however, were not considered to have included whaling (Drucker 1955; Fladmark 1975), an enterprise supposedly restricted to their Nootka neighbours to the south.

The large quantity of whalebone recovered from a selection of sites on the southern Queen Charlotte Islands, however, suggests something quite different. This paper examines the archaeological and ethnological evidence for, and possible role of whaling among the Kunghit Haida of the southern Queen Charlotte Islands, using techniques generally described as analogic and ethnohistorical. The implications are potentially far reaching, not only touching upon questions of origin and age of whaling on the Northwest coast, but more importantly, of Haida settlement pattern and subsistence strategies. While the data are insufficient to resolve such questions, the evidence gives renewed attention to these problem areas.

To explore the possibility of whaling by the Haida the faunal assemblage from two Kunghit sites is compared with the Nootkan sites of Ozette and Hesquiat Harbour, where whaling was known to have occurred. A second line of enquiry involved the review of ethnographic and historical data for references to hunting and the use of whales by the Haida. Archival sources consulted included the journals and logs of early explorers and traders, as well as the later accounts of government agents, missionaries, and the work of ethnographers.

The extent and manner which ethnographic observation may account for and explain archaeological phenomena is a recurrent theme with seemingly little agreement in the literature. While the use of analogy in both its direct historical and general comparative forms has a long tradition among North American archaeologists, it has been a troubled association fraught with theoretical and methodological ambiguities (cf. Wylie 1982, 1985). The fact that ethnographic descriptions are invariably "many generations removed from the aboriginal condition" (Fladmark 1986:119), is often cited as a major weakness of ethnographic analogue in archaeological interpretation. Ostensibly, this line of reasoning was expressed by Binford (1968:13), among others, who claimed that explanation by analogy, whether direct historical or general comparative, denied the possibility of prehistoric cultural forms outside those known ethnographically. Arguments by analogy, however, are as much concerned with similarities as differences between the historical and archaeological record. Analogic argument is susceptible to the kinds of systematic testing that critics have claimed for nonanalogical forms of inference, as both Gould (1980) has unwittingly demonstrated with his *argument by anomaly*, and Binford (1987) concedes with the use of *ambiguity* in his *middle-range theory*.

The Kunghit Haida or 'Island End People', were one of four major Haida divisions who inhabited the southern end of an archipelago of some 150 islands named the Queen Charlotte Islands located 80 kilometres off the coast of British Columbia (Figure 1). Characteristic of Pacific Northwest maritime hunter-gatherer groups generally, the Kunghit Haida achieved a level of social organization, ceremonial complexity, and cultural inventory more typical of surplus producing agrarian societies and were themselves distinguished amongst neighbouring coastal groups for the arts, warfare and trade. Traditionally, they lived in coastal villages of large, well-built, plank houses. In the absence of both state organisation and agriculture, there existed among these people an historically well-defined socio-economic class structure. Chiefs acted as trustees for the jealously guarded territory and resources owned by their lineage, as well as coordinated the political and ceremonial affairs of the lineage group, which centered largely on the institution of the potlatch (Murdock 1934, 1936; Swanton 1905).

STUDY AREA

The Queen Charlotte Islands are the inclusive name for an island group lying at the western edge of the continental shelf, and cover some 9000 square kilometres. Much of the coast is subjected to sustained, heavy wave action with the southern islands being especially vulnerable to frequent winter gales which generate formidable seas. A sinuous, steep, rocky shoreline with a high relief intertidal zone characterizes much of traditional Kunghit territory. Scattered along this coast are the 'town' sites of the nine Kunghit lineages including the large, historic multi-lineage village of Ninstints, located on Anthony Island, and a second major historic village at Benjamin Point. Sheltered waters and small estuaries are confined to a few major inlets, including Flamingo, Louscoone, and Rose, as well as to Houston Stewart Channel and the deeper bays along the east coast of Moresby and Kunghit Island. These features and the numerous small offshore islands contribute to a varied coastal setting rich in marine resources. At least twelve whale species were known to frequent the waters surrounding the southern Queen Charlotte Islands with the Pacific gray whale (Eschrichtius robustus) annually migrating along both the east and west shores of the archipelago. Others species include the humpback (Megaptera novaeangliae), killer (Orcinus orcas), minke (Balaenoptera acutorostrata), finback (Balaenoptera physalus), the now rare sperm (Physeter catadon), sei (Balaenoptera borealis), blue (Balaenoptera musculus), right (Eubalaena sieboldi), giant beaked (Berardus bairdii), stejneger's beaked (Mesoplodon stejnegeri), and goose-beaked whale (Ziphius cavirostris) (Bamfield 1974; Leatherwood et al. 1988).

THE APPROACH

The question of whether the Haida hunted whales arose during the course of a detailed archaeological investigation designed to obtain, through a programme of survey and test excavations, a representative sample of archaeological sites and assemblages for the southern Queen Charlotte area. A systematic inventory was conducted along a 245 kilometre section of coastline from Nagas Point on the west coast of south Moresby Island to Benjamin Point on the east, encompassing all of Kunghit Island and adjacent waters of Houston Stewart Channel, plus the smaller offshore islands (Figure 2). A 20 per cent disproportional stratified random sample of the 84 habitation sites then identified in the survey was selected for subsequent test excavations. One other site was judgementally selected for a total of 18.

FAUNAL RECORD

The fauna has been analyzed from 13 sites, totaling 82,236 bones. Of these, 25,846 specimens were identified with 87% being fish bones, 9% bird and 4% mammal. Salmon, rockfish and halibut are the main fish species caught with little variation among the sites. With the exception of two sites, FaTt 9 and FaTt 22a, the main mammal species are sea otter

(Enhydra lutris) and harbour seal (Phoca vitulina), found in about equal quantities. The dominant birds are the small alcids, such as the ancient and marbled murrelets. The only noticeable vertical change within the sites is an increase in the number of salmon bone and a decline in the number of rockfish bones from the oldest to the recent levels in four sites, including FaTt 9. Interpretation of this is not complete, but it appears not to be taphonomic and probably indicates an actual shift in subsistence activity.

FaTt 9 is likely Tc!u'uga ['to go for cedar'] Town (Swanton 1905:270, 277), consisting of three or four house sites and associated shell midden on Louscoone Point at the entrance to Louscoone Inlet on the west side of Moresby Island. The village site lies at the head of a long narrow bay fronted by a series of small tidal islets. The bay affords protected marine access, sheltering the beach from the incessant swell of the open Pacific. FaTt 22a is similarly located on the exposed west coast of Moresby Island at Cape Freeman. This somewhat smaller shell midden site is situated on a large lagoon-like bay protected by a ring of rocky basalt islets. Both sites predate the contact period with radiocarbon estimates of 980+/-65 (WAT 1637) for FaTt 9 and 1140+/-80 years B.P. (WAT 1621) for FaTt 22a.

At FaTt 22a the dominant mammal taxon is whale. The site mammal NISP is 249, of which whalebones comprise 70%. Harbour seal and sea otter are a distant second and third at 16 and 8% respectively. A somewhat similar situation exists for some units of FaTt 9. Two units were placed within a house feature and from these units 188 mammal bones were identified. The NISP for whale is 70, 37% of the total, with sea otter and harbour seal in second and third places at 35% and 16% respectively (Table 1). None of the other sites show whale in any significant amount from the test excavations, although several have whalebones as a minor component of the mammal assemblage (see Table 1).

Since the Haida were not known to practice whaling historically, the immediate interpretation is that the whales were salvaged by the residents. It is possible that dead or dying gray whales were available in greater numbers on this part of the coast as those fatally wounded by Nootkan whalers on Vancouver Island continued or drifted northward (Mitchell pers. comm. 1986). However, this same amount of whalebone recovered from a Nootka site would have, as a matter of course, been attributed to active whale hunting rather than the salvaging of dead animals by the residents.

There have been few detailed archaeological investigations on the Queen Charlotte Islands, and fewer yet that have dealt with faunal assemblages. While little quantified faunal data is available, whalebone is a persistent element of excavated shell middens. Fladmark's (1973:70) excavation of an early 19th century Haida house at Tlell (FjTx 1), Graham Island identified 132 small fragments of whalebone scattered over the length of the exposed living floor area. Here, Fladmark concluded that the fragments, amounting to no more than 2 complete bones, were being used as raw material for tool manufacture. At the historic Kunghit village of Ninstints, Duff and Kew (1958:51) observed "large amounts of whalebone" (ribs and vertebrae) on the surface and upper levels of the site while removing a number of poles. Other more recent, but limited excavations have uncovered a number of pieces from around the base of the poles at Ninstints (Abbott per. comm. 1986; Acheson n.d.). Again on Graham Island, Severs (1974) mentions whalebone for the Blue Jackets Creek site (FlUa 4). Her preliminary reports (n.d.) on the excavations at Tow Hill (GaTw 5) and Masset (GaUb 7), unfortunately, do not provide any species breakdown of the sea mammal bone recovered, but one can reasonably expect that whalebone is present.

Much better data is available on Nootkan sites for comparison with the southern Queen Charlotte material. In this instance, however, NISP was viewed as the simplest and most easily compared measure of abundance since MNI figures available for the Nootkan sites were calculated in quite different ways.

The Hesquiat Harbour site complex is located on the northwest coast of Vancouver Island. Three sites were excavated in the harbour, DiSo 9, DiSo 1 and DiSo 16, dating from the historic period to about 100 A.D. (Calvert 1980). DiSo 9 and DiSo 16 both had whalebones in very low percentages, less than 10%. However, from DiSo 1 a total of 635 whale bones were recovered, 40% of the total mammal NISP of 1604. This is comparable to the FaTt 9 house units, but substantially less than the proportion of whale found at FaTt 22a (Figure 3).

Another site where whalebones have been recovered in substantial numbers is Ozette, a Makah village site on the northwest coast of Washington. This is a water-logged site with several houses and some associated midden dating from the historical period to 400 years ago. Data on the number of whalebones recovered to the number of mammal bones identified are spread among several publications. In Area B70 52,938 mammal bones have been identified (Huelsbeck 1983) and 2,328 whalebones were identified from the same area (Huelsbeck n.d.). Using these numbers the proportion of whalebone to total mammal NISP is 4.2%. Huelsbeck also states that identification of mammal bones (non-whale) is not complete and could add another 30,000 identified bones to the total NISP which would lower the percentage of whale even farther. Other sites in Makah territory show little or no whalebone (Friedman 1976). The pattern is similar to that of Hesquiat Harbour sites.

Despite this very low percentage of whalebones in the assemblage, there is no doubt that whales were hunted by the Ozette residents and constituted a major food source. According to Huelsbeck (1983; 1988a; 1988b), whale products may have accounted for as much as 83% of the consumable food represented in the midden. There is both historical data as well as good archaeological data available, including whaling harpoons and whalebone with embedded fragments of harpoon blades. A whaling harpoon was also recovered at Hesquiat and there is good historical data on Nootkan whaling generally, although not specific to this locale. The conspicuous absence of whalebone at many sites in the Hesquiat and Ozette locales, then, may be explained by the practice of skeletons having been left on the beach. Walker, for example, sighted 11 complete whale skeletons on the beach fronting a large Nootka village in 1786 (Fisher and Bumsted 1982:47) (See Table 2).

It is not possible to identify any of the whalebone from the Kunghit Haida sites to species. Two teeth were identified as belonging to a toothed whale, possibly killer whale. The majority of bones that could be identified from the Ozette assemblage were from gray and humpback whales. As well, small numbers of bones from right, finback, killer and sperm whales were identified. All these whales would have been available in the region of the Queen Charlotte Islands, in addition to at least six other species, and were also the most likely species to be used by the Kunghit.

The conclusion to be drawn from the faunal data when compared with the Hesquiat and Ozette sites is that the amount of whalebone recovered from FaTt 9 and FaTt 22a is certainly enough to suggest whale hunting and, at the very least, whales were a measureable part of the subsistence round. Historical records were then examined, as the next logical step, for evidence in support of this argument.

HISTORICAL RECORD

In turning to the ethnographic and historical literature on the Haida one is struck by the uneveness and paucity of information, particularly on subsistence. Swanton's (1905) singularly important ethnographic study devotes less than a page to the subject and makes no reference to the Haida's use of whales. The general lack of critical research on Haida subsistence behaviour is perhaps symptomatic of the paucity of historical documentation on the subject. The patent acceptance that the Haida never hunted whales prehistorically is but one small example.

Dawson was unable to learn at the time of his visit to the Queen Charlotte Islands in 1878 whether the Haida hunted whales but notes that carcasses which drifted ashore were utilized. To quote:

> "The whale and hair-seal . . . abound in the waters surrounding the islands. I cannot learn that the former were ever systematically pursued as they were by the Makah Indians of Cape Flattery and Ahts of the west coast of Vancouver Island. When, however, by chance one of these comes ashore it is a great prize to the owner of the particular strip of beach on which it may be stranded" (Dawson 1880:111 B).

The operative word is "systematically" for in Fladmark's (1975:83) later review of Dawson's list of major food resources of the Haida in a landmark study "A Paleoecological Model for the Northwest Coast," this adverb is replaced with "deliberately." It is an unfortunate choice, perpetuating a less than substantiated claim that the Haida did not pursue the whale. Drucker (1955:49) was even more emphatic stating that neither the Tlingit, Tsimshian nor Haida knew anything about the whaling techniques of their neighbours to the north, the Eskimo and Aleut, let alone the Nootka. Reportedly, the Tlingit went so far as to spurn the eating of whale meat.

Interestingly enough, much of the Eskimo whaling complex, including many ritual elements, paralleled Nootkan whaling practices. Similarities with the Aleut were not as great, except with respect to ritual behaviour (Drucker 1955:46-49). The Aleuts used poisoned slate blades mounted on lances without the attached lines and sealskin floats typical of the Nootkan whaling kit. Instead of towing the carcass back to the village they were left to drift ashore. From this, Drucker surmised an early link between the Nootka and subarctic and arctic cultures to the exclusion of the Haida and neighbouring Tlingit and Tsimshian. But in fact there are references to whaling by all three groups.

For the Tsimshian, the Fort Simpson Post Journal (Hudson's Bay Company n.d.) for January 26, 1843 reports: "Several of the Chym [Tsimshian] started from here this evening to Dundass Island after a whale which they caught there . . ." McNeary's Niska informants claimed that the coastal Tsimshian harpooned whales using cedar bark lines and sea lion stomach floats (McNeary 1976:107). And, although lacking in graphic detail, Fleurieu (1801:249) did observe whale hunting by the Tlingit in 1791. He wrote:

In whale hunting they use a barbed bone harpoon with a long shaft. When they come to the spot where they last saw him dive, they slow up their boats and play slowly on the surface of the water with their paddles and as soon as he appears, the harpooner reaches for his harpoon and throws it at the monster.

Historical records are somewhat ambiguous on whether the Tlingit did consume whale meat. Several accounts (Langsdorff 1813/14:111; Holmberg 1856:22) report that with the exception of the Yakutat Tlingit, they disdained whale meat. Krause (1956:124-125), on the other hand, found quite the contrary with the Killisnoo Tlingit in 1881-82.

Turning to the Queen Charlotte Islands, James Colnett on his arrival among the Kunghit Haida in 1787, also suggests something quite different: "Their fishing Instruments are confined within a very narrow Compass; besides those for striking Whales & Otters, . . ." Four years later Hoskins remarked on the Kunghit: "they procure fish of different sorts; such as whale, large peices [sic] of which I have seen them eating in their canoes . . . " adding "they also get sharks, which are here very large; . . ." (Hoskins 1791 in Howay 1941:206). The latter remark contradicts Dawson's reference to sharks, reiterated by Fladmark (1975), that large sharks were "much feared by the Haidas who allege that they frequently break their canoes . . . " (Dawson 1880:111 B). Collison (1915:244) remarked from his experiences among the Masset [Northern Haida] in the late 1800's that in "their expeditions, whether hunting or fighting, . . . they required the same outfit: a good canoe, with bows and arrows, spears, clubs, harpoons, golf-hooks, with which they could either attack an enemy or kill a whale." An even more conclusive account of whaling by the Haida is provided by James Deans following his 1884 summer trip to the west coast of the Queen Charlotte Islands. To quote:

> "These waters abounded with whales which frequently came into the long, shallow bays and inlets which indented their coasts. To those people a whale was a God-send because on it they depended not only for food, but for many of the necessaries of life. When one was seen the united forces of these villages was generally required to effect its capture. After the excitement of the chase was over . . . they did not stop to wrangle over the ownership of the fish. . . . These peoples canoes were large enough to seat from 25 to 30 people, and each canoe was provided with long cedar bark ropes which they took and tied on the fish, so many to the head, and so many to the tail" (Deans 1888:42).

And more recently, Blackman (1981:9) stated on the basis of informant information that whales were "occasionally hunted as well as utilized when they drifted ashore." According to her Masset informant, the Haida pursued the humpback whale because of their relatively small size, and of their habit of frequenting bays and sheltered waters where they could be more easily taken. The statement parallels Kool's (1982) findings when having re-examined the ethnographic literature on Nootka whaling the humpback emerges as having been far more important than the larger gray whale.

At the other end of the spectrum were killer whales which, according to Blackman (n.d.), were neither hunted nor economically important to the Northern Haida. Here the humpback were hunted in the spring along the bays of Langara Island using a toggleheaded harpoon, kittu, made of hemlock (Blackman 1979:54). While no diagnostic whaling implements have been recovered from the few Haida sites that have been examined, composite toggling harpoon elements of a size that could be used for this purpose do occur archaeologically on the Queen Charlotte Islands. Whaling equipment generally is poorly represented at Nootka sites where the most common whaling artifact is the small valve component belonging to the sealskin float and not harpoon elements (Marshall n.d.).

Even more invisible archaeologically is the traffic in whale blubber and oil. The Fort Simpson Journals (Hudson's Bay Company n.d.) reveal a modest trade in whale oil by the Haida, and neighbouring groups, with the fort. Near continuous records for the years 1836 to 1863 show various Haida groups trading as little as 10 to as much as 1030 gallons of whale oil annually in addition to whalebone [baleen] (Table 2).

The volume of whale products traded by the Haida is certainly insufficient to prove their hunting of whales especially when a single humpback could yield anywhere between 850 to 1650 gallons of oil (Wolman 1978). However, it would not be unrealistic to expect, as with the sea otter trade, that the European whale oil trade similarly relied in the beginning on co-opting native expertise and traditional technology in whaling for an external market. While this may be difficult to substantiate, the trade does give some indication of the relative importance of whales to the Haida, let alone Hudson's Bay Company interests. In the interest of maintaining a trade monopoly over the area, Charles Dodd wrote to the Board of Management, Western Department of the Hudson's Bay Company on October 26, 1857:

A great deal of oil, Whalebone etc. now traded at Fort Simpson come from Queen Charlotte's Island and the quantity I have no doubt could be much increased by trading it from the Indians on the spot (Hudson's Bay Company B 226/c/1, fos. 472-473d).

An indication of the volume of this trade in the late 1840s, a period which the Fort Simpson Journals are silent, is found in the records for Fort Vancouver (see Table 3) (Fort Vancouver, Columbia Department, District Fur Returns 1844-1849, Hudson's Bay Company).

Even for those Nootkan groups where there is reasonable, quantifiable data in the historical record, the significance of whale in the prehistoric economy is only now being recognized (Huelsbeck n.d.). Drucker's (1951:49) claim that Nootkan whaling was a prestigious occupation of minimal economic importance finds little support in the historical record (Cavanagh 1983; Inglis and Haggarty n.d.; Marshall n.d.). Inglis and Haggarty's analysis of historical documents of the late eighteenth and early nineteenth centuries show whaling to be a major economic activity of at least nine Nootkan groups from March through September. They add that five of these groups were successful enough to provide for their own needs as well as generate a trade surplus. Can a similar conclusion be drawn in the Haida oil trade with Fort Simpson? The small quantities of oil being traded in contrast to what can be extracted from a single humpback, may well represent just that, a small trade surplus.

DISCUSSION

Some of the discrepancies in the ethnographic and historical literature on Haida subsistence pursuits may reflect regional variation and/or a shifting economic orientation during the historical period. Dawson's observations were primarily of the Central and Northern Haida at a time of drastic population loss and re-adjustment to a new political and economic environment for all Haida groups. Historical records attest to the presence of smallpox among the Haida in 1791 (Fleurieu 1801:294) and possibly as early as 1788 (Colnett n.d.). This, coupled with the lucrative sea otter trade in this period, could have substantially altered resource activities, particularly when this trade was conducted during the time of year normally devoted to sea mammal hunting and offshore fishing. As Deans (1888:43) remarked, the west coast Haida had abandoned whaling by the time of his visit in 1884 owing to that group's declining population "through troubles with tribes on other parts of the islands and other things." From the historical record then a potentially complex, even disjointed picture emerges where, on the one hand, certain traditional subsistence pursuits were disrupted and in some cases abandoned, while others were intensified.

The richness of the ethnographic and historical literature on Nootkan whaling overshadows all that can be said for the Haida. In fact, the lack of whaling ritual and ceremonialism among the Haida has perhaps been the single most common justification for discounting their hunting of whales. The lack of a ritual complex associated with whaling does not in itself, however, preclude such activity. Rather it poses the possibility that it simply was not ritually important to the Haida. Otherwise, we are faced with the more difficult question of why the Haida failed to exploit this resource, particularly in light of the biotic similarities and geographical proximity of the two regions. The striking similarity in the distribution of whalebone within some Nootkan and southern Queen Charlotte Islands sites suggests they did. Whether Nootka whaling has an Eskimo-Aleut origin as the diffusionists have claimed (Lantiss 1938, 1940; Borden 1962; Swanson 1956), or was independently invented (Dewhirst 1977:1-2), the arguments are the same with population pressure upon limited salmon resources being the common denominator. This same argument would hold for the Haida.

When turning to the use of ethnographic and historical records the fundamental concern, as critics of ethnographic analogue have argued (Bettinger 1980; Freeman 1968; Gould 1980), is whether ethnographic descriptions can ever accurately reflect the aboriginal condition for the purpose of archaeological interpretation. Late 19th century ethnographic descriptions of a culture subjected to new economic relations, a catastrophic decline in population, and the compelling work of missionaries, admittedly limit their content and ability to accurately reflect precontact conditions. It is precisely this variability, or even discontinuity between ethnographic and archaeological data, however, that offers a means of assessing the types of changes and factors contributing to change otherwise invisible to archaeological scrutiny. An enriched, potentially more accurate view of the archaeological record is the result.

To return to Fladmark's earlier review of Dawson, there is sufficient evidence to argue that the Kunghit did "deliberately" pursue whales. Dawson's statement that whales were not "systematically pursued as they were by the Makah" is probably quite correct. Whaling may never have been a major subsistence activity of the Kunghit at any time in their history, but they may well have taken whales as the archaeological record suggests and rather offhand remarks from the historical record imply. It can be cautiously concluded from the present evidence that whales and whaling were an integral part of their subsistence round. To this extent, this paper is a modest call for a re-evaluation of some rather long-held and generally not well substantiated notions on the relative importance of various subsistence pursuits among lesser known Pacific Northwest coast cultures.

ACKNOWLEDGEMENTS

I wish to express my appreciation to the Skidegate Band Council for their support of the archaeological field work on the Queen Charlotte Islands which prompted this paper. Petro-Canada Resources Ltd. and the British Columbia Heritage Trust generously funded the research. Rebecca Wigen co-authored an earlier version of this paper and much is owed to her for compiling the faunal data.

BIBLIOGRAPHY

Acheson, S., n.d. Archaeological Investigations: SgA'ngwa-i lnaga'-i. Ms. on file *Ministry Library, Ministry of Municipal Affairs*, Recreation and Culture, Victoria.

Bamfield, A.W.F., 1974. The Mammals of Canada. University of Toronto Press, Toronto .

Bettinger, R.L.,1980. Explanatory/Predictive Models of Hunter-Gatherer Adaptation. In Advances in Archaeological Method and Theory, M. Schiffer (ed.), Vol. 3:189-255. *Academic Press*, New York.

Binford, L.R.,1968. Archaeological Perspectives. In New Perspectives in Archaeology, L.R. Binford and S.R. Binford (eds.), pp. 5-32. *Aldine*, Chicago.

Binford, L.R.,1987. Researching Ambiguity: Frames of Reference and Site Structure. In Method and Theory for Active Area Research :An Ethnoarchaeological Approach, Susan Kent (ed.), pp. 449-512.*Columbia University Press*, New York.

Blackman, M., n.d. Northern Haida Land and Resource Utilization. Ms. on file, *Ethnology, RBCM*, Victoria.

Blackman, M., 1979. Northern Haida Land and Resource Utilization: A Preliminary Overview. In Tales from the Queen Charlotte Islands. *D.W. Friesen & Sons*, Cloverdale .

Blackman, M. 1981. Window on the Past: The Photographic Ethnohistory of the Northern and Kaigani Haida. National Museum of Man, *Mercury Series* (Ethnology) No. 74, Ottawa.

Borden, C.E., 1962. West Coast Crossties with Alaska. In Prehistoric Cultural Relations Between the Arctic and Temperate Zones of North America. *Arctic Institute of North America Technical Paper* Number 11:9-19. Montreal.

Calvert, S. G., 1980. A cultural analysis of faunal remains from three archaeological sites in Hesquiat Harbour, British Columbia. Unpublished Ph.D. dissertation, *Department of Anthropology and Sociology*, University of British Columbia.

Cavanagh, D. M., 1983. Northwest Coast Whaling: A New Perspective. Unpublished M.A. thesis, University of British Columbia.

Colnett, J., n.d. A Voyage to the N.W. Side of America: 1786-1788. *Journal in the Public Record Office*, London.

Dawson, G. M., 1880. Report on the Queen Charlotte Islands. *Geological Survey of Canada*, Report of Progress for 1878-79.

Deans, J., 1888. A Strange Way of Preserving Peace Amongst Neighbors. *American Antiquarian and Oriental Journal* 10:42-43.

Dewhirst, J., 1977. The Origins of Nootkan Whaling: A Definition of Northern and Central Nootkan Ecological Orientation for the Past Four Millennia. Paper presented at the *Canadian Archaeological Association 10th Annual Meeting*, May 1977. Ottawa.

Dodd, C., n.d. Letter to the Board of Management, Western Department, October 26, 1857, B 226/c/1, fos. 472- 473d. *Hudson's Bay Company Archives*, Winnipeg.

Drucker, P., 1951. The Northern and Central Nootkan Tribes. *Bureau of American Ethnology*, Bulletin 144, Smithsonian Institution.

Drucker, P., 1955. Indians of the Northwest Coast. *The Natural History Press*, New York.

Duff, W. and Michael K., 1958. Anthony Island: A Home of the Haidas. *British Columbia Provincial Museum of Natural History and Anthropology Report*, 1957, pp. 37-64, Victoria.

Fisher, R. and Bumsted, J.M.,1982. An Account of a Voyage to the Northwest Coast of America by Alexander Walker. *Douglas and McIntyre*, Vancouver .

Fladmark, K., 1973. The Richardson Ranch Site: A 19th Century Haida House. In Historical Archaeology in the Northwest North America, K. Fladmark and R. Getty (eds.), pp. 53-107. *University of Calagary Archaelogical Association*, Calgary.

Fladmark, K., 1975. Paleoecological Model for Northwest Coast Prehistory. National Museum of Man, *Mercury Series* No. 43, Ottawa.

Fladmark, K., 1986. British Columbia Prehistory. National Museums of Canada, *Runge Press*, Ottawa.

Fleurieu, C.P. Claret, 1801. A Voyage Round the World Performed during the Years 1790, 1791 and 1792 by Etienne Marchand. 2 Vols. *T.N. Longman and O. Rees*, London.

Freeman, L.G., 1968. A Theoretical Framework for Interpreting Archaeological Remains. In Man the Hunter, R.B. Lee and I. DeVore (eds.), pp. 262-267. *Aldine*, Chicago.

Friedman, E., 1976. An Archaeological Survey of Makah Territory: A Study in Resource Utilization. Ph.D. dissertation, *Department of Anthropology*, W.S.U., Pullman, WA.

Gould, S.J., 1980. *Living Archaeology*. Cambridge University Press, Cambridge.

Holmberg, Heinrich I., 1856. Ethnographische Skizzen Über die VÖlker des Russischen Amerika. *Acta Societatis Scientiarum Fennicae*. Vol. 4:281-421. Helsingfors.

Howay, F.W. , 1941. Voyages of the "Columbia" to the Northwest Coast 1787-1790. *Massachusetts Historical Society*, Boston .

Hudson's Bay Company, n.d. Fort Simpson Post Journal, 1834-38, 1838-40, 1840, 1841-42, 1852-53 1855-59, 1863-66. *Hudson's Bay Company Archives*, Winnipeg.

Hudson's Bay Company, n.d. Fort Simpson Post Journal, 1842-43, 1859-62. *Provincial Archives of British Columbia*, Victoria.

Hudson's Bay Company, n.d. Fort Vancouver, Columbia Department, District Fur Returns 1844-1849, B 223/h/1. *Hudson's Bay Company Archives*, Winnipeg.

Huelsbeck, D. R., 1983. Mammals and Fish in the Subsistence Economy of Ozette. Unpublished Ph.D. dissertation, *Department of Anthropology*, W.S.U., Pullman, WA.

Huelsbeck, D. R., n.d. The Economic Context of Whaling at Ozette. Ms. presented at the *11th ICAES Conference*, Vancouver, B.C.

Huelsbeck, D. R., 1988a. Whaling in the Precontact Economy of the Central Northwest Coast. *Arctic Anthropology* in press.

Huelsbeck, D. R., 1988b. The Surplus Economy of the Central Northwest Coast. In Prehistoric Economies of the Pacific Northwest Coast. Research in Economic Anthropology Supplement 3:149-178, B.L. Isaac (ed.). *JAI Press*, Greenwich.

Inglis, R. I. and J.C. Haggarty, n.d. Provisions or Prestige: A Re-evaluation of the Economic Importance of Nooka Whaling. Ms. presented at the *11th ICAES Conference*, Vancouver, B.C.

Kool, R., 1982. Northwest Coast Indian Whaling: New Considerations. *Canadian Journal of Anthropology* 3:31-44.

Krause, A., 1956 The Tlingit Indians: Results of a Trip to the Northwest Coast of America and the Bering Straits. Translated by Erna Gunther, American Ethnological Society. Seattle: University of Washington Press.

Langsdorff, von, G.H. 1813. Voyages and Travels in Various parts of the World, 1814 during the Years 1803, 1804, 1805, 1806, and 1807. 2 Vol. *Henry Colburn, English and Foreign Public Library*, London.

Lantiss, M., 1938. The Alaskan Whale Cult and its Affinities. *American Anthropologist* 40:438-464.

Lantiss, M., 1940. Note on the Alaskan Whale Cult and its Affinities. *American Anthropologist* 42:366-368.

Leatherwood, S., Reeves, R.R., Perrin,W.F. and W.E. Evans, 1988. Whales, Dolphins, and Porpoises of the Eastern North Pacific and Adjacent Waters: A Guide to Their Identification. *Dover Publications*, New York.

McNeary, S. A., 1976. Where Fire Came Down: Social and Economic Life of the Niska. Unpublished Ph.D. dissertation, *Bryn Mawr College*.

Marshall, Y., n.d. Whaling, Subsistence and Settlement on the Westcoast of Vancouver Island. In Saying so Doesn't Make It So: Essays in Honour of B. Foss Leach, D.G. Sutton (ed.), *N.Z.A.A. Monograph* 17, in press.

Murdock, G, P., 1934 Kinship and Social Behaviour Among the Haida. *American Anthropologist* 36:355-385.

Murdock, G, P., 1936. Rank and Potlatch Among the Haida.*Yale University Publications in Anthropology* 13:1-20.

Newcombe, C.F., n.d. Miscellaneous papers for years 1897, 1901 and 1903 Vol. 35, *British Columbia Provincial Archives*, Victoria.

Severs, P., n.d. Preliminary Report on the Archaeological Investigation of FlUa 4, the Site of Blue Jackets Creek, Queen Charlotte Is. Ms. on file *Ministry Libary, Ministry of Municipal Affairs*, Recreation and Culture, Victoria.

Severs, P., n.d. Preliminary Report on Archaeological Investigations at Tow Hill, GaTw 5, in Naikoon Park, Queen Charlotte Islands. Ms. on file *Ministry Library, Ministry of Municipal Affairs*, Recreation and Culture, Victoria.

Severs, P., 1974. Resume of 1973 Field Season at Blue Jackets Creek, FlUa 4, Queen Charlotte Islands, B.C. In Archaeological Salvage Projects 1973, *National Museum of Man, Mercury Series* No. 26:131-141.

Swanson, E.H., 1956. Nootka and the California Gray Whale. *Pacific Contributions to Knowledge* Number 220, Vol. 6, Article 8:1-108. Washington.

Swanton, J, R.,1905. Contributions to the Ethnology of the Haida. *Memoir of the American Museum of Natural History*, Vol. 5, New York.

Wolman, A.A., 1978 Humpback Whale. In Marine Mammals, D. Haley (ed.), pp. 46-53. *Pacific Search Press*, Seattle.

Wylie, A., 1982. An Analogy by Any Other Name is Just as Analogical: A Commentary on the Gould-Watson Dialogue. *Journal of Anthropological Archaeology* 1:382-401.

Wylie, A., 1985. The Reaction Against Analogy. In Advances in Archaeological Method and Theory, M. Schiffer (ed.), Vol. 8:63-111. *Academic Press*, New York.

Table 1

**Whalebone Recovered from Various
Haida and Nootkan Sites**

	Whale Total NISP	Mammal NISP	% Whale
FaTt 9	70	188	37%
FaTt 22a	175	249	70%
FjTx 1 (Tlell)	132	277	47.7%
DiSo 1 (Hesquiat)	635	1604	39.6%
Ozette	2328	52938	4.2%

Table 2

Haida Whale Oil Trade with Fort Simpson

Year	Month	Group	Remarks
1836	May	Skidegate/Cumshewa	16 pieces whalebone
1837	April	Skidegate	183 gallons whale oil
1838	June	Skidegate	300 gallons whale oil and bone
	June	North Island/ Masset	20 gallons
1839	September		"have got little or no oil [whale] this season."
1840	March	Haida	"some whalebone and whale oil"
	July 13	Haida	"3 gns whale oil and 100 pd walebone".
	September	Haida	"50ps whalebone, 7gns whale oil
1841	July 1	Haida	220 gallons whale oil and 100 pieces whalebone
	July 20	Haida	10 gallons whale oil / 61 pieces whalebone
	September	Masset 17 gallons whale oil	
1842	June	Skidegate	90 gallons whale oil
1853	May	Skidegate	a quantity of whale and seal oil
1856	June	Skidegate/Kilkits	580 gallons whale oil
1857	April	Kaigani	a quantity of whale oil
	June	Skidegate/Kilkits	1030 gallons whale oil
	August	Kaigani	a quantity of whale oil
1858	July	Skidegate	150 gallons whale oil
1859	April	Skidegate	"traded whale oil"
	August 6	Haida	200 gallons oil
	August 31	Haida	7 casks of oil
1862	June	Masset	"trading oil"
	July	Skidegate	[90 gallons dogfish oil]
1863	March	Masset	a quantity of whale oil

(Source: Hudson's Bay Company n.d.)

Table   2

Table 3

**The Hudson's Bay Company Trade in Whale Products
Years 1846, 1847, 1849, and 1850**

Year	Commodity	Origin	Distination
1846	387 gals whale oil	Fort Simpson	London
1847	174 lbs whalebone	Fort Stikeen	London
1849	230 lbs whalebone	Fort Simpson	London
1850	560 lbs whalebone	Fort Simpson	Londcn

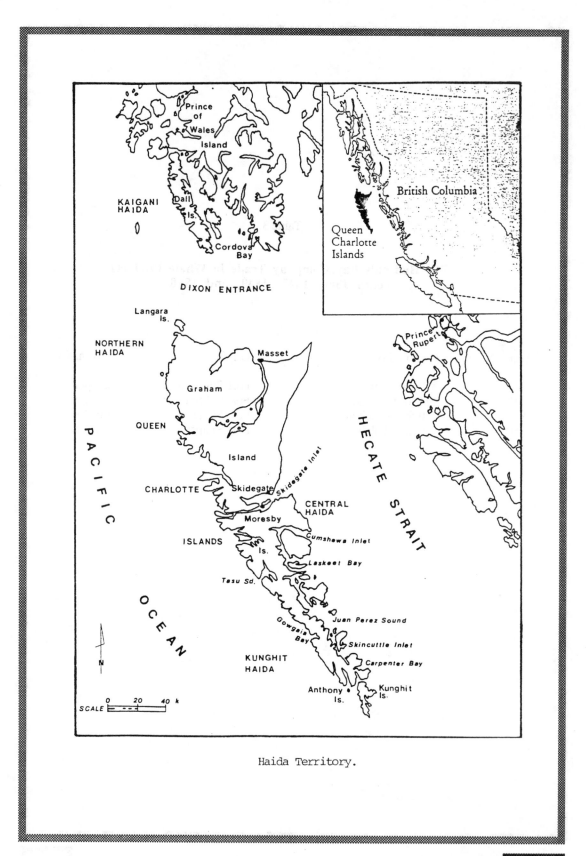

Haida Territory.

DCATT&T   Figure   1

362

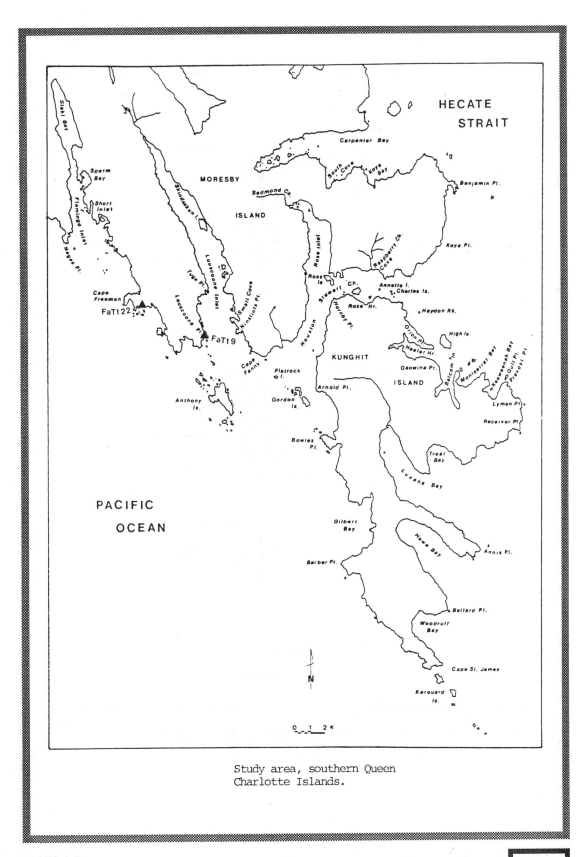

HECATE
STRAIT

Carpenter Bay

MORESBY

ISLAND

Siaki Bay

Sperm Bay

Short Inlet

Flamingo Inlet

Negas Pt.

Cape Freeman

Skindaskun I.

Louscoone Inlet

Tuga Pt.

Louscoone Pt.

Small Cove

Winstints Pt.

Cape Fanny

Flatrock I.

Gordon Is.

Anthony Is.

Sedmond Ck.

Rose Inlet

Rose Is.

Stewart Ch.

Houston

Hornby Pt.

Arnold Pt.

KUNGHIT

ISLAND

Bowles Pt.

South Cove

Koya Bay

Raspberry Ck.

Annette I.

Charles Is.

Rose Hr.

Orion Pt.

Heater Hr.

Gaowina Pt.

Balcom In.

Haydon Rk.

High Is.

Montserrat Bay

Seewenenah Bay

Quill Pt.

Prevost Pt.

Lyman Pt.

Receiver Pt.

Treat Bay

Luxana Bay

Benjamin Pt.

Koya Pt.

FaTt 22

FaTt 9

PACIFIC

OCEAN

Gilbert Bay

Barber Pt.

Howe Bay

Annis Pt.

Ballard Pt.

Woodruff Bay

Cape St. James

Kerouard Is.

0   1   2 K

N

Study area, southern Queen
Charlotte Islands.

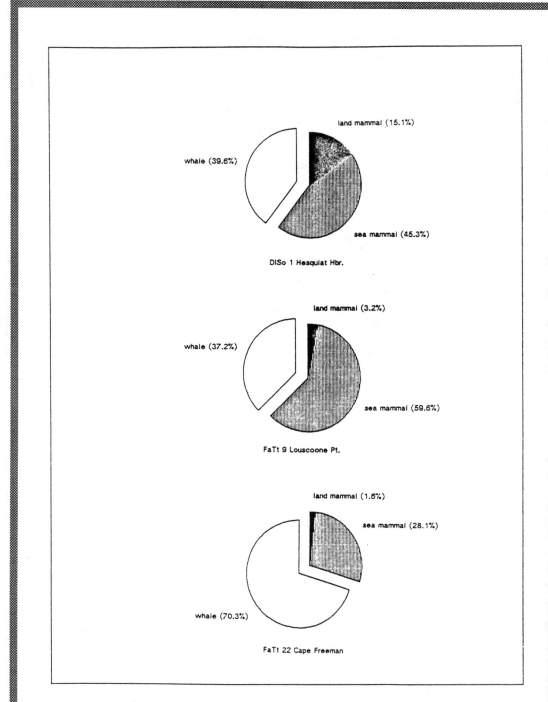

Figure 3. Distribution of mammal assemblages (NISP).

ARCHAEOLOGICAL TECHNIQUES, TECHNOLOGY AND THEORY

L'IMMAGINE FEMMINILE NELLE STATUE-MENHIRS

ROMOLO FORMENTINI
Via dei Colli, 6
19100 La Spezia,
Italy.

RESUMEN

Premesse utili alla migliore comprensione della comunicazione:

DEFINIZIONE DELL STAUE-MENHIR

La statua menhir, o statua stele, è una scultura preistorica antropomorfica, legata ad uno spazio di terreno pianeggiante, per destinazione (e cioè per la forma appuntita in basso che la rende idonea ad essere confitta al suolo) o per natura (e cioè in quanto eseguita su di uns superficie di roccia affiorante o su un grande masso la cui collocazione non sia dovuta alla mano dell'uomo, ma a cause naturali).

UNITARIETA DEL FENOMENO CULTURALE
Riteniamo che oggi si accetti generalemente il quidizio di sostanziale comunanza di funzioni, di significato e di origine fra tutti i gruppi di monumenti di tale tipo, almeno nei limiti del territorio europeo.

LEGAME CERTO CON UN RITO FUNERARIO

La somma delle osservazioni relative ai singoli gruppi di monumenti è certamente sufficiente a confermare il legame con un rito funerario anche per quei gruppi che sono privi di qualsiasi contesto archeologico.

SOSTANZIALE UNITARIETA DEL RITO

Malgrado la apparente diversità del rito funerario per i singoli gruppi di monumenti, o forse meglio per le singole regioni, soprattutto per quel che riguarda le strutture funerarie, il loro tipo, e addirittura la loro non infrequente totale assenza, le stresse ragioni che ci hanno convinti della unitarietà generale di funzione, significato e origine, rafforzata dalla constatazione della ripetizione continua nelle figurazioni di temi e motivi particolari che non possono non avere un significato comune e concorde, ci induce a credere alla sostanziale unitarietà del rito funerario praticato.

IPOTESI DI DEFINIZIONE DEL RITO FUNERARIO

Per quella che è ora soltanto una ipotesi personale, noi proponiamo il rito della doppia deposizione, nel quale le statue-menhirs avrebbero avuto la loro funzione primaria, nella fase del primo interramento, como segnacoli della posizione del cadavere, e soprattutto come custodi del defunto stesso, nel senso di impedire il suo pericoloso ritorno nel mondo dei vivi, tramite l'effette di seduzione della figura femminile; mentre nella fase della definitiva collocazione, alle statue è toccata talvolta la funzione, certamente secondaria, di elementi costitutivi delle strutture lapidee funerarie.

LA FIGURA DEL GUERRIERO

L'interpretazione della figura di un guerriero, divenuta ormai tradizionale, è suggerita certamente dalla rappresentazione di un'arma che appare sicuramente mettalica, ed è particolarmente, ed abbondantemente, presente nei gruppi di monumenti della regione alpina e della Val di Magra, ma pure rintracciabile in Corsica, in Sardegna, e più raremente anche altrove.

A noi non pare però che la rappresentazione di una sola arma, per di più di assai incerta definizione tipologica, basti a personalizzare il concetto del querriero, umano o divino, pur nell'assenza di ogni altro attributo più significativo, come tutto l'apparato di armi difensive (elmo, scudo, corazza). E, constatando come sia frequente il caso di statue che mostrano, al di là di ogni dubbio, i carratteri della più inequivocabile femminità, e cioè il seno, o addirittura il segno vulvare, e tuttavia portano be chiara la rapresentazione di uno più elementi apparentemente contrastanti con questi caratteri (scure, martello, piccozza, bastonee appuntito, arc con frecce), riteniamo più probabile che questo tipo di arma impropria, e cioè di strumento che, pur avendo per sua destinazione tutt'altra funzione practica, può assumere anche cuella occasionale di arma offensiva, sia stato più tardi interpretato per equivoco come arma da guerra, giustificando la individuazione della figura di un guerriero che doveve essere più accetta alla mentalita maschilista di nuove genti venute da lontano.

LA FIGURA FEMMINILE

Abbiamo rilevato altrove (Formentini 1988) che non esiste un solo elemento della serie di rappresentazione antropomorfe del tipo statue-menhir o statua stele (fino al limite della I Età del ferro) in cui sia manifests l'intenzione di rappresentare una figura virile: mentre crediamo di poter riconoscere una serie svariata di attributi e di segni che dovrebbero rivelare l'intenzione di rappresentare una figura femminile.

Tali segni, che vogliamo definire genericamente femminilizzant, sono di tanto grande varietà tipologica che ci è parso opportuno distinguerli non solo in base all'oggetto della rappresentazione, ma anche considerando il grado di certezza della interpretazione del significato, per i segni espressi con minore realism o, per qualche motivo, sospetti di aver subito una trasformazione che ne possa rendere equivoca una definizione troppo affrettata e superficiale.

Abbiamo dunque proceduto alla distinzione e classificazione de segni femminilizzanti delle statue menhir, partendo dai più sicuri e significativi, o cioèo da quelli che costituiscono una rappresentazione, più o meno realistica, degli attributi concreti della femminilità, quali la vulva ed il seno; per passare a quelli che si riferiscano a particolari meno sicuri, quali la lunghezza della capigliatura o i particlari anatomici volti a sottolineare l'esuberanza delle forme, ed ai veri o presunti oggetti ornamentali, quali orecchini, pendagli o amuleti, con particolare riguardo per quei segni ai quali orecchinisi dà solitamente il nome di collana, quasi sempre multipla, accettando una interpretatzione tutt'altro che certa per quel problematico motivo dei solchi paralleli che vedremo applicato a tanti e svariti temi, non solo nella scultura preistorica, ma anche in quella altomedioevale, con la serie dei nodi e degli intrecci viminei delle chiese romaniche.

E per il particolare disegno di una serie di archi concentrici aperti solitamente verso l'alto (ma talvolta anche, in assurdo contrasto con la definizione di collana, verso il basso) abbiamo proposto, anche richiamandoci alle incisioni delle sepolture megalitiche della Bretagna e dell'Irlanda (Gavrinis e Knowth)., l'interpretatzione di un fondamentale segno vulvare, particolarmente significativo in Valcamonica, e ancor più in Valtellina, ma ravvisabile, pur se più raramente, anche altrove, nella Penisola Iberica per esempio, e perfino fuori dell'Europa, in Etiopia e nel Marocco.

Ne abbiamo trascurato di considerare l'atteggiamento delle braccia e delle mani, spesso accennanti significativamente alla esibizone del seno o della vulva, anche in assenza del disegno esplicito degli stessi attributi.

Abbiamo quindi constatato che la grande maggioranza dei monumenti del tipo menhir o stele finora noti, quando conservati per intero, o almeno in parte così consistente da dare una buona probabilità di permettere il riconoscimento dei più significativi caratteri particolari, esibiscone uno, o più d'uno, di quelli che abbiamo definito, ragionatamente, segni femminilizzanti.

Abbiamo infine formulato, per trarne una giustificazioni alla sproporzione che intercorre in alcuni tipi di statue fra la dimensione del presunto segno vulvare e la statura della figura antropomorfa, particolarmente evidente nelle statue còrse, in quelle sarde, ed in altre ancora, compreso un importante gruppe di stele etiopiche, l'ipotesi ardita di una fusione fra due diverse tipologie rappresentative, che, in un livello cronologico prossimo a quello delle statue ciotttolo di Lepenski Vir, avrebbero prodotto un tipo di statua menhir in cui si sarebbero insieme combinati gli elementi costitutivi della reppresentazione antropomorfica e del segno vulvare isolato, che a Lepenski Vir coesistono, svolgendo evidentemente una medesima funzione.

E tale ipotesi ci ha fornito anche la possibile spiegazione per un fenomeno che avevamo sempre considerato con perplessità: quello cioè della scarsa rilevanza del disegno della testa, particolarmente ravvisabile nelle statue-menhirs francesi, nelle stele di Sion e di Aosta, e nelle statue della regione nordpontica; permettendoci di supporre che nel processo di fusione la silhouette della nuova figura antropomorfizzata potesse avere conservato, in qualche caso, il profilo del segno vulvare, che se del tipo en ècusson (a scudo), si conclude in alto ad arco ribassato, rialzato al centro in una breve sporgenza ad arco più rilevato, proprio come accade per alcune statue russe (Novocerkassk, Tiritaki, Natalevka) e per tutte le stele di Sion e di Aosta, e se del tipo ad archi paralleli aperti verso l'alto, risparmia una zona semiellittica, proprio simile a quella in cui è disegnato il volto di molte statues-menhirs francesi.

Ed abbiamo concluso con una ipotesi di lavoro, che a noi pare ragionevole, e meritevole di più ampia verifica, anche a prescindere dalla fondatezza dell'ultimo ragionamento che trovo spunto nella distinzione fra le due tipologie dei monumenti di Lepenski Vir.

La motivazione originale degli autori delle statue stele preistoriche è stata, almeno fino all'Età del ferro, quella di produrre una immagine, non soltanto femminile, ma di una talmente pregnante ed enfatizzata femminilità, da essere questo carattere appunto a deterninarne sicuramente la funzione, che dovrebbe essere, come si è accennato nelle premesse, quella di placare, tramite l'effetto di seduzione della figura femminile, lo spirito inquieto del morto, onde evitarne il minaccioso ritorno nel mondo dei vivi.

L'Immagine Femminile Nelle Statue-Menhirs
R. Formentini

A la grande varietà tipologica di segni che vogliamo definire genericamente *femminilizzanti* della rappresentazione antropomorfa nella scultura preistorica in generale, e nelle statue menhirs in particolare, ci convince della opportunità di organizzare l'esame dell'argomento, distinguendoli non solo in base all' *oggetto* della rappresentazione, ma anche considerando il grado di certezza della interpretazione del significato per i segni espressi con minor realismo o, per qualche motivo, sospetti di aver subito una trasformazione che ne possa rendere equivoca una definizione troppo affrettata e superficiale.

Facciamo, per miglior chiarezza, alcuni esempi dei casi più significativi: il disegno del seno, articolato nella coppia di protuberanze delle mammelle, o anche nella fin schematica rappresentazione di due dischi, o di due cerchi, nella posizione corrispondente, è normalmente da considerare inequivocabile per quanto riguarda il suo significato, e quindi per il suo valore *femminilizzante*, ma quando noi volessimo attribuire questa definizione ai due circoli che affiancano, solo un poco più in basso, il cerchio maggiore che sta in alto in alcune delle stele piùù significative della Valtellina, dovremmo anche giustificare con altri argcomenti questa interpretazione altrimenti non pienamente accettabile, ma da considerarsi solo una ipotesi. Ed i segni, cosi svariati tipologicamente, che in qualche modo sembrano suggerire una, talvolta assai astratta, rappresentazione dell'organo sessuale femminile, e cioè i cosi detti segni vulvari, sono praticamente certi nella loro interpretazione quando posti nella parte pertinente della figura antropomorfa, e ancor piùù sicuramente se accompagnati da altri attributi *femminilizzanti*, ma lo sono assai meno, anche se tipologicamente molto somiglianti, quando i trovano per sempio disegnati in alto sul petto, magari addirittura al i sopra della rappresentazione del seno, oppure quando, pur rimanendo sostanzialmente somiglianti alla tipologia generale, mostrano chiaramente, come l'*objet* delle statue menhirs francesi, di essere stati interpretati, forse in una fase più tarda della loro evoluzione rappresentativa, con altro, e ben diverso, significato dagli stessi costruttori dei monumenti. E ancora, l'atteggiamento delle braccia e delle mani levate nel gesto della esibizione del seno, o viceversa portate sul grembo a circoscrivere, o anche, più da lontano, soltanto accennare alla posizione el sesso, rappresenta di per una forte suggestione di intenzione *femminilizzante*, che diventa per praticamente certezza solo per l'aggiungersi di altri elementi di giudizio, quali, per esempiùo, la ripetizione su diversi esemplari dello stesso gruppo, o la presenza di altri caratteri significativi in tale senso, come gli orecchini ad anello, la *collana* multipla o il disegno di una fluente capigliatura (Figura 1a-1b).

L'assunto di questo lavoro non per soltanto quello di dimostrare che l'individuazione della rappresentazione femminile almeno presente con certezza in ognuno dei gruppi, e neppure di provare, come abbiamo fatto recentemente in uno studio dedicato alla rappresentazione di armi (Formentini 1988), che non esiste neppure uno fra gli elementi statuari singoli, almeno fino alla prima Età del ferro, che si possa considerare una inequivocabile rappresentazione virile; ma di convincere che la massima probabilit di verità va riconosciuta all'ipotesi che l'intenzione originale di dare un significato di rappresentazione femminile sia a attribuirsi, fino alla piena

369

Età del ferro, a *tutti* gli elementi singoli della sterminata serie delle statue menhirs e statue stele.

E veniamo dunque alla distinzione e classificazione dei *segni femminilizzanti* delle statue menhirs, partendo dai più sicuri e significativi, e cioè da quelli che costituiscono una rappresentazione, più o meno realistica, degli attributi concreti della femminilit; quali la vulva e il seno, per passare a quelli che si riferiscono a particolari meno sicuri, ma pur sempre ben caratteristici, quali la lungchezza della capigliatura, la rotondit delle forme, a largchezza dei fianchi, peraltro tutti non così evidenti nelle statue in pietra, quanto lo sono invece nelle statuette di terracotta, ed ai veri o presunti elementi ornamentali, quali orecchini, pendagli o amuleti, giungendo a quei segni ai quali si d solitamente il nome di *collana*, più spesso multipla, accettando una interpretazione tutt'altro che certa.

LA RAPPRESENTAZIONE DEL SENO

Il segno più sicuro è dato dalla rappresentazione della coppi di mammelle, che si trovano, *in ogni caso*, collocate al loro naturale posto, sull'alto del petto; mentre non di rado il segno vulvare si sposta assai più in alto, certamente per raggiungere una posizione di maggiore rilievo *emblematico*, arrivando talvolta, come vedremo, a collocarsi addirittura al di sopra del seno (Figura 1c).

Naturalmente il massimo livello di certezza della interpretazione si raggiunge quando la rappresentazione realistica, come avviene particolarmente in alcune statue della Val di Magra; ma anche la forma a dischi o a *pastiglie* quasi altrettanto sicura; e l'equivoco sul valore della forma a circoletti incavati, talvolta definiti *borchie o comunque elementi dell'armamento difensivo*, è basato sul pregiudizio, di cui abbiamo già trattato nello studio dedicato appunto alle armi, per il quale si vuole identificare la statua *armata* soltanto con la figura, ovviamente virile, di un guerriero; come accadrà alla statua di Sibioara in Romania, che la manifestamente successiva aggiunta del disegno di un pugnale dell'Età del ferro ha mutato appunto in un *guerriero*, al quale non si può naturalmente riconoscere l'attributo, molto femminile invero, della rappresentazione del seno (Figura 1d).

Anche accettando comunque di abbandonare la statua di Sibioara alla sua definizione di *guerriero*, che peraltro la toglierebbe dal novero delle stele più antiche, rimangono ben numerose ovunque le statue di cui non si discute la femminilit attestata, principalmente almeno, dalla rappresentazione del seno: in Val di Magra, dove la rappresentazione talvolta di un sorprendente realismo; nella regione gallica, tanto nel Rouergue che nel Garde nel bacino parigino, fino alla Bretagna e all'isola di Guernesey, della Manica, dove la rappresentazione spesso più decisamente realistica, quasi come in Val di Magra, e frequentemente, in Bretagna in particolare, isolata dal resto della figura antropomorfa, bastando a rappresentarla nel suo insieme; a Castelluccio dei Sauri, in Puglia, con tre elementi statuari gradualmente differenziantisi da un relativo realismo alla stilizzazione più astratta; in Alto Adige, con un solo esemplare abbastanza vivacemente naturalistico; nella regione nordpontica, della Russia Meridionale, dove però le rappresentazioni esplicite sono pure poco numerose; in Sardegna, con la rappresentazione realistica della serie di menhirs mammati di Paulilatino, e con quella più schematica delle stele della regione di Laconi; e ancora, più sporadicamente, con la per ora unica stele di Ciamannacce in Corsica e con quella di Larissa in Grecia.

Alle quali tutte dovrebbe, secondo noi, aggiungersi la serie delle stele di Caven, in Valtellina, nelle quali si notano, nella posizione genericamente *competente* della arte superiore, ai lati del cerchio maggiore, che sembrerebbe rappresentare la testa, due cerchi minori, che ben potrebbero rappresentare appunto i seni (Figura 1e).

Ma una categoria ancora più numerosa e geograficamente diffusa di monumenti in cui praticamente certa l'allusione alla presenza del seno, anche se non esplicitamente rappresentato, quella in cui l'atteggiamento delle mani chiaramente sottintende tale presenza, che da intendersi come celata dalla rappresentazione delle mani aperte sulla sommit del petto, ad imitazione della figura femminile, cos diffusa nel bacino orientale del Mediterraneo, nella quale il disegno dei seni, probabilmente per merito di na più evoluta capacit tecnica dell'artista, si distingue dalla rappresentazione delle mani.

E questo tipo di presenza *sottintesa*, ma certamente altretanto significativa, lo riconosciamo partiolarmente ai due estremi dell'area di diffusione dei monumenti: ad Occidente nella regione gallica, especialmente nel Gard (Rosseironne, St.Bénézet), e ad Oriente, dalla regione Nord el Mar Nero (Natalievka, Belogrudova) fino alla Siria (Abu Irayn).

Ci che viene a dare appoggio a quella tesi della maggior antichità delle manifestazioni presenti nelle aree laterali, che probabilmente non da ritenersi applicabile soltanto alla linguistica (Figura 2a-2e).

LA RAPPRESENTAZIONE DEL SESSO

Il modo di rappresentare il esso femminile presenta, fin dalla Preistoria, il più ampio e svariato repertorio di tipi, che vanno dal disegno sostanzialmente realistico, anche se ridotto di solito alla semplificazione delle sue linee essenziali, fino alla stilizzazione più astratta; mentre solo assai più tardi, a partire cioè dalle civiltà protostoriche, si iunge, in particolare nell'arte popolare spontanea, al mascheramento dietro una rappresentazione realistica di un *oggetto* simbolo, come la conchiglia o la foglia polilobata.

Per quanto riguarda per la statuaria preistorica in pietra, la stessa difficolt di lavorazione el materiale basta a limitare strettamente la tipologia della rappresentazione, riducendola a questa casistica:

Disegno esplicito - al giusto posto.
Disegno esplicito -fuori posto (in posizione emblematica).
Rappresentazione sottintesa" (e cio indicata dall'atteggia- mento delle mani) con due varianti: - mani che inquadrano - mani che accennano.

La appresentazione esplicita, al giusto posto, è presente soltanto, e assai raramente, nelle streme aree laterali (Penisola Iberica e regione a Nord el Mar Nero); mentre fuori posto, cio situata nella posizione di emblema centrale fondamentale del monumento, si trover soprattutto in gran parte della Regione Gallica ed in Sardegna (Figura 3a-3b).

La appresentazione sottintesa, cioè suggerita dall'atteggiamento delle mani, anche se presente pure, sporadicamente, in molti gruppi di monumenti, soprattutto nella tipologia delle *mani che accennano*, è particolarmente caratteristica della Val di Magra, dove talvolta le mani della figura femminile, incontrandosi sul grembo, affiancate o affrontate, danno forma ad un solco la cui immagine, recepita isolata dal contesto, può suggerire, anche per la sua giusta posizione, una rappresentazione esplicita del segno vulvare Figura 3c-3d).

Un altro segno sicuro di femminilizzazione la cosiddetta collana, semplice multipla, che ben raramente compiùe il completo giro del collo, limitandosi invece alla zona pettorale, nella quale si interrompe lasciando i vari giri aperti verso l'alto, o anche talvolta, assurdamente verso il basso, dando cos fondamento alla interpretazione di segno vulvare, soprattutto per la corrispondenza, quando semplice, con le incisioni rupestri a *ferro di avallo* a *impronta di animale* della Penisola Iberica (es. Pedra de Ferraduras da Benfeitas, in Portogallo), e con l'elemento ad U el complesso seni-collana della Regione Gallica (es. Laniscar); entre quando multipla il richiamo, forse ancor più suggestivo, rivolto alle *composizioni* di solchi paralleli caratteristiche delle tombe megalitiche della Bretagna e dell'Irlanda (es. Gavrinis e Knowth). Altri segni femminilizzanti (Fura 4a-4e).

ALTRI SEGNI FEMMINILIZZANTI

Altro segno ancora fortemente sospetto di un valore femminilizzante, è quello delle due cavit circolari ai lati dello schema essenziale del volto, talvolta precisato nel disegno di due anelli in rilievo, che difficile rifiutare di riconoscere come una rappresentazione di orecchini a cerchio, soprattutto considerando l'analogia con gli anelli appunto formati a tutto tondo appesi alle orecchie delle statuet te in terracotta neolitiche diffuse in cos grande numero fra le coste orientali el Mediterraneo e l'India (es. Mesopotamia e Moenjodaro), e considerando anche la scarsa credibilit di una rappresentazione delle orecchie in uno schema facciale sul quale frequentemente assente la stessa raffigurazione della bocca (Figura 5a-5b).

Nè meno convincente l'interpretazione dell'intenzione di rappresentare una capigliatura tipicamente femminile, non solo quando, come nelle stele provenzali, e forse anche, sia pure con minor sicurezza, in quelle di Sion e di Aosta, si copre la parte superiore delle statue con un disegno finemente intrecciato, suggestivamente allusivo alla disposizione di una capigliatura fluente e ondulata o ricciuta; ma anche quando si taglia di netto, in alto, il profilo laterale della figura umana, producendo l'effetto del cosiddetto *cappello di gendarme*, ma anche del taglio di capelli pareggiato al di sopra delle spalle che caratteristico delle figure femminili nella statuaria dell'antico Egitto; soprattutto se si tiene presente a suggestiva impressione rappresentata, in ambedue i casi, dall'esempio delle tavolette di Okuniev, in Siberia, nelle quali il realistico disegno della lunga capigliatura ricadente sulle spalle, e addirittura riportata sul davanti a ricoprire il petto, de la immediata certezza visiva di una rappresentazione inequivocabilmente femminile (Figura 5c-5d).

Ma anche un'altra, piccola ma svariata, serie di segni va considerata a tale riguardo; e si tratta di particolari notazioni anatomiche, che testimoniano altres l'attenta considerazione che l'artista preistorico dedica al suo modello, del quale evidentemente sente tutta la suggestione ed il fascino.

Ed ecco quindi la rilevanza della linea clavicolare, praticamente sempre evidente nelle stele della Val di Magra, e caratteristica della struttura somatica femminile; ecco la serie di solchi paralleli sulla faccia anteriore del collo, comunemente interpretata come il disegno di una collana, o meglio di un collare multiplo, del tutto diversa dalla *collana festone,* che per noi, come dicevamo più sopra, un possibile segno vulvare, ed invece probabilmente da interpretare come la realistica raffigurazione di una caratteristica tipica di un tipo femminile dotato di quella abbastanza rilevante pinguedine che pare fosse considerata nella preistoria una dote positiva di attrazione, come lo ancora nei tempi assai prossimi, e forse ancor oggi, in molti Paesi, fra i quali sono sicuramenteda comprendere quelli in cui si sono prodotte qulle meravigliose sculture, antiche na certamente non preistoriche, di cui è rimasta traccia nell'arte nigeriana (Ife, Benin); ecco più raramente il segno dell'ombelico, che nel gruppo dei monumenti nigeriani almeno, dare destinato, per la sua enfatizzazione, a dare rilievo alla forte sporgenza del ventre ignudo; ecco infine, proprio nella statua di Sibioara, che pure ciononostante si continua ad interpretare come maschile, per via della certamente tardiva aggiunta el disegno di n'arma dell'Età el ferro, e malgrado a resenza dell'inequivocabile rappresentazione dei seni, un segno che a noi pare ripetere un particolare abbastanza frequente nelle stauette ceramiche soprattutto nella regione del Vicino Oriente, cio le due fossette poste all'attacco delle masse muscolari dei glutei, la cui presenza pure un altro dei *sintomi* di una rilevante pinguedine (Figura 5e).

IL SESSO DELLE STATUE MENHIR

Se ogliamo ora giungere ad una conclusione, sia pure provvisoria, è cioè valida solo fino alla eventuale scoperta di nuovi elementi di giudizio, evitando di fare la fine di quei saggi che sono rimasti celebri per il loro vano discettare sul sesso degli angeli, dobbiamo cercare di riassumere la questione in termini concreti e concisi.

Abbiamo rilevato che non esiste un solo lemento della serie di rappresentazioni antropomorfe scolpite nella pietra in Età preistorica (fino al limited ella I Età del ferro) in cui sia manifesta l'intenzione di rappresentare una figura virile; mentre con 'Età del ferro appunto tale intenzione si concretizza spesso, non solo con la raffigurazione di armi rispondenti a concreti modelli attribuibili ad una particolare, localizzabile, e databile, cultura, ma anche, più ecisamente, con la raffigurazione esplicita del membro virile.

Abbiamo per contro reduto di riconoscere una serie svariata di attributi e di segni che dovrebbero rivelare l'intenzione diappresentare una figura femminile.

Constatiamo che la grande maggioranza dei monumenti di tale tipo finora noti, quando conservati per intero, o almeno in parte così consistente da dare una buona probabilit di permettere il riconoscimento di tutti i caratteri particolari, esibiscono uno, o più d'uno, di quelli che abbiamo definito, ragionatamente, segni femminilizzanti.

Vediamo ora la rilevanza statistica dei monumenti non definiti, basandoci sulla serie più numerosa di elementi figurati posti in allineamento unico ritrovati ancora allineati e integri (tranne i due elementi estremi), e cio le nove stele di Pontevecchio in Val di Magra:

La aggiore per dimensioni imponenza, porta ben tre dei caratteri femminilizzanti (seni, collare, atteggiamento delle mani, affrontate a definire il sesso), altre due mostrano sicuramente i seni (e forse anche l'atteggiamento delle mani), una quarta gli orecchini e le mani sul grembo, altre tre soltanto gli orecchini, una ancora, piccola e all'estremo ella fila stata decapiùtata sembra deliberatamente), soltanto una, per quanto integra, non mostra alcuno dei segni femminilizzanti, restando peraltro il sospetto che il disegno di un pugnale a pomolo semicircolare, che altri ritengono una aggiunta successiva, possa aver alterato l'atteggiamento elle mani che vengono ora tagliate dal solco che definisce il contorno del pugnale. E comunque, anche se questa ultima ipotesi non dovesse essere valida, e se altre tanto fosse per l'altra ipotesi da noi avanzata qualche pagina più sopra proposto del possibile valore femminilizzante dello stesso disegno el pugnale, si tratterebbe pur sempre di un unico caso su nove, e si potrebbe facilmente giustificarlo considerando come ragionevolmente non necessaria la specificazione del sesso di gni singolo elemento in una serie omogenea di statue femminili, ella quale avrebbe dovuto piuttosto essere evidenziata la eventuale eccezione.

Ci pare cio di poter supporre, data l'abbondanza della sicura attestazione di caratteri femminili, che la statua stele sia stata sempre, fino all'Età del ferro, concepita come rappresentazione appunto femminile; è tale principio non possa considerarsi contraddetto dalla semplice casuale missione anche di tuttii caratteri specifici, specialmente quando non si tratti di un elemento isolato ma di una serie in cui tali caratteri sono abbondantemente rappresentati.

Cosicch quando rileviamo che, per esempio, nelle statue della regione a Nord el Mar Nero abbondano i connotati chiaramente femminili, quali a rappresentazione del seno (esplicita o suggerita dalla posizione delle mani) o della *natura*, e che tali caratteri non sono incompatibili con il disegno di quelle che abbiamo più sopra definito armi improprie (scure, arco con frecce, mazze ecc.), non ci sogniamo neppure di considerare come raffigurazioni virili quelle statue in cui non di fatto ravvisabile alcuno di tali elementi; perch pensiamo che chi avesse dovuto, o comunque voluto, rappresentare, per una ragione specifica, quella che sarebbe stata l'eccezione di una figura maschile, lo avrebbe dovuto fare dando particolare evidenza ad un elemento sicuramente virile.

E lo stesso ragionamento facciamo anche per le statue menhir francesi (in generale), pur rilevando la complicazione portata in quel caso dalla frequente presenza dell'equivoco *objet*, che in un certo momento (o in un certo ambiente) assume probabilmente il significato di una vera propria arma offensiva, dismettendo quello originale, che era secondo noi di segno vulvare; è viene pertanto porsi in contrasto con il disegno del seno, con il quale si alterna, talvolta in ripetuta vicenda, quando vengono in contattto le due culture, a più antica (e autoctona), che nella statua evidenzia le attrattive sessuali femminili, la meno antica (e allogena), che, quivocando, ritiene la rappresentazione femminile una manifestazione di culto (quale sar poi veramente, ma soltanto nelle più volute società urbane), e vuole contrapporle la figura del guerriero divino.

Nè diverso, almeno nella sua conclusione, il ragionamento da fare, a questo riguardo, nel caso del grande gruppo di statue a *betilo* della regione del Ghedeo, nel Sud Ovest dell'Etiopia: un centinaio di monumenti, alcuni dei quali (poco meno i una ventina) sono stati trasferiti a Francoforte, e sono esposti nel locale Museo Etnografico.

Pochi di essi ortano, più o meno chiaramente riconoscibile, il disegno del seno, ma tutti mostrano, sempre più o meno chiaro, ma comunque nella massima evidenza, un motivo figurativo complesso, che in qualche singolo elemento statuario si precisa inequivocabilmente in una rappresentazione vulvare. Ed è ovvio che tale significato, considerata la sostanziale analogia del disegno, va riconosciuto anche nei casi in cui il giudizio basato sulla considerazione dei singoli elementi solati non sarebbe completamente sicuro; e che a tessa soluzione sar anche favorita nella spiegazione di altri segni riscontrabili, nella posizione analoga, e on decise somiglianze nell'impiùanto generale, su numerosi altri monumenti di altri gruppi regionali dell'Etiopia, i cui elementi si contano addirittura a migliaia.

Aggiungiamo ancora, per non mostrare di voler evitare un caso per il quale la stessa conclusione otrebbe sembrare scarsamente convincente, e cioè al riguardo delle stele della Corsica, che la nostra convinzione di analogo significato di rappresentazione, almeno originalmente, femminile era fino a pochi anni or sono la coraggiosa, e qualcuno potrebbe anche dire temeraria, affermazione di un principiùo generale, che trovava una facile obiezione ella constatazione ella resenza, quasi senza eccezione, ella rappresentazione di un'arma da combattimento, quale appunto la lunga spada, talvolta anche di n'arma più breve, non molto dissimile dal pugnale alpino.

La scoperta ella statua di Ciamannacce, in cui alla stessa lunga spada si associa il disegno inequivocabile dei seni, ci assicura oggi sulla compatibilit dei due motivi, e ci consente, anche se a qualcuno potr sembrare questa una ulteriore prova di pervicace temerariet, di proporre anche per il segno della spada quella tessa potesi di un significato originale di segno vulvare al quale abbiamo gi creduto di poter far cenno relativamente al pugnale alpino ed all'*objet* francese.

E questo accostamento, che assicuriamo essere el tutto casuale, fra i monumenti della Corsica e quelli dell'Etiopia, ed in particolare della regione del Ghedeo, ci suggerisce un argcomento che ci pare molto suggestivo per la suluzione di un problema, che non eravamo mai riusciti ad inquadrare.

Diciamo subito quale l'analogia che ci ha colpiti fra i due tipi, apparentemente cos diversi fra loro:

Alla stretta banda verticale, che appresenta nelle stele corse la lunga spada, corrisponde nelle statue tiopiche un altrettanto esageratamente lungo solco, al quale abbiamo creduto di poter attribuire il significato di una appresentazione del sesso femminile, proponendo pure di trasferire lo tesso significato anche al disegno originale che si sarebbe trasformato in seguito nella rappresentazione della spada còrsa (figura 6 a).

L'accostamento però, provocando l'occasione dui n confronto visivo, ci ha suggerito una osservazione che forse merita di essere discussa:

Il egno verticale, che va in qualche aso addirittura dal mento della figura antropomorfa fino quasi alla parte interrata, veramente di una lungchezza spropositata, sia come rappresentazione di una spada, sia, e ancor di più, comerappresentazione della fessura vulvare. E difficilmente la spiegazione di questo singolare *errore di rospettiva* potrebbe essere diversa per i due tipi.

Avevamo d'altra parte gi più volte considerato, con una certa perplessit, il fencomeno della riduzione nella misura della sporgenza della rappresentazione della testa, riscontrabile nelle statue appartenenti a gruppi diversi, e lontani, come le stele russe e quelle di Sion e di Aosta, in cui la sporgena delle testa appunto minima, e ridotta quasi ad una protuberanza nella linea delle spalle, o le statue menhir francesi in cui, quasi sistematicamente, a rappresentazione del olto completamente inserita nel profilo del tronco che si conclude in alto d arco ribassato (Figura 6b).

E ci eravamo posto il problema del motivo di una cos strana valutazione dell'importanza della rappresentazione del capo in statue che avrebbero dovuto essere, a giudicare da tanti altri particolari, impostate su di una realistica rappresentazione antropomorfa.

Per quale misterioso motivo, ci chiedevamo, la silhouette della figura umana può non corrispondere alla realt in un particolare di tale importanza quale quello della proporzione del capo rispetto alla misura del tronco e degli arti?

E ci venne il sospetto che si potesse trattare, originariamente, della antropomorfizzazione sommaria di una figura vente altro e diverso significato; come per il pugnale *oculato*ella statua di Villar e Ala, come per l'altro pseudo pugnale dell'incisione rupestre di Caneda de Morillas, che a noi pare piuttosto un chiaro segno vulvare, umanizzato con l'aggiunta di re punti (occhi bocca?), posti nella zona che dovrebbe corrispondere al clitoride, e che in tal modo si trasforma nella figura del volto (Figura 6c).

Ma questo ultimo sempio, particolarmente, tanto vicino al problema che nasce dalla considerazione delle proporzioni dei particolari figurati sulle statue della Corsica e di Etiopia, che non pu mancare di suggerire una soluzione analoga anche per questi monumenti, magari er l'altra questione, cui abbiamo accennato, della dimensione della testa nelle statue russe ed alpine, e della sua autonomia figurativa, nelle statue francesi.

Anche nelle statue Etiopiche, e, se vale il nostro ragionamento, in quelle còrse, il solco verticale (e la spada) sarebbere un elemento fondamentale di segno vulvare, fra i più elementari, e cio il disegno del taglio nella figurazione del sesso femminile del tipo a *chicco di grano*.

Per cui si dovrebbe immaginare tale linea come passante, per tutta (o quasi tutta) la sua lungchezza, nel mezzo di una ellisse, più o meno appuntita alle estremit; e questa figura di ellisse, mancante del disegno interno alla statua, potrebbe essere ragionevolmente, e più proporzionatamente, costituita dal profilo generale della statua tessa, che prima di essere tale sarebbe stata appunto una grande scultura vulvare.

Le statue-ciottolo di Lepenski Vir, per fare un solo esempio, peraltro assai suggestivo, si distinguono infatti in due tipi: quelle che rappresentano chiaramente una figura femminile, anche se si parlato, al momento del loro rinvenimento, di figure di pesce, come immagini di una divinit fluviale; e quelle che rappresentano, talvolta in modo assolutamente inequivocabile, il sesso femminile (Figura 6d).

E questo non può avere altra piegazione che quella della equivalenza, di funzione e di importanza, dei due tipi. Per cui si pu pensare che le raffigurazioni della totale immagine antropomorfa, gi in questo livello cronologico intorno al VI millennio a.C.), fossero originate dall'impegno di dare un più suggestivo effetto alla schematica rappresentazione del sesso (Figura 6e).

Un processo di tale tipo ben potrebbe essere alla base della formazione del tipo di figurazione antropomorfa che trova il suo momento di maggiore diffusione, qualche millennio più tardi, nelle statue stele e statue menhirs dell'intero mondo bitato. E si potrebbe trovare in questa ipotesi il motivo della centralit emblematica dell'essenziale segno vulvare, cha sarebbe giustificata dalla sua posizione ella rappresentazione limitata alla esibizione del sesso.

Per ui, per esempio, il disegno del *capovolto* dei menhir sardi, da interpretarsi, secondo noi, come un tipiùco segno vulvare classificabile nella serie tipologica, assai comune, alla quale appartengono anche un certo gruppo di stele Etiopiche, oltre ad una serie di simboli apotropaici medievali el tipo *fiordaliso*, conserverebbe nella figura antropomorfa la posizione centrale che gi gli spettava nella presumibile fase di rappresentazione esclusivamente vulvare, anzich assumere quella che dovrebbe spettargli in qualit di semplice particolare anatomico nella figura umana.

E d'altra parte la silhouette della figura antropomorfizzata potrebbe aver conservato il profilo del segno vulvare, di cui sarebbe una elaborazione successiva; ciò che potrebbe giustificare da una parte la riduzione della rappresentazione del capo nelle stele russe ed alpine, e dall'altra l'utilizzazione, per la affigurazione el volto, di uno spazio rimasto libero all'interno di quella che era diventata nel profilo superiore la linea delle spalle; dovendosi supporre che nel primo caso il disegno simbolico fosse del tipo che i francesi definiscono *en ècusson* (a scudo), nel quale il profilo superiore ad arco ribassato si rialza al centro in una breve sporgenza ad arco più rilevato, proprio come accade per alcune statue russe (Novocerkassk; Tiritaki, Natalevka) e per tutte le stele di Sion e di Aosta; che nell'altro caso si trattasse del motivo ad archi paralleli, aperti, come più comune, verso l'alto, nel quale viene ad essere risparmiata una zona semi-ellittica, simile a quella in cui é disegnato il volto di molte statue menhir francesi.

Ma lasciamo ora ad altri l'impegno, ed il divertimento, di verificare la credibilit delle nostre ipotesi anche relativamente ai gruppi di monumenti che non abbiamo esplicitamente considerato in questo sommario studio, tenendo presente che i casi i invenimenti sporadici ed esolati non possono costituire valida prova in senso negativo, e cio per la eventuale mancanza di sicuri segni di femminilizzazione; e viceversa possono valere come utili elementi di conferma quando questi segni sono resenti; come el esto avviene non rare volte: i seni della statua di Larissa, in Grecia, il probabile disegno di una capigliatura ricciuta nella stele i Troia, la *collana multipla* della tele di Pfutzthal, nell'Eisleben, l'atteggiamento delle mani e la rappresentazione del *bastone da scavo*nella stele di Lumbrein, nei Grigioni (7a-7b).

E veniamo ad una conclusione pratica, e operativa, del nostro ragionamento sui segni femminilizzanti nelle statue menhir, affermando che ci pare lecito a questo punto rinunciare a produrre altre *prove* che sarebbero soltanto ripetitive, e proponendo la seguente, ragionevole, *ipotesi di lavoro*:

La motivazione originale degli autori di tale tipo di monumenti preistorici stata certamente, almeno fino all'Età del ferro, quella di riprodurre un'immagine, non soltanto femminile, ma di una talmente pregnante ed enfatizzata femminilit, da essere questo carattere a determinarne, sicuramente, a funzione, che dovrebbe essere quella di placare, tramite l'effetto di seduzione della figura femminile, lo spirito inquieto del morto, onde evitarne il minaccioso ritorno nel mondo dei vivi (Figura 7c).

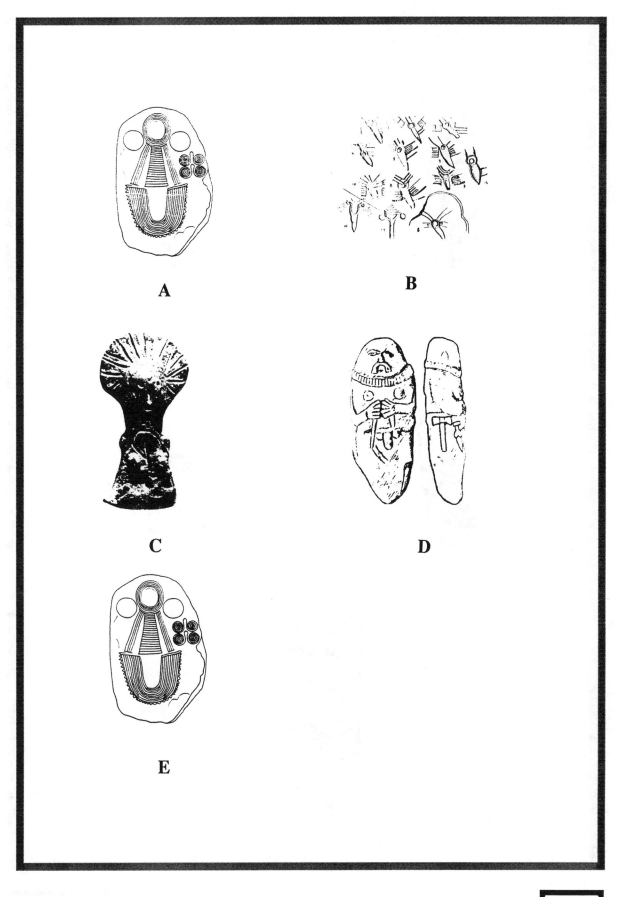

A

B

C

D

E

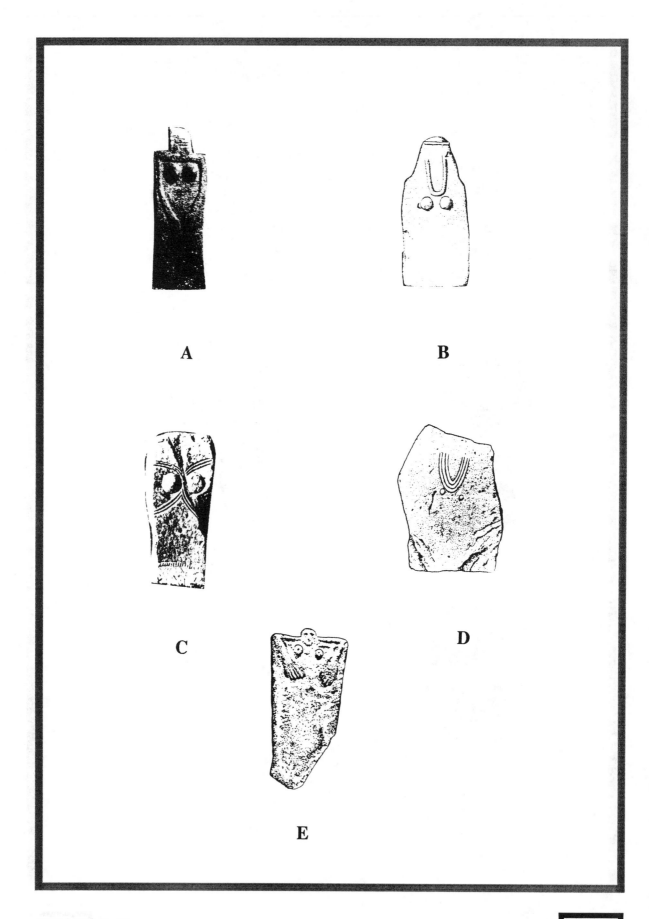

A

B

C

D

E

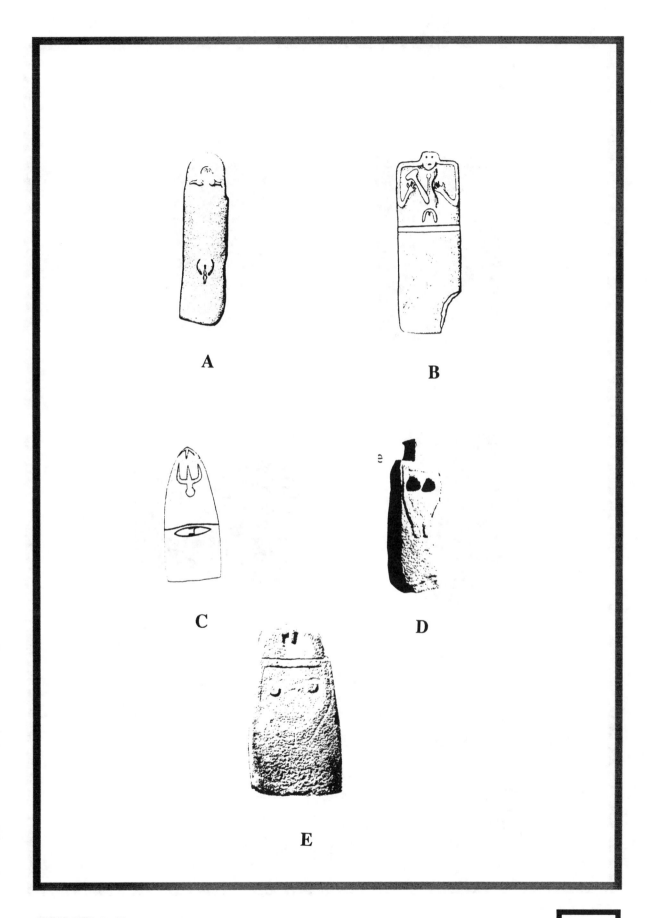

A

B

C

D

E

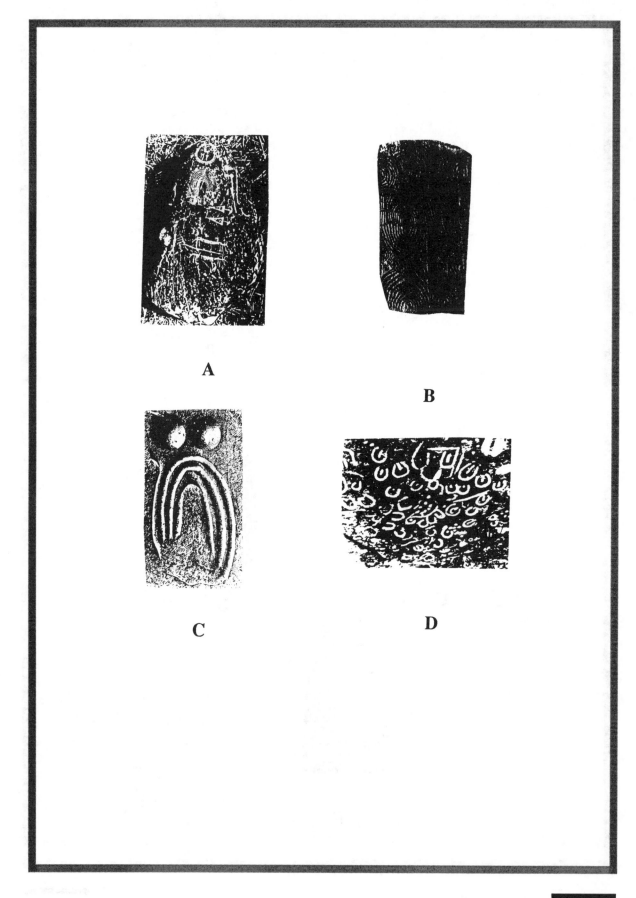

A

B

C

D

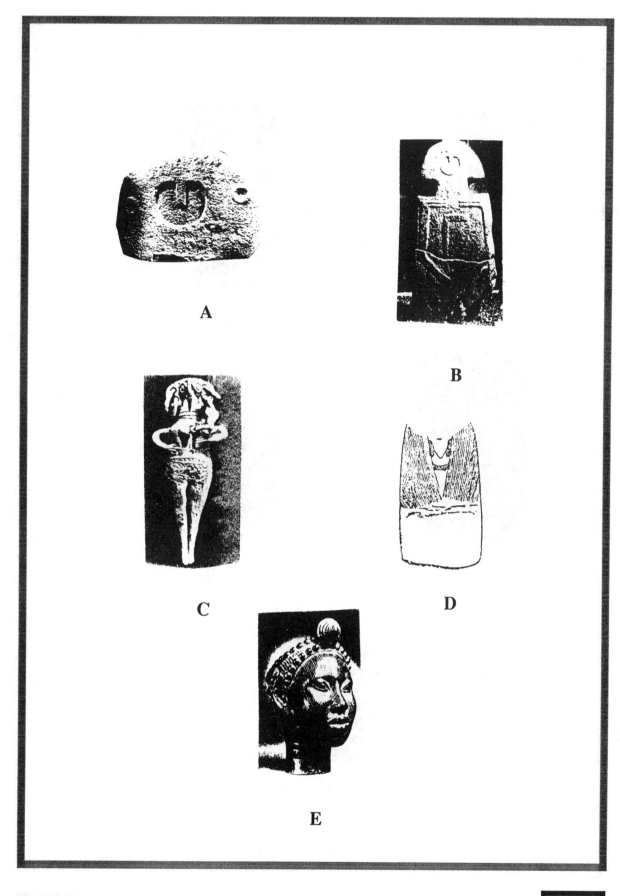

A

B

C

D

E

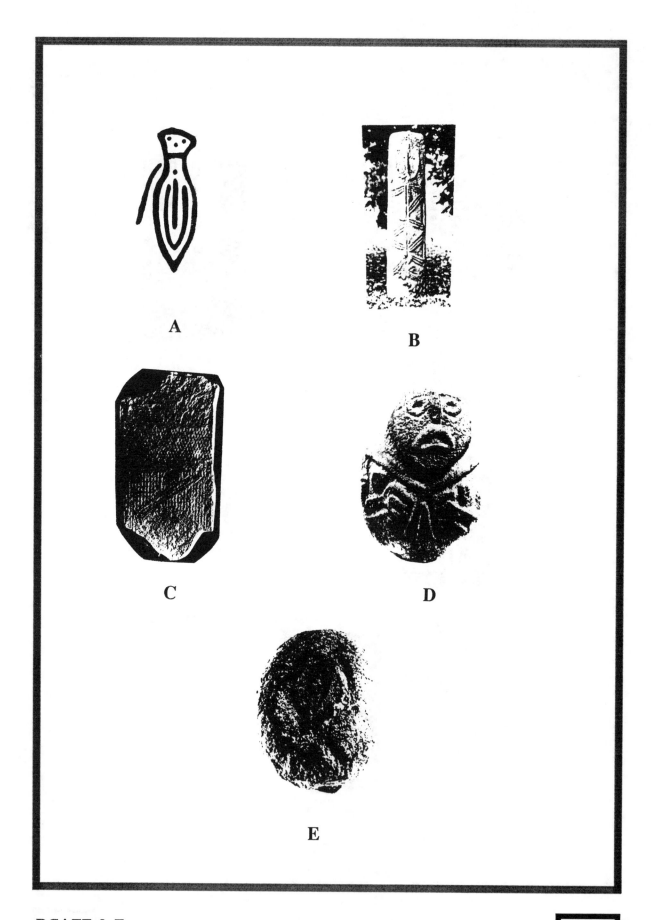

A

B

C

D

E

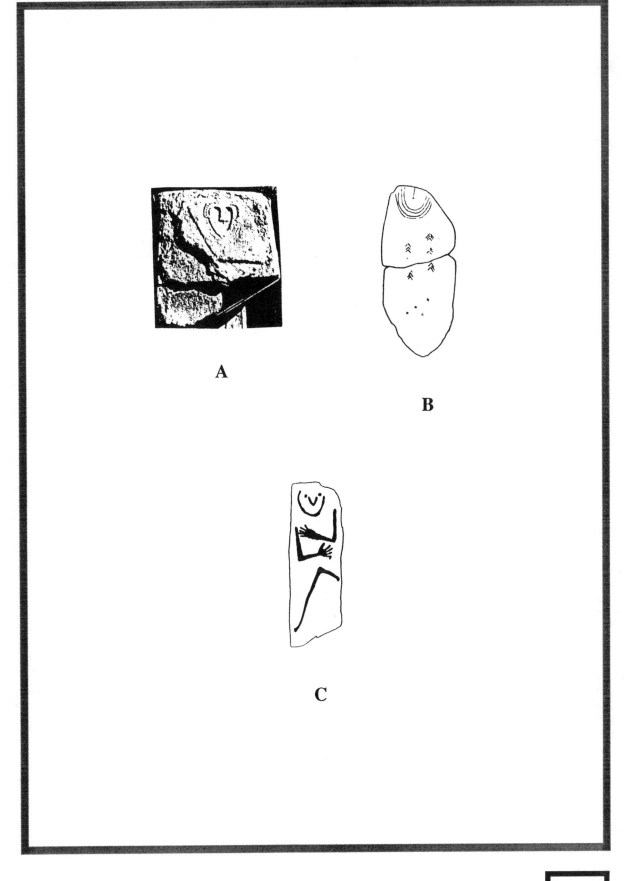

A

B

C

ARCHAEOLOGICAL TECHNIQUES, TECHNOLOGY AND THEORY

MESOLITHIC METAPHYSICS: SOME PHILOSOPHICAL ISSUES INVOLVED IN DEFINING THE MESOLITHIC PERIOD

JOHN CASTLEFORD
Department of Ethnology and Prehistory
University of Oxford
Oxford OX2 6PN, England

RESUME

Despite considerable research into mesolithic archaeology to date, no-one seems able to define what the Mesolithic Period is.

We know essentially what is meant by the term Mesolithic. We know that chronologically it follows the {alaeolithic and precedes the Neolithic, and we also know that the period essentially encompasses a hunting and gathering way of life in a relatively rapid sequence of environmental changes following climatic amelioration. So why should there be so much difficulty in providing a concise yet unequivocal definition?

Whilst this seems to be a fairly straightfortward archaeological problem, its resolution necessitates consideration of some interesting philosophical issues. Reflection on this explicitly theoretical problem warrants attention because of the implications that obtain from the search for theoretical and conceptual parameters .

I propose to examine first the general nature of the difficulties of definition, and then broaden the scope of the problem to ponder the wider view. I have no definitive answer to the problem I address, but proffer them in the earnest aspiration that, by keeping them current, they may serve to clarify thinking about the wider philosophical tenets and canons which underlie and influence the way we think.

Mesolithic Metaphysics: Some Philosophical Issues Involved in Defining the Mesolithic Period
John Castleford

INTRODUCTION

The history of Mesolithic archaeology spans some six decades, yet in all that time no-one has satisfactorily defined "Mesolithic". In recent years there has occurred a tremendous degree of interest in the Mesolithic period, and many important economic and social questions about the nature of postglacial cultural adaptations have been addressed. One would have thought, then, that the provision of a universally acceptable definition of the Mesolithic would be simple and straightforward. Not so; it actually turns out to be an intractable and implacable impasse.

This is not the first paper to discuss the difficulties of defining the Mesolithic (cf. Czarnik, 1976; Clark, 1978; Mellars, 1981; Castleford, 1986; Zvelebi, 1986). However, most of this debate focuses only on one level, that of archaeological categorisation *per se*. But the very fact that the Mesolithic is proving so difficult to define indicates that the problem has deeper roots which touch on some interesting theoretical aspects of conceptual parameters in archaeology. I contend that the nature and scope of the difficulty is such that it cannot be dealt with in purely archaeological terms. It is also epistemological, and as such pertains to how we know what we know. So what appears, on the one level, to be an exercise in archaeological semantics also acts as a metaphor for a deeper philosophical problem, and this is what I explore in this paper.

I begin by surveying the definitions of the Mesolithic period encountered in the literature to date and consider some of the complications which arise. To see how the discussion goes from there, read on...

THE QUEST FOR A DEFINITION OF THE MESOLITHIC PERIOD

The earliest [1] use of the term Mesolithic in an archaeological context is that by Torell in 1874 at a meeting in Stockholm, Sweden, of the International Congress of Anthropology and Prehistoric Archaeology.

> Le jour viendra aussi, sans nul doute, où l'on sera mis en demeure de distinguisher dans le vaste âge de la pierre une subdivision nouvelle, la periode mésolithique (Torell, 1876:876). [2]

The first appearance of the term Mesolithic in English is attributed to Hodder Westropp (1872:65) when he differentiates between the Palaeolithic ("flint implements of the gravel drift, and of the cave period, evidently used by man in his lowest and most barbarous grade") and Neolithic ages ("ground and polished stone implements which mark a more advanced stage, and which are associated with traces of a pastoral age"). The intermediate stage, termed the Mesolithic, is denoted by flint implements (the flint flakes, and the chipped flints) found on the surface in England, Ireland, Denmark, and other countries, which belonged to a people who lived by the chase (ibid).

John Allen Brown also used the term to denote stone objects intermediate between "the drift period and that of polished stone" (1893:93). The concept was slow to diffuse, however. Even though Montelius had been present at the congress when torell first introduced the notion of a new subdivision in the Stone Age, Oscar Montelius did not make use of it in his book on Swedish prehistory, even though he refers to material which we now know to be mesolithic (1888:8-11).

Not everyone had the same conceptions of prehistory as is evident from some interesting early concepts which arose at this time. For example, there were even those who were quite prepared to deny the existence of a Stone Age. In 1865 Sir John Lubbock (later Lord Avebury) cites the view of one of his contemporaries, a Mr Wright, "learned secretary of the Ethnological Society":

> there may have been a period when society was in so barbarous a state that sticks and stones were the only implements with which men knew how to furnish themselves

who then went on to doubt whether "the antiquary has yet found any evidence of such a period" (Lubbock, 1913:75). So much for close ties between anthropology and archaeology.

But, well into the twentieth century, even for a slightly more enlightened antiquary like Miles Burkitt, the evidence for the Mesolithic was still sparse, and little of worth could be inferred:

> The wonderful late palaeolithic cultures ... vanished and were replaced by a series far inferior in cultural development (1932:240).

Almost two decades later, the perception of postglacial community life as a dour and disconsolate existence had not changed much. Hawkes and Hawkes state:

> If Mesolithic adaptations show no advance on Palaeolithic cultural standards, but indeed in many ways, as in the loss of art, a decline, they did at least allow the old human stocks to survive in Europe (1949:20).

> Any modern visitor to Mesolithic Britain....would see poor little groups of hunters and food gatherers scattered round the fringes and in the clearings of the dripping forests (1949:23-24).

In discussing the evidence for postglacial culture in Europe in the mid-1950s, Childe still retained much the position he had held three decades earlier when he concluded that

> Mesolithic groups appear in general isolated and poorly equipped in contrast to the Magdalenian and Predmostians....Several of the Mesolithic cultures are clearly just the responses of Palaeolithic survivors to the new environment (1957:3).

This early view of European Mesolithic communities was one of woeful and wretched strandloopers, mere survivors from the Palaeolithic, eking out a perilous hand to mouth existence, waiting to be rescued and elevated into civilisation by influences emanating from the Orient. The assumption that there was a long cultural hiatus between the Palaeolithic and the Neolithic held universal currency until the pioneering work of Grahame Clark (1932, 1933, 1952) and others gradually began to establish the Mesolithic as an archaeological period in its own right. However, even in the recent literature, one still encounters a minimal view of the Mesolithic, as Rowley-Conwy (1986:23) observes.

The early definitions reflect a recognition that the material culture of the Mesolithic was sufficiently distinctive to be differentiated temporally from the preceding Palaeolithic and the succeeding Neolithic, but there was no attempt to imply anything in the way of genetic relationships. In both of Clark's early books on the period the use of the expression "Mesolithic" is strictly chronological (1932:2-3; 1936:xiv).

Subsequently, it became clear that the new material was correlated with environmental characteristics of the postglacial period, but the cultural significance of this was slow to surface. Childe still only ever regarded the Mesolithic folk as mere survivors from an Upper Palaeolithic way of life - a relict culture with arboreal tendencies (cf. 1931; 1940:26; 1957:9;). But eventually the occurrence in the early Holocene of rapid and widespread environmental change, and the effect it had on cultural developments, became the focus of attention. This change of emphasis marked an opportunity to move away from the somewhat sterile realms afforded by flint typology. Consequently, the new definitions became more ecologically oriented in their attempts to highlight the relationship between cultural adaptations and the environmental setting in which they occurred:

> Cultural adaptations by the resident hunter-gatherer societies to the environmental changes of the early post-Pleistocene period (Clark, 1962:100).

This type of definition became standard, and indeed, is still current:

> Chronicle of the adaptation to the late glaciation population of western Europe to the rapid ecological change which marked the Pleistocene/Holocene border (Newell, 1984:71).

Other definitions of the Mesolithic focus on cultural features. Possibly illustrative of East European attitudes generally, Dolukhanov (1979,1981) simply correlates period and pottery: theMesolithic was aceramic while the presence of pottery defines theNeolithic. In similar vein, but in contrast to David Clarke(1976) who advocated less emphasis on hunting and more on gathering, Rozoy (1984:14-15; 1986) also takes a single cultural trait -- hunting -- and equivocally characterises the Mesolithic period as "the age of Red Deer or of Bowmen", leaving the reader to decide whether the definitive characteristic should be predator or prey.

Many of the definitions on offer endeavour to stress differences between the Palaeolithic and the Mesolithic. But not everyone feels the Mesolithic Period is sufficiently dissimilar from the Upper Palaeolithic to warrant undue differentiation from it (cf. Gamble 1986). For others, the key feature of the Mesolithic Period remains solely one of chronology. Mellars (1981) suggests that the period should be defined in strictly chronological terms, beginning at 10,000±years BP (1981:14).

A final category of definitions are a blend of cultural, environmental and chronological factors. In his review of Clark's *Mesolithic Prelude* (1980), Price notes Clark's observation that the Palaeolithic and Neolithic had originally been defined by Lubbock in 1865 in terms of technology, economy and chronology, but proposes that now

> the term "Mesolithic" in Europe must simply be defined as that period of time when Postglacial hunter-gatherers occupy the Continent (of Europe) prior to the introduction of agriculture (Price, 1984:18).

Bray and Trump had already furnished something similar in their dictionary definition:

> The period of transition between the Palaeolithic and Neolithic, with persistence of the old Palaeolithic hunting and collecting way of life in the new environment created by the withdrawal of the Pleistocene ice sheets around 8300 bc (1982:156).

Note that a further ingredient, transition, is now in evidence, a point to which I shall return later.

As an alternative to the problem of juggling traits and characteristics in the search for a common denominator, Binford (1968: 317-8) presented an inventory of six features which, for him, characterised the Mesolithic period. These include changes in demographic patterns and lithic styles, greater geographicalvariety, increased exploitation of aquatic resources and small game, and a general cultural decline compared to the Upper Palaeolithic. Kolowski and Kolowski (1986:96) also define the Mesolithic Period in terms of several aspects: chronologically 8000-4500/4350 bc; ecologically and economically centred on specialised niche exploitation of postglacial forests; culturally by standardisation and microlithisation of lithic industries.

Zvelebil proposes that if the term *Mesolithic* is to be retained, then it should be "deliberately broad, yet socioeconomically meaningful" (1986:6). He then offers an extensive, but somewhat inelegant definition (perhaps descriptive portrayal is a better term), too lengthy to include here, but which articulates many of the multi-facetted features mentioned above. Whilst there will be probably be broad agreement that Zvelebil has identified accurately the principal attributes of the period, as indeed have Binford and the Kolowskis, there seems little likelihood that his discourse will be adopted as the definitive definition, although, to be fair, Zvelebil did advance his definition more as a "contributory notion"(*ibid*).

DISCUSSION

A wide variety of definitions has been encountered in this brief review. As already noted on page 1, this diversity has been subject to occasional debate from time to time (e.g. Castleford 1986 Czarnik1976; Mellars 1981; Zvelebil 1986), the keynote of which is that many of the definitions proposed were reactions to existing definitions deemed deficient and inadequate. The absence of a universal "winner", a definitive definition (with consequent immortality in the citation stakes), indicates that there are indeed considerable difficulties involved in categorising an extinct prehistoric age or phase. Attempts to elicit the ethos of the Mesolithic period have drawn on a variety of cultural and ecological factors, particularly those of a technological or economic nature.

The various definitional candidates invariably highlight some central features, but often at the expense of others. This is perhaps symptomatic of the aspiration to emulate colleagues in the natural sciences, and play the "$E = mc^2$ game" by reducing the number of words to an absolute minimum whilst still being able to provide the quintessence of the period in a simple yet elegant concept. The ultimate in reductionist approaches is reached in some quarters by those who feel that perhaps the Mesolithic is best defined simply as post-Palaeolithic and Pre-Neolithic. Here the difficulties encountered in the search for the right blend of elements are all swept aside in one fell swoop by omitting them all! Thus the Mesolithic is defined not in terms of itself, but in terms of what it is not.

In retrospect, we clearly see at work a process of reduction in which attempts are made to subsume six millennia of cultural developments within brief yet meaningful statements of the relationship between several integral elements, variously social, economic, technological and ecological. While there are certain commonalities in many of these definitions, there is no consensus and occasionally even uncertainty. The search for a universally acceptable lowest common denominator is, of course, an exercise in modelling; but although several designs have been proposed, we still lack a universally acclaimed definitive definition.

All prehistorians (and even some archaeologists) know essentially what is meant by the term "Mesolithic". Chronologically it followed the Palaeolithic and preceded the Neolithic; it encompassed a hunting and gathering way of life in the context of a relatively rapid sequence of the environmental changes following climatic amelioration, and the lithic industries became microlithic. So why should there be so much difficulty in providing a concise yet unequivocal archaeological definition of the period which would satisfy everyone?

One may feel that *ex cathedra* pronouncements from the specialists have an inherent advantage, and that the greater the distinction of the individual, the more he/she must know about that of which they speak. However, somewhat paradoxically, the most eminent mesolithicists seem to have had the most difficulty of all in furnishing a definition. Interestingly enough, it is Grahame Clark, the doyen of Mesolithic scholars, who seems most ambivalent when it comes to defining the period. In the preface to his last specialist book, *Mesolithic Prelude*, just when we might have hoped for the fitting climax to an illustrious career of musing mesolithically -- in the form of the definitive definition -- we find only references to "the Mesolithic, Archaic or intermediate phase of the stone age in the history of mankind" (1980:vii). The "Archaic" is, of course, the North American Postglacial period. Slightly earlier, he had warmed to the idea of using the term "Neothermal" to connote the period (1978). If someone as eminent as Clark should have such difficulties in defining the Mesolithic, the situation is indeed problematic.

CONTEXTUAL CONSIDERATIONS.

All ideas are a function of the intellectual milieu in which they arise, and a comprehensive appreciation of the problem being considered here necessitates a consideration of the context. There are a number of reasons why difficulties of definition have emerged, not the least of which is the relatively nascent status of mesolithic archaeology. The concept of a Mesolithic period was not a custom-built innovation but was, as Czarnik noted, merely a residual category

> utilised to embrace empirical archaeological data that could not be adequately handled by either the Palaeolithic or the Neolithic (Czarnik, 1976:60)

which was appended to existing prehistoric taxa: the Stone Age, Bronze Age and Iron Age. While this typology has never received more than grudging acceptance in recent times, it is firmly entrenched in the literature. Its continued duration is recognised generally to be of little more value than a disposable label, but its persistence obtains in the absence of a suitable replacement. Thus the first appearance of the concept of the Mesolithic was not in terms of itself, but as an implant, slotted in between Lubbock's (1913:2-3, orig. 1865) definitions of the Palaeolithic (= extinct Pleistocene fauna) which preceded it in time, and the Neolithic (= polished stone) which followed. In retrospect we can see what a shaky edifice this was.

As was common to many intellectual pursuits of the time, anthropology and archaeology in the late nineteenth century was very much the preserve of a wealthy elite of gentlefolk who were influenced by a ubiquitous undercurrent of unilinear evolution. They believed that their own social strata represented the pinnacle of human development, and that this consummate achievement had been preceded by a succession of lesser stages which marked the slow but inexorable progress upward from the lowliest form of social life: Stone Age savagery. Predicated on such canons, the archaeology being undertaken in this climate was largely concerned with the finer points of chronological detail. The nature of the past was known; the ultimate objective of archaeology was merely to chart this human progress.

The conceptual foundations of prehistory were laid down when there was obviously limited evidence to play with, and any judgments contrived in Victorian times about the structure of the phases of the past must be seen in the light of the information then available, as well as in terms of the theories which held sway. The accumulation of the evidence has generally been a process of slow accretion, and, prior to the emergence of academic archaeology, and in complete contrast to the "Information Age" in which we now live, the means for disseminating knowledge were often fragmented and infrequent. Public discourse a century ago was represented by little more than occasional meetings and intermittent publications. It was not until the increased provision of academic posts in archaeology that the evidence became more concentrated, the means to study it gradually evolved, and a more expansive view was facilitated.

The concept of a Mesolithic phase, then, did not erupt with explosive force, but grew almost imperceptively. It has taken many decades for the present corpus of evidence to accumulate, but in comparison with other prehistoric periods, such evidence is often much more subtle in character, and perhaps the attraction of Mesolithic archaeology is fully appreciated only by a discerning few. Clark provides a nice metaphor for the situation when he suggests that it can be symbolised by the hallmark of the Mesolithic, the microlith: small and insignificant (1978:3).

As noted above, many people had (and some still have) a minimal view of the period, when it comes to be contrasted with the artistic brilliance of the Palaeolithic and the revolutionary status of the Neolithic. Because the ultimate roots of the problem of defining the Mesolithic period can be traced to Thomsen's tripartite division of Stone Age, Bronze Age and Iron Age, it was predestined to flounder decades before the concept of Mesolithic had even been engendered. The preceptual foundation was shaky to begin with, and subsequent attempts to improve on earlier definitions merely compounded the problem.

WHAT NEXT ?

All the various attributes, ingredients and constituent elements of the Mesolithic period have been juggled and shuffled around in a multiplicity of combinations and permutations, but still the embodiment of the quintessence of the Mesolithic in one succinct expression remains elusive. Just as we don't seem to know "what is this thing called love" but soon discover what "love" is when we fall in it, we know what we mean when we say "Mesolithic" but we cannot provide a definition of what we mean.

So, what to do ? There would seem to be two possible avenues available. The first is more pragmatic, and basically ignores the problem, concentrating instead on more resolvable and immediate concerns of a practical day to day nature. The modern secular parallel would be concerning ourselves less with the meaning of life as the living of it. Proponents of this view would likely feel that as everyone involved "knows" what constitutes the Mesolithic, the provision of the definitive definition is merely a word game.

An alternative approach is to accept that this issue is worth considering, in which case the problem seems not so much a question of shuffling the "right" combination of words around, as examining how and why the problem has arisen. That this paper does not end here indicates that I consider the problem worth considering further. That you are still reading suggests you concur. So, instead of indulging in circumlocutory tautology by re-hashing earlier definitions, we need to expand the scope of the problem, and see it in wider terms.

We can begin by asking how necessary is it to even have a universally acceptable definition of the Mesolithic ? After all, major concepts remain undefined in other realms of social science. Psychologists have yet to arrive at a universally accepted definition of "intelligence", obliquely referring instead to "that which intelligence tests purport to measure". Similarly, anthropologists have spent much time trying to provide a single, all embracing definition of "culture", apparently without success. "Learned, patterned behaviour" (Selby, 1975) comes close to being the favoured choice to inaugurate most introductory anthropology texts, although Leslie White's offer of "an extrasomatic temporal continuum dependent on symbolling" (1959) might not be without some merit if it were not bound up in such execrable jargon. These are but two definitions of culture on offer; the interested reader will find the full narrative in Kroeber (1952) and Kroeber and Kluckhohn (1952). The *ad hoc* definition of culture is a compromise which parallels that adopted by psychologists for their definition of intelligence "culture is that which is described in ethnographic accounts".

Are the disciplines of anthropology and psychology handicapped by the lack of definitions of key concepts ? Apparently not. The burgeoning literature in anthropology and psychology attests to a dynamic disciplinary disposition, seemingly unconstrained, if not wholly indifferent to the explicit delineation of fundamental precepts so necessary in the natural sciences.

However, the social sciences and natural sciences differ in a number of ways, not the least of which is the highly variable nature of the subject matter. In social science the focus of enquiry is nothing less than humanity and all the unwieldy variation and diversity that it represents, as against a range of more unitary and constant phenomena encountered in the natural sciences. Physicists would need precisely to define "light" and "energy: but social scientist could not hope to do the same with "love" and "power".

Nevertheless, even though the demarcation of concepts is problematic in many areas of social science in general, and prehistoric archaeology in particular, it is obviously unacceptable to have words mean whatever we want them to mean. There must be some degree of concurrence, otherwise our discipline will degenerate into a semiotic morass. The more cynical reader may consider that this already characterises much of the present debate on theory in archaeology.

There are clearly conceptual parallels between "Mesolithic" and "Culture". Both elude definition, yet "Culture" and the Mesolithic Period (a specific instance of a prehistoric culture, and therefore a subset of "Culture") manifest themselves through certain recognisable phenomena. It is not difficult to recognise these manifestations when we encounter them. We recognise postglacial microliths as Mesolithic and kinship systems as cultural. Indications of such phenomena can be readily appreciated; what evades us is comprehending definitively what these are manifestations of.

Let us consider some basic epistemological issues in relation to actual archaeological data -- mesolithic manifestations -- which are often concrete in nature but may also need to be interpreted. I suggested above that all processes of categorisation is an exercise in modelling. But, as we have seen, there is no consensus in deciding which of the mesolithic ingredients should be included, and which can be left out. What is called for now, then, is a careful consideration of what genuine commonalities there are, and what is open to interpretation.

Let us take as an example the fact of the microlith. It exists physically in time and space. To this physical item we can assign certain attributes. We can recognise properties of a concrete nature: it is small, it has a particular shape, it was made from a particular lithic material in a particular way. We can associate it with other data. We can classify it according to *à priori* systems as a member of a pre-ordained class of items which share a set of given properties. Mesolithicists may debate which are the most appropriate attributes and which typological systems are the best, but all would agree that the microlith is a microlith. But what does it mean ? What do its properties signify? What are the implications of this microlith ? It is only when questions of interpretation arise that complications inexorably ensue.

CONCEPTUAL FRAMEWORKS

It has been recognised for many decades that the data of social science cannot be meaningfully interpreted except by means of an appropriate conceptual framework. As Kluckhohn observed:

> Facts only have meaning when ordered in terms of a system of categories, and any system of categories is inevitably bound up with definite assumptions about the nature of things (1936:159).

There are basically two ways of looking at the world. One can adopt either a monistic or dualistic perspective. For the monist:

> the world of appearance is the only world there is; truth, and ... reason itself (are) created by people in the course of their interaction....Man is the measure of all things (Leaf 1979:7).

Monism has widespread intellectual appeal, predicated as it is on the belief that everything can be reduced to one ultimate reality "presenting the universe as all of one piece" (Edwards 1973:176). In contrast, the dualist denies the existence of objective truths and prefers instead a deductive approach involving "concepts of form and matter which are hierarchically arranged in a series of increasingly dichotomised generalities" (Leaf 1979:9). What is the nature of reality - archaeological or otherwise? Does it have en existence independent of our perception of it ? Or not ? Whether one sides with the monist or the dualist is a matter for personal consideration, but the implications of whatever choice is made will always have a bearing.

Recourse is often made to the eyrie of objectivity, often for no better reason, apparently, than that one way out of subjective difficulties is to adopt a "more scientific" approach. But the dualistic / monistic dichotomy throws into whole question of how objective objectivity can be. Subjectively speaking.

That so many archaeologists fervently desire that archaeology be incontrovertibly elevated to the status of a science implies allegiance to "scientific principles". Most archaeologists would consider themselves scientists of a type, and Embree (1987) considers archaeology to be "the most basic science of all". Of course, it depends on what we mean by science. If we assume science to be the systematic formulation and accumulation of knowledge, and hold scientists to be those who make observations and use objective logic in pursuit of their conclusions, then archaeology can be said to be a science. But in order to understand how scientific approaches work, we need to consider the principles on which science is built, and for that we need to examine the doctrines of Descartes, for it is these which constitute the foundations of western science.

In the Cartesian scheme of things, the world is a domain of separate and alienated entities and elements. Analysis of the world therefore involves a reductive approach by studying its constituent parts. As Levins and Lewontin (1985) state:

> It is an explicit objective of Cartesian reductionism to find a very small set of independent pathways or "factors" that can be used to reconstruct a larger domain of phenomena... The error of reductionism is ... that it supposes the higher-dimensional object is somehow "composed" of its lower dimensional projections which have ontological primacy and which exist in isolation, the "natural" parts of which the whole is composed (1985:271, emphasis in original).

In case the reader is wondering what all this has to do with matters mesolithic, the threads of my argument will soon be drawn together. The point to make is simply that the Cartesian perception of things is nothing less than the notion that the world consists of the sum of its parts. But a Cartesian approach is more than merely a method, it is a perception of how the world is. [3]

Uncritical adoption of Cartesian principles will therefore have important implications. Thus, if we take the view that the Mesolithic Period can be said to be all those things which comprised it, and therefore is the sum of its parts, we are adopting a Cartesian outlook.

However, the question then arises as to how appropriate it is to break down the world into reductive elements. Obviously it is impractical to deal in totalities; the available data are far too unmanageable to be dealt with as a whole. If we accept that the world consists of the sum of its parts, then it is a tacit assumption that a representative sample of those parts will enable us to reconstruct the whole. Archaeologists certainly have the problem of taking isolated material remains and using them in order to infer the nature and structure of the cultures which produced them.

Mechanistic reduction has had considerable success in the natural sciences, and particularly so in physics and chemistry. Natural scientists tend to view natural phenomena as the consequences of the interaction of constituent parts, each with their own properties which thereby determine the shape and form of the whole. Indeed, one of the cardinal issues in contemporary physics is the search for the fundamental nature of matter (Hawking, 1988:63 ff.). But it is in molecular biology that Cartesianism has been embraced most vigorously, in the demonstration that all biological characteristics and traits are able ultimately to be reduced to protein chains and human thought to electrical impulses. Proponents of sociobiology advocate that even human behaviour has its roots in our DNA.

It is unlikely that human behaviour is epistemologically in the same camp as the normative phenomena of physics and chemistry, and therefore debatable whether the methods of hard science are appropriate in cultural settings other than those of the petri-dish variety. Clearly it is imprudent to apply uncritically Cartesian principles to all phenomena, yet those in archaeology who most fervently advocate a "scientific" approach do not always demonstrate such circumspection.

BEYOND MECHANISTIC REDUCTION

Most social scientists soon came to appreciate the limitations of Cartesianism once they recognised that their sphere of interest comprised not only individual entities, but also the relationships that obtained between them. Consequently, the next paradigmatic shift (*sensu* Kuhn [1972]) was to cybernetic principles and general systems theory. The basic premise insystems theory is that primacy is given to the integrated and interactive relationships between elements rather than the autonomous properties of the elements themselves (von Bertalanffy, 1968). The adoption of cybernetic principles in human science was, in many ways, a considerable epistemological advance, and it was not long before many archaeologists recognised the utility of regarding culture in terms of processes and systems (cf. Friedman and Rowlands, 1977).

Many archaeologists, particularly those concerned with prehistory, grasped enthusiastically the concept of ecological systems. As we know, ecological approaches in Mesolithic archaeology have been pursued with considerable success (Welinder, 1978), following the pioneering endeavours of J.G.D. Clark (1936, 1952, 1954, 1972), and, to paraphrase Gamble (1981), this paradigm has been of inestimable value in prehistoric archaeology, providing one goes a bit further than merely retrorse meteorology, getting help from palynologists and pedologists, and taking inventories of faunal specimens. Butzer (1971, 1987) and Gjessing (1980), to cite but two, contend that the most germane paradigm for archaeology is one of societies functioning in both a social and physical environment, and ecological orientations in prehistoric archaeology are now well established.

While it makes sense to regard ecological relationships as important, we should not lose sight of the fact that such relationships are only part of the story. Uncritical and injudicious application of ecological techniques borrowed wholesale from bio-geography and elsewhere is as imprudent as it is untenable, and Flannery and Marcus provide astute counsel when they advocate"neither mindless ecology nor a glorification of mind divorced from the land" (1976:383). A cultural foundation underpins all human ecological relationships.

THE CULTURAL FACTOR

What is often implied, but not always made explicit, is the cultural basis of the Mesolithic. Artefacts are often taken to be both cultural items in their own right as well as symbols of the culture in which they originated, and it is not always clear exactly how the concept of culture is being applied. But that is hardly surprising. As noted above, those who specialise in the study of culture and cultures -- anthropologists -- are seemingly unable to define "culture". In fact, as even the current state of anthropological theory will show (Barrett 1984; Leaf 1979), not only is there a lack of consensus on how to define culture, and how to deal with it, there is a widespread difference of opinion regarding even basic notions of what culture actually is. So, if anthropologists are unable to form a consensus as to the nature of contemporary culture and cultural manifestations, what hope is there for archaeologists dealing with cultural phenomena many millennia removed ? Obviously compromises have to be made between an anthropological view of culture and an archaeological one, and the notion of "material culture" reflects this.

But if we exclude even a compromise notion of culture from our concept of the Mesolithic, then we surely deny its essence. If the Mesolithic is only microliths, then it is dead in more senses than one. The cultural factor is fundamental and indispensable; it has a dynamic integrity which is central to human adaptiveness and cultural evolution. Any attempt to define the Mesolithic period has to take this firmly into account, and in practise only archaeological dinosaurs would consider divorcing the mesolithic from its cultural basis, as typological mesolithicists sometimes seem to do.

Archaeologists are obviously unable to utilise retrospective participant observation, and any inferences about mesolithic culture have to be made only indirectly. But even so, in contrast to the attitudes prevalent only a few decades ago, mesolithic folk are now being treated with the understanding they deserve. Once considered to be only chronological stop-gaps, they have now been imbued with ecological tendencies. However, as Richard Bradley noticed, social relationships did not begin until the Neolithic; the only social interactions Mesolithic folk had were with hazelnuts (1978:11). But that's not really fair, and even those who hold a minimal view of the Mesolithic agree that the period was an interval in which the human stock was able to keep going (cf. Hawkes and Hawkes,1949:20, cited above) until farming (and stockbreeding proper) could begin in earnest. One can just imagine the scene in the fringes of the dripping forests: satiated on hazel nuts and birch-bark soup (which is what you got when your arrow missed the auroch and only hit a tree), the mighty hunter rolls over and asks his mate if she wants to keep the population going. She says she'd love to, but can't because they're not supposed to have any social relations...

THE CONCEPT OF INTEGRATIVE LEVELS

I digress. If the Mesolithic was a cultural phenomenon, any representation of it has to be in analogous terms. Anthropologists, although unable to define culture, have traditionally found favour with organic analogues (cf. Sahlins and Service, 1960). An organism consists of cells, groups of cells, and organs, and the integrated nature of these constituent elements comprise a dynamic functioning, interactive system. Although an organic analogue provides a useful model, to what extent can it be employed ? The nature of the relationship between human culture and its biological base is problematic, but this question has been considered in a rarely cited paper by Novikoff (1945) which may well be of use in the context of the problem being considered here.

Novikoff's thesis is a systematic analysis of the nature of integrated levels, which from a biologist's philosophical perspective, clearly illuminates an area of some conceptual confusion. He suggests that although evolutionary processes can affect inanimate, organic and social phenomena, such progress is a function of laws which are applicable to each level at each level. The main points are worth citing at length.

> In the continued evolution of matter, new levels of increasing complexity are superimposed on the individual units by the organization and integration of these units into a single system....Each level of organization possesses unique properties of structure and behaviour, which though dependent on the properties of the constituent elements, appear only when these elements are combined in the new system. Knowledge of the laws of the lower level is necessary for a full understanding of the higher level; yet the unique properties of the higher level can not be predicted a priori, from the laws of the lower level....Full recognition of both units and whole leads to a more adequate understanding of the whole (1945:208).

Novikoff also anticipated Czarnik's point, noted above, about the need to avoid imposing a classificatory model which eclipses transitions:

> No boundary in nature are fixed, and no category air-tight. "Meso-forms" are found at the transition point of one level of organization to the next....Yet the absence of rigid demarcation between the two levels does not make the difference between them any less clear or fundamental (*ibid*).

Implicit in Novikoff's discourse is the danger of mechanistic reductionism. Properties and attributes of parts have to be seen in terms not only of the parts, but also as a consequence of their integration at a higher level. The crux of the problem, if not the key to its resolution, would seem to concern the way in which the principal mesolithic characteristics are meaningfully integrated. Parts and wholes, and the relationship that they have with each other are basic concepts with which we must deal, But perhaps the difficulty has been that "wholes" have only been thought of as an end product. It seems more sensible to think in terms of a dialectical relationship between parts and wholes, not a unitary compound. Parts are obviously parts of wholes, but, using the organic analogy above, some wholes can be seen as parts of still bigger wholes.

Using Novikoff's holistic perspective, the constituent features are not the sole problem, it is the nature of the structure of which we intend they become part. This perspective is clearly dialectical and, as such it may have the potential to signpost a way out of the impasse with which we are here concerned.

To summarise thus far then, I have briefly reviewed some of the perspectives which affect how we see the world. Whereas archaeology once dealt with available specimens, the modern synthesis now uses available and generated data -- the physical item and its properties in the context of the wider networks of integrated relationships. What were once seen as alienated parts of wholes are now regarded as systemic elements.

But difficulties remain. While the systems paradigm has been embraced by many patrons of processual archaeology, post-processual archaeology, ecological archaeology, and other assorted sects, the systems approach has not been free from a number of criticism. Principal among these seem to be the contentions that systems theory is (a) often infused with a mechanistic perspective which fails adequately to appropriate the social dimension, and (b) is tautological, in that it focuses on how systems maintain themselves, not why systems change into other systems (cf. Bender, 1978; 1981; Friedman and Rowlands, 1977; Ingold, 1981; Wiessner, 1982). Conceptual difficulties relating to structure could perhaps be ameliorated by using a concept of integrative levels, rather than a linear arrangements of systemic elements. But the overall structure needs to apprehend and be responsive to diachronic as well as synchronic phenomena.

THE NOTION OF TIME AND TRANSITIONS

Much of archaeology is concerned with describing and explaining cultural change over time, and it is now time to consider time. Mesolithic archaeology occupies a unique niche between two million years of hunting and gathering, on the one hand, and the Neolithic revolution on the other. The nature of the transition from one major system to another is clearly of pivotal concern. But, mindful of the criticisms noted above, for a systemic paradigm to work, it must have the capacity and structure to deal with both socio-cultural stasis and change.

But further epistemological difficulties may now arise, this time of a teleological nature. The thinking goes thus: because the Mesolithic changed into the Neolithic, the nature of mesolithic adaptations must have been geared towards the goals it eventually achieved. Obviously this is erroneous reasoning; mesolithic cultural behaviour cannot be envisioned as goal-directed. The Mesolithic period occupies fully half of the entire postglacial period to date, and as such had a sufficiently extensive and tangible existence to warrant being regarded as an entity in its own right, and not merely as a vehicle for change.

But if mesolithic communities were not there just to be harnessed by external forces to bring about future changes, what are we to make of the transition ? The answer remains elusive; evolutionary changes in cultural systems are problematic in general, and particularly so in the case of the Mesolithic where crucial data which impinge on the transitional process(es) are so sparse. In his analysis of the history of mesolithic archaeology, Czarnik (1976) concluded that because the Mesolithic was essentially a cultural entity in transition, and because traditional definitions focused on phenomena at a single point in time, the definitions failed to encapsulate the essence of the period. Even though it is necessary to characterise and classify the stages in an adaptive process, the very process of classification and typology involves stasis -- freezing in time -- but this inevitably conceals and eclipses the very adaptive process the characterisation is intended to encompass (Czarnik, 1976:65). A paradox is evident, added to which is the need to see the Mesolithic in terms of itself, as six millennia of adaptive stability, and not merely as the means by which change was facilitated. One possible solution would be to develop a classificatory process which emphasises the adaptive process without obscuring it. In order to design effectively a suitable classificatory apparatus we need carefully to consider the present structure of the archaeology we are intending to harness.

As Spaulding (1960) once noted, the three principal dimensions of archaeology are form, space and time, and this observation provides us with a standard definition of archaeology: the study of past cultural material distributed in space and time. I suggest that many of the epistemological difficulties have arisen because we have combined these dimensions in standard Cartesian fashion; we have not integrated them. Many of the early definitions in prehistory have been simple combinations or correlations of prominent features. For example, as was noted above, Lubbock defined the Palaeolithic by correlating Pleistocene geology and extinct fauna, and a moment's reflection will show that while these characteristics have been correctly identified as prominent and present, they do not of themselves betoken very much of the essential character of the period, although they are important aspects of it. Similarly, the presence of the Palaeolithic period as a chronological precursor to the Mesolithic period (whether genetically antecedent or not is another matter), identifies a temporal marker. The two are correlated. But is there a relationship present beyond chronological contiguity, or are the two periods merely adjoining intervals in time?

Time is a difficult concept to deal with, and perhaps chronology and the nature of time have been the least well understood of archaeology's three dimensions. As Aristotle is reputed to have said, "if I am not asked what time is, I know; if I am asked, I do not know". I suggest that by becoming period specialists archaeologists have essentially avoided dealing with the real questions of chronology. These go far beyond identifying dates, or points in time, and treat relationships between temporally distinct phenomena. Merely identifying dates only provides an heuristic framework which enables us to establish order and intervals by a labelling process. But the dates themselves do not bespeak nor treat veritable affinities and linkages. Archaeology is, by definition, concerned with time, and with events in the past. It is the archaeological identification of change over time, then, which makes archaeology what it is. Some of the most intensive archaeological interest converges on changes from one social situation to another, and the transition from hunting and gathering to food production is a classic example. Indeed much of the preoccupation with matters mesolithic is predicated on precisely this concern.

But in archaeology generally the time dimension has often been effectively disregarded, often because of the specialist nature of contemporary archaeology which is almost exclusively period-orientated. Archaeologists pigeonhole themselves as Iron-Age specialists, Medievalists or Upper Palaeolithicists. The professional shoveller in one particular region may well have to cope with a wider temporal range, but in the academic ivory towers, from whence commeth all great theoretical innovations, the period specialists sited comfortably in their specialist nests do not have to contend overmuch with the concept of time.

THE INTELLECTUAL STATE OF ARCHAEOLOGY

It would be most unkind, as well as illogical, to blame atheoretical archaeologists for not having provided the answer to a difficult theoretical problem like the nature of time and transitions. But just as historically derived ideas have to be seen in the context of the intellectual milieu which prevailed at the time, so too could the present dearth of ideas be related to the present theoretical (or atheoretical) state of the discipline.

It could be said that such is the intellectual sociology ofarchaeology that perhaps only a very few archaeologists contend overmuch with concepts of any kind and many remain mercifully bereft of the ravages of theory. It's not hard to understand why. In a discipline dominated by artefact-orientated archaeologists, the tacit assumption prevails that because they exist in a real physical sense, sherds, lithics and postholes have a real life of their own, and there is simply no need for recourse to conceptual and interpretative stances. Why contemplate epistemology when grasping a polished hand axe or some incised ceramic microlithic fragment? Why bother with how we know what we know when we know we have the artefacts in what we know to be the palm of our hand.

After all, for many archaeologists, archaeology is fundamentally about things of a material nature, and this seems implicitly to impede and inhibit inroads into ideational realms. There seems to be something mutually exclusive about the world of things and the world of ideas. And that too is a Cartesian principle from which one can trace the origin of the dichotomy of the material and the ideational. Often, carefully and effectively insulated from intellectual cross-fertilisation with such other social scientists as anthropologists, sociologists and human geographers, many archaeologists decline to commune with the conceptual and concentrate instead on material realities.

Those who do have theoretical tendencies within the discipline are often perceived to be little more than voluble jargon-vendors, and certainly, their case is not helped by a predilection for big words when small ones will do. Interesting ideas occasionally do emerge, however, but while intellectual eunuchs hold sway, theoretical arenas remain relatively sparsely populated [4], in contrast to other disciplines in the social sciences, where theoretical endeavours are pursued far more vigorously.

But all is not lost. The situation in prehistoric archaeology is less affected by these difficulties than seems to the case in other branches of archaeology such as classical archaeology, where there often exists a hierarchical structure headed by established scholars immersed in entrenched scholastic traditions. This invariably conditions and constrains the thinking of subordinates who spend long periods in indentured apprenticeship before being allowed to exercise any degree of independent control of their own (cf. Hanbury-Tenison, 1986:110).When finally possessed of sufficient seniority, the conditioning process has had its effect.

In contrast to classical archaeology, barbarian archaeology appears to be more liberated and less constrained. Prehistorians, not unlike the hunter-gatherers they study, seem to be more egalitarian, more independent, and freer to develop and implement their own approaches and strategies. Additionally, hunter-gatherer contexts are generally less encumbered by the sociological complexities associated with later archaeological periods. Furthermore, the literature on hunter-gatherer archaeology is less extensive, and a wider number of methodological and theoretical approaches are represented (cf. Bailey, 1983; Sheridan and Bailey, 1981; Wobst, 1983). There may be difficulties of the sort with which this paper is concerned, but that in itself attests to a healthy state of intellectual opportunity. So even though the problem prevails, we can remain optimistic for its resolution. For ideas to germinate and flourish, there has to be a suitable intellectual climate. That archaeological theory is lacking attests to the sequacious disposition of the discipline overall as well as flaws in the present state of the theoretical offerings themselves. To summarise the point then: it's all very good in practise, but will it work in theory ? And do we care? But we must not be dogmatic!!

CONCLUSION

There will be no conclusion. The problem remains. I end this paper, but hopefully not the debate, with the original question unanswered.

How can the diagnostic features of the Mesolithic be integrated into a corpus or entity that both defines the period in terms of itself and the processes which gave rise to genetic relationships with antecedents and subsequent cultural entities ?

For there to be any hope of success we need to establish exactly what we want the Mesolithic to be. The Mesolithic no longer survives as itself. The past is, by definition, past, and it is one of the great myths of archaeology that the past can reconstructed. The Mesolithic was once alive, and dynamic, but no longer. What is alive is the array of concepts shared by prehistorians which embody the period. Just as a bottle of liquid can be both half full and half empty at the same time, so too can different notions and concepts be applied to both the symbols of the past which survive to the present and the attributes we impose upon them. Just as history belongs to those that write it, the Mesolithic can only ever be what we consider it to be. Mesolithic archaeology is very much an activity of the present, and one can always hold out hope for a general consensus, but archaeologists can never hold in common a single and unitary set of ideas about what happened in the past: too many different perspectives are available. Similarly, there never was, nor ever could have been a single, unitary perception by Mesolithic people as to the nature of their social milieu; every individual has a unique perception of the world, and just as our world is 'all things to all men', so too the Mesolithic, notwithstanding a common fund of ideals, mores rules and traditions, would have differed from individual to individual, from group to group, and from area to area. Consequently, while there may be commonalities in technology, and such features of social organisation as are detectable from the few remaining items of mesolithic material culture, interpretations of the archaeological record will always be problematic (cf. Binford, 1986).

The problem of taking isolated material remains and using these to infer the nature and structure of the cultures which produced them involves a complex range of perspectives, but the question remains - which ones are the most appropriate for our purposes?

There are many avenues we could pursue; my own preference is for something akin to Darwinian principles of hereditability using more of an evolutionary approach to mesolithic archaeology (cf. Mithen, 1989, but on its own terms, and not as a reaction to perceived mis-perceptions of others). After all, one of the characteristic features of the Mesolithic was adaptiveness, and adaptations are central to evolutionary processes. If cultural systems can be dealt with in terms of behavioural choices that have been selected for, and if we can find a way of utilising such principles archaeologically, then perhaps we can move closer to apprehending more clearly the essential meaning of the mesolithic by utilising an evolutionary perspective. But that is a task for the future.

Although the lack of a vibrant intellectual tradition in archaeology may be an accessory to the problem of definition and epistemology, suffice it so say that this, of itself, is no bar to potential resolution of the problems; indeed, anyone who cares to attempt a solution will have precious little competition.

However, the process of defining something necessarily involves setting out precise limits. The absence of a definitive definition for a complex interactive phenomenon like the Mesolithic ensures that it has not been reduced to a lowest common denominator. Mesolithic archaeology does not appear to have been unduly constrained by the lack of a definition for the period. But the quest for one has led to some useful insights.

ACKNOWLEDGEMENTS

As an impecunious student I was unable to attend the 1989 Deià conference, present this paper, and cure the delgates' insomnia. I'm very grateful to Bill Waldren to allow me (so much) space in which to set out these ideas.

NOTES

1- There is an earlier reference; Roy Lankester (1867:12) uses the word in a geological context when he speaks of "The Mesolithic or Mesozoic period" in Haekel's *History of Creation* II, xv:12.

2- My Translation: The day will come, without a doubt, that one will be in a position to distinguish within the vast stone age a new subdivision, the Mesolithic period.

3- Parenthetically, Descartes may have been building on a philosophy that was already current, and had been so for centuries. Thomas Aquinas, in his *Summa Theologica* (1265) introduced the literary techniques which prevail today. Complex thoughts are successively broken down into component elements, and presented in a literary form which parallels the organisation of thought: book, chapter, section, paragraph, sentence. The literary devices we use to convey our thoughts themselves serve to both influence and reflect the organisation of thought, and have done so for many centuries.

4- How many archaeologists have actually read Analytical Archaeology? Be honest!

404

REFERENCES

Aquinas,Thomas, 1981. (Orig.1275) *Summa Theologica*. (Translated by F. Copplestone). Middlesex: Penguin Books.

Bailey, Geoff, (ed.) 1983. *Hunter Gatherer Economy in Prehistory*. Cambridge, Cambridge University Press.

Barrett, Stanley, 1984. *The Rebirth of Anthropological Theory*. Toronto University Press.

Bender, Barbara, 1978. Gatherer-Hunter to farmer: a social perspective. *World Archaeology* 10, pp. 205-222.

Bender, Barbara, 1981.Gatherer-Hunter intensification. In *Economic Archaeology* (eds. Alison Sheridan and Geoff. Bailey), pp. 149-157, Oxford: British Archaeological Report No.96.

Bertanffly, L. von,1968. *General Systems Theory*, New York.

Binford, Lewis R.,1968. Post-pleistocene adaptations. In *New Perspectives in Archaeology* (eds. Lewis Binford and Sally Binford), pp. 313-341. Chicago: Aldine.

Binford, Lewis R.,1986. Data, relativism and Archaeological Science. *Man* 22:391-404.

Bradley, Richard, 1978. *The Prehistoric Foundations of Britain*., London: Routledge and Kegan Paul.

Bray, Warwick and David Trump, 1982. *The Penguin Dictionary of Archaeology* (2nd ed.), Harmondsworth, Middlesex: Penguin Books.

Brown, J. Allen, 1893. On the Continuity of the Palaeolithic and Neolithic periods. *Journal of the Royal Anthropological Institute* XXII:66-98.

Burkitt, Miles, 1932. *The Old Stone Age*. Cambridge: Cambridge University Press.

Butzer, K., 1971. *Environment and Archaeology*. Chicago: Aldine.

Butzer, K., 1987. *Archaeology as Human Ecology*. Cambridge: Cambridge University Press.

Brown, J Allen, 1893. On the Continuity of the Palaeolithic and Neolithic periods. *Journal of the Royal Anthropological Institute* XXII:66-98.

Castleford, John, 1986. Away from a definition of the Mesolithic. *Mesolithic Miscellany* 7 (2):1-3.

Childe, V. G, 1931. The forest cultures of northern Europe: a study in evolution and diffusion. *Journal of the Royal Anthropological Institute* 61:328-328.

Childe, V. G, 1940. *Prehistoric Communities of the British Isles*. Edinburgh: W. & R. Chambers.

Childe, V. G, 1957.*The Dawn of European Civilization*. London: Routledge & Kegan Paul.

Clark, J. Grahame, 1932. *The Mesolithic Age in Britain*. Cambridge: Cambridge University Press.

Clark, J. Grahame, 1936. *The Mesolithic Settlement of Europe*. Cambridge: Cambridge University Press.

Clark, J. Grahame, 1952. *Prehistoric Europe: the Economic Basis*. Methuen: London.

Clark, J. Grahame, 1954. *Star Carr*. Cambridge: Cambridge University Press.

Clark, J. Grahame, 1956. *Prehistoric Europe: The Economic Basis*. Stanford University Press.

Clark, J. Grahame, 1962. A survey of the Mesolithic phase. In The Prehistory of Europe and South-west Asia, pp. 97-111. Atti VI Congresso Internazionale Scienze Preistoriche e Protostoriche, Rome.

Clark, J. Grahame, 1978. Neothermal Orientations. In *The Early Post Glacial Settlement of Northern Europe* (ed. P. A. Mellars), pp. 1-10.London, Duckworth.

Clark, J. Grahame,1980. *Mesolithic Prelude*. Edinburgh University Press.

Clarke, David L.,1976. *Mesolithic Europe: The Economic Basis*. In Problems in Economic and Social Archaeology (eds. G. de G. Sieveking, I. H. Longworth and K. E. Wilson), pp.449-481. London: Duckworth.

Czarnik, Stanley, 1976. The Theory of the Mesolic in European Archaeology. *Proceedings of the American Philosophical Society* 120 (1):59-66.

Dolukhanov, P., 1979. *Ecology and Economy in Neolithic Eastern Europe*. London: Duckworth.

Edwards, Paul and Arthur Pap, 1973. *A Modern Introduction to Philosophy*. London: Free Press.

Embree, Lester, 1987. Archaeology: the most basic science of all. *Antiquity* 61:75-8.

Flannery, K., and J. Marcus, 1976. Formative Oaxaca and the Zapotec cosmos. *The American Scientist* 64:374-383.

Friedman, Jonathan and Michael J. Rowlands, 1977. *The Evolution of Social Systems*. London: Duckworth.

Gamble, Clive, 1981. Review of R. Foley, (1981) Off-site Archaeology and Human Adaptation in Eastern Africa. Cambridge Monographs in African Archaeology No. 3. Oxford, British Archaeological Reports, International Series 97, *Proceedings of the Prehistoric Society* 48:529-530.

Gamble, Clive, 1986. The mesolithic sandwich: ecological approaches and the archaeological record of the early postglacial. In *Hunters in Transition* (ed. M. Zvelebil), pp. 33-42. Cambridge: Cambridge University Press.

Gjessing, G., 1980. Ideas around prehistoric societies. *Norwegian Archaeological Review* 13 (2):119-120.

Hanbury-Tenison, J., 1986. Hegel in prehistory. *Antiquity* 60:108-114.

Hawkes, C.F.C. and J. Hawkes, 1949. *Prehistoric Britain*. London: Chatto and Windus.

Hawking, Stephen,1988. *A Brief History of Time*. London: Guild Publishing.

Ingold, Tim, 1981. The hunter and his spear: notes on the cultural mediation of social and ecological systems. In *Economic Archaeology* (eds. Alison Sheridan and Geoff. Bailey), pp. 119-1130, Oxford: British Archaeological Report No. 96.

Kluckhohn, Clyde, 1939. Some reflections on the method and theory of the Kulturkreislehre. *American Anthropologist* 38(2):157-196.

Kroeber, Alfred, 1952. *The Nature of Culture*. Chicago: University of Chicago Press.

Kroeber, Alfred and Clyde Kluckhohn, 1952. Culture: a critical review of concepts and definitons. *Papers of the Peabody Museum of American Archaeology and Ethnology*, vol XLVII, No. 1. Harvard University.

Koslowski, Janus K. and Stefan Koslowski, 1986. Foragers of Central Europe and their acculturation. In *Hunters in Transition* (ed. M. Zvelebil), pp. 95-108. Cambridge: Cambridge University Press.

Kuhn, T., 1972. *The Structure of Scientific Revolutions*. Chicago: University of Chicago Press.

Leaf, Murray, 1979. *Man, Mind and Science*. New York: Columbia University Press.

Levins, Richard and Richard Lewontin, 1985. The *Dialectical Biologist*. New York: Academic Press.

Lubbock, Sir John, (Lord Avebury) 1913. (orig 1865) *Prehistoric Times*. London: Williams and Norgate.

Mellars, Paul, 1981. Towards a definition of the Mesolithic. *Mesolithic Miscellany* 2 (2):13-16.

Mithen, Steven, 1989. Evolutionary theory and post-processual archaeology *Antiquity* 63:483-494.

Montelius, Oscar,1888. *The Civilisation of Sweden in Heathen Times*. London: MacMillan.

Newell, R.,1984. On the Mesolithic contribution to the social evolution of Western European society. In *Contributions to Social Evolution* (ed. John Bintliff) pp. 69-82. Bradford: University of Bradford Press.

Novikoff, Alex, 1945. The concept of integrative models in biology. *Science* 101 (2618): 209-215.

Price, T. D., 1984. Review of Grahame Clark's Mesolithic Prelude (Edinburgh University Press, 1980), in *Mesolithic Miscellany* 5(1):15-19.

Rowley-Conwy, Peter, 1986. Between cave painters and crop planters: aspects of the temperate European Mesolithic. In *Hunters inTransition*, (ed. Marek Zvelebil) pp. 17-32. Cambridge: Cambridge University Press.

Selby, Henry, 1975. *Social Organization: Symbol, Structure and Setting*. Dubuque, Iowa: W.C. Brown.

Sahlins, Marshall and Elman Service, (eds.),1960. *Evolution and Culture*. Ann Arbor: University of Michigan Press.

Rozoy, Jean-Georges, 1984. The age of red deer or bowmen. *Mesolithic Miscellany* 3 (1):14-15.

Sheridan, Alison and Geoff Bailey, (eds.), 1981. *Economi Archaeology*. Oxford: British Archaeological Report No. 96.

Spaulding, Albert, 1960. The dimensions of archaeology. In *Essays in the Science of Culture in Honor of Leslie A. White* (eds. G. Dole and R. Carneiro), pp.437-456, New York: Thomas Crowell.

Torrell, M. Otto, 1876. Sur les traces plus anciennes de l'existence de l'Homme en Suede. *Congrès International D'Anthropologie & D'Archaéologie Préhistoriques.* Compte Rendu 7e session, Vol II. Stockholm: Imprimerie Centrale 1876.

White, Leslie, 1949. *The Science of Culture*. New York: Grove Press.

Welinder, Stig. 1978. The concept of "ecology" in Mesolithic research. In *Early Post Glacial Settlement of Northern Europe* (ed. P. A. Mellars), pp. 11-25. London, Duckworth.

Westropp, Hodder M.,1872. *Prehistoric Phases*. London: Bell and Daldy.

Wiessner, P., 1982. Beyond Willow Smoke and Dogs' Tails: a comment on Binford's analysis of hunter-gatherer systems. *American Antiquity* 47 (19):171-178.

Winnick, Charles, 1977. *Dictionary of Anthropology*. Totowa, New Jersey: Littlefield & Adams.

Wobst, Martin,1983. Palaeolithic archaeology: some problems with form, space and time. In *Hunter Gatherer Economy in Prehistory*, (ed. Geoff. Bailey), pp. 220-225. Cambridge, Cambridge University Press.

Zvelebil, Marek, 1986 Mesolithic prelude and neolithic revolution. In *Hunters in Transition*, (ed. Marek Zvelebil) pp. 5-15. Cambridge: Cambridge University Press.

ARCHAEOLOGICAL TECHNIQUES, TECHNOLOGY AND THEORY

LOS MILLARES: NUEVAS PERSPECTIVAS

ANTONIO ARRIBAS PALAU and FERNANDO MOLINA
University of the Balearics, Palma, Mallorca and University of Granada, Granada, Spain.

RESUME

This paper attempts to explain the processes of changes that took place in the Almerian Culture during the Later Neolithic and finishing with the highly stratified societies of the Bronze Age (Culture of the El Argar). Various hypotheses over the years have been put forward to explain these changes. Most of the explanations for socialogical or economic change in the southeast have included colonial or evolutionary considerations reinforced by other theoretical concepts or processes such as functionalism, marxism or cultural materialism.

The majority of these in turn have been derived from evidence of climatic alterations that took place from the III millenium forward in the southeast, and have been interpreted as projections of past geographic patterns and environmental conditions. Such theories have leaned heavily on this evidence as the major determinants in the social process and other development in the area. In contrast, other more direct alternatives have been suggested, where the processes of change have been reduced to single major factors: capitalisation or control of a subsistence economy based on the regulation, development of metallurgy and intercommunal competition, etc. This paper examines the difficulties and shortcomings of most of these hypotheses, especially when taken in consideration with new evidence.

Los Millares: Nuevas Perspectivas
A. Arribas Palau y F. Molina

Con la idea de explicar el proceso de cambio que desde la Cultura de Almería, durante el Neolítico final, alcanza hasta las sociedades fuertemente estratificadas de la Edad del Bronce (cultura de El Argar) en los últimos años se han sugerido varias hipótesis. Frente a la propuesta explicativa de las *colonias* las hipótesis *evolucionistas* han buscado el apoyo d e argumentaciones teóricas más explícitas para el desarrollo cultural del Sudeste desde unas perspectivas funcionalistas, marxistas o materialistas culturales (1).

La mayor parte de ellas han partido de la evidencia climática, proyectando hacia el III milenio a.C. los patrones geográficos y medioambientales actuales del Sudeste y se han apoyado en los condicionantes ecológicos como determinantes del proceso social. Por otra parte las alternativas que se presentan suelen reducir a un sólo factor principal la explicación del proceso de cambio: capitalización o control de una economía subsistencial basada en el regadío, desarrollo de la metalurgia, competencia intercomunal, etc.

Así se hacen evidentes las debilidades empíricas cuando se soslayan aspectos tales como:

1) los resultados de los estudios faunísticos ya publicados que ponen de relieve la abundancia en la zona durante la Edad del Cobre, de animales salvajes cuyo biotopo contrasta radicalmente con el del paisaje desértico actual y

2) el desarollo durante la Edad del Cobre de modelos de poblamiento muy semejantes a los del Sudeste (Cultura de Vilanova de San Pedro) en regiones que, ni por su situación geográfica ni por su ecología actual pudieron sufrir unas condiciones climáticas rigurosas.

Dentro de esta problemática hemos programado un Proyecto de Investigación que, partiendo de un principio similar al de las propuestas *evolucionistas* previas - la autonomía de la Edad de Cobre del Sudeste peninsular -, se apoya en una hipótesis multivariable para explicar el proceso que tuvo lugar en el Sudeste durante la Prehistoria Reciente.

En líneas generales las evidencias del registro arqueológico de las que hemos partido son las siguientes:

1) el medio ambiente de la región ha cambiado sustancialmente en los últimos milenios;

2) presión del progresivo crecimiento demográfico que, a tenor del número de yacimientos arqueológicos, se observaba en las regiones bajas del Almería desde el Neolítico final a la Edad del Bronce.

3) posible jerarquización del poblamiento en la época del Cobre, según la clara diferenciación en dimensiones y complejidad de los asentamientos.

4) nuclearización del poblamiento y cierto control del territorio a nivel de unidades regionales.

5) desarrollos desiguales en el poblamiento, teniendo en cuenta la existencia de campos megalíticos dolménicos situados en los alrededores de núcleos como Los Millares con necrópolis concentradadas de sepulturas circulares (tholoi).

6) especialización artesanal en sectores económicos no subsistenciales, como es el caso del sector de la metalurgia.

7) importante intercambio a nivel inter e intraregional.

8) posible inicio de la descomposición del sistema social igualitario a lo largo de la Edad del Cobre, con la aparición y desarrollo de elites, acaso linajes, que tuvieron un acceso diferenciado a la riqueza, según se desprendía no sólo del análisis de la necrópolis de Los Millars, realizado por R. Chapman, sino de la existencia de grandes obras de carácter público en este yacimiento.

A partir de estas variables elaboramos una hipótesis explicativa de la dinámica prehistórica del Sudeste, implicando en el proceso diversos factores causales como la demografía, la explotación de recursos no subsistenciales, la nuclearización del poblamiento con la aparición de asentamientos centrales que comenzarán a dirigir el proceso, el desarrollo de la desigualdad y acceso diferenciado al status y a la riqueza y, por último, el desarrollo desigual de poblaciones vecinas que mantienen estructuras económicas muy distintas.

La medida de la importancia de cada uno de estos factores, su interrelación y la adecuación del proceso en todas sus fases son los principales elementos que tienen que ser contrastados en el desarrollo de este Proyecto.

METODOLOGIA Y ACTUACIONES

El análisis se ha establecido en tres ámbitos distintos:

a) Dos grandes áreas regionales (cuenca del rio Andarax en las tierras bajas de Almería y el pasillo de Cúllar-Baza/Chirivel/Vélez Rubio en la zona más oriental de la Alta Andalucía) son el marco regional de amplitud obligada cuando se desea analizar procesos de cambio cultural. Fenómenos tales como la distribución del poblamiento, cambios demográficos, explotación de recursos específicos como la minería y el comercio quedarían oscurecidos en el caso de que se limitara el análisis a territorios reducidos.

b) Varias unidades geográficas de extensión limitada, resultantes de la división de las dos áreas regionales, cuya prospección sistemática posibilita el estudio de patrones de asentamiento, ordenaciones del poblamiento, distribución de recursos potenciales, adaptaciones a nichos ecológicos concretos, etc.

c) Estudio de yacimientos concretos y de su área de captación, seleccionando dos de ellos (Los Millares y El Malagón) que son objeto de excavación sistemática y un número mayor que será motivo de sondeos estratigráficos con el fin de contrastar los desarrollos secuenciales y obtener muestreos con miras a la reconstrucción paleoambiental de cada área.

A continuación indicamos los tipos de actuación realizados a lo largo de los últimos años, explicando sus planteamientos metodológicos básicos.

Tres tipos de PROSPECCION SISTEMATICA han sido utilizados:

A. *Prospección selectiva* Las áreas prospectadas han sido:

    a) estuario y curso bajo del rio Andarax (1985, 1986).

    b) curso alto del Andarax (1986).

    c) pasillo de Chirivel/Cúllar-Baza (1985).

    d) región de los Vélez (1986-1987) (2).

Metodología: Partiendo de un cuerpo de hipótesis previas, diferenciadas según la época, acerca de los rasgos geográficos, geológicos y espaciales esperados en la distribución de los asentamientos, la prospección se ha centrado en aquellos puntos o áreas donde se presupone la existencia potencial de yacimientos. A una mayor rapidez y menor costo de la prospección se ha unido una menor representatividad de la muestra obtenida, como mayor inconveniente de este tipo de actuación. Valga como ejemplo la prospección realizada en 1985, en la margen derecha del rio Andarax, que proporcionó 44 yacimientos - prehistóricos e ibero-romanos - que representan una densidad aprox. de 0,2 yacimientos por km^2.

B. *Prospección intensiva.* Las áreas prospectadas han sido:

    a) pasillo de Tabernas (1985-1987).

    b) Rambla de Gergal (1987).

    c) pasillo de Fiñana (1987) (3).

Metodología: Supone la aplicación de una analítica de muestreo al estudio del territorio, con una metodología explícita a nivel de la cobertura del terreno y de la recuperación del material, siguiendo los siguientes pasos:

    1) selección en el territorio a estudiar de diversas áreas de prospección de dimensiones limitadas, atendiendo a espacios geométricos "transects" rectangulares, de 2 a 4 km. de anchura o naturales (p.ej. ramblas o valles).

    2) utilización de una sistema de cobertura exhaustiva del área prospectada, mediante recorridos longitudinales paralelos que mantienen una equidistancia de unos 50 a 75 m.

    3) recuperación sistemática de la información en cada uno de los yacimientos localizados mediante la aplicación de una ficha con diversas variables geográficas, ecológicas y morfológicos y con un sistema de registro exhaustivo del material superficial, recogido según sistemas de muestro.

    4) se ha procurado tomar en consideración las transformaciones geomorfológicas en los asentamientos y los fenómenos erosivos y antrópicos que han afectado a los mismos. Como ejemplo, la prospección realizada en el pasillo de Tabernas durante 1985 proporcionó 142 yacimientos que suponen una densidad de 1,3 por km^2.

C. *Prospección de fuentes de materias primas.* Areas propectadas: a) pasillo de Chirivel/Cúllar-Baza (rocas silíceas: 1985-1987; rocas no silíceas: 1985-1986) (4).

Este tipo de actuaciones encaminado a la localización de las fuentes de suministro y estudio de las áreas de captación de rocas silíceas necesarias para la talla y rocas no silíceas utilizadas para la fabricación de utensilios de piedra no tallada, ha contado con sus propios estrategias y técnicas operativas que, por su complejidad, no vamos a reseñar aquí.

En CONCLUSION estos trabajos han dado por resultado la documentación de una gran variabilidad en los patrones de asentamiento y cultura material de las poblaciones que ocupan el Sudeste durante la Edad del Cobre. A "grosso modo" se distinguen dos tipos de asentamientos:

1) poblados tipo Los Millares, fortificados, situados en las zonas bajas de los rios, en los que las necrópolis con sepulcros de camara circular aparecen concentradas y

2) poblados de pequeñas dimensiones, asociados a necrópolis dispersas de tipo dolménico, con sepulcros de corredor de planta trapezoidal, rectangular o poligonal. Muy sugestiva, por sus ricas implicaciones, es la constatación de que el territorio de Los Millares queda compartido por diversos grupos de poblaciónes contemporáneas con rasgos bien diferenciados.

Los SONDEOS ESTRATIGRAFICOS Y EXCAVACIONES SISTEMATICAS han estado centrados en los siguientes yacimientos:

a) Los Millares (1985, 1987);

b) El Malagón (1986);

c) Cerro de la Virgen (1986);

d) Cerro de los López (1986).

PROGRAMA DE EXCAVACION EN LOS MILLARES

Presentamos a continuación el programa metodológico utilizado en Los Millares (5), exclusivamente. Dicho programa se ha estructurado a partir de los pasos siguientes:

1) Planteamiento de cortes muy amplios, que en una primera fase han sido rebajados superficialmente, dejando al descubierto la capa superior de los derrumbes y depósitos sedimentarios no removidos, así como el techo de las construcciones. Con esta actuación se posibilita la definición y visión de los rasgos estructurales esenciales del espacio arqueológico.

2) En una segunda fase se han replanteado las zonas motivo de excavación, rebajándose en profundidad pequeños sectores. Con ello se ha pretendido documentar la secuencia y los rasgos esenciales de la sedimentación arqueológica.

3) Excavación en extensión. En una fase siguiente de excavación se ha utilizado un programa de registro diferenciado, distinguiendo entre espacios estructurales cerrados (torres, viviendas etc.) y espacios abiertos. En los primeros la superficie interna se ha dividido al menos en cuatro cuadrantes, cuya excavación ha permitido la obtención de dos secciones estratigráficas perpendiculares. Se ha intentado aislar techo y base de cada una de las unidades sedimentarias y se ha extremado la recogida de información sobre sus componentes materiales (industrias y ecofactos). En las áreas abiertas los espacios se han dividido en sectores regulares, localizándose tridimensionalmente sólo aquéllos

elementos que ofrecen un mayor potencial informativo. En algunos sectores se han aislado techo y base, mientras que en otros se ha trabajado con alzadas artificiales.

4) Con este programa se han logrado aislar diversos espacios conductuales, que ofrecen distribuciones materiales características y diferenciadas y que proporcionan un alto potencial inferencial sobre los patrones de comportamiento desarrollados en el interior del asentamiento. Quedan de esta manera aislados espacios domésticos, áreas de producción especializada, zonas de paso, vertederos etc.

RESULTADOS GENERALES

La fase I de investigación, cuyo término está previsto para 1989, ha tenido como finalidad principal el estudio de los sistemas de fortificación en tanto en cuanto representan las lineas maestras de la distribución espacial en el poblado.

Se han obtenidos datos en especial en estructuras cercanas a los cortes de la muralla exterior, con respecto a viviendas y a zonas especializadas en activadades de trabajo y zonas públicas.

La organización del poblado:

a) *Los sistemas de defensa:* Desde 1978 hemos venido trabajando en este campo de actuación y son ya numerosas las publicaciones en las que hemos expuesto los resultados obtenidos. En síntesis han quedado al descubierto cuatro lineas de murallas, de las cuales la exterior y de mayor perímetro se ha investigado en su totalidad. La presencia de varios bastiones, el complejo sistema de puerta y barbacana con saeteras y la existencia de un foso delante de la muralla son los resultados más notables de estas actuaciones.

b) *Zona de vivienda:* Las cabañas con zócalo de planta circular situadas en el interior del poblado y que se han descubierto en la fase de estudio de los sistemas de defensa, adjuntas a la muralla exterior unas y dispersas por las terrazas interiores otras, atestiguan su función como lugares de vivienda por la presencia de hogares, recintos adosados y de molinos. En la II fase de nuestro Proyecto se prevé la intensificación del estudio sistemático de las viviendas del interior del poblado.

c) *Los fortines.* El descubrimiento de un buen número de fortines situados en la linea de colinas que domina el poblado y los trabajos realizados en el mayor y más completo de ellos (Fortín no. 1) permite en la actualidad asegurar que sus funciones fuéron de indole varia:

1) De defensa y de control visual, como queda atestiguado en la reconstrucción con bastiones (con sus saeteras), puertas y fosos profundos cortados en la roca.

2) De control de áreas de producción agrícola de la zona de Los Millares, situados en zonas de barrancas con aterrazamientos naturales que permiten el mejor control del agua de lluvia, en cultivos de secano. Acaso la producción quedó suplementada con pequeñas huertas de regadío, cuya importancia, a juzgar por los datos que se han obtenido respecto al paleoambiente, no debe ser enfatizada.

3) De vivienda y de molienda de cereal y almacenamiento del mismo así como también de centro de re-distribución.

La especialización artesanal:

Con los datos obtenidos en el registro arqueológico de Los Millares creemos estar en condiciones de demostrar la existencia de una creciente división sectorial del trabajo durante la Edad del Cobre.

La complejidad en la manufactura de ciertos productos como p.ej. los objetos de cobre arsenicado, determinadas cerámicas de lujo, como las denominadas "de superficie anaranjada", o los campaniformes de carácter local que sustituyen a los marítimos de importación), las estatuillas antropomorficas de marfíl, hueso y alabastro, etc. se pueden interpretar como muestras de una clara producción de carácter artesanal.

Los tipos de hallazgos esperados en el caso de la existencia de una producción artesanal son:

    1) talleres o áreas especializadas para dichas actividades.

    2) equipos de utillaje especializado.

    3) áreas dedicadas al almacenamiento de los productos.

    4) explotación regular de recursos concretos.

    5) intercambio y comercio de los productos elaborados (6).

Estas expectativas se han cumplido ostensiblemente en el caso de la producción metalúrgica y, hasta el momento, sólo en parte en la producción de la cerámica artística y de las figurillas antropomorfas.

Producción metalúrgica:

Se han iniciado los trabajos preliminares del amplio Proyecto de Investigación Arqueo-metalúrgica, planteado en colaboración con el Institute for Archaeometallurgical Studies del Institute of Archaeology de Londres y el British Museum, con el análisis de unas 200 piezas metálicas procedentes de distintas excavaciones realizadas por el Departamento de la Universidad de Granada (7).

Estos análisis proporcionan ya importantes inferencias sobre el inicio y el desarrollo de la metalurgia en el Sudeste. Entre otros resultados se plantean argumentos de peso para demostrar el carácter intencional de la aleación del cobre y el arsénico. En el caso concreto de El Malagón las 14 piezas manufacturadas que han sido analizadas ofrecen siempre porcentajes de arsénico que oscilan entre un 0,55 y 3,5%.

El análisis de trozos de mineral y de fragmentos calentados de malaquita, demuestra que el cobre existente en los filones situados junto al yacimiento no contiene arsénico. Esto sugiere un enriquecimiento intencionada de arsenico, que puede bien demostrada con respecto a la metalurgia de la Cultura de El Argar. Aquí, las hojas de los puñales muestran siempre un incremento notable en el porcentaje de arsénico que alcanza entre un 4 y un 6%, frente al 1-3% existente en las restantes piezas, incluídos los remaches de estos mismo puñales.

La envergadura de las actividades metalúrgicas realizadas en Los Millares es evidente si analizamos los datos que han proporcionada las últimas campañas de excavación. Dichas actividades pueden sintetizarse en los siguientes apartados:

1) Producción a gran escala en amplios talleres, como el que se ha localizado intramuros de la tercera linea de fortificación, donde puede seguirse con detalle todo el proceso del trabajo metalúrgico.

2) Zonas de refinamiento del metal en áreas más limitadas (bastiones cerrados de la fortificación exterior).

3) Areas de almacenamiento (depósitos de gotas de cobre en el Fortín no. 1)

Intercambio:

En este terreno no podemos aportar por el momento una mayor documentación que la ya publicada. Existe un importante desarrollo de tipo comercial de productos como el marfíl, cerámicas campaniforme y "naranja", metal, silex, huevos de avestruz y otras materias primas exóticas con contactos a larga distancia y a nivel interregional entre el área de Los Millares, la Alta Andalucía, el Suroeste peninsular, el estuario del Tajo y el Norte de Africa.

Estos resultados preliminares de la investigación de Los Millares y de otros asentamientos del Sudeste demuestran las posibilidades de contrasstación de las hipótesis planteadas previamente y el interés que puede ofrecer el desarrollo de nuestro Proyecto de investigación a corto y medio plazo.

NOTAS

(1) Chapman, R.W.: The evidence for prehistoric water control in South-East Spain, *Journal of Arid Environments* 1, 1978, pp. 261-274. Chapman, R.W.: Autonomy, ranking and resources in Iberian prehistory, *Ranking, Resource and Exchange. Aspects of the Archaeology of Early European Society* (C. Renfrew y S. Shennan, Eds.), Cambridge University Press, Cambridge, 1982, pp. 46-51. Chapman, R., V. Lull, M. Picazo y M.E. Sanahuja (Eds.): *Proyecto Gatas. Sociedad y Economía en el Sudeste de España c. 2500-800 a.n.e. 1. La Prospección Arqueoecológica*, BAR International Series 348, London, 1987. Gilman, A.: Bronze Age Dynamics in Southeast Spain, *Dialectical Anthropology* 1, 1976 pp. 307-319. Gilman, A.: The Development of Social Stratification in Bronze Age Europe, *Current Anthropology* 22, 1981, pp. 1-23. Gilman, A.: Regadío y conflicto en sociedades acéfalas, *Boletín del Seminario de Estudios de Arte y Arqueología* LIII, 1987, pp. 59-72. Gilman, A.: El análisis de clase en la Prehistoria del Sureste, *Trabajos de Prehistoria* 44, 1987, pp. 27-34. Mathers, C.: Beyond the grave: The Context and wider Implications of mortuary practice in south-eastern Spain, *Papers in Iberian Archaeology* (T.F.C. Blagg, R.F.J. Jones y S.J. Keay, Eds.), I, BAR International Series 193 (i), Oxford, 1984, pp. 13-46. Ramos Millan, A.: Interpretaciones secuenciales y culturales de la Edad del Cobre en la zona meridional de la Península Ibérica. La aternativa del materialismo cultural, *Cuadernos de Prehistoria de la Universidad de Granada* 6, 1981, pp. 203-256.

(2) Cara Barrionuevo, L y M. Carrilero Millan: Prospección arqueológica superficial del Estuario del Andarax y piedemonte de la Sierra de Gádor (Almería), 1985 *Anuario Arqueológico de Andalucía 1985*, II, 1987, pp. 63-66. Moreno Onorato, A., A. Ramos Millan y J. Martinez Garcia: Prospección arqueológica superficial de las zonas occidental y central del Pasillo de Chirivel/Vélez-Rubio (Almería), 1985, *Anuario Arqueológico de Andalucía 1985*, II, 1987, pp. 19-25. L. Cara Barrionuevo y J. Mª Rodriguez Lopez: Prospección arqueológica superficial del Valle Medio del Rio Andarax (Almería), *Anuario Arqueológico de Andalucía 1986*, II, 1987, pp. 58-61. M. Carrilero Millan Y otros: Memoria de la prospección arqueológica superficial del Bajo Andarax (Fase 2), y piedemonte de Sierra Alhamilla (Almería), *Anuario Arqueológico de Andalucia 1986*, II, 1987, pp. 66-68.

(3) F. Alcaraz Hernandez y otros: Proyecto de prospección arqueológica superficial llevado a cabo en el Pasillo de Tabernas (Almería), *Anuario Arqueológico de Andalucía, 1986*, II, 1987, pp. 62-65.

(4) Moreno Onorato, A., A. Ramos Millan y J. Martinez Garcia: Prospección arqueológica superficial de las zonas occidental y central del Pasillo de Chirivel/Vélez-Rubio (Almería), 1985, *Anuario Arqueológico de Andalucia 1985*, II, 1987, pp. 19-25. A. Ramos Millan: Prospección geoarqueológica de fuentes de rocas silíceas en el entorno geológico del poblado eneolítico de El Malagón (Cúllar-Baza, Granada), *Anuario Arqueológico de Andalucia 1986*, II, 1987, pp. 69-72.

(5) Arribas, A. y F. Molina: The Latest Excavations of the Copper Settlement of Los Millares, Almeria, Spain, *The Deya Conference of Prehistory. Early Settlement in the Western Mediterranean Islands and the Peripheral Areas* (W.H. Waldren, R. Chapman, J. Lewthwaite y R-C. Kennard, Eds.), BAR Intern. Series 229, pp. 1029-1050. Arribas, A. y otros: Informe preliminar de los resultados obtenidos durante la VI campaña de excavaciones en el poblado de Los Millares (Santa Fé de Mondújar, Almería), 1985, *Anuario Arqueológico de Andalucía, 1985*, II, 1987, pp. 245-262. Molina Gonzalez, F. y otros: Programa de recuperación del registro arqueológico del Fortín 1 de Los

Millares. Análisis preliminar de la organización del espacio, *Arqueología Espacial* 8, Coloquio sobre el microespacio-2, Teruel, 1986, pp. 175-201.

(6) Evans, R.K.: Early Craft Specialization: An Example from the Balkan Chacolithic, *Social Archaeology. Beyond Subsistence and Dating* (C.L. Redman y otros, Eds.), New York, 1978, pp. 113-130.

(7) Hook, D.R. y otros: Copper and Silver in Bronze Age Spain, *Bell Beakers of the Western Mediterranean* (W.H. Waldren y R-C. Kennard, Eds.), BAR International Series 331 (i), 1987, pp. 147-162.

PIES DE LAMINAS

Lam. I.   - Los Millares, 1985. Vista aerea del poblado. En primer término área de la puerta principal en la muralla exterior, excavada en profundidad.

Lam. II.   - Los Millares, 1981. El Fortín 1, tras la excavación superficial.

Lam. III.   - Los Millares, 1983. Sondeos en profundidad en el Fortín 1.

Lam. IV.   - Los Millares, 1985. El Fortín 1, tras la excavación en profundidad del área oriental.

Lam. I. - Los Millares, 1985. Vista aerea del poblado. En primer término área de la puerta principal en la muralla exterior, excavada en profundidad.

Lam. II. - Los Millares, 1981. El Fortín 1, tras la excavación superficial.

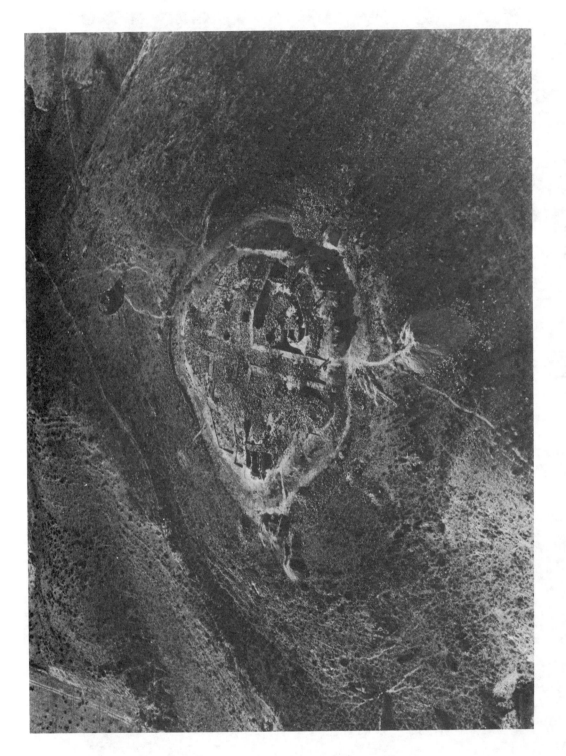

Lam. III. - Los Millares, 1983. Sondeos en profundidad en el Fortín 1.

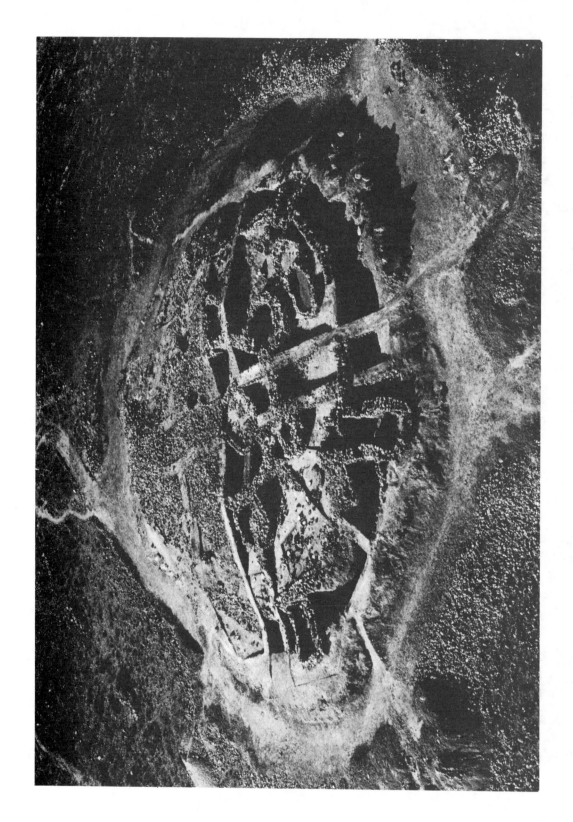

Lam. IV. - Los Millares, 1985. El Fortín 1, tras la excavación en profundidad del área oriental.